TOURISM AND POLITICS:

GLOBAL FRAMEWORKS AND LOCAL REALITIES

ADVANCES IN TOURISM RESEARCH

Series Editor: **Professor Stephen J. Page**
University of Stirling, UK
s.j.page@stir.ac.uk

Advances in Tourism Research series publishes monographs and edited volumes that comprise state-of-the-art research findings, written and edited by leading researchers working in the wider field of tourism studies. The series has been designed to provide a cutting edge focus for researchers interested in tourism, particularly the management issues now facing decision-makers, policy analysts and the public sector. The audience is much wider than just academics and each book seeks to make a significant contribution to the literature in the field of study by not only reviewing the state of knowledge relating to each topic but also questioning some of the prevailing assumptions and research paradigms which currently exist in tourism research. The series also aims to provide a platform for further studies in each area by highlighting key research agendas which will stimulate further debate and interest in the expanding area of tourism research. The series is always willing to consider new ideas for innovative and scholarly books, inquiries should be made directly to the Series Editor.

Published:

Benchmarking National Tourism Organisations and Agencies
LENNON, SMITH, COCKEREL & TREW

Extreme Tourism: Lessons from the World's Cold Water Islands
BALDACCHINO

Tourism Local Systems and Networking
LAZZERETTI & PETRILLO

An International Handbook on Tourism Education
AIREY & TRIBE

Tourism in Turbulent Times
WILKS, PENDERGAST & LEGGAT

Taking Tourism to the Limits
RYAN, PAGE & AICKEN

Tourism and Social Identities
BURNS & NOVELLI

Micro-Clusters and Networks
MICHAEL

Forthcoming titles include:

Tourism in the New Europe
THOMAS & AUGUSTYN

Hospitality: A Social Lens
LASHLEY, LYNCH & MORRISON

For other titles in the series visit: www.elsevier.com/locate/series/aitr

Related Elsevier Journals – sample copies available on request

Annals of Tourism Research
International Journal of Hospitality Management
Tourism Management

TOURISM AND POLITICS:

GLOBAL FRAMEWORKS AND LOCAL REALITIES

EDITED BY

PETER M. BURNS

Centre for Tourism Policy Studies, University of Brighton, UK

MARINA NOVELLI

Centre for Tourism Policy Studies, University of Brighton, UK

ELSEVIER

Amsterdam • Boston • Heidelberg • London • New York • Oxford
Paris • San Diego • San Francisco • Singapore • Sydney • Tokyo

Elsevier
The Boulevard, Langford Lane, Kidlington, Oxford OX5 1GB, UK
Radarweg 29, PO Box 211, 1000 AE Amsterdam, The Netherlands

First edition 2007

Notice
No responsibility is assumed by the publisher for any injury and/or damage to persons
or property as a matter of products liability, negligence or otherwise, or from any
use or operation of any methods, products, instructions or ideas contained in the material
herein. Because of rapid advances in the medical sciences, in particular, independent
verification of diagnoses and drug dosages should be made

British Library Cataloguing in Publication Data
A catalogue record for this book is available from the British Library

Library of Congress Cataloguing in Publication Data
A catalogue record for this book is available from the Library of Congress

ISBN-13: 978-0-08-045075-9
ISBN-10: 0-08-045075-X

For information on all Elsevier publications
visit our website at books.elsevier.com

Printed and bound in The Netherlands

07 08 09 10 11 10 9 8 7 6 5 4 3 2 1

Contents

List of Figures   ix

List of Tables   xi

About the Authors   xiii

Acknowledgements   xix

Tourism and Politics: Introduction   1
P. M. Burns and M. Novelli

1   Democracy and Tourism: Exploring the Nature of an
    Inconsistent Relationship   5
    Linda K. Richter

Section I   Politics, Democracy, and Organisations   **17**

2   Tourism as Political Platform: Residents'
    Perceptions of Tourism and Voting Behaviour   19
    Reil G. Cruz and Lisa Grace S. Bersales

3   Privatisation during Market Economy
    Transformation as a Motor of Development   33
    Heike Bähre

4   Group Politics and Tourism Interest
    Representation at the Supranational Level:
    Evidence from the European Union   59
    Constantia Anastasiadou

5   The Politics of Exclusion? Japanese
    Cultural Reactions and the Government's
    Desire to Double Inbound Tourism   71
    Malcolm Cooper, Radaslawa Jankowska and Jeremy Eades

6   Taming Tourism: Indigenous Rights as a Check to
Unbridled Tourism   83
Freya Higgins-Desbiolles

7   Celebrating or Marketing the Indigenous? International Rights
Organisations, National Governments and Tourism Creation   109
Susan Keitumetse

8   The Politics of Institution Building and European
Co-operation: Reflections on an EC TEMPUS Project on
Tourism and Culture in Bosnia-Herzegovina   123
Tom Selwyn and Jonathan Karkut

Section II   Scapes, Mobility and Space   **147**

9   Towards the Responsible Management of the Socio-cultural
Impact of Township Tourism   149
Pranill Ramchander

10 Hegemony, Globalisation and Tourism Policies in
Developing Countries   175
Andrea Giampiccoli

11 The Politics of Tourism: Ethnic Chinese Spaces in Malaysia   193
K. Thirumaran

12 Preparing Now for Tomorrow: The Future for Tourism in
Scotland up to 2015   211
Una McMahon-Beattie and Ian Yeoman

13 Governing Tourism Monoculture: Mediterranean Mass
Tourism Destinations and Governance Networks   235
Giorgio Conti and Carlo Perelli

14 The MTV Europe Music Awards Edinburgh03: Delivering
Local Inclusion?   263
Gavin Reid

15 The Lost Gardens and Airport Expansion: Focalisation
in Heritage Landscapes   279
M. W. J. Spaul

Section III   Circulation, Flows and Security   **291**

16 The War Is Over So Let the Games Begin   293
Adrian Devine, Robert Connor and Frances Devine

17 Hostile Meeting Grounds: Encounters between the Wretched
    of the Earth and the Tourist through Tourism and
    Terrorism in the 21st Century   309
    Freya Higgins-Desbiolles

18 Defending Voyeurism: Dark Tourism and the Problem
    of Global Security   333
    Debbie Lisle

19 Rethinking Globalization Theory in Tourism   347
    Ana María Munar

20 The End of Tourism, the Beginning of Law?   369
    Brian Simpson and Cheryl Simpson

    Author Index   389

    Subject Index   399

List of Figures

Figure 3.1:   Flow chart depicting political fields and sector transformation
               paths, with respect to the reorganisation of sector-specific
               property rights according to Lehmbruch and Czada. *Source*: Own
               depiction (with reference to Gade & Lehmbruch (eds.) 1998).   37

Figure 3.2:   The development of the proportion of foreign travel of all
               holiday travel. *Source*: Own depiction in accordance with the
               tourism analysis (RA) of Studienkreis für Tourismus and FUR
               (Holiday and Travel Research Group), various years.   48

Figure 3.3:   A comparison between the number of beds and occupancy
               rates in the new federal states and eastern Berlin. *Source*: Own
               calculations (1992 = 100), based on: Statistisches Bundesamt
               (German Federal Office of Statistics): Tourismus in Zahlen,
               various years.   50

Figure 3.4:   A comparison of full occupancy in the hotel industry between
               the new federal states (and eastern Berlin) and former
               West Germany. *Source*: Statistiches Bundesamt (German Federal
               Office of Statistics): Tourismus in Zahlen 2000/2001, p.135.   50

Figure 3.5:   A comparison of beds per capita between the new federal
               states (and eastern Berlin) and former West Germany.
               Source: Own calculations, according to Statistisches
               Bundesamt (German Federal Office of Statistics: Tourismus in
               Zahlen, various years.   51

Figure 3.6:   Own depiction, according to Bähre (2003).   52

Figure 3.7:   The Hotel Metropol in Binz on the island of Rügen in
               1993 and 2003. *Source*: Permission to publish granted by Helfer
               (IGU, 2004).   53

Figure 7.1:   The impact of conflicting ideologies on cultural consumption of
               the indigenous (Keitumetse, January 2006).   110

Figure 7.2:   Marketing distortion as reality: Excerpts from Lonely Planet
              publications marketing the San/"Bushmen" in southern Africa:
              The marketing phrases hold on to the "difference" as provided
              for by the "time immemorial" and "scarcity" principles.   117

Figure 9.1:   Soweto map (Travel Companion Gauteng, GTA, Johannesburg, 2003).   154

Figure 9.2:   Soweto pictures of everyday life and historical landmarks.   157

Figure 10.1: The linkage between hegemony and convergence/
              divergence effects.   178

Figure 10.2: Hegemony structure in global tourism.   182

Figure 11.1: The statue of Admiral Zheng He.   203

Figure 12.1: Strategy map.   229

Figure 13.1: The location of Rimini.   236

Figure 18.1: The post-war model of conflict and tourism.   339

List of Tables

Table 2.1:   Sampled respondents by barangay.   25

Table 2.2:   Respondent voting data.   26

Table 2.3:   Factor analysis.   27

Table 2.4:   Impacts data analysis.   28

Table 3.1:   Travel agencies in eastern Germany in 1991.   43

Table 4.1:   Some classifications of interest groups.   60

Table 4.2:   Single voice versus common voice.   66

Table 5.1:   Number of non-japanese residents in Japan by country 2004.   73

Table 5.2:   Inbound tourists to Japan 2000–2004.   79

Table 9.1:   The most positively perceived attitude statements.   166

Table 9.2:   The most negatively perceived attitude statements.   167

Table 12.1: Contributors to Scotland 2015.   214

Table 12.2: Short break destination – the value of tourism in 2015.   216

Table 12.3: Short break destination scotland – spending patterns.   216

Table 12.4: Yesterday's destination – the value of tourism in 2015.   221

Table 12.5: Yesterday's destination – spending patterns.   221

Table 12.6: Weekend getaway – opportunities and challenges.   223

Table 12.7: Yesterday's destinations – opportunities and challenges.   227

Table 13.1: Rimini, the PCI, local elections
             results, 1946–1990.   243

Table 13.2: Tourism diversification strategies after 1989 environmental crisis. 248

Table 16.1: Awareness of GAA.   300

Table 16.2: Nationality and awareness of GAA.   301

Table 16.3: Respondents interested in playing or watching a sport
            unique to the Island of Ireland.   301

Table 16.4: Respondents who are interested in a sport.   301

Table 16.5: Sex of respondents and interest in sport.   302

Table 16.6: Purpose of visit and interest in sport.   302

Table 16.7: Respondents interested in the Scor.   303

Table 16.8: Sex of respondent and their interest in the Scor.   303

Table 19.1: The three approaches method and tourism.   363

About the Authors

Peter M. Burns (PhD) is Professor of International Tourism and Development and Director of the Centre for Tourism Policy Studies (CENTOPS) at the University of Brighton. He is former Director of the Fiji Hotel School and Head of Department of Sport, Leisure and Tourism, The Business School, University of Luton. He is a consultant anthropologist specialising in strategic policy-making/implementation for tourism's human resources and identifying insightful solutions to the cultural impacts of tourism. He has extensive international experience in institutional strengthening and working with communities helping them achieve better education, participation, and training opportunities. He is the founding chair of the Association of Tourism and Leisure Studies (ATLAS), special interest group on Tourism and Social Identities, Vice Chair of the ATLAS committee, member of the World Tourism Organisation Education Committee and one of the first tourism scholars to be elected as an Academician of the Academy of Learned Societies for the Social Sciences.

Marina Novelli (PhD) is a Senior Lecturer in Tourism Development and Management at the CENTOPS, University of Brighton. Her main research interests include regional development and tourism, tourism planning and management, niche tourism and rural tourism markets development and management. She recently edited the volume *Niche Tourism: Contemporary Issues, Trends and Cases* (2005, Oxford: Elsevier) and completed a monograph commissioned by the Italian Ministry of Environment on the "Gargano National Park, Apulia, Italy". Her most recent research activity focuses on consumptive versus non-consumptive tourism, community-based tourism and tourism cluster development. She has been previously involved in a variety of European regional planning and tourism management consulting projects and is currently co-ordinator of the special interest group *Tourism and the Local Economy*.

Constantia Anastasiadou (PhD) has wide ranging research interests in national and supranational tourism policy, and in particular in the European Union, tourism and regional development, tourism in peripheral regions and cross border tourism development. She has worked in the travel industry in Europe and has worked as a qualitative social researcher on tourism-related and employability projects. She is a Lecturer at Napier University, UK and a research fellow in the Center of Excellence for Research in Tourism and Services (CERTS), Universiti Putra Malaysia. She gained an MSc and a PhD in Tourism from the Scottish Hotel School, University of Strathclyde, UK and a BA Hons in Economics from the University of Macedonia, Greece.

Heike Bähre (PhD) research focus and field of activity lie in the new German federal States as well as in Middle and Eastern Europe. Dr. Bähre was closely involved in the transition process of the new federal states in creating effective structures for Eastern German tourism economy and helped to develop them. For more than 7 years she served as an assistant/seminar project head at the central training academy of the German tourism industry, the German Tourism Institute (DSFT), before beginning a doctoral programme in 1999 with an assistantship at the chair of the Economics of Tourism at the Technische Universität Dresden. Dr. Bähre took part in the special projects of the German Tourism Institute Berlin (DSFT) for further training of disseminators (of opinions/information) in the countries of central and eastern Europe for the Federal Ministry of Economics. Mrs. Bähre planned several programmes of professional training in the form of seminars and conventions, drew up documentations and contributed articles. She teaches tourism marketing at the Berufsakademie (BA), a branch of the Berlin School of Economics (Fachhochschule für Wirtschaft (FH) Berlin), and tourism sciences at the Euro-Business-College Dresden.

Dr. Bähre is the owner and managing director of the iNTEGRON Institute for Tourism and Policy Councelling in Berlin, Germany.

Lisa Grace S. Bersales (PhD) is Professor of Statistics at the University of the Philippines in Diliman, Quezon City where she earned her BS, MS, and PhD (Statistics) degrees. She has been with the University for 24 years and is currently the Dean of the University's School of Statistics. She has also served as a statistical consultant for various government and international institutions. Her areas of interest are econometrics, time series analysis and statistical modeling in general. She has also served as survey statistician for the World Bank Baseline Survey of the Philippine government's poverty alleviation program, KALAHI-CIDSS and the World Bank-SAGRIC-Supreme Court Survey on Users' Experience and Perception on the Judiciary. She is as trainer in various trainings such as the Bangko Sentral ng Pilipinas statistical training programs, UN-SEAMEO-SEARCA Impact Assessment trainings, UNSIAP-Statistical Research and Training Center Research Based Training Programs in 2004 and 2005. She heads the Technical Committee on Seasonal Adjustment of Philippine Time Series under the National Statistical Coordination Board. She is a member of the International Statistical Institute and the Philippine Statistical Association.

Robert Connor is a Lecturer in the School of Hotel, Leisure and Tourism. He mainly lectures in Marketing Management to final year undergraduate students in Hospitality, Tourism, Travel and Tourism, Hotel and Tourism, Consumer Studies and Leisure, Events and Cultural Management. He also lectures to Masters students who are studying International Hotel and Tourism management. His main research interest at present is in hospitality and tourism marketing and in service quality in the private and public sectors of service industries.

Giorgio Conti is Associate Professor of Territorial Planning, University Ca' Foscari of Venice, Department of Environmental Sciences. In the past he has been working at IUAV University (Venice), and in Alger, Salerno, Ancona. He is responsible in charge for the scientific coordination of the International Meeting "Image et Science" in Paris organised by the CNRS, Centre National de la Recherche Scientifique.

Malcolm Cooper (PhD) holds the position of Vice President (Research and International Cooperation) and is Professor of Tourism in the Graduate School of Asia Pacific Studies at Ritsumeikan Asia Pacific University, Beppu, Japan. He is a specialist in tourism management and development, cultural tourism, ecotourism, sustainable tourism and environmental law. Dr. Cooper is the Asia Pacific regional editor for Tourism Research International and sits on the Editorial Boards of other international academic tourism journals. He has held previous appointments at the Universities of New England, Adelaide and Southern Queensland (Australia), and Waiariki Institute of Technology (New Zealand) and has worked in the tourism policy and environmental planning areas for Federal, State and Local Governments in Australia, and as a private consultant.

Reil G. Cruz is an Assistant Professor at the University of the Philippines Diliman Asian Institute of Tourism with more than 20 years of teaching experience. He served as Dean of the Institute from 2001–2004. He is currently (2005–2006) the Chief Technical Adviser for Tourism Human Resource Development Capacity Building Project for Mt. Chilbo, DPR Korea working under the UN World Tourism Organization. The project is funded by the United Nations Development Programme.

Adrian Devine is a Lecturer in the School of Hotel, Leisure and Tourism, University of Ulster. He mainly lecturers in the areas of Tourism Policy, Sports Tourism and Leisure Management. Adrian is currently researching the level of collaboration between the public sector organisations involved in sports tourism policy.

Frances Devine is a Lecturer in the School of Hotel, Leisure and Tourism, University of Ulster. She mainly lecturers in the areas of Human Resources and Organisational Studies. Frances is actively involved in researching Human Resource issues in hospitality and tourism, focusing particularly on cultural diversity – the characteristics of migrant workers, place–people– imagery and the importance of investing in education of cultural awareness in people.

Jeremy S. Eades (PhD) is Professor of Asia Pacific Studies at Ritsumeikan Asia Pacific University, researching the impact of globalisation on the Asia Pacific Region. His most recent books are "*The Making of Anthropology in East and Southeast Asia*" (co-edited with Shinji Yamashita and Joseph Bosco, Berghahn, 2005) and The "Big Bang" in Japanese Higher Education (co-edited with Roger Goodman & Yumiko Hada, Trans Pacific Press, 2005).

Andrea Giampiccoli is a PhD student in Geography at the University of KwaZulu-Natal, Durban, South Africa. He holds an undergraduate degree from the State University of Milan (Italy) and a Masters degree from Leeds University (England). His research interests are political–economy and globalisation issues in tourism, community-based tourism and ecotourism in relation to developing countries and the development of poor communities. His PhD research investigates the relationship between globalisation and community-based tourism in rural Pondoland, South Africa.

Freya Higgins-Desbiolles is a Lecturer in Tourism with the School of Management of the University of South Australia. She is also completing a PhD thesis on the topic of

"Tourism, Globalisation and the Responsible Alternative" with the School of Political and International Studies of the Flinders University of South Australia. She is committed to the principle that tourism can be a positive social force and she is active in endeavours to direct it to such ends. She currently serves on the Executive Committee of the Australian chapter of the International Institute for Peace through Tourism. She has worked with the Ngarrindjeri community for some 7 years.

Radaslawa Jankowska is a graduate of the College of Asia Pacific Studies at Ritsumeikan Asia Pacific University. Her graduation thesis research focused on discrimination and the politics of exclusion in contemporary Japan.

Jonathan Karkut specialises in project development, design and management with particular reference to the Balkans and Eastern Mediterranean. He is a project manager for the European Union Mediterranean Heritage programme entitled "Mediterranean Voices". He also manages an EU TEMPUS tourism institution building project in Bosnia-Herzegovina.

Susan Keitumetse (PhD) has recently been appointed as Research Fellow in Cultural Tourism at the University of Botswana. She completed her PhD at the Department of Archaeology, University of Cambridge on "Sustainable Development and Archaeological Heritage Management: Local Community Participation and Monument Tourism in Botswana". She is affiliated scholar of the Department of Archaeology at the University of Cambridge.

Debbie Lisle (PhD) is a Lecturer in Politics and Cultural Studies at the School of Politics, International Studies and Philosophy in Queens University Belfast. Her interdisciplinary research examines the connections between global politics, cultural formations and mobility. She has published work on war films, contemporary travel writing and the relationship between tourism and conflict.

Una McMahon-Beattie is a Lecturer and researcher at the University of Ulster. Her research interests include revenue management, tourism marketing and tourism futures and she has published widely both in the UK and internationally in these areas. She is co-editor of four books in the field of tourism management and she is currently the Practice Editor for the *Journal of Revenue and Pricing Management*.

Ana María Munar is a political scientist, Director of the Office for European Convergence and Harmonization of the University of the Balearic Islands (UIB). Prior to this, she was a faculty member of the Department of Applied Economics, Associate Director of the Master in Tourism and Environmental Economics and a teacher of the Tourism School of the UIB. Her research areas are globalisation theory, tourism globalisation, European education policy and trends in higher education.

Carlo Perelli (PhD) has recently completed his PhD at University Cà Foscari, IDEAS (Interdepartmental Centre for Dynamic Interactions between Economy, Environment and Society) and SSAV (School for Advanced Studies in Venice Foundation), Venice. He is currently working as consultant for an Italian tour operator.

Pranill Ramchander (PhD) is a senior management professional with 13 years experience in the field of strategic tourism development, management and planning, event management and promotions tourism development research, marketing, advertising, publishing, lecturing, consulting, public and media relations, corporate communications, commissioning and brand building. Dr Ramchander has acquired strong management and interpersonal skills, excellent research and writing skills in his working career thus far. He has been able to secure international scholarships and secure research funding from the National Research Foundation in South Africa. As a result he has published a range of articles, research reports in the field of Tourism Development and has attended and delivered academic papers internationally. He is actively involved in the corporate sector and higher education sector in SA, and is an external examiner for courses in Tourism Management and Development for Johannesburg University, University of South Africa (UNISA) and Tswane University.

Gavin Reid (PhD) is a Lecturer in Sports Management at the University of Edinburgh with a particular research interest in the politics of post-devolution leisure policy. After completing a Recreation degree from Edinburgh's Moray House College of Physical Education in 1992 he moved to Glasgow Caledonian University where, after obtaining his PhD, he lectured for several years. He has recently published work on charitable leisure trusts and is currently researching Scottish political parties' leisure policies and the Scottish Executive's Active Schools initiative.

Linda K. Richter (PhD) is Professor of political science at Kansas State University in the US where she teaches public policy and gender politics. She has authored *Land Reform and Tourism Development: Policymaking in the Philippines*, *The Politics of Tourism in Asia*, and has published widely on tourism politics both in the US and abroad. She was the academic representative to the US Travel and Tourism Administration, an associate editor of the Annals of Tourism Research and the Encyclopedia of Tourism. She was a member of International Academy for the Study of Tourism. She received graduate degrees from the East–West Center of the University of Hawaii and the University of Kansas. She has done field research in India, the Philippines and Pakistan and has lectured on international tourism in 19 countries. Her current research concerns international health, security and tourism policies.

Tom Selwyn (PhD) is Professor of Anthropology, specialising in the anthropology of tourism, at London Metropolitan University. His interests include the role of tourism in economic development, tourism in post-conflict regions, imagery, memory and memorialisation, landscape, and coasts. He widely published in these areas. He directed the EC's TEMPUS project on tourism and the cultural industries in Bosnia-Herzegovina described in the present volume, presently directs a TEMPUS project on pilgrimage and tourism in Palestine, and was member of the co-ordinating team of the MED-VOICES project in the Mediterranean. His geographical areas of interest are the Mediterranean, in particular Bosnia-Herzegovina and Israel/Palestine. He is on the Editorial Board of Annals of Tourism Research, Tourism Studies, and the *Scandinavian Journal of Hospitality*. He is also Honorary Librarian of the Royal Anthropological Institute (RAI), and Chair of the RAI's Achives and Manuscripts Committee.

Brian Simpson is an Associate Professor in the School of Law, University of New England, Australia. He was formerly a Senior Lecturer in the School of Law at Keele University, UK. In addition to his legal background, he also has post-graduate qualifications in urban planning. His research interests include children's rights in the media and cyberspace, the place of marginalised people in urban space and the intersection between tourism and human rights. Brian taught a course in Law, State and Tourism for a number of years at Flinders University of South Australia. He is currently writing (with Cheryl Simpson) a book titled *From Heritage to Terrorism: Regulating Tourism in an Age of Uncertainty* (to be published by Glasshouse Press), which explores the role of law in regulating and defining the tourist experience.

Cheryl Simpson is a Lecturer in Legal Studies at the Flinders University of South Australia. She is an editor of *Ways of Resistance: Social Control and Young People in Australia* (1995), *Law and Cultural Heritage* (1996) and *Cultural Heritage: Values and Rights* (1998). She has also published papers on cultural heritage and the law and social justice issues. Cheryl is the South Australian convenor for the *Alternative Law Journal* and has edited a number of issues of the journal. Her current research is on cultural heritage, tourism and the law.

Martin Spaul holds an MA and PhD in philosophy from the University of Cambridge. Having found himself, following crook'd and diverse ways, teaching multimedia computing, he specialises in the poetics of multimedia, drawing theory from literature, film studies and art history. His research interests are in multimedia heritage interpretation, especially the interpretation of heritage landscapes, and the semiotics of designed landscapes. His recent publications include: (2003) Straight Ways and Loss: The Tourist Encounter with Woodlands and Forests; in Crouch, D. and Lubbren, N. (Eds) *Visual Culture and Tourism*, Berg Publishers, Oxford (with S.H. Evans), and (2005) Historic Landscapes, Cultural Capital and Sustainability: Interpreting Ancient Woodlands, *Current Issues in Tourism*, *8*(2) (with S.H. Evans).

K. Thirumaran is a PhD candidate in the Southeast Asian Studies Programme at the National University of Singapore. He has over 7 years of practical experience in the tourism industry. His research interests centre on the development of performing arts tourism in Bali and Singapore, the concept of cultural affinity in tourism and the experiences of Indian and Chinese tourists in Southeast Asia.

Ian Yeoman is the Scenario Planner at VisitScotland, the National Tourism Organisation where he is responsible for economic forecasting, scenario construction and trends analysis. He is the founding editor of the *Journal of Revenue and Pricing Management* and co-editor of six books in the field of tourism management. His latest book *Tomorrows Tourist* is due to be published by Elsevier in 2007. Ian has a PhD in Management Science from Napier University, Edinburgh, and was recently appointed to the UN World Tourism Organisation expert panel.

Acknowledgements

A number of people have contributed significantly to the realisation of this book. First of all, we would like to thank Mercedita (Merz) Hoare for her meticulous attention to details and her good-natured way of dealing with our tiresome demands of her. Secondly, we are appreciative of Mary Beth Gouthro, Michael O'Regan and Christina Koutra's editorial assistance.

We are particularly grateful to all those colleagues who have refereed the chapters contained in this volume, whose name remains anonymous for the purpose of maintaining integrity.

Tourism and Politics: Introduction

P. M. Burns and M. Novelli

Tourism is a powerful mix of cultural, economic and political phenomena; it has multiple meanings and applications loaded with the ambiguities encapsulated by Zygmunt Bauman's concept of liquid modernity (Bauman, 2005). Its continuing growth is exposing tourists to a bewildering array of images, destinations and decisions on a scale hitherto undreamt. Since 9/11, global inventions of the "other" have increasingly taken on a heightened political dimension especially in the sphere of travel and the tourism, so that these stereotyped constructions meet constantly shifting local frameworks and global realities (Scraton, 2002). The consequences cannot be reduced to the simplistic idea of place and space becoming occupied only by vapid tourists and congenial, compliant local populations: tourism is simply too political, important and valuable to be so dismissed. For instance, how is tourism and its related sectors to deal with passports, borders, mobility and the politics of exclusion (migrant versus tourists) in the light of increased (some say draconian) travel security measures (Montanari & Tomas, 2005).

Tourism is often described as the world's biggest industry: this is simplistic at best and disingenuous at worst. Many, including the present authors, doubt this proposition as there is no clear idea upon what premise it is made and what is included in or taken out of tourism. Even so, doubt about the exact size does not lead to concomitant doubts over the scale of tourism: we can all agree that tourism is hugely significant in terms of environmental, socio-economical and political implications. It does not require detailed empirical investigation to see the ways in which the regional and transnational flows of tourists as well as the various scapes created by its sectors (airlines, hotels, e-businesses, etc.) making up the tourism "industry" are reordering the world (Franklin, 2004). The intersections of people on the move, geographical space and compressed time as characterised in the globalisation debates and illustrated by affordable airfares and opening up of new destinations are clearly framed by politics and ideologies (Burns, 2004) resulting from economic imperatives.

The potent but unstable mix of politics, ideologies and economic principles become even fuzzier when culture and heritage are thrown into the pot as frequently happens with the development of tourism (Selwyn, 1996). Where culture and heritage become politicised, as increased competition, accompanied by the intensification of market forces, exacerbates existing tensions and forms of co-operation between regions and nations, as well as creating new ones, the area of cultural politics is revealed. Socially constructed consensus about the nature and shape of tourism at a destination, and perhaps more importantly, the consensus by which cultures acquire symbolic value, may reflect political imperatives and ideological currents, and thus can be directly linked to questions of democracy, power and citizenship.

Issues of politics, risk and security are illustrated by the events of the New York 9/11 and London 7/7 and more explicit attacks on tourists. These acts of terror offer a stark reminder that the "unhindered" mobility upon which travel depends can be easily shattered. In a sense, tourism is predicated on freedom of mobility, the politics of security and the negotiation of risk (Hall, Timothy & Duval, 2003), thus challenging the very idea that tourism can be separated from other areas of policy-making.

The local interactions of tourism with politics and democracy are increasingly being framed by global realities such as General Agreement and Tariffs and Trade (GATT), General Agreement on Trade and Services (GATS), World Trade Organization and corporate alliances. The result is often the privatisation of tourism spaces, erosion of labour rights, and a new cultural politics of identity (Enloe, 1989; Lippard, 1999). A clear understanding of the political nature of tourism is an essential precursor for innovation and co-operation within the sector. Given tourism's propensity towards micro and Small and Medium Enterprises (SMEs), and its local location within a context of international competitiveness, the creation of an environment free from relative restriction balanced with human (community) rights should be seen (in an era of corporate social responsibility) as part of tourism's product development.

Tourism development itself is political in terms of policy decision about public expenditure (e.g. on human capital and physical resource development), together with support and mediation on the sustainable use of resources. The introduction of new labour patterns that reflect tourism's seasonality and the accompanying 24/7 service ideology adds further political complexities as traditional cultures try to adjust to new pressures and challenges without resorting to the "bunker mentality" of resistance to change. Finally, it could be argued that the act of marketing a country as a destination is political in the fact that decisions will be made in terms of what images to project, what (whose) stories to tell and who to include (and thus exclude) in the constructed and projected identities chosen to represent the space involved.

The first contribution by Linda Richter has been intentionally chosen as the introductory chapter setting the scene for the entire volume. It offers some really thoughtful considerations on the democratisation of tourism within the framework of globalisation and focuses on general issues such as power, security, terrorism, global heath and decision-makers' position in their regards. The insights Linda brings to the volume are thus reflected in several of the other chapters.

The first section contains seven chapters discussing the themes of "Politics, Democracy and Organisations", with Chapter 2 by Cruz examining the relationship between the perceived impacts (mainly positive) of tourism development among the local residents of Intramuros, Manila and their voting behaviour being influenced by the tourism friendly political decisions of one particular candidate. The local insights provided help us to locate the global trends identified at the beginning of the present chapter. By using data related to the Eastern Germany's experience, Bähre (Chapter 3), outlines the effects of privatisation during market economy transformation, highlighting the implication that this can generate in terms of tourism SMEs and economic development in general. Using empirical evidence drawn from a study on the European Union (EU) tourism policy environment, Anastasiadou (Chapter 4) discusses the difficult role and challenging work of interest groups at supranational level. Cooper's Chapter 5 investigates the changes occurring in the Japanese tourism sector opening up to inbound tourism and analyses the new consensus on how the country's culture can engage with the foreign "other" but be protected from its influence. Higgins-Desbiolles' Chapter 6 focuses on the implications of an "Indigenous rights regime for tourism" and narrates the efforts of the Ngarrindjeri community of South Australia to reach an agreement with Australian federal, state and local government bodies in order to preserve their indigenous rights against any form of homogenisation belonging to the word of capitalist globalisation. Drawing from research conducted in Botswana on the San community, Chapter 7 by Keitumetse offers another perspective on indigenous rights, by looking at the role and activity of an international advocacy organisation (Survival International) and by investigating the different perception of "indigeneity" by international advocacy organisations and national governments. The last chapter (Chapter 8) of this section offers a powerful piece of narrative by Selwyn and Karkut on a 3-year training, research and development project in tourism and the cultural industries in Bosnia-Herzegovina within the EU TEMPUS framework. This unique contribution offers discussion on issues of ethnic dissonance and division, consideration on the nature of the organisation of TEMPUS projects, questions about the role of universities in development and about the team work of international, national, regional and local institutions; all of this is outlined in a very critical and pragmatic way through the description of the authors' personal experience.

The second section also contains seven chapters and highlights experiences from themes related to what can be summarised as "Scapes, Mobility and Space". Chapter 9 offers results from research conducted by Ramchander in post-apartheid Soweto and highlights the socio-cultural implications of a recent niche segment called "township tourism", as perceived by the host population and aiming at supporting the government and other decision-making institutions. In Chapter 10, by using as a background the Gramscian theory of hegemony and convergence/divergence model, Giampiccoli explores the direction of contemporary tourism development in poor contexts, such as the Southern African, and the effects of the currently dominant neo-liberal paradigm. Chapter 11 by Thirumaran presents a perspective on Malaysia's tourism policies in relation to Malay–Chinese relations and suggest that local–global political economy affects the commodification of ethnic Chinese heritage for tourism in Malaysia. By focusing on experience on Scotland, McMahon-Beattie and Yeoman's Chapter 12 highlight best practice in terms of scenario planning and policy development in tourism. Using the case of Rimini, one of the Italian leading coastal destinations, Chapter 13 by Conti and Perelli adopts an urban regime approach to analyse governance mechanisms in traditional mass tourism destinations in the Mediterranean. Chapter 14 by Reid discusses the MTV Europe Music Awards event's contribution to Edinburgh's re-imaging and local inclusion also looking at its politicisation in terms of public subsidy allocation. By using the case of London's Stansted Airport expansion plans, Chapter 15 by Spaul highlights those landscape utilisation conflicts arising from the need for airport's expansions and the pre-existence of countryside resources such as the Gardens of Easton Lodge benefiting attracting a steady flow of visitors.

The third section offers five chapters related to the themes of "Circulation, Flows and Security". Chapter 16 by Devine, Connor and Devine examines Northern Ireland opportunities in sport tourism, one of the world's fastest growing niche markets. In Chapter 17, using the dichotomy of "tourist" versus "terrorist", Higgins-Desbiolles utilises the style of polemic essay in order to expose some controversial truths about the contemporary state of word affairs in travel and tourism. By critical assessing the literature on dark tourism, in Chapter 18 Lisle analyses the overlaps between tourism and conflicts in relation to issues of global security. Chapter 19 by Munar offers a rethink of the relationship between tourism and globalisation by placing tourism research in the broader theoretical frame of globalisation theory. By analysing the issue of "global movement of people", Simpson and Simpson (Chapter 20) offer considerations on the relationship between "law" and the "vague and shifting definitions" of travel and tourism.

The very least that the analysis above reveal is that tourism deserves a more nuanced analysis than familiar binary divisions ("left–right", "good–bad", "right–wrong", "North–South", "authentic-staged" and indeed "hosts–guests") can provide. By looking at an eclectic set of case studies, this book provides a platform for critical discourse and reflection on tourism, politics, democracy and the deriving chaotic web of power relations.

References

Bauman, Z. (2005). *Liquid life*. Cambridge: Polity Press.

Burns, P. (2004). Social identity globalization and the cultural politics of tourism. In: W. Theobald (Ed.), *Global tourism* (pp. 391–405). Oxford: Butterworth-Heinemann.

Enloe, C. (1989). *Banas, beaches and bases: Making feminist sense of international politics*. London: Pandora.

Franklin, A. (2004). Tourism as an ordering: Towards a new ontology of tourism. *Tourism Studies*, *4*(3), 277–301.

Hall, C. M., Timothy, D., & Duval, D. (Eds) (2003). Editorial: Security and freedom, towards a new understanding? *Journal of Travel and Tourism Marketing*, *15*(2/3/4), 1–18.

Lippard, L. (1999). *On the beaten track: Tourism, art, and place*. New York: The New Press.

Montanari, A. & Tomas, P. S. (Eds) (2005). Editorial, special edition: Human mobility in a globalising world. *Belgeo: Belgian Journal of Geography*, *1*(2), 3–6.

Scraton, P. (Ed.) (2002). *Beyond September 11: An anthology of dissent*. London: Pluto.

Selwyn, T. (Ed.) (1996). *The tourist image: Myths and myth making in tourism*. Chichester: Wiley.

Chapter 1

Democracy and Tourism: Exploring the Nature of an Inconsistent Relationship

Linda K. Richter

Introduction

There has been an implicit if not explicit assumption in much of the national rhetoric of developed nations and their tourism industries that there is a basic relationship between the freedom to travel, the welcome of visitors from abroad and democracy. The now defunct US Travel and Tourism Administration used to have as its slogan: "Travel: The Perfect Freedom." It was designed to highlight the mobility of Americans and the openness of American society in contrast with dictatorships, especially those of the USSR and its satellite nations.

The Helsinki Accords carried this assumption further by declaring travel to be a basic human right and monitoring freedom of movement was essential to assuring compliance. Again, the USSR and Eastern bloc nations were pressured to open up their societies to outsiders and to allow their own nationals freedom to travel. Democratization was to some extent being measured by the right to travel abroad. Internal support for the leisure of workers and provision for their holidays was not on the international agenda, though by that standard the then socialist nations would have ranked much higher than many capitalist governments.

What is the relationship if any between tourism and democracy and is there a way to investigate it? The answer this chapter suggests is that there are many relationships but they are not neatly a function of political arrangements or level of analysis. Tourism may nudge democratic institutions sometimes as an independent variable, but equally often elite decision-making shapes tourism.

The literature, case studies, and aggregate statistics seem to draw conclusions about this topic, but not in a consistent direction (Burns, 1999; Jurowski & Gursoy, 2004; Murphy, 1985). Tourism research tends to fall into two broad camps: those writers that see tourism as a positive good, a symbol of freedom, culture and well-being, a force for peace and understanding, and an economic force for development and heritage preservation (Richter, 2000; Richter & Richter, 2001). Tourism can promote the desirability of leisure, of education through travel, and break down artificial barriers that ignorance and isolation have established.

The other perspective tends to offer a critique that contains all or some of the following: tourism is an elite activity, enjoyed primarily by elites, controlled almost exclusively by elites, and one increasingly divorced from the control of those most affected. It exacerbates cultural tensions, bastardizes some heritage, and ignores other claimants for preservation of culture. It despoils the environment and disrupts local life. It creates unhealthy dependency on outsiders' demands for sex, increases gender and racial disparities, and creates shortages of scarce resources like water and energy (CONTOURS, 1985–present; Richter, 1995; World, 1978). It spreads disease from tourists to local populations and from destinations to tourist-generating countries (Garrett, 2000; 1996; Richter, 2003).

Tourism can be easily sabotaged by terrorism (Neumayer, 2004; Richter, 1991; Richter & Waugh, 1991). It creates a demonstration effect that brings home the inequalities of the leisure tourist compared to the employees of the tourist industry (Fisher, 2004). Familiarity breeds contempt and envy, not understanding. It breaks down family cohesion and encourages bad habits among the residents whether in the form of gambling, immodesty, prostitution, pedophilia, begging, truancy, or crime (Richter, 1989).

Given these disparate perspectives, it is rather daunting to investigate how tourism and democracy might be related. To say it all depends is probably accurate but not very helpful. Even when there is a strong positive relationship, it is not necessarily good for the majority. For example, there are some places so dependent on tourism that a majority might willingly develop tourism in ways that will create future water and energy shortages or result in increased school dropouts, addiction, etc. Las Vegas comes to mind.

Unfortunately, there are also some places like Pagsanjan Falls in the Philippines where the selling or renting of children to pedophile tourists is very common (Richter, 1989). The situation got so bad that the Philippine Department of Tourism left the falls off the tourism maps to thwart pedophiles and punish the locals for selling their children (Personal Interview, 1987).

To say that elite decisions and behaviors have often been better than the majority in protecting democratic values is to go against the basic premise of majority rule and to beg for clarification. The political writings of Thomas Dye and Harmon Zeigler have often noted that it is the elites in many societies that are the protector of liberties and civil rights that the majority might willingly sacrifice (Dye & Zeigler, 2000).

From a touristic standpoint, a majority of Americans would probably rather remember a tourist site like Pearl Harbor than Hiroshima. The former details the Japanese attack on the US that brought the US into World War II in 1941. More controversial in the US is the Enola Gay, one of the two planes that dropped atomic bombs on Hiroshima and Nagasaki, ending World War II. The plane, was highly controversial for years. Funding for the Smithsonian Museum that wanted to display the Enola Gay, was threatened by Congress until it was taken off display, only to return years later with more innocuous labeling.

Given that the relationship between democracy and tourism is ambiguous at best, this writer has opted simply to call it untidy or inconsistent.

Democracy Defined and Evolved

In recent years, democracy has come to be defended by the US in ways that have added much ideological baggage to the key term. Webster defines "democracy" as "a form of government for the people, by the will of the majority of the people; a state having this form of government" (Allee, 1977, p. 89). By this standard there are few pure democracies; certainly not in the US where the Electoral College prevents a popular vote from necessarily determining the outcome of Presidential races, for example the election of 2000 where Al Gore won over 500,000 more popular votes, but lost the electoral vote, by means fair or foul (Moore, 2001).

Even without an arcane gimmick like the Electoral College attached to the counting of ballots, the number not voting in many countries means that there can be no assurance of majority will prevailing. Nor would most of us be content with such a brief definition for it allows no recognition of any rights at all for the minority or minorities be they on the basis of race, gender, ethnicity, economic condition, religion, or geography. Nor does it contain the notion of representative democracy which most developed nations have. The fact that those actually making policy are rarely a mirror of the society at large further illustrates the difficulty of assuming that money, education, media access, and other factors do not trump representativeness. This was brought home during the current invasion of Iraq, when it was noted that only four members of the US Congress had a child in the military, and that some of the most enthusiastic proponents of the Iraqi invasion had never served in the military – the so-called "chicken hawks," like then Assistant Secretary of Defense Paul Wolfowitz and Vice-President Dick Cheney.

Democracy has clearly evolved in the popular media to include so much more than government by the majority. Minority rights, civil liberties, and policy-making ostensibly by elected representatives of the people have come to be part of the equation.

International organizations attempting to measure how people fare in various nations include certain criteria to come at a definition of "Freedom in the World." Freedom House (2004; 2001), for example, assigns a rating for each country "based on a checklist of questions on political rights and civil liberties. … Each country is assigned a rating … based on a scale of 1 to 7, with 1 representing the highest degree of freedom present. … The combined average of each country's political rights and civil liberties ratings determines an overall status of Free, Partly Free, or Not Free" (Freedom House Country Ratings, http://www.freedomhouse.org/ratings/index.htm).

By their definition one finds substantial tourism in a variety of nations they classify ranging from free to non-free. More salient for the volume of tourism seems to be the stability of the government rather than its form of government (Neumayer, 2004). As one talks of democratization, it is easy to forget that some of the earliest popular destinations for mass tourism were Franco's Spain, Salazar's Portugal, and Batista's Cuba. Nice beaches may be more relevant to tourists than human rights!

Other bodies regularly measure the fairness of elections, level of corruption, and incidents of domestic violence and civil strife (Neumayer, 2004). One might expect tourism to be positively related to low levels of corruption and domestic violence, but this hypothesis deserves more research. Corruption and violence kept away from the tourist belt or at a level of bureaucratic accounting and police control that is not obvious may not deter arrivals as much as the threat of disease. The latter usually warrants a warning from many tourist-generating countries (Richter, 2003).

National elections may impact tourism policy as in Costa Rica's decisions to commit 25% of its land to national parks or in its decisions as to how to develop sustainable tourism, but for larger and more complex nations, tourism issues are seldom important electoral issues

(Richter, 1998). Ironically, in some countries the tensions surrounding national elections may in fact depress rather than encourage tourism, because tourists fear violence, terrorism, or simply the absence of normality.

In recent years democratization has also taken on economic as well as political elements not fully appreciated by the makers of dictionaries. Though the process started much earlier in post-World War II societies and accelerated in the administrations of US President Ronald Reagan and UK Prime Minister Margaret Thatcher it would be encapsulated in the book *Reinventing Government*. It argued for government to allow the individual and the private sector to flourish by setting them free of "oppressive" regulation and Big Government (Osborne & Gaebler, 1992).

Thus, deregulation, privatization, and free trade were seen as hallmarks of progressive (read democratic) societies. In societies, not already considered democratic, democratization in terms of free elections, competitive media and civil liberties were made a part of the recipe (Richter & Richter, 1995). Societies that had popular state-run airlines, trains, hotels and inns, and medical, educational, and poverty programs were seen as perhaps well-meaning but on the wrong side of history.

This newer elaboration supported by conservative administrations around the world has resulted in increased opportunities for businesses including the tourist industry to operate with fewer regulations and more opportunities for mergers, lower taxation, and reduced environmental requirements. Government-owned airlines have been broken up and privatized in most instances. Aeroflot, once the world's largest airline, is now in more than 400 pieces.

Depending on the sector tourism has become more competitive, freer, and there has been even some equalization of large and small operations given the Internet. Incomes of those in the tourism sector, however, have been stagnant and guaranteed vacation and health care benefits more illusory than ever. Generalizations about democracies and tourism a few decades ago would have emphasized the rights of workers to paid vacations and the recognition of leisure in the constitutions of European nations.

The importance of school children taking "field trips" or even longer trips to major educational venues would have been seen as part of their political socialization to their nation and supportive of their sense of citizenship. Today cutbacks and fears about health and safety in many democratic societies have meant fewer "frills" like school trips and have made sport and recreation as well as basic education dependent on corporate scholarships. Today, the Gini Index of Inequality would show a widening gulf between the rich and the poor, and the International Labor Organization would show a decline in the power of organized labor.

Surprisingly the decrease in leisure would be most marked in those nations like the US that promoted the linkages of economic changes to democracy. The average American receives a little over 2 weeks paid vacation – far less than is true of most developed countries. Moreover, some 37% of those took none of their vacation and in 2003 the average American vacation totaled 8.1 days (Smith, 2004, Schor, 1991).

Ironically, the breakup of the USSR and the emergence of capitalism in Eastern Europe have increased freedom of travel while reducing the right to leisure, economic security, and health care. Eastern Europe and Russia are increasing destinations for Western travelers but the intra Eastern Bloc travel that prevailed in the era of Soviet hegemony has been in some places reduced by the increased cost of travel and the lack of workplace retreats, and guaranteed leisure once widespread in socialist countries.

The trends in tourism policy development and control have been in terms of devolution of control and planning. While never as centralized in its tourism policy as most democracies, the US did have over 40 federal agencies that dealt with tourism (Richter, 1985). In recent years the federal government has abolished the US Travel and Tourism Administration and its advisory bodies, reduced support for national parks and recreation sites, and has instead made the hurdles for in-bound travel increasingly convoluted and cumbersome. These measures preceded terrorism concerns and were intended to assure that "visitors" to the US not remain as illegal aliens (Personal observation while member of the USTTA, 1990–1994).

Complicating the discussion of democracy still further is the increasing marginalization of the nation-state. Terrorism, tourism, and trade flow over borders in ways that until recently have been hindered by national boundaries. At the international level, one may hear talk of democracy and the right to leisure and freedom to travel but no enforcement mechanism exists to make that a reality.

Moreover, political definitions of democracy have given way to definitions that associate democracy with free trade, globalization, deregulation, decentralization, and increasingly privatization. These policies do not flow from a definition of democracy, but they do flow from the economic and political clout of the largest so-called democracies. They ironically allow increased control by the few over the many whether measured in terms of individual clout, corporate strength, or media access.

Thus, one finds a contrary economic trend prevailing which promotes economic concentration through deregulation of barriers against mergers existing alongside rhetoric urging decentralization. It also means that as private economic interests grow vis-à-vis the nations, the ability of the government weakens as it seeks to protect itself from privatization of activities once deemed too important to the public to be in private hands. The new mantra of globalization has been appended to what democratic nations should pursue. Decentralization and deregulation have been added to the democratic equation as well.

Democracy and Tourism: Odd Couple or Natural Allies?

Tourism is profoundly affected by the international order, but as we have seen, international tourism is not under the control of an international public body. Transnational organizations dominate in the international arena with respect to many tourism issues.

The World Health Organization (WHO) has little power except that of persuasion and it was not until the threat of SARS (or more recently Avian flu) that it was considered a key player in controlling the spread of disease. The critical role tourism plays in the spread of disease has become obvious in only the past few years. The WHO has pathetic resources and mainly begging rights vis-à-vis nations (Garrett, 2000; 1996; Richter, 2003a).

The World Tourism Organization is a new UN affiliate but it lacks the stature, let alone budget, to speak on behalf of nations, the travel industry, or the general population. It has rightly condemned sexual exploitation and trafficking in women and children and has espoused a code of ethics for tourism. The UNWTO supports sustainable tourism initiatives and attention to heritage protection. These pronouncements illustrate a rhetorical regard for host communities but for implementation of its goals the UNWTO must depend on the tourist industry and interested governments – neither group having established a record for self-policing or a desire for increased regulation (Richter, 2003b; 2004a,b).

Issues of global warming, the conditions of the oceans, and even the control of acid rain are issues, complicated by tourism – especially in the case of beach development and cruise ship pollution, but each cries out for regulation, supranational agreements, an international court, and a variety of controls totally at odds with the current political climate in the most powerful countries (Langewiesche, 2003).

Cost–benefit analysis discourages any single nation taking action, yet, in the absence of collective action all countries lose. Majority will may be thwarted if all refuse to participate. Sometimes developing nations feel they cannot afford some of the environmental and other sustainability programs many countries favor. Their reluctance gives other governments an excuse to refuse to go along in their absence.

Such is the Tragedy of the Commons – in this case, air, water, energy. Initiatives like the Kyoto Protocol have been ratified by many nations but many others have waited, excused by US inaction. Even so, some in the expanded European Community have moved on select issues rather than wait for the dominant US to assume leadership it has evidently forfeited.

Too little attention has been paid to the increasingly numerous regional efforts of nations to include tourism as one of the generally economic issues about which they agree to consult, negotiate, and in some cases organize. Three early examples are the Pacific Area Travel Association (PATA), the Association of Southeast Asian Nations (ASEAN), and the Organization of Economic Cooperation and Development (OECD). Each was the product of elite interests rather than majority organization, but in regards to tourism, each undertook some activities that can be said to benefit the majority.

PATA, the only one of the three to be exclusively interested in tourism, was probably the first international regional association to encourage heritage protection of tourist sites and to award groups that had taken steps to protect local and national built heritage. You could say its interest was ultimately self-serving, but they were steps that could be valuable to protecting national identity (Richter, 1995; 2000).

ASEAN established a subsection concerned with tourism that originally sought to assure that there were airline connections among all members. That may seem like a small tourist measure, but consider that even in recent times in Africa, it is sometimes necessary to fly from an African country back to Paris, Rome or London in order to get to other African countries by air (Richter, 1989). The OECD has also been active on issues of air and water pollution in and surrounding member nations. The Mediterranean and the Black Sea have been particular areas of concern.

Their early and not wholly successful efforts also put in place smaller but more active regional tourism marketing cooperation that built a region rather than a nation into a destination. Singapore, with capitalist savvy and political stability has built its attractiveness to some extent around its geographic proximity and cooperative agreements with Malaysia and Indonesia (Chang, 2004).

South Asia has also had similar efforts, but these have been largely failed elite attempts that have ignored the hostility, border closures, civil war, and outright nuclear threats that have crippled their efforts to make South Asia a regional destination both among neighbors and long-haul traffic from the major tourist-generating centers of Europe, North America, etc. (Richter, 1989).

Except for a very few economically undiversified nations that are overwhelmingly dependent on tourism, this situation is not a national issue of public debate. For a few nations that regulated the freedom of nations to travel, for example the former nations of the Soviet Union, Eastern Europe, or those like Korea and Taiwan who did not allow draft age men to go abroad, the decisions about international travel were national but elite actions.

One could say those countries had until recently lacked basic freedom of movement. Other countries simply have controlled in-bound travel (e.g. Saudi Arabia, Bhutan, and Brunei). Each fear the "cultural pollution" of outsiders. Bhutan, however, saw in tourism a means to keep its majority culture and monarchy intact. It came to this realization after another nearby princely state, Sikkim, was annexed by India in 1973. By limiting tourism to a few affluent visitors, Bhutan has reinforced its image as a separate nation while limiting the cultural impact (Richter, 1989).

More complicated is the case of the US, where the national government has always contrasted the freedom to travel of its citizens with that of the former USSR. But in fact, many nations have been off-limits to Americans. Yemen and Libya were often on the banned list. For nearly 40 years travel to Cuba has been severely restricted. Travel to China was also not permitted for most Americans for over 30 years following the Communist takeover in 1949. Today, China enjoys most favored nation status with the US despite remaining a communist government while Cuba is increasingly off-limits to Americans.

In fact the tightening of controls on travel to Cuba may be seen as a reflection of the growing importance of the conservative Cuban exile vote to Florida politics. The importance of Florida to the Bush Presidency led to an unusual degree of responsiveness by the national government to the will of the people in that state. That state's Governor, Presidential brother Jeb Bush was also able to prevent off-shore oil drilling that might impact the important tourism industry of the state.

The US has also unilaterally tightened restrictions on travel to the US. It has made visas more expensive and has required more elaborate passports from abroad. This has triggered reactions to US, visitors by some other countries like Brazil. Ostensibly the reason for such US action has been to deter terrorism or to appear to do so for domestic consumption.

The tourist industry has been appalled but has been unable to mobilize public reaction and a consistent opposition to these moves. Since about 96% of US tourism is domestic, there is little risk politically or economically for the Bush administration even if its policies are at odds with deregulation and free trade. Indeed, except for Japan, the US does not have a positive balance of tourist trade with any other nation. Thus, to the extent other nations retaliate or the Bush administration ratchets up the fears of terrorism, more US tourists simply stay home which eases the American balance of payments crisis.

National governments do set visa policies, health policies, transport policies, and occasionally even national tourism plans that impact tourism, but to the extent they do so, these decisions are made without much public debate and with few opportunities for public input. Thus, it can be said rather generally that there is little democracy associated with national tourism policies.

But perhaps democracy and tourism are linked at other levels and what looks chaotic is simply a level of analysis question. Indeed, at the subnational and local level in many nations there are tourism plans of one kind or another that have provided case studies of local and regional activism vis á vis tourism. Spain, for example has begun a process of devolution of power and decentralization of tourism. It was hoped that efficiencies could be realized, that there would be greater sensitivity to local cultures and greater privatization of tourism assets. Early indications are that it has been less than a success (Baidal, 2004).

Christopher Pforr's study of attempts to devolve tourism decisions and be more inclusive of indigenous Australians – surely democratic goals – has also shown that it is hard to erase the history of exclusion by a simple invitation to aborigines to participate. Moreover, there is little indication that the powers that be were doing more than going through the motions of inclusion (Pforr, 2003).

The activist organization, Equations, has for years in India and in Goa particularly sought to force government and the tourism industry to consider locals and the environment in their development plans. They have had demonstrations and articles, but their success has been limited and their inclusion in formal decision-making processes over the past 25 years less than decisive.

A major problem associated with the devolution of power is that it often exacerbates the very problem it is intended to address. At the national level, even despotic governments need to balance a range of issues to be successful in maintaining political stability and keeping tourists and other investments forthcoming. As decision-making moves closer to the grassroots, unless there is an extraordinary degree of equality and activism, fewer and fewer interests dominate. Decisions tend to be made by the dominant elite.

James Madison argued in Federalist No. 10, one of several letters written to newspapers in favor of ratification of the US Constitution, that far from losing individual liberty by the growth of a stronger national government, one actually assures that more interests are balanced in decisions and fewer local elites dominate (Patterson, 1990).

This would seem to be ever more likely as communication and technology have made getting local issues heard at higher levels more feasible. But does it pertain to tourism? Maybe. Again, it depends on who owns those grassroots! Some would note how one local US community in the 1980s stopped the Winter Olympics from being held in their Colorado town. But this particular town was a wealthy enclave that did not want the riffraff and construction let alone crowds the Winter Olympics would entail. The rest of the state was far more sanguine about the money that would come to the state and at the national level hosting the Winter Olympics sounded like an even better idea because of all the money tourists would also spend in other states. The infusion of funds from the preparations was also a factor in the different responses to be found at different levels of government. Local democracy triumphed, but it was scarcely because of a fondness for the masses.

Atlanta, Georgia's poor people were not so able to control the demolition of their housing for the 1996 Summer Olympics. Who wins and who loses from such mega events? Perhaps the Summer Olympics in Greece in 2004 or the 2006 Winter Olympics in Torino will get a thorough scrutiny by some researcher. Tourist receipts, media exposure, and increased numbers of jobs in everything from construction to security are supposed to pay off for the host venue.

Perhaps democracy's impact is not just a level of analysis problem but a function of whether one is talking about a special event or a permanent tourist attraction. Perhaps tourism's impact on democracy depends on the type of tourism, the scale, the pace, and the overall carrying capacity of a destination. All of these issues have been investigated to some degree, but no definitive conclusions have specifically linked the degree of democratization over the process and the success of tourism for the majority most impacted.

That would in any case be hard to do. Tourism is so easy to destroy, so dependent on political stability that even a few can disrupt it (Richter, 1982; 1989; Richter & Waugh, 1991). Some have done so to protest an illegitimate regime that squandered billions on tourism while the population suffered as in the Philippines under President Marcos. The Light a Fire Movement specifically targeted tourism and utilized arson as a way to get international publicity focused on the regime (Richter, 1982). In those instances, many perhaps approved the daring of a few, because the industry had so few benefits for anyone but Marcos cronies.

In 1986, a peaceful People Power revolution overthrew the Marcos regime following a corrupted election and the very excesses of the regime and the places where millions confronted the tanks of the government became tourist attractions and places of pilgrimage (Richter, 1989).

In fact, one place where we can assuredly say that democracy and tourism are increasingly intersecting is in terms of tourist attractions highlighting the ability of the masses to prevail over threats of tyranny and actual despotism. A new travel book by Jim Carrier highlights travel to sites linked to the US civil rights movement (Carrier, 2004). It turns out there are hundreds and surely they play a role in the political socialization of those who visit them, but who decided the interpretation of the site, what would be left in and left out, what sites would be recognized, and what ones ignored is not necessarily a reflection of democracy so much as clout (Richter, 1995).

The People Power Tour in the Philippines very explicitly was used to justify the overthrow of President Marcos as well as provide new and interesting tourist venues. "Roots tours," based on Alex Haley's powerful book, *Roots* and the subsequent TV miniseries, also have flourished in parts of West Africa that figured prominently in the slave trade. Similarly Robin Island and other places central to the life of Nelson Mandela have been historical markers remembered for their role in his fight against white supremacy in South Africa.

The interpretation of these sites, their development and control, the land development, and employment associated with the sites – all these need to be the subject of extended analysis. Is a new theme merely being packaged by a few or is such development linked to the growing inclusiveness of the society and encouraged by the majority and minority alike? (Richter, 2003c). Is tourism expanded by democracy, enriched by democracy? Examples differ. Does tourism further democracy by promoting the freedom of travel, by bringing peoples of different cultures together? Can it pressure societies to open up or become more inclusive and free? Sometimes.

Over 200 major US organizations used the boycott of certain states for their conventions to pressure those key states to ratify the Equal Rights Amendment. They took their annual confabs to other states. It was a very powerful economic tool impacting St. Louis, Atlanta, Kansas City, New Orleans, Salt Lake City, and Miami to name just a few popular convention venues. But the technique was applied too late and it mainly penalized the more liberal urban parts of the unratified states instead of the rural opposition. Black convention planners and increasingly gay and lesbian groups are picking their conference sites and travel plans according to political criteria. Both markets have become enormous within the American tourism scene (Richter, 1995; 2000).

Aung San Suu Kyi, Nobel Peace Prize winner and leader of the Burmese opposition in Myanmar, has urged tour groups and individual travelers to boycott Myanmar because of its abysmal human rights violations. Arrival figures suggest she may have had some effect, but the country is calm and removed from terrorism which may ultimately make its human rights abuses less salient to travelers. Such was the case in China after the government's crackdown in Beijing in 1989. International tourism plummeted, but within 4 years was back to pre-1989 levels.

Tourists have also acted as advocates for oppressed peoples in undemocratic societies by documenting and publicizing their plight; but in general tourists are attracted to nations more by the sights and the exchange rate than by risking their freedom ferreting out abuses (Hall & O'Sullivan, 1996; Richter, 2001a).

Finally, pilgrimage tourism is unfortunately associated with several particularly undemocratic nations – Saudi Arabia, Israel, Pakistan, etc. All restrict freedom of passage to devotees of several faiths while encouraging the dominant faithful or useful allies to visit. Tourism has not trumped political rivalries in such settings.

Conclusion

In this chapter, more questions and hypotheses have been suggested than relationships established exploring democracy's links to tourism. What can be said is that tourism sometimes is an independent variable influencing democratic values and promoting the celebration and visitation of markers in the struggle for civil rights.

In other cases, tourism is a dependent variable possibly impacted by democracy under some conditions, but more often by political stability. International agreements and accords are beginning to push tourism development toward more sensitivity to more groups in its marketing, in accessibility for the elderly and disabled (Richter & Richter, 2003), in protection of the environment, and in helping to control the exploitation of women and children (Richter, 2003b; 2004a).

We have seen that there are various ways to investigate this topic. Analysis from different levels of government offer insights on how democracy and tourism may be linked. Using macro data sets like the Correlates of War Studies, Freedom House assessments, and US State Department reports also offer information on the nature of the societies being visited (Gibney, 2002; Neumayer, 2004). Aggregate tourism statistics from any number of sources also help to explore some of the tantalizing potential relationships.

Case studies of privatization, of participatory planning, of deregulation also add to our understanding. Studying strategic planning efforts and looking at implementation efforts to link the two concepts also offer more nuanced assumptions. Ultimately, we are led back to the old questions of what constitutes democracy and who gets what when and where within it? (Lasswell, 1936). And who already has what? (Parenti, 1988). Beyond this one must ask: "who cares?" Without a level playing field and without an aroused citizenry eager to engage on issues of tourism policy, the relationship between democracy and tourism seems tragically irrelevant.

Acknowledgments

The author wishes to thank Kansas State University and the political science and women's studies departments for their support. And, I am most grateful for careful assistance of my graduate assistance, Teola Dorsey, in the final preparation of this manuscript.

References

Allee, J. G. (1977). *Webster's dictionary.* US: Ottenheimer Publishers.

Baidal, J. A. (2004). Tourism planning in Spain, evolution and perspectives. *Annals of Tourism Research, 31*(2), 313–333.

Burns, P. (1999). Paradoxes in planning: Tourism elitism or brutalism? *Annals of Tourism Research, 26,* 329–348.

Carrier, J. (2004). *A Traveler's Guide to the Civil Rights Movement.* Orlando, FL: Harcourt.

Chang, T. C. (2004). Tourism in a "Borderless" World: The Singapore Experience. *Asia Pacific Issues, 73,* May, Honolulu, East–West Center.

CONTOURS (1985–present). Publication of the Ecumenical Coalition of Third World Tourism.

Dye, T., & Zeigler, H. (2000). *The irony of democracy.* Millennium Edition Fortworth, Texas: Harcourt Brace.

Fisher, D. (2004). The demonstration effect revisited. *Annals of Tourism Research, 31*(2), 428–446.

Freedom House (2001). *Annual Surveys of Freedom Country Ratings (1972–1973) (2000–2001).* New York: Freedom House.

Freedom House (2004). *Freedom House Country Ratings,* March 12. http://www.freedomhouse.org/ratings/index.htm

Garrett, L. (2000). *Betrayal of trust: The decline of global public health.* New York: Hyperion.

Garrett, L. (1996). The return of infectious disease. *Foreign Affairs, 75*(1), 66–79.

Gibney, M. (2002). *Political terror scales dataset.* Ashville: University of North Carolina.

Hall, C. M., & O'Sullivan, V. (1996). In: Abraham Pizam & Yoel Mansfield (Eds), *Tourism, political instability and violence. tourism, crime and international security issues* (pp. 105–121). New York: John Wiley.

Jurowski, C., & Gursoy, D. (2004). Distance effects on residents' attitudes toward tourism. *Annals of Tourism Research, 31*(2), 296–312.

Langewiesche, W. (2003). Anarchy at sea. *Atlantic Monthly,* September, 50–80.

Lasswell, H. (1936). *Politics: Who gets what, when and how.* New York: McGraw Hill.

Moore, M. (2001). *Stupid white men.* New York: Regan Books.

Murphy, P. (1985). *Tourism: A community approach.* New York: Metheun.

Neumayer, E. (2004). The impact of political violence on tourism. *Journal of Conflict Resolution, 48*(2), 259–281.

Osborne, D. E., & Gaeble, T. (1992). *Reinventing government: How the entrepreneurial spirit is transforming the public sector.* Reading, MA: Addison-Wesley.

Parenti, M. (1988). *Democracy for the few.* New York: St. Martin's Press.

Patterson, T. (1990). *The American democracy.* New York: McGraw Hill, 31.

Pforr, C. (2003). *Tourism policy in Australia's Northern Territory: A policy process analysis of its Tourism Development Masterplan.* Unpublished doctoral dissertation. University of the Northern Territories, Australia.

Richter, L. K. (2003a). International tourism and its global health consequences. *Journal of Travel Research, 41,* May, 340–347.

Richter, L. K. (2003b). Not a minor problem: International issues surrounding the traveling child. A paper given at the *International Academy for the Study of Tourism Biennial Conference in Savonlinna,* Finland, June (Forthcoming in *Tourism Analysis*).

Richter, L. K. (2003c). *The* politics of negotiating ethnicity in tourism. A paper given at the *Global tourism, local realities conference,* Eastbourne, UK, September.

Richter, L. K. (2004b). Not home alone. *Tourism, Recreation, Research, 29*(1), 27–35.

Richter, L. K. (2001a). Tourism challenges in developing nations: Continuity and change at the millennium. In: D. Harrison (Ed), *Tourism and the less developed world: Issues and case studies* (pp. 47–60). UK: CABI Publishers.

Richter, L. K. (2001b). Political lessons of Philippine tourism development. In: V. Smith & M. Brent (Eds.), *Hosts and guests revisited* (pp. 283–297). New York: Cognizant Publications.

Richter, L. K. (2000). The politics of heritage tourism. In: D. Pearce, & R. Butler (Eds), *Emerging issues for the new millennium* (pp. 108–126). London: Routledge.

Richter, L. K. (1999a). Ethics challenges, health, safety and accessibility issues in international travel and tourism. *Public Personnel Management, 61*(28), 4.

Richter, L. K. (1999b). After political turmoil: Lessons in rebuilding tourism in three Asian countries. *Journal of Travel Research, 38*(4), 41–46.

Richter, L. K. (1998). Exploring the political role of gender in tourism research. In: W. Theobald (Ed.), *Global tourism* (2nd ed., pp. 391–404). Indiana, Purdue University Press.

Richter, L. K. (1995). Gender and race: Neglected variables in tourism research. In: R. Butler, & D. Pearce (Eds), *Change in tourism* (pp. 71–91). London: Routledge.

Richter, L. K. (1992). Political instability and tourism in the Third World. In: D. Harrison (Ed.), *Tourism in the less developed countries* (pp. 35–46). London: Belhaven Press.

Richter, L. K. (1989). *The politics of tourism in Asia*. Honolulu: University of Hawaii Press.

Richter, L. K. (1985). Fragmented politics of US tourism. *Tourism Management, 6*(3), September, 162–174.

Richter, L. K. (1983). Tourism and political science: A case of not so benign neglect. *Annals of Tourism Research*, October–December.

Richter, L. K. (1982). *Land reform and tourism development: Policy-making in the Philippines.* Cambridge, MA: Schenkman.

Richter, L. K., & Richter, W. L. (2001). Back from the edge: Rebuilding a public heritage: A case study of Dubrovnik, Croatia. In: S. Nagel & A. Robb (Ed.), *Handbook of global social policy* (pp. 357–375). New York: Marcel Dekker.

Richter, L., & Richter, W. L. (1995). Reinventing government abroad. A paper presented at the *National American society for public administration conference*, San Antonio, July.

Richter, L. K., & Richter, W.L. (1991). Terrorism and tourism as logical companions. In: S. Medlik (Ed.), *Managing tourism* (pp. 318–326). London: Butterworth Heinemann.

Richter, W. L., & Richter, L. K. (2003). Human Trafficking, Globalization and Ethics. *PA Times, 26*(2), February, 4.

Schor, J. (1991). The overworked American: The unexpected decline of leisure. New York: Basic Books.

Smith, L. (2004). Take a vacation or die. *Kansas City Star*, E4, July 15.

World (1978). *Who Pays for Paradise?* Video.

SECTION I:

POLITICS, DEMOCRACY, AND ORGANISATIONS

Chapter 2

Tourism as Political Platform: Residents' Perceptions of Tourism and Voting Behaviour

Reil G. Cruz and Lisa Grace S. Bersales

Introduction

Richter (1989 in Cheong & Miller, 2000, p. 373) observed that there is often a political agenda ... underlying an explicit tourism programme. Cheong and Miller (2000) have noted that there has been very little research on tourism's political dimension. Ludwig Rieder's (1997) article on how the Marcoses of the Philippines used tourism to serve political ends is one of the few articles in current literature to have examined this area. Hardly any work has been devoted to examining residents' attitudes in developing countries, especially at the inception stage when the support and involvement of the local community is critical (Teye, Sonmez & Sirikaya, 2002). Moreover, the bulk of US-based research has been on rural (rather than urban) residents' attitudes towards tourism (Madrigal, 1995 in Teye et al., 2002, p. 669).

This study fills many of the aforementioned gaps. It extends the theory by examining voting behaviour as a function of residents' perceptions of tourism. The study area is in an urban setting in a developing country involving a tourism product that is relatively new. In previous studies concerning resident perceptions of tourism, the emphasis has been on the factors that affect such perceptions. In other words, perception has been the dependent variable. In this research, residents' perception of tourism is used as the independent variable in order to analyze its effect on voting behaviour. This is also the first time that the role of tourism in the success of a politician is being studied. It is hypothesized that a positive perception of a tourism project will result to the residents' voting for the candidate that has been responsible for that tourism project. On the other hand, a negative perception of the tourism project will result to the residents' not voting for the candidate involved.

Background

Richard Gordon, the immediate past secretary of the Department of Tourism, ran as senator in the Philippine national elections of 10 May 2004. He won, placing fifth overall out of twelve possible seats. He now heads the Philippine Senate's Committee on Tourism. He was unique in the sense that he was the first senatorial candidate who ever used tourism as the major political platform. Platform is defined by New World Dictionary as "a statement of principles and policies [of a political candidate]".

As Olongapo City mayor in the 1970s, he created the local version of Mardi Gras Festival, which made the city famous as the entertainment capital of the Philippines. As Chairman of Subic Bay[1] Metropolitan Authority in the 1990s, he developed the former US military base into a world-class multi-attraction tourist destination. It became known as the only place in the Philippines where traffic and anti-littering rules were strictly enforced.

In the May 2004 electoral campaign, Gordon seemed to ride on the WOW[2] Philippines publicity. Tarpaulin billboards on major thoroughfares showed him white-water rafting with President Gloria Arroyo and her husband. Gordon focused on the theme "Tourism Means Jobs". "WOW" was used to create top-of-the-mind awareness, as in WOW Gordon! Prime-time television commercials had ordinary vendors offer testimonials of how Gordon's effective leadership has generated jobs and increased income for themselves and their families. Estimates placed the number of jobs generated by the project WOW Philippines – The Best of the Regions between 2800 and 4000, many as street sweepers and security personnel. Many others sold various products. Gordon convinced local politicians to underwrite some of the costs of producing posters for their respective provinces and put up exhibits and send cultural performers to WOW Philippines.

Intramuros is a must-see tourist destination because of its historical and architectural significance. Intramuros consists of about 88 hectares (Santiago, 2003). It was actually the core of the city of Manila during the Spanish period (16th to 20th century). Some of the famous attractions in Intramuros are San Agustin Church, Manila Cathedral, Fort Santiago, and Intramuros Golf Course.

The survey respondents were from the five *barangays*[3] in Intramuros. The five barangays have a total voting population of 8000 according to local officials.

Limitation of the Study

This study has some limitations. The questionnaire was not thoroughly pretested. The respondents were homogenous in socio-economic status (mostly belonging to the lower economic class) and therefore not representative of the Intramuros population. Lastly, the method used was quota sampling, whose results may not be as conclusive as that of random sampling. But nonetheless the results have produced some interesting if particularized insights into the relationship between local politics and tourism.

---

[1] Subic Bay was the site of the biggest US Naval Base outside the US. Olongapo used to serve as entertainment post for the servicemen until the base's closure in 1991.
[2] WOW Philippines was the brand and international advertising campaign adopted by the Philippine Department of Tourism during the term of Richard Gordon as Secretary of Tourism. "WOW" in WOW Philippines stands for several things: Wealth of Wonders, which was the main meaning, Wacko over Wildlife, Warm over Winter, Wear our Wares, and Watch our Whales. One of these, Walk our Walls, pertains to the historical Walled City of Intramuros.
[3] Roughly translated as village, barangay is the smallest unit in Philippine political structure. Several barangays make up a district.

Literature Review

Residents' perceptions and attitudes have constituted a major area of tourism research. They are important considerations if tourism programmes and projects were to be sustainable (Ap, 1992; Ap & Crompton, 1998; Allen, Long, Perdue & Kieselbach, 1988; Belisle & Hoy, 1980; Doxey, 1975; Lankford, 1994 in Brunt & Courtney, 1999, p. 494; Maddox, 1985; Murphy, 1983 in Williams & Lawson, 2001, p. 270). Williams and Lawson (2001) noted that perceptions of tourism have significant implications on the residents' (perceived) quality of life.

Numerous studies have identified the factors that affect perceptions. These are intrinsic and extrinsic variables (Faulkner & Tideswell, 1997 in Fredline & Faulkner, 2000, p. 765). Intrinsic variables include demographic characteristics, geographical proximity, activity concentration and involvement in tourism (Ap, 1992; Brougham & Butler, 1981; Milman & Pizam, 1988; Pizam, 1978; Pizam, Milman & King, 1994; in Fredline & Faulkner, 2000, p. 766; Teo, 1994). Extrinsic factors refer to product life cycle stage, seasonality and cultural differences between tourists and residents (Butler, 1980; Butler, 1975 in Fredline & Faulkner, 2000, p. 766; Belisle & Hoy, 1980; Doxey, 1975; Sheldon & Var, 1984).

In their extensive review, Williams and Lawson (2001) presented a long list of variables that affect residents' attitudes towards tourism. These are (a) distance of respondents' home from tourism centre, (b) attachment to the community, (c) knowledge of the effects of tourism, (d) length of residency in the community, (e) being native born, (f) ethnicity, (g) retail activity attributable to tourism as a proportion of total retail activity, (h) level of knowledge about tourism and the local economy, (i) level of contact with tourists, (j) perceived impact on local recreation opportunities, (k) perceived ability to influence tourism planning decisions, and (l) gender.

In general, socioeconomic variables have been found to have little relationship to resident perceptions of tourism (Liu & Var, 1986; Madrigal, 1993; Pizam, 1978 in Madrigal, 1995, p. 87), while heavy tourism concentration (Madrigal, 1993; Pizam, 1978), greater length of residency in the community (Liu & Var, 1986; Madrigal, 1993; Pizam, 1978; Um & Crompton, 1987), and native-born status (Canaan & Hennessy, 1989; Davis, Allen & Cosenza, 1988; Um & Crompton, 1987) have been found to be linked to greater negative perception of tourism (Madrigal, 1995, p. 86). Economic reliance has been linked to more positive perceptions of tourism (Madrigal, 1993; Milman & Pizam, 1988; Pizam, 1978 in Madrigal 1995, pp. 86–87). Belisle and Hoy (1980) reported a positive relationship between distance of residence from the central tourism zone and perceptions (Madrigal, 1995, p. 87). Lindberg and Johnson's 1997 studies of value-attitude models showed that residents who place importance on a growing economy are likely to have positive attitudes towards tourism. They also concluded that beliefs about tourism's effect on congestion have greater effect on resident attitudes than beliefs of its effect on crime.

Doxey (1975) developed the Irritation Index (Irridex) Model (Mercer, 1998, p. 122; Pearce, 1998, p. 141) that suggests residents' attitudes to tourists deteriorate over time. Doxey assumed that residents react uniformly at every stage of tourism development. Smith and Krannich (1998) found that increasing levels of tourism dependence in a community are associated with increasingly negative attitudes towards its further development, as well as lower levels of local satisfaction, and higher levels of crime concern. Mason and Cheyne (2000), on the other hand, found that there was a significant opposition to proposed development, contrary to Doxey's theory that residents would greet tourism with euphoria at the inception stage. Ap (1992) established that response to tourism development was not necessarily a function of the product life cycle. Using social exchange theory as theoretical framework, Ap concluded that people's attitudes towards tourism were instead a function of the perceived benefit that they derive from it (Fredline & Faulkner, 2000, p. 766). In essence, social exchange theory presupposes that people will have a more positive attitude to tourism if the costs that it (tourism) might entail (congestion, extended hospitality to tourists, etc.) will be commensurate to the benefits (employment, improved infrastructure, etc.) that they can derive from it (Madrigal, 1995). Gursoy, Jurowski, and Uysal (2002) found that community support for tourism development is affected by the level of community concern, the utilization of tourism resource base by local residents, level of ecocentric values of residents, the state of local economy, the perceived costs and perceived benefits of tourism development. In Teye et al., research (2002) however, the main conclusion was that it is the nature of the employment and the context within which this employment occurs that is more theoretically important. They found that those working in the tourism industry had actually very negative attitude about tourism because the expectations for tourism as a vehicle for economic development were not realized. Frustrations were caused by the predominance of organized tours, the lack of attractions that can be offered to tourists, the seasonal character of tourism, low occupancy, high leakage, low wages, and long work hours.

Studies that used social representations theory as theoretical framework showed that resident perceptions are a function of the cluster or groups in which residents belong. Muscovici (1963) defined social representations as "the elaborating of a social object by the community for the purpose of behaving and communicating ... They are like theories or systems of knowledge that include values, ideas, and guides for behaviour that allow communities to make sense of their social world" (Pearce, 1998, p. 143). The main sources of social representations are direct experience, social interactions, and the media (Fredline & Faulkner, 2000, pp. 767–768).

Weaver and Lawton (2001) found that any particular stage of tourism development seems to be accompanied by a bell-curve of resident perceptions as revealed in cluster analysis rather than a uniform response as proposed by Doxey. They found that people who are most cynical about tourism rate community issues more highly than other issues; people who are most positive about tourism rate community issues lowest. They conclude further that its implication for public policy lies in that rather than highlighting economic incentives, authorities should emphasize how tourism provides better facilities for local people to enjoy and provides incentives to protect the natural environment, and how the planning authorities take the views of local residents seriously.

So far none of the literature has dealt with finding the relationship between perception of tourism impacts and voting behaviour.

Methodology

The objectives of this study are to determine how perception of tourism affects residents' voting behaviour, and what factors are significant in affecting this behaviour.

Data collection was done by personal interview using a questionnaire. The questionnaire contained the following parts:

1 Demographic characteristics, such as barangay of residence, age, sex, educational attainment, civil status, period of residence in Intramuros, place of birth, occupation, and place of work.
2 Knowledge of WOW Philippines – what was it about and whose project it was.
3 The senators the respondent voted for (list of senators presented to the respondent included Richard Gordon, with other names used only as decoys).
4 Perceptions on the effects of WOW Philippines – environmental effects, economic effects, socio-cultural effects.
5 Question on whether the respondent's income increased or decreased with the introduction of WOW Philippines in Intramuros.

Perceptions on the effects of WOW Philippines were measured using a five-point Likert scale: (1) strongly disagree, (2) disagree, (3) neutral, (4) agree, (5) strongly agree. These items totalled 28 – with 6 items on environmental effects, 9 items on economic effects, and 13 items on socio-cultural effects. The items for the questionnaire were derived from the review of literature and personal interviews of initial respondents.

Because of WOW Philippines…	Factor
1. I was able to get a job.	Economic
2. The amount of litter increased.	Environmental
3. My income increased.	Economic
4. The roads in (the special district of) Intramuros were improved.	Environmental
5. My life became better.	Socio-cultural
6. The price of goods increased.	Economic
7. I was able to establish my own business.	Economic
8. Our lives were disturbed because of tourists.	Socio-cultural
9. Our place began to stink.	Environmental
10. Cultural attractions have been maintained.	Socio-cultural
11. I became poorer.	Economic
12. I became prouder of Intramuros.	Socio-cultural
13. My knowledge about Intramuros increased.	Socio-cultural
14. Intramuros became more peaceful.	Socio-cultural
15. The variety of recreational activities increased.	Socio-cultural
16. Rent for stalls increased.	Economic
17. Real estate taxes that I am paying increased.	Economic
18. The number of outside investors increased.	Economic
19. Traffic inside Intramuros improved.	Environmental
20. Parking became more difficult.	Environmental
21. Intramuros became a nicer place to visit.	Environmental
22. Snatchers and gangs increased.	Socio-cultural
23. Prostitution became rampant.	Socio-cultural

24.	Rumbles increased.	Socio-cultural
25.	Intramuros residents became united.	Socio-cultural
26.	I learned more about the cultures of the regions in the Philippines.	Socio-cultural
27.	The architectural heritage of Intramuros has been maintained.	Socio-cultural
28.	The number of my customers increased.	Economic

Factor analysis was performed to look for factors that reflect the perceptions of the respondents in the items of the questionnaires. Logistic regression analysis was done to determine what demographic characteristics and which voters' perceptions are significantly related to residents' tendency to vote for Gordon.

Items which had non-responses of more than 10% were not included in factor analysis and logistic regression since they would decrease the observations actually used in the estimation and statistical tests. Thus, only 17 perception items were retained in the statistical analyses. These are:

Because of WOW Philippines...

1. The amount of litter increased.
2. The roads in Intramuros were improved.
3. My life became better.
4. The price of goods increased.
5. Our lives were disturbed because of tourists.
6. Our place began to stink.
7. Cultural attractions have been maintained.
8. I became poorer.
9. I became prouder of Intramuros.
10. My knowledge about Intramuros increased.
11. Intramuros became more peaceful.
12. The variety of recreational activities increased.
11. Traffic inside Intramuros improved.
14. Parking became more difficult.
15. Intramuros became a nicer place to visit.
16. I learned more about the cultures of the regions in the Philippines.
17. The architectural heritage of Intramuros has been maintained.

The authors initially attempted to conduct a stratified random sampling of the voting population. Problems, such as, our survey-takers not being entertained by the residents of the big houses in the area and labyrinthine arrangement of households in the squatter sections, forced the authors to adopt a quota sample instead. The quota sample was proportionate to the population of voters in each of the five barangays. A total sample size of 96 was deemed adequate for the population (8000) involved. In the sampling, care was taken in order not to get more than one respondent per household. Computations were done using SPSS and EVIEWS statistical software.

Table 2.1: Sampled respondents by barangay.

	Barangay	**Frequency**	**%**
Valid	654	10	10.4
	655	21	21.9
	656	24	25.0
	657	16	16.7
	658	25	26.0
Total		96	100.0

Table 2.1 shows the distribution of sampled respondents by barangay.

The study area chosen was Intramuros, the site of the event. Intramuros offered the advantages of smallness and easy access. According to Capenerhurst (1994), small communities are likely to react more strongly to (tourism) development as it will be far more visible to them… It is at the local level where facilities are seen to be built, where land and other resources are allocated between competing users, and where the wishes of permanent residents need to be accommodated as well as visitors (Mason & Cheyne, 2000, p. 395).

Findings

Majority of the respondents are females (57%), born in Luzon Island (52%), have lived in Intramuros since 1987 (53%), finished at most high school education (58%), are married (66%), employed (75%), and work in Intramuros (83%). Most (46%) are 39-year old and below. The voters surveyed were homogeneous with respect to socio-economic status. Almost all are in marginal jobs or in small-scale businesses such as vendors, pedicab drivers, and variety store owners.

When asked if their incomes increased because of WOW Philippines, 18% of Intramuros residents surveyed said yes, 3% said they incurred losses; the rest either did not respond or said that their incomes were not dependent on WOW Philippines.

All the respondents have knowledge of WOW Philippines. This is expected since Intramuros is the site of the event and is also a major tourist area being promoted by the said project. About 9 in 10 respondents (86 people or 90%) attributed the project to Gordon. The other persons and agencies mentioned were President Arroyo, Manila Mayor Atienza, Intramuros Administration General Manager Ferrer, the Department of Tourism, Philippine Tourism Authority, and Intramuros Administration.

Majority (67%) of the respondents voted for Gordon (Table 2.2).

Barangay 655 gave the highest percentage of votes in favor of Gordon, while 656 gave him the lowest percentage of votes. Barangay 655 happens to be the barangay where the core of WOW Philippines facilities is located. It is from Barangay 655 captain where clearances for WOW businesses are obtained. Gordon was highly praised by the barangay officials for his "pro-poor project" which generated jobs for a lot of people from Barangay 655. During the last elections, the Barangay Chairman even placed Gordon's name on his sample ballot (interview with a Barangay Councilor).

Table 2.2: Respondent voting data.

Barangay[D4]	Sample size	Number who voted for Gordon	%
654	10	7	70
655	21	19	90
656	24	8	33
657	16	8	50
658	25	22	88
	96	64	67

Barangay 656 on the other hand is on the fringes of Intramuros and is physically far-thest from the tourism centre. This is the barangay whose residents benefit the least from WOW Philippines. Many of the residents here were displaced due to a fire that gutted their makeshift houses. There are rumours that the fire was deliberately set to drive the residents away to make way for a promenade, shopping arcade, and cafes. Its Barangay Chairman was critical of WOW Philippines Project. He calls it WOW *Mali*! (WOW What A Mistake!). He maintained that the project entailed huge government expenditures that at best created only temporary livelihood opportunities for the people. "And what of the regions? Has there been any monitoring if the regional governments actually made money from this project?" he asked rhetorically. "Gordon used WOW Philippines to advance his senatorial bid. Gordon had only short-term plans for election purposes". The local leader lamented that the welfare of residents was not taken into account in tourism development. "A thorough study must first be carried out before any decision could be adopted", the chairman said.

Factor analysis yielded five main factors that represent 54% of the information that the 17 items gave. These were cultural awareness, sense of well-being, environment, traffic, and economic hardship. These factors were defined mainly by the elements highlighted in Table 2.3.

Overall, residents placed higher importance on socio-cultural and environmental aspects than on the economic.

Logistic regression results showed that the factors that gave significant information on whether a resident voted for Gordon as senator in the 10 May 2004 election were the following:

1 Distance of residence from tourism centre
2 Marital status
3 Factor 1 (cultural awareness)
4 Factor 2 (sense of well-being).

All things being equal, the nearer the residence to the tourism centre, the higher the score that a voter gives to cultural appreciation factor, the higher would be the chance that a resident would vote for Gordon. On the other hand, respondents who are married and those that gave higher scores to quality of life tended not to vote for Gordon.

Table 2.3: Factor analysis.

Factor	(Number in questionnaire) Perception items	Weight
Factor 1	(27) Architectural heritage	0.757
Cultural awareness	(26) Knowledge of local cultures	0.735
	(13) Knowledge about Intramuros	0.714
	(21) Intramuros a nicer place to visit	0.635
Factor 2	(14) Intramuros became peaceful	0.653
Sense of well-being	(15) More variety in recreational activities	0.600
	(5) Better life	0.513
Factor 3	(2) Increased litter	−0.816
Environment	(4) Improved roads	0.520
Factor 4	(19) Improved traffic	0.526
Traffic concerns	(20) Worse parking	−0.443
Factor 5	(11) Became poorer	0.646
Economic hardship	(8) Disturbance from tourists	0.512
and disturbance		

The estimated regression equation is given below:

Logit (probability that voter votes for Gordon) = 3.84 Near − 2.23 Mid − 1.64 Married + 0.69 Factor 1 − 0.71 Factor 2

Where

Near is a dummy variable representing residence in Barangay 655

Mid is a dummy variable representing residence in Barangays 654, 657, 658

Married is a dummy variable representing civil status married

Factor 1 is the factor representing cultural awareness

Factor 2 is the factor representing well-being.

This estimated logistic regression equation has good fit with 92% correct prediction for those who voted for Gordon and 64% correct prediction for those who did not vote for Gordon.

Perception and voting behaviour

To analyze the relationship between perception and voting behaviour, it was necessary to segregate those items that constituted negative impacts from the positive ones. The negative impacts are:

Because of WOW Philippines...

1. The amount of litter increased.
2. The price of goods increased.
3. Our lives were disturbed because of tourists.
4. Our place began to stink.
5. I became poorer.
6. Parking became more difficult.

In determining whether a respondent generally agrees that WOW Philippines generated negative impact, the average of the scores given by each respondent across the 6 negative items was obtained. If the mean score was 3.46 to 5, the respondent is considered to agree that WOW Philippines created negative impacts. (The respondent perceives that WOW Philippines created negative impacts.) If the average score for the 6 items was 1 to 3.45, then the respondent is said not to agree that WOW Philippines created negative impacts.

The same procedure was used for the positive impacts. For each respondent, the average score for the 11 items (Numbers 4, 5, 10, 12, 13, 14, 15, 19, 21, 26, and 27) was obtained. If the mean score was 3.46 to 5, the respondent is considered to agree that WOW Philippines generally created positive impacts. (The resident perceives that WOW

Table 2.4: Impacts data analysis.

Sector	$n = 96$	Married $n = 63$	Non-married $n = 33$	Bgy 655 $n = 21$	Bgy 656 $n = 24$	Bgys except Bgy 655 $n = 75$
Number who perceive WOW Philippines generated negative impacts	12	9	3	2	4	10
Number who did not vote for Gordon	7	6	1	1	2	5
Probability of negative perception leading to non-vote for Gordon	58.3%	66.7%	33.3%	50%	50%	50%
Number who perceive WOW Philippines generated positive impacts	69	46	23	16	11	53
Number who voted for Gordon	54	34	21	15	5	40
Probability of positive perception leading to vote for Gordon	78.3%	73.9%	91.3%	93.8%	45.4%	75.5%

Philippines created positive impacts.) If the average score for the 6 items was 1 to 3.45, then the respondent is said not to agree that WOW Philippines created positive impacts.

- *In the total sample of 96 respondents...*
  Out of the 12 who perceived that WOW Philippines generated negative impact, 7 (58%) did not vote for Gordon. Out of the 84 who perceived that WOW Philippines did not generate negative impacts 59 (70%) voted for Gordon.
  Out of the 69 who perceived that WOW Philippines generated positive impacts, 54 (78%) voted for Gordon. Out of the 27 who perceived that WOW Philippines did not generate positive impacts, 18 (67%) did not vote for Gordon.
- *Among the married respondents (n = 63)...*
  Out of 9 who perceived that WOW Philippines generated negative impacts, 6 (67%) did not vote for Gordon. Out of 54 who perceived that WOW Philippines did not generate negative impacts 35 (65%) voted for Gordon.
  Out of 46 who perceived that WOW Philippines generated positive impacts, 34 (74%) voted for Gordon. Out of 17 who perceived that WOW Philippines did not generate positive impacts, 13 (76%) did not vote for Gordon.
- *Among residents who are single, separated, or widowed (n = 33)...*
  Out of 3 who perceived that WOW Philippines generated negative impacts, 1 (33%) did not vote for Gordon. Out of 30 who perceived that WOW Philippines did not generate negative impacts 23 (77%) voted for Gordon.
  Out of 23 who perceived that WOW Philippines generated positive impacts, 21 (91%) voted for Gordon. Out of 10 who perceived that WOW Philippines did not generate positive impacts, 5 (50%) did not vote for Gordon.
- *Among Bgy 655 residents (n = 21)...*
  Out of 2 who perceived that WOW Philippines generated negative impacts, 1 (50%) did not vote for Gordon. Out of 19 who perceived that WOW Philippines did not generate negative impacts 17 (90%) voted for Gordon.
  Out of 16 who perceived that WOW Philippines generated positive impacts, 15 (94%) voted for Gordon. Out of 5 who perceived that WOW Philippines did not generate positive impacts, 2 (40%) did not vote for Gordon.
- *Among residents Bgy 656, the farthest barangay from the tourism core (n = 24)...*
  Out of 4 who perceived that WOW Philippines generated negative impacts, 2 (50%) did not vote for Gordon. Out of 20 who perceived that WOW Philippines did not generate negative impacts 7 (35%) voted for Gordon.
  Out of 11 who perceived that WOW Philippines generated positive impacts, 5 (45%) voted for Gordon (Table 2.4). Out of 13 who perceived that WOW Philippines did not generate positive impacts, 10 (77%) did not vote for Gordon.

Conclusions

The findings show that distance of residence from tourist centre, marital status, cultural awareness, and sense of well-being were determinants of voting behaviour.

It can be concluded that tourism as a political platform has served Gordon well in catapulting him to the Philippine Senate, mainly because of the positive perceptions of WOW

Philippines – The Best of the Regions, and his being closely identified with the successful project. However, the reasons for the positive perception were non-economic (as Gordon flaunted during the campaign) but factors relating to cultural awareness and sense of well-being.

There was an overwhelming general perception among Intramuros residents that tourism activity (WOW Philippines) generated positive impacts more than negative impacts.

The results show a significant relationship between residents' perception of tourism and voting behaviour. Positive perceptions of tourism tended to result to a vote for Gordon, negative perceptions of tourism tended to result to non-vote for Gordon. However, positive perception in general is more predictive of positive voter behaviour than negative perception is of negative voting behaviour.

Among the married respondents, the probability of not voting for Gordon as a result of perceived negative impacts was higher than for those who are single, separated, or widowed. The probability of voting for Gordon as a result of positive impacts was lower among married respondents than among those who are either single, separated, or widowed. It could be that married individuals are more affected and acutely aware of quality of life factors than those who are non-married individuals.

It is also noted that compared with Bgy 655 residents, Bgy 656 residents were more critical of tourism with higher percentage perceiving tourism generating negative impacts and lower percentage perceiving tourism generating positive impacts. The probability of voting for Gordon was lower in Bgy 656 than in Bgy 655.

In order to validate the results of this study, it may be necessary to replicate this in similarly situated communities during an election time. The problem of course will be finding a candidate who will build his platform around tourism. For Intramuros, using a random sampling methodology might be able to prove or disprove the results of this present research.

Acknowledgements

The authors wish to thank the University of the Philippines for the faculty research dissemination grant. They would also like to acknowledge the assistance extended by their colleagues at the UP Asian Institute of Tourism Division of Tourism Research and Extension Services for helping out in the field survey in Intramuros, Manila. Finally, we wish to express our gratitude to everyone who has been part of the review process leading to the publication of this article as a book chapter.

References

Brunt, P., & Courtney, P. (1999). Host perceptions of sociocultural impacts. *Annals of Tourism Research, 26*(3), 493–515.

Cheong, S., & Miller, M. (2000). Power and tourism: A Foucaldian observation. *Annals of Tourism Research, 27*(2), 371–390.

Fredline, E., & Faulkner, B. (2000). Host community reactions: A cluster analysis. *Annals of Tourism Research, 27*(3), 763–784.

Gursoy, D., Jurowski, C., & Uysal, M. (2002). Resident attitudes: A structural modeling approach. *Annals of Tourism Research, 29*(1), 79–105.

Lindberg, K., & Johnson, R. (1997). Modeling resident attitudes toward tourism. *Annals of Tourism Research, 24*(2), 402–424.

Madrigal, R. (1995). Residents' Perceptions and the role of government. *Annals of Tourism Research, 22*(1), 86–105.

Mason, P., & Cheyne, J. (2000). Residents' attitudes to proposed tourism development. *Annals of Tourism Research, 27*(2), 391–411.

Mercer, D. (1998). The uneasy relationship between tourism and native peoples: The Australian experience. In: W. Theobald (Ed.), *Global tourism* (pp. 98–128). Oxford: Butterworth-Heinemann.

Pearce, P. (1998). The relationship between residents and tourists: The research literature and management directions. In: W. Theobald (Ed.), *Global tourism* (pp. 129–149). Oxford: Butterworth-Heinemann.

Rieder, L. (1997). The development of Philippine tourism in the post-marcos era. In: Go, F., & Jenkins, C. (Eds.), *Tourism and economic development in Asia and Australasia* (pp. 222–236). London: Cassell.

Santiago, A. M. (2003). The restoration of historic Intramuros: A case study in plan implementation. *Quezon City: School of urban and regional planning* (pp. 1, 45–57). University of the Philippines and UP Planning and Development Research Foundation, Inc.

Smith, M., & Krannich, R. (1998). Tourism dependence and resident attitudes. *Annals of Tourism Research, 25*(4), 783–802.

Teye, V., Sonmez, S., & Sirikaya, E. (2002). Resident attitudes toward tourism development. *Annals of Tourism Research, 29*(3), 668–688.

Weaver, D., & Lawton, L. (2001). Resident perceptions in the urban–rural fringe. *Annals of Tourism Research, 28*(2), 439–458.

Williams, J., & Lawson, R. (2001). Community issues and resident opinions of tourism. *Annals of Tourism Research, 28*(2), 269–290.

Chapter 3

Privatisation during Market Economy Transformation as a Motor of Development

Heike Bähre

Introduction

Privatisation as a reform of property rights, the rights of disposal included, is considered the basis for market economy transformation. Especially for the tourism industry market transformation is seen to play a special role in creating small- and middle-sized businesses as a motor of economic development. From the viewpoint of transformation research and tourism science, this chapter discusses aspects of privatisation as a requirement of a national tourism policy in a market economy transformation of the tourism sector. Market economy transformation is always analysed from the point of view of a necessary democratisation of society.

System Transformation, the Reform of Property Rights and Tourism Politics

Systems Theory, Transformation Research and Tourism Science

The theoretical foundation of this chapter concerning property transformation in the tourism sector is systems theory. Systems theory is an auxiliary construct for the systematisation of the complex human environment. A system comparison brings into relief the qualitative and also the quantitative differences between different social systems and furthermore permits changes between the old and new structures of a social system to be illustrated over time. The formulations of institutional economics allow the models of systems theory additionally to take on a dynamic dimension, making it possible to differentiate between formal regulations and the more gradually changing informal rules or norms, focussing upon the interaction of parliamentary democracy, interest groups and administrative structures in economic politics within the framework of market-economy and democratic system transformation.

Transformation can be concisely described as a "transition from one system state to another". If a new quality is achieved in the state of a society or socio-economic system, so it is possible to observe a new quality or "quality jump" (see Bähre, 2003, p. 65; Hanel, 2000, p. 153; Wrobel, 1999, p. 139).

Like transformation research, tourism science is concerned with complex phenomena. To do justice to the complexity of the market economy transformation of the tourism sector, a diversity of methods is required rather than an exclusive decision for one single scientific method. Geographical maps enable the geographical distribution of tourism supply and demand to be depicted in the individual destinations and thus permit the destinations to be ranked at the beginning of and during the transformation process. Historical chronological tables illustrate the process of transformation and the institutional changes in tourism occurring during that process. Official statistics and regular tourism surveys of tourism supply and demand not only assist in monitoring tourism development but also illustrate changes in the individual branch segments of tourism, such as business and holiday travel or within the accommodation sector.

Economic Systems According to Ownership and Planning, Economic and Tourism Policy and the Role of the State

Economic systems can be differentiated according to planning and ownership. For Marxists, ownership of the means of production by itself characterises the economic system (cf. Blum, 2000, p. 519). However, the constitution of ownership (known also as the property system) is generally assigned the central role, as it is considered to be the heart of any economic and social system. The constitution of ownership determines the manner in which property rights to economic goods are distributed. Thus, sellers and buyers on the market are not only exchanging goods for money: each transaction also involves an exchange of rights. Ownership and disposal rights describe rights and duties that are determined by the existence of limited resources. These rights are also the prerequisite for the rational use of resources. Within the context of the free market legal system, the use of ownership and disposal rights is limited whenever general interests are affected.

Economics makes a distinction between a centrally controlled or command economy and a market economy. Owing to the interdependence of the political and the economic subsystems within a social system (of the socio-economic system), these two basic types (centrally controlled economy and market economy) can be combined with different basic political system types. Thus the centrally controlled economies of yesterday and today were and are almost always characterised by a dictatorship or an oligarchic system of government (cf. Bernholz & Breyer, 1993, p. 230). In formal terms, with reference to the "dictatorship versus democracy" dichotomy, there are the following combinations (cf. Wrobel, 1999, pp. 62–63):

1 Market economy and democracy
2 Market economy and dictatorship
3 Centrally controlled economy and democracy
4 Centrally controlled economy and dictatorship.

In the long term, a centrally controlled economy cannot be conceived without a dictatorship. On the other hand, however, a market economy is compatible with a dictatorship, at least in the medium term (cf. Wrobel, 1999, p. 63, after Schwarz, 1992 and Leipold, 1994).

Economic policy objectives are derived from fundamental social values. In many Western industrial nations, freedom, justice and security can today be considered the principal fundamental social values. In contrast to Western democracies, in the former so-called socialist countries, the freedom paradigm was entirely under the influence of the diktat of Marxist/ Leninist social theory and the ideological control of the institutions established to serve it. Protection of nature is now becoming increasingly more important and is situated alongside the three above-mentioned negatives in its role as the fourth determinant of economic development (cf. Bähre, 2003, p. 35; Klump, 1992, p. 148).

In market economy systems, governmental authority penetrates into those areas in which economic policy objectives are influenced by super-ordinate objectives and by fundamental social values (e.g. the areas of education, defence/security and public health). Lehmbruch (1998) notes that governmental activity has been sectorised since the beginnings of the interventionalist and welfare state, as testified by the classification according to policy domains contained in Lorenz von Stein's eight-volume work entitled *Verwaltungslehre* (Administration Science) (1865–1884) (cf. Lehmbruch, 1998, p. 24).

Privatisation and Institutional Change Within the Market Economy Transformation

Transformation – Endogenous and Exogenous Institutional Change

In a state obligated to a "doctrine of salvation" (e.g. Marxist/Leninist dogma), all areas of society, including permitted parties, organisations and state administration (bureaucracy), and all policy domains are subordinate to this doctrine elevated to a governmental doctrine. This doctrine also determines the social values concerning the tourism sector and tourism policy. In contrast to a dictatorship, in a democratic system, acceptance of the individual's interest is a constituent part of that system. The democratic society is legitimised by the ties between decisions concerning society as a whole and individual interests. The legitimacy of democratic systems is based on the functioning communication of interests (cf. Teuber, 2001, p. 65, with reference to Abromeit, 1993, p. 7). Interest groups, also known as lobby or pressure groups, are typical as far as parliamentary democracies are concerned, but are alien to dictatorships. Analyses from the field of transformation research have shown that institutional change in respect to the post-socialist transformation of the remaining central and eastern European countries must occur (largely) endogenously (i.e. from the inside), while as far as the accession of the German Democratic Republic (GDR) to the Federal Republic of Germany (FRG) was concerned, there was the possibility of "extensive institutional transfer" (Lehmbruch, 1991) (i.e. exogenous institutional change). During the reunification of Germany, "transformation and reunification overlapped and mingled" (Czada, 1997).

The Sector Concept, Political Fields and the Explanation of Sector Transformation Paths According to Lehmbruch and Czada

In order to illuminate the market economic transformation of the tourism industry within the context of the transformation of ownership, it is necessary to consider the subdivision of the economy in accordance with the three-sector model commonly used in Germany. This model distinguishes between:

- the primary sector: agriculture (production factor: soil, soil intensive);
- the secondary sector: industry (production factor: capital, capital intensive);
- the tertiary sector: services (production factors: work and knowledge, work (knowledge) intensive).

While the tourism industry is generally assigned to the services sector, it is not actually an "industry" in the sense of economic production. Rather, the tourism industry is a functional category for the use of economic production, to which many industries contribute, and in which all economic sectors participate indirectly, through the demand for tourism goods (see DIW, 1999, pp. 5–6).

In general, the conceptual constructs "primary, secondary and tertiary sectors" combine very heterogeneous economic sectors, but these descriptive aggregates do not represent social structures (cf. Lehmbruch, 1998, p. 26). The "Governance Principle" (Williamson, 1975; 1985) flowing from the new institutional economy takes into account the social structures within and among the various economic sectors. In their transformational analysis, which focuses on a reorganisation of ownership rights, Lehmbruch and Czada discover sector-specific regularities, or "sectoral paths of transformation" [Lehmbruch 1998, Czada (eds)] (Figure 3.1). In their view, sectors are distinguished not only by the equivalent and related products and services which they produce or offer and the common technical and management features which emerge as a result (cf. Lehmbruch, 1998, pp. 26–27), the authors also point out that real market economies are comprised not only of sectors determined by the free market alone and sectors which are "potentially or actually in competition with each other", but also of sectors which rank high on a state intervention scale in free market societies as well, and which are determined by "policy domains" (cf. Lehmbruch, 1998, p. 30, with reference to Laumann & Knoke, 1987).

In summary, there are three types of sectors with a high degree of state intervention with respect to the reorganisation of sector-specific property rights:

- sectors with a proximity to the state, in which the state, even in western Germany, far beyond the definition of framework conditions or basic institutions, has long specified the concrete structure of sector-specific property rights in detail;
- sectors with a relatively high proximity to the market, which are characterised by a high degree of state intervention, even in western Germany;
- sectors consisting of state-owned businesses (a comparable GDR term is the "societal ownership of the means of production").

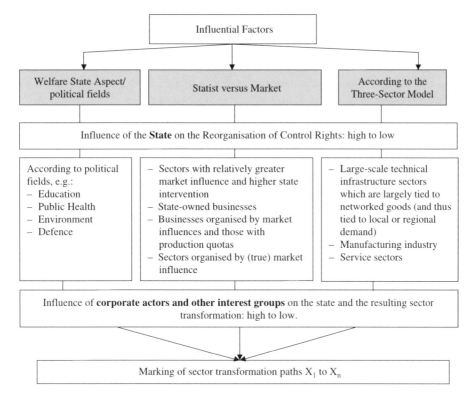

Figure 3.1: Flow chart depicting political fields and sector transformation paths, with respect to the reorganisation of sector-specific property rights according to Lehmbruch and Czada. *Source*: Own depiction (with reference to Czada & Lehmbruch (eds.) 1998).

There are three further categories of economic sectors with a unique type of transformation (a specific path of transformation):

- large-scale technical infrastructure sectors,
- the manufacturing industry,
- service sectors (cf. Czada, 1997).

Large-scale technical infrastructure sectors (such as telecommunications, water management, energy supply) provide semi-public, largely network-bound goods. They are relatively statist in nature. Negotiations at the state level are made possible through regulatory specifications, direct public participation and cartel-like self-organisation. Pure monopoly structures, such as potassium carbonate mining in Germany, are even more open to intervention. The transformation of eastern German potassium carbonate mining was determined by a single broad privatisation contract signed by the *Treuhandanstalt* – the state's official agency for privatisation – and the western German firm *Kali und Salze*. Like the service sector, the infrastructure sectors profit from their own regional and local demand: businesses must invest locally in order to serve their customers. In state-organised sectors and sectors with a close relationship to the state, the government can make use of existing planning measures. Given that the postal service, telecommunications and railroad were still under federal administration at the time of reunification, the state was able to decree paths of transformation for these sectors. The industrial sectors closely tied to the market (e.g. mechanical engineering), as well as those so-called "sectors" that are organised closely to the market and subject to a collective mass regulation (e.g. shipbuilding) offer a stark contrast to the above. The transformational function of these branches is to modernise and create private, extremely robust businesses that can survive global competition (cf. Czada, 1997, pp. 7–8, with reference to Hoffmann, 1993; Wegner, 1996; Welfens, 1996).

With respect to the reconstruction of the service sectors, subsections trading and banking, in eastern Germany, rapid progress has been observed, primarily in the form of an extension of the market territories of western German providers. Any related changes in managerial structures are primarily tied to market developments rather than to reunification. For example, during the construction of shopping centres in eastern Germany, investors were able to shift to outlying areas without restraint, while in the West they would have had to face earnest protests from the relevant municipalities (cf. Czada, 1997, p. 7). This example serves to illustrate that the development of the trading sector is not unaffected by changes in other areas, such as local government.

In cases of rapid transformation the configuration of sectors is particularly susceptible to negative developments (cf. Czada, 1997, p. 6). The transformational result in eastern Germany is ultimately contingent upon the extent to which the basic institutions of the market economy penetrate the new organisation of eastern German sector institutions. The more the sector governance structure has been marked by markets or market-similar mechanisms, the greater the transformational result has been influenced by the dominant corporate and institutional members of the relevant sector in the former Federal Republic. The sector transfer of institutions was more successful in those instances when the state was able to suspend free market mechanisms during the reorganisation of disposal rights (cf. Lehmbruch, 2000, p. 123f.). Because the German state has not generally implemented governance measures in respect to restructuring property rights as the basis for creating a highly competitive market structure (Czada & Lehmbruch, 1998), in many regions of eastern Germany it has not yet been possible to establish a self-supporting economic structure. A transfer economy has come into existence. Financially, eastern Germany is still drip fed by western Germany today.

The sectoral paths of transformation that Czada and Lehmbruch uncovered can also be observed in the restructuring of property and disposal rights, as well as in the reorganisation of the tourism industry. However, because the tourism industry is unique, there are multiple possible transformation paths, depending on the particular kind and forms of tourism.

Provisions for the Restructuring of Disposal and Property Rights in the Market Transformation of Eastern Germany

Article 10 of the GDR's constitution defined different types of property: "property belonging to society as a whole, cooperative common property of workers' collectives and property belonging to social organisations of citizens" (*gesamtgesellschaftliches Volkseigentum, genossenschaftliches Gemeineigentum werktätiger Kollektive und Eigentum gesellschaftlicher Organisationen der Bürger)* (cf. Constitution of the GDR).

In the process of restructuring and reinstating property rights along the principles of the unification treaty and the laws enacted in connection with that treaty, both while the GDR still existed and after, property was to be reorganised as follows:

- Municipal property (i.e. property of municipalities and regional corporations within the framework of municipalisation).
- Property of parties and organisations. In this instance a special Independent Commission *(Unabhängige Kommission)* was founded that would determine whether, according to the GDR's Party Law (PartG-DDR), said parties and organisations had acquired their property legally. This process entailed property allocation and the restoration to previous owners (reprivatisation). The actual goal, however, was not privatisation; rather it was to involve the removal of privileges in cases where property had been acquired or used illegally.
- Property of private persons and legal persons (i.e. privatisation and reprivatisation).
- Special assets of the federal government or owners used by the government, as for the GDR's Deutsche Post (postal service, see Article 27 of the unification treaty) and the Deutsche Reichsbahn (the GDR's railway service, see Article 26).

In addition there were irregularities during the transformation of collective property, which will not be discussed here. The legal provisions made the short-term exploitation of property belonging to the Party and other organisations very difficult. Under the law, the *Treuhandanstalt* was compelled to work with the consent of the Independent Commission and the *Bundesamt zur Regelung offener Vermögensfragen* (Federal Office for the Settlement of Property Issues, or BARoV).

The *Ur-Treuhandanstalt* (the original trust authority) existed from March to June 1990, based on the Modrow government. The first 120 employees of the *Ur-Treuhandanstalt* were culled from GDR ministries (cf. Czada, 1993, p. 155). On 1 July 1990, the Law for the Privatisation and Reorganisation of State-Owned Property, or the Trust Act (*Gesetz zur Privatisierung und Reorganisation des volkseigenen Vermögens, or Treuhandgesetz – THG*), removed the legal jurisdiction of the *Modrow* interim government and thus ended the *Ur-Treuhandanstalt*. The Unification Treaty of 31 August 1990 transformed the *Treuhandanstalt* into a legal federal institution in public law.

While the *Ur-Treuhandanstalt's* primary mission had essentially been to preserve state-owned property, the Treuhandanstalt's focus was on reorganising the economic structure of the new federal states through privatisation.

Once they had created a management board and supervisory board, lawmakers created a constitution for the *Treuhandanstalt*, which resembled that of a joint-stock company. According to the Trust Act, as well as the Round Table's conceptualisation, state-owned property (designated in the GDR as "people's property") should henceforth truly become the property of the people of the GDR (cf. Kloepfer & Unger, 1993, p. 55, with reference to Busche, 1993). The ultimate disregard of trust companies was in technical violation of the law, though it did transpire with official (political) sanction (cf. idem: 77. For more information see Seibel & Kapferer, 1993, pp. 117ff).

Since reunification, the restructuring of sector property rights through the *Treuhandanstalt* has been largely determined by western German elites. The broad transfer of institutions from western to eastern Germany accompanied a replacement of former East German officials by West Germans. The *Treuhand's* management board was replaced after the Day of Unity on 3 October 1990, and all fifteen regional *Treuhand* directors from the former GDR were dismissed (cf. for more information see Bähre, 2003, p. 313, with reference to Neugebauer & Hüning, 1992, pp. 14–18). At the end of May 1991 the last former high-ranking state functionary of the GDR, Dr. Gunter Halm, left the *Treuhandanstalt's* board of directors. All leadership positions in the Treuhandanstalt were now filled with West German officials, with the exception of one member of the management board, Wolfram Krause (a former member of the State Planning Commission of the GDR) (cf. Seibel & Kapferer, 1993, p. 115).

Through the *Treuhandanstalt* a number of polymorphic informal contacts developed in addition to the formal contacts and branch offices. This stemmed from the *Treuhandanstalt* hiring over 4000 employees in a very short period of time – many of them maintained professional contacts with their former businesses, administrations, states and friends in the old Federal Republic. These contacts were even decisive in hiring at the managerial level (cf. Czada, 1993, p. 149).

The *Treuhandanstalt* continued to exist by 31 December 1994. By this time the process of privatisation had been largely completed. Five successor institutions assumed the remaining process of privatisation, particularly concerning real estate; of these five institutions, only two continue to exist today.

Reconstruction of Disposal and Property Rights in the Tourism Industry and Intra-sector Transformation Paths in Tourism Industry Branches

Introduction

In the reform of property rights within different subsectors of the eastern German tourism industry governmental influence depended in particular upon three aspects:

- the aspect of the welfare state (e.g. in respect to the policy fields of education, public health and environmental protection);
- the closeness of the sector's relationship to the state (e.g. in rail transportation or aviation);
- in accordance with the three-sector model, most particularly depending upon whether the demand is local or regional (i.e. whether the tourism goods are bound to a net or not).

Intra-sector Paths of Transformation in the Tourism Industry in Light of the Welfare State

The state may also retain greater influence on market systems through welfare state aspects, such as in child and youth tourism within the context of educational or social tourism, or in the spa system in the context of public health.

Child and youth tourism institutions in the GDR entailed not only youth hostels and youth tourist hotels; there were also 51 Central Pioneer Camps and roughly 5000 holiday camps, the former organised by GDR enterprises and institutions. The end of the GDR signified the end of these holiday camps. The camps last took place in the summer of 1990. Privatisation was implemented through the *Treuhandanstalt* with the assistance of municipalities as "company assets not essential for operations", insofar as the camps consisted of properties used expressly for this purpose or which were in the company's possession. In four new federal states, parts of the Central Pioneer Camps developed into so-called Children's and Holiday Centres (*Kinder- und Erholungszentren*, or *KiEZe*). These are specific institutional successors to the GDR's large-scale tourist accommodations for children and youth, with intra-regional significance and institutional funding from their respective federal states. In the new federal states, the *KiEZe* developed endogenously alongside the exogenous institutions that modelled themselves after those of the old federal states (e.g. school-holiday retreats, church and other socially affiliated leisure organisations, as well as federal- and state-sponsored youth hostels).

In the FRG the public health sector is subject to a high level of state intervention. German spas and resorts are dominated by a small number of clinical groups. Within a short span of time, the privatisation of clinics was implemented by the *Treuhandanstalt* in Berlin, under the considerable influence of the Federal Ministry of Health and the relevant West German lobbies. No voice was granted to the East German municipalities in negotiations with the clinic investor. The East German clinic sites were rapidly parcelled out to West German clinical groups. Only in rare cases were East German bidders granted the purchasing contract.

By 1994, the municipalisation of the infrastructure, the settlement of ownership issues and the creation of a legal framework for a qualitative, highly developed organisation of spas had largely been achieved. Despite the influential exogenous transformation process, eastern German spas and recreational centres have largely been able to prevent their baths from following the more clinical model in the old federal states. Their resistance was facilitated by the process of municipalisation, which had given them jurisdiction over establishments within the local infrastructure, and by state funds. The jurisdiction included the individual spas that already belonged to the resorts, as well as the transfer of natural remedies (e.g. salt springs).

The privatisation of former state-owned forestry property is directly tied to the "National Park Programme for Eastern Germany" (*Nationalparkprogramm für den Osten Deutschlands*), concluded shortly before German reunification. According to a decree issued by the GDR's cabinet council on 12 September 1990, 6835 km^2 were temporarily secured. This represents approximately 10% of East Germany (cf. Godau, 1991, p. 177). On this legal basis, environmental laws were enacted in all the new federal states through 1993, which form the basis for the use (and sale) of land in these areas.

The Travel Industry (Travel Agencies and Tour Organisers)

When the border between East and West Germany opened, eastern Germany experienced a boom in travel agencies (for more detail see Bähre, 2003, pp. 328–333), along with a rush of educational tours and training programmes for eastern German travel agents offered by the West German (later unified German) travel industry associations (e.g. *Deutscher Reisebüroverband DRV e.V.*). In West Germany, travel agency chains began to expand their retail offices and many tour organisers began to take an interest in the new markets. While the development of eastern Germany by western German tour organisers and their retail partners was in full swing, the *Treuhandanstalt* focused on the sale of the three former East German state-owned travel companies (which had enjoyed a monopoly in the GDR): the German tour organiser and travel agency of the GDR *Deutsches Reisebüro der DDR*, the youth travel organiser *Jugendtourist* and the retail stores belonging to the East German travel service of the Free German Federation of Unions (*Freie Deutsche Gewerkschaftsbund, or FDGB*), referred to as "FEDI" in 1990.

In the spring of 1991 the eastern German "mid-size businessman" Frank Enzmann formally acquired the 51 offices of the FDGB travel service. Through travel agency agreements, Enzmann had already become a partner with Touristik Union International GmbH & Co. KG (TUI), the leading western German tour organiser. He later affiliated shares of his travel agency *Reisebüro Enzmann GmbH* with the capital-related firms TUI and *Deutsches Reisebüro GmbH* (*DER*) (cf. also Schneider, 2001, p. 321).

In May 1991 there were already 1525 (!) travel agencies in eastern Germany (Table 3.1). The offices of the GDR state travel agencies *Reisewelt* and *Jugendtourist* and their tour organiser branches were still for sale.

On 19 July 1991 the Independent Commission determined that the travel agency *Jugendtourist* had ties to the GDR's youth organisation Free German Youth (FDJ). Thus *Jugendtourist* was subordinated to the Independent Commission. Based on a contract of 24 September 1991, the travel industry giant ITS (International Tourist Services) *Länderreisedienste* GmbH (an affiliate of *Kaufhof* Holding AG Cologne, and presently the third largest western German travel group) acquired a portion of the *Jugendtourist* tour organiser's and travel agency's investment on 1 October 1991 for 1,318,000 DM. The acquisition included the 35 branch offices (idem, 1991) as well as the name (cf. BT 13/5377, pp. 71–74). The acquired offices were to offer a full range of services. At this point ITS already owned 31 additional travel agencies in the former GDR (idem, 1991, p. 17). *Kaufhof* AG Holding Cologne, the parent organisation, assumed control over the state trade organisation's Centrum-*Warenhäuser* department stores and its travel offices. At that time the executive director of *Kaufhof*, Dr. Jens Odewald, was the President of the Board of Directors of the *Treuhandanstalt* (from 20 August 1990 to 20 April 1993).

By January 1992 the following had resulted from the former East German state travel agency *Reisewelt* (a part of the former *Reisebüro der DDR*):

- only 28 branches were sold to employees, whereby three quarters of these sales invoked the aid of the European Recovery Programme (ERP);
- an additional 11 branches were transferred to the West Berlin tour organisers *Wolters Reisen* and *Germania Reisen*;
- nine branches were closed because they were considered unprofitable or because of a lack of potential buyers (cf. Hempel, 1994, p. 635).

With consent of the German Cartel Office (*Kartellamt*), the branch giant ITS was given the contract to purchase the remaining 75 offices, as well as the subsequently formed tour organiser *TrendReisen* (the other part of the former *Reisebüro der DDR*). After incremental

Table 3.1: Travel agencies in eastern Germany in 1991.

Organisers	Total number of agencies	Types of agencies			Aspired agency network with the following number of travel agencies
		Company-owned agencies	Chains	Agencies located in department stores	
TUI	327	–	188[b]	–	600–700
NUR	472	15	153[c]	38	800–900
ITS	300	20	106[d]	206[f]	In each Kaufhof and Hertie department store
LTT	200[a]	–	100	–	400
DER	226	–	129[e]	2	–

[a] An agreement with *Reisewelt* is nearing completion.
[b] 130 *Reisewelt* agencies, 22 *Buchtours* agencies, 36 *Reiseland* agencies.
[c] 106 *Jugendtourist* branches, 10 *Allkauf* agencies, 10 agencies of the *Thüringer Reisebüro*, 26 *Palmtouristik* agencies.
[d] All *Jugendtourist*.
[e] All *Reisewelt*, of these 58 are DER/DB agencies.
[f] 16 *Kaufhof*, 16 *Hertie*.
Source: Bremkes (1991), Travel Agencies in the Former GDR, Touristik-Report 5/1991, cited in Kaub Consult, 1991, p. 57.

development the ITS travel agencies have now been united under the ITS-REWE name of *Atlas-Reisebüros* (for more on this subject see Bähre, 2003, pp. 330–335).

By 31 December 1992 the entire former state travel industry of the former GDR had become disaggregated and privatised and was owned nearly completely by western German entities. No independent, trans-regional eastern German tour organiser has been able to establish itself in a unified German market (cf. also Kaiser, 2000, p. 124). After purchase, the buyers ceased travel production in offices acquired from the former GDR, developing eastern Germany into a market for sales, not production (cf. Bähre, 2003, p. 334, with reference to the Vice President of *Deutsches Reisebüro GmbH* (Frankfurt/Main), Werner Sülberg).

The possibilities for development of the eastern German travel market triggered by reunification fit in with the horizontal and increasingly vertical integration of German travel organisers amidst the consolidation trends evident since the mid-1990s. Where there were once four west German travel market giants in 1990 – Touristik Union International GmbH & Co. KG (TUI), *NUR Touristik GmbH, LTT-Lufttransport-Touristik GmbH & Co. KG* (a subsidiary of LTU) and ITS *Länderreisedienst GmbH & Co. KG* – there are now three large vertically integrated European travel groups:

- the REWE Group (composed among others of DER, ITS, *Atlas-Reisebüros*, LTT);
- TUI, which belongs to Preussag AG (since 2002 renamed TUI AG);
- Thomas Cook AG, which emerged from NUR (*Neckermann*).

In 1992 there began a 2-year consolidation and takeover wave in eastern Germany, with small, newly founded travel agencies purchased by travel agency chains and partnerships, as well as by now vertically integrated travel groups operating from western Germany.

The Reorganisation of the Transportation Sector

Transportation services are rendered with the aid of transportation authorities on a municipal, state or federal system of roads, waterways, railways and motorways. Harbours and airports also form key components of the infrastructure.

At this point, *Deutsche Lufthansa*, like the *Deutsche Bundesbahn*, still counted as federal property. It was therefore subject to a high level of state intervention. Although an initial cooperative agreement had been reached between the two state enterprises Lufthansa and the East German Interflug in January 1990, after unification on 15 October 1990 Lufthansa withdrew its notification of the cooperation in anti-trust law at the German Cartel Office. On 1 March 1991 the *Treuhandanstalt* announced a liquidation resolution for Interflug GmbH. The liquidator employed, who wanted to preserve and privatise a part of Interflug (commercial and charter) as the most cost-effective solution and to maintain employment, was dismissed by the *Treuhandanstalt* on 7 March 1991, 6 days after he had been hired. Shortly thereafter the *Treuhandanstalt* hired his successor along with a team of consultants, who were provided by the Interflug-partner-turned-competitor Lufthansa. The East German airline market was thus open for takeover by the West German Lufthansa.

By the end of 1991 all four commercial airports (Berlin-Schönefeld, Leipzig-Halle, Dresden and Erfurt) as well as the agrarian aviation companies had been transferred to the federal states (*Länder*) and municipalities. A rapid modernisation of airports followed. This led to a staggering increase in the numbers of flight passengers at eastern German and Berlin airports. Another result was an increased preference for airline travel over other means of vacation travel among eastern Germans.

The fifteen-volume *Treuhandanstalt* documentation illustrates that 56% of all companies were sold to entrepreneurs from the new federal states, while 11% were acquired jointly by both eastern and western Germans. This "makes clear an extraordinarily high recognition of eastern German businesses" (cf. *Treuhandanstalt*, 1994/Band 8, p. 140). Compared to shipbuilding and many other sectors, this is truly a high percentage. However, this high recognition of eastern German applicants was required by federal transportation laws, as well as by the local and regional concentration of demand. During reunification, federal law on public transportation (ÖPNV) gave preference to local applicants. Generally, many bus companies are engaged in local transit, group transport as well as tourism. The legal provisions hindered a large-scale market takeover by western German companies and thus fostered the development of a local bus industry (for more detail see Bähre, 2003, pp. 354–357). These provisions are also relevant to youth tourism which is decisively determined not only by the usage of bus tourism (more an issue of local and regional demand), but also by educational tours as well as various provisions of the *Länder* Ministries of Education. Moreover, there is a significant number of middle-class eastern German providers offering child and youth tours today.

Like tourism transportation, taxi companies are also tied locally, through demand, which has ultimately fostered a consideration of eastern German applicants.

The Hotel and Restaurant Industry

The restaurant industry As with travel agencies, a lack of commercial space was initially the leading obstacle to the establishment of restaurants (cf. Kaub Consult, 1991, p. 39). The initial outlay required for restaurants is far less than that required in the hotel industry. Similar to travel agencies, restaurants can be opened rapidly on the basis of leases. Banks are not the only possible sources of credit. In cooperation with their in-house banks, convenience providers and breweries provide financing concepts and marketing know-how to interested entrepreneurs as a way of increasing their sales. Within the context of the developing market, the growth of breweries, bottling companies and convenience producers, as well as restaurant franchise systems and catering firms was accompanied by rapid modernisation. But this also conceals a risk for tourism that travel destinations will appear to be increasingly interchangeable, at least from a culinary point of view.

The privatisation of restaurants belonging to the state trade organisation (*Handelsorganisation*, or *HO*) has been considered complete since 1991, and that of other restaurant facilities, except for establishments belonging to the vacation service of the Unions (*Feriendienst der Gewerkschaften*, or *FEDI*), since 1992.

Overall it is evident that the sector paths of transformation of travel agencies and restaurants are comparable to the path of transformation for the retail sector, and these two segments are in fact are often classified as part of the retail sector. On the other hand, western German businesses executed a hostile takeover in the tour organiser segment, which is dominated by air travel, with the termination of production in eastern Germany, a development which was similar to that observed in other market-oriented sectors, such as the eastern German mechanical engineering sector.

The hotel industry   Aside from lease and operator models, financing expenses in the hotel industry are much higher. Between 1990 and 1992 existing eastern German hotels did not meet with much competition. The rapid establishment of competition was blocked by as-yet-unresolved questions concerning property ownership, a chaotic land registry and an undeveloped real estate market.

Depending on whether the relevant properties belonged to the GDR's political parties or mass organisations, the competent authority for the reorganisation of the eastern German hotel industry was either the trust authority (the *Treuhandanstalt*) alone, or the *Treuhandanstalt* working together with the Independent Commission.

In 1990 the GDR's Interhotel chain had over 34 hotels with 9951 rooms and, with respect to number of rooms, was the 16th largest (of 25) western European-based hotel chain in the world (cf. Lembke, 1994, p. 893, only in reference to its presence in western Europe). Due to the cooperation with foreign construction companies in building the *Interhotels*, the chain's quality was more in line with international hotel standards than other East German hotels. Interhotel, which had become a joint-stock company in April 1990, had opted for a common holding company with the West German Steigenberger GmbH in July 1990. However, Munich attorney Dr. Ralf Corsten, who was appointed managing director on the day after reunification, declared this resolution invalid. The privatisation of Deutsche Interhotel AG was conclusively decided on 22 November 1991, and the sale of Deutsche Interhotel AG's stock package of 28 hotels to the West Berlin investment group Groenke & Guttmann GmbH for 2.2 billion DM became a done deal. The *Treuhandanstalt* sold five hotels to other bidders for 346 million DM. Only one of these bidders was East German, when the Interhotel director purchased "her" hotel through an MBO (Management-Buy-Out) agreement with the aid of an ERP credit.

The privatisation of SED's nine Cicero Hotels was completed in 1992, with one hotel going to its original owner. (The Socialist Unity Party (*Sozialistische Einheitspartei/ SED*) was the leading state party in the political system of the GDR.) In addition, of the 420 hotels belonging to the state's Commerce Organisation (*Handelsorganisation, or HO*), the *Treuhandanstalt* privatised 160 in the autumn of 1993. Of the remaining approximately 100 hotels belonging to the Parties and Mass Organisations (*Parteien und Massenorganisationen*), only 17 were sold by the autumn of 1993 for barely 200 million DM (cf. Bähre, 2003, pp. 342–356 and the works cited therein).

In addition the question as to ownership of the 35 hotels from the former GDR's state-owned *Reisebüro der DDR* chain "Travel Hotels", with a capacity of 2000 beds, was settled by 1993. Five hotels were returned to their original owners. An international German-language investment group purchased another 25 of the hotels. The Travel Hotels have since developed into three-to-five star establishments of the "Travel Charme" brand. Ten years after the purchase, the Travel Charme group operates 13 hotels in eastern Germany.

Former state-owned company holiday and training facilities made up the highest percentage of accommodations in eastern Germany (cf. Bähre, 2003, p. 243, author's own calculations based on the GDR's hotel data). Beginning in March 1992, properties with a value of less than 1 million DM were offered primarily to entrepreneurs from the new federal states and eastern Berlin. However, 550 of the 850 properties intended for sale had to be taken off the market because of their unsuitability. Through October 1993, only 300 properties had been sold at favourable terms to entrepreneurs, as intended, together with state grants (cf. idem, 1993, p. 28). In sum, the market viability of many properties was overrated (cf. Melzow, 2000, p. 42).

The GDR's parties and organisations had properties that they actually owned (private property), as well as those that they merely used ("legal entity properties"). Of relevance were 2983 private properties and 3343 legal entity properties. Among these, 580 private properties and 252 legal entity properties were under the jurisdiction of the unions' (FDGB) travel service (FEDI). After reunification, in the third supplementary budget, the Federal Ministry of Finance cancelled the subsidies (in the amount of 91 million DM) that the de Maizière government had promised the FDGB's travel service for the fourth quarter of 1990 (cf. Passow, 1996, p. 45). This resulted in the temporary closing of many FEDI properties. Not until May 1991, prompted by the communal works *Aufschwung Ost* (the eastern Boom) case, did the *Treuhandanstalt* act on the federal government's recommendation to offer municipalities the option of assuming the management and use of these facilities. The municipalities accepted this offer for 672 of 832 properties, which represented approximately 80% of all the properties. It was now municipalities' responsibility to do everything necessary to ensure the proper management and use of their vacation properties. These actions proved to be far too late for the 1991 tourist season. Demand collapsed entirely in eastern German tourism destinations and resulted in rampant unemployment there.

Through 31 December 1995, a total of 155 FEDI (FDGB) properties were subject to restitution, and an additional 718 FEDI properties were sold (91 of these properties sold based on § 3a of the Property Act, i.e. the priority investment procedures). All FEDI properties have since been sold (cf. Passow, 1996, pp. 73–74). The Dutch Euromill Properties GmbH & Co. KG (financed by a Thai bank consortium) was one of these buyers which acquired 10 of the FDGB's 18 vacation homes (nearly 5300 rooms) that were sold as hotels. However, the Euromill hotel chain was forced to declare bankruptcy in 1999; most of the acquired hotels have since closed.

Through 1995, the privatisation of the hotel industry proceeded relatively quickly, given its somewhat complex measurement and asset situation (cf. Melzow, 2000, pp. 41–42). Hotels with a clear location-related advantage, offering relatively good facilities and attractive locations, were sold most quickly. At the beginning of the 1990s this was especially true for hotels accommodating business travellers.

It should also be kept in mind that, since the summer of 1990, eastern German tourism destinations have faced competition from western German and foreign destinations. In contrast to the populations of the other post-socialist (referred to in western English-language literature as "the former communist") countries, East Germans had a freely convertible currency and a means of payment recognised worldwide on 1 July 1990, when monetary, economic and social union came into force. The rapid development of sales in package tour holidays by western German tour organisers and the swift expansion of airports in eastern Germany made a significant contribution to a situation wherein, as early as 1992, more eastern Germans were going on holiday abroad than to German destinations. Eastern Germans were now able to enjoy the foreign holidays they had never dared to dream about before the fall of the inner-German borders (Figure 3.2).

Figure 3.2: The development of the proportion of foreign travel of all holiday travel.
Source: Own depiction in accordance with the tourism analysis (RA) of Studienkreis für
Tourismus and FUR (Holiday and Travel Research Group), various years.

The Joint Task Assistance Programme and the Bedding Boom in the Eastern German Hotel Industry

Given the overwhelming political events of 3 October 1990, the Federal Ministry of
Economics, which was now also responsible for tourism in eastern Germany, did not have
a master plan for tourism policy. The predominant opinion was that the transition from a
planned economy to a market economy generally could not be planned. The administrative
structures in the new federal states and Berlin were changing on all levels, while the new
regional, state and local tourism associations' structures were being created. During routine
reviews, especially on the basis of GDR secret service files, many former East German functionaries were disqualified from the newly formed eastern German civil service due to their
previous close association with the state socialist system. Newcomers set the tone, along
with western German officials coming to aid in reconstruction.

As the agency charged by the federal government with privatising the eastern German
tourism industry, the trust authority (the *Treuhandanstalt*) was completely overwhelmed in
regard to setting a course towards a socially responsible, ecologically friendly and economically sustainable tourism policy in eastern German tourism destinations, especially since its
only task was to complete the privatisation, and that as rapidly as possible. As mentioned
above, municipalities were required to present tourism and utilisation concepts to trust

authority representatives and potential investors beginning in spring 1991. The costs associated with these tourism concepts were covered by governmental assistance programmes. The eastern German municipalities received the western German advisers, many of them self-proclaimed "tourism experts", with open arms. The word "tourism" evoked for most local politicians visions of the excess demand during the time of the GDR. Even the federal government believed that eastern German tourism would serve as the motor for a developing middle class and set great stock in its ability to generate a rapid economic recovery.

In view of the western German hotel industry's reputation: overcapacity, hotel failures, missing guests, banks were generally reluctant to grant loans to the sector in eastern Germany, particularly when the entrepreneurial groups were eastern Germans. Eastern Germans were even required to pay higher interest rates than western German applicants, in order to offset the increased risk due to their lack of entrepreneurial expertise. However, contrary to developments in other post-socialist states, the influx of funds to eastern Germany as a means for renewing capital stock in real estate was not a serious problem. Tax write-offs and other incentives created very attractive opportunities for western Germans willing to make money available to companies investing in the east. During the 1990s, interest rates dropped on the world market, resulting in lower interest rates in Germany as well, with interest rates in the east higher than in the west. Rather than paying taxes on credit interest, many western Germans preferred to invest in mixed-use properties, hotels, clinics or apartments in order to make use of the special tax write-offs available in eastern Germany.

Contrary to developments in the other post-socialist states, the reconstruction of eastern German infrastructure was financially secured by German and European structural development funds. The most important source of financing for the tourism infrastructure was the *Gemeinschaftsaufgabe* (Joint Task) assistance programme for the "improvement of the regional economic structure". While the amount of Joint Task subsidies for "improvement of the regional economic structure" was limited to 30% in the commercial sector (e.g. hotels), Joint Task subsidies could total between 50% and 70% in the municipal sector. The remainder of the necessary financing volume had to be provided by the municipalities themselves. Joint Task assistance for the overall and tourism infrastructure has made it possible to advance and secure a qualitatively more highly developed tourism industry in eastern Germany during the free market transformation. More than 8.7 billion DM in Joint Task funding was transferred to the new federal states (not including Berlin) between 1990 and 2000 (cf. OSGV, 2001, p. 77). An analysis of Joint Task subsidies clearly illustrates that both tourism infra- and superstructure were financed between 1993 and 1995. The willingness to invest has declined sharply since 1998, as, for example, the poor state of municipal finances leaves its mark on tourism infrastructure. This has made it difficult to procure the necessary local contributions (cf. OSGV, 2001, p. 78. See also Heuschmid, 2001, p. 299).

Since 1995 the number of beds in the east increased more rapidly than the level of occupancy (Figure 3.3).

Since 1995 occupancy in eastern German hotels has been lower than in western Germany, a fact which remains true in comparing hotels in the new federal states (including Berlin) and the former West Germany (Figure 3.4).

By 1997 the number of beds per capita in East Germany had climbed to levels similar to West Germany. The period of expansion in the hotel industry, particularly hotels, largely ended in 1998 (cf. OSGV, 2001, pp. 78–79) (Figure 3.5).

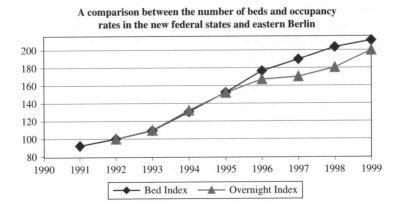

A comparison between the number of beds and occupancy rates in the new federal states and eastern Berlin

Figure 3.3: A comparison between the number of beds and occupancy rates in the new federal states and eastern Berlin. *Source*: Own calculations (1992 = 100), based on: Statistisches Bundesamt (German Federal Office of Statistics): Tourismus in Zahlen, various years.

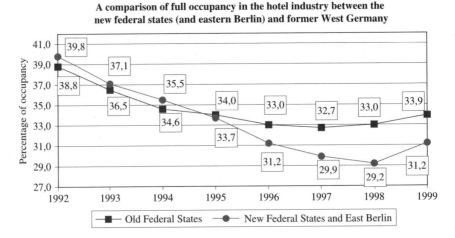

A comparison of full occupancy in the hotel industry between the new federal states (and eastern Berlin) and former West Germany

Figure 3.4: A comparison of full occupancy in the hotel industry between the new federal states (and eastern Berlin) and former West Germany. *Source*: Statistiches Bundesamt (German Federal Office of Statistics): Tourismus in Zahlen 2000/2001, p.135.

Unrestrained growth generated by tax incentives for investors in the property sector led to a surplus in the eastern German accommodation market, as was observed during the 1980s in West German tourist areas (cf. Meyer-Schwieckerath, 1990). Since then, the saturation tendencies of western German tourist areas have further increased. Ten years after German reunification, more western Germans (3.2 million) than eastern Germans (2.4 million) are now holidaying in eastern German tourist areas. With respect to their preferences for foreign holiday destinations, eastern Germans have aligned their travel behaviour to that of western Germans and, in the year 2000, took only 4.2 million holidays within Germany

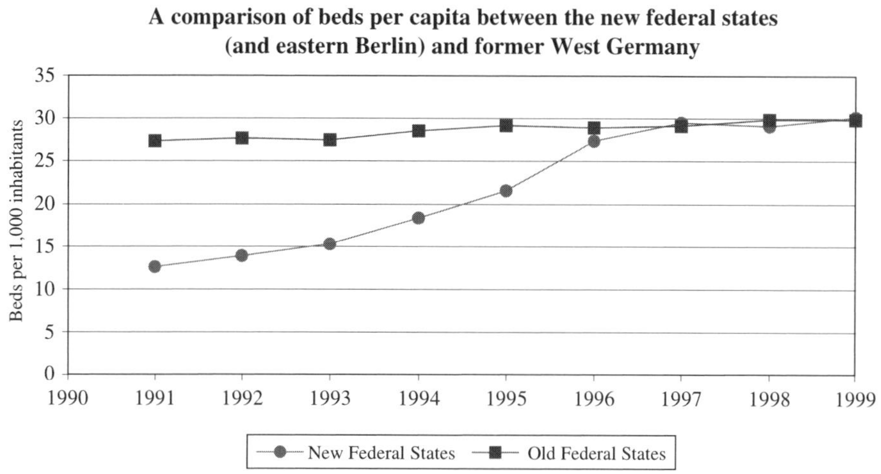

A comparison of beds per capita between the new federal states (and eastern Berlin) and former West Germany

Figure 3.5: A comparison of beds per capita between the new federal states (and eastern Berlin) and former West Germany. *Source*: Own calculations, according to Statistisches Bundesamt (German Federal Office of Statistics: Tourismus in Zahlen, various years.

compared to 9.9 million in the year 1990 (for more information see Bähre, 2003, p. 430, own calculations in accordance with the tourism analyses RA 1990, 1991 and FUR 2001). In the year 2000, experts agreed that there were surplus capacities in eastern Germany and that building continued in excess of demand. Demand in the eastern German *Länder* has yet to "grow into" an excessively high supply of hotels (with reference to Stoll, 2000, p. 70).

The Outcome of Transformation in Some Indices (1989/1990–1999/2000)

An analysis of the geographical distribution of bed occupancy rates achieved, of overnight stays in commercial establishments and private dwellings and the intensity of overnight stays in eastern German tourist areas in the year 1999, that is, 10 years after the fall of the inner-German borders, reveals that development has been most favourable in the traditional tourist areas. These traditional destinations report higher occupancy rates, a higher intensity of overnight stays and higher numbers of overnight stays than the other areas (Figure 3.6). Owing to its promising natural potential for tourism and the now complete modernisation of its general and tourism infrastructure, even after reunification, Mecklenburg-West Pomerania's Baltic coast has asserted its position as eastern Germany's most popular destination for summer holidays.

Today, eastern Germany has become an attractive destination, offering modern industrial parks and shopping centres, impressively restored urban historical districts, as well as health spas and holiday resorts with the most modern leisure infrastructure (see Figure 3.7).

However, the majority of shopping centres, hotels, bed and breakfasts and industrial parks do not belong to local residents; the vast majority of the former state-owned GDR property became western German property.

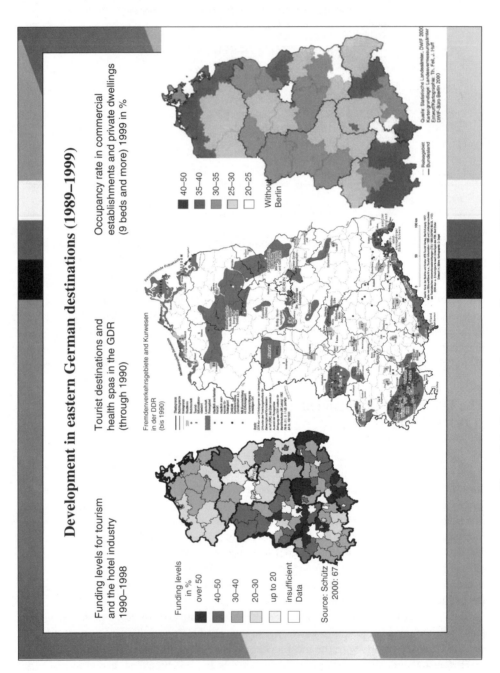

Figure 3.6: Own depiction, according to Bähre (2003).

Figure 3.7: The Hotel Metropol in Binz on the island of Rügen in 1993 and 2003.
Source: Permission to publish granted by Helfer (IGU, 2004).

In the GDR, holidays were statutorily regulated by the constitution and by a collective agreement. It can be assumed that holiday intensity in the GDR was at least 90%, and was almost certainly nearer 100%. Since 1990, holiday intensity in the former East Germany has fallen below that of the former West Germany (in accordance with the tourism analysis (RA) of Studienkreis für Tourismus, FUR, various years). In the new *Länder* and East Berlin, the proportion of persons employed was, in 1999, already lower than in the former FRG (Calculations of the German Federal Office of Statistics, 1999). The unemployment rate in the new *Länder* and East Berlin increased from 11.1% in the year 1991 to 17.6% in the year 1999 with the biggest increase in Saxony-Anhalt (20.3%). During the same period, the unemployment rate in the former FRG rose from 5.7% to 8.8% and across Germany to 10.5% (Greiner, 1998, IAB (German Institute for Employment Research), various years). The unemployed spend demonstrably less money on recreation, entertainment, culture, education and accommodation and travel less (for more detailed information, see Bähre, 2003/Vol. II, Statistics 1.34 and 1.35 in Volume II of the two-volume edition of the same name (Calculations of *Statistisches Bundesamt* (Federal Office of Statistics), Use of Income Survey (EVS) various years). Unemployment and the increasing social distinctions between the inhabitants of the former GDR – an egalitarian, paternalistic society – in the context of its transformation to a pluralistic, Western society had a direct effect on their travel behaviour. In the period 1990–2000, the German population's holiday travel intensity increased over-all. Today, however, western Germans have overtaken eastern Germans (see the tourism analysis (RA) of Studienkreis für Tourismus, FUR, various years).

The lack of a self-supporting economic structure in eastern Germany is the reason why city tourism and business tourism do not yet have any major significance in the context of domestic and foreign demand for eastern Germany and the reason why these sectors do not as yet generate the same level of income as they do in the former FRG (for more detailed information, see Bähre, 2003, pp. 443–446).

Conclusions

Economic policy defines the economic framework of a market economy in tourism to be cre-ated. This is the prerequisite for (re-)establishing private ownership of capital and production resources. It is furthermore the condition for the evolution of competition and for the development of entrepreneurship as the driving force of economic development.

Generally, the tourism industry is often cited in its role as a motor for small businesses, in particular for the evolution of entrepreneurship in market economy transformation. However, the classic alliance of tourism and regional and small businesses policy, which is also applied in EU economic policy, is increasingly being called into question (cf. Bieger, 2001, pp. 16–18). Long-term safeguarding of value creation and thus of the innovative and developmental strength of the tourism industry can only be achieved by ensuring competitive, dynamic and viable products and services and thus attractive jobs and regional value creation and by establishing network requirements (e.g. transport networks, distribution platforms) for other industries (cf. Bieger, 2001, p. 36). A tourism policy of indiscriminate all-round development of infrastructure and tourism causes a relatively even (uniform) and also, if required, rapid, modernisation of the transportation, communications and leisure infrastructures and the image and leisure-time value for the indigenous population is enhanced by this.

However, the desired effects of these measures, such as a rise in earnings, will not occur through tourism if the travel destination does not have any markedly favourable natural or socio-cultural potential for tourism (as a destination for excursions or for domestic and/or foreign tourists) or if the anticipated business tourists fail to materialise as a result of the decline of domestic industry.

It is not solely an issue of the favourable tourism supply but, rather, of the general orientation of tourism development according to national and international demand.

Governmental funding policy must not end with the financing of infrastructure, but must consider marketing concepts; the role of the local economy in destination management must at the same time be strengthened by means of public–private partnership models, and the local economy must (be able to) play its part (cf. Kreilkamp, 2001, pp. 62–64). With respect to the issue of transformation and the associated necessity of developing market economy structures in tourism, this does, however, mean that only with the successful establishment of entrepreneurship can private–public partnership models in destination management be implemented and take effect.

Tourism science and tourism politics as institutions must succeed in playing a part in the transformation of market economies, especially during privatisation. In order to safeguard the common good, tourism science must assert itself as a balance to interest groups and lobbies.

The interaction of parliamentary democracy, interest groups and administrative structures in tourism politics within the framework of market-economy and democratic system transformation should be the focus of further research.

References

Abromeit, H. (1993). Interessenvermittlung zwischen Konkurrenz und Konkordanz: Studienhandbuch zur vergleichenden Lehre politischer Systeme. Opladen: Leske + Budrich.

AIEST (Ed.). (1991). Qualitätstourismus – Konzeption einer gleichermaßen wirtschafts-, sozial-und umweltverträglichen touristischen Entwicklung, Publications de l'AIEST Vol. 33. St. Gallen.

Bähre, H. (2003). Tourismus in der Systemtransformation. Eine Untersuchung zum Reisen in der GDR und zum ostdeutschen Tourismus im Zeitraum 1980 bis 2000. Two-volume edition (Vol. I has the same content as the single-volume edition). Berlin: INTEGRON.

Bernholz, P., & Breyer, F. (1993). Grundlagen der politischen Ökonomie (Edition in 2 volumes), Vol. 1: Theorie der Wirtschaftssysteme, 3rd fully revised edition (1st edition 1972), Tübingen: J.C.B. Mohr (Paul Siebeck).

Bieger, T. (2001). Perspektiven der Tourismuspolitik in traditionellen alpinen Tourismusländern. In: Kreilkamp, E./Pechlaner, H./Steinecke, A. (Eds), Gemachter oder gelebter Tourismus? Destinationsmanagement und Tourismuspolitik, pp. 11–37. Wien: Linde-Verlag.

Blum, U. (2000). Volkswirtschaftslehre. München, Wien: R.Oldenbourg.

Bremkes, W. (1991). Reisebüros in der Ex-DDR. In: Touristik-Report 5/1991, cited in: Dr. Kaub Consult (1991): Strukturkonzept für das Gastgewerbe, p. 57. Düsseldorf/München/ Frankfurt am Main/Hamburg/Berlin/Leipzig.

Brunner, G., Clemm, H., Etzbach, E., et al. (Eds) (1993). *Rechtshandbuch Vermögen und Investitionen in der ehemaligen DDR* (Band I). Zweiter Abschnitt (Teil B). Ordnungsnummer 200 (Stand 1993). München: Beck.

Busche, J. (1993). Gesetz zur Privatisierung und Reorganisation des volkseigenen Vermögens. In: G. Brunner, H. Clemm, E. u.a. Etzbach, (Hrsg). *Rechtshandbuch Vermögen und Investitionen in der ehemaligen DDR*. (Band I). Zweiter Abschnitt (Teil B). Ordnungsnummer 200. München: Beck.

Corsten, M., & Voelzkow, H. (Eds) (1997). Transformation zwischen Markt, Staat und Drittem Sektor. Marburg: Metropolis.

Czada, R. (1993). Die Treuhandanstalt im Umfeld von Politik und Verbänden. In: Fischer, W./Hax, H./Schneider, H.K. (Eds), Treuhandanstalt: Das Unmögliche wagen, pp. 148–173. Berlin: Akademieverlag.

Czada, R. (1997). Vereinigung und Systemtransformation als Governance Problem. In: Corsten, M./Voelzkow, H. (Eds), Transformation zwischen Markt, Staat und Drittem Sektor, pp. 181–210. Marburg: Metropolis.

Czada, R., & Lehmbruch, G. (Eds), (1998). Transformationspfade in Ostdeutschland: Beiträge zur sektoralen Vereinigungspolitik. Frankfurt am Main: Campus.

DIW (Deutsches Institut für Wirtschaftsforschung) (1999). Wirtschaftsfaktor Tourismus: Gutachten im Auftrag des Bundesministers für Wirtschaft und Tedchnologie (Abschlussbericht) [Evaluations for the Federal Minister of Economic Affairs and Technology (Bundesministerium für Wirtschaft und Technologie) (Concluding Report 1999)]. Berlin.

Esser, H. (Ed.) (2000). Der Wandel nach der Wende: Gesellschaft, Wirtschaft, Politik in Ostdeutschland, Wiesbaden: Westdeutscher Verlag.

Fischer, W., Hax, H., & Schneider, H.K. (Eds) (1993). Treuhandanstalt: Das Unmögliche wagen. Berlin: Akademieverlag.

Freyer, W., & Bähre, H. (Eds) (2000). Tourismus in den neuen Bundesländern 10 Jahre nach der deutschen Wiedervereinigung [Conference Volume for the Fourth Dresden Tourism Symposium (4. Dresdner Tourismus-Symposium 2000)]. Dresden: fit-Verlag.

Godau, A. (1991). Nationalparks, Biosphärenreservate und Naturparks in den neuen deutschen Bundesländern – ein reicher Teil des Erbes und eine große Chance für gleichermaßen wirtschafts, sozial- und umweltverträglichen Tourismus, in: AIEST (Ed.), Qualitätstourismus – Konzeption einer gleichermaßen wirtschafts-, sozial- und umweltverträglichen touristischen Entwicklung, Publications de l'AIEST Vol. 33, pp. 175–188. St. Gallen.

Greiner, U. (1998). Zur sozialen Lage in den Neuen Ländern und Berlin-Ost: Arbeitsmarkt und Erwerbsleben, in: Federal Office of Statistics(Ed.), Wirtschaft und Statistik 4/1998, pp. 287–291.

Hanel, U. (2000). Personalmanagement in den Transformationsphasen von der Plan- zur Marktwirtschaft: eine Untersuchung in mittelständischen Unternehmen der neuen Bundesländer, München/Mering: Rainer Hampp Verlag.

Helfer, M. (2004). Transformation des Tourismus in den Neuen Bundesländern: das Beispiel Binz auf Rügen. Conference of the International Geographical Union (IGU) at the University of Greifswald. Unpublished conference paper. Greifswald.

Hempel, R. (1994). VEB Reisebüro – der Rohwedder-Brief als Alarmsignal. In: Treuhandanstalt (Ed.), Dokumentation Treuhandanstalt 1990–1994 in 15 Bänden, Volume 6, pp. 626–639. Berlin.

Hermann-Pillath, C. (Ed.) (1994). Marktwirtschaft als Aufgabe: Wirtschaft und Gesellschaft im Übergang vom Plan zum Markt / [Ludwig-Erhard-Stiftung e.V., Bonn]. Stuttgart, Jena, New York: G. Fischer.

Heuschmid, W. (2001). Geschäftsfeld Tourismus – Herausforderungen für Sparkassen und Kommunen. In: J. Wannhoff, (Ed.), *Sparkassen und Tourismus* (pp. 279–325). Stuttgart: Deutscher Sparkassenverlag.

Hoffmann, L. (1993). Warten auf den Aufschwung. Regensburg: Transfer-Verlag. Dr. Kaub Consult (1991). Strukturkonzept für das Gastgewerbe in den neuen Bundesländern (written at the direction of the German Federal Ministry of Economics), Düsseldorf/München/ Frankfurt am Main/Hamburg/Berlin/Leipzig.

Institut für Länderkunde, Becker, C. & Job, H. (Eds) (1999). Nationalatlas Bundesrepublik Deutschland, (Vol. 10). *Freizeit und Tourismus*, Heidelberg/Berlin: Spektrum Akademischer Verlag.

Kaiser, C. (2000). Reiseveranstalter und Reisemittler. In: Institut für Länderkunde, C. Becker, H. Job (Eds), *Nationalatlas Bundesrepublik Deutschland* (Vol. 10), *Freizeit und Tourismus* (pp. 124–127). Heidelberg/Berlin: Spektrum Akademischer Verlag.

Kloepfer, M., & Unger, J.-F. von (1993). Public-Legal Factors for the Treuhandanstalt. In: Fischer, W./Hax, H./Schneider, H.K. (Eds), Treuhandanstalt: Das Unmögliche wagen, pp. 41–84. Berlin: Akademieverlag.

Klump, R. (1992). Einführung in die Wirtschaftspolitik, 2nd revised edition (1st edition 1989), München: Verlag Franz Vahlen.

Kreilkamp, E. (2001). Zukunftsorientierte Tourismuspolitik in Deutschland. Ergebnisse des 3. Tourismus-Kolloquiums der Deutschen Gesellschaft für Tourismuswissenschaft e.V. In: Kreilkamp, E./Pechlaner, H./Steinecke, A. (Eds), Gemachter oder gelebter Tourismus? Destinationsmanagement und Tourismuspolitik, pp. 57–65. Wien: Linde-Verlag.

Kreilkamp, E., Pechlaner, H., & Steinecke, A. (Eds) (2001). Gemachter oder gelebter Tourismus? In: Kreilkamp, E./Pechlaner, H./Steinecke, A. (Eds), Destinationsmanagement und Tourismuspolitik. Wien: Linde-Verlag.

Laumann, E.O., & Knoke, D. (1987). *The organizational state: social choice in National Policy Domains*. Madison, WI: University of Wisconsin Press.

Lehmbruch, G. (1991). Die deutsche Vereinigung: Strukturen und Strategien. *Politische Vierteljahresschrift, 32*(4), 585–604. Opladen: Westdeutscher Verlag.

Lehmbruch, G. (1998). Zwischen Institutionentransfer und Eigendynamik: sektorale Transformationspfade und ihre Bestimmungsgründe. In: Czada, R./Lehmbruch, G. (Eds), Transformationspfade in Ostdeutschland: Beiträge zur sektoralen Vereinigungspolitik, pp. 17–57. Frankfurt am Main: Campus.

Lehmbruch, G. (2000). Bedingungen sektoralen Institutionenwandels im deutschen Vereinigungsprozess. In: Esser, H. (Ed.), Der Wandel nach der Wende: Gesellschaft, Wirtschaft, Politik in Ostdeutschland, pp. 113–142. Wiesbaden: Westdeutscher Verlag.

Leipold, H. (1994). Interdependenz von wirtschaftlicher und politischer Ordnung. In: Hermann-Pillath, C. (Ed.), Marktwirtschaft als Aufgabe: Wirtschaft und Gesellschaft im Übergang vom Plan zum Markt / [Ludwig-Erhard-Stiftung e.V., Bonn], pp. 723–738. Stuttgart, Jena, New York: G. Fischer.

Lembke, D. (1994). Vereinigung Interhotel: Odyssee einer Hotelkette. In: Treuhandanstalt (Ed.), *Dokumentation Treuhandanstalt 1990–1994 in 15 volumes* (Vol. 6, pp. 885–900). Berlin: Direktorat Kommunikation/Medien.

Melzow, J. (2000). Der Beitrag der Tourismuspolitik auf Bundes- und EU-Ebene zur marktwirtschaftlichen Transformation. In: Freyer, W./Bähre, H. (Eds), Tourismus in den neuen Bundesländern 10 Jahre nach der deutschen Wiedervereinigung (Tagungsband zum 4. Dresdner Tourismus-Symposium 2000), pp. 41–44. Dresden: fit-Verlag.

Meyer-Schwieckerath, M. (1990). Perspektiven des Tourismus in der Bundesrepublik Deutschland – Zur Notwendigkeit eines wirtschaftspolitischen Konzepts. Dissertation at the University of Göttingen. Göttingen.

Neugebauer, G., & Hüning, H. (1992). Privatisierung in der ehemaligen DDR. Materialien zur Arbeit der Treuhandanstalt (Berliner Arbeitshefte und Berichte zur Sozialwissenschaftlichen Forschung No. 58, Zentralinstitut für sozialwissenschaftliche Forschung an der Freien Universität Berlin [Central Institute for Social Science Research at the Free University of Berlin]). Berlin.

No author (1991). ITS übernimmt 35 Jugendtourist-Büros. In: Handelsblatt No. 195 dated 10. 10. 1991, p.17.

No author (1993). Interhotels vorm Untersuchungsausschuss. Hotels und Ferienheime sind nahezu ausverkauft. In: Handelsblatt No. 209 dated 28.10.1993, p. 28.

Ostdeutscher Sparkassen- und Giroverband (OSGV) (Ed.) (2001). Das Tourismusbarometer– Jahresbericht 2001, Berlin.

Passow, U. (1996). Die Eigentumstransformation in Ostdeutschland – Am Beispiel der Neuzuordnung der Feriendienstobjekte (FEDI) – Zur Kritik sozialer und politischer Folgen des rechtlichen Verfahrens im Einigungsprozess als Sonderfall postsozialistischer Transformation (unpublished master's thesis, available at the library of the Eastern European Institute at the Free University of Berlin, Garystraße 55). Berlin.

Schneider, O. (2001). Die Ferien-Macher – Eine grundsätzliche Betrachtung über das Jahrhundert des Tourismus. Hamburg: TourCon Hannelore Niedecken GmbH.

Schütz, W. (2000). Im Osten was Neues? – Daten und Fakten zur Tourismusentwicklung. In: Freyer, W./Bähre, H. (Eds), Tourismus in den neuen Bundesländern 10 Jahre nach der deutschen Wiedervereinigung [Conference Volume for the Fourth Dresden Tourism Symposium (4. Dresdner Tourismus-Symposium 2000)], pp. 54–72. Dresden: fit-Verlag.

Schwarz, G. (1992). Marktwirtschaftliche Reform und Demokratie – eine Hassliebe? Überlegungen zur Interdependenz der Ordnung beim Übergang von der Kommando- zur Wettbewerbswirtschaft. In: ORDO, vol. 43: pp. 65–90.

Seibel, W., & Kapferer, S. (1993). Die organisatorische Entwicklung der Treuhandanstalt. In: Fischer, W./Hax, H./Schneider, H.K. (Eds), Treuhandanstalt: Das Unmögliche wagen, pp. 11–147. Berlin: Akademieverlag.

Statistisches Bundesamt [German Federal Office of Statistics] (Ed.) (1998). Wirtschaft und Statistik 4/1998. Wiesbaden.

Statistisches Bundesamt [German Federal Office of Statistics] (Ed.) (various years). Tourismus in Zahlen (TiZ). Wiesbaden.

Statistisches Bundesamt [German Federal Office of Statistics] (Ed.) (various years). Various series. Wiesbaden.

Stein, von Lorenz (1975). Die Verwaltungslehre (1852–1868), reprint, 8 parts in 10 volumes. Aalen: Scientia Verlag.

Stoll, G. (2000). Wolkig mit wenig Aufheiterungen: Hotelmarkt in den neuen Bundesländern hinkt dem Aufschwung im Westen hinterher. In: fvw International 28/2000 dated 10. 11. 2000. 70–71.

Studienkreis für Tourismus [Study group for tourism (StfT)] (Ed.) (various years up to 1993): Reiseanalyse, Starnberg, various years from 1994: [Forschungsgemeinschaft Urlaub und Reisen (Holiday and travel research group) (FUR)] (Ed.) U + R, Hamburg.

Teuber, J. (2001). Interessenverbände und Lobbying in der Europäischen Union (Europäische Hochschulschriften Reihe 32 Politikwissenschaft, Band 423), Frankfurt am Main/Berlin/Bern/ Brussels/New York/Oxford/Wien: Europäische Hochschulschriften.

Treuhandanstalt (Ed.). (1994). *Dokumentation Treuhandanstalt 1990–1994, 15 volumes*, Berlin.

Treuhandanstalt (Ed.). (1994). *Dokumentation Treuhandanstalt 1990–1994 in 15 volumes*, (Vol. 6). Berlin: Treuhandanstalt, Direktorat Kommunikation/Medien.

Wannhoff, J. (Ed.). (2001). *Sparkassen und Tourismus*. Stuttgart: Deutscher Sparkassenverlag.

Watrin, C. (1989). Wirtschaftssystemreformen in Deutschland. Ein Vergleich zwischen 1948 und 1989. Zeitschrift für Wirtschaftspolitik, 38/3, 77–81.

Wegner, M. (1996). Die deutsche Einigung oder das Ausbleiben des Wunders. Sechs Jahre danach: eine Zwischenbilanz. Politik und Zeitgeschichte, 40/96, pp. 13–23.

Welfens, P. J. J. (Ed.) (1996). *Economic aspects of German unification*. Heidelberg: Springer.

Williamson, O. E. (1975). *Markets and hierarchies: Analysis and antitrust implications*. New York: The Free Press.

Williamson, O. E. (1985). *The economic institutions of capitalism*. New York: The Free Press.

Wrobel, R. M. (1999). Die Bedeutung des Systemwettbewerbs für die Evolution und Transformation von Wirtschaftssystemen (mit einer Analyse des Transformationsprozesses in Estland als Anwendungsbeispiel). Dissertation at the Christian-Albrecht University Kiel, Kiel.

Printed materials from the eleventh through the fourteenth legislative periods of the German Bundestag. In particular:

BT 13/5377 (01.08.96); Report of the Independent Commission for the Examination of the Property of the Parties and Mass Organisations of the GDR (second concluding report) concerning the Free German Youth (FDJ), and reactions of the federal government. Bonn.

Chapter 4

Group Politics and Tourism Interest Representation at the Supranational Level: Evidence from the European Union

Constantia Anastasiadou

Introduction

Group politics have flourished since the mid-20th century, as the result of the changes in the economies and societies in the West, which have seen interest groups increasingly more actively involved in policy-making. The basic premise of interest representation is that individuals can only influence policy-making to a certain degree, therefore organising in some collective form can have much greater impact (Hall & Jenkins, 1995). In recent decades transnational social movements and international non-governmental organisations have also emerged (Axford, 2002), as politics have become increasingly globalised especially in areas such as the environment and human rights.

Nowhere have perhaps interest groups been encouraged to participate more in policy formulation than the European Union (EU). Integration theorists suggested that the establishment of scientific and technical elites was instrumental in the process of European integration (Mazey & Richardson, 1993; 2001) and consequently the organisation of interests at the EU level was actively encouraged and supported by the EU institutions. This support led to an explosion in the numbers and types of interest groups active at the EU level, which have played a key role in the development and growth of EU politics.

Tourism interest groups are also present at the supranational level, as EU regulatory mechanisms have had a profound impact on tourism growth and development (Lickorish, 1994). Just like at the national level, tourism interests strive to make their views known and wish to affect the strategic policy directions, but they are operating in a more complex and dynamic environment which makes representation cumbersome and complicated.

It is difficult to comment on how representation is adjusted at the supranational level, as there has been little systematic study of tourism interest issues in the tourism literature.

Empirical data drawn from an investigation of the institutional arrangements for tourism at the EU level builds a picture of the dynamic of tourism interest representation at the supranational level, and sheds light on their performance and their interaction with the EU institutional setting. Conclusions can then be drawn on how the added complexities and structures of the supranational environment condition the interactions, efficiency and effectiveness of tourism interest groups in agenda setting.

The functions and the influence of interest groups are largely context dependent so it is important to establish the context before their analysis can go further.

The Study Context

A reciprocal relationship between government and interest groups exists. Governments are often dependent on interest groups to receive technical knowledge and expertise, while interest groups establish relationships with the government in an attempt to monitor potential regulation, contribute to the implementation of policy and where feasible, influence it to their advantage. The salience of an issue, its importance to the government and the public can be crucial in getting the group's voice heard (Axford, 2002).

Interests have come to "embody a significant force in European politics, affecting the way agendas are shaped and legislation is made" (Aspinwall & Greenwood, 1997, p. 1). It is practically impossible to be authoritative on the numbers of interest groups that focus their attention on the EU since not all are centrally registered or have offices in Brussels, and for some monitoring the EU activity is only part of their role. There are also different kinds of interest groups and Table 4.1 summarises some of them.

Political thinking and the expansion of the EU areas of activity have conditioned the development of EU level interest representation. Neo-functional theories of integration had asserted that through the closer co-operation and development of scientific and technical elites, European economic and political integration would become a reality (Mazey & Richardson, 2001). Organisation at the European level would influence the speed and success

Table 4.1: Some classifications of interest groups.

Nugent (1999)	**Mazey and Richardson (1999)**
Regional government groups	European associations
	National associations
Private and public companies	Individual firms
	Lobbying consultancy firms
National interest groups	Public bodies such as regional governments and local authorities
Euro-groups	*Ad hoc* coalitions for a single issue
	Organisations of experts and epistemic communities.

of any integration efforts and the establishment of Euro-associations was actively encouraged from the start (Greenwood, 1993).

The gradual expansion, deepening and growth of competencies of the EU, led to an increase in the numbers of interest groups (Aspinwall & Greenwood, 1997). Interest representation displayed a spectacular growth in the years after the signing of the Single European Act (1986) and up to the completion of the Single Market in 1993. The arduous and complicated Single Market process gave rise to a number of regulatory and legislative changes and the Commission and other institutions encouraged the presence of lobbyists in order to facilitate their work. For interest groups lobbying national governments was increasingly inadequate as by this stage the EU had significant powers in several policy domains over the nation-state. In addition, the reform of the EU decision-making process had begun to weaken governments' influence at EU level (Mazey & Richardson, 1993). In order for interest groups to influence policy-making, it was imperative they made their presence and had their views heard at the supranational level.

The EU institutions are now dependent on interests to receive specialist information and knowledge that will assist them to perform their responsibilities more efficiently (Nugent, 2001). The Commission depends on interest groups for information (Greenwood, 1995) and can use them as a measure of public opinion. If interest groups are consulted at the formulation stages of a proposal, the Commission can gauge where it might come up against political difficulties at the national level (Mazey & Richardson, 1993). The European Parliament seeks out regular consultations with experts and interested organisations through public hearings, as a means of gaining and disseminating information (Judge & Earnshaw, 2003) and specialised intergroups. Intergroups give the opportunity to Parliamentarians to focus on issues they are interested in and make contacts with interest groups on an informal basis (Corbett, Jacobs & Shackleton, 2000).

Interest groups have thus, the opportunity to influence decision-making and making their views known through several paths. The activities of the Commission are closely scrutinised by interests who want to be informed of forthcoming legislation and policy development and, where possible, influence it to their benefit. The European Parliament has been the prime target of lobbying from certain types of groups that have had difficulty in accessing the Commission and the national governments such as consumer and environmentalist groups (Mazey & Richardson, 2001). The existence of multiple venues and the wide communication with several players make it impossible for any single interest or association to secure exclusive influence.

However, business interests are by far the most influential (Coen, 1997) and the ability of the Euro-associations to perform their functions has come under questioning (Greenwood, 1997; Mazey & Richardson, 1999). Pijnenburg (1998) commented that Euro-associations are often presented as weak, ineffective and "paper tiger" lobbies but free riding also appears to be a major issue (Mazey & Richardson, 1993). In addition, they suffer from lack of resources, a lack of internal hierarchy and discipline, differences in political culture and approaches to lobbying, too much distance between individual companies and Euro-associations and the attitude by the EU institutions, primarily the Commission, to prefer direct contacts with the business community.

The Commission often bypasses associations in the day-to-day activities because they tend to be broad in their interests (Mazey & Richardson, 1993). The officials prefer to deal with individual associations and firms in order to secure reliable, technical information quickly. In addition, the national industries that the associations represent have different traditions, structures and different competing interests. Associations tend to act as a clearinghouse rather than the aggregate of interest they are representing (Peters, 2001). Consequently, Euro-associations often have to devise compromise policies that are usually of little practical use (lowest common denominator policies) and quite often lack the expertise the Commission needs.

In those sectors where Euro-associations come forward with broadly united and coherent positions, they can greatly assist the Commission by allowing it to deal with aggregated sectoral views (Nugent, 2001). Coherent positions predispose the Commission and Parliament positively about the sector but agreement can only be achieved in those sectors where identification of common issues and the establishment of a joint agenda are possible. The pharmaceutical sector, for instance, is a sector that has secured its priorities with the institutions because of the identification of common issues (Greenwood, 1997) but other sectors, such as tourism, have not.

Characteristics of Tourism Interest Groups

Tourism lobbying has been traditionally problematic not only at European level, but at the national and the subnational levels. Despite the economic importance of tourism, its political influence is limited by the existence of conflicting interests (Greenwood, 1992). Tourism interests do not include only those of the tourism industry but also a wide array of community, public and special interest groups (Hall & Jenkins, 1995). Because of the large number of stakeholders, communication with government is often problematic.

Tourism interest groups can be classified as producer, non-producer and single interest groups (Hall & Jenkins, 1995). Producer groups include business and labour organisations and professional associations and are permanent, well organised and can enjoy key positions in negotiations with government. Non-producer groups such as consumer and environmentalist groups are established on the basis of a shared or common issue, which is of continuing relevance to their members. Single interest groups are developed to lobby for a specific issue and usually disappear once their lobbying efforts have been achieved or are abandoned.

Although business interests have enjoyed more prominence in dealing with the government (Coen, 1997; Greenwood, 1993), increasingly non-producer groups are impacting profoundly on the articulation of the tourism agenda. This certainly holds true at the European level where consumer and environmental groups are very powerful and dynamic. Their influence was present in the Communication on the Future of European Tourism (CEC, 2001) where a lot of what can be described as the environmental agenda for tourism has been adopted as a priority for European tourism.

Given the fragmented nature of the tourism industry it is difficult for business interests to identify common positions on matters of policy (Hall, 1994). Consequently, associations are limited in focusing their efforts in those areas where their members are able to agree, in order to achieve consensus and keep their members satisfied. This in turn affects the possibilities for efficient lobbying and provision of information to the government.

Although there have been attempts to unify the views of the tourism industry and create "one voice" structures there are limits to the extent that these can create a single political voice (Greenwood, 1993). The variety of sectors and interests that constitute tourism simply does not allow for effective "one voice" efforts, as tourism interests are often complementary but rarely integrated (Tyler & Dinan, 2001a).

Problem Area

The role of tourism interest groups in the public policy arena has received limited attention in the tourism literature (Greenwood, 1992; 1993; 1995; Tyler & Dinan 2001a,b). Greenwood studied tourism producer groups in England and in the European Community and suggested that neo-pluralist relationships that favoured some and not all groups had been established. Tyler and Dinan (2000a,b) studied the English tourism policy arena in greater depth focusing as well on tourism producer groups. Their findings suggested that a tourism issue network was emerging in England that remained loose and immature. Commercially oriented interests had established stronger links with the government as evidenced by the dominance of industry-based themes in the national strategy. Their findings confirmed Greenwood's assertion that some associations had formed stronger relationships with the government whereas others had failed.

Little is known of what is happening in tourism interest representation at the European level, as it has received very little reference in the literature (Greenwood, 1992; 1993; 1995). In his study of tourism interest representation at this level, Greenwood noted the presence of a large number of – often overlapping – tourism Euro-groups, which varied in their success in influencing policy-making. Some groups were making substantial contributions, whereas others were little more than nominal associations. Overall, he described tourism interests, as being weak in comparison to other sectors because of the diversity of the tourism sector. He stressed the need for tourism interests to be better organised in order to become more influential. Greenwood (1997) claimed that attempting collective action across a domain that lacks definition, such as tourism, is always likely to be troublesome. The possession of key resources such as expertise, implementation control and economic muscle ultimately conditions the power of interests in public policy-making (Greenwood, 1992). Examining up close the groups would help in determining their influence on agenda setting, but there was no further study than Greenwood's original analysis.

An investigation by the author of the interactions in the EU tourism policy environment unearthed further findings of the characteristics of tourism interest representation (Anastasiadou, 2004), which complement Greenwood's commentary and constitute a basis for a useful comparison to Tyler and Dinan's work. By studying the features and characteristics of tourism interest representation, the influence and impact of tourism interest groups can be seen and any significant comparisons to interest representation at the national level can be made. In addition, the investigation allowed for interest groups to be seen from the perspective of the interest groups and the institutions.

In particular, does working in a policy environment that welcomes and even expects input from interest parties affect how tourism interests are organised? Are there significant differences to interest representation at the national level?

Empirical data drawn from 14 in-depth, elite, face-to-face and phone interview were complemented by a large number of secondary information sources consisting of reports, newsletters, bulletins, statistical data, minutes of meetings, position papers and Commission discussion documents. The perceptions of a range of individuals from tourism interest groups, Commission civil servants and Members of the European Parliament, regarding tourism interest representation were explored. Unlike previous studies, where the focus was exclusively business interest associations, an attempt was made to include representatives from environmental and consumer interest groups but their participation was not secured. As a result, the investigation focused mainly on tourism interests but views were also expressed about the representation ability and approach of other types of groups.

Findings

Interest representation at the supranational level appears to demonstrate similar traits and characteristics to that at the national level. In particular *small size* of interest groups and *fragmentation* are replicated at the supranational level. However, there are also issues relating to how *representative* the various Euro-associations are and *access* to the EU institutions, which is far from being uniform. Each of these features is examined in more detail below.

Small Size

Most of the interest groups are of a small size and have a limited budget because of a limited membership base. The groups' limited resources dictate prioritisation of involvement and consequently, interest groups are obliged to focus their efforts only on those issues that are of direct relevance to them. The large majority of groups do not have sufficient resources to deal with the array of diverse issues that emerge from the Commission and which are influential to tourism, which confirms previous claims in the literature (Greenwood, 1995; Elliot, 1997). Group interests dictate the fashion in which groups organise and lobby and their limited resources condition the extent of their involvement in areas outside their immediate remit.

A safe conclusion can be made then that the more specific the interests represented by an organisation the fewer the areas where it will be active. Potentially the organisation's overall impact might also be limited but a lot will depend on the breadth of its membership base. The broader the base, potentially the wider the membership and consequently the number of areas where a group is active. This is why organisations with a broader base (either in terms of members or interests represented) appear to be more active, for example ETAG, HOTREC and ETOA[1]. Obviously, the larger the membership base the bigger the weight the association will carry in the consultations with the Parliament and the Commission. In short, size matters … a lot.

---

[1] European Tourism Action Group (ETAG); Confederation of the National Associations of Hotel, Restaurants and Similar Establishments in the EU and the EEA (HOTREC); European Tour Operators Association (ETOA).

Overlap and Issues of Representativeness

Overlap was identified as an area of potential conflict between groups. Overlap puts pressure on organisations to prove the added value that being a member brings and creates stiff competition between associations. If the members of an association are not persuaded of the benefits of membership, they are likely to discontinue it or perhaps even worse, move to the rival or overlapping association and thus, further undermine the importance of the first association.

In addition, an attitude of scepticism from their members and from the institutions towards associations is evident, further confirming the difficult position associations may find themselves in. In particular, issues of representativeness are raised. Interviewees suggested that as membership is not mandatory, quite often associations do not represent all the equivalent associations in member states and they might not even represent the majority but rather a section of them. This is a significant difference to what happens at the national level, where competing associations may exist but are not as pronounced.

Perhaps more importantly, it is the authority with which associations are claiming to speak that was questioned and there were implicit accusations of elitism. Some trade associations were perceived as being run by public affairs' professionals rather than professionals from the industry segment they represented and were being pushed aside in favour of people with real experience. The repercussions of these perceptions are very significant as they question the licence with which these organisations present themselves and the weight that is given to their positions. Such perceptions jeopardised the future and relevance of trade associations.

In particular, institutions preferred dealing with larger organisations because this allowed reaching more people with fewer contacts, but even large organisations cannot speak authoritatively for the whole industry; the positions of the large majority of which are small and medium enterprises (SMEs). Tourism interests could then easily be over and under-represented at the European level. This attitude compromised representativeness and fairness over ease of access.

In this setting, representativeness is a two-dimensional question: first, how representative interest groups really are and second, how representative of the sector is the perspective the institutions gain through conversing to selected organisations? Naturally, the absence of uniform access created tension between the interest groups and the institutions, and among the interest groups.

The existence of so many groups with varied agendas and priorities presented further problems to the institutions other than just keeping in regular contact. The groups' tendency to present a fragmented agenda during consultations left institutional representatives unsure of how best to assist the sector. Were the big issues identified, it was claimed, the institutions would be better positioned to assist the sector. Voices for the establishment of a **single voice for tourism** had gained some momentum.

Single Voice or Common Voice?

It was argued that through improved communication and co-operation interest groups would gain a better understanding of their own agendas and reap greater benefits. However, there was a difference of opinion on whether a single voice or common voice approach were feasible or desirable.

The institutional representatives demonstrated a preference towards the establishment of a tourism umbrella group to encompass the entirety of tourism interests become the voice of the sector and act as a single point of reference. They argued, that contrary to tourism interest groups' claims, it was not impossible for the industry groups to establish a single voice and co-ordinate their activities, but rather because of conflict, competition and self-interest, an umbrella group was undesirable.

The tourism interests representatives presented a case of unfeasibility rather than undesirability stating diversity of interest and distinctiveness as defining characteristics of their fragmented industry. However, some displayed a degree of scepticism and considered this degree of institutional involvement as intervention in their own affairs. Some suggested that a single voice for tourism in fact meant a single person that could speak to the Commission on behalf of the tourism industry, which would obviously work against the interests of existing groups.

For these reasons, interest groups representatives suggested that presenting *a common voice* on certain issues rather than a single voice for all issues was a more relevant and realistic proposition. In brief, the common voice approach supported a system of common and individual representation depending on the issue at hand while dismissing the single voice as being unrealistic and unfeasible.

The logic behind the common voice approach was reflected in the joint declaration by the tourism sector "Tourism in Europe: United yet diverse", which brought together private sector industry organisations and public and private sector umbrella groups. The declaration made reference to matters such as taxation, liberalisation, comprehensive policy co-ordination to name few, which were supported by all signatories (ETP, 2000) but failed to receive the recognition of other interest groups.

Declarations had been proffered before and their limited endorsement by the tourism industry was common. For these reasons the institutional representatives considered such attempts unsatisfactory and tended to ignore them and "Tourism in Europe: United yet diverse" was not an exception. For them the notion of a common approach was not novel and was not a solution. Table 4.2 below summarises single voice/common voice debate.

Table 4.2: Single voice versus common voice.

	Single voice		Common voice	
	Opinion	**Problem**	**Opinion**	**Problem**
Institutions	Feasible but not desirable	Conflict self-interest	Impractical	Communication problem remains unresolved
Tourism interest groups	Unfeasible	Diversity makes it impossible	Feasible	Limited areas of agreement due to the nature of tourism

Agenda Setting

If no agreement could be made about the feasibility and relevance of single voice/common voice efforts, maybe the identification of common issues for the whole industry could help improve communication between groups and institutions. Establishing a rudimentary common tourism agenda could be the way forward.

Perhaps surprisingly, is process was initiated by the European Parliament and the tourism industry representatives were asked to identify those issues that were of relevance and importance to all of them. The issues eventually identified included: raising awareness of the importance of travel and tourism, improving tourism infrastructure, people's skills, open skies and taxation.

Addressing these issues at the European level was considered an important step towards assisting the growth of sector but these issues were too far-reaching to be lobbied by tourism interests alone; a wider coalition of interests from a number of more powerful than tourism domains would be necessary.

However, one cannot fail to notice that these issues were only generated as a response to the Parliament's request, rather than the coming together of tourism interest and were put forward because interest groups were asked to produce a list, not because of the prominence of these issues in their own agenda. It is more likely that these were selected as the only issues where they shared similar views; as it is common with tourism issues, once again the lowest common denominator prevailed.

Tourism interests need to assert themselves more with the institutions if they want to have a prominent place and define the EU tourism agenda. While tourism interests remain isolated and fragmented, they will fail to do so but by building more meaningful coalitions they will gradually gain the place they desire.

Conclusions

The main objectives of the chapter were to build on existing findings of tourism interest representation and examine whether tourism interest representation at the supranational and national levels differed significantly.

The literature demonstrated that a complex policy environment exists at the EU level, with formalised relationships between institutions and interest groups and opportunities to use several paths for lobbying. The existence of several, diverse players and multiple venues makes the secure exclusive interests that some groups may enjoy at the national level, practically non-existent at the EU level. In this environment, the sectors that can put together coherent positions are the winners, but with fragmentation being such a defining characteristic of the tourist activity, tourism is clearly not one of them.

Evidence drawn from the practices of tourism interest groups (Greenwood, 1993; 1995; 1997; Tyler & Dinan, 2001a,b) highlighted small size, diversity and fragmentation as defining characteristics of tourism interest representation at the national level. Overlap, issues regarding the representativeness of tourism interests and access to institutions are added to the list at the supranational level. The selection of specific individuals and organisations for regular consultation by institutional representatives was met with criticism but was justified because of the numbers of interests involved and the fragmentation of their agendas. The practice of the institutional representatives to deal directly with the business community posed implications and threats for the SMEs-dominated tourism sector.

Improving communication among interest groups through a single/common voice instrument was deemed necessary but there was a clear divide between institutional and interest group representatives on how this could be best achieved. Attempting to establish a common agenda had not been successful either, as it was largely a by-product of institutional pressure rather than the outcome of the interest groups' conscious efforts. Clearly, the inability of tourism interests to put forward aggregated sectoral views was weakening their bargaining position with the institutions.

Tourism interest representation at the supranational level is thus, weak. Interest groups appear to be reactive to issues largely dictated by the institutions rather than proactive. By implication they are unable to set the tourism agenda and are instead being guided by the very institutions they are trying to influence. Revisiting Greenwood's (1993) notion of power dependence, tourism interests have the expertise but they lack the economic muscle and implementation control that will allow them to make their presence more prominent in EU policy-making. Fragmentation and diversity of interest seriously dampen any attempts for leadership of the sector or collective responses.

Unlike what is happening at the national level where loose issue networks have been reported (Tyler & Dinan, 2001a,b), the internationalisation of tourism issues and priorities appears to be happening only as a nervous reaction. Tourism interest groups appear to be engaged in a damage limitation exercise and setting a supranational agenda for tourism seems to be a low priority perhaps because the relevance of EU involvement remains a contested issue (Anastasiadou, 2006). Instead of being the drivers, tourism interest groups appear to be driven by the process, the speed and direction of which is dictated by the institutional stakeholders and the priorities of non-tourism interests.

The absence of truly global policies for tourism makes tourism interest groups appear to be unsure how to lobby at a complex, supranational environment such as that of the EU. By adopting strategies and lobbying approaches similar to those of their counterparts at the national level, they remain unprepared for the complexities and implications of lobbying at the supranational level. Interest representation is a lot more complex and sophisticated, the institutions rely more on interest groups and the inability of tourism interests to adjust their approach impedes their ability to set or even influence the agenda to their benefit.

As this is a little explored area, it is suggested that more studies of tourism interest representation at the regional, national and subnational levels would help pursue further the points raised in this chapter and help construct a more solid picture of the characteristics of interest representation.

References

Anastasiadou, C. (2004). *Supranational involvement in tourism: The case of the European Union.* Unpublished doctoral dissertation. University of Strathclyde, Glasgow.

Anastasiadou, C. (2006). Tourism and the European Union. In: D. Hall, B. Marciszewska, & M. Smith (Eds), *Tourism in the new Europe: The challenges and opportunities of EU enlargement* (pp. 20–31). London: CABI Publishing.

Aspinwall, M. & Greenwood, J. (1997). *Collective Action in the European Union: Interests and the New Politics of Associability.* London: Routledge.

Axford, B. (2002). Parties, interest groups and public opinion. In: B. Axford, G. K. Browning, R. Huggins, & B. Rosamont (Eds), *Politics: An introduction* (2nd ed., pp. 358–407). London: Routledge.

CEC (2001). *Working together for the future of European tourism.* Brussels: COM (2001) 665 final.

Coen, D. (1997). The European business lobby. *Business Strategy Review, 8*(4), 17–25.

Corbett, R., Jacobs, F., & Shackleton, M. (2000). *The European Parliament* (4th ed.). London: John Harper.

Elliot, J. (1997). *Tourism politics and public sector management.* London: Routledge.

ETP (2000, September 13). Small step or giant leap for European tourism organisations? European travel policy. Retrieved February, 26, 2002 from http://www.europeantravelpolicy.com/010227.htm

Greenwood, J. (1992). Producer interest groups in tourism policy: Case studies from Britain and the European Union. *American Behavioral Scientist, 36*, 236–256.

Greenwood, J. (1993). Business interest groups in tourism governance. *Tourism Management, 14*, 335–348.

Greenwood, J. (1995). Introduction. In: J. Greenwood (Ed.), *European casebook on business alliances* (pp. 1–22). London: Prentice Hall.

Greenwood, J. (1997). *Representing interests in the European Union.* Basingstoke: Macmillan Press Ltd.

Hall, C. M. (1994). *Tourism and politics. Policy, power and place.* Chichester: John Wiley & Sons.

Hall, C. M., & Jenkins, J. (1995). *Tourism and public policy.* London: Routledge.

Judge, D., & Earnshaw, D. (2003). *The European Parliament.* Basingstoke: Palgrave Macmillan.

Lickorish, L. J. (1994). *Developing tourism destinations policies and perspectives.* London: Longman.

Mazey, S., & Richardson, J. (1993). Pressure groups and lobbying in the EC. In: J. Lodge (Ed.), *The European Community and the challenge of the future* (2nd ed., pp. 37–47). New York: St. Martin's Press.

Mazey, S., & Richardson, J. (1999). Interests. In: L. Cram, D. Dinan, & N. Nugent (Eds), *Developments in the European Union* (pp. 105–129). Basingstoke: MacMillan Press Ltd.

Mazey, S., & Richardson, J. (2001). Interest groups and EU policy-making: Organisational logic and venue shopping. In: J. Richardson (Ed.), *European Union power and policy making* (2nd ed., pp. 217–238). London: Routledge.

Nugent, N. (2001). *The European Commission.* Basingstoke: Palgrave.

Peters, G. B. (2001). Agenda setting in the European Union. In: J. Richardson (Ed.), *European Union power and policy making* (2nd ed., pp. 77–94). London: Routledge.

Pijnenburg, B. (1998). EU lobbying by *ad hoc* coalitions: An exploratory case study. *Journal of European Public Policy, 5*, 303–321.

Tyler, D., & Dinan, C. (2001a). The role of interested groups in England's emerging tourism policy network. *Current Issues in Tourism, 4*, 210–252.

Tyler, D., & Dinan, C. (2001b). Trade and associated groups in the English tourism policy arena. *International Journal of Tourism Research, 3*, 459–476.

Chapter 5

The Politics of Exclusion? Japanese Cultural Reactions and the Government's Desire to Double Inbound Tourism

Malcolm Cooper, Radaslawa Jankowska and Jeremy Eades

Introduction

Japan in the 21st century will have to face many challenges: economic, political and social. The well-documented ageing of the Japanese and the other developed societies on a world-wide basis is one such social phenomenon that will heavily influence the economy and social structure of 21st century Japan (Cooper & Eades, 2006). In the case of Japan how-ever, there is another social factor that will also influence the responses of this society to the aging trend to a great extent and in a negative way, the equally well-documented ten-dency for the Japanese to exclude *Gaijin* (foreigners) from full participation in society (Tsuda, 2003). At one level, local communities are interested in the potential of foreign tourists to revitalize their stagnant economies, at other levels, the treatment of foreign vis-itors is more ambiguous. Signs denying foreigners access to *onsen* (spas), traditional hotels and restaurants may be found throughout the country and have proven difficult to remove, despite successful challenges in the Courts. It should not be surprising then that the Japan Tourism Advisory Council's (2003) report on encouraging inbound tourism and the sub-sequent announcement by the government of a target of 10 million international visitors by 2010 occasioned vigorous debate.

Labour mobility and cultural exchange are most important resources on the world stage and can be only gained by cooperating with others. Japan does not seem too keen on such exchanges and this can be felt on many levels: national, local and individual. For the moment this problem is not taken very seriously, especially as the number of foreigners in Japan is low and to date the economy's demand for external labour resources has not been high. However, this does not mean that the question should be ignored, and it is especially important given the stated intention of the government to achieve a target of 10 million international visitors by the year 2010, double that of 2003 (Ministry of Land, Infrastructure and Transport, 2004a).

The main goal of this chapter is to examine the question of exclusion in present day Japan and how this might affect inbound tourism, but as this topic is very wide many aspects have to be left out. For example, the experience of the *zainichi* (permanently resident) foreigner is omitted as this constitutes a separate and very large topic in itself and is not directly related to inbound tourism. Also, the question of illegal immigrants to Japan is not discussed. The chapter however does generalize about the position of foreigners in Japan, irrespective of their legal status or country of origin, in so far as this points to the likely impact of the politics of exclusion on inbound tourists in the future.

The methods used for researching this topic mostly entailed examining already existing published material, and the topical media. This was necessary both to understand the framework of the exclusion discussion and also to report accurately the details of the current debate on the development of inbound tourism to Japan. The material has been collected since the beginning of 2002. In addition, as all of the authors are foreigners living in Japan in a well-known but domestic tourism-based city, some observations and data come directly from our own experiences. Consequently, this is very much work in progress.

Context: The Politics of Exclusion: Japan Style

As globalization continues to spread, spearheaded by tourism, some problems have emerged (Meethan, 2001). One is that people who may have been formerly quite isolated from the outside world are increasingly meeting outsiders, and are becoming more conscious of the growing likelihood of this happening more often. This situation often leads to a feeling of discomfort as people find themselves in unusual situations even in their own home towns. A good example of this is Beppu, a famous domestic spa tourism city on the southern Island of Kyushu in Japan, but one where few foreigners were resident until 2000 and very few inbound tourists visited. After the opening of the Ritsumeikan Asia Pacific University in 2000, the city centre was soon crowded with young people from all over the world (the total is now 2000 students or about 45% of the 2006 university enrolment), and the number of foreign tourists now stands at around 140,000 per year (Beppu Foreign Tourists Information Bureau, 2006). However, not all citizens were happy about these changes, as they were afraid of the potential consequences from a clash of cultures (Prof Masakatsu Ogata, September 2003, personal communication). But by 2006 these fears had largely disappeared, as students and the services that they attract have moved into the local economy in quite a big way, even to the extent of taking over restaurants and introducing new types of food.

This fear of foreigners, and of new diseases, increasing crime, etc., is in its most extreme form *xenophobia* (e.g. Bourdieu, 1999), and is expressed strongly in parts of the Japanese media and in the "beware of foreigners" pronouncements of certain prominent politicians such as the current Governor of Tokyo (http://voyage.typepad.com/china/2005/07/tokyo_governor_.html), but in any form it is always characterized by a strong feeling of *us* versus *them*. One of its central characteristics is also that these feelings have a tendency to get stronger as the number of outsiders increases, as according to the argument's internal logic more outsiders mean even more disease and crime. Also, by meeting outsiders more often locals quite often start thinking about the possible problems more than they did before rather than how nice these strangers actually are, especially if media reports are implying an increasing incidence of foreign crime or similar impacts from their presence.

Ethnocentrism (Korostelina, 2004) is another important aspect of xenophobia and refers to the idea that one culture is superior to another and, moreover that it has the right to impose its own tenets onto another culture. Usually this is connected with a tendency to interpret and evaluate other people's behaviours by the group in question's own standards (Carr, 2003; McKay, 1994). The more ethnocentric a person or society is, the harder it will be to cope with new situation visitation from people foreign to the cultural group. This is also true for the visitors to a new cultural environment (Boyle, 2003, pp. 255–256). If they too are strongly ethnocentric, it will make it difficult for them as outsiders to get used to the new situation, even if they are relatively open-minded. As such movements and inter-actions of people form the major part of tourism, it is important that visitors feel comfort-able in the new environment and also, if they have a good image of the host community, they can provide good publicity when they return to their respective countries of origin. For this reason both the host community and the visitor have to be as culturally relativis-tic as possible, which means that their members should suspend judgment, and to try to understand the way that the cultures being brought together by the act of tourism see the world (Carr, 2003).

In the case of Japan the number of foreign residents is comparatively low compared with the other major industrial countries. This has come about for several reasons includ-ing geographical isolation, long historical seclusion, and more recently strict labour and immigration policies. In 2004 the number of foreigners living in Japan was just 1.7% of the total population or about 2 million, but even that modest figure consists mostly of second- and third-generation Koreans and Chinese whose ancestors were brought to Japan when it maintained colonies on the Asian mainland (Table 5.1).

Table 5.1: Number of non-Japanese residents in Japan by country 2004.

Country of origin	Persons
South Korea and North Korea	607,419
China	487,570
Brazil	286,557
Philippines	199,394
Peru	55,750
USA	48,844
Other countries	288,213
Total	1,973,747

Source: Gaikokujin Torokusha Tokei ni tsuite (Statistics on Foreign Residents), Immigration Bureau, Ministry of Justice (June 2005).

As resident *Gaijin* know all too well, even long-term immigrants face frequent discrimination and are not accepted as real Japanese (Tsuda, 2003). The general image of Japan held outside the country is that it is *far away*, not only in terms of geographical distance, but also in cultural terms. Japan's culture and people are considered different and strange mainly because the Japanese themselves believe in the existence of such differences and do everything to sustain this image by emphasising their culture and by trying to keep their traditional ways of doing things intact, as if they are unique to the world (Hellyer, 2002; Yoneyama, 1999). This leads to the formation of an image of Japan and its culture that is sold externally in which there are still samurais and geishas walking up and down little streets between the kinds of very traditional houses seen in historical films. The problem with this image is that it is so far from reality that it is not conducive to the construction of an open and friendly stay for inbound tourists because it simply does not provide any reference points to describe how to get around modern Japan even for the tourist interested in the country's history.

Two major factors have led to the development of this idea of the difference of Japan. One is historical and the other is cultural. The historical is connected with the long closure of Japan's borders to European *trade* (but not to a number of Europeans or their ideas). The cultural reason is also connected with the historical one: to Westerners, Japanese seem *distant* in their behaviour. This is caused by differences in their way of communicating, and is therefore a simple problem of intercultural communication. As the Japanese communicate in a way that is seen by Westerners as indirect, difficult to understand and so on, the image of them being distant is formed easily. This is clearly also a result of Western people's own ethnocentric way of thinking, more or less like saying "they speak in a different way, so they must be strange". For the same reason, from the Japanese point of view Westerners may seem rude, in their direct behaviour. Naturally, this is not necessarily the case, either.

Nevertheless, there are questions to which cultural differences cannot be applied as an explanation of behaviour. One of the most important is the moral issue of discrimination (Tsuda, 2003). Discrimination in levels of information, in level of services offered or in actual day-to-day treatment can not be ignored just by saying it stem from a country's culture. This is especially true in a time of globalization, when national borders are becoming more and more blurred. However, discrimination needs to be understood before it can be cured, and this topic has become of major importance in the current debate over increasing inbound tourism opportunities for Japan.

Nihonjinron

This section of the chapter concentrates on *Nihonjinron* (a theory of Japanese identity), as it has an important role in this problem of discrimination and therefore of reported cases of xenophobia towards *Gaijin* tourists in Japan. Obviously this discussion can only be partial in a chapter of this length, but we hope to provide an overview of Nihonjinron, its various definitions and history and, paradoxically, how it might be used in creating solutions to the very behavioural problems it appears to be associated with. The whole concept can be viewed with understanding, contempt or a range of other emotions; however this does not change its importance. It affects an influential country, so it cannot be ignored, whatever an observer's feelings towards it are. Its followers are usually regarded as xenophobic and nationalistic, while its opponents are often seen as trying to force on the Japanese people behaviour deriving from foreign sources that is unnatural for them. The supporters say that Japan should not change, as it has to maintain its uniqueness. The opponents think that Japan does not change, and does not *want to* for the ethnocentric reasons supporting Nihonjinron.

There are many alternative terms for the concept of Nihonjinron, such as *Nihon bunkaron*, *Nihon shakairon* and *Nihonron* (Befu, 2001, p. 2). All these expressions concentrate on the idea of *Japanese-ness* and for the purposes of this discussion have been subsumed within the term *Nihonjinron*. Japan and its people are portrayed in these discourses as being unique and as being better than other nations, and the concept of *Nihonjinron* is an attempt to justify this theoretically. There are also a wide variety of definitions of the term, and none of them are universally accepted. For example, Befu (2001) does not give a clear definition of the concept but just calls it "Japan's dominant identity discourse" (Befu, 2001, p. ix), which is a little vague. McDonough calls it "the pseudoscience industry of Japanese uniqueness" (McDonough, 1997). Asami defines it as "the assertion of Japanese uniqueness" (Asami, 1997). Dale labels it as an "intellectual fast food of consumer nationalism" and "the commercialized expression of modern Japanese nationalism" (Dale, 1990, pp. 14–16). Austin classifies *Nihonjinron* as endless debate on "what is and isn't truly Japanese" (Austin, 1996). Similar to this is Ismail's variation, describing Nihonjinron as "discussion of the Japanese" (Ismail, 1996). Another definition given by Ismail partly explains why there is no consensus about the meaning of Nihonjinron: he notes that "The Nihonjinron explains everyday occurrences and current news in terms of culture or cultural ethos considered peculiar to the Japanese. Virtually anything can (therefore) become subject matter for the Nihonjinron". As a result, it may be seen in totally different ways by different groups of people.

For the purposes of this chapter, *Nihonjinron* is defined as a living, popular discourse on Japanese identity, distinguished in terms of contrasts that it tends to draw with other nations and in making the Japanese seem unique. Its importance lies in the extent to which it influences the way the Japanese relate to the world outside Japan and to the foreigners who live in and *visit* the country. There are two levels of Nihonjinron; general and individual. These influence each other all the time. For example if an individual introduces his own ideas on a topic and this is accepted by the social group it can change the general standpoint too. On the other hand general views also influence the individual's opinion as a given person's Nihonjinron model is not a static one but is constantly changing in a sort of feedback loop, being revised over and over as a person's experience increases, and with exposure to more literature or new situations relevant to the formulation of their views on the position of Japan in the world (Befu, 2001, p. 77).

The phenomenon described above means that it is important, *but also possible*, to change the popular usages of *Nihonjinron* on the individual level in order to change the whole way in which the Japanese interact with other nations. Ismail (1996) notes that: "the thinking elites are perceived to be the active producer of knowledge about Nihonjinron and the ordinary Japanese as the passive consumer" in the explanations offered for the success of the concept in Japanese society. This can of course be dangerous: powerful societal elites can change the *Nihonjinron* as they want and thus influence ordinary people to accept their view of the world. They can for example turn it into pure nationalism (Buruma, 1994). On the other hand, they can also turn it into a tool for helping with such social problems as discrimination against foreigners (e.g. Kawasaki, 2004). This process naturally depends to a great extent on the elite's interests, and at the present these interests appear to be aligned towards accepting more tourists from abroad (Japan Association of Travel Agents, 2004; Kajimoto, 2003).

The Purpose of Nihonjinron

One of the characteristics of *Nihonjinron* compared to other world-wide quests for national identity, as Befu (2001) suggests, is its popularity. Rarely do countries other than Japan have so many discussions on their uniqueness and national character in their media; possibly they are being more cautious with this kind of discourse because of a fear of being regarded as xenophobic or overly nationalistic. Another feature of the Japanese concept is how narrowly *Nihonjinron* views differences in cultures: in other countries it is generally known and accepted that there are diverse cultures, but this does not usually lead to interpreting this fact as a proof that they themselves are unique. The more usual deduction from this fact is that *every* culture is unique in some way. An additional aspect of this is that of how the users of *Nihonjinron* reason when establishing its positions. One method lies in the choice of national traits: the supporters of the concept tend to choose for comparison only traits that are different from those of other countries in order to directly counterpoint Japan's uniqueness (Dale, 1990).

Up to this point the basic characteristics of the concept have been discussed, but there is an important question that is still left without an answer. It is about the purpose of *Nihonjinron* in present day Japanese society. The question is what does the concept give that the Japanese are so attached to it, even to the point of observable adverse impacts on inbound tourism? According to Ismail (1996), there are three basic purposes of *Nihonjinron*. The first is to recreate the Japanese identity against external threat; mainly in cultural terms. This means that after Western culture for example intruded in every level of Japanese life (clothing, food, language, etc.) during the 1940s and 1950s and Japanese self-identity was almost destroyed by this, *Nihonjinron* gave an opportunity to the Japanese nation to rebuild, albeit in a heavily modified form. It might thus be argued that the concept thus protected the Japanese way of life and culture from being totally colonized by Western, mainly American culture.

The second function is to explain the unique Japanese economic success throughout history and especially in the 1950s and 1960s, when Japan experienced a level of economic growth not seen before in Asia. The propagators of *Nihonjinron* thought that, given that most of the other Asian countries during their histories had lost many wars and were colonized, Japan was unique because it only lost one war and was never colonized. Also, in other Asian countries the attempts to regain total independence (including economic control) after the colonial period lasted much longer than that in Japan after the American occupation. Explaining the underlying reasons for Japan's success through a largely ethnocentric model could therefore perhaps provide a signpost that could be used in identifying the importance of Japan to other countries.

The third purpose of *Nihonjinron*, as Ismail (1996) sees it, is to unify different groups living together in Japan. This is however a clear denial of the homogenous image of Japan that is one of the basic ideas of the concept. According to Dale (1990) the concept "implicitly assume(s) that the Japanese constitute a culturally and socially homogeneous racial entity, whose essence is virtually unchanged from prehistoric times down to the present day" (Dale, 1990, Introduction), in that it ignores the existence of groups like the Ainu or the Okinawans, not to mention the more recent arrivals the Koreans, Chinese and others. According to this interpretation the Japanese fear diversity so much that they promote uniqueness in order to make the nation as a whole seem more homogeneous and successful.

Befu (2001), on the other hand, thinks that *Nihonjinron* is simply a replacement for the national symbols that lost their meaning after the Pacific War. He says that as the most important national symbols of the Japanese became untenable after 1945 they needed something that would define their identity in contrast to other nations. As the Emperor, the national flag and the national anthem all had some problems relating to their interpretation and underlying meaning as a result of Japanese imperialism in the early 20th century, they had to find a new symbol of national identity. After their defeat the theory that the West was better, stronger and more powerful was confirmed and it became obvious that the Japanese (including the Emperor) were not descendants of Gods and the country was not "God's" chosen nation. Also, because of a fear of renewed nationalism and further defeats, they had to find another way to keep their identity and to give strength to the people to rebuild the country and start all over again without resorting to nationalism and militarism. *Nihonjinron* is strong precisely where symbols are weak: namely, it explicitly defines national identity and explains why one should be proud of one's nation (Befu, 2001, p. 101). Consequently in Befu's interpretation the function of *Nihonjinron* is to replace the former national symbols and to become one itself. As the purpose of national symbols is to make a nation distinct from others and to give a sense of unity and power to its people, the concept can be accepted in these terms.

Nihonjinron and the Future Outlook for Tourism

As already mentioned, the future of Japan in the age of globalization and internationalization depends strongly on how it will relate to others. For this reason it is also important to consider how *Nihonjinron* will influence the way Japanese people think about inbound tourism, as it is clear that is has been a strong force shaping the Japanese way of interacting with foreigners both abroad and within Japan. Ismail (1996) quotes Dr Kosako Yoshino, according to whom "globalization ... can have the unintended consequence of promoting cultural nationalism", as *Nihonjinron* speaks of the Japanese as different or distinct. This is against the main idea of international tourism, which is about finding common points not ones of difference.

There are therefore various points in *Nihonjinron* that could disturb Japanese *kokusaika* or internationalization, especially in relation to inbound tourism. One is "the assumption that uniquely Japanese modes of thinking and behaving are incomprehensible for non-Japanese" (Ismail, 1996). If the Japanese refuse to communicate with foreigners except in line with this assumption there will be no chance for a proper dialogue. And without dialogue, there will be no exchange of information, or at least the flow of it will be one-sided: from the Japanese to the foreigner. Communication control in line with this assumption may be seen in the extremely slow conversion of signage from being solely in Japanese to being multilingual in areas where foreigners might be expected to be found or to require such a service.

The other important point is the question of asserting Japan's ethnic homogeneity. Like virtually all other nations, Japan has never been ethnically homogenous, and yet the *Nihonjinron* concept implies that it is. In this form the concept seems dangerous, since *Nihonjinron* not only tries to convince people of this, but also implies that as Japan always has been a "pure" nation, it has to stay this way for ever and not allow foreign intrusion. By changing this assumption many problems could be solved. Even if the assumption of Japan's (relatively) homogeneous past has to be accepted and only the assertion that for this reason Japan has to stay "pure" is rejected, the situation in relation to *Gaijin* would become much better. For example, the experiences of foreigners living in Japan would improve a lot, and the treatment afforded to tourists would also improve.

In summary then, individual *Nihonjinron* is shaped by that of the elite and in this case this feature can be both detrimental *and* useful, as it makes it possible to modify the tone of the discourse on inbound tourism and by this change the attitudes of the majority of the population. Once the prevailing mindset is altered, it will be easier to promote changes through education and exchange programs, as well as inbound tourism, but until then such measures will have little effect in boosting inbound tourism.

Inbound Tourism: The Welcome Plan 21 and Visit Japan Campaigns

That the problem of Nihonjinron (but equally its usefulness in promoting change) has been recognized, and may be beginning to be modified at least at the political level, is evidenced by the fact that in the late 1990s Japan finally got serious about attracting more foreign visitors to its shores (Kajimoto, 2003). The initial campaign, known as *Welcome Plan 21*, was drawn up in 1996 (Ministry of Land, Infrastructure and Transport, 2004a,b). The new campaign (Visit Japan – 2003) includes setting up information booths at tourism fairs and inviting foreign media, travel agents and other stakeholders to Japan. It is hoped this will promote the country and help create inbound tours in collaboration with the private sector (Kajimoto, 2003). However, there is a long way to go in the promotion of inbound tourism to Japan compared with its outbound tourism (Table 5.2). In 2003 the world's top tourist destinations were France, followed by Spain and the US. Japan meanwhile came in at 32nd – putting it behind such countries as Poland and Croatia. In 2005, 17.4 million Japanese travelled abroad but only 6.8 million foreigners visited Japan (Japan Association of Travel Agents, 2006), creating an international tourism deficit of over 15 billion US dollars.

However, as Japanese national tourism policy was totally outbound-oriented for international tourism, and domestically oriented internally up until at least the late 1990s, there is as yet little expectation of change. Also, the fact that the domestic orientation was also heavily influenced by major land developers interested only in using such forms of tourism as visits to theme parks to make money on the fringe of major urban centres (Hebbert, 1994), meant that little regard for inbound tourism at a local level preceded the change in the government's thinking. For example, while developments under the *Law of Comprehensive Resort Development*

Table 5.2: Inbound tourists to Japan 2000–2004.

Region	2000	2001	2002	2003	2004
Asia	2,854,570	3,085,239	3,263,158	3,511,513	4,208,095
Europe	801,825	615,130	671,495	648,495	726,525
Africa	15,680	17,194	17,156	19,015	19,510
North America	864,842	863,238	835,465	893,971	798,358
South America	35,949	30,672	33,627	25,971	27,238
Oceania	181,570	185,684	200,789	206,994	231,877
Others	2,710	2,209	1,954	1,363	814
Total inbound	4,757,146	4,771,555	5,238,963	5,211,725	6,137,905
Total outbound	17,818,000	16,216,000	16,522,824	13,578,934	16,830,112
Inbound % of total outbound	26.7	29.4	31.6	38.3	36.5

Source: Japan Association of Travel Agents 2005.

(the Resort Law) enacted in 1987 brought about a huge growth in local attractions all over Japan, the development of too many similar attractions frequently occurred and little thought was given to their suitability for inbound tourism. As a result, more than 80% of these resorts are no longer in existence (Shiota, 1999, p. 178) – even though they were of high quality, facilities such as Seagaia (Ocean Dome) in Miyazaki Prefecture (Kyushu), Huis Ten Bosch (Sasebo, Kyushu) and Owani Resort in Aomori Prefecture (North Honshu) were bankrupted because their operating expenses were too high for the domestic tourism market to support. Local governments also built tourism facilities in disadvantaged areas, which became difficult to support because there was no clear market for such businesses. In addition, many developers from urban areas and operating companies were controlled by banks, and consequently suffered in the recession which followed the collapse of the *bubble* economy (NIRA, 2001). Despite little emphasis on or knowledge of how to attract high fee-paying foreign tourists, there has as a result emerged a clear realization that the domestic sector alone cannot support such development except in major cities such as Tokyo and Osaka.

Challenges for Inbound Tourism Development

Apart from the questions raised by *Nihonjinron*, the development of Japanese inbound tourism faces several other disadvantages. Firstly, geographical isolation from the huge inbound tourism potential of Europe requires more and cheaper transportation routes to Japan. Secondly, the perception of high domestic prices is another disadvantage for inbound tourism. While this perception is not entirely correct (Cooper & Lockyer, 2005), especially if the tourist knows where to look for the usual bargains to be found in any community, the relative value of the yen issue will be hard to control by the Japanese government alone given the country's heavy dependence on external terms of trade for manufactured goods and raw materials.

Thirdly, international and domestic marketing and visitor acceptance strategies need attention. The Welcome Plan 21 and Visit Japan Campaign are two of the more successful policies when compared with earlier policies developed after the *Basic Law on Tourism* (1964) was introduced. In spite of this, they are still less effective than the policies of those Countries that enjoy much larger inbound tourism visitor flows, for several reasons. The first problem is budget – promotional expenditure by the Japan National Tourism Organization (JNTO) was only 440 million yen in 2002. On the other hand, expenditures for Australia were at 5530 million yen in 1999, for France 5940 million yen in 2000 and for Canada 9870 million yen in 2001 (Ministry of Land, Infrastructure and Transport, 2004a).

Not only has the promotional budget not been sufficient over time, but the human resources for inbound tourism remain inadequate. For example, authorized tour guides who speak foreign languages are still few in numbers, even for English speakers. Coupled with this low level of resourcing the differing policy reactions by bureaucrats in the Ministries responsible for aspects of the tourism industry or its regulation are also a considerable problem. While the Ministry of Land Infrastructure and Transport is undertaking the Visit Japan Campaign and hopes to invite up to 5 million more inbound visitors from all over the world every year by 2010, the Ministry of Justice (*Homusho*) is still against welcoming overseas visitors because of perceived public peacekeeping issues. As some politicians and mass media use sensationalism to warn of dangers for ethnocentric reasons as noted above, this internal government conflict situation means that local communities are easily led to misunderstand overseas visitors as being dangerous to Japanese society.

The fourth aspect lies in the impact of *glocalization* (globalization + localization – Yamashita, 2003). Strong and vibrant relations between international promotions and local development programs are also needed (Asamizu, 2004). With the Japanese central government now promoting the country as a destination for overseas visitors, then it will perhaps be more successful in attracting these visitors. However, to invite mature repeat visitors local tourism development programs for inbound tourists are also important. In the past local tourism destinations were for domestic tourists and there was not enough information available for overseas visitors. In most parts of the country there are very few signs written in foreign languages despite the fact that there are growing numbers of visitor arrivals from Korea and Taiwan at least. Some tourist towns in Kyushu and Okinawa now have voluntary tour guides who speak foreign languages, but many local destinations still do not have signs in English or *Romaji* (Japanese words in Roman alphabet – Asamizu, 2004).

If a local community wants to manage tourism as a small domestic business the concept of *just think local* as in the past will be fine. However, if tourism is to be treated as an important inbound industry a wider point of view is needed. The problem here is that, even though local people may know the uniqueness of their destination, at times they are unaware of what is attractive for visitors and how to present these unique and attractive characteristics to people outside of their community, especially to inbound tourists. This problem is made even more difficult when the politics of exclusion intervene in its solution.

The Future: A Tentative Conclusion

Cross-cultural understanding and acceptance is important for the development of relationships between Japanese and overseas visitors. *Nihonjinron* is presently an obstacle to this, but may be a blessing in disguise if the government seriously wants to persuade Japanese people of the value of inbound tourism. The globalization of Japanese society is progressing: local universities that were once thought to be strictly domestic institutions for example have welcomed many overseas students because of their need to survive against a dramatic decrease in the number of eligible Japanese youth. Local factories are also hiring foreign workers, legally and illegally, because of Japan's aging society and the increasing lack of qualified native-born labour. Cross-cultural understanding is becoming necessary not only for the academic researcher's satisfaction but also for anyone who belongs to a local community anywhere in Japan.

In the past local tourism was for local people and international tourism was essentially outbound after 1964. The huge number of festivals and special events that exist as a result of the preservation of traditions and the redevelopment of domestic tourism could be as important for inbound tourism as for domestic, and the daily lives of people in remote communities also has possibilities as a cross-cultural resource for tourists. Not only can local, regional and national development be encouraged, but environmental conservation efforts may also enhanced with good local tourism policies based on inbound tourism. Nevertheless, Japanese inbound tourism is still under construction and it may take long time to become a significant destination because of the deleterious impact of *Nihonjinron*. However, the politics of exclusion look like they are finally being replaced by attempts to develop mutual understanding between overseas visitors and the nation as a whole and, if this proceeds as the current Prime Minister wants it to, the image of Japan as being distant and perhaps unfriendly to inbound tourists will finally be replaced by that of a favoured international destination.

References

Austin, G. (1996). Rising Sun acutely sighted. *Hobart Mercury (Australia)*, May 27, 1996. Full-text (online). Dialog Accessed on 3rd May 2003 at website address http://www.yomiuri.co.jp/dy/.

Asami, T. (1997). New form of nationalism emerging. *The Daily Yomiuri*, January 1, 1997. Full-text (online). Dialog (Accessed 3rd May 2003).

Asamizu, M. (2004). The relations between national and local tourism policies in Japan. In globalization and tourism research: East meets West. *Proceedings of the 10th annual APTA conference* (pp. 924–934). Nagasaki Japan, 4–7 July.

Buruma, I. (1994). *The wages of guilt: Memories of war in Germany and Japan*. New York: Farrar, Straus & Giroux.

Bourdieu, P. (1998). *On television*. New York: New Press.

Befu, H. (2001). *Hegemony of homogeneity*. Melbourne, VIC.: Trans Pacific Press.

Boyle, A. (2003). Research and indigenous tourism-cultural collision or collaboration. In: M. Ranga & A. Chandra (Eds), *Tourism and hospitality in the 21st century* (pp. 249–272). New Delhi: Discovery.

Beppu Foreign Tourists Information Bureau. (2006). *Information for foreign tourists*. Beppu: Beppu Foreign Tourists Information Bureau.

Carr, S. (2003). *Social psychology: Context, communication and culture*. Brisbane: John Wiley & Sons Ltd.

Cooper, M. J., & Eades, J. S. (2006). Landscape as theme park: Tourist consumption and identity of place in contemporary Japan under conditions of rapid demographic change. In: W. C. Gartner & C. H. C. Hsu (Eds), *Tourism research: Where have we been, where are we going?* Hong Kong: International Academy for the Study of Tourism, December (in press).

Cooper, M. J., & Lockyer, T. (2005). Price perception and tourism destination decision making. Presented to the 11th annual *APTA conference*, July 8–11, Goyang, Korea.

Dale, P. N. (1990). *The myth of Japanese uniqueness*. Kent: The Nissan Institute/Routledge.

Hebbert, M. (1994). Sen-biki amidst desakota: Urban sprawl and urban planning in Japan. In: P. Shapira, I. Masser & D. W. Edgington (Eds), *Planning for cities and regions in Japan* (pp. 70–92). Liverpool: Liverpool University Press.

Hellyer, R. (2002). Historical and contemporary perspectives on the Sakoku theme in Japanese foreign relations 1600–2000. *Social Science Japan Journal*, 5(2), 255–259.

Ismail, F. (1996). Japanese response to the "world outside". *New Straits Times*, March 19, 1996. Full-text (online). Dialog (Accessed 5th May 2003).

Japan Association of Travel Agents (2004). http://www.jata-net.or.jp/english/materials/2004/materials-list04.htm.

Japan Association of Travel Agents (2005). http://www.jata-net.or.jp/english/materials/2005/materials-list05.htm.

Kajimoto, T. (2003). *Getting serious about tourism – finally. The Japan Times*, April 24.

Kawasaki, T. (2004). *The foreign angle. The Japan Times*, November 16.

Korostelina, K. (2004). The impact of national identity on conflict behavior: Comparative analysis of two ethnic minorities in crimea. *International Journal of Comparative Sociology*, July 1.

McKay, I. (1994). *The quest of the folk: Antimodernism and cultural selection in twentieth-century nova scotia*. Montreal: McGill-Queens University Press.

McDonough, B. (1997). A swing through modern Japan. *The Daily Yomiuri*, July 6, 1997. Full-text (online). Dialog (Accessed 3rd May 2003).

Meethan, K. (2001). *Tourism in global society: Place, culture, consumption*. Basingstoke, Hampshire: Palgrave.

Ministry of Land, Infrastructure and Transport, Government of Japan (2004a). *Making Japan a tourism-based country: A beautiful country*. Retrieved 26/02, 2006, from http://www.mlit.go.jp/english/white-paper/mlit04/p2c2.pdf

Ministry of Land, Infrastructure and Transport, Government of Japan (2004b). *Overview of Japan's tourism policy*. Retrieved 26/02, 2006, from http://www.mlit.go.jp/sogoseisaku/kanko/english/overview.html

National Institute for Research Advancement (2001). Challenges facing Japan in the twenty-first century. *NIRA policy research paper*, Vol. 14, No.5. Tokyo: NIRA.

Ogata, M. (2003). *Personal communication*. September, Beppu: Ritsumeikan Asia Pacific University.

Shiota, M. (1999). *Kanko Gaku Kenkyu II*. Tokyo: Gakujyutsu Sensho.

Tsuda, T. (2003). *Strangers in the ethnic homeland*. New York: Columbia University Press.

Yoneyama, L. (1999). *Hiroshima traces: Time, space and the dialectics of memory*. Berkeley: University of California Press.

Yamashita, S. (2003). Introduction: "Glocalizing" Southeast Asia. In: S. Yamashita & J. S. Eades (Eds), *Globalization in Southeast Asia local, national and transnational perspectives* (pp. 1–17). Oxford: Berghahn.

Additional web-based sources consulted

http://voyage.typepad.com/china/2005/07/tokyo_governor_.html
http://www.crisscross.com/jp/forum/upfiles/33662/802B8B9038534F00BE80138268C0C715.jpg

Chapter 6

Taming Tourism: Indigenous Rights as a Check to Unbridled Tourism

Freya Higgins-Desbiolles

Introduction

The economic focus of tourism studies in the early years of the modern tourism industry has since expanded to accommodate social and environmental concerns as the interests of "host" societies have come to the fore and the various negative impacts accompanying tourism have become more apparent. As a result, the tourism arena has had to engage with considerations of human rights and consider the ethical implications of its development, its operations and its impacts. The assertion of Indigenous rights in the international arena will also present issues for the tourism industry in the future. In particular, the Draft Declaration on the Rights of Indigenous Peoples holds the potential to transform the ways that government, the tourism industry and Indigenous communities interact. This is a force that tourism leaders will need to take heed of. However, this new development has received little attention within academia, and so this analysis offers a case study of the efforts of the Ngarrindjeri community of South Australia as an example of what the aims, processes and outcomes of such a movement might entail in a particular and local context.

Theoretical Perspective and Methodology

Research is a contested terrain, particularly so in the case of Indigenous research.[1] Currently in academia, and within tourism studies itself, there are clear divisions between quantitative,

---

[1] Indigenous people have frequently been the objects of exploitative research by non-indigenous researchers who have been keen to create "expert knowledge of the Other" (Smith, 2005, p. 87). Smith asserts that Indigenous researchers are developing an Indigenous research agenda and methodology which has shifted the perspective from being "passive victims of all research to seeing ourselves as activists engaging in a counterhegemonic struggle over research" (2005, p. 87).

scientific research and qualitative, "soft scholarship", as its opponents describe it (Denzin & Lincoln, 2005). This chapter foregoes the positivist paradigm of quantitative research and opts for qualitative research methods in order to explore how Indigenous people assert their rights in the face of global frameworks of capitalist globalisation which impact upon their local realities of survival as Indigenous people. It approaches this topic from an Indigenous perspective and is told by an engaged, non-Indigenous researcher using the techniques of critical enthnography. Critical theory charges that "claims to truth are always discursively situated and implicated in relations of power" (Kincheloe & McLaren, 2005, p. 327). This chapter describes Indigenous rights in tourism from the standpoint of Indigenous people and recounts the struggle of the Ngarrindjeri people of South Australia to secure their Indigenous rights in an effort to destabilise the power relations in contemporary tourism, often seen as an exploiter of Indigenous people. In the mode of Denzin (2005, p. 950), this work is attempting to respect and follow an Indigenous research ethic which has as its aim the support of Indigenous self-determination. Denzin has described the Indigenous research ethic as calling for a "collaborative social science research model that makes the researcher responsible not to a removed discipline ... but to those studied ... it forcefully aligns the ethics of research with a politics of the oppressed, with a politics of resistance, hope, and freedom" (2005 p. 952). Those that demand scholarly objectivity and neutral assessment of issues from the point of view of the tourism academy might find this chapter objectionable. Those that wish to engage with another perspective of tourism and learn of developments in tourism of concern to those outside the power corridors of industry and government may find this chapter informative.

Discussion

Human Rights and Tourism

The right to tourism and the freedom of movement of tourists are asserted through such declarations as the Universal Declaration of Human Rights and the World Tourism Organisation's (UNWTO) Global Code of Ethics for Tourism, because tourism brings numerous benefits. For instance, the UNWTO envisions tourism's potential as "contributing to economic development, international understanding, peace, prosperity and universal respect for, and observance of, human rights and fundamental freedoms for all" (UNWTO n.d.). Despite such lofty rhetoric, it has been recognised that tourism proponents must address the concerns of "host communities" and the negative impacts of tourism, which have become increasingly evident around the world and have revealed the often conflictual nature of tourism development. The effort to address these concerns is multi-fold: the tourism industry is exhorted to observe principles of corporate social responsibility (CSR) and environmental guidelines, tourists are provided sensitive codes of conduct to inform their consumer choices and guide their holiday activities, governments are instructed to observe community rights and carry out consultations and "host communities" are being apprised of their human rights. The assertion of human rights in tourism is evident both at a pragmatic level through the efforts of non-government organisations (NGOs) and others trying to reign in tourism's ill effects and harness its beneficial ones, and at a theoretical level in the analysis of tourism.

With the global expansion of tourism as an engine of economic development, its various impacts, both positive and negative, became readily apparent (Mathieson & Wall, 1982). As Third World countries became independent and were exhorted to turn to tourism for development, the connection of tourism development with exploitation and human rights violations was exposed. It was also at this time that vocal advocacy for the rights of host communities began, as some of these communities faced displacement, exploitation, enslavement, loss of livelihoods and other negative impacts in the worst cases. NGOs of all stripes, including aid agencies, human rights organisations, church-based groups and dedicated tourism campaigning groups both nationally and globally began to agitate for a human rights agenda in tourism. Noteworthy among the latter are Tourism Concern, the Ecumenical Coalition on Tourism (ECOT) and End Child Prostitution, Child Pornography and Trafficking of Children for Sexual Purposes (ECPAT). Perhaps one of the most interesting examples of debate within the tourism arena about how far the tourism industry should go in its observance of human rights imperatives was the boycott Burma campaign that was initiated when the military government declared the "Visit Myanmar (Burma) Year" in 1996, which was followed by Aung San Suu Kyi's plea for visitors to stay away until democracy was restored in Burma (Mowforth & Munt, 2003, pp. 289–293).[2] In this instance, Lonely Planet publications disagreed with the boycott proposed and debated NGOs such as Tourism Concern on the issue. This example illustrates that consideration of human rights issues is integral to the conduct of the tourism industry and will remain contentious even if tourism operators try to separate business and "politics".

At the theoretical level, academia is weighing into human rights issues in tourism. Mowforth and Munt (2003) in their discussion of "new tourism" in the third world engage with human rights as they illustrate the power discrepancies evident in the conduct of tourism. Ryan claims the UNWTO's global code of ethics for tourism represents a "statement of sets of mutual responsibilities between both host and tourist" (2002, p. 19) that, together with the development of social tourism precepts and stakeholder theory, could secure more equitable and sustainable outcomes in tourism development. Some texts have made a considerable contribution to the discussion. Scheyvens provides a positive consideration of how tourism can best work for real development and specifically addresses a chapter to the new phenomenon of "justice tourism", which is defined as tourism that is "both ethical and equitable" (2002, p. 104).[3] Smith and Duffy have presented a much needed analysis of ethics in tourism (2003). Their discussions of rights, codes of practise, social justice and an ethics of care are particularly relevant to an understanding of how human rights considerations might be used to transform tourism. Their work provides nuanced insight into the complexities

---

[2] Aung San Suu Kyi's National League for Democracy (NLD) won the democratic elections in Burma in 1990 by a landslide but the military through the State Law and Order Council (SLORC) refused to give up power and imprisoned Suu Kyi and other elected NLD representatives. Mowforth and Munt provide a good briefing to the dynamics of the conflict that ensued between Lonely Planet Publications and the NGOs Burma Campaign UK and Tourism Concern for the continued production of the Lonely Planet travel guidebook to Burma (2003, pp. 290–293); but the issue has involved travel agencies, consumers and activists around the world and still continues.

[3] Scheyvens outlines justice tourism's attributes as: "builds solidarity between visitors and those visited; promotes mutual understanding and relationships based on equality, sharing and respect; supports self-sufficiency and self-determination for local communities; and maximises local economic, cultural and social benefits" (2002, p. 104).

of applying ethical frameworks to the conduct of tourism and they conclude that we need numerous and responsive forms of ethics which "must embody an enlightened approach to encountering and understanding the Other" (Smith & Duffy, 2003, pp. 165–166).

This brief and incomplete survey of the topic should not imply that awareness and acceptance of human rights issues in tourism is firmly entrenched in the field. The fact remains that foundational texts such as Weaver and Lawton's *Tourism Management* (2002) and key journals such as the *Annals of Tourism Research* and *Tourism Management* rarely mention human rights in tourism at all. Perhaps this is because many feel uncomfortable linking tourism to such serious political issues. Some see tourism as an "industry" restricted to business and economics. Others view it only as frivolous fun, as is the case of Butcher who laments the "moralisation of tourism" and reminds us "tourism need only be about enjoyment" (2003, p. 143). This largely reflects the wider environment where rights discourses are marginalised in this neoliberal market era with its emphasis on individual choice and consumer freedom. But as globalisation and tourism continue to be dominated by pro-development and economic growth agendas, the human rights agenda in tourism will increasingly be advocated by NGOs and locals in order to restore balance and ensure that such forces are harnessed to meet human needs rather than feed corporate coffers that benefit only an elite minority.[4]

Indigenous Rights in Tourism

A new development set to impact profoundly on the tourism industry is the establishment of an Indigenous rights regime. The concept of Indigenous rights as a related yet separate aspect of human rights is slowly being formulated in international fora. Its potential to circumscribe the way that the powerful forces of the tourism industry interact with often vulnerable Indigenous peoples is profound. It also should exert a positive impact on the lives of Indigenous peoples, which could alleviate some of the appalling statistics of disadvantage that have resulted from their historical dispossession and/or marginalisation in many parts of the world.

The formulation of Indigenous rights has arisen in the milieu of greater respect for, and encoding of, a deep and comprehensive human rights regime during the course of the 20th century. However one significant distinction between human rights and Indigenous rights

---

[4] For example, globalisation analyst Leslie Sklair, argues that capitalist globalisation underpinned by the "culture-ideology of consumerism" should give way to a "culture-ideology of universal human rights" (2002, p. 299). He argues that an imbalance has resulted from over-emphasis on economic imperatives and pro-growth agendas and that balance can be restored by a focus on universal human rights which details not only rights but also responsibilities and applies then to not only the civil and political spheres as currently practised but also to the social and economic spheres as well. He argues that this will eliminate the two crises that capitalist globalisation causes: ecological unsustainability and class polarisation (2002, pp. 299–321). In her analysis of Indigenous rights in tourism, Johnston outlines briefly the sites where contemporary corporate and consumer behaviour impact on the safeguarding of human rights of peoples impacted by tourism (2003, pp. 116–119). Robinson (1999) argues that communities' and Indigenous people's rights have to form an integral part of the sustainability equation. Finally, for a more thorough examination of the dynamics between human rights and globalisation (see Brysk, 2002).

is that the former applies to individuals whereas the latter are communal rights.[5] Because Indigenous rights have grown from the human rights movement, they have been founded in the multitude of human rights protocols drafted at the international level.

One of the important milestones in the enunciation of Indigenous rights is the ILO's 1989 Convention No. 169 entitled Indigenous and Tribal Peoples Convention.[6] This document is viewed as the current minimum standard for the protection of Indigenous peoples around the world, as it establishes many of the precepts that give meaning to the concept of "self-determination" for Indigenous peoples. This important document itemises the steps required to address Indigenous disadvantage and progress towards parity with other citizens of the states in which they reside. It also demands that Indigenous "social, cultural, religious and spiritual values and practices ... shall be recognised and protected" (ILO, 1989). Further, this document delineates such rights as the right to chart their own path to development, the right for their environments to be protected, the right to maintain their own customs and institutions, and the right to access services such as health and education provided in culturally appropriate ways, such as education in Indigenous languages. Considerable attention is given to the issue of Indigenous lands and resources, including ownership of and/or access to their traditional lands, the right to ownership of and/or benefits from their natural resources and required measures of consultation and redress if these rights are infringed. Because of the strength of the statements made within this convention, only 17 states have ratified it to date.

Surpassing the ILO's Convention No. 169 and presenting the future pinnacle of the Indigenous rights regime is the United Nations Draft Declaration on the Rights of Indigenous Peoples (hence forth called the Draft Declaration). It has been described as:

> Perhaps the most representative document that the United Nations has ever produced, representative in the sense that its normative statements reflect in a more than token way, the experience, perspectives and contributions of Indigenous peoples. In a word, it is a document that was produced in a decade long spirit of equal dialogue and mutual recognition. (Representative of the Grand Council of Crees, quoted in Community Aid Abroad, 1999)

Before analysing this important document in greater detail, it would be helpful to briefly chart its origins. The Working Group on Indigenous Populations (WGIP) was the catalyst for the Draft Declaration. The WGIP was formed following a study within the UN Economic and Social Council (ECOSOC) in 1971 which focused upon discrimination against Indigenous peoples. The WGIP held its first meeting in Geneva during 1982 and was charged with two duties:

1 review developments pertaining to the promotion and protection of the human rights and fundamental freedoms of Indigenous populations and

---

[5] Indigenous peoples would hold both sets of rights; they have a right to respect for their individual human rights and the right to recognition of the rights that they hold collectively under the Indigenous rights regime.

[6] This convention was adopted almost fifty years ago with ILO Convention No. 107 of 1957 and this Convention No. 169 of 1989 represents an update.

2   give special attention to the evolution of standards concerning rights of such populations (Aboriginal and Torres Strait Islander Commission, ATSIC n.d.).

The WGIP "reviews developments" by receiving reports from both governments and Indigenous representatives. The WGIP stands out amongst the multitude of international organisations because of the access it gives Indigenous peoples. The WGIP's second task of overseeing
the "evolution of standards" has been partially fulfilled by the effort it has made in creating
and fostering the Draft Declaration since 1985. The Draft Declaration is an evolving document that is being shaped by numerous discussions within the WGIP forum. The WGIP submitted its finalised text to the Commission on Human Rights in 1994. This marked the opening
up of the text to debate particularly on behalf of concerned governments whose support
would be needed to get it adopted by the UN General Assembly (with a target date of 2005,
which marked the close of the UN's International Decade of the World's Indigenous People).
Complex and difficult meetings followed in subsequent years as the Indigenous representatives called for acceptance of the Draft Declaration without amendment while various
government representatives demanded significant change.[7] To date, attempts to secure the
adoption of the Draft Declaration have not yet succeeded but the WGIP renewed its operating mandate in 2005 in order to continue the struggle to achieve its adoption.

One of the most important principles of the Draft Declaration is the right to self-
determination (Article 3),[8] which serves as the foundation of all of the other principles
advocated within the document. This key principle has also been the most opposed, particularly by the United States and Australia,[9] who see it providing Indigenous peoples with
the right of secession from the territorial states in which they reside (Community Aid
Abroad, 1999). It is difficult to see how compromise can be secured on this issue because
Indigenous peoples argue that the right to control their present and future circumstances in all
aspects (social, cultural, environmental, economic and political) is the only path to rectify
past injustices against and dispossession of Indigenous peoples whose rights were violated
as the "First Peoples" of their lands.[10] Unless governments can be persuaded that honour-
ing the rights of Indigenous peoples and remedying the past will not lead to secession and
fragmentation, it is difficult to see how the Draft Declaration can be made meaningful. The

---

[7] These events are well described on the ATSIC web site where extensive materials are available (ATSIC n.d.).
[8] Article 3 states: "Indigenous peoples have the right to self-determination. By virtue of that right they freely
determine their political status and freely pursue their economic, social and cultural development" (UNHCHR &
WGIP, 1999).
[9] Prior to 1995, the Australian government supported the use of the term "self-determination" within the Draft
Declaration, arguing that "the principle of the territorial integrity of states is sufficiently enshrined internationally
that a reference to self-determination in the Draft Declaration would not imply a right to secession" (Butler, 2000).
With the change to the Howard-led Liberal-Coalition government in 1995, the Australian position changed to opposition to the use of this term because of a stated concern with the problem of secession; this government expressed a
preference for the term "self-management" (see Butler, 2000). Community Aid Abroad became so concerned about
Australia's obstructionist role in these discussions that it used its advocacy network called "Polliewatch" to ask its
supporters to lobby the Australian government to support Indigenous rights (see Community Aid Abroad, 1999).
[10] It is a more fundamental argument presented by Indigenous groups that the right to self-determination is a fundamental right of all peoples and thus cannot be denied to Indigenous peoples without being discriminatory and
in breach of their human rights under international law (see Hansen, 2000).

example of engaging with the demand for self-determination set by Canada,[11] which shares similar circumstances to the United States and Australia, offers hope that such states can be persuaded. In the discussions on the Draft Declaration, many Indigenous representatives have repeatedly stated that few Indigenous peoples advocate secession; rather, what they wish is to negotiate a settlement with the peoples with which they co-exist which acknowledges Indigenous peoples' right to govern themselves in the areas vital to their future as Indigenous peoples.[12] To prematurely cut off avenues for such a settlement defeats the entire purpose behind the Draft Declaration.

Nonetheless, the Draft Declaration is important for the recognition it gives to the concerns of Indigenous peoples. It recognises both the collective and individual rights of Indigenous peoples, as many of these peoples come from communal traditions but have adapted to the more individualistic cultures that have come to dominate them. It demands respect for Indigenous customs, laws, traditions, institutions and cultures. It delineates the special relationship that Indigenous people hold with their lands and waters and the "resources" that pertain to these. Within its many articles and statements are clear guidelines for the non-indigenous communities around the globe to come to understand Indigenous aims and negotiate a shared future.

In addition to the thorny issue of self-determination, some states resist signing the document because some of its provisions imply substantial financial costs. These include proper compensation for compulsory acquisition of land or resources, loss of revenues due to protection of Indigenous rights to culture, knowledge and resources,[13] compensation for previous violation of Indigenous property rights and substantial commitment of government revenues and resources to fund their Indigenous peoples adequately to enable them to realise their right to self-determination to its fullest extent.

The Draft Declaration stands to have substantial impact on the interests and the operations of the tourism industry. Some of the relevant principles of potential importance include:

- It cordons off Indigenous culture from economic exploitation by outsiders without permission.[14]
- It demands restitution for improper usurpation of Indigenous culture and knowledge.

---

[11] In 1999, Canada accepted a federal relationship with the Inuit nation of Nunavut marking the "latest development in Canada's nation building" and "a profound shift in how Canada relates to Aboriginal people" (see: http://www.educationcanada.com/facts/index.phtml?sid=nu&a=5&lang=eng). The full position of Canada on the issue of self-determination in the Draft Declaration is provided at http://www.usask.ca/nativelaw/iadir_canada.html

[12] I am grateful for Vesper Tjukonai for pointing out that some Aboriginal and Torres Strait Islander (ATSI) leaders are already asserting their rights to self-determination through such activities as creating the Aboriginal Tent Embassy in Canberra without any concern that official recognition has not followed. This discussion of ATSI contributions to the WGIP does not reflect the diversity of opinions of ATSI leaders nor the multitude of efforts they undertake to secure their Indigenous rights. The Redfern Riots of 2003 cannot be ignored as a sign of the dissatisfaction with the pace of change.

[13] This situation is apparent in the provisions of Article 12, for example, which focuses upon the "right to practise and revitalise their cultural traditions and customs", which could take away the right of non-indigenous tourism operators and non-indigenous artists to interpret Indigenous sites or create art using Indigenous iconography.

[14] This is very important in Australia for example where ATSI cultural tours frequently include a "bush tucker and bush medicine" component and provide a prime opportunity for representatives of pharmaceutical companies to act as tourists and seize this knowledge which can reap profits if patentable.

- It blocks access to and affords protection of Indigenous sacred sites from non-indigenous people.
- Conversely, it demands Indigenous access to sacred sites that are under the ownership of others.
- It potentially could ban or restrict the use of Indigenous words and names by non-indigenous people.
- It advocates the provision of public education and information to non-indigenous people which teaches them of the "dignity and diversity of their (Indigenous peoples) cultures, traditions, histories and aspirations".
- It calls for Indigenous participation in decision making at all levels in the decisions that affect them.
- It advocates for the Indigenous right to maintain and manage their own development and subsistence and calls for compensation when this right is impinged upon.
- It provides a strong statement of the right to ownership and control of their total environments.[15]
- It provides the right to conservation, restoration and protection of their total environment (and thus could limit development projects).
- It describes a right to "full ownership, control and protection of … cultural and intellectual property".
- It states that Indigenous peoples have the right to determine their development strategies and that states must secure their consent[16] before approving development projects affecting their lands and resources (with requirements for fair compensation to address harmful environmental, economic, social, cultural or spiritual impacts).[17]
- It argues that Indigenous peoples have the right to exercise self-determination through their own institutions and structures equating to autonomy or self-government in all matters such as their culture, religion, society, economy and resources.

---

[15] The full wording of Article 26 is worth including: "Indigenous peoples have the right to own, develop, control and use the lands and territories, including the total environment of the lands, air, waters, coastal seas, sea-ice, flora and fauna and other resources which they have traditionally owned or otherwise occupied or used. This includes the right to the full recognition of their laws, traditions and customs, land-tenure systems and institutions for the development and management of resources, and the right to effective measures by States to prevent any interference with, alienation of or encroachment upon these rights" (UNHCHR & WGIP, 1999). Should this article be accepted, it could mean for example that protected area managers who wish to keep their protected areas as "pristine wilderness" for ecotourism could not prevent the Indigenous peoples "owning" a land designated as a protected area from using it for their economic development through practices such as traditional hunting and whaling (which some sensitive ecotourists would find repugnant).

[16] The term "consent" here is very important. Previous government policies have utilised the term "consultation", which is too weak because it in practice can mean processes that give a veneer of respect for Indigenous viewpoints while allowing the developers to conduct "business as usual". Consent means that developers and governments have to negotiate a mutually agreed outcome which shifts power in the favour of the Indigenous peoples concerned. Such issues are highlighted in the case study where the relationship between the Alexandrina Council and the Ngarrindjeri is discussed.

[17] This broad and sensitive acknowledgement of the impacts relevant in an Indigenous cultural context is important in the Ngarrindjeri case study that follows later in this chapter. Their experiences during the Hindmarsh Island bridge (HIB) conflict illustrates the spiritual and cultural damage that an inappropriate development project can wreak upon an Indigenous community. If the provisions of Article 30 of the Draft Declaration were effective, the Ngarrindjeri would have received fair compensation for the impacts of the bridge conflict.

From these brief descriptions of relevant provisions which have great potential impact upon tourism, it is evident that the Draft Declaration is an important document with the potential to shift the balance of power in the tourism encounter in favour of Indigenous peoples.

Assuming that the Draft Declaration will be ratified, its effectiveness will depend on its implementation procedures, found in Section 8 of the Draft. Here the document establishes such requirements as: implementation of appropriate measures within national law to make the Draft Declaration's provisions enforceable, provision of financial and technical support to enable Indigenous peoples to achieve their right to self-determination to its fullest extent, the right to access dispute settlement mechanisms in cases of conflict with states and governments, and the duty of the UN and its agencies to enable the achievement of the Draft Declaration's aims. The Draft Declaration is a "non-binding declaration" and so places no enforceable constraints upon its signatories to adhere to its provisions. Therefore its power rests mainly in its moral authority, which would be backed up only by peer pressure aroused within the community of nations. However, together with the ILO's Convention No. 169 (which is similarly weak due to the paucity of signatories), it is anticipated that the Draft Declaration will contribute to the development of "a growing body of customary international law in the area of Indigenous peoples' rights" (ATSIC n.d.) which could grow increasingly effective over time (Keal, 2003, p. 220).[18]

However, it must be acknowledged that ratification is unlikely in the short term, as the discussions in the UN Commission on Human Rights are still marked by obstructionistic efforts by powerful states to weaken the draft developed by the WGIP (IITC, 2004). Yet, at another level, the effort to formulate the Draft Declaration and secure its passage has been an unqualified success because it has formed a network of communication and support among the world's Indigenous peoples. This outcome is reflected in the words of Mick Dodson, who attended meetings in the mid-1990s as the ATSI Social Justice Commissioner:

> What I found was that I was part of a world community of Indigenous peoples spanning the planet: experiencing the same problems and suffering the same alienation, marginalisation and sense of powerlessness. We had gathered there united by our shared frustration with the dominant systems in our own countries and their consistent failure to deliver justice ... We were looking to and demanding justice from a higher authority. (quoted in Community Aid Abroad, 1999)

Such networking may result in unforeseen and powerful outcomes. For instance, in 2005 an International Forum of Indigenous Nations met to discuss Indigenous Nation-to-Nation treaty-making between Maori, Aboriginal Australians, Canadian First Nations and Native American peoples.

---

[18] Should the Draft Declaration be adopted by the United Nations' General Assembly, it would then become the minimum standard for the protection of Indigenous peoples around the world.

Implications for the Tourism Industry

With the exception of Johnston's work (2000; 2003), little attention has been given to the implications of the development of these Indigenous rights protocols in the tourism field.[19] Most tourism leaders continue to see the nature of their relationship with Indigenous peoples as one of "consultation" with them as one of many "stakeholders" in tourism, as outlined in principles of CSR.[20] Despite this situation, the Indigenous rights regime is set to impact on tourism because of the increasing assertiveness of Indigenous peoples.

Johnston has reflected at length on the implications of the Indigenous rights regime for the processes and conduct of the tourism industry (2000; 2003). Johnston argues that the 1997 Berlin Declaration on Sustainable Tourism, the discussions for the Convention on Biological Diversity (CBD), the ILO Convention No. 169 and the Draft Declaration have shifted the emphasis to Indigenous peoples' right to self-determination (2000; 2003). For Johnston, self-determination in tourism means the right to choose whether and how to engage with tourism, the requirement of "prior informed consent"[21] in negotiations with Indigenous people in the development process, and the right of Indigenous people to protect their sacred sites, know-ledges and spirituality by not sharing them (Johnston, 2003, p. 122). Johnston recommends: building sustainable partnerships by learning and respecting Indigenous values, protocols and processes (2003, pp. 131–132) including the most important value, building relation-ships rather than relying on models and mechanisms of managerial consultation; setting a policy of prior informed consent as the industry standard secured by both legislation and impact assessment protocol (2000, p. 96); respect for Indigenous conservation knowledge; and empowerment of Indigenous peoples to negotiate by provision of appropriate resources and information so that they are able to prepare themselves for the negotiations equally as well as the representatives of industry and government they will face at the negotiating table.[22] She argues that Indigenous peoples are asserting their values through articulation of their Indigenous rights and resisting the tourism industry's propensity to seek to continue

---

[19] Johnston (2000; 2003) is one of the few analysts who have explored the implications of Indigenous rights in tourism to date in the tourism literature. Robinson has advocated the concept of sustainability include a recogni-tion of the rights of communities and Indigenous people to be partners in the tourism development process with the ultimate power to reject tourism (1999). The NGO Indigenous Tourism Rights International seeks to assist Indigenous communities to assert their rights to reject or control tourism by providing them with information, training and networking opportunities as well as carrying out education activities for the wider community and the tourism industry (see: http://www.tourismrights.org). Deborah McLaren, Director of Tourism Rights International, has co-published an article on planeta.com's ecotravel web site which introduced the concept of Indigenous rights to those interested in "green travel" (Pera & McLaren, 1999).

[20] If not committed to CSR, they frequently see Indigenous peoples as simply to be ignored or pushed aside as impediments to progress.

[21] Johnston does not actually provide a definition of this term. But from inductive reading of this chapter, obtain-ing prior informed consent would obligate non-indigenous negotiators to ensure that an Indigenous community has a readiness to negotiate (that negotiations are not forced on them); that the Indigenous community is informed of both the pros and the cons of the proposal; that appropriate Indigenous protocols are followed when negotiations are planned; that relationships are built with the Indigenous people party to the negotiations; and that their con-cerns are not only heard but responded to with an understanding and respect for their rights.

[22] Johnston outlines three Indigenous demands for change in current negotiating practice: (1) the format, agenda and outputs of the negotiations process need to be agreed prior to the start of the process with Indigenous leaders (and

"business as usual". Conversely, the assertion of Indigenous rights at the international level is raising the profile of Indigenous peoples in tourism. Johnston states:

> Gradually, Indigenous peoples are finding that they have a voice in international policy on tourism. The CBD, signed by 175 countries since 1993, has been pivotal in facilitating this breakthrough. It is legally binding and provides clear benchmarks for safeguarding the interests of Indigenous peoples and other local communities. Most significant in this regard is Article 8(j), which obliges governments to protect and promote Indigenous knowledge systems for the conservation and sustainable use of biodiversity, while ensuring the equitable sharing of related benefits. (2003, p. 125)

How is this desire for Indigenous rights expressed by those currently engaging with the tourism phenomenon? It is expressed in the demands for Hawaiian sovereignty in the face of an almost "genocidal" tourism impact on Indigenous Hawaiians ("Tourism in Independent Hawai'i", 1997). It is expressed by Maori tourism academic Shirley Barnett, who claims:

> Maori want to be autonomous, they want to run their own show "... not just be the last three seats on the bus, the optional extra, the clip-on, add-on, tear-off-the-coupon sideline event. We do not want to provide tacked-on plastic Maori experience in the venue of the facilities belonging to others. We want to provide authentic experience, learning experiences, through which we learn too, interacting with our guests." (Barnett, quoting a Maori tourism professional, 2001, p. 84)

It is also seen in the practical policies created by Indigenous communities. For example, the Kuna people of Panama have asserted their Indigenous rights through their 1996 Statute on Tourism which "represents a carefully planned strategy to direct the tourism industry to the needs of the entire Kuna nation" (Snow, 2001, p. 1).

Indigenous peoples are still learning the full implications of Indigenous rights. They are networking globally to support each other in these efforts, for example via the NGO Indigenous Tourism Rights International. Evidence of this comes from such statements as the Oaxaca Declaration from the International Forum on Indigenous Tourism in 2002, which asserts:

> Indigenous Peoples are not mere "stakeholders", but internationally-recognised holders of collective and human rights, including the rights of self-determination, informed consent and effective participation. Tourism is

---

not imposed upon them); (2) funding and resources needs to be provided to Indigenous participants in the negotiations for them to prepare their own analyses to inform their participation in the negotiations and (3) government bodies and other organisations participating in the negotiations need to be required to abide by international Indigenous and human rights codes and standards (as provided by the ILO's Convention No. 169 and the Draft Declaration) (2003, pp. 127–128).

beneficial for Indigenous communities only when it is based on and enhances our self-determination. (McLaren, 2003, p. 3)

The forces of globalisation and tourism are being subjected to the resistance of Indigenous people who hope to tame them through Indigenous rights protocols to serve the needs of Indigenous peoples. A key question for the future is: how will the tourism industry and its supporters react to this situation. Articulate voices in academia are recommending that Indigenous people be listened to. For instance, Robinson's (1999) analysis shows that sustainability will remain elusive as long as the cultural dimension of Indigenous and local people's rights and needs are marginalised in the decision-making processes of tourism development. Even more importantly, the work of Maori academic, Stewart-Harawira (2005, p. 32) suggests Indigenous knowledges "have a profound contribution to make towards an alternative ontology for a just global order".

In order to add to an understanding of this issue and shed light on the dynamics of Indigenous assertions of rights at a local level, this chapter will now recount some of the experiences of the Ngarrindjeri community.

A Case Study: The Ngarrindjeri Effort to Tame Tourism

The Ngarrindjeri are the Aboriginal people of the Lower Murray River, the Lower Lakes and the Coorong[23] of south-eastern South Australia. Like other Aboriginal nations, the Ngarrindjeri have been subjected to a history of dispossession and marginalisation whose effects are still reverberating today.[24] Ngarrindjeri continue to face grave difficulties in asserting their rights, protecting their heritage, maintaining their culture and securing a positive future. In the face of discrimination and marginalisation, the Ngarrindjeri leadership[25] have devised a two-prong strategy that has been forged in the fires of bitter experience. One tactic has been to educate through their facility Camp Coorong Race Relations and Cultural Education Centre in order to foster better relationships between Aboriginal and non-Aboriginal peoples (Hemming, 1993; Higgins-Desbiolles, 2003b). This tactic has been pursued since the mid-1980s and was deemed very successful until its limits were revealed in the conflicts of the 1990s, which will be recounted momentarily. This necessitated another tactic which is to assert their Indigenous rights in the political realm. This is the story that will be narrated within this case study.[26]

---

[23] As Bell states, "the extent of Ngarrindjeri lands and the divisions within their territory are not beyond dispute" (1998, pp. 29). The definition of Ngarrindjeri country is not a static nor an uncontested concept.

[24] This history is not unimportant to this discussion because it explains community differences that facilitated the fragmentation of the community in the Hindmarsh Island conflict (see Bell, 1998).

[25] Through organisations such as the Ngarrindjeri Heritage Committee and the Ngarrindjeri Lands and Progress Association.

[26] This article will not engage with the important events occurring at the federal level in Australia, including the debates among ATSI leaders on the treaty issue, the government's agenda of "practical reconciliation", the complex politics of native title and the abolishment of ATSIC (a body providing a weak level of Indigenous Australian self-governance).

Conflicts as Catalysts to Ngarrindjeri Assertion of Indigenous Rights

The Hindmarsh Island Bridge (HIB) conflict played a pivotal role in Australian politics and has had momentous repercussions for the Ngarrindjeri. This conflict emerged in the early 1990s as a result of a plan to expand a marina and residential development on Hindmarsh Island/Kumarangk.[27] This development sought to capitalise on the island's proximity to the South Australian state capital, Adelaide, and its tourism and recreational drawing potential, strengthened by its proximity to the Coorong National Park (CNP). In order to obtain planning approval, a bridge was required to replace the car ferry that provided access between the town of Goolwa and the island in order to accommodate the heightened traffic the development would attract. The marina development and the bridge that followed were the subject of a tripartite agreement between the developer's company, Binalong Pty Ltd, the South Australian Labour government and the local council at Goolwa, now called the Alexandrina Council (Simons, 2003, p. 60).[28] Opposition to the bridge first emerged from environmentalists, community groups and trade unionists. However, when some of the Ngarrindjeri[29] voiced objections based on sacred sites and the spiritual significance of the island (and in particular, the so-called "secret women's business"[30]), the conflict escalated and drew national and international attention. Unable to get protection under the state government's Heritage Protection legislation (Kenny, 1998, p. 5), the Ngarrindjeri appealed to the federal government to use the *ATSI Heritage Protection Act 1984*. Federal Minister for Aboriginal Affairs Robert Tickner placed a 25-year ban on bridge construction in July 1994 following investigation of Ngarrindjeri claims in an inquiry conducted by Cheryl Saunders.[31] However, an appeal by the developers for a judicial review led to Tickner's ban being overturned.[32] After late 1994, when "a handful" of Ngarrindjeri "dissidents" (Brodie, 2002, p. 151) came forward claiming they had no knowledge of "women's business"

---

[27] Kumarangk is the Ngarrindjeri name for Hindmarsh Island.

[28] It is too difficult to describe fully the complexity of the politics operating behind this issue throughout the 1990s (such as the state government facing collapse of its main financial institution, the State Bank, the rivalries between politicians on the left and right of politics and the dynamics operating in the media). The simplified point made here is that both the state government and the local council were firmly tied up through these agreements to building the bridge. For a more nuanced discussion of these events Simons (2003) is invaluable.

[29] The Ngarrindjeri community fragmented during this event, with the people advocating sacred sites and women's connections with the island being labelled "proponents" and those denying these attributes being labelled "dissidents". Kenny claimed that of the some 2500 Ngarrindjeri, the "vast majority ... support the opposition to the HIB" (1998, p. 3).

[30] The restricted and sacred knowledge that certain Ngarrindjeri women claimed to hold about Hindmarsh Island was referred to in the media as "Secret women's business", which has been picked up in popular discourse much to the offence of Ngarrindjeri proponents.

[31] The Saunders Inquiry was the only inquiry which was given the information on the confidential women's sacred knowledge because Tickner respected the restricted nature of this information and appointed Saunders (a woman) to be informed of its content on his behalf (Kenny, 1998, p. 6).

[32] The ban was overturned because the Notice of Inquiry for the Saunders Inquiry failed to precisely identify the area covered by the application for the protection and because Tickner did not consider the content of the women's knowledge himself and had instead delegated that role to Saunders (Kenny, 1998, p. 6).

(or denied its current validity) and politicians and the media became involved in this split,[33] the state government called a Royal Commission[34] in 1995, which found that the Ngarrindjeri proponents of "secret women's business" were "fabricators" of their stated cultural beliefs. The Ngarrindjeri returned to Tickner with another application under the federal Heritage Act but a change in federal government from Keating's Labour to Howard's Liberal-Coalition government in March 1996 saw the new Aboriginal Affairs Minister John Herron refuse to appoint a female Minister to analyse the women's sacred knowledge and so the Ngarrindjeri proponents refused to cooperate (Kenny, 1998, p. 9). In order to prevent further Ngarrindjeri applications for protection and thus ongoing delays, the HIB Bill 1996 was introduced to parliament. This legislation overrode the provisions of the 1984 *ATSI Heritage Protection Act* specifically for the Hindmarsh Island area and thus terminated avenues for Ngarrindjeri use of the heritage protection legislation to protect their culture (Simons, 2003, pp. 404–405). The Bill passed in May 1997[35] and bridge construction was underway by October 1999. The determination of the SA Royal Commission was called into question by a Federal High Court decision in August 2001 (in a court case brought by the developers of the marina, the Chapmans, against Aboriginal Affairs Minister Tickner and others) in which Justice von Doussa concluded: "I am not satisfied that the restricted women's knowledge was fabricated or that it was not part of genuine Aboriginal traditions" (Barker, 2001).[36] Unfortunately for the Ngarrindjeri proponents, this finding came too late to stop the bridge, which was officially opened on the 4th of March, 2001.

I have written about the HIB conflict in previous writing focusing on the Ngarrindjeri experience as an example of the problematic nature of contemporary tourism's engagement with Indigenous communities (Higgins-Desbiolles, 2003a; 2004). Rather than revisiting that discussion here, it is more useful to explore how the lessons of the Hindmarsh Island experience led the Ngarrindjeri on a determined path to assert their Indigenous rights.

---

[33] The roles of federal liberal politician Ian McLachlan and reporter Chris Kenny to these events was decisive (see Simons, 2003).

[34] Tellingly, the terms of reference set for this Royal Commission were to report on "whether the 'women's business' or any aspect of the 'women's business' was a fabrication and if so (a) the circumstances relating to such a fabrication; (b) the extent of the fabrication and (c) the purpose of such a fabrication" (Stevens, 1995, p. 3). Twenty-three women proponents signed a statement presented to the Commission which in part stated: "We are deeply offended that a Government in this day and age has the audacity to order an inquiry into our secret, sacred, spiritual beliefs. Never before have (sic) any group of people had their spiritual beliefs scrutinised in this way ... Women's business does exist, has existed since time immemorial and will continue to exist where there are Aboriginal women who are able to continue to practise their culture" (Brodie, 2002, p. 151).

[35] The Ngarrindjeri challenged the HIB Act in the High Court on the basis of the amendment to the Australian Constitution of 1967 which gave the Federal government powers to make "special laws" for Aboriginal people (Section 51 (xxvi) – informally referred to as "race power" clause). It was this constitution change which enabled the ATSI Heritage Protection regime to be established in the first place – it was in the spirit of the 1967 referendum which gave Aboriginal people citizenship rights and intended to rectify the wrongs of the past. The Ngarrindjeri's legal team read the "race power" clause in Section 51 (xxvi) as empowering the federal government to only make "special laws" *for the benefit* of Aboriginal people and said that the HIB Act clearly damaged Ngarrindjeri interests. While the court was divided on this matter, the outcome is that the HIB Act and other actions detrimental to Aboriginal people were determined acceptable under the "race powers" clause of the Constitution. See Kenny (1998) for full details.

[36] The Ngarrindjeri proponents hailed this as a vindication of their claims.

One Ngarrindjeri elder, Veronica Brodie, summed up the experience as an assault on Aboriginal people's rights to limit development in their "country":

> Aboriginal people were part of a game of political football. We were being played against one another while the developers and politicians were making as many gains as they could. We now have a better understanding of the issues facing us. The land grab and destruction of Aboriginal sacred sites will continue and we must be sure that the Coorong is protected from the expanding development. (Brodie, 2001, p. 4)[37]

In a speech presented to Ngarrindjeri proponent supporters just after the opening ceremony for the bridge, Ngarrindjeri Elder Tom Trevorrow said:

> My Elders, My People, our friends, brothers and sisters, we are gathered here today in sadness and pain while they up there celebrate the opening of a Genocide Bridge. This bridge has been secured and built upon our land across our waters without our consent. It has been built in a place which is very spiritually and culturally important to our Heritage and Beliefs. It has been secured and built by people who can't understand or don't want to understand other people's Heritage and Beliefs, especially if other people's Heritage and Beliefs interfere with developments that could possibly make big money, or perhaps they fear that to recognise other people's Heritage and Beliefs might mean to recognise their official rights ... We take time today to speak to the spirits of our old people, the spirits of all things upon these lands and under these waters: we are sorry, we tried and tried; we are sorry. (Trevorrow, 2003, p. 63)

The events in the HIB episode indicate important disjunctures between the values of non-Aboriginal and Aboriginal people. The Ngarrindjeri interpreted the outcomes from this event as demonstrative that Ngarrindjeri people and culture could not be protected through the human rights accorded the Ngarrindjeri within the Australian legal process[38] and thus necessitated a resort to their Indigenous rights.[39]

---

[37] This sensibility that the bridge conflict was about curbing growing acceptance of Indigenous rights seems vindicated by events surrounding the development of a federal government green paper on tourism policy in 2003. A headline in the Australian newspaper read "Black law 'poses a threat' to tourism" (Emerson, 2003, p. 5). The National Tourism Alliance chairman Col Hughes argued that environmentalists and "Aboriginals" should not be allowed to block access to culturally or environmentally sensitive areas: "what we don't want is more and more sites being put in a basket saying 'quarantine the bloody things from tourists' ". In this interview he referred to restrictions at Uluru and the Great Barrier Reef as examples of "creeping restrictions on tourism and a lack of certainty for the industry" (Emerson, 2003, p. 5).

[38] Since then, ironically, Ngarrindjeri attachment to the island and the larger region has been promoted as a tourism asset. This suggests that, while the Ngarrindjeri were defeated in their attempts to assert their cultural and spiritual traditions in the political realm, in the aftermath of this defeat they are encouraged to perform these same cultural and spiritual traditions in the tourism realm.

[39] In fact during the conduct of the Royal Commission, the Ngarrindjeri proponent women (but one) refused to participate in the inquiry but instead submitted a written statement in which they said "It is our responsibility as custodians of this knowledge to protect it ... We have a duty to keep Aboriginal law in this country ... We do not recognise you, Madam Commissioner, as a custodian of law in our society. We shall continue to practise our customs and law according to our customs and law as Aboriginal people have since time began and especially since

Another incident that crystallised determination to pursue an Indigenous rights agenda was their experiences relating to the International Year of Ecotourism 2002 (IYE 2002). The IYE 2002 was designated by the United Nations in order to highlight the potential of ecotourism to contribute to economic development and conservation of environments. The right to host the launch of the year's activities in Australia was won by the SATC.

The SATC chose the Coorong in Ngarrindjeri country as the venue in which to showcase the nature-based and ecotourism jewels of South Australia. Their committee[40] chose Godfrey's Landing[41] in the CNP as the site for the event and planned to transport one hundred VIPs from Adelaide to Hindmarsh Island where tour boats would take them past the Murray Mouth before landing at the event site. Although the Ngarrindjeri are recognised throughout tourism brochures and planning documents as the traditional owners of this land and frequent mention is made of the need to consult and involve their community organisations in management, they were not consulted during the planning stages for this significant event. They were only invited along to give the traditional "welcome to country" and for one of their dance troupes to perform some traditional dances (Rigney, 2002, personal communication). This is indicative of the enduring colonial attitudes that linger in the minds of tourism industry players that Indigenous people are exotic performers to add colour and value to tourism events, not Indigenous people with rights that must be respected. In particular, the organising committee should have recognised that the Ngarrindjeri people have a right to have a say about what happens in their country and they should have been represented on the committee at the outset.

A few weeks before the launch, when the Ngarrindjeri received the request to dance at the event, they grew very angry about the lack of respect for proper protocol demonstrated by the SATC.[42] After consulting with the leadership in the state office of the ATSIC, the Ngarrindjeri put the SATC on notice that they were unsatisfied with these events. This resulted in a meeting with representatives of the SATC, including the CEO, Bill Spurr. Here Matt Rigney, Chairperson of the Ngarrindjeri Native Title Committee, said that the Ngarrindjeri were insulted by SATC's conduct and that they wanted to conclude a memorandum of understanding with SATC with agreed protocols that would prevent such difficulties arising in the future and that SATC management should undergo cultural training at Camp Coorong (Rigney, 2004, personal communication).

In light of the conciliatory meeting with SATC and reflecting their desires to use such events to communicate Ngarrindjeri values, they decided to participate in the launch (Rigney, 2004, personal communication). The Ngarrindjeri delegation greeted the VIPs invited to the event with protest banners claiming "You're on Ngarrindjeri country" and "Treaty – Let's get it right". The *Rupelle* of the Ngarrindjeri *Tendi*, George Trevorrow, gave the opening address which was a very powerful oration that had significant impact on the listeners (see Higgins-Desbiolles, 2003a,b for greater detail).

---

the invasion. Our only motivation for protecting our stories is our responsibility to the land and surrounding waters and to our people" (quoted in Langton, 1996, p. 214).

[40] The organising committee included representatives of the SATC, National Parks and Wildlife SA, academics from a local university and tour operators.

[41] This is a very sensitive site for the Ngarrindjeri. However, it is already a heavily used landing point for eco-cruises operating within the CNP.

[42] This anger was caused not only by the lack of proper consultation, but also at the insensitive use of Hindmarsh Island as the transit point for the VIPs to board boats for the Coorong.

So while the planners of the launch can feel pleased that they pulled off the event to the desired effect,[43] the Ngarrindjeri were able in a diplomatic yet effective way to express their concerns, their hopes and their cultural protocols. The reaction of the guests was very warm and supportive, and the communications during the event breached some significant cultural barriers. SATC managers did participate in cross-cultural training at Camp Coorong which by all accounts was successful in heightening awareness that was clearly lacking prior to the IYE 2002 launch. However, the memorandum of understanding containing cultural protocols has yet to be developed. As a result of such conflicts as the Hindmarsh Island issue and the IYE 2002 launch, the Ngarrindjeri have been very assertive of their Indigenous rights.

Ngarrindjeri Paths to Securing their Indigenous Rights

At the height of the HIB conflict when the legal and political struggles afforded little accommodation to the beliefs and values of the Ngarrindjeri proponents, the Ngarrindjeri leaders made a historic move. On Sunday, the 22nd of November 1999 at the construction site of the HIB lying on the Kumarangk/Hindmarsh Island side, after a significant cultural ceremony, Elders Maggie Jacobs and Grace Sumner raised the Ngarrindjeri flag and Matt Rigney presented the Proclamation of Ngarrindjeri Sovereignty (Proclamation, 2000, pp. 11–12). This proclamation recounts the historical fact that at the founding of South Australia the instructions for colonisation from the Crown to the South Australian Colonising Commission acknowledged Aboriginal occupation and rights to land and demanded that consent and compensation for land acquisition be secured. The proclamation then declares "now take notice that Ngarrindjeri have always occupied this place, Ngarrindjeri have never ceded nor sold this land" (2000, p. 12). Additionally, the proclamation asserted two demands: firstly the return of title of Ngarrindjeri lands to Ngarrindjeri people and secondly to stop the construction of the HIB which entailed violation and trespass of Ngarrindjeri rights (2000, p. 12). This proclamation, which the Ngarrindjeri described as "denouncing the unlawful nature and genocidal impact of colonisation and ... asserting ongoing Aboriginal sovereignty in South Australia" (2000, p. 11), was delivered to both the Governor of South Australia (the Crown's representative) and to Her Majesty the Queen of England. While evoking no response from these eminent persons yet and therefore remaining largely symbolic, this proclamation marked the opening salvo in the Ngarrindjeri efforts to secure their Indigenous rights.

In April 2000, two Ngarrindjeri men, Darrell Sumner and Tom Trevorrow, brought a complaint to the United Nations Committee on Social, Economic and Cultural Rights alleging that Australia was failing to live up to its international obligations. In particular, they argued in a media release that the HIB Bill 1997 was "a racist act" and endangered

---

[43] Which seems to have paid off: the SATC secured the hosting rights for the annual Australian conference on ecotourism (supported by the Ecotourism Association of Australia) in 2003 (Eco-tourism Coup, 2001). The SATC has also claimed that the media kit produced for the launch has generated more than $300,000 worth of media exposure for South Australia (see: http://www.ecotourism.org.au/IYE2002/pdfs/SA%20IYE%202002%20Report.pdf).

Ngarrindjeri native title interests in and around Hindmarsh Island and Goolwa (Trevorrow, 2000). Trevorrow complained:

> The government listens to local community concerns except where they are to maintain Native Title and to respect the cultural and spiritual beliefs of Indigenous people. The answer to improving the statistics of Indigenous people in the areas of health, housing and education is to respect and support Indigenous cultural and spiritual beliefs, and to acknowledge the native title owners as equal property owners by right. Having one attitude towards the property rights of non-indigenous people with a lesser approach to the rights of Ngarrindjeri people is wrong. (Trevorrow, 2000)

To date, the major milestone of Ngarrindjeri success in advancing their Indigenous rights has been the *Kungan Ngarrindjeri Yunnan* Agreement (which in English translates as "Listening to Ngarrindjeri People When They Are Talking") negotiated with Alexandrina Council, the local government body in the Goolwa and Hindmarsh Island region. Considering that the Ngarrindjeri lands and waters fall under the jurisdiction of four local councils (Alexandrina, Coorong District, Murray Bridge and Victor Harbor), it is ironic that Alexandrina would be the first to conclude an agreement with the Ngarrindjeri since it is their district which saw the battles over the HIB. As might be anticipated, such a conciliation had unusual origins.

The town of Goolwa is a historic river port that is now trading on this image in its tourism promotions. Accordingly, it hosts an annual Wooden Boat Festival as well as special, one-off events to raise its marine profile, which is enhanced by its proximity to the CNP, the Murray River and the local beaches. In early 2002, the SATC and the Alexandrina Council together committed just over $2.7 million for a redevelopment of the Goolwa wharf precinct (which is in the shadow of the HIB) in order to make it an attractive tourism zone (SATC, 2002) particularly with the then upcoming 2003 Wooden Boat Festival which had been funded and promoted more extensively. During the digging needed for the wharf upgrade, Ngarrindjeri remains were uncovered. Such a discovery brought the provisions of the South Australian *Aboriginal Heritage Act* of 1988 into play and as a result endangered the tight timelines that the wharf redevelopment project was under.[44] Tom Trevorrow of the Ngarrindjeri Heritage Committee said that this difficulty would not be addressed by the community until the Alexandrina Council concluded a proper agreement of protocols to prevent such future violations of Ngarrindjeri heritage. The Alexandrina Council responded to Ngarrindjeri proposals to use this difficult circumstance as an opportunity for forging more cooperative relationships. The results were two very significant precedents: the Alexandrina

---

[44] This unearthing of Ngarrindjeri remains (allegedly dated at 200 years old according to Alexandrina Council's CEO John Coombe, quoted in Debelle, 2002) so close to the foundations of the HIB has been taken as vindication of Ngarrindjeri proponents' claims of the significance of this area for them, contra the findings of the 1995 SA Royal Commission's assertion that "women's business" was fabricated (see Debelle, 2002; Williams, 2002, pp. 1–2). While neither the apology nor the agreement from the council addresses the pain of the HIB conflict, Tom Trevorrow told Debelle that the Ngarrindjeri understood the council's apology to address this problem "not in exact words, but it encompassed everything that happened to us there" (Debelle, 2002).

Council presented the Ngarrindjeri people with a statement of apology and signed the formal *Kungan Ngarrindjeri Yunnan* Agreement.

The Alexandrina Council's statement of "sincere expression of sorrow and apology to the Ngarrindjeri People" (2002) was presented on the 8th of October 2002. It not only expresses sorrow at past injustices but also acknowledges current racism and division and promises to work collaboratively to remove them from the community. The council acknowledges Ngarrindjeri connection to and interests in the lands and waters composing the council area and importantly acknowledges Ngarrindjeri rights to "determine your future". The council makes two important commitments within the document, including to work with the Ngarrindjeri and acknowledge their wisdom and to be "guided by your vision of a future where reconciliation through agreement making may be possible and we can walk together". The former could be viewed as a promise to engage Ngarrindjeri visions in a course of "sustainable development" for the council area and the latter is a pledge of support for the Ngarrindjeri agenda of securing Ngarrindjeri rights through a process of agreement making. The words of the apology contain many words advocating reconciliation such as "work with you", "walk beside you" and "working together", but importantly some phrases imply more than rhetoric such as the phrase "acknowledge your right to determine your future" and "reconciliation with justice".

On the same day as the signing of the historical apology, the Alexandrina Council and the Ngarrindjeri also signed the *Kungan Ngarrindjeri Yunnan* Agreement (henceforth called the Agreement)[45] which furthered sentiments into binding legal commitments.[46] This agreement specifically addresses the difficulties that the unearthing of Ngarrindjeri burials during the Goolwa wharf redevelopment project created but extends its mandate to preventing similar re-occurrences: "the Council and the Ngarrindjeri wish to further protect their Aboriginal sites, objects and remains of significance at the Site (the wharf) and across the Council area" (*Kungan Ngarrindjeri Yunnan* Agreement, 2002). The Agreement provides extensive procedures to ensure that the Goolwa wharf redevelopment could proceed with no further damage to Ngarrindjeri heritage in the project area; including a commitment by the council to allocate $20,000 to fund two Ngarrindjeri site monitors to be on site through the duration of the project with powers to issue stop work orders if the redevelopment again unearthed Ngarrindjeri heritage.[47] Recognising the council's damaging role in the unearthing of the Ngarrindjeri burial sites, the council commits to pay "the reasonable

---

[45] Importantly, the council was persuaded of the need to fund Ngarrindjeri for their participation in the negotiations to form this agreement and continue consultation subsequently, through an argument presented by Councillor Beckett that council paid consultants to inform their decisions and policies and so should similarly treat Ngarrindjeri consultants (Councillor M. Beckett, 2004, personal communication). This is in line with Johnston's recommendations discussed earlier that Indigenous peoples must be adequately resourced for negotiations (2003).

[46] At the time of its conclusion, this agreement would have been a rare phenomenon. However, as federal political circumstances are closing off avenues to self-determination and "treaty", such agreements are increasingly being made at the local and regional level. For insights into the breadth of such agreements see the database provided by the Agreements, Treaties and Negotiated Settlements project funded by an Australian Research Council Linkage grant examining treaty and agreement making with Indigenous Australians, available at: http://www.atns.net.au/atns.html

[47] Appropriate practice under the S A Aboriginal Heritage Act of 1988.

disbursement costs of the reburial".[48] Of the more wide-ranging provisions, two particular sections contain statements indicating significant transformations in council–Ngarrindjeri relationships. In the third section entitled "Acknowledgement", it states:

- The Council acknowledges that the Ngarrindjeri are the Traditional Owners of the Goolwa area and that according to their traditions, customs and spiritual beliefs its lands and waters remain their traditional country.
- The Council also acknowledges and respects the rights, interests and obligations of Ngarrindjeri to speak and care for their traditional country, lands and waters in accordance with their laws, customs, beliefs and traditions.

The fourth section of the documents lays out the following commitments:

- The Parties commit to seek ways together to uphold Ngarrindjeri rights and to advance Ngarrindjeri interests when decisions are being made about their traditional country, lands and waters.
- The Parties commit to work together to advance harmonious community relations and promote the interests of the whole community.
- The Parties commit to develop greater community understanding of Ngarrindjeri traditions, culture, laws and spiritual beliefs in the Council area.
- The Parties commit to work together to determine, and to advance the community recognition of, a framework agreement for the protection of Aboriginal sites, objects and remains in relation to development in the Council area.
- The Parties commit to the formulation of a model or models of best practice for consultation in relation to development assessment within the meaning of the Development Act 1993 (SA) to occur in the Council area, which reflects the rights, interests and obligations of the Ngarrindjeri.
- The Parties commit to formulate a strategy for the Ngarrindjeri to access their lands on, and waters around, Kumarangk (Hindmarsh Island).[49]
- The Parties will establish a joint committee comprising equal numbers of Ngarrindjeri and Council representatives to develop a strategy for the implementation of the commitments expressed herein, whose name will be determined by the committee.

The document specifies the appropriate bodies for consultation on development issues within the Council area, including the Ngarrindjeri Heritage Committee, the Ngarrindjeri Native Title Management Committee and the Ngarrindjeri Tendi ,and the issues each is responsible for so that consultation occurs with only those authorised to do so.

In order to ensure that the agreement does not endanger wider Ngarrindjeri rights, provision 17 states that the agreement does not "affect, extinguish or derogate from any subsisting legal rights, powers, interests or obligations of the Ngarrindjeri People" including sovereign rights, native title rights or rights under the state and federal Aboriginal heritage legislation. Recognising that the Agreement may face future impediments, provision 28 contains

---

[48] These costs included transport of the remains back to Goolwa from Adelaide, the costs of a meeting of Ngarrindjeri Elders and the costs incurred for the attendance of community representatives at the reburial ceremony.
[49] The Ngarrindjeri refuse to cross the bridge and therefore their rights as custodians of Kumarangk are hindered.

the *force majeure* clause which explains the conditions for addressing impediments to cooperation with the provisions of the agreement for either party to the agreement.

After the apology was presented and the *Kungan Ngarrindjeri Yunnan* Agreement was concluded, the Ngarrindjeri arranged a reburial ceremony where the remains were restored to their original resting place in the presence of their Ngarrindjeri descendants and observed by friends from the community and the council. Also, as per the statement in the Agreement and an addendum made on the 18th of November 2002, the council has come forward with monetary support for the Ngarrindjeri ferry project which Ngarrindjeri need in order to return to Kumarangk to perform their duties as custodians.[50] The council committed to match any money raised by Ngarrindjeri up to $75,000 within a period of 18 months of the agreement. Despite expiry of this time limit, the council has provided these funds as the Ngarrindjeri managed to gather support from various sources. The Ngarrindjeri recently purchased an appropriate boat with these funds. As the Ngarrindjeri can now return to Kumarangk in a culturally appropriate way, the *Kungan Ngarrindjeri Yunnan* Agreement can be seen as a journey to healing the divide that the bridge conflict caused.

Both the Ngarrindjeri and the members of the council view the agreement as a living document that can help build better relationships (M. Rigney, 2004, personal communication; Mayor K. McHugh, 2004, personal communication). Mayor Kym McHugh stated: "we've found this very rewarding, building up a good relationship with our Ngarrindjeri people and I think we have a lot of ground to make up for over the years ... and we're very much committed to moving forward with them" (personal communication, 2004). When he was asked if there were any differences of interpretation of the Agreement, Mayor McHugh could only point out the continued need the Ngarrindjeri feel to have their lawyer present at all discussions with the council, which he feels "really does limit and hamper a feeling of trust and some good discussions" (personal communication, 2004). In light of Ngarrindjeri experiences with the bridge conflict and the fact that council attitudes only shifted when lawyers were co-opted in the effort to secure their Indigenous rights,[51] this point of difference is likely to remain. Councillor Mary Beckett arranged for members of the Council to undertake Ngarrindjeri cultural training at Camp Coorong in 2004 to further improve relationships between the Ngarrindjeri and the Council (personal communication, 2004).[52]

The efforts of the Ngarrindjeri to secure their Indigenous rights continue as they seek similar agreements with the other three councils that are situated in Ngarrindjeri country. Additionally, the Ngarrindjeri await negotiations with the SATC to draft a memorandum

---

[50] Additionally, this addendum includes an acknowledgement that the Goolwa wharf area is a site of particular significance to Ngarrindjeri women (contra the charge of "fabrication" made in the 1995 Royal Commission). Additionally the council stated its support of the Ngarrindjeri request that the state government agree to a joint management arrangement for the CNP.

[51] Historian Steve Hemming witnessed much of the conflict surrounding the SATC's IYE 2002 launch and the Ngarrindjeri (discussed previously) and remarked that if the Ngarrindjeri had a lawyer retained then, the launch would not have been allowed to proceed without rectification of the problem to Ngarrindjeri satisfaction because the conduct of the event violated their rights under the state *Aboriginal Heritage Act* (Hemming, 2004, personal communication).

[52] This shows the dual-pronged strategy mentioned earlier in action; Indigenous rights efforts are complemented by Camp Coorong's efforts in offering cultural education thereby improving race relations.

of understanding as first proposed during the negotiations around the IYE 2002 launch discussed earlier. Because the SATC is a state government agency, this aim may have to await success on another Ngarrindjeri front. In December of 2003, the Ngarrindjeri issued the Proclamation of Time Immemorial Ngarrindjeri Dominium and presented it to the Crown's representative. Much of this document is similar to the 1999 proclamation. However, this proclamation notes the illegitimate founding of the State of South Australia and calls upon the government to "enter into a Social Charter with the Ngarrindjeri Nation to inscribe mutual recognition of our dominium as between Ngarrindjeri Nation and the Crown within South Australia" and to present a bill to the state parliament for a Ngarrindjeri treaty. While this sounds unlikely, the state of South Australia has been at the forefront of progressive issues in past decades and may be so again. No such hope can be entertained at the federal level as the Howard government has diverted reconciliation, dismantled ATSIC, denied self-determination and limited the effectiveness of native title.

As the preceding discussion illuminates, the Ngarrindjeri have utilised a dual strategy to assert their Indigenous rights; one tactic is symbolic assertions of sovereignty (which await a more favourable political climate for recognition) and the other is pragmatic agreement-making efforts which are envisioned to cover all institutions and organisations operating on and/or affecting Ngarrindjeri people and country. The ultimate aim of this Ngarrindjeri Indigenous rights agenda is as simple as it is vital; it is to assert an unassailable Ngarrindjeri role in management of their lands and waters, as is made clear in this Ngarrindjeri statement:

> The sense of feeling, sense of belonging, sense of responsibility for the River, Lakes and Coorong experienced by Ngarrindjeri people has survived occupation, dispersal and attempted assimilation. It continues to exist irrespective of where Ngarrindjeri people currently live. The link with the land lies at the heart and soul of Ngarrindjeri culture. A proper relationship and role in management of the land is a fundamental platform in building and maintaining Ngarrindjeri culture and Ngarrindjeri self-respect. Ngarrindjeri believe that their future involvement in the management of the land would be positive and beneficial to all members of the community, not just Ngarrindjeri. It would represent a significant step in the process of reconciliation and co-existence. The strengthening of Ngarrindjeri people and their culture requires a serious involvement in the managing of their traditional lands. (Ngarrindjeri Ramsar Working Group, 1999)

Conclusion

The profile and interests of Indigenous peoples has been raised at the international level through their efforts to assert Indigenous rights. The progress of the Draft Declaration on the Rights of Indigenous Peoples and the outcomes achieved in the talks on the CBD illustrate this. At the same time Indigenous nations such as the Ngarrindjeri are working concertedly to secure their rights at the local level. Together, these macro- and micro-level activities towards Indigenous rights may well point the way to a fundamental change that could sweep the tourism arena and to which it will have to adjust as it has done to activism on human rights and demands for sustainability. It is becoming increasingly apparent that relegating social justice to the backburner in the drive for economic growth through tourism is increasingly no longer acceptable (Scheyvens, 2002). The Ngarrindjeri's efforts demonstrate that local and Indigenous communities are asserting their rights and taming tourism to their needs.

Acknowledgements

I am grateful to the Ngarrindjeri for their willingness to share their experiences and visions for a better future and allow me to write about these. Special thanks are due to Matt Rigney, Vesper Tjukonai, Mayor Kym McHugh and Councillor Mary Beckett. Kate Leeson provided editorial assistance.

References

Aboriginal and Torres Strait Islander Commission (n.d.). *An analysis of the United Nations Draft Declaration on the Rights of Indigenous Peoples.* Retrieved 12 February 2004, from http://www.atsic.gov.au/issues/indigenous_rights/international/draft_declaration/draft_dec_preface.asp

Alexandrina Council (2002). *Sincere expression of sorrow and apology to the Ngarrindjeri people.* Unpublished document.

Barker, A. (2001, August 21). Hindmarsh bridge controversy continues. *7:30 report transcript*, ABC television. Retrieved 12 October 2003, from http://www.abc.net.au/7.30/s350217.htm

Barnett, S. (2001). Manaakitanga: Maori hospitality – A case study of Maori accommodation providers. *Tourism Management, 22*, 83–92.

Bell, D. (1998). *Ngarrindjeri wurruwarrin: A world that is, was and will be.* Melbourne, Vic.: Spinifex.

Brodie, V. (2001, March 21). A devisive bridge. Interview in *The Koori Mail*, 4.

Brodie, V. (2002). *My side of the bridge.* Kent Town, SA: Wakefield Press.

Brysk, A. (Ed.) (2002). *Globalization and human rights.* Berkeley: University of California Press.

Butcher, J. (2003). *The moralisation of tourism: Sun, sand ... and saving the world.* London: Routledge.

Butler, B. (2000). Statement to the UN Commission on Human Rights Working Group on the Declaration on the Rights of Indigenous Peoples (on behalf of ATSIC et al), 1 December 2000. Retrieved 12 February 2004, from http://www.atsic.gov.au/issues/indigenous_rights/international/draft_declaration/draft_dec_preface.asp

Community Aid Abroad (1999). The Draft Declaration on the Rights of Indigenous Peoples, December, *Polliewatch.* Retrieved 12 February 2004, from http://www.caa.org.au/campaigns/polliewatch/ddrip.html

Debelle, P. (2002, December 10). Bones discovery at bridge unearths land-claim proof, *Sydney Morning Herald.* Retrieved 23 May 2003, from http://www.smh.com.au/articles/2002/12/09/1039379788777.html

Denzin, N. K. (2005). Emancipatory discourses and the ethics and politics of participation. In: N. K. Denzin, & Y. S. Lincoln (Eds), *The sage handbook of qualitative research* (3rd ed., pp. 933–958). Thousand Oaks, CA: Sage Publications.

Denzin, N. K., & Lincoln, Y. S. (2005). Introduction: The discipline and practice of qualitative research. In: N. K. Denzin, & Y. S. Lincoln (Eds), *The sage handbook of qualitative research* (3rd ed., pp. 1–32). Thousand Oaks, CA: Sage Publications.

Eco-tourism coup (2001, October 28). *The Advertiser,* 8.

Emerson, S. (2003, August 21). Black law "poses a threat" to tourism. *The Australian*, 5.

Hansen, M. (2000). Statement to the UN Commission on Human Rights Working Group on the Declaration on the Rights of Indigenous Peoples (on behalf of ATSIC et al), 1 December 2000. Retrieved 12 February 2004, from http://www.atsic.gov.au/issues/indigenous_rights/international/draft_declaration/draft_dec_preface.asp

Hemming, S. (1993). Camp Coorong: Combining race relations and cultural education. *Social Alternatives*, *12*(1), 37–41.

Higgins-Desbiolles, F. (2003a). Globalisation and indigenous tourism: Sites of engagement and resistance. In: M. Shanahan & G. Treuren (Eds), *Globalisation: Australian regional perspectives* (pp. 240–262). Adelaide, SA: Wakefield Press.

Higgins-Desbiolles, F. (2003b). Reconciliation tourism: Tourism healing divided societies. *Tourism Recreation Research*, *28*(3), 35–44.

Higgins-Desbiolles, F. (2004). Reconciliation tourism: Challenging the constraints of economic rationalism. In: C. Ryan & M. Aicken (Eds), *Indigenous tourism: The commodification and management of culture* (pp. 223–245). Amsterdam: Elsevier.

International Indian Treaty Council (2004, 15 March–23 April). *Written Intervention submitted to the UN Commission on Human Rights*. Retrieved 6 June 2004, from http://www.treatycouncil.org/IITC%20Item15%20Indigenous%20Issues.pdf

International Labor Organisation (1989). *Convention No. 169: Indigenous and Tribal Peoples Convention*. Retrieved 25 February 2003, from http://www.ilo.org/ilolex/cgi-lex/convde.pl?C169

Johnston, A. (2000). Indigenous peoples and ecotourism: Bringing Indigenous knowledge and rights into the sustainability equation. *Tourism Recreation Research*, *25*(2), 89–96.

Johnston, A. M. (2003). Self-determination: Exercising Indigenous rights in tourism. In: S. Singh., D. J. Timothy & R. K. Dowling (Eds), *Tourism in destination communities* (pp. 115–134). Oxon: CABI.

Keal, P. (2003). *European conquest and the rights of indigenous peoples: The moral backwardness of international society*. Cambridge: Cambridge University Press.

Kenny, S. J. (1998). The Hindmarsh Island Bridge case – implications for native title. AIC Native Title Conference, Brisbane, Qld, 29th April–1st May.

Kincheloe, J. L., & McLaren, P. (2005). Rethinking critical theory and qualitative research. In: N. K. Denzin & Y. S. Lincoln (Eds), *The sage handbook of qualitative research* (3rd ed., pp. 303–342). Thousand Oaks, CA: Sage Publications.

Kungan Ngarrindjeri Agreement (2002). Unpublished document between Alexandrina Council and Ngarrinjderi.

Langton, M. (1996). The Hindmarsh Island Bridge affair: How aboriginal women's religion became an administrable affair. *Australian Feminist Studies*, *11*(24), 211–217.

Mathieson, A., & Wall, G. (1982). *Tourism: Economic, physical and social impacts*. Harlow, UK: Longman Scientific & Technical.

McLaren, D. R. (2003). Indigenous peoples and ecotourism. In: M. Honey & S. Thullen (Eds), *Rights and responsibilities: A compilation of codes of conduct for tourism and Indigenous and local communities*. Retrieved 11 November 2003, from http://ecotourism.org/rights_responsibilities.html

Mowforth, M., & Munt, I. (2003). *Tourism and sustainability: Development and new tourism in the Third World* (2nd ed.). London: Routledge.

Ngarrindjeri Ramsar Working Group (1999). Ngarrindjeri perspectives on Ramsar issues. In South Australian Department for Environment, Heritage and Aboriginal Affairs, *Draft Coorong and Lakes Alexandrina and Albert Ramsar management plan*, (Appendix 8). Adelaide, SA: SADEHAA.

Pera, L., & McLaren, D. (1999). *Globalization, tourism and indigenous peoples: What you should know about the world's largest "industry"*. Retrieved 21 May 2003, from http://www.planeta.com/ecotravel/resources/rtp/globalization.html

Proclamation of Ngarrindjeri sovereignty (2000). *Indigenous Law Bulletin*, *4*(26), 11–12.

Robinson, M. (1999). Collaboration and cultural consent: Refocusing sustainable development. *Journal of Sustainable Development*, *7*(3–4), 379–397.

Ryan, C. (2002). Equity, management, power sharing and sustainability: Issues of the "new tourism". *Tourism Management*, *23*, 17–26.

Scheyvens, R. (2002). *Tourism for development: Empowering communities*. Harlow, UK: Prentice-Hall.

Simons, M. (2003). *The meeting of the waters*. Sydney, NSW: Hodder.

Sklair, L. (2002). *Globalization, capitalism and its alternatives* (3rd ed). Oxford: Oxford University Press.

Smith, L. T. (2005). On tricky ground: Researching the native in the age of uncertainty. In: N. K. Denzin & Y. S. Lincoln (Eds), *The sage handbook of qualitative research* (3rd ed., pp. 85–107). Thousand Oaks, CA: Sage Publications.

Smith, M., & Duffy, R. (2003). *The ethics of tourism development*. London: Routledge.

Snow, S. G. (2001). The Kuna General Congress and the statute on tourism. *Cultural Survival Quarterly*, *24*(4). Retrieved 19 August 2003, from http://www.culturalsurvival.org/publications

South Australian Tourism Commission (2002). Goolwa wharf redevelopment. *SATC Tourism News*. Retrieved 23 September 2002, from http://www.tourism.sa.gov.au/TWA/archives/March2002/tourism_news.htm

Stevens, I. (1995). Hindmarsh Island Bridge Royal Commission, Transcript of Proceedings, 19 July, Adelaide, SA. Retrieved on 27 March 2000, from http://www.library.adelaide.edu.au/gen/H_Islnd/P_1.pdf

Stewart-Harawira, M. (2005). *The new imperial order: Indigenous responses to globalization*. London: Zed Books.

Tourism in Independent Hawai'i (1997). *Contours*, *7*(11–12), 24.

Trevorrow, T. (2000). Unpublished media release with Darrell Sumner.

Trevorrow, T. (2003). A shocking insult. *Overland*, *171*, 62–63.

United Nations Commission on Human Rights and Working Group on Indigenous Populations (1999). *Draft Declaration on the Rights of Indigenous Peoples*. Retrieved 23 September 2003, from http://www.austlii.edu.au/au/other/ahric/treaties/declrip.html

United Nations World Tourism Organization (n.d.). *Global Code of Ethics for Tourism*. Retrieved 8 March 2000, from http://www.world-tourism.org/pressrel/CODEOFE,htm

Weaver, D., & Lawton, L. (2002). *Tourism management*. Milton, Qld: John Wiley & Sons.

Williams, T. (2002, September 10). Bone find may vindicate sacred site. *The Australian*, 1–2.

Personal Informants South Australian Fieldwork

Steve Hemming, 5 February 2004, Adelaide, SA.

Kim McHugh, Mayor Alexandrina Council, 18 June 2004, via phone call.

Matt Rigney, Chair Ngarrindjeri Native Title Committee, 29 January 2002, Meningie and 22 June 2004, Adelaide, SA.

Mary Beckett, Member of Alexandrina Council, 26 June 2004, via phone call.

Chapter 7

Celebrating or Marketing the Indigenous? International Rights Organisations, National Governments and Tourism Creation

Susan Keitumetse

Introduction

This chapter discusses how the variation in perception of the concept of *indigeneity* by national governments and international advocacy organisations impact on the way indigenous communities' heritage is presented in enterprise tourism. The group referred to here is the San, referred to as Basarwa in Botswana and as the Bushmen by the UK-based inter-national advocacy organisation called Survival International (SI).[1] Both Botswana government[2] and SI are referred to here as stakeholders in the management of cultural heritage of the indigenous San.

I argue that conflicting debates about the categorisation of the San as indigenous are perpetuated by a profound failure by the two stakeholders to look at the root of their problem which is variation in perception of what constitutes cultural difference of these communities (Keitumetse, 2004; 2002). The indigenous concept appears to be facing scepticism in other regions as well. Many Asian governments are reluctant to ratify the International Labour Organisation (ILO) No.169 Convention. The same also goes for African countries. The Convention is ratified by only 17 states, although about 76 states have indigenous and tribal populations. Of the 17 only 3 are from the developed world.[3] In particular, Botswana has not ratified this convention even though it has the highest number of San population in Southern Africa.

A biased focus on communities that with time have come to be known as indigenous can be attributed to the 19th century focus of applied anthropology primitivism (Boissevain, 2002;

---

[1] Refer to Survival International website http://www.survival-international.org for a detailed account. "Survival International is a worldwide organisation supporting tribal peoples. It stands for their right to decide their own future and helps them protect their lives, lands and human rights".

[2] Refer Botswana Government website http://www.gov.bw/ for a detailed account. Botswana is a landlocked country in Southern Africa with the highest number of the San population.

[3] http://www.unhchr.ch/html/menu3/b/62.htm

Edwards, 1992; Nolan, 2002; Smith, 1989). The images created from this focus tended to describe these communities as "primitive", "culturally pure", "uncontacted", "stone age" peoples. In turn international legislation such as the 1989 ILO Convention seems to have obliviously followed this guideline which in turn has influenced approaches of international advocacy organisations and some academics working among indigenous communities. However, because their definition and descriptions of what the indigenous means is not reconciled with how they are perceived in their national localities, conflicts ensue, resulting in unsustainable utilisation of these communities' cultural heritage in enterprise tourism.

Drawing from conflicting perceptions of the concept of *indigeneity* by both local (national governments) and global (international advocacy) cultural custodians, this chapter departs from the premises that the sometimes essentialist analyses of tourism as a "... negative phenomenon which, through the process of commodification destroyed or modified the authenticity of other cultures and places" (Meethan, 2001, p. 90) needs to be modified. It is argued that at times tourism is not the sole source for the commodification of cultures. Factors such as the political relationship between national governments and international organisations advocating for communities and their cultural heritage indigenous are identified as one example (Figure 7.1). The commodification of indigenous communities' cultural heritage is here attested to the aggressive implementation of concepts that are adopted at universal level with very little consideration of how they are perceived at national government levels as well as the failure of national governments to endeavour to understand perceptions informing and guiding international Conventions.

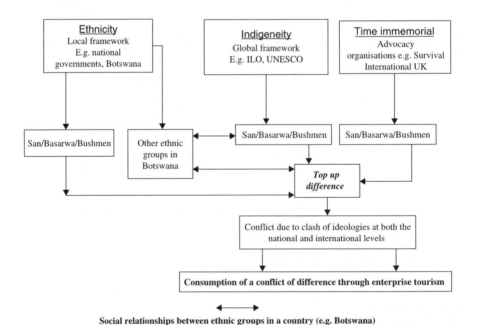

Figure 7.1: The impact of conflicting ideologies on cultural consumption of the indigenous (Keitumetse, January 2006).

Discussion

Indigeneity *and African politics: Global–Local Connections*

In both the developing and the developed worlds *indigeneity* is used today as a marker of cultural difference for certain communities (Berkhofer, 1979; Boyd, 2004; Bonvillain, 2005; Howard, 2003; Saugestad, 2001; http://www.survival-international.org). Phrases such as "native" (2003) and "First Peoples" (First People of the Kalahari in Botswana; Sanders 1995) are commonly used to denote indigenousness.

At the international level the indigenous ideology is spearheaded by the International Labour Organisation's (ILO) *1989 Convention No. 169 concerning Indigenous and Tribal Peoples in Independent Countries*, which was adopted in June 1989 by the General Conference of the ILO at its 76th session. The convention came into force in September 1991.[4] Within the UNESCO, the convention is supported by the *International Decade of the World's Indigenous People*,[5] which was officially launched in December 1994 by the United Nations General Assembly. The UNESCO further plays a key role in the decade, which is intended to strengthen international co-operation for the solution of problems faced by indigenous people in such areas as human rights, the environment, development, education and health (UNESCO, 2001). Unlike most international Conventions, once ratified, the 1989 ILO Convention No.169 is legally binding. The ILO is a United Nations (UN) specialised agency which:

"aims to contribute to the establishment of universal and lasting peace through the promotion of social justice by raising working standards and living standards world-wide, achieving full employment, and promoting training, social security, and other socially desirable objectives" (Jan Osmanczyk, 2003, p. 1109).

Article 1(a) of this convention currently defines the indigenous people as:

"Tribal peoples in independent countries whose social, cultural and economic conditions distinguish them from other sections of the national community, and whose status is regulated wholly or partially by their own customs or traditions or by special laws or regulations".[6]

Article 1 (b) further elaborates that indigenous people are:

"Peoples in independent countries who are regarded as indigenous on account of their descent from the populations which inhabited the country, or a geographical region to which the country belongs, at the time of conquest or colonisation or the establishment of present State boundaries and who, irrespective of their legal status, retain some or all of their own social, economic, cultural and political institutions" (Jan Osmanczyk, 2003, pp. 986–987).[7]

---

[4] http://www.unhchr.ch/html/menu3/b/62.htm
[5] http://www.un.org/rights/indigenous/mediaadv.html
[6] http://www.unhchr.ch/html/menu3/b/62.htm
[7] http://www.unhchr.ch/html/menu3/b/62.htm

The 1989 convention is a revision of the *ILO's 1957 Indigenous and Tribal Populations Convention (No. 107) Concerning the Protection and Integration of Indigenous and Other Tribal and Semi-Tribal Populations in Independent Countries*, that initially advocated for the integrationist approach aimed at assimilating indigenous communities and other natives into civilised society. The 1957 convention was reviewed because with time it became perceived as constituting some ideas that "no longer reflect current thinking" (Jan Osmanczyk, 2003, p. 987). It is significant to highlight that by 1957, almost all of the African states had not gained independence therefore the welfare of communities including indigenous ones was a responsibility of their colonial powers. Assimilation was a priority because most colonial masters were keen to civilise what was viewed as barbaric and uncivilised attitudes on the part of their subjects, be they indigenous or otherwise. Consequently, this civilisation impacted on the cultures of the communities in question. In contrast, the 1989 convention aims to remedy thissituation by persuading independent governments to take responsibility for developing co-ordinated and systematic action to protect indigenous peoples' rights and guarantee respect for their social, economic and cultural integrity. Although only specific to indigenous communities, the convention emphasises cultural diversity as opposed to cultural homogeneity. This approach is crucial for the sustainability of most communities' cultural heritage.

However, the emphasis of this convention on *indigeneity* is now changing the face of the debate, or rather blame. In contemporary African states, the emphasis is shifting from being coloniser/colony or black/white blame to being indigenous groups versus their national governments scenario. Subsequent to this ideological shift, it appears that some African countries have come to perceive international advocacy for the indigenous as being biased in shouldering all the blame on them and capitalising on their post-colonial mistakes rather than acknowledging where necessary that the problem has deeper roots. This perception is perpetuated by the fact that, definitions and descriptions guiding the designation of a community as indigenous contain several loopholes. Until these are addressed it might be difficult for advocacy organisations to call for exclusive focus on a particular group in a nation such as that of Botswana. These loopholes are identified in this chapter as follows; i) the concept of *indigeneity* clashes with already-existing cultural markers such as *ethnicity* (Figure 7.1), ii) economic resources distribution in community-based programmes that follow the *indigeneity* model by default exclude other resources users creating conflict, iii) the designation of the concept ignores both colonial and post-colonial politics; and iv) there is lack of co-ordination between stakeholders that designate, and those that implement the concept.

In African contexts one factor that challenges the basic frameworks within which *indigeneity* is formulated is the concept of ethnicity. The emphasis of the ILO convention that indigenous groups are those "… whose social, cultural and economic conditions distinguish them from other sections of the national community …" seems to apply to all ethnic groups in a country such as Botswana. The already recognised cultural differences in funerary wedding, song, dance, etc. practices at country level constitute distinct cultural expressions of ethnic communities in Botswana. This challenges elements of the ILO convention to demonstrate how *indigeneity* differs from concepts such as ethnicity that is a common and generally accepted indicator of cultural difference at the local (country) level. In general the concept of ethnicity is perceived as a marker of cultural difference (Eriksen, 1993; Smith, 1986) not only in Botswana but also in most, if not all parts of Africa.

In some instances the "from time immemorial" concept has at times been used to support policies of cultural superiority (Franke, 1993; Kohl & Fawcett, 1995). The definitions of *indigeneity* provided above carry undertones of the "time immemorial" concept. An example of this can be extrapolated from a conference titled "*A dialogue of Cultures for sustainable development*" organised by the Commonwealth Human Ecology Council and United Nations Educational Scientific and Cultural Organisation (UNESCO). One speaker working with indigenous communities in Canada elaborated on the characteristics that they used to denote indigenousness. According to Burnstick (1993, p. 145) who worked for the Indian indigenous people, the indigenous fell into two groups:

1 "... the spiritual, traditional people who live based on the land, understanding the land and having traditional spiritual ways that existed before the coming of Columbus to the Americas".
2 "... who have lost a lot of their traditional ways they do not understand anything about their land, or about their traditions and to the point that they no longer even speak their traditional language and have not retained any of their cultural background. We call them conservatives and pro-government Indian peoples".

The speaker indicated that they preferred to work with the indigenous Indians from the first definition not the second definition. It is evident that the latter lacks the qualities associated with the "... before the coming of Columbus ..." and the communities "... have not retained any of their cultural background".

Such approaches seem to be oblivious to the fact that culture is dynamic not static. Any kind of advocacy that argues for static images assumes the halt of the dynamic nature and process of culture thus painting a distorted image of the cultures of the groups in question. Most significantly, such approaches fail to acknowledge that in the 21st century, retaining cultural background sometimes requires one to be "... conservative and pro-government ..." in order to better understand the systems that purport to represent oneself at international law levels in the first place.

In addition, whereas the above examples might be readily applicable in Canada, North America (Morningstorm, 2004) and Australia. In African contexts this might be complicated by the fact that the notion of "independence" in the 1960s focused substantially on nationalism, a concept that still opposes colonialism ideologies that encourage ethnic segregation into superior and inferior categories. Selecting the "indigenous" as the only group that has been negatively impacted upon culturally and economically might not be accommodated by post-colonial governments, resulting in the concept and the cultures it purports to protect being alienated at national government policy levels. The concept of *indigeneity* has therefore gradually become a North–South debate and until this is accounted for prior to implementation of conventions such as the 1989 ILO No. 169, little progress can be achieved. In contrast the approach of such international law poses the danger of conventions being likened to colonial approaches where models of "Development" were simply diffused to the developing world without any assessment as to whether they were compatible with the socio-cultural contexts or not. This automatic diffusion is illustrated by the transition from the ILO Convention No. 107 of 1957 to the ILO Convention No. 169 of 1989 as highlighted above. The swift changes between contrasting ideologies dealing with cultures and communities in sovereign countries, and the expectation that countries should passively oblige could come across as a violation of post-colonial concept of "independence" that is embraced and cherished by all African states.

Another look at the ILO definitions outlined above illustrate that the socio-cultural features identified as exclusive to what I term the *indigenous local* are usually readily applicable to what I shall call the *ordinary local*. For instance, all ethnic groups in Southern Africa lived in colonial circumstances, indigenous or otherwise. They were therefore impacted upon either culturally, socially and economically. The yard-sticks used through *indigeneity* to measure the degree of cultural impact among the *indigenous local* and the *ordinary local* at country level therefore remain open to challenge. Failure by organisations such as the ILO, to justify this exclusive category of indigenousness might cause conflict between national governments such as Botswana and international advocacy organisation such as SI. Also where such conflicts surface, exclusive categorisation of indigenous communities at a country level is likely to attract the question of "why them not us?" particularly where cultural revival results in economic gain through cultural tourism activities. As an example, in Tsodilo World Heritage site in Botswana where the San/Basarwa/Bushmen are found, there are development initiatives by organisations whose mandatory focus is specifically on the San/Basarwa/Bushmen (Kuru Development Trust, 2002). Still in Botswana, the Community Based Natural Resources Management (CBNRM) programme has for a long time focused almost exclusively on San/Basarwa communities. In such cases, when financial benefit is determined along such categories, conflicts could arise, as the *ordinary locals* become excluded following the *indigeneity* model.

While the selection of a community as indigenous might not be too problematic, the indicators used in the ILO convention to advocate *indigeneity* in African contexts leave it open to challenge (Keitumetse, 2004; 2002; Parsons, 2004). In most parts of post-colonial Africa, groups other than the indigenous communities still refer to themselves as having distinct cultural heritage from others although they lived under, and were impacted upon by colonial conditions. Questions of why only indigenous people are assisted in retaining their cultural heritage surface. In the same token, focus on the dichotomy between "authentic" and "non-authentic" cultures and traditions result in the concept denoting some cultures as more valuable than others. In archaeological heritage this compares with the world heritage concept that designates some monuments as more valuable than others (UNESCO, 1972).

Such politics challenge the premises of the convention to consider the basis for advocacy of exclusive conservation of indigenous groups' cultural heritage. Given that the UNESCO and the ILO depend on governments' approval of conventions (Fontein, 2001; UNESCO, 2003; 1972), the frameworks of the convention can only become effective if national governments understand and agree with its context and contents. Currently only 17 countries out of 76 states with indigenous and tribal populations have ratified the convention, with only 3 from the developed world.[8]

Further scepticism surrounding the international context of the concept of *indigeneity* might be explained by its origin in the UN family of organisations. The placement of the convention under the Human Rights concept makes it appear as a form of political advocacy for indigenous communities by the ILO, not as a politically neutral policy framework. Failure

---

[8] http://www.unhchr.ch/html/menu3/b/62.htm

of the convention to explicitly highlight and prioritise the cultural aspect of *indigeneity* further aggravates this scepticism among member states. The Human Rights concept is guided by international law which has been accused of having … a historical role in legitimising the expansion of colonial empires and the acquisition of title to the territory of indigenous peoples and constitute "… exclusive domain of European powers with imperial agendas" (Pritchard, 1998, p. 02). It appears therefore that the environment within which international conventions with implications on cultural heritage management operate have to be assessed to investigate whether such environments benefit *sustainable development* community heritage in particular. The 1989 ILO Convention on indigenous peoples might benefit communities and their cultural heritage if it operates directly under UNESCO which already has a socialised image as a cultural, rather than a civil right organisation.

Findings: *Indigeneity* and Enterprise Tourism

Focus on primitivism of indigenous communities has changed through time. Currently in Southern Africa indigenous communities are portrayed as marginalised, and poor with the main focus placed on their socio-economic needs (Kretch, 2005; Saugestad, 2001). Together with the earlier primitivism model such representation has resulted in a socialised perception of these communities as what I refer to as "objects of pity" by academics, cultural custodians and the governments of their own countries. They are therefore rarely involved as equal participants in the management of their cultures. Instead they are managed together with their cultures as evident from approaches of Botswana government[9] and SI.[10] This is in contrast with situations in the North America where groups of indigenous communities are significantly representing themselves in museums (e.g. Bonvillain, 2005; National Museum of the American Indian in Washington, DC; McIntosh and McIntosh, 2004) and other social institutions. It is therefore evident that the selective focus on these communities by conventions such as the ILO No. 169 directly or indirectly perpetuates some of these stereotyped representations.

   However, the impact of such representations of indigenous communities is even more significant in enterprise tourism. Representation of indigenous communities in tourism is gradually increasing. References to both international advocacy organisations such as SI and the national governments such as that of Botswana are made in these tourism marketing media such as Lonely Planet (Figure 7.2; Hunter, Rhind & Andrew, 2002; Richmond, Murphy, Wildman & Burke, 2002; Swaney, Fitzpatrick, Greenway, Stone & Vaisutis, 2003). Such references support the argument that these stakeholders at times arouse unwanted publicity. The stereotyped images of the indigenous communities are distorted even further in such contexts as indicated in Figure 7.2. I argue that this owes to the debates' exaggerated emphasis on elements of authenticity, scarcity and selectivity in cultures of indigenous communities. Such terminology feeds one of the main ingredients of tourism; in this case being the "scarcity" principle.

---

[9] /www.gov.bw/
[10] /http://www.survival-international.org/

Tourism survives on marketing "scarce" products. The scarcity principle is therefore very important for tourism survival (Smith, 1989). In cultural heritage management cultural difference is an important indicator of the scarcity principle. For indigenous people *indigeneity* in a way provides for this principle. How this happens can be best understood by looking at Beteille's (1983) analysis of the idea of natural inequality, which demonstrates how differences emanate in a socio-cultural context. Betielle posits that:

> "Nature presents us only with differences or potential differences. With human beings these differences do not become inequalities unless and until they are selected, marked out and evaluated by processes that are cultural and not natural ... differences become inequalities only with the application of scales; and the scales ... in a social context are ... culturally constructed by particular human beings under particular historical conditions" (Beteille, 1983, p. 08).

Applying Beteille's theory to the definitions and categories espoused in the ILO Convention, the scale is provided by the indicators contained in the definitions of the indigenous concept, therefore representing markers of cultural difference. In African contexts however, where ethnicity is also a marker of cultural difference, the "difference" provided by the concept of *indigeneity* overlaps significantly with the socio-cultural element such as *ethnicity* that already differentiate communities that I have earlier referred to as *the ordinary local*. Given that the indicators used to denote cultural difference appear to be ubiquitous at the national level the indigenous-based difference appears to be a rather artificial or fictitious indicator or a top-up on the ethnic component (Figure 7.1). The "top-up" is in turn projected through its agents, the San/Bushmen/Basarwa communities. I therefore argue that at times enterprise tourism scavenges from an already existing artificial/superficial/fictitious cultural difference in a bid to hold on to the "long time ago", thus scarce, commodity. The more "authentic" or "time immemorial" label attached to indigenous communities, the more in demand they remain, and the more likely that the communities and their cultures will be negatively exploited in enterprise marketing. Enterprise tourism revisits such anthropological descriptions as "one of the most mysterious peoples of the world ... to find a comparable form of existence you would have to go back to the Stone Age" (Balsan, 1954, p. 83) as indicative of scarcity. In a world devoid of scarcity due to globalisation, tourism recycles nostalgic elements provided by colonial anthropology and replicated in international law (ILO convention No.169) and spearheaded by international advocacy to sustain the "difference" of indigenous cultures for tourists to acquire as "souvenirs of Africa", alongside other commodities. This contributes not only to cultural devaluation but also to cultural and community commodification (Figure 7.2; Hunter et al., 2002; Richmond et al., 2002; Swaney et al., 2003).

Figure 7.2 illustrates that the distorted image represented in the 1989 ILO No. 169 Convention spearheaded by international advocacy is with time recycled, re-appropriated and finally socialised as "reality".

Descriptions carrying the same undertones have been observed in the context of Australian Aboriginal (Waitt, 1999) and the Eskimos (Smith, 1989) who also fall under the indigenous category. Van der Post and Taylor's assertion that "... the Bushman was and, to

---

1. (Hunter et al., 2002, p. 154).[11]
"... indigenous Khwe (Bushmen) who have lived here for at least 30 000 years ... extremely friendly, they welcome visitors ..."

2. (Swaney et al., 2003)
In this publication, supposed "myths" about the San/Bushmen's sense of hearing, eyesight and direction are listed. Although they are referred to as "myths" they are extensively listed without the author expressing any opinion about the political correctness. This indicates that the author is deliberately leaving tourists the space to draw their own conclusions that might be informed by the very knowledge that objectifies such communities, in the process perpetuating the "myths".

3. (Richmond et al., 2002, p. 86)[12]
Description of the San focuses on their physical features as an indicator of difference. Described as having:
"... honey coloured skin, buttocks that can store reserves of fat (most other people store fat on the hips and stomach) and hair that forms tight curls" The Bantu descriptions are language and material culture. No anatomical description indicating the need to reinforce the "scarce difference" of the indigenous people.

Figure 7.2: Marketing distortion as reality: Excerpts from Lonely Planet publications marketing the San/"Bushmen" in Southern Africa: The marketing phrases hold on to the "difference" as provided for by the "time immemorial" and "scarcity" principles.

an extent, remains what we, increasingly cut off from our natural selves and the little that is left of the natural world, can only dream of today" (1984, pp. 134–135) clearly explains the biased focus on descriptions such as above. It can therefore be argued that tourism is not always the sole factor responsible for the commodification of community cultures such as those of the indigenous. It is possible that at times tourism "scavenges" on an already existing exaggerated cultural difference that is obliviously perpetuated by approaches of conventions such as the 1989 ILO Convention and international advocacy organisations.

Theorising the Conflict: Bourdieu's Cultural Capital Theory

One way to explain the contrasting perception and understanding of the indigenous ideology by African governments and international advocacy organisations is by looking at the

---

[11] Descriptions of the San in the Central Kalahari Game Reserve in then Bechuanaland who were moved into the Reserve in the 1960s (Silbabuer, 1965).
[12] Descriptions such as "... one of their most well-known physical peculiarities is the tendency, especially among women, to steatopygy, i.e. the excessive development of fatty tissue on the buttocks" (Forde, 1963, p. 24) can be traced as far back as the early twentieth century and earlier.

French philosopher, Pierre Bourdieu's analysis of university students' social origin and its influence on their choice and understanding of subjects (Bourdieu, 1979). In his book, the *Inheritors*, Bourdieu & Passeron (1979) observed that:

> "Whereas bourgeois students, more assured of their vocations or their abilities, express their real or alleged eclecticism and more or less fruitful dilettantism in the greater diversity of their cultural interests, other students manifest greater dependence on the university. When sociology students are asked whether they would rather study their own society or Third World countries and anthropology, the choice of 'exotic' themes and fields becomes more frequent as social origin rises. Similarly, if the most privileged students are most attracted by fashionable ideas ... this is perhaps because their previously protected experience predisposes them to aspirations guided more by the pleasure principle than the reality principle and because intellectual exoticism and formalistic purity are the symbolic, that is, ostentatious and innocuous, way of liquidating a bourgeois experience while expressing it" (Bourdieu & Passeron 1979, p. 15).

Although this theory was applied to an educational setting a lot can be drawn from it as regards the contested values placed on *indigeneity* by both the local (national) and global (international) institutions. It is possible that the differences in perception of *indigeneity* is indicative of the differences in cultural association and exposure to indigenous communities themselves which then influences perception of what is culturally valuable about them. It appears that the "cultural" value placed on indigenous cultures by international advocacy organisations might be indicative of what in Bourdieu' theory is perception by bourgeois students who, unlike their lower middle class counterparts (represented by African national governments) have already acquired, understood and accepted what *indigeneity* as a concept is. International advocacy organisations can therefore be viewed as possessing the *cultural capital* to understand the point from which international law departs, given that international law originates from the West (Pritchard, 1998). Moreover, international advocacy, organisations "... more assured of their vocations or abilities" as regards the ILO Convention No. 169, can afford to focus on the "pleasure principle" of detached advocacy for the San. African national governments on the other might not view *indigeneity* as a given because to them it is a concept that is evaluated using historical experiences involving, for instance, post-colonial politics. Therefore to some African governments the San might not be viewed as "exotic themes and fields" mainly because the San populations are ubiquitous in those areas. They might therefore view approaches of international advocacy as mostly guided by "fashionable ideas" contained in international law and guided more by the "pleasure principle" of romanticised exoticism, rather than the "reality principle" of dealing with such communities in a national citizenship context. The conflicts surrounding *indigeneity* therefore illustrate not resistance, but rather failure by the two stakeholders to understand and reconcile their variations in cultural tastes of indigenous communities' heritage. This has to be worked on first if international law is to benefit indigenous communities at national levels. As Bourdieu concluded in his study:

> "The reason why these and similar self-evident facts need to be restated is that the successes of a few too often cause it to be forgotten that they have

only been able to overcome their cultural disadvantages by virtue of exceptional abilities and certain exceptional features of their ... backgrounds ...
the relative equality between students selected with very unequal severity
may conceal the inequalities on which it is based" (Bourdieu & Passeron
1979, p. 23).

Likewise, the "near universal" nature of international law conceals the inequality in perception, understanding and value placements by assuming homogenous understanding and
consensus of concepts such as *indigeneity* among member states I argue that the main
focus has to be placed on differences in socio-cultural perception instead.

Without such understanding it appears that focus on approaches of international law
also exclude indigenous groups themselves as they are entangled in "repressive participation" (Baudrillard, 1998; 1981a; Horrocks & Jevtic, 1996) where they become involved in
the process of cherishing a *cultural capital* that has been formulated outside their own
worldview. However, the formulated concept nonetheless remains favourable to indigenous
communities and like any other group made up of ordinary individuals living in a world
influenced by capitalism and global politics, indigenous groups are likely to manipulate this
outside perception of themselves for their own benefits. As highlighted by Boniface and
Fowler (1993, p. 20); "As the neo-colonialist tourist strikes even further from home ... the
'natives' become more restive about interpretive packaging, the 'meaning' of what the
tourist wants to see and what he or she is shown" (Boniface & Fowler, 1993, p. 20).

Conclusion

Tourism has been described as an entity that:

"... feeds on the colonial impulse. Part of the appeal, the frisson, of travelling to strange lands is the opportunity that it may afford to patronize the
poor native unfortunates who may know no better way of life than that of
their homeland. Tourism, in many ways, is a sort of neo-colonialism"
(Boniface & Fowler, 1993, p. 19).

In contrast with this observation, I argue in this chapter that this encounter is at times
contributed to by other sectors from which tourism only "scavenges" an already formulated
image (Figures 7.1 and 7.2). Focus here is on the clash of ideologies of international law,
international advocacy organisations and the ensuing conflicts with national governments.
The outcome of the conflict between the two stakeholders does not benefit indigenous communities' cultural sustainability as the two stakeholders resort to defensive attitudes to sustain
their institutions' image instead of focusing on the interests of the indigenous communities
themselves. For instance although international advocacy institutions such as SI claim to
know the effect of "harmful misconceptions and stereotypes" on indigenous populations, in
practice the organisation has occasionally used such descriptions in its mailing lists (SI News
Release 29 May 2002). Descriptions from the organisation's newsletters and web reports
have contained phrases such as "original inhabitants of the Central Kalahari" (17 June 2003)

"endangered tribes" (6 August 2003), "the oldest inhabitants of Southern Africa", "… this ancient culture" (19 August 2003), "the lands they have lived on for thousands of years (invoking the time immemorial concept). Just as Columbus" landing in the West Indies is still celebrated as the "discovery" (Boniface & Fowler, 1993), the image of the San is still portrayed as primitive, and ancient. Because tourism can be said to be "… a metaphysical search for completeness…" (Meethan, 2001, p. 90), tourism enterprise in general "scavenges" on this nostalgic and distorted image and market it to its clientele who are in search of authentic cultural experiences. On the other hand these descriptions have aroused several political reactions from governments such as that of Botswana. (www.gov.bw). It appears therefore that the image being pursued and perpetuated by international law and international advocacy organisations and rejected by national governments is not perceived in the same way by these institutions, hence the conflict. Van der Post and Taylor (1984, pp. 134–135) accurately described this scenario when he asserted that "Indeed the Bushman was and, to an extent, remains what we, increasingly cut off from our natural selves and the little that is left of the natural world, can only dream of today".

Acknowledgements

I am grateful for the encouraging comments given during earlier version of this chapter. I am indebted to my colleague Dr Sorensen for her encouraging comments at the initial composition of the chapter. Various versions of this chapter have been orally presented at different institutions among them the University of Cambridge's Centre of African Studies, UK 2004; London Metropolitan university's Institute of Tourism, Culture and Development (IITCD) UK, 2005; and the University of Newcastle-upon-Tyne's Centre for Heritage Studies 2004, I am particularly indebted to colleagues at the Smithsonian Institution's Center for Folklife and Cultural Heritage (CFCH), Washington DC, where I had an opportunity to undertake a Rockefeller Humanities Fellowship and reflected more on the issues related to the chapter.

References

Balsan, F. (1954). *Capricorn*. London: Arco.
Baudrillard, J. (1981a). *Simulacra and simulations*, Trans. P. Foss, P. Patton and P. Beitchman, MO: Telos.
Baudrillard, J. 1998. (1970). *The consumer society*. London: Sage.
Beteille, A. (1983). *The idea of natural inequality and other essays*. Oxford: Oxford University Press.
Boniface, P., & Fowler, P. (1993). *Heritage and tourism in "the Global village"*. London: Routledge.
Bonvillain, N. (2005). *The Mohawk: Indians of North America*. Philadelphia: Chelsea House.
Bourdieu, P., & Passeron, J. (1979) (1964). *The inheritors*. Chicago: Chicago University Press.
Burnstick, E. (1993). Concern for indigenous peoples. In: D. Hall et al. (Eds), *A dialogue of cultures for sustainable development* (pp. 145–147). London: Commonwealth Human Ecology Council.
Edwards, E. (Ed.) (1992). *Anthropology and photography* (pp. 1860–1920). London: Yale University Press.

Eriksen, T. H. (1993). *Ethnicity and nationalism: Anthropological perspectives.* London: Pluto Press.

Fontein, J. (2000). *UNESCO, heritage and Africa: An anthropological critique of world heritage.* Edinburgh: Centre of African Studies.

Forde, D. C. (1963). *Habitat, economy and society.* London: Methuen.

Franke, W. (1993). The *indigenous voice in world politics: Since time immemorial.* Sage: New bury Park.

Horrocks, C., & Jevtic, Z. (1996). *Introducing baudrillard.* Duxford: Icon Books.

Howard, B. R. (2003). *Indigenous peoples and the state.* Illinois: Illinois University Press.

Hunter, L., Rhind, S., & Andrew, D. (2002). *Watching wildlife: Southern Africa* (1st ed.). London: Lonely Planet.

Jan Osmanczyk, E. (2003). *Encyclopaedia of the United Nations and international agreements* (3rd ed., Vol. 2). London: Routledge.

Keitumetse, S. (2002). Does survival international represent indigenous communities? *Mmegi Newspaper, 19*(47). 29th November 2002–05th December 2003. Gaborone: Mmegi.

Keitumetse, S. (2004). Who is Indigenous? *Mmegi Newspaper, 19* (47). 29th August 2004. Gaborone: *Mmegi Newspaper,* Available at (www.mmegi.bw).

Keitumetse S. O. (January 2006). *Theorizing community representation: Indigeneity, International law and cultural sustainability.* Unpublished paper submitted as a partial fulfilment of a requirement for a Rockefeller Humanities Fellowship to the Center for Folklife and Cultural Heritage, Smithsonian Institution, Washington, DC.

Kohl, P. L., & Fawcett, C. (1995). Archaeology in the service of the state: Theoretical considerations. In: P. L. Kohl, & C. Fawcett (Eds), *Nationalism, politics, and the practice of archaeology* (pp. 03–18). Cambridge: Cambridge University Press.

Kretch, S. (March 2005). Reflections on conservation, sustainability and environmentalism in Indigenous North America. *American Anthropology, 107*(1), 78–84.

Kuru Development Trust (2002). *Tsodilo community initiative I: A paper outlining proposals by TOCaDI,* May 2002, Revised October 2002 Following a Meeting with Representatives from the National Museum. Unpublished report.

Kuru Development Trust (2002). *Tsodilo community initiative II: Community development alongside flora/fauna conservation. A suggestion to include a comprehensive EIA in the new management plan for Tsodilo Hills, including an evaluation of the herein presented concept,* May 2002, Revised October 2002 following a meeting with representatives from the National Museum. Unpublished report.

Meethan, K. (2001). *Tourism in global society: Peace, culture, and consumption.* Hampshire: Palgrave.

MorningStorm, B. (2004). *The American Indian warrior today: Native Americans in modern US warfare.* Manhattan: Sunflower University Press.

Nolan, R. (2002). *Development anthropology: Encounters in the real world.* London: Westview.

Parsons, N. (2004). This is a myth. *Mmegi Newspaper* Online documents at URL http://www.mmegi.bw/2004/March/Wednesday31/4493554841735.html

Patrick, B. K. (2003). *Native American languages.* Philadelphia, PA: Mason Crest.

Pritchard, S. (1998). The significance of international law. In: S. Pritchard (Ed.), *Indigenous peoples, the United Nations and human rights.* London: Zed Books.

Richmond, S., Murphy, A., Wildman, K., & Burke, A. (2002). *South Africa, Lesotho and Swaziland.* London: Lonely Planet.

Saugestad, S. (2001). The inconvenient indigenous: *Remote Area Development in Botswana, Donor Assistance and the First People of the Kalahari.* Uppsala: Nordic Africa Institute.

Silerbauer, G. B. (1965). *Report to the Government of Bechuanaland on the Bushmen Survey.* Gaberones: Bechuanaland Government.

Smith, A. D. (1986). *The ethnic origins of nations.* Oxford: Blackwell.

Smith, V. L. (1989). Introduction. PP01-17. In *Hosts and guests: The anthropology of tourism* (2nd ed.). Philadelphia, PA: University of Pennsylvania.

Swaney, D., Fitzpatrick, M., Greenway, P., Stone A., & Vaisutis, J. (2003). *Southern Africa*. London: Lonely Planet.

UNESCO (1972). *The general conference of the United Nations Educational, Scientific and Cultural Organisation (UNESCO) meeting*, Paris, 17th October to 21st November 1972, 17th session. *Convention for the protection of the World cultural and natural heritage*, adopted 1972, Paris, France.

UNESCO (2001). *The general conference of the United Nations Educational, Scientific and Cultural Organisation (UNESCO) meeting*, Paris, 2 November 2001, 31st Session. *UNESCO universal declaration on cultural diversity, adopted 02nd November 2001*.

UNESCO (2003). *The general conference of the United Nations Educational, Scientific and Cultural Organisation (UNESCO) meeting*, Paris, 29 September to 17th October 2003, 32nd session. *Convention for the safeguarding of the intangible cultural heritage*, adopted 17th October 2003. Paris, France.

Van der Post, L., & Taylor, J. (1984). *Testament to the Bushmen*. Middlesex: Viking.

Waitt, G. (1999). Naturalizing the "primitive": A critique of marketing Australia's indigenous peoples as "hunter-gatherers". *Tourism Geographies, 1*(2), 142–160.

Internet sources

ILO Convention No. 169 – http://www.unhchr.ch/html/menu3/b/62.htm, Convention (No. 169) Concerning Indigenous and Tribal Peoples in Independent Countries. Adopted on 27 June 1989 by the General Conference of the International Labour Organisation at its seventy-sixth session.

http://www.ilo.org/ilolex/cgi-lex/convde.pl?C107, C107 Indigenous and Tribal Populations Convention, 1957. Convention concerning the Protection and Integration of Indigenous and Other Tribal and Semi-Tribal Populations in Independent Countries. Adopted at the fortieth session.

International Labour Organisation (http://www.unhchr.ch/html/menu3/b/62.htm).

Republic of Botswana – http: //www.gov.bw/

Survival International, UK – http://www.survival-international.org/

http://www.survival-international.org/enews.htm, 29th May 2002. Racist comment on BBC fuels unfounded stereotype of Amazonian tribe.

_____, 17th June 2003. Persecution of Bushmen stepped up: Bushmen charged for entering their ancestral land.

_____, 06th August 2003. Pushed to the edge: Survival marks UN day by naming top three endangered tribes.

_____, 19th August 2003. Kalahari Bushmen thrown off their land as diamond companies move in.

http://www.unhchr.ch/html/menu3/b/62.htm, Convention (No. 169) concerning Indigenous and Tribal Peoples in Independent Countries. Adopted on 27 June 1989 by the General Conference of the International Labour Organisation at its seventy-sixth session.

Chapter 8

The Politics of Institution Building and European Co-operation: Reflections on an EC TEMPUS Project on Tourism and Culture in Bosnia-Herzegovina

Tom Selwyn and Jonathan Karkut

Introduction

The following is an account of a 3-year training, research, and development project in tourism and the cultural industries in Bosnia-Herzegovina (BiH). It was part of the European Commission's (EC's) Trans-European mobility scheme for university studies (TEMPUS) Programme, and was carried out partly in BiH – the non-member "partner country" of the project – and partly in Italy and the UK. The project was managed by a consortium of 13 institutions (see below) from these three participating countries, and was co-ordinated from London Metropolitan University by the authors of the present chapter.

The structure of this chapter is as follows. We start by explaining the aims and objectives of the TEMPUS Programme in general and our project in particular. Since one of the two main priorities of the latter was "institution building" we then describe in some detail the institutions, both within BiH and beyond, with which we chose to work in order to build a national, regional, and international institutional network to serve the future tourism industry in the country. Following this we describe – in two rather different but complementary sections – the course of the project as this was carried through between 2001 and 2005. Here we concentrate on the other main priority of the project, namely the delivery of a post-graduate training course to a cadre of 24 youngish mid-career professionals. Following this we reflect on what the experience of carrying out the project has taught us about institutions in and near the field of tourism and the cultural industries in contemporary BiH. Referring briefly to aspects of the aftermath of the project, we conclude by considering what general lessons might be learnt from our experience about institutions and institutional development in contemporary BiH.

Part I: Institutional Network Building for the Project

The title of our project was "Institutional development in the field of tourism and the cultural industries in Bosnia-Herzegovina" and its aims (to quote from the project's contract document) included the setting up of "a programme of work based upon the universities of Sarajevo and Banja-Luka in order to provide a focus for the advancement of civil society through the development of specific institutions connected with the tourism and cultural industries sector". To accomplish this aim, the intention was to carry out four interlinked activities. The first was to deliver the post-graduate training course referred to above. This was to consist of nine taught course units, each lasting 10 days, and taught, at the campuses of the five universities represented in the project consortium, namely Sarajevo, Banja-Luka, Bologna, the Development Planning Unit (DPU) of University College London, and the then University of North London.[1] The second, as already indicated, was to establish a network of institutions within and beyond BiH with interests in the development of tourism and the cultural industries in the country. The third was to establish a consultative forum – a policy think tank on tourism and the cultural industries – based in BiH but with international affiliates. The fourth was to produce and deliver a short training course capable of being offered to personnel working in the field and taught by the project's newly trained trainees.

It needs to be clarified that, from the outset, the principal aim of the project was not to train personnel in existing tourism related institutions. Rather it was to explore what kind of institutions in the tourism and cultural industries sector might best contribute to the process of economic and social re-integration necessary for any kind of post-war recovery. This aim flowed directly from the larger aims of the TEMPUS Programme itself and it is to these which we will now turn.

European Co-operation: Background to the EC's TEMPUS Programme

The TEMPUS Programme itself, at its inception part of the PHARE aid programme to Eastern Europe, takes two forms. One consists of the development of curricula in subjects identified as priorities by partner countries. The other is concerned with "institution building" in those countries. Our project was of the latter type and was one of the first TEMPUS Institution Building (TIB) projects in South-East Europe. As such it was required to be managed by a consortium of representatives from a broad range of institutions drawn from the university, government, private, public, international, and non-governmental sectors.

The TEMPUS guidelines explain to all prospective project consortia that the background to Institution Building projects lies in the formidable collection of legal texts, the *Acquis Communautaire*, the terms of which need to be fulfilled by member and prospective member

---

[1] Now London Metropolitan University.

states of the European Union (EU). The three principal general foundations of the *Acquis* and thus the necessary underpinnings for all TIB projects are (i) that the candidate country must achieve stability of institutions guaranteeing democracy, the rule of law, human rights, and respect for and protection of minorities. (ii) that there is a functioning market economy in the country, and (iii) that countries have the capacity to take on all other obligations of EU membership.

The guidelines also point out that the concept of Institution Building itself is older and broader than the *Acquis*. They point to the idea having been in existence for decades and being common to most United Nations Development Programme (UNDP) country portfolios. They state that "an institution building project is called for if the need identified is to improve the capacity of an organisation to serve its purpose as part of an institution of the society" – "institution" in this context being defined as "a system of rules and structures evolved to serve a purpose in society". "Institution building", the guidelines tell us, "is a flexible tool which must be tailored to the specific needs identified in the specific context".

Two aspects of these guidelines warrant particular emphases: that institution building pro-grammes are to be directed at social institutions serving the well-being of society, and that they need to be tailored to the specific needs of specific contexts. The latter, in our case, included the institutional context in which tourism development would and could best take shape in BiH.

At the time our project started TIB projects had been going for several years in those Eastern European states which finally joined the EU in 2005. As noted, however, ours was one of the first in a SE-European country. One of the distinguishing features of TIB projects is that they are required by the EC required to ensure a balance between the involvement of academic institutions and non-academic partners. The guidelines further specify that the particular value of TIB programmes is to embed the education and training of administrators and other actors within the theoretical support of universities, to provide extended access to models in EU countries, and to be directed at civil society below the national level.

Finally, the guidelines stress that TIB projects are different from traditional TEMPUS pro-jects in that they have a "bottom up" organisational methodology. They conclude by giving us a significant piece of advice, namely that:

> "The shaping of TIB is an interactive process. The Commission has already elaborated and offered a framework for the TIB projects. Now it is the project consortia's turn; they should design and implement successful TIB projects, thus realising and slightly reshaping the TIB concept at the same time."

Responding to the Challenge: Initial Stages of the Project

The TEMPUS guidelines are extensive and, for present purposes, have been distilled above into the barest outline. Yet it will already be clear that TIB projects are ambitious, complex, and extremely challenging. The rest of this chapter consists of an account of how our own project responded to the challenge.

The aims of the project were spelt out in the inaugural lecture of the project. This was held in the EC's London headquarters and was given by the project's co-ordinator, Tom Selwyn. The lecture was attended by members of the project's teaching team, the newly recruited trainees, representatives from the project management consortium, including Professor Boris Tihi, then Rector of the University of Sarajevo, and Dr Mladen Ivanic – member of the Economics Faculty of Banja-Luka University, at the time Prime Minister of Republika Srpska (RS) and subsequently foreign minister of BiH – and invited guests, including Lord Paddy Ashdown, shortly to become the High Representative in BiH. Selwyn described the underlying aim of the project as being:

> "... to encourage institutions, at various levels of civil society and national and international administration to work effectively and co-operatively in the field of tourism and the cultural industries". The project would approach this task by educating and training a new generation of academics, practitioners and policy-makers in the fields of tourism and the cultural industries in BiH. Once trained, the graduates – who would then be the only post-war trained personnel in the field in BiH – would be able to play leading roles in planning and policy-making processes within the new tourism industry in BiH. "Success in this one sphere", Selwyn added, "may also serve as a model for other spheres of governance. As such it may contribute towards the larger goal of promoting democratic processes generally – with all the benefits for the rule of law, human rights, and respect for minorities that this would imply".

These latter claims might appear overblown and too rhetorical for some tastes. In fact they were designed specifically to draw attention to two of the unique characteristics of the tourism "industry" itself. The first is that tourism's capital and raw material consists of, on the one hand, the land, water, and other natural endowments of the country, and on the other, the people and their social and cultural productions. The second is that in order to preserve and enhance this capital the "industry" is effectively dependent on a wide range of civil actors. Thus, whilst governments may (or may not) frame tourism policies, private and public companies may transport, accommodate, and feed some tourists some of the time, the fact is that behind and beyond these institutions lie a mass of smaller institutions: municipalities, family-run businesses of many kinds, professional associations, trade unions, non-governmental organisations (NGOs), including environmental groups, for example, specialist social clubs, such as mountaineering associations, orchestras, theatres, museums, guides, and universities. No tourism "industry" anywhere in the world can operate without the involvement of these and other civil institutions. Indeed, tourism infrastructure needs to be based on close co-operation between state and such civil institutions as those listed here, as well as between public and private sectors.

The extent to which civil institutions are necessarily embedded within the tourism and cultural industries sector make this field an ideal subject for a project of this kind. The economic necessities of institutional good practice and inter-institutional co-operation form the practical bedrock upon which to build a political and social programme of institution building in Bosnian civil society and in those key departments of government engaged in tourism.

Each of the aims listed above aims derived directly and intentionally from at least three of the main building blocks of the EC's TEMPUS Programme in general. First of all, the project was founded on the principle of *de-centralised co-operation*. Thus although it was set to work co-operatively with departments of government at national and international levels, its primary engagement was with representative institutions under the level of the state. Secondly, it sought to integrate theory (including theories of governance insofar as these related to tourism and the cultural industries) with the practice of tourism development, organisation, and management. Thirdly, it aimed to link institutions in BiH with comparable institutions in the EU in line with the TEMPUS notions of institutional interchanges between member and aspiring states.

Building the Project Consortium

The building blocks for our project began as far back as 1998 when the project manager, Jonathan Karkut, conducted the first research on the state of the tourism industry in BiH. At that stage the principle issue was to discover which international, national, entity, and civil institutions were involved in the development of tourism in BiH, and how they were organised and related to each other.

In those relatively early days after the Dayton peace accords, the focus of the international community was upon physical reconstruction. When pressed to discuss the possibility of tourism playing a part in the reconstruction of the Bosnian economy, the general response was that such activity could only happen once there was a stable political environment and when the huge impact of landmines and un-exploded ordinance was cleared from the cities and countryside. On more than one occasion it was stated that those circumstances would only arrive in a generation or more time.

Within the Bosnian institutions working in tourism and the cultural industries, the responses at that time were slightly more positive. The memory of the successful organisation of the 1984 Olympics in Sarajevo remained fresh. However, there was an overwhelming tendency to look back to the organisations and structures that managed the industry when BiH was part of Yugoslavia. Little or nothing was being done either to respond to current or future trends in tourism or to re-structure, re-train, and re-educate in a country that was now an independent state with new and highly complicated political structures. In the past the industry in BiH was guided by expertise grown from research and educational centres in what are now the independent states of Croatia and Slovenia. Those centres were no longer internal and effectively left BiH in a huge vacuum when it came to a strategy to guide tourism development. Furthermore, there was no response to the fact that industry in BiH was highly fragmented, with no overarching policy or planning. Instead what was found were individual clusters of organisations which operated independently from each other and were simply concerned with surviving until tourist flows started up again and the approaches to tourism applied in the former Yugoslavia would be simply jump started and imposed on these new clients.

It was therefore, quite clear that any initiative into capacity building required the involvement of as wide a range of stakeholders as possible and to encourage co-operation between them. The other major challenge was to imagine how institutions might move away from the past and to work towards installing methods of approaching a contemporary vision of tourism development in BiH. The following is a brief account of the various sectors in which we looked for institutions from which to draw appropriate institutional members of the project's management consortium.

The university sector   The EC required our TEMPUS project to be anchored in universities. Having visited all the universities in BiH it became clear that the Economics Faculties of the Universities of Sarajevo and Banja-Luka were the most appropriate academic partners although neither had post-graduate provision in the tourism field at the time. Two university departments in European member states that stood out as being natural partners were the *Istituto per l'Europa Centro – Orientale e Balcanica* at the University of Bologna, Italy, and the Development Planning Unit (DPU) at University College, London. The former had been engaged, through the work of Stefano Bianchini and Francesco Privitera for many years in a raft of initiatives in BiH in general and at the University of Sarajevo in particular. Furthermore the *Centro* enjoyed extensive links within the region of Emilia-Romagna, through which the consortium and trainees would have the opportunity to establish relations with a wide range of institutions across this region. The latter, mainly through its well-established research and training track record in cosmopolitan development and the involvement by Michael Safier in urban development programmes in Sarajevo and elsewhere in BiH, had a demonstrable interest in the project. Together with the co-ordinating institution, the now London Metropolitan University, the project had five academic institutions in its emerging consortium.

Government institutions   One of the key aspects of the programme as stipulated in the guidelines was to build greater linkages between education and public and private institutions. It was thus decided to establish a partnership with the ministries of trade and tourism within each of the two political "entities" that had been created by the Dayton agreements, the Federation of Bosnia and Herzegovina (FbiH) (hereafter the Federation) and RS.

The private sector   With respect to the private sector the issue was more problematic. Around 1999–2000 when the bid was being drafted, there were very few agencies working in tourism and those that did exist were concerned more or less exclusively with the outbound market. No significant companies had even begun to think of BiH as an inbound market. There were however, a few organisations inherited from the centrally planned system that were used as a bridge between the public and private sectors. Although, as will be discussed at greater depth later in this chapter, there was not a clear-cut separation between those two sectors in the Yugoslav model of "self-management". Nonetheless, the Tourism Association of Sarajevo Canton (which later became part of the BiH Tourism Association) and the BiH Chamber of Commerce did nominally represent clusters of private businesses and had a wide range of contacts. They were both thus seen as appropriate partners to become involved in the project and, thanks to the enthusiasm of a few individuals, became involved in the consortium.

In addition to the Tourism Association and the Chamber we were fortunate to be able to recruit an independent tour operator based in the UK. Regent Holidays had a long-standing relationship with such destinations as China, Cuba, Albania, and the Baltic states and thus was a natural partner for our project consortium. Another private company based in BiH, Harlequin Leisure, joined the consortium in the early days but withdrew as the project commenced.

The non-governmental sector   The final piece in the jigsaw was to locate a partner drawn from the non-governmental sector, an area that had grown rapidly in BiH since the end of the war and the arrival of the huge international presence. Again, it was found that no organisations were working solely in the field of tourism, but a few were active in urban development and so the Sarajevo based NGO "Urbforum" which had an interest in the role of tourism as a development tool, was invited into the project.

International agencies   In post-war BiH a major role was being played by a host of international agencies. As mentioned earlier, these were initially present in the country as part of efforts physically to reconstruct the devastated country as well as to ensure the warring factions were disarmed and kept apart. Additionally, work was carried out in attempts to facilitate greater political stability, through a process of "democratisation". Until this point there was little direct involvement by international agencies in economic reforms and the building up of investment opportunities.

Partly because of Karkut's previous experience of work in BiH for the Organisation of European Co-operation and Development (OSCE) and partly because the OSCE was the largest international body in BiH at the time, the project approached this institution and successfully persuaded them to join the consortium.

We thus started the project with a management consortium of 13 institutions: five university departments (two in BiH, one in Italy, two in the UK), two ministries (one in each of the two Bosnian entities), the BiH Chamber of Commerce, two private tour operators/leisure companies (one in BiH, one in the UK), a tourism association representing businesses in BiH, an NGO based in BiH, and an international organisation.

Our intentions for the work of the consortium in the 3 years of the project directly followed our interpretation of the role assigned to project consortia in TIB projects by the TEMPUS guidelines. We thus expected the members of our consortia to come together co-operatively in a coherent programme of work to advance the capacity of the institutions they represented, to encourage greater co-operation between those institutions for the benefit of tourism and cultural development in BiH, to engage with the institutions outside the project – in BiH itself, within the Balkan region, and in our partner countries, Italy and the UK – and strongly to support, encourage, and to work with the trainees undertaking our course.

At this stage we will run ahead of ourselves in order to return to the narration of the story of the project shortly. As already noted we felt it necessary and appropriate to make links with a raft of institutions beyond the boundaries of the project consortium itself. As we have indicated our hope and expectation was that they too would become integrated into our work and thus contribute to the development of tourism in BiH and that some of them would help project a nascent tourism industry into the wider world. For present purposes the account is necessarily brief.

Institutions Beyond the Consortium

As before, we group our "affiliate" institutions into several categories.

Inter-governmental agencies   The vast bulk of international assistance for the reconstruction, and now sustainable development of BiH, has come through international agencies. The project therefore established communication with the key United Nations bodies in BiH, the UNDP, the United Nations Environmental Programme (UNEP) and the UN/EC Office of the High Representative (OHR), the latter being the most powerful authority in the country and seat for 3 years of Ashdown. The other major player in the region was the EC itself, so contacts were established with the EC delegation to BiH. Furthermore, the project itself was fully funded through the TEMPUS strand of what had become the Community Assistance for Reconstruction, Development and Stabilisation (CARDS) Programme.

These inter-governmental organisations were involved in assisting with infra-structural projects (connecting BiH railways into the regional international network being one nice example). They were also central in helping bring Bosnian institutions closer to EU norms and standards. Amongst other things this has included the bringing together of public and private agencies to identify and work to remove obstacles to investment and economic development.

At a regional level, the project also established links with the Central European Initiative (CEI), working group on tourism, a grouping of institutions aiming to encourage greater co-operation with neighbouring states in the sub-region such as Croatia and Serbia-Montenegro.

International financial bodies   Early on in the course of the project the co-ordinators established links with the European Bank for Reconstruction & Development (EBRD), and the World Bank mission to BiH. The World Bank in particular was involved in the establishing of national plans such as the national environmental plan and the Poverty reduction strategy programme (PRSP).

Governmental agencies   It was crucial though for the institutions associated with tourism and the cultural industries in BiH, to demonstrate how they could take the lead in development of the country by also linking with bi-lateral donors. The most obvious first port of call in seeking such bi-lateral relations was through the national embassies in Sarajevo. Communication has thus established with amongst others the Embassies of the United Kingdom, Netherlands, United States of America, Japan, and Australia. In so doing, the embassies become more aware of the significance of tourism in BiH's developmental plans and where potential sites of investment were located. Conversely, the project consortia was alerted to strands of relevant bi-lateral funding or of existing initiatives in the sector.

Local and regional institutions in neighbouring countries and the UK   As will become clear we took the opportunity throughout the 3 years to make links with potentially relevant institutions in the sector in the two European member state members of our project.

These included; the Ravenna provincial chamber of commerce, the *Unione di prodotto costa* (a public–private partnership (PPP) established by the Emilia-Romagna government); the municipalities of Bologna, Forli, Faenza, Ravenna, and Cervia; and the International Ceramics museum of Faenza.

Tourism has played a major role in the development of Emilia-Romagna for many decades now, and through the links with the organisations listed above, the project was able to observe at first hand some relevant examples of "best practice". One of the important demonstrations was to examine how the region had attempted to diversify its tourism product. Tourism in the region had frequently taken the form of mass movements to traditional coastal resorts such as Rimini, Cervia, and Cesenatico. This meant that the hinterland regions have seen limited benefits from tourism up until recently. However, with new trends towards niche markets and the possibilities that have arisen with the arrival of cut-price airlines such as Ryanair and Easyjet to small provincial airports, Emilia-Romagna has responded vigorously. Promotion of a new range of destinations now centres also on artistic and monumental cities, spa resorts, picturesque hill towns, and the traditional organic produce grown across the region. These responses are highly relevant for BiH as it only possesses a narrow strip of the Adriatic coast, so it too will need to look at a range of ways to develop and present its more mountainous hinterland.

Another timely experience was generated through meetings with the *Unione di prodotto costa*. The *Unione* is one of four created in 1998 by the regional government to create sectoral PPP. They have brought together all interested municipalities, provinces, with private sector bodies such as the hotels association, and created a powerful block to co-ordinate development, promotion, and marketing. With the hurried pace of privatisation in BiH, an understanding of such PPP initiatives could offer a viable alternative to the Bosnian government, instead of the selling off all its prime tourism assets to foreign direct investors. Additionally, co-ordinated PPP initiatives such as the *Unione*, could act as a useful model to demonstrate how to limit duplication in activities by neighbouring/competing municipalities or cantons.

Contacts made with the various chambers of commerce in Emilia-Romagna also offered the potential for creating bi-lateral commercial links. The same applied to our relations with municipalities in the region. These have certain responsibilities for external affairs, especially with neighbouring states to the East across Adriatic Sea, and thus contained the potential to pass on their extensive experience of tourism and the cultural industries to BiH.

Tourism enterprises and attractions As BiH has been urged to move rapidly towards becoming a market economy, it was vital for the project to be able to related to private enterprise in BiH and in EU countries. This allowed trainees to gain first hand experience of both how businesses are finding their way in the highly competitive world of European tourism today, and to consider how business links and proposals can be set up. Exchanges of ideas have been made with independent tour operators in the UK and in BiH, national airlines, an organisation running a narrow gauge railway, and several museums. These exchanges have explored numerous possibilities for future collaborations, such as; establishing of direct links and city break packages to BiH from the UK; participating in museum networks; creating regional tourist itineraries; and opening up international cross-border tourist attractions.

Local and international media and publishers The project consortium also made considerable inroads in connecting with both local and international media and publishers. Amongst others, communications were made with local newspapers, BiH TV, the *Times Higher Education Supplement* (UK), *Euroinvest* magazine (Europe wide), *Bradt*, and *Lonely Planet* guidebooks.

One of the key results of this media networking was to disseminate the project activities, and to raise awareness of the position that tourism can take in the future of development in BiH. With coverage outside BiH it allowed the broadcasting of much needed positive news stories about the country, as opposed to the near endless stream of reports on political instability, corruption, and reliance on donor aid. Furthermore, articles ensured that a wide audience of readers and potential backers could find out about the range of investment opportunities opening up in the tourism sector in BiH. Furthermore, a carefully composed travel article can act as a powerful marketing tool. Virtually free marketing through the fostering of a good relationship with the media, can thus end up proving to be a far more effective means of promotion than through a traditional and less cost effective marketing campaign.

Information concerning tourism and the cultural industries in BiH had also been very limited. For instance for the duration of much of the project there were no English language guidebooks about the country, and even basic travel, accommodation, and entertainment listings were absent. In a bid to plug this information gap, the project facilitated the first meetings between a British publisher and a Bosnian based writer, with the result that the first English language guidebook to BiH was produced by Bradt in the Spring of 2004. This was a very important step. As research by Jeff Jarvis of Monash University showed, considerably more tourists already touring the region would be interested in venturing into BiH if they were able to access the basic information provided in a guidebook.

Some of the institutions listed above will be well known to readers of this chapter. Nevertheless, it might be useful very briefly and selectively to underline what we thought we were doing in introducing them to our project. The work of UNDP, UNEP, and, of course, the EC itself, includes the generation of funds for research and policy-making, support for environmental programmes, and policy-related contact in Europe and the wider world that the OHR enjoyed in BiH itself. Regional co-operation is encouraged by the CEI and the EC itself. The EBRD might have be expected to offer facilities for European funding and investment for a sector such as tourism and the cultural industries in one of Europe's most needy developing and transitional economies, whilst foreign government representatives have growing track records in the articulation of research and consultancy in the field. The Italian institutions had an unrivalled store of regional experience in Italy and in the Adriatic border-states, including BiH, whilst the British institutions had an abundance of specialist and relevant experience in the field. The media contacts were, and remain, critical to the marketing of tourism and the more general re-education of Europeans about the nature of BiH.

The Project's Institutional Network: A Summary

By ensuring that the work of the project was not simply restricted to those in and around the consortium, networking allowed the activities, ideas, and initiatives to be placed in a regional, European and global context. With linkages to similar functioning institutions in the rest of Europe, the project sought to encourage the construction of an institutional infrastructure that was fully aware and familiar with current trends in tourism. It also aimed to bring together the scattered and often competing or overlapping fragments that had evolved in the aftermath of the war and associated peace agreements, and encouraged them to function and contribute effectively to the industry in BiH.

We thus put together a network of institutions, inside and outside the consortium, which we imagined could come together to make a substantial contribution to a sustainable, environmentally sound, socially equitable and beneficial, and profitable tourism system in BiH, based upon the best theory and practice in the field.

Part II: Project Delivery: Training, Networking, Mobilising Support, and Strategic planning

Section 1: Expurgated Version

Having put the process of institution building in motion, a process that was to continue throughout the project, and having recruited members of our management consortium, our principal task was to devise and deliver a 3-year training course for a selected cadre of trainees. The following pages describe how this was carried out.

Having recruited our 24 trainees (drawn from various parts of the country including Sarjevo, Banja-Luka, and Mostar) by way of a process that was greatly more complicated than we had imagined (see Section 2) we commenced the delivery of the training course.

The first of the nine modules was held in London, mainly at the co-ordinating university. At the inaugural lecture of the module, given in the EC's London headquarters, two iconic buildings in BiH were adopted as determining symbols of the project. These were the National Library in Sarajevo and the bridge at Mostar.

The main intention of the lecture was to locate the project within a commitment to the cosmopolitan future we imagined would form the basis not only post-war BiH itself but of the country's tourism offer: hence the adoption of the two talismanic symbols. The Library was the first building to have been bombed by the besieging army, the majority of the collection of priceless written treasures being burnt in 1992. The latter had been completely destroyed. Both clearly "stood for" cosmopolitan co-existence in the eyes of those whose aims was put such cultural pluralism to an end in the name of ethnic purification.

The National and University Library of BiH, to give its full title, is one of the most prominent buildings in Sarajevo. It was built as the City Hall in 1896 by the Austro-Hungarian authorities in what is now termed a "pseudo-Moorish" style – following two visits by its architect to Cairo. Between 1910–1914 it housed the Bosnian parliament. It was first established as a library by Tito in 1945 and became part of the University in 1957. Following the burning of its collection by incendiary bombs, the roof was repaired shortly after the war by the Austrian government. The building presently stands empty with a large board outside it, placed there by the EU authorities, announcing that a programme of rebuilding and refurbishment is being undertaken, or perhaps that it is about to be undertaken (such boards are sometimes not entirely clear) by the EU.

The Library's former director, Enis Kujundic (personal Communication) has described the library's former collection in terms of its Bosniak, Croatian, Serbian, and Jewish provenance, recording that the collection had consisted of works in Latin, English, German, Italian, French, Turkish, Persian, Hebrew, and Arabic, amongst other languages, and written in various scripts including Latin, Cyrillic, Old Bosnian, Glagolithic, Church Slavonic, Hebrew, and an adapted Arabic script, *Alhamijado*.

As for the bridge, most people in Northern and Western Europe are aware that the bridge over the Neretva river at Mostar was destroyed in November 1993. Many would agree with Misha Glenny's (1999, p. 646) observation that the single act of its destruction "seemed to represent the utter senselessness and misery of the entire conflict".

For us the significance of adopting the Mostar bridge as a guiding symbol of our thinking about tourism and the reconstruction of civil society in BiH was captured by the distinguished Sarajevan painter, Afan Ramic, who addressed an assembly of Mostar citizens shortly after the bridge's destruction thus:

> "Besides its architectural beauty, the Mostar bridge linked not only two river banks but two civilisations that intertwine at precisely the point where the cultures of East and West have been destined to permeate each other for centuries. That mutual permeation of cultures embodies the dignity of the peoples who know BiH as their only shared country … the bridge is in and

of itself the link between everything that exists between these two cultures." He concluded his oration by asserting that despite the fact that the bridge had been physically destroyed "the thought (of the bridge) will live on because it is inscribed in eternity".

We took these words as particularly appropriate mobilising sentiments for the project.

Having selected our icons the remainder of the module consisted of an introduction to what, following the work of Burns and Holden[2] (1995) we called the "tourism system". Members of the course team,[3] including Scott, Harrison, and Bianchi from the University of North London, and Safier from UCL, explored the infra-structural requirements for tourism development in various fields including transport, accommodation, catering, administrative and institutional networks, and the co-operative structures needed to link public and private sectors.

The module also introduced the early threads of a theme that would accompany us through-out the project, namely the relationship between tourism, culture (in particular the cosmopol-itan culture characteristic of pre-war BiH), and the cultural productions of a cosmopolitan culture.

The second module was held in Sarajevo and consisted of an assessment, with the help of colleagues from various departments of the University, of the emerging forms of tourism in BiH. The importance of this module lay partly in the description from our Bosnian colleagues of the importance to tourism of flora and fauna, of the urban architectural heritage, of cultural festivals, as well as the winter sports facilities in the nearby mountains. Two members of the course team, Jarvis from Monash University and Bell from the London-based tourism-marketing firm, Hills Balfour, also participated in the module. Jarvis observed that by far the most significant category of future tourist to BiH was independent backpackers which would visit BiH for a wide variety of reasons associated with interests in particular aspects of the country's flora, fauna, society, and culture. Bell suggested that the essence of tourism mar-keting for BiH lay not so much in the formal set piece travel markets, such as those in London and Berlin, but in highly focussed niche publications aimed at the specialist tourists Jarvis had identified.

The third module, held at the University of Banja-Luka, was concerned with the relation between tourism and the natural environment. A prominent theme concerned the necessity and mode of participation by civil institutions in environmental protection. A visiting lecturer from the OHR, Van Eekelen, reported on the various tourism initiatives which at that time were being carried out by the OHR under the aegis of the then HR, Ashdown.

The fourth and fifth modules were held in the Italian province of Emilia-Romagna, one in Forli, the hometown of the *Centro*, the other in the small seaside resort of Cervia. In these modules we not only conducted extensive visits to the Italian institutions described in part 1,

---

[2] Both Burns and Holden were members of the course team and made valuable contributions to the strategic plan-ning document.

[3] The regulations of the TEMPUS Programme make provision for teachers of modules to be drawn from the partner institutions of projects as well as nominated others approved by the EC.

but also immersed ourselves in such cultural institutions as theatres, museums, and spas, and the fashion and retailing industries in Bologna itself. We were also guided within the Jewish museum in Ferrara by a member of the course team, Clark, a specialist in European Jewish museums – in particular the museum in Bologna.

During the second of the Italian modules we took the first steps in composing a strategic plan for tourism and the cultural industries in BiH.

Module six took place in Banja-Luka. Much of this meeting was taken up with making progress on the composition of our strategic document and was thus dominated by policy and planning issues.

Module seven, held in Sarajevo, consisted of seven intense days of preparation of the composition and presentation of our strategic plan. We presented this on the eighth day to a large audience in the University of Sarajevo made up of representatives of several embassies, most of the international aid organisations, the OHR, as well as the press and the general public.

Our Strategic Plan[4] still at the time of writing this chapter by far the most comprehensive tourism planning document that has been produced in post-war BiH, consisted of six research papers covering the tourism offer of the country, the geographical and environmental programmes necessary to accompany and deliver the offer, a marketing plan, a consideration of the economy of tourism and the cultural industries in BiH, a lengthy analysis of the social consequences of tourism, and – finally, but for our project, centrally – an analysis of what institutional support the industry would need in the future. These research papers were summarised in a 15 page executive summary. In this latter document four continuing research, training, and institution building projects were signalled as worthwhile additions to future work in BiH on policy and planning in the field. These consisted of the setting up of an institute for the study of tourism and the cultural industries, a research programme on the role of design in tourism, a tourism awareness programme, and a programme of work aimed at restoring the library system in the country.

The Plan was formulated by our trainee body (they alone are credited with its authorship) supervised by the course team including Safier from UCL, Taylor from Regent Holidays, Bell from Hills Balfour, with the assistance of our external assessor, the anthropologist Jeremy Boissevain from the University of Amsterdam, in addition to the two present authors. It was, in effect, the outcome of over a year's work on the part of students and teachers alike.

The eighth module consisted of a research visit to various parts of the country we had identified in our Strategic Plan. In each of the places we visited (including Sutjeska national park, the city of Mostar, the Catholic pilgrimage site of Medugorje, the only seaside resort in the country, Neum, and two towns in Herzegovina, Trebinje and Stolac) we met representatives of local religious and political authorities.

The ninth and final module took place in London, mainly at the DPU, with visits to York and to the Greater London Assembly (GLA). In the former we were guests of the city's Tourist Board, whilst the purpose of visiting the GLA was to become familiar with London's cultural policy.

---

[4] Obtainable from London Metropolitan University from j.karkut@londonmet.ac.uk

The Training Course: Summary

Two of the aims of the course, closely overlapping, of the course were central. The first was were to educate and train a cadre of young professionals in tourism and the cultural industries – bearing in mind that they would, when trained, constitute the *only* professionally qualified persons in the field in the country. The second was to prepare our trainees to take their place as leaders in the field, to which end we expected them to work with the institutions represented on the consortium as well as with those institutions beyond the consortium we had incorporated into our work. In these two ways we hoped appropriately to respond to the TEMPUS Programme's injunction to help develop that "system of rules and structures" best able to address the "specific needs identified in the specific context" (in our case the tourism and cultural industries sector).

Section 2: Unexpurgated Version

So far the account of the project has been selective and dryly factual. We change registers now and consider other aspects of the project. This part is still selective and factual but less dry.

At the first management consortium management meeting, held in March 2001 in an elderly, comfortable, and well-provisioned family-run hotel in Forli, there took place the first of a series of personal, professional, and political confrontations that were to become a routine and regular feature of the project. The co-ordinator opened the meeting with a comprehensive description of the aims and objectives of the project arguing that the work ahead would make a valuable contribution to the growth of tourism, employment generation, as well as general revival in civil society in BiH. In the discussion period which followed a professionally senior female member of the group of Bosnian colleagues asked, simply and justifiably, how the co-ordinator knew that the various desirable consequences of the project he had just outlined would actually take place. At this stage a senior Italian consortium colleague stood up and, pointing his forefinger with clearly forceful intent, berated the questioner for her intervention, concluding his response by saying:

> "You don't live in Tito's Yugoslavia any more. Now you have to make things work yourselves."

Not surprisingly the questioner dissolved into tears, her colleagues coming vigorously to her support. The incident left a shadow on the remainder of the 2 days of the meeting, and the issues it raised were to live with us in more ways than one throughout the next 3 years.

Towards the conclusion of the meeting the consortium took a collective decision that, not altogether unlinked to the previous incident, was ultimately to prove even more structurally explosive. Having asked the consortium members to find potentially qualified trainees for the post-graduate course amongst their employees, and having received a blank response, the decision was taken to advertise in local newspapers for applicants. It was also agreed, *nem con*, to announce that the course was to lead to a Masters degree. The co-ordinator promised to seek permission from the Brussels TEMPUS Unit to offer the MA (up to then no TIB project had included such provision) and to put in motion its validation from the co-ordinating institution. As instructed by the consortium the co-ordinator fulfilled both of these tasks. The TEMPUS Unit in Brussels agreed that an MA could be awarded and the co-ordinating institution commenced the process of validation. Following a period of advertising for trainees and a careful and comprehensive interviewing process in BiH trainees/students were recruited and the course commenced, as already noted, the following November.

During one of the seminars of the first module, a certain (completely understandable) spatial distance was evident between those trainees (mainly Muslim Bosniaks from Sarajevo, together with one Catholic from Mostar) from the Federation and those (Serbs) from RS. One of the consortium members from Sarajevo, who had somehow become inserted into the student body, publicly and provocatively demanded from the Serb colleagues what "they" had thought when the *Ferhadia* mosque had been blown up in Banja-Luka during the war. After a pause one of the more senior Serb students said, with very considerable dignity:

"We felt that we had lost a part of our heritage."

This exchange calls to mind the claim made by the former Bosnian President Alija Izetbegovic in 1997 when he addressed a meeting of planners in Mostar. He started his speech by suggesting that there was no sense in speaking of social or cultural divisions in Bosnia because:

"... there is only one division which does make sense: a division which will remain – it is the division between the people who destroy bridges and the ones who build them".

Whilst founding our own project on sentiments such as these, it is just as relevant to observe that our Serbian trainee in London was in the financial services sector and that, whatever else his observation signalled, it reflected the growth at that time of cross-entity economic linkages and relationships.

By the second module in the University of Sarajevo it was noticeable that the group was becoming more unified, although the opportunities to provoke divisions were still present. As if scripted in advance an incident took place that was (in the opinion of more than one observer) designed to do precisely that. During a lecture by an academic professor from Sarajevo who was much involved in the organisation of increasingly successful festivals in the city, one of the consortium members (from Sarajevo) strode into the classroom and announced that in the "next door" lecture theatre there was an event that the students should attend. This turned out to be a televised meeting marking the anniversary of the start of the war and containing relatively strong pro-Bosniak and anti-Serb pronouncements. All the teachers present (including those from London and Sarajevo) were outraged – not by the expression of the kinds of sentiments we have described but by a clear breach of academic etiquette. This had consisted of the disruption of a planned teaching session and (worse) the transformation of a "third space" (i.e. a space in which participants might feel safe to come together from different political/ethnic/religious sides) into a partisan space in which some were necessarily included and others excluded. Not surprisingly some of the students from the RS were both angry and hurt.

Once again, not unrelated to this incident, there was a much more potentially disruptive one a few days later. On this occasion the representative of the EC's TEMPUS office in Sarajevo arrived at the university (during the course of teaching) and requested a meeting with the co-ordinating team and as many consortium members that were available. The representative asked the consortium members to explain why they had recruited students by public advertisement rather than seek course participants from the consortium own institutions. The nub of the issue was that our project was about institution building whilst what we seemed to be doing was teaching an academic Masters degree unrelated to the institutions represented on the consortium.

We would pause at this point to draw attention to three related issues. The first was the attempt by a consortium member to divide the trainees on ethnic/religious grounds. The second was the objection (by an EC representative) that the consortium was training the "wrong" trainees (all of whom should, according to him, to have been recruited from the institutions represented in the consortium). The third was the implied objection (by the same EC representative) that we were teaching students on a Masters programme.

The TEMPUS participants were one of the first, possibly the first, post-war group of ethnically "mixed" students to be taught in the University of Banja-Luka (during module 3). During this module RS consortium colleagues had arranged, quite appropriately, a visit to a natural park. However, it came to be known by the group that this park was on, or near, the site of the infamous camp of *Omarska*, where many hundreds of Bosniak Muslims had been tortured and killed during the war. The Muslim students considered their position and decided that they should go to the park despite its connotations. It was only following an abrasive exchange between a member of the university, unconnected with the TEMPUS project but who had heard our students discussing the issue and who had decided to tell them to cease talking about such things "which probably did not happen anyway", that our Muslim students decided to decline the offer of the visit. Once again the same trainee who was involved in the cross-questioning in London about the *Ferhadija* mosque, discussed the issues with his student colleagues in a way that helped the group to come together.

By now the issue of the MA being offered in a TIB and the fact that we were said to be teaching the "wrong" students came spectacularly to the surface. A combination of actions (seeming to some to be co-ordinated) by one consortium member and the local TEMPUS representative's office placed severe strains on the integrity of the consortium. A deluge of messages swept into the E-mail in-boxes of the co-ordinator and other members of the consortium. The co-ordinator himself was accused of "mobbing and Stalinist behaviour" amongst many other things. The implication was floated that the project might be asked to return all the EC's funds. The combined objective of the alliance seemed to be to bring the project to a halt and to re-position it as a much more pragmatic training course for employees in the institutions represented in the consortium. The issue of a new co-ordinating team was raised. The consortium came under considerable pressure and might well have broken under the strain.

The response from Brussels was to freeze all project activity and to initiate an enquiry.

Let us make it clear at this point that we interpreted the dispute, as we still do, as being one in which both parties held quite legitimate views. On our side we were clear that we had, first of all, consulted the consortium quite properly and democratically, about the recruitment of trainees. Secondly, as a consequence of there apparently being *no* appropriate candidates in the consortium's own institutions, we were also clear that the consortium had been right to issue an open call for candidates. Thirdly, once we had been through the rigorous process of CV selection and interview, we were unequivocally clear that our primary loyalty – which would and could be unwavering – was to our group of student/trainees. On the other side the local EC representative was perfectly justified in querying the consortium's decision to support the validation and award an MA degree to trainees in a TIB project. It was also understandable that he should feel we were favouring a relatively small number of privileged students rather than a larger number of employees in, for example, a government ministry. We would not, moreover, like to blame the consortium member for taking these views – although we did not, nor do we now, agree with any of them.

In the event the matter was solved more by hubris than design. A partner from the Brussels TEMPUS Unit, together with a colleague from the Italian technical assistance office, came to take statements from the students and members of the course team at a module held in Italy. (The module was permitted by the TEMPUS Unit had on the grounds that an enquiry could only proceed with a substantial number of student, staff, and consortium members present.) The central feature of the meeting, however, was that neither of the two main protagonists, the consortium member, and the local BiH TEMPUS representative, managed to attend. In their absence, there was a clear majority of participants who felt the project should proceed – and so it did.

There is a single further point to be made. Had it been within the power of the consortium to resolve by majority voting to expel one of its members on the grounds, not of deliberate *malfaisance* but that much damage was being done to the project, however justified the various views held, then that decision would have been made. But the consortium did not have that power and it thus was the Brussels TEMPUS Unit alone that had the power to determine the future of the project. In this regard it needs stressing that both the TEMPUS representative from Brussels and his colleague from the technical assistance office were at once courteous, thorough in their taking of evidence, and extremely fair in their dealings with the staff and students of the project.

Institutions, the Consortium, and the Course: A Summary

A fuller and more considered account of the project success (or lack of it) in "institution-building" for the tourism and cultural industries sector in BiH and the Balkan, SE-European, and European levels is being prepared for publication in book form. In the present context we may make the following summary observations. First of all, our students were indeed trained according to what we considered the highest standards of European Masters level teaching in tourism and the cultural industries. Apart from anything else our MA used several of the most experienced European teachers in the field. Secondly, we did indeed also construct the space for institution building in BiH partly by assembling what seemed to be the principal institutional players in the field into our project consortium, partly by introducing a wide range of regional, European, and global institutional players to ongoing work of the project, and partly by creating the means for a body of trainees undergoing education and training to become engaged with (and/or to become engaged by) our partner institutions in order for them to evolve into professional organisations fit for the challenges of the newly emerging post-war economy. Thirdly, however, as we look back at the project now, we cannot say that the promise of Bosnian institutional development in the sector has advanced to anything like the degree we might have hoped for.

We may put the matter more bluntly. The war and the economic transitions that followed left many of the institutions represented in our consortium weak and shaped by forces that promoted, and promote, personal over public interests. Furthermore the fragmented structure of governance bequeathed by the Dayton Peace Agreement (e.g., how can two ministries of trade/tourism in a relatively small country possibly work for the overall well-being of the sector?) has clearly allowed the kind of institutional stagnation we witnessed in our project to continue. Such stagnation benefits nobody except those who privately gain from weak institutions. In our case such institutional weakness runs directly counter to the interests of our students and the sector that they might reasonably be expected now to lead.

To obtain a more general view of the specific institutional experiences we have had in our project we may usefully look a rather wider institutional field.

Part III: Lessons about Institutions from the Project and Beyond

A growing body of publications has now been written to reflect upon the development of tourism in the transition economies in Central and Eastern Europe (Hall, 1995; 1998; 2004; Light & Dumbraveanu, 1999; Roberts & Simpson, 1999), but as a very new comer to the field there has been very little presented on the nascent industry in BiH. This section therefore, draws upon the numerous meetings, interviews, and observations conducted by the present authors over the period from 1998-present, in an effort to describe the structures and directions taken by those institutions currently involved in the organisation of tourism in BiH today.

When reflecting upon the political, social, and economic situation within BiH, it is easy to be sucked into the complexity of institutions and layers of governance created by the Washington and Dayton peace accords that brought about peace but not an easily functioning state. As the vast bulk of agencies are wartime or post-war creations this is not that surprising. However, within those agencies the dominating theme in terms of policy, management and networks is one of continuity from the pre-war state-organised models that functioned in the former Yugoslavia.

For instance when discussing approaches to tourism, interviews showed that until very recently much of the language was drawn from the Yugoslav model. So in BiH that primarily meant "transit tourism", meaning the flow of then domestic tourists travelling from inland areas of the country via BiH to the coastal resorts in Croatia and Montenegro, or "spa tourism", meaning the flow of socially organised trips to spas for factory groups or sports clubs where they would be accommodated in large functional hotels linked to medical facilities within the spa resort. Little was thus done to update approaches that barely recognised the dramatic changes in the regional geo-politics, such as the fact that people wishing to "transit" would now have to pass into BiH via international rather than internal borders.

Equally, the public sector that dominated in the pre-war socialist period continues to play the dominant role, but within a far more fragmented structure. So we find two "entity" ministries covering tourism (the Ministry of trade & tourism in RS and the newly created Ministry of Environment & Tourism in the FbiH), up to 10 Cantonal ministries in the FbiH and numerous municipal departments all across the country. Inside those agencies even though they are on paper "new", many of the key senior staff were working in the public sector before the war. As there is minimal influx of fresh blood in terms of recently qualified and skilled staff, then the management structures with rigid vertical hierarchies remain virtually unchanged. This has lead to a situation where opportunities to build up internal training and pass on recently acquired knowledge and skills are severely limited.

Thus when the participating Bosnian institutions were asked at the beginning of our capacity building TEMPUS project to nominate candidates to participate in the programme there was a stony silence followed by the response that the agencies "did not have any appropriate staff" to take up such a proposal. This was partially understandable due to the demographics of the Yugoslav economy. Within the tourism sector in the former Yugoslavia as the industry and its organising bodies centred in Croatia, Slovenia, and Montenegro (all which now lie outside of BiHs international borders), the newly created Bosnian institutions had only a very narrow expertise base to draw upon. Nonetheless, those institutions certainly had more than a sufficient number of staff to allow at least a small cluster the chance to bring in such sorely needed skills. So perhaps the turning down of this opportunity was due to other factors.

Certainly one element became very apparent from the early responses of both those managing the existing tourism institutions and from the cohort of trainees within the capacity building project. That was in the reply to the question: "what needs doing to the Bosnian tourism industry to help it function in this new market economy?". Both groups immediately stated that the first thing to do was to create new laws. This reflects what the Berlin based think tank, ESI have described as one of clearest indications of a continuity from the pre-war socialist era to the present, in terms of understanding:

> "… of what good governance actually means. Faced with the enormous problems of today, an important part of the Bosnian élite is falling prone to an authoritarian temptation – the belief that policy (mainly understood as legislation) can best be formulated outside the political process, and imposed on society without the participation of stakeholders" (ESI, 2004).

Further evidence of this ingrained understanding of governance was found in the responses to the creation of a "bulldozer" committee in 2003. This was a body of commanders from Bosnian business asked to propose 50 reforms to help private enterprise by removing "pointless bureaucratic barriers to doing business in Bosnia-Herzegovina". Instead of coming up with ways of re-structuring malfunctioning institutions, building up expertise through training and education or sharing information and strategy through networking, the key reforms suggested by the cream of the Bosnian business world were again to request changes in laws to be drawn up. So for example in this chapter to help the tourism sector the first requests were for:

> "Improving mechanism of tourism and catering inspection in FbiH."

A further telling outcome of the Bulldozer process, was the request for the:

> "Rationalisation of tourism company contributions and accommodation tax in FbiH."

Although such a move could certainly help in clearing away red tape, it could also function as a way of clearing away opposition and an opportunity to consolidate power in the hands of an existing élite. In becoming the point of funding to cantonal tourism associations "contingent on the satisfactory performance of these associations", as long as "satisfactory performance" was not further defined, then one organisation would become sole distributor of funds without any scrutiny as to why decisions were made.

This lack of direct accountability was a feature that figured in the Yugoslav political sphere and has shown few signs of altering in the present BiH (ESI, 2004). With very little transparency, there is virtually no understanding outside the institutions of what they actually do. But at the same time there are no pressure groups within the non-governmental sector worked to redress this situation either. In the country as a whole there are around 195 NGOs registered in the International Council of Voluntary Agencies annual publication for 2005/2006 (ICVA, 2006), but none are working directly to progress or influence the role of tourism and tourism institutions.

In contrast, particularly since 2003 significant projects and grants have been established within a wide range of the international NGOs and aid agencies working in BiH. So we can reflect on major inputs from the EC (via the EU-RED and TEMPUS programmes), USAid, GTZ of Germany and JICA of Japan amongst others. However, the bulk of those projects have been run in pilot areas, mirroring the fragmented nature of tourism development as demonstrated by Bosnian public agencies. There has been no push to bring together or network across initiatives and pool together to any form of state level strategy.

This has meant that day-to-day decisions are being directed by weak policy or narrow objectives. Of huge importance is the simple fact that the information base to feed into policy is severely limited. One of the principle factors behind this is because there is virtually no empirical research being conducted in any aspect of tourism. As mentioned earlier, the centres of education for the tourism industry as it stood pre-war were located outside of BiH. Subsequently there has been a slow reaction to fill this vacuum. As within other institutions, the universities in BiH have demonstrated little capacity for dynamic change. So, once again drawing from our experiences in co-ordinating the TEMPUS capacity building project, we saw that when offered with an opportunity to embed the newly created training course as a functioning post-graduate degree, the Bosnian universities found it a too complicated structural and bureaucratic process to allow the course to be validated. This happened even though there was a clear acknowledgement of the urgent need to create full tourism courses in higher education centres.

Compounding the situation in the area of research, is what little information that is gathered is jealously guarded and rarely disseminated to all stakeholders. Thus for instance when colleagues attempted to compile a comprehensive list of accommodation to present in a new guidebook (something that would benefit all involved in the sector), they had to trawl through hundreds of phone calls and meetings rather than turn simply to a central database. The data was finally collected and demonstrated that:

> "The shortage of information in Bosnia is not primarily a problem of supply, however. The results of investigations, fact-finding missions or institutional audits undertaken by foreign or local consultants in the post-war period add up to a substantial body of knowledge. The problem is in the way this information is used within the policy process – in the demand for information.

Across the different areas we have examined, there is a remarkable absence of goal-oriented approaches to solving real-world problems. This is a reflection of a profoundly distorted political process, which generates little demand for tangible social and economic policy outcomes." (ESI, 2004)

However, a complete stasis has not been observed either. What appears to have taken shape in BiH are the creation of structures that operate on new tiers of governance, function principally along pre-war modes of policy but additionally have reacted to the rapid pushes toward creating a market driven economy. This final aspect has taken place in the form of attempts at rapidly undertaken privatisation. However, in the tourism industry as with most other sectors, privatisation has taken place within a policy vacuum and one where planning is completely uncoordinated across cantons or entities. The result of this is something of a free for all.

The current authors had a first hand opportunity to investigate this situation when they were asked in 2004 by the UK government to conduct an audit to identify key local and international stakeholders in the tourism and cultural industries field, to identify the principle areas of the BiH tourism offer, to conduct a local needs analysis of facilities in the field, to assess the opportunities for UK investment arising from these needs and to make an indicative survey of UK interests in the field. The audit was conducted by communicating with a wide range of stakeholders across the country. The conclusions from that report were that there certainly were many potential situations for British expertise to play a major role at assisting the building up of viable and profitable tourism assets in BiH. The investments should be firstly within the areas of governance, training, development of policy, networking, and partnering between public and private agencies. Thus individual private sector attractions could find their niche within a coherent statewide strategy for development.

Two years later on, the Bosnian Agency for Investment Promotion (FIPA) staged a tourism investment conference at the BiH embassy in London. They provided a substantial list of projects proposed by Bosnian partners. That list addressed none of the major policy related issues but instead sought to quickly sell off land and allow, "cherry picking" of the most attractive tourism assets in the country. A more unsustainable proposition could not be imagined and this currently sums up the position within the country. Institutions combine the worst of the patronage systems of the pre-war era, with a chaotic and poorly informed "dog-eat-dog" attitude to opportunities thrown up by the thrust towards the production of a market economy.

Parts of the private sector however, have shown small ways to move ahead and succeed regardless of the lack of support from public bodies. One example of this is the new mainly family-run hotels and guesthouses that have been set up in several towns. These draw upon long traditions of hospitality and demonstrate an awareness of what customers/tourists are eager to see. They stand in stark contrast to the mothballed state or recently privatised hotels where lack of motivation dominates the attitude in service.

Part IV: Interpretations and Conclusions

What might be learned from this narrative?

The first issue concerns ethnic dissonance and divisions. Although we witnessed attempts to divide participants on these grounds, and although some nationalist rhetoric was used at certain times, it became very clear that the participants in our group of trainees were consistently more concerned with the professional issues of tourism development in the country – with all the (state level) associated state-level implications for employment and economic growth. The "battleground" in our particular experience (we are not making generalisations here) was not, and is not, in that space.

The second issue concerns the nature of the organisation of TEMPUS projects. Although the Guidelines state quite specifically that it is for project consortia to shape the direction of the programme, it was our experience that in order actually to do this we had, quite literally, to fight for the life of our project in the face of determined opposition from the quarters we have outlined. The fact is that project consortia do not really have a great deal of real decision-making power. In some, if not all, senses this makes the emphasis on de-centralised co-operation more rhetorical than substantial.

The third question concerns the role of universities in development. Clearly, we are strong advocates of such a role – and would applaud the whole emphasis of the TEMPUS (as well as other projects articulated by the EC) is giving universities this role. However, after 3 years of unremitting work, we cannot see that the universities are actually able either to assume such a role themselves or are genuinely supported to take that role by political authorities at any level, including the level of the EU. They simply lack the power in an increasingly privatising economy. Where planning or policy-making (one preserve of academically trained advisors) actually fits into this "post-socialist", "free market" economy, and society is still, in our particular experience, unclear.

The fourth issue concerns institutions. We took the view that, faced with a clearly defined economic and social sector, tourism and cultural industries, there are two choices. The first is to take the TEMPUS guidelines at face value and to imagine (with all the necessary research and experience) a set of local, national, regional, and international institutions that are "fit for purpose" or, in the words of the TEMPUS authorities, able to "serve a particular purpose", namely the delivery of a sustainable, profitable, and equitably organised tourism industry. The other is simply to take the line of least resistance and to drift along with existing institutions that have been inherited from the past and transformed in the way we have described to serve themselves and those who run them. How the latter choice can be accurately associated with any genuine "institution building" programme remains a mystery to us.

Which brings us, finally, to the "market economy" itself. Here again there are two choices. The first is simply to become submerged uncritically in the rhetoric and practices of privatisation and liberalisation. In this case the work of FIPA, accompanied by the kind of weak inherited institutions some of which we have described, appears appropriate and inevitable. Why should anyone be concerned that the way ahead for tourism in BiH should be shaped by golf courses, holiday villas in resorts built by foreign companies, and casinos? The other flows from the appreciation that the tourist "capital" of the country is its natural and cultural resources, and that the conservation and preservation of these, and the way they become articulated in the tourist economy of the future, is complex and requires strong institutional involvement. Such a view would also include the understanding that such involvement and building up of institutions needs to be based on the kind of research, experience, and planning dispositions that our project attempted to encourage. Indeed the overall lesson of the project might be summed up thus: unless the future tourism and cultural industries sector in BiH is organised and managed by highly professional and efficiently run public and civil institutions the likelihood is that a type of investment will take place in the field that will benefit no-one except largely foreign interests. In our rather particular field that would amount to a case of "capital against capital".

References

Burns, P., & Holden, A. (1995). *Tourism: A new perspective*. Hemel Hemstead: Prentice Hall.

ESI (2004). *Governance and Democracy in Bosnia and Herzegovina: Post-Industrial Society and the Authoritarian Temptation*. Available at http://www.esiweb.org/index.php?lang=en&id=156&document_ID=63

Glenny, M. (1999). *The Balkans 1804–1999: Nationalism, war and the great powers*. London: Granta.

Hall, D. (1995). Tourism change in Central and Eastern Europe. In: A. Montanari & A. M. Williams (Eds), *European tourism, regions, spaces and restructuring* (pp. 221–244). Chichester, UK: John Wiley & Sons.

Hall, D. (1998). Tourism development and sustainability issues in Central and South-Eastern Europe. *Tourism Management, 19*(5), 423–431.

Hall, D. (Ed.) (2004). *Tourism and transition: Governance, transformation and development*. Wallingford, UK: CAB International.

ICVA (2006). The ICVA Directory. Available at http://www.icva-bh.org/eng/publications.wbsp

Light, D., & Dumbraveanu, D. (1999). Romanian tourism in post-communist period. *Annals of Tourism Research, 26*(4).

Roberts, L., & Simpson, F. (1999). Developing partnership approaches to tourism in Central and Eastern Europe. *Journal of Sustainable Tourism, 7*(3/4), 314–330.

SECTION II:

SCAPES, MOBILITY AND SPACE

Chapter 9

Towards the Responsible Management of the Socio-cultural Impact of Township Tourism

Pranill Ramchander

Introduction

Literature Review

South Africa's cultural resources post-1994 Traditionally, in terms of tourism, South Africa's unique selling points have been scenic beauty, wildlife and climate. Before the first democratic elections of 1994, 30% of visitors came to South Africa for its scenic beauty, while 26% were drawn by its wildlife (Gauteng Tourism Authority, 2002; Lubbe, 2003). Yet, in the words of Goudie Khan, and Killian (1999, p. 24), with the demise of apartheid, "increasing emphasis has been placed on the role of township tourism as a catalyst for social change and healing in South Africa by the state, the private sector, and community organisations". In similar vein, Lubbe (2003, p. 96) notes that "[a]fter 1994, 27% came to see the 'new South Africa', while 21% came to view our cultural attractions that is, 48% of tourists coming to South Africa with a cultural motivation." In a more recent survey, the number of tourists whose motivation for visiting South Africa is cultural or socio-cultural has risen to 46% (Lubbe, 2003).

South Africa consists of a remarkable mix of cultures, with African, European and Asian influences intermingled to create a unique South African multi-cultural society. The many-faceted heritage bequeathed by this mixture of exotic and indigenous culture is inextricably bound up with the social and political history of the country (Parker, 1997). Although cultural tourism in South Africa is still in its infancy, the political changes of 1994 have stimulated increased interest in the fascinating mix of cultures found in townships. In this melting pot, some things have remained unchanged, while other new and unique cultural expressions have evolved. Many forms of dance, music, song, theatre and cuisine, both traditional and modern, from every cultural group may be encountered. Festivals, concerts and performances reflecting lifestyles and regional interests are numerous. History and heritage are preserved in existing and newly developing museums and monuments in townships, living cultural villages and places where the freedom struggle took place (Damer, 1997). There is also the wealth of art and crafts produced by talented South Africans for sale in craft centres and open-air markets in townships (Gold Reef Guides, 2003; Soweto Tours 2003a).

The urban black townships in South Africa differ from other deprived areas in the world largely as a result of the circumstances which prevailed under the ruling white minority during apartheid (Ramchander, 2003). To achieve social segregation, the National Party implemented a broad range of Acts and ordinances ensuring that different races could not come into contact with each other, even in their free time (Soweto SA, 2003; Soweto Tours, 2003a). The segregation of housing, education, and health and leisure facilities such as beaches, hotels, restaurants, libraries, cinemas, camping sites and national parks was an elaborate and humiliating system often entrenched with force, and which extended to the development of the townships as dormitory towns as a means of segregating black labour. Townships were established far away from the central business districts, and from the white urban areas; and were not allowed to develop as an integral part of the white city (Mabogane & Callaghan, 2002; Ramchander, 2003). Many black townships, in particular, have suffered as a result of the perception that they are places of violence and squalor.

Tourists over the past decade have exercised a preference for travel that involves broadening the mind and learning, as opposed to the mass tourism culture of relaxation in the sun. The 1990s saw the emergence of various types of popular tourism, such as green, alternative, sustainable, cultural, adventure, health and eco-tourism, with each destination marketing its own unique offering (Poon, 1993). In South Africa cultural tourism, which is a component of special-interest tourism, has primarily taken the form of township tourism and cultural village tourism (Dondolo, 2001; Ramchander, 2004). Township tours present themselves primarily as offering insights into post-apartheid progress and development, and cite attractions such as beer makers, traditional healers, traditional dancing, arts and craft centres, taverns, bed and breakfast establishments, crèches, political landmarks and shanty towns (Chapman, 2003; Ramchander, 2003; Wolf, 2002). Township tourism is growing rapidly as international tourists are eager to see how South Africa has progressed since its first democratic elections in 1994 (Ramchander, 2004; Sithole, 2003). Tourists are interested in townships that reflect past and present human experiences; they want to see the "real" people and witness their daily life, their present developments and their cultural heritage (South Africa Online Travel Guide, 2002). Seeing that the township tourism involves tourists motivated by interests in other people's cultures and a search for the different, it falls incontrovertibly within the body of cultural tourism.

However, as a new and unique tourism phenomenon, little research has been undertaken into the development or planning of township tourism, or of its impact on the resident community. This study seeks to ascertain the degree of meaningful community participation and concomitant empowerment that have resulted from township tourism and to gain an insight into residents' perceptions of its social and cultural impacts.

The study concludes with the author discussing the challenge of responsibly managing sustainable township tourism. Principles and guidelines are discussed which can be applied to the management of responsible township tourism in South Africa, so as to create the basis necessary for good practice for any community cultural tourism project.

Township Tourism

Township tourism involves travelling for the purpose of observing the cultural expression and lifestyles of black South Africans, and offers first-hand experience of the practices of another culture (Mabogane & Callaghan, 2002; Ramchander, 2004). Tourists are typically transported in a microbus accommodating no more than fifteen people at a time. Many tourists visit South Africa's most famous townships because they symbolise political freedom and because visits to the sprawling townships fit in perfectly with the new paradigm of special-interest tourism. Political violence may have made black townships no-go areas for foreign tourists in the days of apartheid, but 1976 and the political strife of the 1980s subsequently made townships such as Soweto world-famous (Mabogane & Callaghan, 2002; Ramchander, 2004), and it is not surprising that township tourism has increased significantly since the first democratic elections in South Africa in 1994. Their legacy of violence and pain has made townships unlikely tourist destinations, yet busloads of visitors arrive every day to sample the renewed vitality of township life (Joburg Gateway to Africa, 2001; Sithole, 2003). Most leave with a very different impression from the one with which they arrived, having gained new insights following tours led by local entrepreneurs, and discovering that townships are not depraved areas of violent crime, but vibrant centres populated by friendly people with inspirational stories to tell (Chapman, 2003; City of Johannesburg, 2003). Tourists are given a glimpse of local residents' daily lives and living conditions. There is the mandatory visit to a few carefully selected people in their homes, which range from a small tin and wood house to a room in a hostel (Ian, 1999; Latherwick, 1999). A day-care centre is chosen to put on a daily performance for the tourists. A short walk through a series of designated streets, under the watchful eye of the guide, is intended to impart the "feel" of the townships (Ramchander, 2004). At a craft centre tourists are able to satisfy their expectation of encountering work and development, and at the same time feel they have made a contribution by purchasing what appears to be a hand-made memento of Africa. Finally there is the social experience, set up in a "safe" shebeen, where the tourists will be able to partake of township life without being harassed by drunken and disorderly clientele (Chapman, 2003).

Despite urbanisation, displacement and modernisation, people in the townships hold their customs and traditions dear (CNN-TravelGuide, 2003), and township tours also include visits to traditional healers. Traditional healers are a source of health care to which Africans have turned throughout the ages, and even with the expansion of modern medicine, healers are still popular (Wolf, 2002).

Like other forms of community tourism development in the rest of the world, township tourism is increasingly being seen as an important economic activity with the potential to enhance the local economy. The term "tourism impact" has become increasingly prominent in the tourism literature (Allen, Long & Kieselbach, 1988; Ap, 1990; Brunt & Courtney, 1999; Brown, 2000; Pearce, 1989; Ratz, 2003), as the literature has demonstrated, at least to some, that tourism development has both negative and positive outcomes at the local level. Tourism development is usually justified on the basis of economic benefit, and challenged on the grounds of social, cultural, or environmental destruction.

The actual contribution made by tourism in a development programme has come increasing into question because of an alleged meagreness of actual benefits, an inequality of benefit distribution, and the high social costs exacted by tourism (Ashley & Roe, 1998). Further, economic benefits traditionally associated with tourism development are now being measured against its potential for social disruption. Some governments are now starting to realise that the welfare of the public should be considered along with the needs of tourists and investors.

Whilst the South African White Paper on Responsible Tourism (South Africa, 1996), addresses the development, management and promotion style of tourism development in the country, there is nevertheless a lack of information on the potential socio-cultural impacts that township tourism may have on the host destination. This very lack opens the way to the research problem to which this study will attempt to provide a solution.

Problem Investigated

Township tourism is a new and unique tourism product that is rapidly gaining currency in South Africa, with little or no research on its development, planning and impacts.

Research in this domain would be particularly enriched by the debates concerning the way in which the culture and lifestyle of people in townships are marketed and commodified through cultural tourism in post-apartheid South Africa. There is a clear need to look beyond the obvious economic networks associated with the tourism industry to a deeper understanding of the issues of power, access, empowerment, and participation. Focusing on residents' perceptions of the socio-cultural impacts of township tourism, the researcher in this study assesses some of the challenges associated with the development of more responsible and socially sensitive township tourism in South Africa. Using Soweto as a case study the researcher examines the opportunities for and constraints on tourism development and the influences of these factors on township residents, questioning how tourism can be practised in these areas in a way that ensures that benefits reach locals without being detrimental to their social and cultural heritage.

In the past, few black South Africans were allowed access to the tourism industry, either as tourists, operators or managers. At worst, black cultures were ignored or repressed; at best they became stereotyped and trivialised commodities (Beavon, 1982; Goudie Khan & Killian, 1999; Ian, 1999). An analysis of the township tourism market should therefore necessarily be extended to include the perceptions of the host community towards this new form of tourism that has engulfed their communities. As already mentioned, tourism research reveals increased attention to the social impacts of tourism on local communities, particularly marginalised indigenous groups. Urry (2002) contends that the process of creating a commercial tourism product from local cultures involves the careful selection, as well as screening, of cultural elements but these products are never simple mirror images of reality. A constant struggle, he argues, has emerged between market viability and authentic representations of local cultures, frequently resulting in a commercial (and political) screening and packaging of reality. Urry suggests that what tourists are guided through are more often than not profitable "pseudo-events" that are reflective of neither past nor present realities.

This raises important questions in South Africa about the social and cultural representation of township residents, and makes an examination of township tourism in South Africa particularly relevant. Black alienation and exclusion from mainstream tourism in the past has meant that most black South Africans have lacked control over the way in which their diverse cultures have been portrayed (Wolf, 2002). Yet the extent to which South Africa, like other developing countries, is benefiting by showcasing indigenous or marginalised communities as part of a cultural tourism strategy must be investigated. Are the desired side effects of cultural tourism, such as job creation, the upliftment of communities and the preservation of cultural lifestyles and expressions truly being realised, or have cultural expressions in fact changed and adapted to suit the demand and needs of the consumer tourist? Further subjects for debate are whether the ownership of cultural products should lie in the hands of the community or the developer, and whether the township community is exploited in the practice of cultural tourism as a result of its need for consumer goods and financial gain.

Many authors stress that cultural tourism brings about the gradual demise of traditional forms of art, craft and design, or its replacement with reproductions (Fladmark, 1994; Nash & Smith 1991; Pearce, 1995). The deterioration and commercialisation of non-material forms of culture has been a matter of major research concern, and the marketing of culture appears to be most prevalent in developing countries. The staging of contrived experience to compensate for the lack of real cultural experiences is another development that has become an accepted outgrowth of contemporary tourism (MacCannell 1973; Pearce & Moscardo 1986; Robinson & Boniface, 1998). Communities living in and around townships and cultural villages fall within the category of host populations, and so are included among those affected by cultural tourism. Socio-cultural impacts in these areas, however, are less well documented.

Research Objectives

The purpose of this study is to document township tourism and to investigate the socio-cultural impacts of township tourism in Soweto as perceived by the host population and to examine the extent to which these coincide with the classifications in the literature. The study aims specifically to examine local residents' perceptions of and attitudes towards tourism, without measuring the actual social effects of tourism development on the area. Results from the study may provide the basis for formulating responsible tourism guidelines that will shape appropriate policies and measures intended to prevent negative tourism impacts and reinforce positive ones.

Soweto: The Study Area

Soweto (originally an acronym for South Western Townships) is an urban area near Johannesburg, South Africa. During the apartheid regime, Soweto was constructed for the specific purpose of housing African people who were then living in areas designated by the government for white settlement. Today it remains an overwhelmingly black-dominated city (Figure 9.1).

Soweto gained the world's attention when it became the centre of the anti-apartheid movement. With a population of over 2 million, the township is the biggest black urban

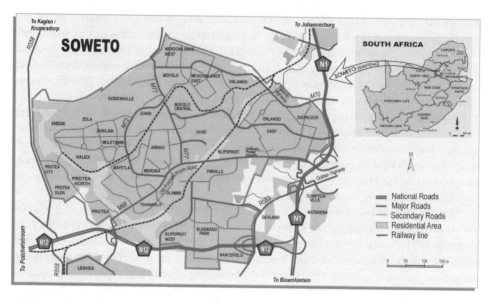

Figure 9.1: Soweto map (Travel Companion Gauteng, GTA, Johannesburg, 2003).

settlement in Africa with a rich political history. Soweto was the centre of political campaigns aimed at the overthrow of the apartheid state. The 1976 student uprising, also
known as the Soweto uprising, started in Soweto and spread to the rest of the country.
Black students protested against the introduction of Afrikaans as medium of instruction at
black high schools. Onto this legacy of repression and resistance Soweto tourism has
grafted a sense of cultural Africanness.

Although reports of crime in the townships have caused many travellers to bypass them,
more visitors are now taking tours. Many visitors take driving tours that let them see the
world of the township from a van window. But there are tours that allow you to get out and
interact with the locals.

Reasons for Selecting Soweto as the Study Area

There are townships located on the outskirts of all major cities in all nine provinces of the
country, and in selecting a study area the researcher recognised that an investigation of the
socio-cultural impacts of cultural tourism spanning all townships in South Africa would
have proved excessive in scope. Since the researcher is situated in Johannesburg, Soweto
constituted the most practical and accessible choice of site for a study of this kind. The
researcher was further led to select Soweto as the site for the present study because it is
representative of South African black townships, while simultaneously being an icon: "Soweto
has developed from a mere geographical concept into an international symbol of victory

over oppression. Throughout the world there are monuments condemning fascism, tyranny and abuse of human rights, with the implicit message: let this never happen again. Soweto like townships around South Africa represents living proof that, with determination, spirit and a just cause, an ordinary community can make a difference" (City of Johannesburg, 2003). This sentiment was reiterated by Mrs M.J. Woods, Director of City of Johannesburg's Tourism & Marketing during an interview conducted on 21 August 2003; in her view, Soweto is internationally known and is South Africa's most famous township because it symbolises political freedom to people around the world. As a result, with little or no marketing, and despite a great deal of adverse publicity, it has established itself as a major destination for foreign tourists in South Africa. Thus, because of both Soweto's representativeness and what it represents, the researcher considered that findings and conclusions reached from this study could be applicable to other townships in South Africa.

Woods (2003) describes Soweto as an unusual tourist destination because the events for which it is famous took place within recent living memory and the people responsible for these events are ordinary Sowetans. In this sense, Soweto is not an artefact or a museum, but a living place. It is not just another tourist destination; it is in part a memorial to those who died for freedom and in part a celebration of what human beings can achieve (Soweto SA, 2003, Woods, 2003). Soweto boasts special attractions as it is home to people who resisted the apartheid system. Tourists therefore visit sites that were the frontiers of anti-apartheid battles and today hold memories of that struggle (Mabogane & Callaghan, 2002). Cultural tourism is therefore an integral element of all tourism in Soweto.

A final compelling reason for selecting Soweto as the site for this study is its very popularity as a tourist destination. Soweto has drawn innumerable visitors because international tourism trends for South Africa have also moved to cultural tourism patterns, and the sprawling township satisfies the new paradigm. Despite a scarcity of precise data on tourism markets and marketing relating to Soweto, evidence suggests that the majority of tourists originate from Europe. The perception is that they want to make contact with local people and experience the Sowetan way of life. National tourism statistics suggest that 8% of all visitors who visit South Africa's main attractions visit Soweto. Soweto holds joint fourteenth position on the list of the most popular attractions in South Africa, and is one of only eight attractions to have drawn an increased number of tourists over the past year (SA Tourism, 2003a).

According to a report from the Gauteng Tourism Authority (2002), the number of visitors who pay to enter the Hector Peterson Memorial site is an indication that an average of 1498 tourists visit Soweto each month. However, as not all tours visit the memorial square, this figure is likely to be conservative. Mr W. Radebe, tour guide employed by Jimmy's Face to Face Tours, the largest tour operator in Soweto, explained in an interview on 12 June 2003 that the enterprise takes approximately 3000 tourists to Soweto per month. Three smaller operators take in the region of 1000 visitors to Soweto per month between them (Radebe, 2003).

In an interview conducted on 15 September 2003, Mr K. Sithole, research manager of the Gauteng Tourism Authority estimated the total number of foreign and domestic tourists entering Soweto daily at 800. This figure does not take into account those not participating in official tours.

The Soweto Township Tourism Trail

A small, but growing number of foreigners are overnighting in the homes of middle-class and working-class families in Soweto, seeing the rhythms and routines of the new era at first hand. Most tourists come from Europe, and some from the United States (South Africa Online Travel Guide, 2002). The most infrequent visitors, tour operators say, are white South Africans (Chapman, 2003).

Mabogane and Callaghan (2002) describe Soweto as containing lively hubs of humanity. It is not merely a place for squatters, criminals and the poverty-stricken – amidst the apparently grim living circumstances, there is hospitality and hope, and even beauty. Soweto has always had a small and thriving middle class. The professionals – the teachers, doctors, shopkeepers and civil servants – have taken pains to build comfortable double-storey houses with roses in the gardens, satellite dishes on the roofs, and, in some instances, luxury cars parked in the driveway (Ramchander, 2003).

Local tour operators are of the opinion that at present tourists are generally not interested in cultural villages, as they are beginning to realise that cultural villages offer no more than staged authenticity (Ramchander, 2003). These villages commercialise the culture(s) of the people who are on display and have no spiritual links with the real culture of the people whatsoever, as they have been established expressly for the purposes of tourism (Dondolo, 2001; Witz, 2001). By contrast, however, the number of tourists visiting the townships is increasing, as tourists want to see the "real" people. They are more interested in townships as reflections of past and present human experience, and in people's daily life as an amalgam of current developments and their cultural heritage (Ramchander, 2003; Witz, 2001).

Mrs J. Briscoe, CEO of Gold Reef Guides, in an interview conducted on 23 May 2003, cited the fact that a number of entrepreneurs from Soweto have established tour operations or shuttle services. The relatively high start-up costs, as well as the difficulties involved in obtaining tour operators' licences and competition from large players in the field have meant that only the most determined have endured. They are now well organised: tours are conducted in air-conditioned vehicles with cell-phone contact by trained guides and staff.

Popular stops during tours include the opportunity to view the huge mansion built by Winnie Mandela for her estranged husband, the tomb of Hector Peterson, the first victim of the 1976 riots, and the recently constructed Hector Peterson Museum, which offers visitors a detailed account of the events of 1976, including visuals and eyewitness accounts. Further stops are the Regina Mundi Catholic Parish Church, formerly the venue of protest meetings; the street on which stands the house that former President Nelson Mandela occupied prior to his imprisonment, and the home formerly occupied by Dr Desmond Tutu (Soweto Tours, 2003a). Tourists also have the opportunity to peek into old hostels, visit Freedom Square, which commemorates the struggle for liberty, pay a call on merchants selling traditional African medicines, and savour typical African dishes (Gold Reef Guides, 2003). The Credo Mutwa Cultural Village, built by Credo Mutwa, herbalist, author, diviner and sangoma (traditional healer), features a number of impressive mythical statues within its grounds, and provides the ideal setting to learn about the different dimensions of Soweto's cultural heritage (Farrow, 1999; Joburg Gateway to Africa, 2001; Soweto Tours 2003b).

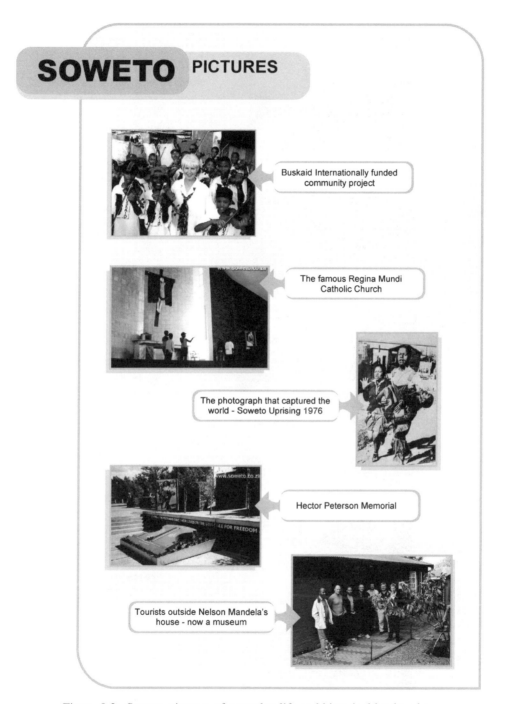

Figure 9.2: Soweto pictures of everyday life and historical landmarks.

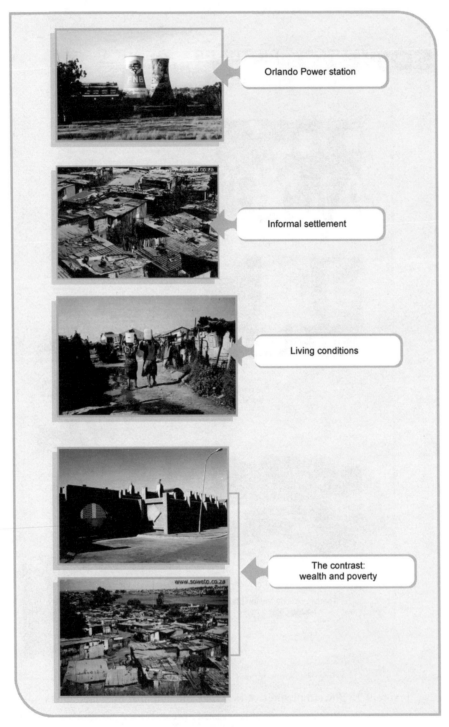

Figure 9.2: (Continued)

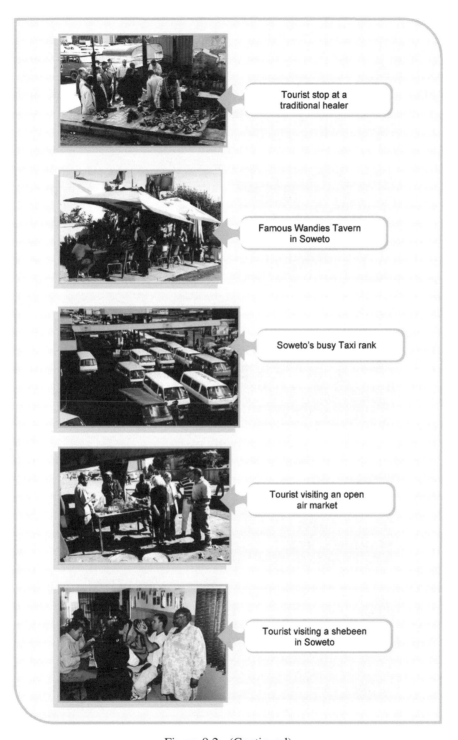

Figure 9.2: (Continued)

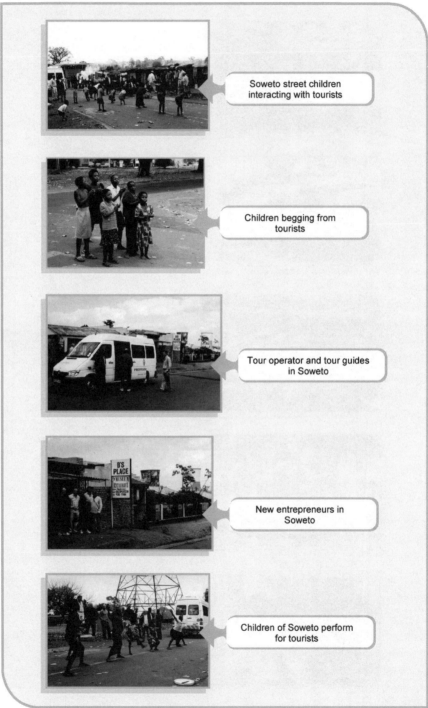

Figure 9.2: (Continued)

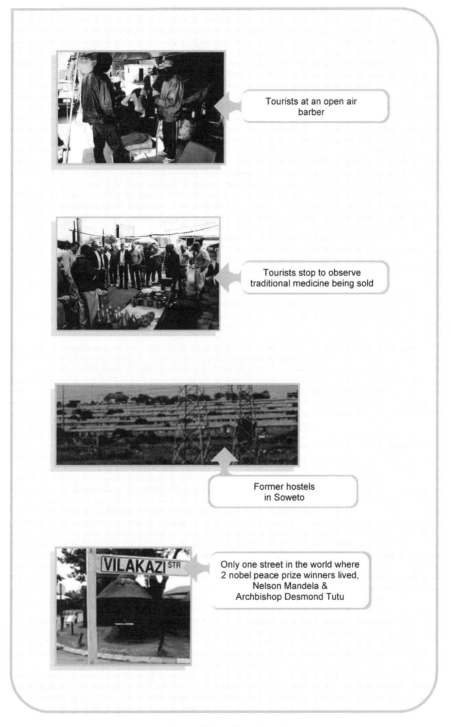

Figure 9.2: (Continued)

Township Tourism Blessing or Blight?

Township residents say tourism has been a mixed blessing – some see it as an intrusion, while others are benefiting from the financial and cultural exchanges the tours offer. Because cultural tourists are presumably motivated by a desire to experience local cultures when choosing to visit a particular location, they are perceived as both a blessing and a blight in terms of their social and cultural impact. Some authors suggest that culturally motivated tourists are desirable because they tend to be relatively few in number and are also more sympathetic in their approach to the local population and its culture than other tourists (Smith, 1989). Other have suggested that it is precisely this cultural motivation that makes cultural tourists less desirable in some areas. "Alternative" tourists seeking authentic cultural experiences can open up culturally fragile areas, clearing the way for potentially more damaging mass tourism (Burns & Holden, 1995). Cultural tourists can also severely damage (in terms of socio-cultural impact) local communities. Those in search of active contact with the local population are likely to cause far more disturbance by seeking out "local" places where their presence may cause friction with the local population. Local culture may become commercialised and the youth may begin to copy the behaviour and styles of foreign tourists. An increasing presence of tourists may lead to inflated prices.

Townships are the new tourist trend in South Africa, where the emphasis is on cultural tourism. Townships are meant to provide a more authentic and non-performative experience, depicting "real" history, "real" people and the "real" South Africa (Witz et al., 1999, p. 17). Township tours are presented as an alternative to cultural village performances where tourists are invited to see the local residents in the townships as more authentic and in a non-performative environment. Despite the claim that township tours are non-performative, the local people do perform for tourists in different ways, for instance in pre-schools that are visited by tourists, shebeens, open-air meat markets and some cultural groups also perform for visitors. This is the experience of a township tour package provided by many township tour operators (Dondolo, 2001).

During the researcher's fieldwork, local entrepreneur Lekau had this to say about the tours: "What you have to understand, is that that township people do not always like the tours that now pass regularly through this place. Some of these give them the feeling that they are living in a zoo." Lekau has therefore been "educating" her neighbours to make sure they welcome her guests, ensuring that they know that the more visitors she receives, the more they – as local suppliers – will benefit. Some feel that tour operators and guides who live in the township should interact more with the local people.

On the downside, tour guides say too many companies run safari-style drive-through tours, where tourists snap photos and peer at the surrounding poverty from air-conditioned buses. After snapping up their postcards and African masks, most tourists leave with only the most fleeting of contacts with the local people. An unnamed resident, says she saw one guide stop his bus in the township and allow tourists to throw money at the people below. Another guide was embarrassed by two guests who demanded that local children dance for their cameras.

Many township residents are still alarmed by visitors in their neighbourhood. According to a tourism development officer working in the area, the tours have had some negative impact. There has been an invasion of privacy, for example people barging into homes, which is not taken to kindly by the community. But guides insist the tours are not an attempt to make a voyeuristic theme park out of poverty, saying they brief tourists on acceptable behaviour and offer them an opportunity to interact with residents.

There are the more enlightened tour operators, however, who allow tourists to meet locals in the township taverns, jazz clubs and restaurants, and encourage them to support local artists and community projects. Some residents say they are being exposed to the rest of the world's people and cultures through these tourists.

A local bed and breakfast entrepreneur says: "Some days, I have two buses full of people. There's no room to sit down, so I have people in my kitchen and everywhere, just talking about everything. They come from Germany, Ireland, Florida, Michigan, Denver, Denmark. Because of apartheid, we never had the opportunity to share our cultures before."

Communities living in and around townships and cultural villages are thus affected by township tourism to some extent, both negatively or positively. Its socio-cultural effects in these areas, however, are less well documented.

Robinson and Boniface (1998) argue that the positive and negative consequences of contact fostered by tourism have been closely linked to debates about authenticity. It is well documented that the concept of authenticity in tourism studies has been shaped by the work of MacCannell (1973, 1976), who first made the connection between a formal concept of authenticity and tourist motivation, suggesting that tourists seek authentic experiences which they can no longer find in their everyday lives. MacCannell proposes that, for Western tourists, the primary motivation for travel lies in a quest for authenticity.

MacCannell (1973, 1976) notes that although tourists demand authenticity, it may be difficult to distinguish between true authenticity and what he terms "staged" authenticity, where a situation has been contrived so as to seem authentic. MacCannell argues that attractions vary in terms of the degree to which they are staged, and suggests that tourists today seek "backstage" (genuine or non-contrived) experiences, since modern tourists demand true authenticity (MacCannell, 1988). MacCannell further argues that "backstage" is where the real life of the community is carried out and authentic culture is maintained. The front stage, by contrast, is where commercial and modified performances and displays are offered to the mass of the visitors, and it is this area that tourists try to get beyond in their search for authenticity (Richards, 1997). Ramchander (2003) comments that in South Africa, both front stage and backstage authenticity are evident, for instance in cultural villages, where locals "perform" culture for the tourist in the front stage area, returning to the backstage area when they return to their real homes at the end of the day and carry out their normal cultural activities.

Townships as destinations are intended to reflect what in MacCannell's terms is the backstage. In the South African context, a visit backstage reveals the effects of racially discriminatory laws on the past and present human experiences, while front stage experiences involve purely favourable images. However, Dondolo (2001) argues that not all of the township tour package is authentically based. Rather, part of the package is carefully constructed, structured, and well planned.

The link between the issue of authenticity in tourism and township tourism is the topic of active debate, and has a direct bearing on the manner in which residents perceive tourism in townships. It is necessary to distinguish, however, between township tourism situations that involve a purely visual display of arts, crafts and political landmarks and those that involve visitors in a genuine context, such as visits to people's homes, traditional healers and active dance (Ramchander, 2003). While the country often benefits by showcasing township communities, it is important to understand how tourists and the host community feel about such cultural experiences.

Research Methodology

In selecting a suitable methodology for this study, the benefits and shortcomings of various methodologies were considered and a decision taken to employ methodological triangulation, which combines elements of both qualitative and quantitative techniques, making a convergence of results possible. In-depth semi-structured personal interviews, participant observation and a Likert scale questionnaire were used to assess residents' perceptions of township tourism development in Soweto. A sample of 350 respondents represented the host community (residents) of Soweto living around the 14 main tourism hubs of Soweto. On the basis of the literature review 57 socio-cultural impact variables were selected and used to formulate item statements designed to determine respondents' perceptions of township tourism in Soweto. A five-point Likert scale was used to measure the levels of agreement and disagreement with each statement, with 1 = strongly disagree and 5 = strongly agree. This scale was selected as reflecting a better conceptual framework with regard to perceived tourism impact. Content validity of the scale was first secured through a pre-test and evaluation by Unisa staff members and students resident in Soweto.

Social exchange theory provided the theoretical background for this study. In the tourism context Ap (1990) incorporates social exchange theory into a conceptual framework using the social exchange processing model as a theoretical basis to assist scholars in understanding why residents have positive and negative perceptions of tourism. Social exchange theory articulates that residents will be inclined to exchange their resources with tourists if they can acquire benefits without incurring unacceptable costs. This theory articulates further that those who perceive the benefits of tourism to be greater than the costs may be more amenable to participating in the exchange and giving full-fledged support for tourism development – other words, if residents perceive themselves as receiving more benefits through the exchange process, they will tend to more loyally support their community tourism business.

Profile of Respondents

For both quantitative and qualitative data collection methodologies, the sample was selected from the following categories:

Type 1: Residents who are in constant and direct contact with township tourists; because they depend on township tourism and would perhaps be unemployed without it, they welcome visitors.
Type 2: Township residents who have no contact with tourists or see them only in passing and whose household income is not derived from township tourism.

The rationale behind selecting different categories of respondents was to allow key comparisons to be made.

Data Analysis

Quantitative data collected was initially coded into numerical representations so that statistical analysis using the software package called SAS version 8 could be performed. Analysis techniques used included single frequency distributions and means, standard deviations (central tendencies) as tools for descriptive analysis, univariate analysis and correlations as instruments of bivariate analysis, and factor analysis as means of multivariate data analysis techniques. Section C of the survey questionnaire as well as qualitative data collected through interview schedules were coded and repeated themes (responses) recorded and then sorted into categories as they emerged. The above analysis would assist the researcher to describe trends in the data and also determine whether there are relationships between variables.

Discussion of Principal Results

The Most Positively Perceived Socio-Cultural Impacts

Frequency distribution and measurements in the form of means and standard deviations (SD) for the most positively perceived impact variables are reflected in the tables below. A higher mean indicates a stronger level of agreement with the statement. Table 9.1 reflects higher mean values for both groups of respondents (type 1 and type 2), indicating an overall strong agreement with the positive impact statements.

Type 1: Respondents with household income derived from tourism
Type 2: Respondents with household income not derived from tourism
V = The socio-cultural variable number on the questionnaire

The Most Negatively Perceived Socio-Cultural Impacts

Frequency distribution and measurements in the form of means and standard deviations for the most negatively perceived impact variables are reflected in the tables below. A higher mean indicates a stronger level of agreement with the statement. In Table 9.2, there are higher mean values for both groups of respondents (type 1 and type 2), showing an overall strong agreement with the negative impact statements.

It was found that the Soweto community's perceptions of township tourism and tourists fluctuate continuously between the negative and the positive. Findings revealed that the host community's support for township tourism was affected by three factors: socio-economic, cultural and physical, and participation in benefits. One of the most important theoretical contributions of this study is the confirmation by the findings of the usefulness of exchange theory principles in explaining residents' perceptions of tourism. The factors thought to directly influence support for tourism actually influence the perceptions of its costs and benefits. Perceptions and expectations of township tourism in Soweto can therefore be very different depending on which group of residents is being considered. Those respondents in continuous contact with tourists and who depend on tourism viewed tourism favourably, and those who have no contact with tourists or see them only in passing exhibited a range of attitudes.

Table 9.1: The most positively perceived attitude statements.

V	Positive attitude statement	Type 1		Type 2	
		Mean	Standard deviation	Mean	Standard deviation
20	Township tourism has resulted in a greater demand for female labour.	3.56	1.20	3.30	1.32
34	Tourism development increases the development of recreational facilities and amenities for residents.	4.01	0.79	3.89	0.94
37	Township tourism has made residents more conscious of the need to maintain and improve the appearance of the area.	3.93	0.94	3.58	1.15
40	The development of township tourism has generally improved the appearance of Soweto.	3.75	0.99	3.46	1.29
42	Tourist interest in culture has resulted in a strengthening of traditional activities and cultural pride.	4.07	0.81	3.99	0.94
44	Township tourism has stimulated the locals' interest in participating in traditional art forms.	3.86	0.76	3.92	0.90
45	Local culture is being renewed as a result of township tourism.	3.67	0.98	3.64	1.18
47	Township tourist show respect for the cultural lifestyle of local people.	4.14	0.82	3.82	1.03
49	Tourism encourages a variety of cultural activities by the local population.	4.00	0.59	3.90	0.86
50	Township tourism helps to conserve the cultural identity and heritage of the host population.	4.08	0.73	3.85	1.05
53	Meeting tourists promotes cross-cultural exchange (greater mutual understanding and respect one another's culture).	3.90	0.98	3.84	1.15
56	By creating jobs and generating income, township tourism promotes an increase in the social well-being of residents.	4.02	0.72	3.72	1.11
57	Township tourism has lead to more people leaving their former jobs for new opportunities in tourism.	3.10	1.15	2.68	1.22
59	Township tourism provides many worthwhile employment opportunities for Soweto residents.	3.79	0.88	3.28	1.25
60	Township tourism holds great promise for Soweto's economic future.	4.08	0.71	3.65	1.14

1: Strongly disagree; 2: disagree; 3: undecided; 4: agree; 5: strongly agree.

Table 9.2: The most negatively perceived attitude statements

V	Negative attitude statement	Type 1		Type 2	
		Mean	**Standard deviation**	**Mean**	**Standard deviation**
22	Township tourism will gradually result in an increase in municipal rates and taxes.	3.10	1.01	3.26	1.25
48	Traditional African culture in Soweto is being commercialised (sold) for the sake of tourists.	3.29	1.02	3.35	1.36
51	Locals often respond to tourist needs by adapting traditional practices to enhance their commercial value.	3.79	0.72	3.84	0.94
52	Township tourism causes changes in the traditional culture of local residents.	2.82	0.98	3.30	1.25
54	Only a small minority of Soweto residents benefit economically from tourism.	3.59	0.04	4.16	0.96
62	The development of township tourism in Soweto benefits the visitors more than the locals.	2.99	1.13	3.54	1.21
64	Township tourism in Soweto is in the hands of a few operators only.	3.83	1.01	4.04	1.07

1: Strongly disagree; 2: disagree; 3: undecided; 4: agree; 5: strongly agree.

Respondents demonstrated a predominantly positive attitude towards a number of socio-cultural impacts and agreed strongly that township tourism in Soweto is dismantling the stereotypical perceptions of townships as dangerous and a haven for criminals and hijackers; increases the development of recreational facilities and amenities for residents; has increased their awareness of tourism and hospitality and the need to maintain and improve the appearance of the area; has fostered a renewed interest in local art, craft and traditions; has instilled a sense of pride in locals concerning their heritage and culture; broadens their knowledge about international tourism, foreign places and people due to the cross-cultural exchange of learning taking place, and leads to the conservation of cultural practices and political landmarks.

Appreciation was shown for the employment benefits generated by tourism, which has resulted in a greater demand for female labour and offered new career opportunities in tourism by creating opportunities for locals to enter the industry as tour guides, tour operators and entrepreneurs. Respondents further believed that the creation of employment through tourism holds a great promise for Soweto's economic future.

Whilst township residents demonstrated a predominantly positive attitude towards tourists and township tourism, they were also able to point out some specific socio-cultural costs. Not all residents were of the opinion that tourism had a positive influence on local culture. Older respondents in particular voiced the concern that traditional African culture was being commercialised and claimed that certain locals sell or trivialise their culture to make a profit.

Residents argued that certain tourists and tour operators do not show acceptable standards of behaviour, and cited intrusion as a significant problem. Some residents expressed concern about the escalation of crime in tourism hubs. Residents further cited inadequate consultation about township tourism development and planning as a negative aspect. Moreover, the benefits of township tourism appeared to accrue to only a small elite within the Soweto community. Respondents were in strong agreement that township tourism benefits only a small minority of Soweto residents, with those with the most power, education and language skills or those who happen to live in the right place being most likely to get new jobs, set up enterprises, make deals with outsiders, or control collective income earned by the community. Increasing disparities in income can exacerbate conflicts within a community and has led to resentment between local people who have started tourism businesses and those who have not, and antipathy between residents not benefiting from tourism and tourists.

A broad conclusion drawn from this study is that township residents who benefit economically from township tourism are supportive of it, and this support is associated with a belief that township tourism causes mostly positive benefits. As a corollary, those without a commercial interest in township tourism tend to regard its impacts in a negative light. In keeping with this argument, Soweto residents who expressed the view that township tourism attracts organised crime and causes traffic congestion, for example, would almost automatically be opposed to tourism.

The identification of Soweto as a tourism destination has undoubtedly affected the quality of life of local residents. Effects of township tourism include an increased number of people, increased use of roads, and various economic and employment-based effects. Because Soweto is in the early stages of its life cycle as a tourism destination, Soweto residents seem to do and accept everything that is demanded by outsiders, ranging from the tourist trade and tourism promoters to their own government and entrepreneurs. They believe the promises when they are told that tourism is their big chance, and that it is of vital importance for the region, and, indeed, for the whole country. Yet no-one has taken the trouble of asking Soweto residents whether township tourism clashes with their own values and ideas. No-one mentions the negative socio-cultural aspects. Tourism development in Soweto appears to take place over the heads of the majority of residents, and few Soweto residents participate in tourism development as equal partners with tourism developers.

While success in this industry depends upon attractions and services, it requires the hospitality of local residents. If the tensions as mentioned by the respondents in this study are not adequately addressed, and the host community gradually reaches the stage of antagonism as identified in Doxey's Irridex model, tourists to Soweto will cease to be perceived by residents as individuals on holiday who may be talked to or who may be interesting. Instead, tourists will be seen simply as unidentifiable components within the mass. In a sense they will then be dehumanised, and as such become fair game for anyone who wishes to cheat, ridicule or even rob them. The hosts' anger, antipathy or mistrust will ultimately be conveyed to the tourists, and is likely to make them reluctant to visit places where they feel unwelcome.

Conclusions

The tourism industry in post-apartheid South Africa has placed the responsibility for constructing, packaging and transmitting images and representations of the "new" South African society and its past in the hands of a limited number of stakeholders within the public and private sector. The alienation and exclusion of black people from mainstream tourism both in the past and currently has meant that most township residents have lacked control over the way in which their diverse cultures are portrayed. While the tourism industry has been recognised both locally and internationally as a substantial and attractive source of economic benefits, problems such as those relating to the representation of and participation by the township community experienced by Soweto residents have been identified.

If we accept that township tourism in South Africa is going to increase, then we face the challenge of finding the balance between consumption and conservation; in other words, the challenge of achieving sustainable township tourism. The present study reveals that township tourism has become a complex phenomenon of unprecedented proportions, which can constitute either an opportunity or a threat with regard to culture, depending on how tourism is managed. Planning and managing township tourism requires that a number of issues be dealt with. For those involved in the preservation of culture, the challenge lies in understanding and working effectively with the tourism industry. For those in the tourism sector, there is a need to understand the needs of host communities as well as the principles and concerns that are a part of cultural heritage preservation (McKercher & Du Cros, 2002). Township tourism as a phenomenon is not about to disappear, and poorly managed township destinations will have a negative effect on both local communities and the tourism industry if cultural resources and values are degraded. The challenge is not to stop township tourism, but rather for stakeholders to work together in achieving sustainable planning and responsible management.

Responsible township tourism development presents many challenges, and policy-makers and communities will have to meet these challenges if they are to achieve comprehensive and sustainable township tourism development (Bramwell & Sharman, 1999; Bramwell & Lane, 2000). Tourism development is dependent on destination area resources and the goodwill of the communities involved. In utilising cultural and natural resources, the tourism industry has a responsibility towards the community in that these resources are being exposed and sold as by-products; these actions affect the lives of everyone involved in such activities (Mann, 2000). It is therefore important that at the local level, township tourism planning should be based on the development goals, priorities, participation and capacities as identified by, and to the mutual benefit of, its residents (Mann, 2000). Community-based planning is a local area planning approach that involves full participation by the local community, drawing on local skills and expertise, and providing for empowerment of the local community through the development and implementation of the resultant plan (Mann, 2000; Singh, Timothy, & Dowling, 2003). This is essentially a bottom-up approach to planning, the objective of which is to build effective communities where residents or neighbouring communities have a high quality of life, and contribute to community well-being and cultural development.

If township tourism is to be encouraged as a new basis for cultural tourism development, the active collaboration of local cultures is required. The literature is clear on the fact that collaboration should address issues such as the redistribution of tourism revenue and the need to involve host cultures in ownership and management roles in the community. Unfortunately the reality for most communities is that outside forces usually determine the speed and direction of tourism development, and local people are seldom consulted. False expectations are often raised among the people when they are promised that the arrival of tourists will bring new wealth to the community. They soon discover that the real economic gain from tourism goes to the organisers and entrepreneurs.

Non-governmental organisations, governments and private initiatives therefore need to work more closely with the townships to develop sustainable cultural tourism that will benefit the community as a whole, and not just the handful of residents who live around tourism hubs or political landmarks. Empowering the locals and giving them the means to develop their culture in their own way must be seen as the key to solving the township tourism problem. It should be up to the local people to decide the limits of tourism. In general it can be said that the more the local community is able to participate in the decisions affecting their own tourist development, the less they will be socially affected by the rapid changes.

Even though South Africa celebrated a decade of democracy in 2004, the South African society continues to face enormous social, cultural and economic challenges in its attempts to confront the legacies of previous generations. For cultural tourism, this challenge lies not only in product development, but also in the issues relating to the impact of culture that are central to development, education, training, marketing and management. Cultural tourism presents a very good opportunity to generate economic growth and development that can be sustainable in the long term. For the previously marginalised groups this constitutes a much yearned for injection of development infrastructure and brings the hope of real economic development, job creation, education and training.

Township tourists need information to enable them to behave in a responsible and sensitive way, both before they depart for their destination and at the destination itself. The tourism industry has the responsibility to provide township tourists with accurate information about local cultures and appropriate behaviour. Host communities need to understand why township tourism is important, how tourism works, its benefits and costs, and how they can participate. Important questions to be asked regarding township tourism in South Africa are: "Who should control township tourism?" and "What should be controlled?"

Resident perceptions are undoubtedly a key component in the identification, measurement and analysis of township tourism impacts. However, investigation of community perceptions of township tourism is not just an academic exercise. These perceptions are also important in terms of the determination of local policy, planning and responsible management responses to township tourism development and in establishing the extent to which public support exists for township tourism.

Cultural diversity and authenticity are central aspects to the township tourism experience. Township tourism requires a higher level of community involvement than most other forms of tourism and offers greater opportunities for local communities. Supporting services and products can be equally rewarding and add local flavour to the experience through the showcasing of local goods and customs. Support for the revival and maintenance of traditional cultural skills and practices, as well as new cultural products, is an integral part of the development of cultural tourism. At the same time, awareness of the various economic, social and cultural opportunities associated with township tourism should be created amongst locals.

Township tourism ventures need to involve local communities through a community tourism approach and should be developed through a process of consultation and negotiation, ensuring opportunities for locals to participate in and determine decisions about the nature of their involvement. Prior to any township tourism development, assessment of both future as well as present needs and expectations of the community should be undertaken. Proper development for township tourism should be informed by both market requirements and societal needs and development objectives. Socially, environmentally and economically beneficial responsible township tourism development requires achieving a balance between commercial success, the maintenance of cultural integrity and social cohesion, and the maintenance of the physical environment.

Acknowledgements

I wish to express my appreciation to the following people and organisation for their contributions to making this research possible.

- The South African National Research Foundation for the funding awarded to me.
- All the fieldworkers and respondents in Soweto who participated in the qualitative and quantitative components of the study.
- Gauteng Tourism Authority, Johannesburg Tourism and the many tour guides and tour operators with whom I interacted for all their valuable assistance and time made available to me.

References

Allen, L., Long, P. R. & Kieselbach, S. (1988). The impacts of tourism development on residents' perceptions of community life. *Journal of Travel Research, 27*(1), 16–21.

Ap, J. (1990). Residents' perceptions research on the social impacts of tourism. *Annals of Tourism Research, 17*, 610–616.

Ashley, C. & Roe, D. (1998). *Enhancing community involvement in wildlife tourism: issues and challenges.* London: International Institute for Environment and Development.

Beavon, K. S. O. (1982). Black townships in South Africa: terra incognita for urban geographers. *South African Geographical Journal, 64*(1), 2–20.

Bramwell, B. & Sharman, A. (1999). Collaboration in local tourism policy making. Annals of Tourism Research, 26, 392–415.

Bramwell, B. & Lane, B. (Eds) (2000). *Tourism collaboration and partnerships: politics, practice and sustainability.* Clevedon: Channel View.

Briscoe, J. (2003). Verbal communication with the author on 23 May. Johannesburg. (Notes in possession of author.)

Brown, F. (2000). *Tourism reassessed: blight or blessing?* Oxford: Butterworth Heinemann.

Brunt, P. & Courtney, P. (1999). Host perceptions and socio-cultural impacts. *Annals of Tourism Research, 26*(3), 493–515.

Burns, P. & Holden, A. (1995). *Tourism: a new perspective.* Englewood Cliffs, NJ: Prentice-Hall.

Chapman, K. (2003). Township tours offer glimpse of "Mandela's country". [Online] Available from: http://www.cnn.com/SPECIALS/1999/safrican.elections/stories/township.tours/ [Accessed: 2003-03-15].

City of Johannesburg (2003). Soweto. [Online] Available from: http://www/joburg.org.za/soweto/index.stm [Accessed: 2003-08-23].

CNN-TravelGuide (2003). Experiencing Soweto. Poverty lingers but things are changing in Mandela's birthplace. [Online] Available from: http://www.cnn.com/TRAVEL/DESTINATIONS/9810/safrica.2/soweto.html [Accessed: 2003-04-13].

Damer, B. (1997). *Soweto township, South Africa.* Johannesburg: South African Picture Gallery.

Dondolo, L. (2001). Depicting history at Sivuyile Township Tourism Center. Paper presented at the Mapping Alternatives: Debating New Heritage Practices Conference, University of Cape Town, 26–27 September.

Farrow, P. (1999). Soweto: the complete township guide. Houghton: Soweto Spaza CC.

Fladmark, F.M. (Ed.) (1994). *Cultural tourism.* London: Donhead.

Gauteng Tourism Authority (2002). Soweto tourism strategy implementation plan. Johannesburg: Heritage Agency CC.

Gold Reef Guides (2003). Township tour – memorable in every way. [Online] Available from: http://www.goldreefguides.co.za/TownshipTour.htm [Accessed: 2003-05-04].

Goudie, S. S., Khan, F. & Killian, D. (1999). Transforming tourism: black empowerment, heritage and identity beyond apartheid. *South African Geographical Journal, 81*(1), 23–31.

Ian, F. (1999). Where apartheid ruled, tourists are swarming. *New York Times, 149,* 4–8.

Joburg Gateway to Africa (2001). A tourist guide to visiting Soweto. [Online] Available from: http://www.goafrica.co.za/joburg/november/soweto.stm [Accessed: 2003-07-06].

Latherwick, P. (1999). Soweto Township Picture Gallery. [Online] Available from: http://www.damer.com/pictures/travels/southafrica/phils-pix/index.html [Accessed: 2003-07-23].

Lubbe, B. A. (2003). *Tourism management in Southern Africa.* Cape Town: Pearson Education South Africa.

Mabogane, M. & Callaghan, R. (2002). Swinging safaris in Soweto. [Online] Available from: http://www.mg.co.za/mg/africa/soweto.html [Accessed: 2002-11-19].

MacCannell, D. (1973). Staged authenticity: arrangements of social space in tourist settings. *American Journal of Sociology, 79,* 589–603.

MacCannell, D. (1976). *The tourist: a new theory of leisure class.* New York: Schocken Books.

MacCannell, D. (1988). *The tourist: a new theory of leisure class* (2nd ed.). Berkeley: University of California Press.

Mann, M. (2000). *The community tourism guide.* London: Earthscan Publications.

McKercher, B. & Du Cros, H. (2002). *Cultural tourism: the partnership between tourism and cultural heritage management.* New York: Haworth Press.

Nash, D. & Smith, V. (1991). Anthropology and tourism. *Annals of Tourism Research, 18*(1), 12–25.

Parker, S. (1997). Discussion paper: Culture and heritage tourism and their potential impact on local communities: the challenges of ownership, developments and other requirements. Department of Arts, Culture, Science and Technology. Pretoria: Government Press.

Pearce, P. L. (1989). Social impacts of tourism. *The social, cultural and environmental impacts of tourism.* Australia: New South Wales Tourism Commission.

Pearce, P. L. (1995). From culture shock and cultural arrogance to culture exchange: ideas towards sustainable socio-cultural tourism. *Journal of Sustainable Tourism, 3*(3), 143–154.

Pearce, P. L. & Moscardo, G. M. (1986). The concept of authenticity in tourists' experiences. *Australian and New Zealand Journal of Sociology, 22,* 121–132.

Poon, A. (1993). *Tourism, technology and competitive strategies.* Wallingford: CAB International.

Radebe, W. (2003). Verbal communication with the author on 12 June 2003. Johannesburg (Notes in possesion of the author).

Ramchander, P. (2003). Township tourism – blessing or blight: The case of Soweto. Paper presented at the ATLAS Expert Cultural Tourism Group Conference on Cultural Tourism: Globalising the Local – Localising the Global, Barcelona, 1 November.

Ramchander, P. (2004). Soweto set to lure tourists. In: A. Bennett & R. George, (Eds), *South African travel and tourism cases*. Pretoria: Van Schaik.

Ratz, T. (2003). The socio-cultural impacts of tourism. Case of Lake Balaton, Hungary. [Online] Available from: http://www.ratztamara.com/balimp.html [Accessed 2003-01-06].

Richards, G. (Ed.) (1997). *Cultural tourism in Europe*. Wallingford: CABI.

Robinson, M. & Boniface, P. (Eds) (1998). *Tourism and cultural conflicts*. Wallington: CAB International.

SA Tourism (2003a). Quarterly reports – quarter two 2003. [Online] Available from: http://www.southafrica.net/index.cfm?SitepageID=223 [Accessed: 2004-01-12].

Singh, S., Timothy, D. J. & Dowling, R. K. (2003). *Tourism in destination communities*. Wallingford: CABI.

Sithole, K. (2003). Verbal communication with the author on 15 September. Johannesburg. (Field notes in possession of author.)

Smith, V. L. (1989). *Hosts and guests: the anthropology of tourism*. Philadelphia: University of Philadelphia Press.

South Africa. Department of Environmental Affairs and Tourism (1996). White Paper on the Development and Promotion of Tourism in South Africa. Pretoria: Government Printer.

South Africa Online Travel Guide (2002). Soweto Johannesburg. [Online] Available from: http://southafrica-travel.net/north/aljohb06.htm [Accessed: 2003-04-16].

Soweto SA. (2003). Soweto: South African history. [Online] Available from: http://www. sowetosa.co.za/soweto.history.html [Accessed: 2003-04-11].

Soweto Tours (2003a). Soweto, an overview. [Online] Available from: http://www.soweto.co.za/ html/history.htm [Accessed: 2003-09-16].

Soweto Tours (2003b). Soweto tours and picture gallery. [Online] Available from: http://www.soweto.co.za/html/gallery.htm [Accessed: 2003-09-16].

Urry, J. (2002). *The tourist gaze: leisure and travel in contemporary sciences*. 2nd ed. London: Sage.

Witz, L. (2001). Repackaging the past for S.A. tourism. Proceedings of the American Academy of Arts and Science. *Daedalus, 130*(1), 277.

Witz, L., Rassool, C. & Minkley, G. (1999). Tourism in African Renaissance. Paper presented at the conference entitled Public History, Forgotten History, University of Namibia, 22–23 August.

Wolf, L. (2002). Beyond the shacks: the vibrant world of the townships. [Online] Available from: http://www.travel.iafrica.com/activities/townships/212881.htm [Accessed: 2002-09-12].

Woods, M. J. (2003). Verbal communication with the author on 21 August. Johannesburg. (Notes in possession of author.)

Chapter 10

Hegemony, Globalisation and Tourism Policies in Developing Countries

Andrea Giampiccoli

Introduction

Globally, the tourism economic sector is regarded as one avenue for boosting socio-economic development. In developed countries, attempts are often made to convert former industrial areas and impoverished rural areas to a tourism economy in order to overcome structural decay. Developing countries also follow this trend in stressing the importance of tourism, assuming it can boost national development. Yet contemporary tourism as an economic, cultural and social activity is embedded in the globalisation process. As Michael Hall suggests:

> Tourism development is an essentially political concept. The pursuit by governments around the world of various states of tourism development, and the perceived benefits of such development, raise questions about the economic, social and political manner in which overt and covert development objectives are pursued at the expense of other objectives. Political philosophy and ideology will have a substantial impact on tourism development processes (Hall, 1998, p. 110).

This chapter sets out to investigate the intersection between trends in the global cultural, economic and political milieux on the one hand, and the tourism industry in developing countries on the other. Globalisation is obviously an important concept to interrogate in this regard. In addition, this chapter employs the concepts of hegemony and processes of divergence/convergence to illuminate the issues. The critique developed in this work is not about globalisation as such, as an objective historical process, but rather some of its parts, specifically the neo-liberal agenda. The point of view adopted is similar to that of Peet, who cautioned: "… we are dealing with neo-liberal globalization, not just globalization as a neutral spatial process … neo-liberal globalization is the focus of our critique, not globalization in general, and certainly not as potential" (Peet, 2003, p. 3).

Tourism and Development

The increasingly global role of the tourism industry is evident in much recent literature as well as in policy statements. For example, the World Bank (WB) has recently noted that: "There is an increasing role for international development institutions, such as theWB, to play in the tourism industry" (Dickinson in WB, n.d.). As stated in Lindberg, Molstad, Hawkins and Jamieson (2001, p. 508), international development assistance is of growing significance in sourcing funding for global tourism development and management. Indeed, "Everything seems to suggest that developing countries look upon tourism consumption as manna from heaven that can provide a solution to all their foreign settlement difficulties" (Erbes in Dieke, 2000, p. 287).

Contemporary tourism development occurs in a world that is integrated at a number of levels. In tourism as in other arenas of global exchange, Teo, Chang and Ho (2001, p. 1) insist that: "Interactions between the local, national, regional and global arenas have thrust multiple structures and agents together so that an understanding of the process underpinning globalisation must be examined *across* rather than within scales." In the case of tourism, these agents are thrown together in part through the transactional nature of neo-liberal capitalism. For Milne and Ateljevic:

> Tourism […] must be viewed as a transaction process which is at once driven by the global priorities of multi-national corporations, geo-political forces and broader forces of economic change, and the complexities of the local – where residents, visitors, workers, government and entrepreneurs interact at the industry 'coal-face' (Milne & Ateljevic, 2001, p. 371).

It is within this context that we observe an increasing imperative to promote tourism as a development tool. The concept of development used here originates from the works of Dudley Seers (1969) and Goulet (1988). Development is here recognised to be holistic and multidimensional – a people-centred concept – and taking into account different historical-geographic situations. Furthermore and in a tourism context it is crucial to grasp the basic facts of "who gets what, when, where, and how?" (Sofield, 2003, p. 92). Britton (1981, p. 19) reminds us that "The emphasis … is not whether tourism is economically advantageous in aggregate terms, but to whom do these advantages accrue." Who benefits from tourism initiatives in poor countries?

Clearly the concept of development must also be linked to power relations. In the case of Latin America, commentators note that the term "development" has become pejorative in its connotation and that "liberation" is increasingly the preferred term. This is understood as liberation from "domination by capitalist countries" (Gutierrez in Goulet, 1988, p. 480).

Hegemony, Globalisation and Divergence/Convergence

The modern concept of hegemony theory is usually attributed to the Italian Marxist Antonio Gramsci (1891–1937) and is mainly concerned with the instruments used by a dominant group to persuade other groups of the legitimacy of the operational political and socio-economic system. Hegemony is understood as "a social condition in which all aspects of social reality are dominated by or supportive of a single class" (Mayo, 1999, p. 35). In hegemony theory, the emphasis is often on the actions of the ruling class in guiding the broader cultural milieu. This cultural factor can be linked to the active agency of organic intellectuals belonging to the ruling class (Macey, 2000), who are also supported by the academic-institutional-media complex (Peet, 2002). Yet aspects other than the cultural remain of crucial importance. For Gramsci (in Forgacs, 1988, p. 423), "though hegemony is ethico-political, it must also be economic, must necessarily be based on the decisive function exercised by the leading group in the decisive nucleus of economic activity".

Hegemony thus covers the cultural, the political and the economic spheres. These three levels of hegemony in the contemporary global milieu can be briefly summarised as follows:

1 Cultural hegemony is seen as linked to what can be termed the TINA (There is no Alternative) syndrome/paralysis. This flows in part from the Fukuyama thesis of "The End of History" which appears to find much support in the contemporary "Davos Culture".[1]
2 Economic hegemony consists of the dual control of private capital (enterprises, banks, etc.) and public capital (loans, grants, etc. by public institutions/organisations).
3 Political hegemony covers the control of policy-making and co-operative institutions/organisations at international, regional and national levels.

The term globalisation gained prominence during the 1980s due to the economic counter-revolution which, critics argue, has pushed the world system towards neo-liberal policies. Associated with a boost in transport, communication and information technologies and the change in the type of management of organisations and companies, globalisation was deepened and entrenched in particular forms. In general, three different levels of global-isation have been recognised by scholars:

1 Economic globalisation is concerned with the decreased relevance attributed to geo-graphical localisation in economic activities. This allows large corporations to distrib-ute their production activities in different geographical locations depending on their convenience and cost.
2 Cultural globalisation is related to the assumption that the world is moving toward a homogeneous global culture, identified with a Western (mostly North American) pattern of consumption and lifestyle. It is possible to identify within this a particular political-economic cultural creed, notably individualistic neo-liberalism.

---

[1] The Davos Culture, after Huntington (1999), is a homogeneous set of values based on the beliefs of individu-alism, market economy and political democracy epitomised by the participants in the World Economic Forum (WEF) in Davos. In addition, these people "control virtually all international institutions, many of the world's governments, and the bulk of the world's economic and military capabilities" (Huntington, 1999).

3 Political globalisation and associated internationalisation "is regarded as leading to the erosion of the former role and power of the nation state" (Potter, Binns, Elliott & Smith, 1999, p. 75).

These theoretical assumptions about globalisation lead us to enquire if the world is tending towards a convergence or divergence process. The concept of convergence refers to the supposition that the world is going toward a uniform global culture with a standardised pattern of consumption and lifestyle. Cultural convergence can also be seen in countries' alignment with the same political-economic creed. In the contemporary context, this may apply particularly to developing countries in the sense that the political autonomy of such countries is often eroded by external policy-making institutions.

The divergence concept, on the other hand, refers to the fact that "increasing international division of labour, and increasing salience of TNCs [Trans-National Corporations] are leading to enhanced heterogeneity or divergence between nations with respect to their patterns of production, capital accumulation and ownership" (Potter, 2002, p. 193). In other words, in a divergence pattern, "aspects of production and ownership are becoming more unevenly spread, and are generally being concentrated in *specific nodes*" (Potter, 2002, p. 194). Politically it is possible to recognise a divergence tendency where the decision-making process is more concentrated in a few localities and in a few powerful political institutions, which, peacefully or through force, can influence and control national and/or local policies.

In the contemporary world, the existence of economic and political divergence together with cultural convergence is closely linked to the globalisation process and to Gramsci's idea of hegemony. A linear-consequential, but historical-geographic and flexible connection can be drawn between these three arguments (see Figure 10.1).

As stated by Gramsci (in Arrighi, 1993, p. 149) "A social group can, and indeed must, already exercise 'leadership' before winning governmental power (this indeed is one of the principal conditions for winning such power)". Historically there are identifiable sequences

Hegemony	Cultural	Pre-conditions	D
	Political		I
	Economic		S
Globalisation	Cultural	Processes	C
	Political		O
	Economic		U
Convergence	Cultural	Effects	R
Divergence	Political		S
	Economic		E

Figure 10.1: The linkage between hegemony and convergence/divergence effects.

of "global" hegemonic countries/classes.[2] In the modern period, the specific occupiers of the hegemonic throne have often changed, but the socio-economic group in each instance has largely remained that of the "capitalist" class. Spain, the Netherlands, England and the United States were in sequence the power holders. The current "free-enterprise" system has, according to Arrighi:

> … considerably restricted the right and powers of sovereign states. The prin-ciples, norms, and rules to which states must submit have increased in number and become tighter, while a growing number of supranational organisations have acquired an autonomous power to overrule the interstate system (Arrighi, 1993, p. 182).

The main point to note is that these supranational institutions are controlled/managed by a handful of powerful countries. As Brohman (1997, p. 142) points out, key decisions are generally made by the "group of five" (USA, UK, Germany, France and Japan). In the view of some critics, the chief reason why power is skewed in the interests of particular countries is because "decisions at the IMF [International Monetary Fund] and WB are taken on the basis of 'one dollar, one vote' guaranteeing the dominance of both by the US government" (Green in Mowforth & Munt, 1998, p. 290).

After the Second World War, as the "winds of change" blew over the formerly colonised world, a new form of global structure began to emerge which came to be termed neo-colonialism. Neo-colonialism describes a situation in which, crudely put:

> "Colonial powers of the First World and transnational corporations (TNCs) dictated the main thrust of economic policy through the Third World. The IMF, World Bank and other supranational lending agencies along with the TNCs took over the mechanism of power from the former colonial powers" (Mowforth & Munt, 1998, p. 291).

Developed countries' economies expand in part through investing in developing countries and acquiring "raw material" (which includes both environment and culture) in the context of these established labour reserves. In so doing the developed world "transfers the contra-dictions [of capitalism] to a wider sphere, and gives them greater latitude" (Marx in Harvey, 1996, p. 612).

Tourism, seen as a leading global economic sector, can also be analysed as a sector serv-ing or attempting to aid the historical expansion of capitalism. Lefebvre in *The Production of Space* identified the leisure sector as a new one for capitalist exploitation:

> … capitalism, and more generally development, have demonstrated that their survival depends on their being able to extend their reach to space in its entirety: to the *land* (in the process absorbing the towns and agriculture,

---

[2] This phrasing ("countries/classes") is intended to make the point that not all people living in the Western world belong to the hegemonic social class, in the same way that not everyone living in developing countries belong to non-hegemonic social groups.

an outcome already foreseeable in the nineteenth century, but also, and less predictably, creating a new sector altogether – notably that of leisure) ... (Lefebvre, 2002, p. 325).

In this regard, tourism has also been described as a force of neo-colonialism because "it may take the form of exogenous development, controlled by overseas interests with a large proportion of income leaking overseas rather than benefit the host nation" (Page, Brunt, Busby & Connell, 2001, p. 397). One often-cited example is the emergence of certain air carriers to service the former colonial empire and dependencies. The network inherited by airlines like British Airways, Lufthansa, Air France, American Airlines and KLM gave them an advantage in the period of booming air transportation in the 1960s and 1970s (Rodrigue, n.d.).

Critics argue that global policies – including tourism policies – are influenced and even controlled by international institutions that are, in turn, influenced and controlled by the neo-liberal creed. A key institution is the World Trade Organisation (WTO). Worth argues that the WTO was "devised structurally to oversee the practices of global trade", setting itself up in response to the changing economic climate as the institutional "'regulator' of the globalisation process" (Worth, 2003, p. 3). Global tourism policies, being structured under the GATS (General Agreement on Trade in Services), are also embedded within this framework.

The focus on the IMF, WB and WTO comes from the fact that they are recognised as dominant international institutions and they share, with minor differences, a common ideology which they use to gain political leverage to force compliance by most countries (Peet, 2003). It is crucial to note that, central to the spread of the ideology that facilitates neo-liberal globalisation, is the formation and management of a prevalent discourse. As Peet (2003, p. 17) argues:

> The depth of a hegemony resides in the ability of a discursive formation to specify the parameters of the practical, the realistic and the sensible among a group of theoreticians, political practitioners and policy makers [and] where critical discussion is limited to variants of a given discourse.[3]

This viewpoint owes much to the Foucauldian analysis of power. Following Foucault, Sheridan (in Ritzer, 2000, p. 594) contends that the ideas espoused in Foucault's *Archaeology of Knowledge* involve a search for "a set of rules that determine the conditions of possibility for all can be said within the particular discourse at any given time". Peet and Watts also underline the point that:

> For Foucault each society has its *regime of truth*, with control of the 'political economy of truth' constituting part of the power of the great political and economic apparatuses. These diffuse 'truth', particularly in the modern form of 'scientific discourse', through the social body, in a process infused with social

---

[3] In his *Archaeology of Knowledge*, discourse-fields are subject to deep re-interpretation: "we must grasp the statement in the exact specificity of its occurrence; determine its conditions of existence, fix at least its limits, establish its correlation with other statements that may be connected with it, and show what other forms of statements it excludes" (Foucault, 1972, p. 28).

confrontation. In the post-structural view, then, truths are statements within socially produced discourses, rather than facts about reality (Peet & Watts, 1993, p. 228).

Gosovic argues strongly that "intellectual hegemony" exercised at the global level may become a form of "intellectual totalitarianism" due to the limited ability of the less powerful to resist (Gosovic, 2001, p. 134). For Gosovic, there is a clear relationship between this discourse and the current course of world development:

> The intention is to defuse issues and preempt any probing questions that may be posed. They (these discourses) are also meant to convey the basic soundness of the system, suggesting that it is the only possible one, the "best of all possible worlds", and non-controversial with respect to basic structural issues (Gosovic, 2001, p. 138).

In Gosovic's view, much has already been done "through the skilled use of words and terminology both to bolster the dominant paradigm and the current order and to endow it with positive qualities, while belittling, discrediting, or demonising any questioning, challenge, or possible alternatives" (Gosovic, 2000, p. 450). The effect of this global intellectual hegemony has been to shift attention from the relevant structural issues, to "case-by-case or sector-by-sector approaches, that is the focus is on the 'tree' instead on the 'forest' " – a particularly fashionable "tree" at present being "poverty alleviation" (Gosovic, 2001, p. 139).[4]

In the next section the consequential divergence/convergence process will be analysed as an outcome of the capacity of rich countries, through the control of key policy-making institutions, to influence/control tourism development in developing countries. Cultural convergence is indicated by a homogenising process towards a global "Davos culture" and, from a tourist perspective, the standardisation of the tourist product and the policies that derive from this culture. Economic divergence is strongly suggested by the always-greater concentration of wealth and power in fewer tourism companies. Political divergence is emphasised by the concentration of policy making in fewer powerful institutions that are controlled by rich countries and that follow the cultural, economic and political needs and wants of the ruling class of developed countries (hence the erosion of political autonomy of developing countries by external policy-making institutions). Given the search by many developing countries to find ways to develop the tourism sector, it can be argued that the latter is deeply embedded in the effects of divergence/convergence.

Hegemony, Globalisation, Divergence and Tourism

Within the tourism sector it is possible to schematically visualise the structure of tourism within this hegemonic framework (see Figure 10.2). This should be understood in relation

---

[4] It is worth reminding the reader that "Tourism and Poverty Alleviation" is the title of the WTO-OMT report in 2002.

Hegemony	Context	Outcome	Expressions	In tourism
Cultural	Western thought Development/ environmental paradigms	Neo-liberalism Conservation/ commodification of nature	"Davos culture" Lifestyle	Tourism demand
Political	Public institutions/ organisations	International/ national institutions/ organisations	World bank World trade Organisation IMF UN, UNDP, EU, SADC, etc. WTO-OMT governments non-governmental organisations	Tourism policies/ programmes/ projects
Economic	Private capital "Public capital"	Multinational/ national/ local private capital	Hotels, tour operators airlines WTO-OMT, WTTC, WB, etc.	Tourism supply

Figure 10.2: Hegemony structure in global tourism.

to the globalisation process and in particular to the position of developing countries in terms of the convergence/divergence paradigm. As seen in Figure 10.2, the cultural, political and economic hegemonies are organised both through their "conceptual" factors – that is, the cultural influence in lifestyle and political-economic creeds which in turn shape the parameters of the tourism market, particularly those of favoured destination and activities – and "material" factors. The latter include political institutions/organisations, tourism policy-making stakeholders, private capital enterprises and their agents, operators and suppliers.

These three levels of hegemony are, of course, interdependent. Each "hegemony" is supportive of and supported by the other two, leading to a reinforcement of the imbalance in relations of power in the tourism sector specifically and in the global structure more generally. Moreover, they exist within an overlapping matrix where finance-capital can belong to both private and public sources. Consequently these hegemonies are able to lead global tourism in a direction beneficial to their interests, leading to further convergence/divergence.

Against this structural backdrop, western controlled international institutions in the tourism sector have significant power. The views of international agencies such as the WB, the IMF and the European Development Fund, involved in implementing programmes in developing countries, is used to "justify the creation and promotion of investment opportunities, especially those for transnational corporations" (Mowforth & Munt, 1998, p. 104). As Scheyvens points out, indebted countries subject to IMF and WB sponsored Structural Adjustment Programmes "have felt pressure to earn foreign exchange through the growth of tourism" (Scheyvens, 2002, p. 25).

Furthermore, tourism policies in developing countries continue to follow:

> Technocratic models of tourism master planning [that constitute] one component amongst a cluster of tourism-related policies which aimed to promote a particular kind of tourism rooted in a Western economic rationality (Bianchi, 2002, p. 273).

The consequence is that to obtain loans, developing countries must respect conditions imposed by the international funding institutions just mentioned.

It appears that the contemporary neo-liberal policy trend is now established as the preferred practice in tourism development in the context of developing countries. This is clear from the policies of the GATS under which the tourism industry lies. The GATS falls under the umbrella of the WTO and its aim is to "*de*-regulate" the service industry. The GATS is said to represent "perhaps the most important single development in the multi-lateral trading system since the GATT [General Agreement and Tariffs and Trade] itself came into effect in 1948" (WTO in Equations, 2002, p. 6).

Critics argue however that that the GATS cannot be considered as a "fair play" agreement because, "Pushed in the 1980s by developed countries and their corporate lobbies, it is an agreement in which developing countries have played a marginal and defensive role" (WTO in Equations, 2002, p. 6). Honey notes that the agreement "opens up signatory countries to 100% foreign investment in tourism and services", while it rules out the introduction of any protectionist measures (Honey, 1999, p. 32). Its effect may well be to edge out small, independent enterprises, as TNCs and their affiliates with the advantage of financial resources and technology, "muscle their way in to control the tourist trade in countries in the South" (Pleumarom in Honey, 1999, p. 32).

The WTO-OMT (World Tourism Organisation) describes the logic behind the GATS as follows:

> In order to do business as effectively as possible, companies need level playing fields so that they can have equal access to natural resources, expertise, technologies and investment, both within countries and across borders (WTO-OMT in Equations, 2002, p. 6).

The "Millennium Vision" of the WTTC (World Travel and Tourism Council) offers a parallel view, captured in the following imperatives:

1. Get governments to accept travel and tourism as a strategic economic development and employment priority.
2. Move towards open and competitive markets by supporting the implementation of GATS, liberalise air transport and de-regulate telecommunications in international markets.
3. Eliminate barriers to tourism growth, which involves the expansion and improvement of infrastructure – for example, the increase of airport capacity, construction and modernisation of airports, roads and tourist facilities (Pleumarom, n.d. a).

The Economic Commission for Africa report on the GATS policies for Africa notes: "First of all, there may be need for greater liberalisation in all sectors that directly or indirectly impinge on tourism development" (Gauci, Gerosa & Mwalwanda, 2002, p. 21). Here the connection between economic and political hegemonies is clear and both are under the "prestigious" cultural hegemony custody of the capitalist free market, what may be termed the "Davos culture".[5]

The Southern African Context and Comparative Examples

In Southern Africa, as elsewhere in the developing world, tourism is also seen as a new panacea to boost socio-economic development, thanks especially to foreign currency earnings. This section will suggest that the neo-liberal dogma embedded in the international policy-making institutions, twinned with the selective use of discourse, is contributing to align the regional, national and local tourism development paradigms in this region with the global neo-liberal framework.

At a regional level the general agenda of NEPAD (New Economic Partnership for Africa's Development) "is based on national and regional priorities and development plans that must be prepared through participatory processes involving the people" (AU/NEPAD, 2005, p. 4). Tourism has been identified by NEPAD as an important vehicle to address development challenges in the African context, in particular market access and private sector development. Tourism promotion is considered to have significant potential to diversify economic opportunities and generate foreign exchange earnings. According to the AU/NEPAD, in addition to developing local economies, a government-led and private sector-driven tourism industry can "unlock the potential of local communities" (AU/NEPAD, 2005, p. 4).

At a general level, NEPAD recognises five sections where actions have to be focused. These actions include:

- Forging partnerships to maximise the benefits of information sharing and co-operative action.
- Providing Africans, particularly communities, with opportunities to participate in, and benefit from the tourism sector.
- Paying particular attention to issues of safety and security.
- Marketing tourism products in specific areas, such as adventure tourism and eco-tourism.
- Increasing the regional co-ordination of tourism activities and maximising the benefits of the strong inter-regional demand for tourism activities, by developing specialised consumer-targeted marketing campaigns. (AU/NEPAD, 2005, p. 7)

The familiar emphasis on the potentialities of tourism and its reliance on the private sector is noticeable. Moreover, currently *en vogue* Public-Private Partnerships are also invoked in the phraseology of a *government-led and private sector driven tourism industry*. As Honey warns, however, this term ("private–public partnership") "often turns out to be a euphemism for state-provided subsides and services for the private sector" (Honey, 1999, p. 18).

---

[5] "Big tourism-related companies are strongly represented in the WEF – a very powerful and largely unaccountable body where global political and economic policies are often fermented. The WEF also played a key role in initiating the GATT and WTO-OMT" (Pleumarom, n.d. b). Pleumarom regards it as no coincidence that at its 2000 annual meeting in Davos, Switzerland, the WEF gave a special backing to tourism "as a contributor to global prosperity" (Pleumarom, n.d. b).

In Zambia, for example, the "Zambia Poverty Reduction Strategy Paper" notes that "Poverty Reduction Strategy Papers (PRSPs) are prepared in broad consultation with stakeholders and development partners, including the staffs of the WB and IMF" (IMF, 2002). The tourism sector is described in Chapter 7 of this document. Three key issues (from IMF, 2002) demonstrate how closely the outcome falls within neo-liberal principles. Each is considered in turn.

- "For tourism to contribute effectively to the national GDP [Gross Domestic Product], foreign exchange earnings and poverty reduction, there is a need to have a conductive environment for private sector participation, environmentally sustainable growth and good governance".

This statement should be questioned. While private capital can boost national GDP and foreign exchange earnings, there is doubt about the resulting capacity to foster poverty reduction, which should be the first goal of developing countries. The association between development and numerical measurement of economic growth is questionable since it has long been recognised that "Growth without development" (Clover in Binns, 1995, p. 306) can be the (undesirable) result.

- "Large-scale investments have economic linkages, which stimulate and strengthen the creation of small- and medium-scale enterprises".

Here private capital remains pivotal to development, the emphasis being on Transactional Tourism Corporations (TNCs). However, international tourism literature "highlights the many constrains on SMME [Small, Medium and Micro-Enterprises] development in the tourism industry, due to the dominance of large enterprises in the mass tourism industry" (Kirsten & Rogerson, 2002, p. 35).

- "*Land tenure*: The process of acquiring land for infrastructure development is slow, thus inhibiting investment in the sector".

Inevitably in southern Africa, land becomes a main focus of privatisation within the tourism sector. This follows the trend to privatise the means of production, and also basic needs such as health, education, transport and so on, while "social discourses are now frowned upon and have virtually disappeared from official usage" – and one of these discourses is land reform (Gosovic, 2000, p. 450).

Finally the Zambian document (IMF, 2002) summarises the three key elements of the tourism policy framework:

- The emphasis is private sector driven development.
- The sector encourages environmentally sustainable growth.
- The government's policy in the tourism sector is to create an enabling environment for private sector participation; provide adequate infrastructure and legislation for the growth of the sector; and encourage *balanced* community involvement aimed at poverty reduction in rural areas (emphasis added) (IMF, 2002, p. 68).

Again the role of the government seems to facilitate profit opportunities for private sector with the *balanced* involvement of the local community, instead of a focus on the local

community and tackling the roots of poverty through land reform and community empowerment, where tourism can contribute parallel to other sectors of the economy.

The WTTC report on South African Tourism (WTTC, 1998, p. 3) states, in barely dis-
guised alignment with the above, that "It should be read with regard towards globalisation,
privatisation, regionalisation and public/private sector driven market economies". This is
the context for the following quote from the Tourism Planning framework for the O R
Tambo District Municipality, a policy drafted by the European Union (EU)-supported Wild
Coast Programme:

> The private sector have a very important role to play, and a significant amount
> of effort should go into establishing more effective working relationships
> with existing private sector operators (even if they are mostly white) and in
> developing black entrepreneurs in tourism (as opposed to focussing too
> much on the community tourism model) (Norton, 2003, p. 32).

In his work on the recent history of international co-operation in tourism development in
the South Pacific Region, Sofield develops an apposite analysis of foreign (and specifically
EU) involvement in tourism projects. Sofield underlines that the "three areas of colonial
domination of the political, economic and cultural may be interpreted as a manifestation
of dependency theory" (Sofield, 2003, p. 164).[6] In his analysis:

> Core-periphery dependency in a new guise is insinuated into the region …
> There is an alternative assessment which suggests that the degree of European
> Community control over the regional tourism development program has
> itself been neo-colonialist, notwithstanding the various achievement of the
> South Pacific Tourism Organisation (Sofield, 2003, pp. 185, 188).

Possible Ways Forward

While alternative solutions could come from co-operation between developing countries, it
may be that this is no longer enough. For example, the India–Brazil–South Africa (IBSA)
Dialogue Forum (IBSA, n.d.), under the tourism section, noted that "the three countries
agreed to pursue a common approach with regard to the activities of the World Tourism
Organisation (WTO) and other relevant multi-lateral fora". However this situation is unlikely
to effect any real change on a fundamentally neo-liberal approach that undermines the possibility of alternative developmental discourses. Regional co-operation can be seen as a
friendly re-arrangement of the neo-liberal global system, a mere smokescreen. It seems, in
a World Order Approach, "part of and reinforces the prevailing hegemonic order, based on
the neo-liberal project and 'there is little evidence that new identities are challenging old,
or that cultural barriers and stereotype are being broken down'" (Söderbaum, 2002, p. 12;
Kearns & Hook in Söderbaum, 2002, p. 12).

---

[6] Note that these are the three areas featured in Figure 10.1 and much of the first section of this article is devoted
to discussing them.

Essentially permitting the process to operate largely unhindered, is a cross-cutting alliance between ruling classes within and between countries. Crucial to understanding the process is the proverbial straightjacket in which elites in developing countries often find themselves. Some elites might be consciously complicit, but in many cases:

> ... local elites are complicit in the underdevelopment of their states, not as an instrument of capital but as a result of the prevailing ideological climate of privatisation and deregulation in which the range of development options available to them has became even more constrained (Bianchi, 2002, p. 289).

Not that there is blindness to the danger. President Thabo Mbeki addressed the SI (Socialist International) and drew specific attention to the organisation's principles, specifically, that there is a duty to "...oppose the neo-liberal market ideology, the neo-conservative agenda and the unilateral approach" (Mbeki, 2004, p. 168). Echoing President Mbeki in an article entitled "Refocusing its intervention" (Eastern Cape Province, 2004, p. 155), the Eastern Cape Provincial authorities concluded, encouragingly that "Shifting power relations are at the heart of poverty eradication". Critics of the current tourism policy in Lesotho voice similar concerns:

> ... it has to be born in mind that the current emphasis on privatisation and private sector driven tourism militates against wider community participation in preference for individual private initiative which is championed for efficiency [consequently] it is also necessary to re-visit privatisation in tourism planning and management (Mashinini, 2003, pp. 91, 92).

Nevertheless, the case of the tourism sector remains deeply problematic. As this modest contribution has shown, different levels of political power all seem to adhere to the TINA climate that "regulates" contemporary political development discourse. Development co-operation and aid, both between and within countries (or a group of countries) should, of course, *continue and possibly intensify*. The issue is to change the rules of co-operation, not to eliminate it. A radical shift may be needed.

This shift is required on two geographical levels. Internationally, regional co-operation should be built as an alternative in which countries have the institutional space to work together. In practice this could mean the provision of multi-lateral fora in which development discourse is re-examined in the light of alternative approaches and solutions which better fit local realities, and where there exists a more democratic arrangement in terms of power relations within such newly formed institutions. The impression continues that "post-modern" (case-by-case) approach has been and continues to enjoy much support within the "modern" homogeneous policy-making institutions. It is this one-dimensional, case-by-case approach that needs to be questioned. What is needed is a "collective perception and a joint stand with respect to the global challenges, structures, regimes and indeed the intellectual paradigm that underpin them" (Gosovic, 2001, p. 144).

At a national level, stress should be placed on the co-operation between public structures and the communities they serve, by-passing the focus on private capital investment, which is often unrelenting in its pursuit of self-sustaining profit at the expense of holistic development approaches.[7] A public sector community alliance should be remodeled followed by the development of a more differentiated and comprehensive tourism development model.

Two problems relating to community involvement and public institutions need to be addressed briefly here. First, the situation in which community involvement is essentially top-down – that is, where the limit of involvement is pre-determined by policy-making institutions – needs to be avoided. Instead, we need to consider long-term empowerment. It should be a process of "insertion" into the hegemonic development *ideology*, not a process where the community is involved in a mere organisational capacity, subject to directives and a governing framework that has originated and is managed externally. Mere involvement or participation in projects is little more than window-dressing, often deepening the process of homogenisation and furthering a hegemonic ideology.

Facilitation, on the other hand, encourages and diversifies approaches whereby each community can promote its own vision of development. The facilitation process should serve to promote genuine community empowerment. Socio-economic instruments (e.g. education, health, energy infrastructures and land reform/possession) ought to generate development from within, a kind indigenous self-development.

Second, as Sofield notes, "A break may occur between policy implementation and actual result, the so-called 'implementation gap', in which a continuing lack of empowerment frustrates effective action" (Dunsire in Sofield, 2003, p. 191). The need here is to establish *ad hoc* institutions that can facilitate the process. Public institutions should be at the forefront of this process because there is the need for "genuine and enduring (sustainable) empowerment to be based on a constitutionally recognised right and sanctioned within an environment supported by the state" (Sofield, 2003, p. 222).

Conclusion

This chapter has shown how international policy-making institutions under a neo-liberal culture, and its links with private capital, can influence the development process. The tourism sector is particularly well equipped to enhance development in particular historical-geographic contexts, as well as being a vector of intercultural change and understanding. In addition, tourism is capable of stimulating an improvement in sustainable development given that tourism itself depends on its environmental, cultural and socio-economic sustainability.

Nevertheless, as this chapter has tried to demonstrate, a certain discursive hegemony, regulated under the umbrella of policy-making institutions, is able to exert undue influence over the tourism sector. The conclusion of this modest contribution on the role of tourism

---

[7] The author would like to underline that the advocated change in policy framework does not mean the abolition of the private sector *tout court* – especially (but not only) small local family owned and run enterprises such as retail shops and craftsmanship – but rather the transformation of the general framework in which they work. In addition private companies should be limited in their power to control specific sectors of public importance such as water, energy, health, education and so on. A mixed or differentiated economy is advocated.

in developing countries' development is that contemporary tourism in developing countries, managed and organised within a neo-liberal logic, is perpetuating the gap between rich and poor (and this, both between *and* within countries). This is traced to non-localised control of the decision-making process.

This is valid for traditional mass tourism as well as alternative tourism, a form of tourism often seen as a more "redistributive". As noted, in the case of alternative forms of tourism such as community-based eco-tourism:

> Eco-tourism is far from fulfilling its promise to transform the way in which modern, conventional tourism is conducted. With few exceptions, it has not succeeded in moving beyond a narrow niche market to a set of principles and practices that infuses the entire tourism industry (Honey, 1999, p. 394).

There are alternatives and they need to be supported. Certainly in a "geo-political context in which left alternatives to free market capitalism, whether communist or social democratic [or any other alternative political perspective], have all but disappeared as viable possibilities" (Peet, 2002, p. 78), it is worth reminding ourselves that as Raymond Williams insisted, "the hegemonic" is neither total nor exclusive:

> … hegemony is not singular; indeed … its own internal structures are highly complex, and have continually to be renewed, recreated and defended; and by the same token … they can be continually challenged and in certain respects modified (Williams, 1976, p. 205).

As Gosovic points out, "Any specific global intellectual hegemony is a passing phenomenon, for hegemonies in general do not last," (Gosovic, 2001, p. 143). Rather, oppositional cultures continue to exist (Peet, 2003, p. 21). We need to confront the monolithic perspective on the meaning of development, re-proposing the active role of public structures – in conjunction with stressing the role of civil society in the decision-making process of development planning.

> "I obviously do not deny the struggle for existence, but I maintain that the progressive development of the animal kingdom, and especially of mankind, is favoured much more by mutual support than by mutual struggle". (Kessler in Kropotkin, 1902).

Acknowledgements

The author would like to acknowledge the support of the Faculty of Humanities of the University of KwaZulu-Natal. The author would like to thank Dr. Shirley Brooks for providing help and support in completing this article. He would also like to thank Professor Robert Preston-Whyte for comments on an initial draft.

References

Arrighi, G. (1993). The three hegemonies of historical capitalism. In: S. Gill (Ed), *Gramsci, historical materialism and international relations* (pp. 148–187). Cambridge: Cambridge University Press.

AU/NEPAD (2005). African Union/New Partnership for Africa's Development Tourism Action Plan.

Bianchi, R. V. (2002). Toward a new political economy of global tourism. In: R. Sharpley, & D. J. Telfer (Eds), *Tourism and development concepts and issues* (pp. 265–299). Clevedon: Channel View Publications.

Binns, T. (1995). Geography in development: Development in geography. *Geography, 80*(4), 303–322.

Britton, S. G. (1981). *Tourism, dependency and development: A mode of analysis.* Occasional Paper no. 23. Australian National University Press, Canberra.

Brohman, J. (1997). *Popular development. Rethinking the theory and practice of development.* Oxford: Blackwell.

Dieke, P. U. C. (2000). *The political economy of tourism in Africa.* Elmsford: Cognizant Communication Corporation.

Eastern Cape Province (2004). Refocusing its intervention. New Agenda, 15, 154–155.

Equations (2002). Weighing the GATS on a development. The Case of Tourism in Goa, India. Available at http://www.somo.nl [Accessed 10-03-2003].

Forgacs, D. (1998). *A Gramsci reader selected writing 1916–1935.* London: Lawrence and Wishart.

Foucault, M. (1972). *The archeology of knowledge.* New York: Harper and Row.

Gauci, A., Gerosa, V., & Mwalwanda, C. (2002). *Tourism in Africa and the multilateral trading system: Challenges and opportunities.* Economic Commission for Africa.

Gosovic, B. (2000). Global intellectual hegemony and the international development agenda. *International Social Science Journal, 166*(52), 447–456.

Gosovic, B. (2001). Global intellectual hegemony and the international development Agenda. Available at http://tcdc.undp.org/coopsouth/2001_2/132-146.pdf [Accessed 2-08-2005].

Goulet, D. (1988). "Development" – or liberation. In: C. K. Wilber (Ed.), *The political economy of development and underdevelopment.* New York: Random House Business Division.

Hall, M. C. (1998). *Tourism and politics policy, power and place.* Chichester: John Wiley & Sons.

Harvey, D. (1996). The geography of capitalist accumulation. In: J. Agnew, D. N. Livingstone, & Rogers A. (Eds), *Human geography an essential anthology.* Oxford: Blackwell.

Honey, M. (1999). *Ecotourism and sustainable development who owns paradise?* Washington, DC: Island Press.

Huntington, S. P. (1999). Keynote Address. Presented at the *Colorado College's 125th Anniversary Symposium.* Cultures in the 21st Century: Conflict and Convergence. Available at http://www.coloradocollege.edu [Accessed 3-31-2006].

IBSA. India–Brazil–South Africa (IBSA) Dialogue Forum: Plan of Action. Available at http://www.dfa.gov.za [Accessed 23-03-2004].

IMF (2002). Zambia Poverty Reduction Strategy paper. Available at http://www.imf.org/External/NP/prsp/2002/zmb/01 [Accessed 2003-08-07].

Kirsten, M., & Rogerson, C. M. (2002). Tourism, business linkages and small enterprise development in South Africa. *Development Southern Africa, 19*(1), 29–60.

Kropotkin, P. (1902). Mutual aid: A factor of evolution. Available at http://www.calresco.org [Accessed 9-25-2003].

Lefebvre, H. (2002). *The production of space.* Oxford: Blackwell.

Lindberg, K., Molstad, A., Hawkins, D., & Jamieson, W. (2001). International development assistance in tourism. *Annals of Tourism Research, 28*(2), 508–511.

Macey, D. (2000). *The penguin dictionary of critical theory.* Harmondsworth: Penguin Books.

Mashinini, V. (2003). Tourism policies and strategies in Lesotho. A critical appraisal. *Africa Insight*, *33*(1/2), 87–92.

Mayo, P. (1999). *Gramsci, Freire and Adult Education*. London: Zed Book.

Mbeki, T. (2004). A people-centred new world order, October 2003. *New Agenda*, *15*, 165–168.

Milne, S., & Ateljevic, I. (2001). Tourism, economic development and the global-local nexus: Theory embracing complexity. *Tourism Geographies*, *3*(4), 369–393.

Mowforth, M., & Munt, I. (1998). *Tourism and sustainability new tourism in the Third World*. London: Routledge.

Norton, P. (2003). Tourism planning framework for the O R Tambo District Municipality, supported by *The EU Wild Coast Programme*. Prepared by Peter Norton & Associates cc.

Page, S. J., Brunt, P., Busby, G., & Connell, J. (2001). *Tourism: A modern synthesis*. London: Thomson Learning.

Peet, R. (2002). Ideology, discourse and the geography of hegemony: From socialist to neoliberal development in postapartheid South Africa. *Antipode*, *34*(1), 54–84.

Peet, R. (2003). *Unholy Trinity: The IMF, World Bank and WTO*. London: Zed Book.

Peet, R., & Watts, M. (1993). Introduction: Development theory and environment in the age of market triumphalism. *Economic Geography*, *1*, 227–253.

Pleumarom, A. (n.d. a). Tourism, globalisation and sustainable development, Available at http://www.twnside.or.sg [Accessed 14-07-2002].

Pleumarom, A. (n.d. b). Campaign on Corporate Power in Tourism. Available at http://www.twnside.org.sg [Accessed 14-07-2002].

Potter, R. B. (2002). Global convergence, divergence and development. In: V. Desai, & R. B. Potter (Eds), *The companion to development studies* (192–196). London: Arnold.

Potter, R. B., Binns, T., Elliott, J., & Smith, D. (1999). *Geographies of development*. Harlow: Longman.

Ritzer, G. (2000). *Sociological theory*. New York: McGraw-Hill Higher Education.

Rodrigue, J. P. (n.d.) Air transport. Available at http://people.hofstra.edu/geotrans [Accessed 24-02-2003].

Scheyvens, R. (2002). *Tourism for development empowering community*. Harlow: Prentice Hall.

Seers, D. (1969). The meaning of development. *International Development Review*, *11*(4), 2–6.

Söderbaum, F. (2002). Rethinking the New Regionalism. Paper for the *XIII Nordic Political Science Association meeting*, Aalborg 15–17 August Workshop Session 23: Regions and Regionalization.

Sofield, T. H. B. (2003). *Empowerment for sustainable tourism development*. Oxford: Pergamon.

Teo, P., Chang, T. C., & Ho, K. C. (2001). Introduction: Globalisation and interconnectedness in Southeast Asian Tourism. In: Teo, P, Chang T. C., & Ho K. C. (Eds), *Interconnected worlds. Tourism in Southeast Asia* (pp. 1–9). Amsterdam: Pergamon.

Williams, R. (1976). Base and superstructure in Marxist cultural theory. In: Dale, R., Esland, G., & MacDonald, M. (Eds), *Schooling and capitalism. A sociological reader* (pp. 202–210). Maidenhead: The Open University Press.

World Bank (n.d.), World Bank revisits role of tourism in development. Available at http://web.worldbank.org [Accessed 17-03-2003].

Worth, O. (2003). Making sense of globalisation: A neo-Gramscian analysis of the practices of neoliberalism. No. 6. Available at http://www.politics.ul.ie

WTO-OMT (2002). *Tourism and poverty alleviation*. World Tourism Organization. Available at http://www.world-tourism.org. Accessed on 20 October 2003.

WTTC (1998). South Africa's travel and tourism economic driver for the 21st century.

Chapter 11

The Politics of Tourism: Ethnic Chinese Spaces in Malaysia

K. Thirumaran

Introduction

Southeast Asia is experiencing an era of strong growths in Chinese tourist arrivals.[1] Malaysia like many countries in the region has numerous ethnic Chinese heritage sites that reflect over 6 centuries of relations with China.[2] However, the Malaysian government turned its attention only recently, to the potential use of ethnic Chinese heritage for the purposes of tourism. A confluence of intensifying relations with China and the dynamics of Malay majority and ethnic Chinese minority politics in Malaysia appears to have an impact on the tourism landscape. This chapter argues that Malaysia's tourism policy has crossed the Rubicon of Malay ethno-nationalism, which comes to terms with global realignments and local political realities that allows for ethnic Chinese heritage to emerge in the tourism landscape.

A periodized examination of the local–global politics clarifies the limits of national tourism space for Malaysia's ethnic Chinese citizens. The period from 1957 (independence) to 1990 (election year) analyses the limited space provided to ethnic Chinese Malaysians in national tourism efforts. The period from 1991 to May 2005 reveals a transforming nation-scape that recognizes and allows for greater ethnic Chinese space in the tourism industry.[3] Issues related to tourism in Malaysia raises two critical questions about the use of Chinese

---

[1] Between 1996–2000, East Asian and South Asian tourist arrivals into Thailand, Malaysia and Singapore have more than doubled. Tourists from China and India are courted by all three countries with numerous country offices and frequently changing marketing efforts aimed at attracting these tourists (WTO, 2002, pp. 517–518, 796–797, 724–726; WTO, 2001, pp. 79–82, 89–92 and 93–95; Day, 2004 and see also King, 1993, p. 109).

[2] The phrase "ethnic Chinese" throughout this chapter refers to the citizens of Malaysia who are of Chinese descent. The word "Chinese" when used by itself, refers to citizens of China or tourists originating from China.

[3] I use the word "transforming" rather than "transformed" to imply that the extension of tourism space for ethnic Chinese heritage is a slow process that is peppered with caution and a project that is ongoing.

---

heritage. First, how does Malaysia's domestic politics and economic pragmatism affect the way ethnic Chinese spaces expand or contract? Second, does a benevolent and capitalist oriented China have a direct impact on Malaysia's ethnic Chinese heritage and tourism development? I contend that local response to tourism opportunities that China presents is dependent on Malaysia's domestic majority–minority politics and the nature of China's international relations.

Literature

Tourism is an exchange, which involves both local and international politics (Hall, 1994). The argument that governments participate in tourism strategies for economic gains (Elliott, 1997) does not fully explain the nuances behind the State's purposeful presence. Beyond economic importance, the State becomes the manager or policy initiator to reconcile national and tourists interest. Many of the governments in the Caribbean "assist" through state funds to internationalize local cultural festivals (Robertson, 1988, p. 33). These local festivals such as the Jamaica Festival and the Barbados Crop-Over festivities are directed towards international tourism with an ultimate goal to increase foreign reserves and employment for the small states (*ibid.*).

There are always social and political ramifications for the government if the State isolates from the market processes. As Richter (1989) points out, the political dimensions of tourism usually call for managed tourism. Governments posses formidable authority to shape marketing efforts and selection of tourism assets for presentation. Often than not tourism assets are intertwined with local socio-cultural elements which requires delicate dealing given the circumstances of the country as is the case of Malaysia. There are also tourism products that chiefly target resident visitors rather than tourists. The complexities of local concerns may also provide sufficient ground for governments to ensure presentations do not transgress national interests.

Of the many reasons, governments also use tourism as a symbol of close friendship between two countries (Craik, 1997; Richter, 1989). Tourism certainly reflects the level of diplomatic relations and people-to-people relations. These relations bring forth security as well as economic benefits for both countries involved. Therefore, tourism is "inherently political" (Hall, 1994, p. 3) because it is embedded with power dimensions within the local and between the local and global forces.

Methodology

Said (1993, p. xv) posits that cultural studies should not be "antiseptically quarantined from its worldly affiliations but as an extraordinarily varied field of endeavour." My aim is to draw on history and place specificity to highlight conditions of local–global negotiation to accentuate the nuances and to articulate the new paradigm in Malaysia's heritage and tourism policy. I use periodization as a methodology to analyse the complexity of the use of heritage by politicians in a majority–minority relationship between Malay and ethnic

Chinese citizens in order to show how these interactions reflect a transforming tourism landscape. The fieldwork emanates from 6 years of industry experience in the region that involved bringing tourists from Singapore to Malaysia. As a participant observer on guided tours and with frequent site inspections in Malacca, Kuala Lumpur and Penang (prominent Malaysian destinations), I was able to solicit information from a wide circle of ground operators. The first part of the chapter examines the genealogy of Malaysian politics and tourism since independence. The second part of the chapter analyses the critical phases of ethnic Chinese transformations and the China nexus. Finally, the chapter looks at the ambiguous political and tourism energy that reverberates amongst the ethnic Chinese and Malay communities in Malaysia.

Discussion and Analysis

Colonial Legacy

Two critical factors that made an indelible mark on the political and tourism landscape are the historical legacy of colonialism and migration patterns. Prior to Western colonialism, Southeast Asian kingdoms and trading centres like Malacca had tributary relationship with China (Abraham et al., 2002; Cartier, 2001; 1998; Wang, 1992). China's internal dynastic struggles and changes in perceptions resulted in periodic absence of Sino-Southeast Asian binding ties. Part of the Malay Peninsula (Malacca) was colonized by the Portuguese in 1511 and thereafter it changed hands to the Dutch and later to the British who eventually assumed authority for the whole peninsula including Singapore and parts of Borneo island (Brunei, Sabah and Sarawak) in the South China Sea. Colonization also left an uneasy socio-political structure among the different Malay and Chinese communities.

The ethnic Chinese migrants and their descendants of pre-colonial Malaya are known as *Peranakans* or Straits Chinese. These are ethnic Chinese who had acculturalized to local Malay ways of life by adopting some features of the Malay dressing, delicacy, language and customs. The second wave of immigrants came during the colonial period in search of jobs and a better life. Many intended to return home after saving enough. Operational needs of tin mines and rubber plantations accelerated migration of workers from China. Most of the Chinese who came during colonial period settled in Malaysia and became citizens of then newly independent Malaysia in 1957.

Malaysia's independence was marked by regional and global tensions: communists against democrats, Greater Indonesia against independent Malaysia, British desires to withdraw from the "East" and realignments along the East–West ideological grid, issues related to power sharing between majority–minority and indigenous-immigrant citizens (Stockwell, 2003; Worden, 2003). Malaysia perceived communism and China as threats during the Cold War. Despite the presence of many Malays in the Malayan Communist Party (MCP), the dominant member of the ruling coalition – United Malays National Organization (UMNO) used British lenses to project the MCP as a Chinese menace (Cheah, 1979). The MCP argued for dual Malaysia and Chinese citizenship (Heng, 1998), which ran contrary to postcolonial nation-building objectives of Malaysia. The Malaysian "state of emergency" ended in 1960 and the communists dwindled to a small band of guerrilla fighters.

Malaysia initially restricted and even prevented people-to-people relations and cultural exchanges with China. Ibrahim (1998), a social anthropologist, reckons that the pattern of colonial bureaucracy and services rendered has left a legacy of racial taxonomies adopted and internalized by the new Malay plutocrats of independent Malaysia.

Yet Malaysia was the first ASEAN (Association of Southeast Asian Nations) member state to establish diplomatic ties with China in 1974.[4] While the West portrayed the Soviet Union as the biggest threat to the region during the Cold War, Southeast Asian countries perceived the Chinese as the main threat. Asian communist movements came under the influence of communist China (Brimmel, 1959). Nian's (1993) study of literary works and mass media suggests strong nationalistic fervour oriented towards China in the early years following independence. Books and magazines published in the People's Republic of China were banned and materials from China were carefully vetted before allowed to circulate in Malaysia. Only a few scholars had access to restricted publications originating from China (Wang, 2002). According to Tsing (2003, p. 46), from the mid-1960s to the early 1970s, Malaysian Chinese dance skits conformed much to the patterns of the Cultural Revolution (1966–1977) in China. The study of Chinese language was discouraged and Malay became the medium of instruction in public schools (Tan, 2000). Heng (1998), political scientist, observed that ethnic Chinese Malaysians following independence had deep attachment to Chinese identity. Their leadership was mainly through the merchant class. On the other hand, Malay hegemony was concerned with the extent Malaysia's ethnic Chinese had connections to "motherland" China.

Worden (2003, p. 31) argues that in the 1970s and 1980s, Malaysia embarked on distinguishing the Malay history within territorial Malaysia and promoted national heritage that excluded the "wider Malay World" and the other ethnic groups. This process entailed a systematic division of the ethnic groups into the orientalist categories of race: Malays, Chinese, Indians and others. In 1971, the National Congress on Culture defined Malaysian culture as having core elements of Malay culture and complementary elements selected from the non-indigenous and Islamic based genres (Din, 1997, pp. 109–110). The State encouraged Malay and indigenous cultural performances. Until recently, national tourism marketing efforts promoted Malay and indigenous cultures. Nevertheless, there was a concerted effort within the tourism industry dominated by Chinese travel agents to display the multitudinous Malaysian culture that included Chinese, Indian and Malay attractions. In the 1980s, the government promoted Malay involvement in the tourism business as part of a larger effort to increase distribution of national wealth that favoured the economically disadvantaged Malays (Khalifah & Tahir, 1997, p. 177). The Malay hegemonic project also included the facilitation of Malay travel agents in an ethnic Chinese dominated industry (Richter, 1993, p. 192). The more capital-oriented elements of the industry such as coach and hotel businesses continued to be mainly ethnic Chinese owned. Malay involvement in the tourism business did not affect Chinese dominance in the industry as it coincided with the promotion of Malaysia as a tourist destination for Muslims in the region and the Middle East.

---

[4] In 1974, ASEAN comprised only Malaysia, Thailand, Philippines, Indonesia and Singapore. Today its membership includes Brunei Darrulsalem, Myanmar, Vietnam, Laos and Cambodia.

International Politics Affecting Local Responses

The former Soviet Union underwent changes in the 1980s with the ascendance of Gorbachev. Gorbachev instituted political openness (*glasnost*) and economic reforms (*perestroika*) at home and conducted a benevolent foreign policy. Communism as an alternative political ideology waned. Both China and the former Soviet Union and later known as the Russian Federation withdrew support to many of the communist insurgents the world over. The communist insurgents in Malaysia dominated by ethnic Chinese had one less ally.

In 1980, the late supreme leader of China, Deng Xiaoping introduced the citizenship law which barred ethnic Chinese from another country to claim Chinese citizenship. The MCP abandoned violent struggles in 1989. China's sterling economy is emerging as one of the power houses of Asia which offers Southeast Asian countries with economic opportunities and stronger political ties. The Western power projections–Asian reception paradigm has transformed into a multi-faceted grid which now seem premised on an emerging powers–Asian enterprise era. Modern China is both a source of labour as well as tourists (Lau, 2004). Its role in ASEAN Regional Forum (ARF) and as a member of World Trade Organisation brings China into a highly respectable and desirable relationships for countries seeking both market opportunities and at the same time rear-guarding competition (see also Ott, 2004).

The emergence of a neighbourly China as viewed by Malaysia and fragmentation of Malay politics from the 1980s concurrently led to a shift in national cultural policy. The Malaysian government in 1980s under the Mahathir administration was not too keen to give a cultural space to the Chinese in the earlier part of his premiership. By the mid-1980s, Malaysia allowed bona fide professionals to conduct business with China. Wong (2002, pp. 37–38), a social anthropologist, ascribes a list of entities belonging to the "China Circle" which curiously does not include the ethnic Chinese citizens of Malaysia, Indonesia and Thailand. His list includes Singapore, Macao, Taiwan and Hong Kong as part of a network of capital enterprises with potential sources of power as counter to the West. This further illustrates the successful disconnections the Malaysian State has weaved into commercial ties and further distanced Malaysia's ethnic Chinese affinities with mainland China since independence.

By the 1990s, on the international front, Malaysia and China had moved towards a degree of people-to-people contacts with greater freedom to study, travel and conduct business with each other (Curley & Lie, 2002; Tan, 2004). As far as education tourism is concerned, over 9000 Chinese students study in Malaysia and form the largest group of foreign students (Hong, 2005). This is a marked increase from 4725 Chinese students in 2002 (Ahmad, 2004b). Another 4000 skilled Chinese labourers from China work in the ceramics and furniture industries of Malaysia (Lau, 2004). More recently, the Chinese embassy has even worked with many local institutions to promote Chinese culture and links to China. For example, in conjunction with Malaysia's 55th National Day celebration and the Chinese Cultural Heritage Festival (Malaysia), the Peoples Republic of China's embassy collaborated closely with the Corporate Communication students from Kuala Lumpur Infrastructure University College (KLIUC) to present cultural performances and exhibitions (KLIUC drums up, 2004). These interrelationships between China and Malaysian ethnic Chinese is also favoured by the Malaysian government's desire to promote ethnic Chinese heritage found in Malacca to Chinese visitors (Ganesan, 2003).

Local Political Alignments

Fragmentation in local Malay politics and the absence of the China factor in insurgency movements converge to open a heritage tourism space previously not viable because of Malay fears, cultural hegemony and Cold War politics.

Management of ethnic minority relations in Malaysia is characterized by Malay hegemony and accommodation (see also Suryadinata, 2000). In 2005, Malaysia's population mix totalled 27 million people. Some 35% of them are ethnic Chinese citizens, 8% are of Indian origins and the remaining majority of 47% compose of Malays and other indigenous groups (Kuppusamy, 2005, p. 15). Most ethnic Chinese consider themselves as citizens of Malaysia rather than as overseas Chinese. Many Malaysian Chinese wield recognizable economic influence but limited political and cultural power. These ethnic Chinese are themselves not a homogenous group; there are some eight different sub-groups of dialects and a socio-culturally distinct group known as the *Peranakans*. The ethnic Chinese are politically a disparate group and divided between the Gerakan and Malaysian Chinese Association (MCA) political parties and not to mention the so-called multi-racial party of Democratic Action Party (DAP).[5] This fragmentation is significant when compared with the Indian minority, whose members are mostly under a single party called Malaysian Indian Congress (MIC) aligned to the ruling coalition of Barisan National (BN).[6]

Kahn (2001, pp. 125–126), posits the Chinese as absent in the Malay imaginary and just as the "British viewed the Chinese as a threat to the Malays," the views of the Malays too are synonymous with the British. On the contrary, Mandal (2002, p. 63) believes that there exist brotherhood between the majority Malay and Chinese minority which is evident in theatrical plays. In the Malaysian political landscape, it was not until after the 1991 elections, that the Malay leaders expressed closer cooperation with ethnic Chinese politicians and their constituents. The gravitation to court Chinese votes was due to an increase in the split of the Malay votes between UMNO – the dominant member of the ruling party and the Parti Islam Se Malaysia (PAS) – the opposition party.[7] With Malay support eroding in Malay majority constituencies, the 1990s witnessed Malay political elites easing and warming up to the Chinese resulting in a new Chinese university and a relaxed language policy. During his administration, former Prime Minister Mahathir even suggested the possibility of a non-Malay becoming Prime Minister (Liu, 2000).

In the last decade, cultural policy in Malaysia shifted with fragmentation of Malay political support. The Islamic based party-PAS had strengthened their parliamentary presence and popularity among Malay voters over UMNO in the 1999 general election. On the other hand, the coalition partners within the BN, such as Gerakan and MCA garnered strong support from the assigned precincts, some of which has a minority of Malay voters. The majority of Malays formed the support base of UMNO's political power. In the 1990s,

---

[5] The MCA and Gerakan parties are ethnic Chinese based parties. They are also part of the umbrella group called Barisan National (BN). The BN also consists of UMNO – a Malay based party, which is the dominant and leading partner in the coalition government. The DAP portrays itself as multi-ethnic group but is dominated by ethnic Chinese and is one of the main opposition parties.

[6] Several other parties from the state of Sabah and Sarawak also add on to the list of BN members.

[7] Both UMNO and PAS are Malay based parties.

the Malays who formed the majority electorates were disenfranchised with UMNO, the premier political party within BN. Hence, UMNO sought to favour greater integration with the Chinese community to balance out the loss of Malay support base. BN candidates had to rely more heavily on Chinese voters to win the 1999 elections (Ho, 2002). Within the first few weeks of becoming Prime Minister of Malaysia in 2003, Abdullah Badawi high-lighted his Chinese ancestry by inviting his distant relatives from China to visit him in Malaysia. The fact that this took place so close to the national elections reveal that politi-cally the ethnic Chinese are important in the power configurations that divide the Malay mass as well as the two opposing Malay based parties: UMNO and PAS.[8]

Courting the Chinese Vote through Heritage Tourism

Next, we explore the tourism landscape in Malacca (one of 13 Malaysian States) to illus-trate the manifestation of local–global politics. Malacca is where Malaysia's first Prime Minister, Tunku Abdul Rahman read the declaration of independence on February 20, 1956. Ambiguity may still linger in State policies towards ethnic Chinese heritage in Malaysia on some instances. However, dialogues and initiatives appear to open spaces for ethnic Chinese heritage presentation especially during politically charged periods like a general election. Three key attractions from the historic city of Malacca highlight a close relationship between politics and tourism. They are the manner in which tours are con-ducted in Malacca, creation of the Zheng He Gallery and the Light and Sound attraction. This interconnection between local politics and development of ethnic Chinese heritage in the name of tourism further elaborates the confluence of politics and tourism.

Tours in Malacca

The city of Malacca is rich with heritage sites spanning from the period of Malay Kingdom to the colonial era. On a typical city tour, tour commentaries follow state discourses that emphasize the history of European conquests, colonial heritage and Malay legendary heroes like Hang Tuah and Hang Jebat.[9] Tour Guides mostly choose to talk about the his-torical legacy of the westerners but miss out information about the *Bukit Cina* cemetery in Malacca and the intermarriage of Chinese and Malays during the period of Malacca Sultanate.[10]

Historically, the Malay royalty readily accepted and even married members of the Chinese community without the present prisms of ethno-religious demarcations and restrictions.

---

[8] There was also a third political party known as Keadilan which is a party formed by the former Deputy Prime Minister Anwar Ibrahim's wife following his sacking from UMNO. This party too attracted a large number of Malay voters, thus creating further divisions.

[9] On six different occasions and each consisting of a 3.5 hours guided tour between 1996–2004, I found that Malaysian Tourism Board licensed tour guides did not expound on ethnic Chinese heritage in Malacca much. Only one tourist guide touched on the topic of mixed marriages between the Chinese courtiers and local princes prior to the arrival of the Portuguese in 1511 and later the British in 1826.

[10] In 1984, the State government was determined to redevelop this historical cemetery. According to Cartier, a multi-cultural opposition successfully articulated the place's "collective identity formation and symbolic national

As Cartier (1998, p. 76) points out, the *Bukit Cina* tussle of the mid-1980s raises an important issue about the gap between the State's vision of national culture and the vernacular lived experience and perception. The state government's plans to develop the cemetery land in the 1980s met with strong community as well as national opposition. Community leaders had also approached China to add diplomatic pressure on the Malaysian government for reconsideration.[11] This act goes to show that ethnic Chinese in Malaysia have a strong sense of pride for their heritage and at times may call on China to assist in their local causes. Ethnic Chinese from all over Malaysia showed common cause to defend the sacred hill from being flattened. The Ethnic Chinese perceived the Malay led state had neglected Chinese heritage in the town altogether (Worden, 2003, p. 38). Attempts to register Malacca City as UNESCO (United Nations Educational Scientific and Cultural Organisation) World Heritage Site have thus far failed. UNESCO's disapproval stems from lack of preservation and promotion of contributions of ethnic Chinese in Malacca (Worden, 2003, p. 39). In early 2006, the state government expressed its desire to gazette a number of heritage sites (Tan, 2006a,b). However, *Bukit Cina* is not in the list and remains unclassified as a heritage site.

The inclusion of the Cheng Hoon Teng Temple (considered the oldest in Malacca) and exclusion of the Peranakan museums in a typical seat-in-coach Malacca city tour are also telling. Tour operators and hotels which are mostly Chinese owned and some tourist guides who are ethnic Chinese may also have had a role in the itinerary choice of the tour operators. Nevertheless, accounts were either superficial or completely left out by tourist guides concerning the historical legacy of *Bukit Cina* and stories of the early Chinese settlers and their mixed marriages with local princes.[12] While the national discourse was to promote heritage with Malay elements, which would include the Peranakan culture, the tourism experience on the ground could be diametrically different for organized group tours.

Within Malacca city, the colonial buildings by St. Paul's Hill house Malay cultural and historical artefacts. Once again, Malay culture gains prominence despite the presence of ethnic Chinese and "Eurasian" heritage.[13] The Baba Nyonya Heritage Museum exhibiting the pre-colonial *Baba* or *Peranakan* Chinese culture is one of the few attractions given a role in heritage tourism. Worden (2003), observes that the heritage of the ethnic Chinese who came during the colonial period lacked representation in the tourism landscape.

Two key factors affect and shape the dynamics of Chinese tourists to Malaysia. The first factor relates to the keen interests of Chinese tourists to visit sites in another country where there are remnants of Chinese heritage. Chinese tourists mostly include a visit to Chinatown when in Singapore and Kuala Lumpur. Apart from Chinese food, Chinatowns in many cities

---

culture" and thwarted all plans to develop the hill, sacred to the ethnic Chinese. In fact, there are also burials of Malay leaders from the earliest days of the 15th century (Cartier, 1998, p. 71). For example, on the peak of Bukit Tempurung, one of the three hills on Bukit China, in the direction of Northeast is the site of the Keramat Panjang Mausoleum. Two of these graves supposedly belong to a famous Achehnese warrior known as Panglima Pidi and his companion Syamsuddin Al-Sumaratani killed during a failed attack against the Portuguese in the early 17th century. People often visit this gravesite to ask for divine help.

[11] This information is based on interviews with community leaders in Malacca.

[12] Findings based on six tours with different tour operators and tourist guides of the city of Malacca.

[13] Eurasians are people of mixed parentage between locals and Europeans.

in Southeast Asia offer a flavour of overseas Chinese life style. The Cheng Hoon Teng and Sam Po Temples and parts of Bukit China in Malacca are also popular amongst Chinese tourists. A sense of pride and awe encapsulates these Chinese tourists when visiting heritage sites that reveal histories of relations with China. Therefore, cities and countries with Chinese heritage possess the potential to utilize such sites to entice tourist visits from China.

The second characteristic about tourists from mainland China is the "zero dollar" tourists package business model. Previously, under this scheme the Chinese travellers paid the full travel cost to their mainland Chinese travel agents. The travel agents in China may only pay for the hotel but not for ground transport at the destination even though it is supposedly included in the package. Hence, on arrival these Malaysian consortiums of travel agents welcome the Chinese tourists and usher them with a busy schedule mainly to shopping stops. The respective Malaysian ground operators use the commission and rebates received from the shopping and restaurant outlets to breakeven on the cost of accommodation, tours and transport incurred by the Chinese tourists. The Chinese travellers to Malaysia are highly sophisticated, they often try to break away from the tour group's programme and explore the attractions on their own. Sometimes, it is a risk to Malaysian travel agents, as the Chinese tourists may not necessarily join the group and a few of these tourists disappear altogether from the hotel in search of a job (Kuppusamy, 2005). The risk of "losing" Chinese tourists discourages many Malaysian travel agents to venture into business relations with their counterparts in China. More recently, the Chinese government has clamped down on such business operations and has established official and approved travel agent list where Chinese tourists travelling overseas are fully serviced for the package paid. With this new official list, more Chinese travel agents are paying their Malaysian counterparts for ground services such as airport and hotel transfers as well as the cost of sightseeing tours.

Chinese tourists to Malaysia dwindled to 350,000 last year compared to 550,000 in 2004 following negative reports on the way Chinese tourists were treated while they were in Malaysia (Liew, 2006). A balanced national emphasis since 1991 continues to woo Muslim tourists from the Middle East and Chinese tourists from East Asia (Liew, 2004, p. 1). Chinese tourists spent RM1,478.5 million in 2002 and were second only to Singaporean tourists who spent RM13,401 million followed by Indonesian tourists RM1,221.2 million and Thailand RM1,002.9 million (Gunaratnam, 2004). Tourism revenue at RM29.7 billion (US$8.04 billion) in 2004 remains importantly the second largest foreign exchange after the manufacturing sector (Tourism to contribute, 2006).

Light and Sound: Protecting Malay Rights

One attraction known as the *Cahaya dan Bunyi* (Light and Sound) reveals a little more of the political psychology of the Malays towards the ethnic Chinese minority. Visitors sit through a 45 minutes show in a makeshift open auditorium facing the historic St. Paul's Hill. The Porta de Santiago commands the height and by the foothill are the *Memorial Pengistyharan Kemerdekaan* (Memorial Hall of Independence), *Muzium Budaya* (Cultural Museum) and other museums depicting Malaysia's cultures and history. The commentary walk tourists through the history of Malacca and Malaysia with lights and sound adding to the dramatic effect to the historical attractions, all located within the historically important St. Paul's Hill. At one point, the commentary promoted Malay unity drawing a lesson from history. The commentary suggested that Malay disunity would mean a similar experience to Malacca's tragic defeat by the Portuguese in 1511.[14] It highlights the event immediately following the 1949 Japanese surrender in which the Kuomintang flag (KMT – China's nationalist party) was raised by ethnic Chinese in Malacca as an example of how Malay stakes to their own land risk hijacked or deprived by "others" with an implicit reference to the ethnic Chinese Malaysians.[15] This *Cahaya Dan Bunyi* show rallies the Malays to unite and look forward to a progressive country.

Hence, tourism assets and places are subject to manipulation and interpretation by historical experiences by different groups within a society. The more powerful and politically dominant ruling group may have control over the wherewithal to ensure a specific political narrative. The *Cahaya Dan Bunyi* show is also telling. The commentary appears targeted at the domestic visitors but it gives tourists a flavour of the internal political sentiments.

Zheng He Gallery

On 10 January 2004, Malacca again became the focal point for acknowledging Chinese heritage with the official opening of the Zheng He Gallery at the Studthuys. Previously, the museum only exhibited Malay cultural artefacts. Prior to the end of the 1970s, the citizens of China were not allowed to go overseas for tourism and they did not have the means to do so, hence Chinese tourists flow was not an issue at all for Malaysian politics. The Malaysian cabinet made a decision and gave directions for an official opening of the gallery with a notice of 2 weeks for the preparations to coincide with the visit of a deputy minister for culture from China.[16] Both countries also used the opportunity to sign an agreement to have cultural exchanges and non-governmental interactions.[17] The 30 years Malaysia–China friendship does not exactly coincide with the 600 years of Zheng He's voyages to Malaysia but the "big bang" signalled the importance in the frenzied months preceding the elections.[18] The Malacca Chinese Chamber of Commerce and Industry bought the granite statue and transferred ownership to a cultural organization named Malacca Chinese Assembly Hall (MCAH). The statue had for many months stood by a business premise with no proper home. By sheer "coincidence" of political and tourism events, the MCAH later contributed to the Studthuys museum complex that houses the Zheng He Gallery.

---

[14] Infighting within the Malacca Sultanate also contributed to its eventual demise when the Portuguese attacked.

[15] KMT is the nationalist party that ruled China from 1911 to 1949. It was deposed by the Chinese Communist Party, which currently rules China. The KMT eventually retreated to Taiwan and continues to be an important political force in Taiwanese politics.

[16] Interview with Dr. Badriyah Bte Haj Salleh, *Pengurus Besar* (General Manager) of *Pebadanan Muzium Melaka* (Melaka Museums Corporation) conducted on 16 March 2004.

[17] Cited from the Malaysian Tourism Promotion Board, http://www.tourism.gov.my/newsletter/index.htm accessed on 15 October 2004.

[18] Zheng He also known as Cheng Ho was a Chinese admiral of Muslim descent who was born in 1371 in Yunan, a southwestern province in China. Over 28 years, he visited around 30 territories going as far as the Middle East. He kept a detailed logbook and made nautical charts of each voyage, which involved an armada of 300 ships carrying 27,000 sailors and soldiers. Some historians claim it was he and not Italian Christopher Columbus who was the world's first ocean navigator as his seven voyages were made between 1405 and 1433.

Figure 11.1: The statue of Admiral Zheng He.

Today, a 4.5 metres solid granite statue of Admiral Zheng He costing some RM20,000 (US$5400) stands outside the gallery of the Stadthuys museum complex (Ahmad, 2004a). It stands as a reminder that strong ties had pre-existed and that ethnic Chinese culture in Malaysia predates inherited colonial constructs of racialized politics and cultural space. Between 1411 and the 1480s, eight sultans of Malacca visited China no less than 11 times, enhancing trade and cultural ties. Relations peaked when Sultan Mansur Shah (1458–1477) married Chinese princess Hang Li Poh and built a palace for her in Bukit Cina in Malacca City.[19] But to restate the politics of this event is important. The exact 600th anniversary should have been in 2005 but celebrations were brought forward a year earlier to coincide with the 2004 general elections. Many countries in the region, Singapore in particular have had plans to commemorate the historical visit with events lined up. Therefore, it is suspect that the Malaysian cabinet sought mileage through the opening of the Zheng He Gallery as a 600 years commemoration falling in 2004. This is one year ahead of the actual year 2005. In a forward to the opening of the Zheng He Gallery, the then Minister of Culture, Arts and Tourism, Datuk Paduka Abdul Kadir Haji Sheikh Fadzir said:

> This colourful event shows the tourism sector in Malaysia has common cultural interests with The People's Republic of China, which have been

---

[19] The word "Cina" in Bukit Cina is pronounced as Cheena.

developed many years ago. Today, they are translated in the forms of various tourists activities such as historical and cultural programmes conducted at state, national and international levels. I am confident that cooperations such as these between Malaysia and the People's Republic of China in the tourism sector will further strengthen our diplomatic relations.[20]

Hence, heritage development in this instance showcases the Malaysian government's effort to court China's goodwill. By linking tourism to heritage and diplomatic relations, common interests are nurtured. The heritage here concerns historical Chinese records and figures connected to Malaysia and the use of it for the purposes of tourism is one step towards better relations with China. Rather than conform to the rubrics of colonial taxonomies and Malay hegemonic designs, tourism as a source promoting ethnic Chinese heritage serves as a positive contribution. More importantly, moves such as the opening of the Zheng He Gallery signals that Malays themselves have arrived at a comfort zone in accepting the ethnic Chinese among their community. Second, this effort to commodify and touristify Chinese culture is significant. Therefore, Malaysia has succeeded under politically diffi-cult and different circumstances to breakout of the nomenclature of majority–minority hegemonic thinking and transcends Malay nationalistic feelings to exercise economic rationality and cultural pluralism when it concerns tourism.

With the recent tourism slogan: *Malaysia Truly Asia*, there is also a sense that the country's multi-cultural image to the world continues to be self-orientalizing by depicting pictures of the different "races." Ethnic Chinese celebrity, Michelle Yeoh is the first non-Malay to represent the face of Malaysia in major tourism campaigns and advertisements, hence cap-italizing on her popularity since her debut in a James Bond movie – "Tomorrow Never Dies" (Lau, 2002). One such advertisement records her saying "Malaysia – Truly Asia," the current marketing brand used by the country to promote inbound tourism. She was also a Miss Malaysia at the age of 21 and has received the title of *Datukship*, one of the high-est honorary title endowed by the King of Malaysia (Zissu, 2005). One such advertisement records her saying "Malaysia – Truly Asia," the current marketing brand used by the coun-try to promote inbound tourism. The fact that an ethnic Chinese citizen is given the space to present Malaysia to the world speaks volume of the Malay majority state's acceptance of ethnic Chinese citizens as part of their national make-up.

The challenges of an election year did not hamper but aided the propping up of ethnic Chinese identity that has long been in the shadow. With the hand-over of power from Mahathir Mohammad to Abdullah Badawi, Malaysia's cultural policy in tourism took a decisive turn. Crossing the Rubicon, the Abdullah administration had come to terms with Malaysia's historical past, its rich ethnic Chinese and Peranakan heritage. In the election year of 2004, the opposition party-PAS espoused Islamic values and was concerned exclu-sively with the Malay electorates. PAS narrow reach to the Malay base was felt as a threat to the ruling party-UMNO's own traditional base. However, PAS failed to gain any kind of alliance from other non-Malay opposition political parties. The fear of losing the Malay

---

[20] Published in a booklet commemorating the event entitled *Tahun Persahabatan Malaysia Republik Rakyat China Sambutan 30 Tahun Hubungan Diplomatik Malaysia – Republik Rakyat China Dan 600 Tahun Ekspedisi Zheng He Ke Melaka*. 2004, Malacca Museum Corporation.

base to PAS, left UMNO with the task to woo the ethnic Chinese, the largest minority group to counterbalance potential loss of the Malay votes. UMNO in 2004 pressed on the theme of economic progress for the Malays and balanced the campaign to promote ethnic Chinese heritage in Malaysia (Chinese community urged, 2004). Hence, the opening of the Zheng He Gallery was carefully crafted to coincide with the promotion of attracting tourists from China.[21]

The 2004 election resulted in an increase support for the government's Chinese based parties: Gerakan and MCA. In 1999, these two parties held a total of 35 parliamentary seats. In the 2004 elections, the number of seats increased to 41 which reflected a strong support for the ruling coalition government dominated by UMNO of which MCA and Gerakan are partners. An accumulative effect at efforts to woo the ethnic Chinese support for the ruling government appears to have worked. Of the 202 seats contested, the ruling coalition government won 181 seats (Balasubramaniam, 2005). This is not to suggest that heritage and outward tourism promotions for Chinese tourists were the only factors which created the strong wins. More than those, local realities of individual constituencies and national politics also played a role. However, the government's efforts to appear promoting ethnic Chinese heritage in Malaysia created favourable impressions and added to the firm support of ethnic Chinese political support (Ahmad, 2004b).

Conclusion

Broadening Horizons and Accelerating Transitions

In the geocultural exchange, a single perspective juxtaposed between Malaysia and China in a multi-dimensional discourse would fail if it does not consider western impositions and eastern iconic powers. I have taken a flexible approach to analyse cultural tourism and the political circumstances explaining it. The high and low tides of Malay politics may have had a real impact on ethnic Chinese spaces in Malaysian national tourism policies. But the question of Malaysia's economic pragmatism and the magnetic power that China's economy yields need further considerations.

Developments in China always have had an impact on Southeast Asia. In a period of rapid economic growth and market reforms, it appears that China will emerge as an important engine for growth and continue to affect the region in diverse ways. The Taiwanese sovereignty issue, Spratly islands disputes with several ASEAN countries and China's political ideology will be important sources of concern for Malaysia as it welcomes the tourists flow originating from China. As long as efforts to welcome Chinese tourists to Malaysia does not affect local political and cultural (imbalances) constructions, tourism might further aid in creating spaces for ethnic Chinese in Malaysia. This might even contribute to the revival of more ethnic Chinese heritage and development of related tourism assets.

With the overwhelming success of the ruling coalition government in the 2004 General Elections, the political repercussions on tourism policy and ethnic Chinese space raises new considerations. Was the official opening of the Zheng He Gallery a momentary political

---

[21] Based on interviews with key personnel Melaka Museums Corporation (PERZIM) and Melaka Heritage Trust.

response to highlighting ethnic Chinese heritage? Is it an electioneering stunt or a real attempt to harness a minority group's heritage for economic gains? Will tourism lead to greater authenticity and presentation of non-Malay sites? The opening of Zheng He Gallery may be a small albeit a positive step. Unless more is done with similar enthusiasm, the answer would be obvious. Will competition from neighbouring countries nudge Malaysian tourism policies to converge favourably with economic development and cultural policy? While democracy is a vehicle for the exercise of equal citizenship rights, the use of tourism resources rests on the power dimensions of such outcome. The ethnic Chinese citizens possess full democratic rights but they do not easily translate to active use of available cultural assets for tourism purposes.

Malay hegemonic projects to "tame" the minority groups in the country rest on the observation that the ethnic Chinese must first be compartmentalized, denied all cultural and political links to China and wherever possible encourage those practices and heritage that have Malay cultural elements.[22] Fragmentation in Malay electoral politics and an evolution of a distinct Malaysian Chinese identity far removed from China are important indicators because it is debatable if Malaysia will continue this open and inclusive path to pluralism in heritage tourism. Thus, tourism may also be a phenomenon in which communities in host countries achieve political power parity (Smith, 1990).

The spill-over effects of Malay political dominance and ethnic Chinese heritage in tourism is premised on a rationale of power relations, and they reflect an extensive tradition of cultural complexes, spatial relations and institutional frameworks of the state and society. One social anthropologist analysing Malaysia's modernity, posits that it is part of the political ideology of the state to work within the context of a larger nation-building project (Goh, 2002). China's continued fairwind in developing friendly ties with Southeast Asian countries also contributes to the transforming benefits of ethnic Chinese in Malaysia. The development of heritage tourism with a China dimension as discussed fits this description. King (1993) suggests that Malaysian culture in reality transcends official representations. Changing political conditions from within Malaysia will determine how the Malaysian state dominated by Malay elites allows minority ethnic groups to showcase their heritage as part of tourism (see also Kahn, 1997).

The extent to which the ethnic minorities are included in the national tourism landscape is dependent on domestic Malay politics and the economic importance of China. One cannot dismiss in the same breathe the comfort sense indigenous Malays must feel towards the ethnic Chinese commitment to the Malay or Malaysian nation-building project. Only then, would the tourism landscape be even for the presentation of Malaysia's multi-cultural heritage for Malaysians and tourists consumption.

Acknowledgement

I thank Professors John N. Miksic, Goh Beng Lan and Joel S. Kahn for their invaluable comments and suggestions that had made this research and writing process an enriching experience.

---

[22] An example of this is Peranakan culture and heritage.

References

Abraham, S., Liu, J. H., Lawrence, B., & Ward, C. (2002). Social representations of history in Malaysia and Singapore: On the relationship between national and ethnic identity. *Asian Journal of Social Psychology*, 5(1), 3–20.

Ahmad, R. (2004a). Malaysia turns to history to woo tourists. *The Straits Times*, 12 January, A8.

Ahmad, R. (2004b). State of the Malaysian States. *The Straits Times*, 11 March, A8.

Balasubramaniam, V. (2005). The politics of locality and temporality in the 2004 Malaysian parliamentary elections. *Contemporary Southeast Asia*, 27(1), 44–64.

Brimmel, J. H. (1959). *Communism in southeast Asia: A political analysis*. London: Oxford University Press.

Cartier, C. L. (1998). Preserving Bukit China: The cultural politics of landscape interpretation in Melaka's Chinese cemetery. In E. Sinn (Ed.), *The last half century of Chinese Overseas* (pp. 65–79). Aberdeen: Hong Kong University Press.

Cartier, C. L. (2001). *Globalizing South China*. Oxford: Blackwell.

Cheah, B. K. (1979). *The masked comrades: A study of the Communist United Front in Malaya, 1945–48*. Singapore: Times Books International.

Chinese Community Urged to Vote BN (2004). *Bernama*, 11 January, p. 1.

Craik, M. (1997). The culture of tourism. In: C. Rojek, & J. Urry (Eds), *Touring cultures: Transformations of travel and theory* (pp. 113–137). London: Routledge.

Curley, M. G., & Liu, H. (Eds) (2002). *China and Southeast Asia: Changing socio-cultural interactions*. Hong Kong: The University of Hong Kong.

Day, P. (2004). Singapore leads India charge: Southeast Asian nations hope to avert overreliance on China. *Wall Street Journal*, 5 April, A.17.

Din, K. H. (1997). Tourism and cultural development in Malaysia: Issues for a new agenda. In: Shinji Yamashita et al. (Eds), *Tourism and cultural development in Asia and Oceania* (pp. 104–108). Bangi: University Kebangsaan Malaysia.

Elliott, J. (1997). *Tourism: Politics and public sector management*. London: Routledge.

Ganesan, V. (2003). Malaysia should tap tourism marts in China, India, Indonesia. *Business Times*, 28 November, 5.

Goh, B. L. (2002). Rethinking modernity: State, ethnicity and class in the forging of a modern urban Malaysia. In: C. J. W.-L. Wee (Ed.), *Local cultures and the new Asia: The state, culture and capitalism in Southeast Asia* (pp. 184–216). Singapore: Institute of Southeast Asian Studies.

Gunaratnam, S. (2004). A country of festivals, carnivals and continuous merriment. *New Straits Times*, 11 February, 4.

Hall, C. M. (1994). *Tourism and politics: Policy, power and place*. Chichester: John Wiley and Sons.

Heng, P. K. (1998). Chinese responses to Malay hegemony in peninsular Malaysia (1957–1996). In: Z. Ibrahim (Ed.), *Cultural contestations: Mediating identities in a changing Malaysian society* (pp. 51–82). London: ASEAN Academic Press.

Ho, K. L. (2002).S Bureaucratic participation and political mobilization: Comparing pre and post 1970 Malaysian Chinese political participation. In: L. Suryadinata (Ed.), *Singapore and Malaysia: A dialogue between tradition and modernity* (pp. 137–154). Singapore: Times Academic Press.

Hong, C. (2005). Malaysian students heading for China. *The Straits Times*, 28 February, p. n/a.

Ibrahim, Z. (Ed.) (1998). *Cultural contestations: Mediating identities in a changing Malaysian society*. London: ASEAN Academic Press.

Kahn, J. S. (1997). Culturalizing Malaysia: Globalism, tourism, heritage, and the city in Georgetown. In M. Picard, & R. E. Wood (Eds), *Tourism, ethnicity, and the state in Asian and Pacific societies* (pp. 99–127). Honolulu: University of Hawai'i Press.

Kahn, J. S. (2001). *Modernity and exclusion*. London: Sage.

Khalifah, Z., & Tahir, S. (1997). Malaysia: Tourism in perspective. In: M. G. Frank, & L. J. Carson (Eds), *Tourism and economic development in Asia and Australia* (pp. 176–196). London: Cassell.

King, V. T. (1993). Tourism and culture in Malaysia. In: M. Hitchcock et al. (Eds), *Tourism in Southeast Asia* (pp. 99–116). London: Routledge.

KLUIC drums up support with Chinese embassy (2004). *New Straits Times*, 13 October, 12.

Kuppusamy, B. (2005). Police told to find 50,000 missing Chinese tourists. *South China Morning Post*, 22 November, 15.

Lau, L. (2002). Malaysia goes all out to woo tourists from booming China. *The Straits Times*, 15 December.

Lau, L. (2004). China students flock to Malaysian town. *The Straits Times*, 29 June. Available at http://web.lexis-nexis.com.libproxy1.nus.edu.sg/universe/document?_m=45d6ecbcd 838811cc7bc2853ebc57841&_docnum=2&wchp=dGLbVzzzSkVb&_md5=9dad19ec4b349 ebb8c77e5e51497a706 (Accessed 7-10-2004).

Liew, L. (2004). One-third of Middle East tourists from Saudi – tourism Malaysia. *Bernama*, 2 June, 1.

Liew, W. C. (2006). Drop in Chinese tourists to M'sia only temporary, says Lim. *Bernama*, 19 March.

Liu, H. (2000). Sino-Southeast Asian studies: Toward a new analytical paradigm. Singapore: National University of Singapore.

Mandal, S. K. (2002). Transethnic solidarities in a racialised context. *Journal of Contemporary Asia*, *32*(3), 50–68.

Nian, Y. S. (1993). Chinese language literature in Malaya and Singapore (1919–1942). In: L. Suryadinata (Ed.), *Adaptation and diversity: Essays on society and literature in Indonesia, Malaysia and Singapore* (pp. 169–180). Singapore: Singapore University Press.

Ott, M. (2004). S-E Asia must wake up to the rise of the dragon. *The Straits Times*, 8 September, 15.

Richter, L. K. (1993). Terrorism policy – making in Southeast Asia. In: M. Hitchcock et al. (Eds), *Tourism in Southeast Asia* (pp. 79–199). London: Routledge.

Richter, L. K. (1989). *The politics of tourism in Asia*. Honolulu: University of Hawaii Press.

Robertson, J. M. (1988). Traditional music: Place in Caribbean tourism. In: *Come Mek Me Hol' Yu Han'* (Ed.), *The impact of tourism on traditional music colloqium* (pp. 29–36). Jamaica: Jamaica Memory Bank.

Said, E. W. (1993). *Culture and imperialism*. London: Chatto and Windus.

Smith, A. D. (1990). Towards a global culture. In: M. Featherstone (Ed.), Global culture – nationalism, globalization and modernity (pp. 171–193). London: Sage Publications.

Stockwell, A. J. (2003). Malaysia: The making of a grand design. *Asian Affairs*, *34*(3), 227–242.

Suryadinata, L. (2000). Ethnic Chinese and the nation-state in Southeast Asia. In: A. S. Teresita (Ed.), Intercultural relations, cultural transformation and identity – The ethnic Chinese Manila (pp. 308–327). Manila: Kaisa Para Sa Kaunlaran.

Tan, C. C. (2006a). Heritage sites to be gazetted. *New Straits Times*, 18 March, 23.

Tan, C. C. (2006b). Conservation efforts undermined by "sins". *New Straits Times*, 21 March, 06.

Tan, E. (2000). Ghettoization of Citizen-Chinese: State management of ethnic Chinese minority in Indonesia and Malaya. In: A. S. Teresita (Ed.), *Intercultural relations, cultural transformation and identity – The ethnic Chinese* (pp. 371–412). Manila: Kaisa Para Sa Kaunlaran.

Tan, J. (2004). From Ping-Pong to KL-Beijing Rapport. *The Straits Times*, 10 February, 14.

Tourism to contribute RM44 Bln next year – Wee. (2006). *Bernama*, 18 February 2006. Accessed on 18 February 2006, http://global.factiva.com.libproxy1.nus.edu.sg/aa/default.aspx?pp

Tsing, M. C. (2003). Tracing the beginning of Chinese contemporary dance in Malaysia. In: Mohd Anis Md Nor (Ed.), Diversity in motion (pp. 43–56). Kuala Lumpur: University of Malaya.

Wang, G. (1992). *China and the Chinese Overseas*. Singapore: Times Academic Press.

Wang, G. (2002). Reflections on networks and structures in Asia. In: M. G. Curley, & H. Liu (Eds), *China and Southeast Asia: Changing socio-cultural interactions* (pp. 13–26). Hong Kong: The University of Hong Kong.

Wong, P. N. (2002). Constructing the "China Circle" in China and Southeast Asia: State policy, the presence of Chinese overseas and globalisation. In: R. K. H. Chan, et al. (Eds), *Development in Southeast: Review and prospects* (pp. 37–55). Hampshire: Ashgate.

Worden, N. (2003). National identity and heritage tourism in Melaka. *Indonesia and the Malay World*, *31*(89), 31–43.

World Tourism Organization (WTO) (1997). Yearbook of Tourism Statistics. World Tourism Organization *2*(49).World Tourism Organization. Yearbook of Tourism Statistics.

Zissu, A. (2005). Tireless, curious, exuberant, irrepressible bunch. *Travel Magazine*, September 25, 76.

Chapter 12

Preparing Now for Tomorrow: The Future for Tourism in Scotland up to 2015

Una McMahon-Beattie and Ian Yeoman

Introduction

Tourism seems to be one of those industries that is always under political review (Kerr, Barron & Wood, 2001; Lederer, 2004; Smith, 1998). In fact, if there is a problem, politicians always seem to want to review it. Such reviews tend to be more of the same, where nothing really changes. The effect of such reviews on policy makers and stakeholders in the industry, means they tend to concentrate on now or the short-term rather than dealing with the long-term view and the uncertainties of the future.

As the future is uncertain, there is a need to prepare and ask "What if" questions such as, "What if, Scotland's economy does not grow as expected and how will this effect tourism?" This kind of thinking, which is at the very heart of scenario planning made famous by Shell International (Heijden, Bradfield, Burt, Cairns, & Wright, 2002), is rare in tourism public policy because it is politically unpalatable (Yeoman & McMahon-Beattie, 2004). The best questions in scenario thinking are the awkward questions, which pose the challenge. How is Scotland's demographic problem going to impact on fiscal spending and how will this shape tourism? What would be consequences of changes to the Barnett formula[1] on tourism spending or do we really need state intervention for destination marketing when we have so little influence over products and consumer choice? The real value in this type of thinking is firstly, to help us to device short-term and tactical plans, just in case everyone assumes that it does not happen, but it does. An example of this is contingency planning and crisis management. Secondly, and more importantly, it helps us to understand the long-term

---

[1] The Barnett formula, named after Joel Barnett the Chief Secretary to the Treasury (1974–1979), stipulates that for every pound of *extra* spending in England each year, Scotland will get an increase in their block grant proportionate to their relative populations. This means that Scotland gets a higher per capita grant than any other region of the UK.

---

and strategic decisions that are needed for the future. Thirdly, it helps us to understand what sorts of actions will be necessary whatever happens in the future, these actions that will remain robust throughout a range of possible future developments.

This chapter presents two scenarios for Scotland, *Short Break Destination* and *Yesterday's Destination* and the consequential policy implications for tourism up to and roundabout the year 2015. The purpose of this chapter is to help those in the tourism industry to consider, what *could* happen over the longer term (hence roundabout 2015), in order to plan effectively for what *should* happen.

Scotland is going to face a range of challenging issues in the longer term, in particular changing demographics will lead to a critical dependency ratio when there are more people over 65 years than under 21 years in Scotland. The impact of this means Scotland's economic performance will start to decline, as there will not be enough people in work to support those out of work. In addition to this there are the challenges of changing tourists' expectations, the quality of our labour supply and worldwide competition for tourists. Scottish tourism industry faces many challenges.

None of the scenarios presented below will happen as described, but it is important to learn and understand the implications of these scenarios in order to improve the accuracy of the prediction. Taken together the scenarios represent a wide range of issues and possibilities, which hopefully will produce constructive thinking about the future of tourism in Scotland. Such thinking leads to "what would happen to tourism policy in this environment" or "what strategies are necessary to guide us through these uncertainties and still meet the expectations of public and private sector stakeholders".

VisitScotland is the national tourism organisation of Scotland whose legislative basis is incorporated under the Development of Tourism Act of 1969 and 1984. It is the lead organisation for tourism in Scotland, responsible to the Minister for Tourism in the Scottish Executive for destination marketing, tourism policy issues and economic advice.

Tourism in Scotland accounts for £4.5 billion – 5% of Scotland's gross domestic product (GDP) – and 8% of employment (Hay, 2002). Scotland is predominately a domestic UK short break destination with 92% of trips coming from those living in Scotland, North of England and London and the South East of England. UK domestic tourism to Scotland represents £3.7 billion, whereas overseas tourism represents £811 million. The main overseas markets are North America, Germany, France and the Benelux countries.

Scenario-Planning Methodology

A scenario-planning process was used in order to create a range of alternative plausible futures and stimulate a strategic conversation (Heijden et al., 2002) about the future of Scottish tourism. Scenario planning is a process of painting pictures rather than a forecast of the future. It is a process in which possible worlds could unfold that are presently unimaginable, unthinkable and unpredictable (Woulde, Damgaard, Hegge, Soholt & Bunkers, 2003). But scenarios represent futures that are plausible based upon trends and a range of assumptions about the future. The principles and history of scenario planning are well documented (Heijden et al., 2002) as a means of developing strategic futures at Shell International. Shell's interest in scenarios arose from the increasing failures of planning, based upon forecasts in the mid-1960s. Scenarios were initially developed as a way to plan without having to predict things that everyone knew were unpredictable.

Key to the success of scenario planning is actioning change. This means working with stakeholders and actors who have the power and influence to create change, otherwise the process of scenario planning is viewed as academic and a failure by stakeholders (Heijden et al., 2002). A number of authors in the tourism industry (Hall & Jenkins, 1995; Ryan, 2002; Sautter & Leisen, 1999) identify stakeholder theory as the essential ingredient in policy development. The politics and power of change must be captured in the process, otherwise those that have influence and power who are left outside the process will ensure usually that the policies fail. Heijden et al. (2002), Ringland (2002) and Eden and Ackerman (1999) note that scenario planning is a process rather than an outcome. Stakeholders must actively engage in the process in order to shift their mindset of the situation. It is through a process of dialogue that stakeholders learn and change their actions. Flood and Romm (1996) calls this triple loop learning. Here stakeholders, through participation move towards "big picture" understandings rather than "finite details".

Based upon this ethos a scenario-planning group has been set up in order to embrace the organisation and industry. By involving these stakeholders in the group, they can act out the scenarios and action change. This group is not about a one-off project but initially a 3-year process in which the group attempts to answer the following core question:

> What actions does VisitScotland and its stakeholders need to take to ensure
> that tourism grows by 50% by 2015?

In addressing this question, more detailed questions include:

(i)   Which markets will thrive and which will decline to 2015?
(ii)   Which product offers will thrive and decline to 2015?
(iii) How will consumer needs and wants change to 2015?
(iv)   How will supply side and structural issues assist or hinder the development of Scottish tourism to 2015?

In answering these questions the scenario-planning group will identify a number of actions in order to create change that is necessary for the future. The group members include representative of government bodies such as Historic Scotland and Scottish Enterprise, transport companies such as CalMac and hotel companies such as Gleneagles and Apex Hotels. The members pay a subscription in order to pay project costs but more importantly a subscription model means group members will take the scenarios seriously.

Scenario Construction

The scenarios were constructed from 60 individual interviews that represented a sample of stakeholders, tourism businesses, bystanders, experts, members of VisitScotland's Board and remarkable people (see Table 12.1). Remarkable people are those that will challenge conventional understandings and attitudes. These people were selected for their leading-edge abilities, creative thinking and challenging reputations and they brought foresight to the process. The interviews were supported by four workshops. In total, over 120 people where consulted about the future of Scottish tourism.

Table 12.1: Contributors to Scotland 2015.

Sector interviews
Airlines
Public sector agencies
Hotels
Visitor attractions
Students
Retail tourism
Lobby groups
Education
Restaurants
Local government
Regional government
Politicians
Travel tour operators
Banks
Rail operators
Ferry operators
Bus operators
Workshops
Younger audience (under 30)
Senior Managers at VisitScotland
Business Leaders × 2

The scenarios were constructed from individual interviews using a range of projection questions and metaphors (Heijden et al., 2002) to surface an interviewee's perception of the external world and how that influenced tourism. Conversations were captured using a tape recorder where possible but certain interviewees declined or it was felt inappropriate to use a tape recorder. Conversations were analysed using *Nvivo* (Richards, 1999) and *Decision Explorer* (Jones, 1993) as a means to code transcripts and interviews. These tools allowed the researcher to "search", "build", "play", "interpret" and "generate" conclusions from the interviews. Scenarios or stories are drawn from a poststructuralist paradigm of research (Flowers, 2003; Hardin, 2003) in which language of stories accesses readers episodic memory and tacit feeling (Sparrow, 1998), bringing a rich sculpted narrative in which readers can make sense in a more personal, easier understand format compared to positivist methodologies and methods. Scenario planning is able to construct a shared language, in which meanings are exchanged and accessed based upon a framework of everyday language.

The group workshops used a visual thinking technique called Hexagons (Hodgson, 1992). Fundamentally, issues are noted down on magnetic, coloured hexagons, which are placed onto wipe-boards and clustered to show related concepts and connections. This allowed participants to play and interact with each other. This stimulated conversation and ideas. The hexagons and conversations were captured using a software package called *IDONS*, allowing the researcher to analyse and build scenarios from workshops. Scenarios were then constructed using Shell's approach to scenario planning as set out in *The sixth sense: accelerating organisational learning with scenarios* (Heijden et al., 2002).

In order to find an economic value for each scenario, consideration was given to the use of econometrics and computable general equilibrium (CGE) modelling (Blake et al., 2006; Devarajan & Robinson, 2003). However, there are problems with both of these approaches. First, there is a time distance problem in econometrics that is the further you forecast into the future the higher the degree of error. Also, CGE modelling cannot be considered as methodologically sound when accounting for major shocks or changes to economic structures, as input–output tables would need to be recalibrated to account for a new economic environment. It was therefore considered appropriate to use a backcasting (Partidario & Vergragt, 2002; Roorda, 2001) and Delphi technique (Evans, Rogers, McGraw, Battle & Furniss, 2004; Hardy et al., 2004) in order to derive an economic value.

Backcasting (Roorda, 2001) states what the future will be as if you have already arrived there and looks back on the journey that you have would have had to take to get to the future. The importance of this in scenario planning and strategic management is that it allows decision makers to identify circumstances and strategies that would be required to get to a future point. When backcasting is used in conjunction with the Delphi technique, a structured process of obtaining opinions from experts and stakeholders about the economic values of tourism in each of the scenarios is obtained.

Two Plausible Futures

Using a range of drivers (governance, fiscal policy, disposable income, price sensitivity, transport, destination image, media environment demographics, history and disruptions) two scenarios have been constructed, *Short Break Destination* and *Yesterday's Destination*. In the *Short Break Destination* tourism is based upon consumerism and play, driven by the short break holidays and European tourists. Scotland offers a diversity of products and experience, which cater for a broad spectrum of visitors. The *Short Break Destination* is very much about disposable income and competing demands for consumers' leisure time. Falling airfare and hotel prices make it so much easier to get Scotland and it is so affordable that a weekend away almost becomes an impulse purchase. But the weekender is not an easy option, as many other destinations offer similar products and experiences.

In the *Yesterday's Destination* scenario, tourism is based upon the past, a world of icons and complacency. Scotland dreams of glory and the past. The problem is, the past is not quite good enough. Tourism is still here but unfavourable exchange rates make Scotland an uncompetitive and Second Division Destination.

These two scenarios, *The Short Break Destination* and *Yesterday's Destinations*, describe two alternative environments, one where Scotland succeeds and one where it just fails. The margin of error between the two scenarios is very tight, just 3.4% revenue growth per annum. But this is a difference between a £7.6 billion and £5.1 billion tourism industry. Together the scenarios presented below represent a spectrum of possibilities of what may happen. The purpose of the scenarios is to make policy makers and stakeholders think about the consequences. In a rapidly changing world, policy makers in tourism must be able to adapt and find appropriate solutions that can make a difference. In order to address the issues and challenges in the scenarios, it is important to ask the right questions. Such questions are:

- What are the primary issues in the scenarios?
- What short-term and long-term actionable responses and policies would be needed to encourage growth and avoid failure?

Scenario 1: Short Break Destination

Scotland is positioned as a Short Break Destination, in which tourism is based upon consumerism, culture and play. We are very much seen as a short break and European destination. Scotland offers a diversity of products and experiences that cater for a broad spectrum of visitors. The Short Break Destination is very much about disposable income and competing demands for consumers' leisure time. Falling airfares and hotel prices make it so much easier to get here, and so affordable, that a weekend away almost becomes an impulse purchase. The Short Break Destination is not an easy option, as many other destinations offer similar products and experiences.

Tourism is now a £7.2 billion industry (see Tables 12.2 and 12.3), which has grown at a steady pace of 4% per annum since 2003. The UK market is worth £5.8 billion, whereas

Table 12.2: Short break destination – the value of tourism in 2015.

Expenditure type	UK tourism £m	%	Overseas tourism £m	%	Total	%
Holidays	3878	70	827	50	4705	65
Business	997	18	331	20	1328	18
Visiting, friends and relatives market (VFR)	554	10	430	26	984	14
Other	111	2	66	4	177	3
Total	5540	100	1654	100	7194	100

Table 12.3: Short break destination Scotland – spending patterns.

Spend	£m	%
Leisure spending	1799	25
Eating and drinking	1870	26
Travel	1367	19
Accommodation	1799	25
Other	360	5
Total	7195	100

overseas tourism is worth £1.7 billion. Tourism employs 250,000 people, making it Scotland's first employer in the private sector. The growth in the domestic market has been driven by transport infrastructure improvements in which tourists leave their office anywhere in the UK at 5.00 p.m. on a Friday night and are in Scotland by 8.00 p.m. We saw substantial growth come from the South East of England, based upon Scotland being an emotional and accessible destination. More budget carriers and continued investment in rail infrastructure allowed Scotland to become a leading weekend destination. In fact, Scotland no longer perceives itself as a tourism destination, rather as the provider of leisure services and goods. It understands that the "weekender" is about "disposable income" and "leisure spend", which is driving growth.

Ever increasing levels of disposal income mean a sophisticated and demanding tourist. Sophisticated tourists are well educated with a strong interest in cultural arts and festivals. The cities of Scotland are destinations in themselves, with lots of social cachet and cultural capital. This is recognised in many destination reviews and media commentators, as these cities are easily accessible, based upon a low-cost transport model. The tourist thinks nothing of spending a weekend away, as long as easyJet are flying there!

Competition however is not restricted to other destinations but includes all non-essential spending such as DIY activity, entertainment durables and other forms of leisure activity. But the Scottish tourism product edge is that it is an experience rather than a material good. The "weekender" is not an easy option as visitors are in an environment of disinflation meaning yields on accommodation and travel are always falling, but spending on retail and activities is rising. Visitors are always looking for good value but do not mind spending more on indulgence so spending on luxury accommodation and travel is growing.

Scotland's accessibility has resulted in a focus on European markets rather than long-haul tourists. Contemporary cities mean that Scotland is more competitive and desirable than destinations such as Paris, Warsaw, Rome and Madrid. A tartan renaissance, in which many European citizens, as far as a field as Poland in the east and Iceland in the west, identified with our enduring proposition of play, freedom, romance and creativity. There is a strong product portfolio: *Food and Drink, Playful Scotland, Culture and Art, Conventions, Rural and Gaelic Scotland, City Breaks.*

By 2015, business tourism has changed. Companies are spending less on travel year on year and video-conferencing technology came of age in 2012. Continued investment in exhibition space and the perception of Scotland as a safe and accessible destination, meant that growth came from the associations and conventions rather than business-to-business transactions.

Tourism was perceived as the *soaring eagle* of the Scottish economy. A sector that had ambition and continuously grew when other industries where in decline such as manufacturing, electronics and fisheries. Whatever people said about tourism, including those early septics and doomsday merchants who said the "product lacked quality", "the destination was too expensive" and "service was poor". They were all proved wrong. A determination to soar above the problem, like an eagle, in order that the products, branding, quality and marketing where right, ensured that Scottish tourism grew at 4% per annum when other destinations showed slower growth or decline.

In a competitive environment, in which consumers have plenty of choice, Scotland realised that a programme of continuous investment was necessary in order to continually grow. Initiatives included:

- A *fitness to practice quality assurance programme*, in which all tourism businesses were required to show competencies in order to gain a license to operate. The programme had two parts, a compulsory certificate that covered all of the legal requirements such as health and safety, customer care, hygiene and training and the diploma stage encompassed more advanced subjects, that is revenue management and innovation. The fitness to practice programme was an important development, as quality was seen by the consumer as a "hygiene factor" rather than a "distinguishing factor", as every destination had invested in quality. The result of such a programme ensured that businesses which were competitive survived, and those that were not, simply died. The assurance element of the programme ensured a *100% guarantee* to the consumer. Your money back if not completely satisfied.
- *Making tourism everyone's business*, was a programme that was born out of the fact that Scottish tourism could not afford to fail – as the competition grew, a realisation occurred that tourism must become the language and values of the people of Scotland. Therefore by putting tourism at the core everything in Scotland, a service ethos emerged that drove change. At Scotland's Thistle Awards in 2013 – Dundee's *Big Issue* vendors won the best ambassadors award. Whereas, the *Partick Thistle* won the prize for Asian Product of Year for the innovative football and tourism initiative.
- The *Schmenner²* project grasped the problem of demographic change and its implications on tourism. This initiative was different from others, instead of beating the same old drum about the "lack of people entering the industry" or "more training is required", the tourism innovation group set about designing products and creative solutions to the problem. New products and gadgets were designed that overcame the problem of labour supply. The Munro Satellite Positioning Watch (MSPW) enabled walkers to climb mountains without the need of a guide or map. The watch was popular with semi – experienced walkers as, in popular resorts such as Glencoe, there was always a shortage of experienced guides. It also allowed Scottish Natural Heritage to monitor tourist flows, enabling them to understand and manage tourism hot spots. The MSPW would send out messages to tourists to tell them to avoid certain areas where queues where forming due too many tourists. This way, a tourism distribution policy was enacted for rural destinations. For the tourist it meant no crowds and more personal space.
- The *Estonia Centre of Excellence* was a new training model. Instead of creating a centre of excellence in Scotland – it was decided to create one in Estonia, as the future of the Scottish tourism labour force was going to be Eastern European rather than Scottish. Here butlers were trained in neuro-linguistic programming. The programme was so successful that even King William recruited his Balmoral Butler from the course. Scotland now has the best-trained Butler Corps and respected force in the world.

---

² Named after Professor Roger Schmenner, whose *Challenges for Service Managers* idea allowed product designers to find solutions for problems based upon the degree of customerisation, interaction and labour intensity.

- By 2015, the Scottish tourism industries *initiative for every household in Scotland to take a short break in Scotland* proved to be a winner – 80% of all households did so. Even General Practitioners in Scotland signed up to the scheme, as the NHS was prescribing short breaks instead of tranquilisers for obesity and mental health problems. *Scotland for Health* was approved by the National Institute for Clinical Excellence as an alternative therapy.
- In order to pay for the growth in tourism, the *Tourism Development Act of 2014* allowed destinations within Scotland to introduce bed and/or ecology tax as means to develop sustainable tourism policies and market their own destinations. Edinburgh was the first city to introduce a bed tax to pay for the development of tourism within the city. Whereas the Orkney Isles introduced a £1000 visitor tax in order balance sustainability with popularity.

Between 2005 and 2010, we saw a number of developments and changes in tourism products and markets. For example, the accommodation sector polarised between two markets. First of all, accommodation providers in suburbia found that consumers wanted basic, safe and comfortable accommodation without all of the frills. The budget accommodation sector thrived as the hotel bedroom became the "spare guest bed" for urban populations spurred on by growth in the numbers of visiting friends and relatives and the need for thrifty accommodation. Even in traditional holiday destinations, visitors were spurning service for self-catering flats. Accommodation in these markets, like many other products in a disinflation economy, was now a commodity. Accommodation providers who had a five star status or a boutique nature grew because mass affluent consumer still wanted to be pampered. It was the providers who were perceived as a traditional three star hotel, or in seasonal locations, that were squeezed between rising costs and falling yields. In this scenario, tourism is *everyone's business*.

Scenario 2: Yesterday's Destination

Scottish Tourism is based upon the past, a world of icons and complacency. We dream of glory and the past. We dream of touring on an old classic. The problem is, the past is not quite good enough. Scotland is an uncompetitive and Second Division Destination, which has consistently not met the expectations of the sophisticated consumer. Although there are examples of good experiences, often there is no consistency. Failure to take tourism seriously, means the destination lacks innovation and social cachet. Basically the competition is better value for money. Tourism is still here, but there are fewer tourists every year and they spend less money.

A 1970s Command and Control Economy

Scotland's path to 2015 is based upon how the past shapes the future. Many business leaders describe the Scottish Executive's economic policy as *Stupid and Unsuccessful Scotland*. Scotland is a nation that lacks confidence and glories in failure. It is restrained by its history in which change is a recycling of previous attempts, reviews and grand ideas. Scotland's economy is only growing at 1% per annum, when measured in Gross Value Added (GVA) terms. Scotland is a command and control economy in which the Scottish Executive thinks they know best, trying a range of investment strategies that attract industries in the short term, but with no long-term success.

The basic problem in Scotland is that it is an ageing nation that is stifled by regulation, which makes the manufacturing of goods expensive. It is as if we cannot learn any lessons from the past, we keep making the same mistakes. Many of Scotland's leading companies such as The Royal Bank of Scotland and HBOS have now been taken over or have decided to move their head quarters to another country leaving only a token presence in Scotland. The effect of globalisation has tended to draw people and businesses away from Scotland. Scotland is seeing a slow decline and drain on resources. Lack of venture capital limits Scotland's economic potential – this is a nation that is shackled to the past. In 2015, Scotland's burgeoning public sector now contributes 65% of GVA. This burden means the nation lacks innovation and ambition. It has a crisis of confidence – a vicious circle that is difficult to change. Risk aversion seems to be the norm in business today. Regulation, fear of failure and litigation forces many businesses to close – they simply cannot afford the insurance premiums or got lost in risk assessment procedures.

Most international companies now perceive Scotland as a branch and regional economy, not a nation. Scotland is more heavily dependent upon the UK for services than at any other time.

An ageing population continues to stifle economic growth, with Scotland having the oldest population in the UK. Scotland's ageing population is bleeding public services, with more and more money being ring fenced for health and social care. In fact, Scotland is perceived as a retirement home. We have the highest number of economically inactive citizens compared to other regions of the UK. On the brighter side, Scotland also has more millionaires than anywhere else in the UK, but their average age is 62 years. Scotland's sophisticated and educated consumers have disposable income but prefer not to spend it in Scotland as other destinations offer better value for money and better experiences.

Scotland is a parochial country in which the culture is strong and distinctive, but often backward looking. The problem is, the young people want to leave and this is taking the real heart out of the country.

Yesterday's Destination – Tourism in 2015

Scottish Tourism is a £5.1 billion industry (see Tables 12.4 and 12.5), which has grown at a rate of 1% per annum since 2003. The tourism industry directly employs 180,000 people and represents 2.5% of GVA still making it one of Scotland's important industries, but it is in slow decline. It is the "old dog" of the economy, as its value and contribution is diminishing in real terms. Scotland is a Second Division Destination that is struggling and uncompetitive.

Scotland's product portfolio concentrates on *Party Scotland, Families Holidays, Health and Well-Being, Rural Scotland, Seniors and Authentic Scotland.* Scotland's tourism market is very clear, it is associated with domestic tourists and traditional experiences. Visitors are segmented as grey and mature or with young families (Scotland is still a safe destination). Health tourism and small family centres have been the success stories of Scottish tourism but these successes could not make up for the decline in the short break market due to increases in outbound tourism to international destinations. Business tourism, once the growing sector of Scottish tourism, is now in decline due to less business travel, new technologies and a poor business product. The impact of risk assessment legislation killed off Scotland's adventure

Table 12.4: Yesterday's destination – the value of tourism in 2015.

Expenditure type	UK tourism £m	%	Overseas tourism £m	%	Total	%
Holidays	2878	66	430	56	3308	65
Business	740	17	115	15	855	17
VFR	650	15	155	20	805	16
Other	75	2	70	9	145	3
Total	4343	100	770	100	5113	100

Table 12.5: Yesterday's destination – spending patterns.

Spend	£m	%
Leisure spending	1240	24
Eating and drinking	1150	22
Travel	1075	21
Accommodation	1060	21
Other	588	12
Total	5113	100

sports industry – most sports tourists now go to Bulgaria – Europe's Outdoor Capital. Service is inconsistent – many tourists complain it is hot and cold, sometimes outstanding but usually dreadful.

People are not holidaying as often in Scotland – the product, the price and the service just are not quite right. In an environment of price-sensitive consumers, value-for-money and destination image are important drivers. You can now get direct flights from Dundee to Prague for less than you could 20 years ago – but Czechs do not seem to want to come here! But plenty of Scots want to leave. Scotland remains a high-cost destination in a price-sensitive world. Although it is cheap to get here, it is expensive to stay here.

The tourism industry introduced compulsory quality to practice license schemes in 2009. Such a scheme, focused on the product quality, was well meaning, but actually added to industries costs and stifled innovation. VisitScotland, who were responsible for the scheme, were always viewed as policemen by the industry.

As the population has aged, there is still some demand for nostalgia of the past. The bread and butter of Scottish tourism is still about haggis, bagpipes and tartan (many of these items are made in China). Tourism still makes a significant, if declining, contribution to the Scottish economy, but it is not seen as a driver of economic growth. In mid-summer, the high streets of Pitlochry and St. Andrews are still crowded with tourists – but those tourists are spending less, every year there are fewer of them, and for how much longer will they keep returning?

In this Scenario, tourism is a second-class experience and a second-class product.

Discussion: Actions and Outcomes

Heijden et al. (2002) states that the main purpose of scenario planning is to create a strategic conversation about a subject in order to action change. Scenarios are a means by which policy makers and politicians can engage in a thinking process which brings sense making and order to a complicated world. The most important outcome from the scenario process was the creation of a common language between stakeholders, policy makers and industry which highlighted the need for change. Senior directors at VisitScotland and political leaders within Scotland realised that they needed to avoid the *Yesterday's Destination* scenario and create strategy and policy that lead to the *Short Break Destination* scenario. Therefore it is important to answer the following questions:

Question 1: What are the opportunities and challenges for the tourism industry in each scenario?

Question 2: What actions should tourism industry leaders be taking today in order to prepare for the future?

Question 1: What are the opportunities and challenges for the tourism industry in each scenario?

Scenario 1: The Weekend Getaway – 2015

Within the Weekend Getaway the world is *doing* tourism. Research by ebookers (McGinty, 2005) states that destinations such as Morocco to the south and Dubai to the east are quickly establishing themselves as destinations catering for both the long- and short-haul market. The trends of greater affluence and the desire to visit far away places with different cultures or with a luxury offer make these destinations more attractive to tourists. The attraction of sand and sun is obvious. This is something which Scotland cannot compete with. According to the WTO (Yeoman et al., 2006) the future tourist is going to be more discerning and looking for more fulfilling experiences. The sophisticated tourist phenomenon is happening now – it describes someone that is educated, well travelled, price sensitive, liberal, concerned about life and changing values. The number of these sophisticated tourists will grow over time. Scotland's diversity of experiences, rich culture, authentic products and choices of rural and city destinations should make Scotland a natural choice in this scenario. But this is not an easy option, because as already mentioned, other destinations are *doing* tourism, so competition for these affluent high yield sophisticated tourists is intensive. In this scenario there is a constant battle to succeed – as the margin of failure is extremely small. Questions are also raised in this scenario about who pays for this and what should be the strategic policy? So what are the opportunities and challenges in this scenario (see Table 12.6).

Scenario 2: Yesterday's Destination – 2015

In this scenario, Scottish tourism has grown at a rate of 1% per annum to 2015. We have been too complacent and just not quite good enough. Therefore, we have being demoted to the

Table 12.6: Weekend getaway – opportunities and challenges.

Issue	Opportunities	Challenges	Area
Transport	Provide direct links to ensure a 3 hour journey Provide luxury travel solutions. Sustainable transport policy.	All transport must be integrated. Improve the transport infrastructure road, rail, ferry network and ensure linkage with. aircraft hubs. Attracting tourists from London and the SE may prove difficult because choices are greater. How can you make Scotland stand out from the competition? Pollution taxes – will they prove a turn off to potential markets? What is the potential harm caused by increasing air travel prices as a result of oil price increases? Development of new transport links continually delayed by planning and enquiry process – how can this be improved? How can the conflict of tourist transport meet the needs of local/native transport needs?	Supply factor
Fiscal autonomy	Scotland would be responsible for spending the money it raises in taxes. Potential as a result for increased investment in tourism. As a result Scotland would be relieved of the vicious circle of dependency culture/low risk/over analytical psyche	Tourism cannot win the strategic argument and is likely to lose out and not get the adequate funds. It is unlikely the private sector could pick up the slack because of inherent short termism.	Supply factor
Making tourism every one's business	Moving tourism into all spheres of business within Scotland and promoting the value and worth of tourism within Scotland would benefit tourism and economic performance of Scotland overall. Need to create a strategic conversation about the value of tourism, showing tourism equal to health and finance.	Tourism seen as a second rate industry with no depth or breadth – need to counter this, for example, with a proper career structure.	Supply factor
Tourism taxes	Can we ring fence the proceeds of a bed tax/environmental tax and spend specifically on	Taxes may cause loss of tourists to other destinations?	Supply factor

(Continued)

Table 12.6: (Continued)

Issue	Opportunities	Challenges	Area
	sustainability and development in tourism and meet the needs of increased demand? Can we use taxes to manage demand – good for sustainability overall?	Would government have the confidence to do it – witness congestion charge in Edinburgh?	
Rise of cultural capital	Scotland has the innate resources that can provide those nuggets of culture that will allow people to differentiate themselves more in the future.	Scotland must innovate to keep up with the demand for new experiences, need to continually invest in new cultural demands and not rely on existing attractions and icons.	Products
Time sensitive immediacy	VisitScotland.com can become the number one integrated booking facility for tourism in Scotland, available 24/7.	The current systems are not efficient enough public sector innovation cycles are too slow to keep up with private sector.	Products
Price-sensitive consumers	Scottish tourism can offer packages that are perceived to be of value at all ends of the spectrum. Diversity in a range of accommodation from budget to luxury. Integrate the transport fares, promote special offers.	Scotland perceived as too expensive. Can't deliver the joined up packages in transport because of political infighting and defensive positioning.	Products
BRIC nations, for example China ADS	Increasing numbers of affluent travellers from new markets. There is the potential for a link with British Council and other educational bodies.	Lack of presence in many of these markets, for example China at present. VisitBritain is under resourced There is no proximity with the new markets – they are more likely to travel to destinations within closer proximities to themselves. Lack of language skills, for example Scotland only has one Mandarin speaking Blue Guide	Markets
Expansion of the EU	Increasing numbers of affluent travellers in the EU Good proximity to Scotland. Many already have good air travel links.	Need direct connections. Need to prioritise markets – must not spread effort too thinly. Need to know the scale of opportunity for each of the markets.	Markets
Ageing population	Increase in the size of the current core market. This group have a higher disposable income. Higher correlation with cultural values that	Need plan to face increasing competition. This group tend to be more price sensitive. Scotland is perceived as an expensive destination. They are a highly competitive market for tourism.	Markets

	Scotland is highly associated with. Opportunity to harness word of mouth to promote Scotland.	The desire for new experiences will be accompanied by a decline in repeat visits. Long-term potential squeeze on disposable income for this group as a result of the "savings gap".	Consumer area
Sophisticated consumers and quality	Scotland has lots of basic qualities that will attract sophisticated consumers. There is a good match with future demands for example, authenticity, cultural capital, new experiences.	They tend to be sophisticated, experienced consumers with high demands – negative word of mouth a continual threat. Quality becomes a hygiene factor – current variation in quality in Scotland means that Scotland could lose sophisticated consumers. They are more demanding consumers and will not repeat visits, if needs not met on first visit. Less forgiving of failure.	Consumer area
Personalisation of authority	Already have advocates out there promoting Scotland in different markets. There is substantial celebrity endorsement of Scotland.	Negative word of mouth spreads much faster than positive. People could potentially trust VisitScotland less because it is a public sector body perceived as being linked with politicians.	Consumer area
Liberal consumers and tolerance	Scotland has a strong education system. There is a history of liberalism and philosophy. The Edinburgh festival is already the height of liberalism.	Scotland is perceived as having high levels of state intervention and over regulation, married with a lack of leadership. There is a perception of lower levels of tolerance in Scotland, it lacks a multicultural society, is perceived as a parochial nation with an ageing population – this does not match with the liberal consumer. There is a divide in religious allegiances across Scotland – Presbyterian heritage goes against the trend to increased tolerance.	

lower divisions of tourism destinations. Although tourism is still an important industry, service quality is patchy and inconsistent. Basically, we have not met the expectations of the sophisticated consumer. Failure to action change and take tourism seriously means the destination lacks innovation and social cachet. There is still opportunity in this scenario as highlighted by the Ella Stewart Family Centres and the mass creative class – but these cases are the isolated rather than ubiquitous. What then are the opportunities and challenges in this scenario (see Table 12.7)?

Question 2: What actions should tourism industry leaders be taking today in order to prepare for the future?

After exploring the challenges and opportunities posed by the scenarios the question turns to actions. These actions are the strategic imperatives that guide future strategies and decision-making (Figure 12.1).

Building a strategic conversation

1 These tourism scenarios will be used to paint a picture of success. By focusing on success extra value is created from the dimensions of economic value, political will, social responsibility, technological needs and a sustainable industry. Success shows the importance and value of tourism for Scotland.
2 Tourism must be everyone's business. In order to show the economic value of tourism and its relationship to the other sectors, a tourism satellite account (TSA) approach will be used. A series of tourism indicators will be published to show the economic value of tourism in the Scottish economy. This will be complemented by a number of educational and community programmes that place tourism at the heart of the Scottish economy. Scotland has a strong Diaspora and history and these together will lead to a "tartan renaissance". By using such an approach the values of Scotland cannot be separated from Scotland.
3 The tourist has to be the central focus to any tourism economy. This means providing a warm welcome and professional service to all visitors that step foot in Scotland. The industry needs to be further professionalised through certification, innovation and regulation.
4 Scotland's ambition to grow tourism by 50% by 2015 needs to be embedded in everyday conversation especially amongst the political and business leaders of Scotland. Therefore, it is necessary that a communications strategy deliver this promise. Scottish tourism also needs strong and confident leadership in order to move tourism up the economic, social and political agenda.

Required Policy Actions

1 Develop a sustainable transport policy in which tourism is a core driver. The foundation of this policy should facilitate the 3-hour journey time, ease of access to Scotland's markets

Table 12.7: Yesterday's Destinations – opportunities and challenges.

Issue	Opportunity	Challenge	Area
Economic stagnation	More focussed markets. Tourism could be more attractive industry to the Scottish executive as a result of decline in other sectors.	How to ensure that tourism moves up the agenda when everything else is declining?	Supply side
Political psyche and short termism	Opportunity for quick wins seized upon that bring in money quickly – quick ROI.	Not a sustainable policy. No joined up thinking. Consensus politics with a lack of leadership leads to stagnation and no innovation. There is a widespread lack of confidence and parochialism.	Supply side
Emigration	Increase to Diaspora.	Labour supply reduced. Lack of dynamism in the economy. Poor dependency ratios.	Supply side
Expensive destination	Focus on exclusive and best practice in tourism and distinction.	General long-term decline in numbers of visitors.	Supply side
Tacky destination	Allows short-term profits to be made.	Not sustainable – drives away sophisticated consumer. Not a sophisticated destination. Over development, wrong development and a lack of good development – spoil offer. Over development of icons destroy authenticity and cultural significance and cachet.	Supply side
Traditional Scotland	Focus on authenticity meets some of the demands of sophisticated tourists.	A lack of innovation and reliance on what done before, does not meet the demand for new experiences.	Supply side

(Continued)

Table 12.7: (Continued)

Issue	Opportunity	Challenge	Area
Scottish food	Good quality products, unique products meet people's demands for new, authentic experiences.	Does not meet perception of Scottish food – home of the deep fried mars bar. Challenge to provide a kite mark and investment in place names, authentic, assured provenance of products.	Supply side products
Tourism in the community	Promotion of tourism as everyone's business. Extend the social value of tourism. All of which widens the reach and impact of tourism.	Making it happen will be difficult – not much to build upon.	Supply side products
Climate change	Potential for new markets and products.	Adaptation strategies need to be in place. Environmental strategies needed to be in place to protect attractions. Difficult to understand the implications of climatic change.	Supply side markets products
Anxiety society	Scotland perceived as a safe destination – can build on this perception.	Over regulation ends in an assault on pleasure. Unaffordability of risk assessment and. increasingly litigious society. Direct threat on adventure tourism. Scotland an expensive destination already and this could make it too expensive. Anxiety society makes tourism in Scotland more susceptible to shocks. Dampens innovation. Negative impact on tourism overall.	Consumer trend and products
Family networks	Family holiday centres can meet need for multigenerational family holidays. Scotland safe and easy destination to reach.	Weather not good for families. Potential difficulties of meeting intergenerational demands.	Consumer trend and products

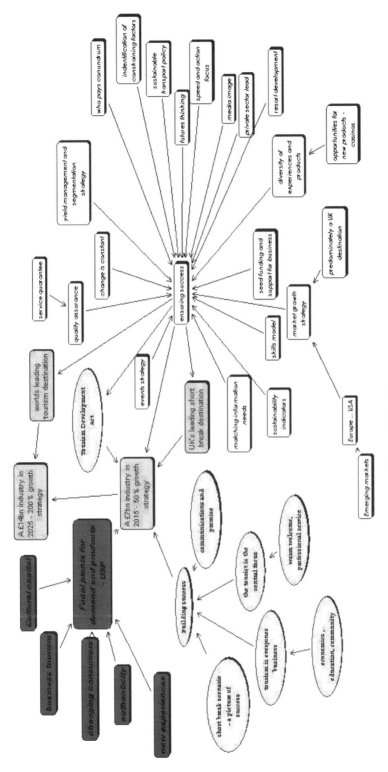

Figure 12.1: Strategy map.

and integration of the transport network. This policy needs to be balanced against future constraining factors and the impact on the environment.

2   Decisions need to be made about "who pays" for the future growth of Scottish tourism. Whether these are local bed taxes to pay for destination marketing or ecology taxes to account for the sustainability of Scottish tourism. This "who pays" conundrum means the development of a payment ratio between industry–the tourist–government.

3   The development of a Scottish tourism proposition based upon the following key drivers: the desire for authenticity delivered in an innovative way; the growth of new experiences that meet and exceed consumer expectations; the need to ensure that tourism is full of cultural capital; and the facilitation of the growth of business tourism. The authenticity of the Scottish tourism product is reflected in its strong built heritage environment. The importance of cultural capital is associated with its international festivals and arts programmes. New experiences will emerge from its strong adventure tourism portfolio. Business tourism will be enhanced through the development of Glasgow's Scottish Exhibition and Conference Centre (SECC). These drivers distinguish Scotland from its competitors and should be the basis for competitive advantage, destination image, brand and marketing strategy and product offering.

4   Over the next 10 years Scotland will be predominantly a UK market based tourism destination with UK tourism representing £5.5 billion. The core overseas markets will be North America and Europe. As the European Union expands eastward it is envisaged that Scotland will be predominately more a European destination that a North American one. This is based upon proximity, rising affluence and Scotland as an English-speaking country. The value of international tourism will be £1.6 billion. The growing significance of emergence of new long-haul markets such as India and China means the development of an emergent market strategy. Additionally, Eastern European markets will stretch to Russia and Turkey. The total value of Scottish tourism by 2015 will be £7.2 billion. This represents an annual growth rate of 4% per annum until that time.

5   As Scottish tourism is to grow by 50% over the next 10 years, a range of sustainability factors or indicators will be established in order to measure the impact of this growth.

6   Scottish tourism will continue to invest in quality assurance as this is now a hygiene factor rather than a distinguishing factor. It will deliver a unified quality assurance programme that guarantees quality of service.

7   The breath of its tourism products and markets represents the vibrancy of a tourism destination. Scottish tourism will prioritise markets and products based upon scale of opportunity and investment potential. The importance of this diversity is significant in a post 9/11 world as markets react in different ways to different "shocks".

8   A study will be undertaken that identifies the constraining factors of growth in order to develop strategies that overcome these factors or facilitate alternative directions. Such a study will explore such factors as accommodation supply, labour supply and transport infrastructure.

9   If Scottish tourism is to grow by 50% by 2015 it is recognised that there will be a skills gap. This will be compounded further by falling demographics. Therefore it is imperative to use a skills model based upon an overseas labour market and industry rather than education must have responsibility for this delivery.

10   Scotland will continue to support an events strategy based upon culture and sport that maintains international appeal.

11   Provision of seed funding that allows entrepreneurs to develop new tourism products and services. To offer support for new start-ups and existing businesses.

12   A reappraisal of information networks based upon changing technology, 24-hour society, and an immediacy culture. This means a Tourism Information Centre (TIC) network that needs to match the demand for tourism services. VisitScotland.com needs to be commercially vibrant in order to compete with other Internet intermediaries.

13   To achieve its growth target, Scottish tourism requires a yield management strategy for the economy that will deliver the right type of growth in line with sustainability and capacity constraints. Scotland must know which type of tourists it wants, what they should be doing and how much they are spending. As it must be remembered that too many of the wrong types of tourist will spoil Scotland's tourism proposition for the future.

14   In order to deliver success Scotland must be seen as an international tourism destination where international tourism companies want to invest and build. Therefore, a resort development programme is needed that balances regulation, sustainability and economic development. Over regulation must not be a barrier to economic development. Processes are needed to speed up planning regulation. Time constrained, comprehensive decisions need to be made rather than longitudinal reviews. In line with this, an independent policy unit is needed to assess the consequences of change and development and improve the knowledge underlying investment decisions.

15   By using the process of futures thinking and scenario planning, the industry needs to anticipate new trends that will lead to the development of products and services that will surprise the customer. Additionally, environmental factors such as climatic change and natural disasters need to be accounted for and contingency plans drawn up.

16   The Scottish tourism industry should be lead by the private sector will have total responsibility for demand side factors such as destination marketing. Therefore, from 2010, the state will start to withdraw its involvement in these areas.

17   A Tourism Development Act is required to enshrine policy initiatives that take into account considerations such as sustainability, national strategy, regulation and certification.

Conclusions

Ringland (2002) notes that the purpose of scenarios in public policy is to create an environment for surfacing and discussing the future. This chapter demonstrates how scenario planning and thinking can be effective. The real outcome of the scenario-planning process was to create a shared language between VisitScotland and its stakeholders, in particular, the political and industrial leaders of Scotland. This created a strategic conversation that change was necessary, and that a plan for change should be developed. Heijden et al. (2002) notes that there is no point in creating scenarios unless change is actioned on the basis of them. Many scenarios planning exercises fail because the outcomes are not implemented, making the exercise academic from a stakeholder's perspective. This case study, however, is an example of best practice in which scenario planning has enabled stakeholders to talk about the future and action the future in a structured and feasible manner. The value of the process links Scottish tourism's ambition to grow the industry by 50% with the scenarios and actionable policies.

References

Blake, A., Dubarry, R., Eugenio-Martin, J., Gooroochurn, N., Lennon, J., Sinclair, M. T., Hay, B., Sugiyarto, G., & Yeoman, I. (2006). Integrating forecasting and CGE models: The case of tourism in Scotland. *Tourism Management*, 27(2), 292–305.

Devarajan, S., & Robinson, S. (2003). *The influence of computable general equilibrium models on policy, trade and macro economics division.* International Food Policy Research Institute. Available at www.cgiar.org/ifpri/divs/tmd/dp

Eden, C., & Ackermann, F. (1998). *Journey making.* London: Sage.

Evans, C., Rogers, S., McGraw, C., Battle, G., & Furniss, L. (2004). Using consensus methods to establish multidisciplinary perspectives methods on research priorities for primary care. *Primary Health Care Research and Development*, 5(1), 52–59.

Flood, R. A., & Romm, N. R. A. (1996). *Diversity management: Triple loop learning.* Chichester: John Wiley & Sons Ltd.

Flowers, B. S. (2003 February). The art and strategy of scenario writing. *Strategy and Leadership*, 31(2), 29–33.

Hall, C. M., & Jenkins, J. M. (1995). *Tourism and policy.* London: Routledge.

Hardin, P. K. (2003 March). Constructing experience in individual interviews, autographies and on accounts: A poststructuralist approach. *Journal of Advanced Nursing*, 41(6), 536–544.

Hardy, D. J., O'Brien, A., Gaskin, C. J., O'Brien, A. J. Morrison-Ngatal, E., Skews, G., Ryan, T., & McNulty, N. (2004). Practical application of the Delphi technique in a bicultural mental health nursing study in New Zealand. *Journal of Advance Nursing*, 46(1), 95–109.

Hay, B. (2002). A vision of tourism in 2020. In: N. Hood, J. Peat, E. Peters & S. Young (Eds), *Scotland in a global economy: The 2020 vision.* Basingstoke: Palgrave.

Heijden, K., Bradfield, R., Burt, G., Cairns, G., & Wright, G. (2002). The sixth sense: Accelerated organizational learning with scenarios. Chichester: Wiley.

Hodgson, A. M. (1992). Hexagons for systems thinking. *European Journal of Operational Research*, 59, 220–230.

Jones, M. (1993). *Decision explorer: Reference manual version 3.1.* Glasgow: Banxia Software Limited.

Kerr, B., Barron, G., & Wood, R. (2001). Politics, policy and regional tourism administration: A case examination of Scottish area tourist board funding. *Tourism Management*, 22(6), 649–657.

Kerr, W. R. (2003). *Tourism public policy, and the strategic management of failure.* London: Pergamon.

Lederer, P. (2004 April). *Our ambition for Scottish tourism.* The Moffatt Lecture, Glasgow Caledonian University.

McGinity, S. (2005). *Far away places now mini break places.* Scotsman, 1st April. Accessed at http://news.scotsman.com/international.cfm?id=342742005

Partidario, P. J., & Vergragt, P. (2002). Planning of strategic innovation aimed at environmental sustainability, actor networks, scenario acceptance and backcasting analysis with a polymeric coating. *Futures*, 34(9), 841–861.

Richards, L. (1999). *Using Nvivo in qualitative research.* Melbourne, Vic.: Qualitative Solutions and Research Pty Ltd.

Ringland, G. (2002). *Scenarios in Public Policy.* Chichester: Wiley.

Roorda, N. (2001). Backcasting the future. *International Journal of Sustainability in Higher Education*, 2(1), 63–69.

Ryan, C. (2002). Equity, management, power sharing and sustainability – issues of the "new tourism". *Tourism Management*, 23(1), 17–26.

Sautter, E. T., & Leisen, B. (1999). Managing stakeholders a tourism planning model. *Annals of Tourism Research*, 26(2), 312–328.

Smith, R. (1998). Public policy for tourism in Scotland. In: R. MacLellan & R. Smith (Eds), *Tourism in Scotland*. London: Thomson Business Press.

Sparrow, J. (1998). Knowledge in organizations: Access to thinking at work. London: Sage.

Woulde, D., Damgaard, G., Hegge, M., Soholt, D., & Bunkers, S. (2003). The unfolding scenario planning in nursing. *Nursing Science Quarterly*, *16*(1), 27–35.

Yeoman, I., & McMahon-Beattie, U. (2004). Designing a scenario planning process using a blank piece of paper. *Hospitality and Tourism Research*, *6*(1), 273–284.

Yeoman, I., Munro, C., & McMahon-Beattie, U. (2006). Tomorrow's world, consumer, tourist. *Journal of Vacation Marketing*, *15* (Issue to be decided).

Chapter 13

Governing Tourism Monoculture: Mediterranean Mass Tourism Destinations and Governance Networks

Giorgio Conti and Carlo Perelli

Introduction

North-Mediterranean mass tourism destinations represent a consolidated research subject. During the past 50 years an increasing concentration of tourism destinations all along the coast line has been attracting consistent international tourism flows. In 1990 according to the European Environment Agency 135 million tourists chose the Mediterranean Sea and the same agency forecasts for the year 2025 between 235 and 350 million tourists in the region (EEA, 2003). Different authors have been focusing their attention on mass tourism destinations facing a stagnation phase (Agarwal, 2002; Knowles & Curtis, 1999; Priestley & Mundet, 1998) and supporting a rejuvenation process (Butler, 1980). Nowadays an attention to tourism diversification processes is generally observable between policy-makers (Bianchi, 2004; Bramwell, 2004) and the rhetoric of sustainable tourism provides the dominant strategic horizon of contemporary tourism policies in the region in opposition to the risk of a De-Mediterraneanization of the Mediterranean (Selwyn, 2000).

Tourism policies and planning strategies in the tourism sector have been traditionally conditioned by the traditional perception of tourism as an environmental friendly industry. Furthermore the hegemony of economic growth-based discourses among local decision-makers have been conditioning the tourism policies and planning evolution toward an integrated framework including environmental and social priorities. Short range and economic drove priorities has been traditionally limiting the capacity to implement strategic planning tools supporting longstanding integrated development policies. Adopting Getz (1987) and Hall (2000) schematization of different approaches to tourism planning we can easily recognize

Tourism and politics
© 2007 Published by Elsevier Ltd.
ISBN: 0-08-045075-X

in the past years the dominance of *boosterism* and *industry-oriented approaches* or, following Burns (2004) a *tourism first* attitude.

Traditional mass tourism destinations in the Mediterranean are nowadays trying to react to the difficulties of the local tourism system by the introduction of new modes of governing the tourism phenomena. Two driving forces (occasionally integrated) are reshaping the traditional approaches to tourism policies and planning strategies: the dominant discourse on the sustainability of tourism and the attention for innovative governance processes. If on the one hand the literature exploring the relationship between tourism and sustainability principles is flourished during the last 15 years, on the other the attention to governance issues characterizing tourism phenomena is relatively reduced. Some interesting exceptions are represented by researches focusing on the implementation of collaboration strategies (Bramwell & Sharman, 1999; Buhalis & Cooper, 1998; Jamal & Getz, 1995), on power (Bianchi, 2003; Cheong & Miller, 2000), community participation in the decision-making process (Murphy, 1985; Pearce et al., 1996; Reed, 1997), and on the political dimension of tourism phenomena at the destination scale (Bianchi, 2004; Boissevain & Selwyn, 2004; Kousis, 2000).

This chapter focuses on the role of governance processes in the development, consolidation, and diversification phases of coastal tourism systems traditionally marked by a tourism monoculture and particularly in the analysis of Rimini case (Figure 13.1), historically the leading Italian coastal destination.

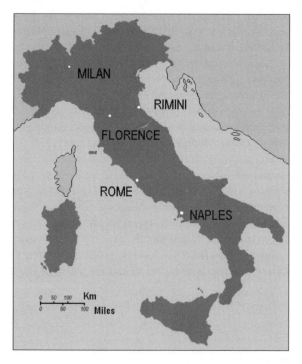

Figure 13.1: The location of Rimini.

As showed by Rhodes (2000; 1997) there are multiple definitions of governance.[1] We agree with the definition stating that governance is about *new process of governing* (Rhodes, 1997). At the same time can be important to underline the fact that the contemporary attention to governance processes is supporting the attempt to reconceptualize the traditional debate on government forms under new conceptual categories. In this sense the conceptual opposition government versus governance is in our view to be reconsidered sharing the two concepts, the core object of research. The case of networking strategies in an urban policy-making scenario clearly describes this process. Our analysis wants to investigate the origins and the contemporary consistency of networking strategies that constituted in the past the main reason of Rimini tourism system success. The analysis adopts as a theoretical framework the urban regimes analysis approach.

Defining Urban Regimes

At the end of the 1980s (Elkin, 1987; Stone, 1989) the emergence of urban regime theories in the US has been introducing interesting elements in the urban governance debate. Aiming to focus on the nature of networking experiences in urban governance processes regimes analysis has been obtaining more and more attention also in Europe (Dowding, 2001; Harding, 1997; John, 2001; Stoker, 1995; Stoker & Mossberger, 1994).

Adopting a very general definition we can see urban regimes as *informal but stable coalitions governing the city*. This definition introduces us to some basics characteristics of a regime. First the existence of an informal network involving local government and non-governmental actors and influencing local decision-making processes. As a condition to identify a regime the non-governmental partners of the networks have to participate with own resources to the policy-making process. If not the policy-implementation process can be considered as the simple exercise of governmental functions by local government institutions.

The nature of network agreement is informal and founded on a collaborative approach between the partners (Stone, 1993). A coercive participation to a network rarely originates a stable regime being the collaboration on shared strategic purposes the founding condition of the existence of a regime. Similarly a bureaucratic cooperation between governmental actors and non-governmental partners is generally not effective if not founded on really shared visions (Davies, 2003). In this sense Stoker (1995) individuates regimes as cooperation networks different from coercive systems of participation and collaboration but also from a traditional system of cooperation merely based on market rules.

Second, the stability of the coalition is measured by the capability to provide a widely shared agenda, a strategy capable to group a relevant network of partners and to provide broad consensus on a governing vision. The agenda have not to cover the totality of the domains of the governing actions but the capability to provide a clear and shared strategy in a domain perceived as strategic by the local community can determine a long-lasting

---

[1] According to the author at least seven main definitions of the concept can be individuated notably: Corporate Governance; Governance as the New Public Management; Governance as "Good Governance"; Governance as International Interdependence; Governance as a Socio-cybernetic System; Governance as the New Political Economy; and Governance as Networks.

urban regime. In this sense the consensus over a shared strategy is not strictly coincident with shared goals. Governing coalition can exists also in presence of not equally shared goals (Stone, 2004a). Networking processes are more exactly based on congruent goals being very common the case of the concurrent presence of shared goals, conflicting goals, and competing priorities between coalition partners.

Third, agenda feasibility can determine the stability of a regime. This condition is strongly related to the consistency of the resources the coalition is able to activate to support the agenda purposes (Stoker, 1995). In this sense the consistency of the governing network agenda and the access to resources (public or private) are unequivocally related. A dynamic equilibrium between the creation of a broad consensus on the agenda and the implementation of the strategy is generally needed to support an urban regime. Agenda feasibility is commonly dependent by agenda credibility expressed by the *interdependence* idea, meaning the capability to combine congruent purposes and adequate resources to legitimate the governing agenda.

Even lacking of the character of a complete and coherent theory of government and power relationships, urban regime theory provides an interesting analysis tool to investigate local politics. The attention for the characteristics of governing networks and the modalities of the adhesion to the governing strategies provides a useful set of variables for the researcher. Being the finality of such an approach to verify the existence and the conditions of stable governing networks and being the basic characteristics of a regime very difficult to be achieved is very common that a regime analysis will lead to the conclusion of the absence of a regime. As clearly explained by Stone:

"Over time, I have come to feel strongly that asking whether a given locality or set of localities pass a litmus test to qualify as urban regimes is the wrong question. Enquiry needs to focus on the character of local governing arrangements, what enables them to pursue an agenda, and what shapes the strength and direction of a locality's problem-solving efforts. Put in general terms, as urban actors construct their responses to the problems and challenges around them, how do governing arrangements take shape? What matters as urban actors adapt their political and civic relationships to the task of governance?"(Stone, 2004a, p. 9)

Regime analysis has been criticized by several authors both for adopting a localistic focus and to underestimate the role of the State in local governance mechanism, especially in Europe (Davies, 2002b; 2003; Harding, 1994). Nevertheless the local scale of the analyses does not exclude the evident influence of external influences on coalitions governing the city but simply focuses on the observation of the mechanism adopted by local networks to constitute long-lasting governing alliances. The fact to consider as a framework the external influences on local governance patterns is not due to an underestimation of the local–global connections characterizing contemporary societies but only to the choice of a bottom-up approach to the analysis of governance mechanisms. The need to integrate this approach with a top-down analysis of the international actors contributing to shape local policies is not on discussion but it's simply out of the finality of a regime analysis approach. Furthermore a better understanding of local governance mechanism can contribute to clarify part of the governance mechanisms puzzle also in a comparative perspective (Stone, 2004b).

Urban regime analysis can be of some utility in the analysis of tourism destinations. An interesting example of the application of an urban regime approach in tourism research is provided by Long's study on London inner city fringe (Long, 1999) or Thomas and Thomas

(2005) research on small and medium enterprises impact on tourism policies. The choice to adopt this approach in the analysis of traditional mass tourism destinations like Rimini is due by several reasons. First is commonly observable in this kind of destinations the consolidation of long-lasting phases where tourism growth is characterized by a wide consensus and local economy is developed around what can be defined as a tourism monoculture. What is generally not investigated is what kind of alliances has been creating the conditions for such a general consensus on *tourism first* growth strategies and what kind of governance mechanism has been founding the governing actions.

Second, consequently to the reorganization process of contemporary tourism industry traditional tourism destinations in the Mediterranean are facing similar difficulties in supporting tourism diversification policies and in activate a rejuvenation process to confirm their leading position in the international tourism market. This change of paradigm in local tourism policies involves the rethinking of traditional governing schemes and commonly causes the emerging of conflicting positions between traditional tourism sector actors and new emerging priorities in tourism organizational patterns. A regime analysis can help to identify and investigate conflicting positions and shared strategies.

Third, the characteristics of European tourism sector justify an increasing attention to networking strategies. According to the European Union (EU) Commission (2004) about 60% of the holidays with at least four overnight stays are spent in seaside destinations and during the period April–October. Furthermore in 2000 about 99% of the enterprises in tourism sector and related activities were small (from 10 to 49 employees) and medium enterprises (from 50 to 250). These characteristics are strongly dominant in southern Europe nations being for instance one-third of the big enterprises (more than 250 employees) concentrated in UK. At the destination level this scenario involves a consolidated tradition of political mediation with tourism businesses networks, business categories representatives, sector Unions, and Chambers of Commerce. In some cases Parties or religious representatives can represent a relevant actor in local governance processes. Urban regimes analysis can help to identify governing alliances and strategies starting from the analysis of the evolution of tourism policies and planning strategies. Differently from Structuralist class analysis for instance, urban regime approach focuses on the form governing coalitions assume by *doing things*, being the effectiveness of the agenda adopted a key element for the identification of a regime.

Methodology Remarks

Our research has been conducted between September 2003 and January 2006. The fact that one of the authors is born in Rimini and during his professional life has been directly and indirectly in contact with tourism officials, entrepreneurs but also what can be defined as the local civil society inevitably advantaged and conditioned the documentation phase and more generally the research plan. During the research phase apart from the inclusion of data derived from newspapers archives, primary and secondary literature, official city, and provincial data we worked in direct contact with the functionaries of the local Provincial Institution in charge for the tourism sector and the Sustainable Development division. We participated in three workshops organized by the Province to coordinate the Local Agenda

21 activities and to create a national network of local authorities implementing tourism-related LA21 processes.

In parallel, informal meetings with local Parties representatives, academicians, and tourism sector operators has been organized aiming to select significant issues and to organize the following interviews phase. The direct interviews have been conducted in October 2005. We selected 20 peoples trying to include also relevant actors normally obtaining marginal positions in the local debate and in media consideration. The interviews involved representatives from local Institutions (Municipality, Province but also Trade Unions), tourism entrepreneurs, local representatives of Parties, local associations, and among the others the President of the local Fair and the Director of the regional Tourism Office. During the same period we organized two workshops with the aim of discuss the findings of the research and stimulate useful suggestions on the research structure.

The first took place in the Province offices involving functionaries working in tourism-related sectors for the Regional, Provincial and Municipal authorities, local University professors, the local Chamber of Commerce, and with the participation of the Province Councillor for the tourism sector. The second workshop has been organized in collaboration with two different local informal networks (one involved more in the local political dimension and in local associations, the second grouping local citizens working in different ways in the local public life and in cultural activities) and we obtained to involve around 25 peoples from very different backgrounds[2] animating an interesting debate on city strategic views.

The Formation of a Seaside Tourism Monoculture

The evolution of Rimini from small town with an established economy based on agriculture and handicraft to one of the European capitals of coastal tourism has occurred through a series of phases. The analysis of these evolutionary moments enables us to emphasize the governance mechanism supporting the formation, consolidation, and crisis of the tourist system based on the seaside tourism monoculture. This system has determined until today the evolution of the Riminese territory, going through different political phases almost undamaged until the 1980s.

Rimini has been historically one of the main city of the area mainly for the key position at the cross road between coast, plane, and inner mountains territories as testified by the strategic role of the city in the Roman Empire communication system. Today Rimini is included in the Emilia–Romagna region and with the surrounding coastal tourism system is one of the main tourism area in the EU, with around 45 million overnight stays each year. The first nucleus of the future tourism industry was born in 1843 with the opening of the *Stabilimento Privilegiato dei Bagni Marittimi*, 20 years after the inauguration of the establishment in Viareggio, Italy's first seaside resort. Rimini in those years accounted for about 30.000 inhabitants. It was situated in the *Stato Pontificio*, under the Pope's dominion, in a backward economic reality based on agricultural incomes. Its strategic geographical position and its healthy coast – free from malaria – led some members of the rising urban middle class of the town to

---

[2] From Academicians to citizens formerly involved in local politics, from local Parties representatives to school teachers or leading tourism attractions managers, from cultural events responsible to local opinion-makers.

undertake the venture, with the support of some progressive nobles. It was basically thera-peutic tourism. The idea of opening the public baths initially met with the determined opposi-tion by the notables men of the town and that of the municipality representing their interests: the new middle class drive disagreed with the static economic system of the time based on agricultural estate incomes. This scenario will not change with the adhesion of Rimini in 1860 to the *Regno di Sardegna*, the original form of what will become the unified Italian state.

The completion of the Bologna–Ancona railway line in 1860 and the intuition of future profits induced the municipality to buy the baths in 1869 after the economic failure of the first ownership. The same year a travelling expedition set out on a cruise in the Mediterranean Sea (Tuscany, Liguria, and the French Riviera) to visit and learn from the most developed tourism destinations in Mediterranean Sea. The appearance of the public management determines the transition from a pioneering phase marked by private industries initiative to the development of a seaside building sector which paralysed the newborn tourist indus-try. The investments strategy focusing on the baths, the therapeutic tourism, and on the hotels sector was given up in favour of an economic development based on land revenue incomes and real estate speculation under the influence of local governing elite. In 1873 the building sector society *Società Anonima Edificatrice Riminese* was established, sub-sidized by the local bank *Cassa di Risparmio* that represented the interests of estate ventures and promoted the building of detached houses, of the Kursaal, and of the new hydrothera-peutic resort. A concept of holiday was born, and with it the littoral town marked by detached houses (Conti & Pasini, 2000). The strategic partnership between municipality and real estate speculators, supported by the local bank will represent the key variable in local governance processes during the following 100 years.

In 1907 the first municipality regulation for the building of detached houses on the beach was approved and in 1908 the municipality sold the management of the littoral area to private individuals. The tourism business started to attract external capitals and entrepreneurs from Milan (grouped in the SMARA Company, *Società Milanese Alberghi Ristoranti e Affini*) chose to built in Rimini the *Grand Hotel Hungaria* aiming to attract elite tourism flows. During the following 40 years the debate on the opportunity to support an elite tourism will be dominant in the local scenario and only with the mass tourism boom of the 1950s Rimini chose its definitive position in the international tourism market. In 1910 the tourism tax was instituted (lasting until 1989) and in this first phase was controlled by the municipality and mainly final-ized to assure investments on tourism sector as well as on the urban quality improvement. It originated on the other hand a long-lasting quarrel and a harsh political contrast over the des-tination of the resources. In 1912 the first town-planning scheme was brought into existence. The philosophy of the plan was clearly oriented to the creation of an elite tourism destin-ation, a coastal garden city with a seaside promenade that resisted in its basic structure until today. If considered under an urban planning point of view such a scheme adopted a low profile aiming only to rationalize a posteriori, the spontaneous littoral urban expansion.

After the First World War all factories of foreign ownership were forced to close. Furthermore the existence of Italian chemical factories was contrasted. The debate over the choice between a seaside-estate economy and the industrial development as axis of prior-ity development let the interests of real estate incomes prevail. The final closing of the *Stabilimento Idroterapico* (Hydrotherapy Resort) in 1920 confirmed the monocultural orienta-tion of the destination development.

In 1922 Rimini was under Fascist control, but the change of regime did not invert the direction of the seaside-real estate development. It was a period of very high taxation levels. In the early 1930s one-third of the inhabitants fed themselves on the town soup-kitchen (Conti & Pasini, 2000). The fragility of the monoculture had reached its apex: most industries were nearly abolished, the tourism season was short and, in spite of the increased number of people who went on holiday, only a few benefited from the tourist industry.

As the *Azienda di Cura, Soggiorno e Turismo* (Tourism Office) was established in 1926, and all the decision-makers represented the Fascist regime as well as its interests. The control over the municipality and the Tourism Office by the same individual, the Fascist regime representative *Podestà*, symbolically embodied the apex of the seaside tourism monoculture. In 1931 the ownership and management of the Grand Hotel and the surrounding bathing establishments are acquired under the control of the municipality. Mussolini spent his holidays in Riccione and the Adriatic Riviera becomes the favourite beach of Fascism. In order to popularize holidays special trains and seaside camps for children were created by the Fascism (De Grazia, 1981). Holiday time becomes part of the rhetoric discourses supporting the regime ideology and in the mid-1930s around 2.5 millions stays are reported in the Adriatic Riviera. Touring had been given a boost together with boarding houses and hotels suitable for both the middle and working class.

This first development phase shows some interesting elements that will support the mass tourism boom, the consolidation of the tourism monoculture but also the emergence of what can be defined as a regime according to the characteristics described before. First the exponential growth of the built areas in the seaside and the consolidation of a privileged relationship between the municipality and the local real estate sector. The consequent urban sprawl in absence of effective planning tools will guarantee in the following decades a justification for an unlimited urban growth philosophy being the urban structure impossible to be radically modified after the pioneering years expansion. Second, the choice to support tourism sector development despite of the industrial factories on the one hand will prevent environmental damages and on the other will create the conditions for the development of a broad hospitality culture in the year of reconstruction after the Second World War. Again can be interesting to note that even crossing different political phases and governing regimes (the unitary Italian state as like the Fascist regime), the support to the consolidation of a seaside tourism monoculture has been representing a constant characterization of the city-governing strategies.

Mass Tourism and the Creation of Rimini Model

After the Second World War, Rimini had lost more than 80% of its buildings because of the bombings (Fabbri, 1992), but it quickly took back its role as Italy's leading seaside tourism destination. The Italian Communist Party (PCI) won the 1946 elections with 37.5 of the votes and strategically decided not to interfere with the recovery process of the city. Consequently no urban planning tools were adopted whereas particular investments were strongly supported. In 1947 the local bank Cassa di Risparmio financed a renewal project for the seaside area and the demolition of the Kursaal the symbol of the former elite tourism season conflicting with the development plans of PCI.

In 1951 tourists exceeded 1 million stays (Dall'Ara, 2002) and starting from 1954 foreign tour operators started to sell the Adriatic Riviera destinations in north European countries. However, the transformation into a mass tourism destination coincided with the agricultural reform in the first half of the 1950s. The National Government abolished the institution of the sharecropper, representing the usual form of agricultural organization in the area at the time. As a result the local government had to face the disintegration of the traditional economic base for inland families. The social block grouping former sharecroppers, farmers and craftsman families constituted the basis for the newly born Riminese tourism industry.

Two elements have been characterizing the decade 1948–1958 that represented the key moment in the consolidation process of the seaside tourism monoculture. The economic scenario was marked at the same time by the urgency of reactivate the local economy after the destructions of the Second World War, by an increasing demand for holiday in the society and by the availability of the working force expulsed from the traditional economic sectors and mainly the agriculture. On the other hand the political scenario was characterized by an impressive consensus around a new generation of decision-makers animating the local PCI.

The Communist Party governed the city uninterrupted from 1946 to the 1980s. As shown in Table 13.1 the traditional diffusion of socialist movements in the Emilia–Romagna region has been legitimating an emerging group of young politicians that showed a remarkable ability in creating a broad consensus on their development project.

We can resume their philosophy with the expression "*from proletariats to owners*". This paradigmatic change has been realized in a very short period of time. More and less in two decades a new hospitality sector has been formed supporting private entrepreneurship in the creation of new hotels in the seaside area despite any hypothesis of planning rationalization of the area. More importantly this new entrepreneurship without capitals has been supported by the local financial system (with a leading role of the bank *Cassa di Risparmio*) that assured the capitals for starting the business and to expand the structures literally one floor each year. The bills system sustained by the increasing holidays demand

Table 13.1: Rimini, the PCI, local elections results, 1946–1990.

Elections year	Votes (%)
1946	37.47
1951	31.16
1956	33.18
1957	35.23
1961	38.05
1965	43.22
1970	36.25
1975	44.07
1980	42.41
1985	39.89
1990	33.62

Source: Zaghini, 1999.

and two decades of sold out tourism seasons has been the engine of an impressive quantitative growth (from around 80 hotels in 1947 to 1.466 in 1961 in Rimini municipality).

The pragmatism showed by the communist leadership in choosing and supporting the seaside tourism monoculture has been sustained by the city only in part for ideological reasons. The real exceptionality of the development model in discussion is the fact that has been capable to group communist, socialist and catholic-oriented entrepreneurship, local finance and at the end of the day two Parties ideologically conflicting like the Christian Democrat Party and the Communist Party. The confrontation between the municipality (governed either by Socialist or Communist Parties) and the *Azienda di Soggiorno* (Tourism Office) of liberal orientation, led by the Central Government of the centre-right wing has been animating the local political debate for long time. The confrontation ended only in 1974 with the election of a member of the PCI to the guide of the *Azienda di Soggiorno*. But only in a first phase the opposition concerned the local development strategy. In the early 1950s in fact the alternative between popular tourism versus elite tourism created the condition for a confrontation opposing municipality and hoteliers supporting a popular tourism and on the other hand the Tourism Office and, indirectly, the national Government that in this phase did not support mass tourism.

The Communist Party became a unifying force sustaining the seaside tourism monoculture in which the working class and the new popular entrepreneurial class met (Zaghini, 1999). The relevance of the mediation process results more significant if we consider that the Italian political debate was characterized by that political phase known as of *Bipolarismo Imperfetto* (Galli, 1966) when Communist Party not legitimated by the political forces as possible alternative for the Government on a national scale made itself known as government force in the local institutions. In those years, in the electoral results emerged a predominance of the Christian Democrat Party in the national political elections and that of the PCI in the administrative elections in the so-called *Regioni Rosse* areas of Central Italy like Emilia–Romagna. Can be interesting to note that during the 1957 local elections Rimini becomes a national case being one of the few Italian areas where the USSR invasion of Hungary in 1956 had not implied the fall but rather the rise of votes for the PCI.

The dominance of local politics in tourism strategies analysis is clearly explainable by shortly analysing the role of tourism sector in the national political scenario. The normative framework approved after the end of the Second World War on the one hand has been supporting the administrative decentralization of tourism-related issues to regional Governments but on the other hand has been creating a Commissary for Tourism in 1947 and then a Ministry of Tourism in 1959 aiming to centralize the control over tourism policies (De Salvo, 2003). The contradictory nature of such a regulation strategy and the fact that Italian Regions has been effectively operating only starting from the 1970s led to a scenario where for long time the local Tourism Offices has been representing the most effective tool of intervention for the national Governments. Other collateral sectors like the regulation of beach use permissions have been more strictly dependent from national level politics. In some cases like in 1954 large coalitions of Member of Parliament (from Communist, Socialist, Social Democrat, and Liberal Parties) advanced the request for a Special Law supporting the Riviera Adriatica tourism system. But the Tourism Offices as a consequence of the relevant power derived by the control over the tourism tax money played constantly a central role in the implementation of local tourism policies. In Rimini the consensus over the development model created the conditions for a shared agreement on the key issues even in presence of a continuous confrontation on tourism policies implementation. Furthermore the Tourism Office has been adopting a mediation strategy also with the hoteliers starting from 1955 grouped in an autonomous category association. It is well-known for instance the fact that at least until the 1960s an informal agreement fixed the amount of the tourism tax as an annual total determined regardless of the effective tourists stays.

In the first half of the 1960s, while several Spanish and Greek mass tourism destinations were given birth, the local tourism model took its distinctive character. The 1965 *Piano Regolatore Generale* (general town-planning scheme) is an interesting example of the strategic horizon sustaining the local development policies. For the first time it was decided a renewal of hotel sector toward a greater quality of the services blocking the quantitative growth of the hospitality sector structures, that is to say the core variable of the economic growth in the post-war period. The expectations of the PRG had to be partly frustrated missing the opportunity to invert the course which led to a crisis in the following decades (Fabbri, 1992) and validating the monocultural vocation of the urban development.

In 1966 the motorway connecting Rimini with Bologna was ameliorated creating the condition for a growth also in week end breaks tourism flows. In 1967 the airport of Miramare 3494 aircrafts had landing with 204,438 travellers from northern Europe. Rimini reached the apex of foreign tourists stays. Starting from the end of the 1960s the international tour operators began to choose other destinations because of the characteristics of local hotel sector management model. The family business model was no more able to ensure qualitative and quantitative standards appropriate to the support tour operator's supply. The Italian tourism replaced the international tourism flows. The family full board hotels with one or two stars became the drive of the system but the lack of coordination between tourism operators on the one hand originated a process of specialization and customization of the local tourism supply but at the same time weakened the possibility of effective tourism marketing strategies at the destination level.

The evolutionary process of the local tourism system has been only marginally affecting the consolidated governing structure and the consensus over the development model. On the contrary, the left-wing municipality kept a conservative attitude and pushed to the pursuit of the monoculture model. A new political subject supported the consolidation of the consensus base on development policies. The Cooperatives Societies even if historically less strong in Rimini than in the rest of Emilia–Romagna were characterized by a strong ideological adherence, Catholic and Socialist/Communist oriented. They represented the attempt to create coalitions between the economical operators, and became relevant consensus tools. The Cooperatives has been operating in different sectors. The CORIAL for instance grouped more than 100 hoteliers aiming to obtain better conditions for hotels purchasing. Probably the most successful example of this bottom-up networking strategies was represented by the Cooperative Society *Promozione Alberghiera* constituted in 1968 and conditioning at least until the 1980s the tourism policies strategies. Created by few local hoteliers the Cooperative grouped in some periods more than 300 hoteliers and represented the first attempt to rationalize tourism marketing and commercialization strategies. Furthermore the Cooperative has been supporting both the extension of the traditional summer season and the diversification of the destination supply by the development of the conferences sector.

The Cooperative Societies were connected with influent national-based associations and introduced the themes of the national political debate in the local governing scenario. At the same time the experience of the Cooperative Societies in Rimini has been providing an organizational framework at the national scale. The *Promozione Alberghiera* success was at the base of the constitution of a national-based federation of Cooperatives called *Federturismo* supported by the Christian Democrat Party. On the other hand the Communist Party supported in 1974 the creation of a Cooperative called *Cooptur* that started operating in the social tourism sector.

The emerging role of local networking experiences introduced interesting innovation in tourism policies implementation. Concluded the boom phase of the 1950s and 1960s the left-winged governing coalitions started supporting a tourism diversification process. The loss of attractiveness toward international tourism flows (representing around 40% of the arrivals at the end of the 1960s) if on the one hand did not produce a reduction of total stays for the presence of a new national demand for holidays on the other created the conditions for an economic loss for the reduced spending capacity of Italian tourists. Starting from this phase seasonality, tourism diversification and quality standards become the key variables of the following 40 years tourism policies. The most important diversification experience is represented by the local Fair opened in 1968. The Fair managed by the municipality, the Tourism Office, and the Chamber of Commerce has been supporting conference and events tourism development creating the conditions for the modernization of the sector in collaboration with the emerging Cooperative Societies representing the innovation force of the local tourism system.

During the 1970s a continuous confrontation between the Unions and the tourism industry anticipated the general debate on the development model opened during the 1980s. Interestingly both the Christian and left-winged Unions started to discuss the viability of the seaside tourism development model contesting the tourism sector working conditions. This reflection concerned first of all Rimini and its peculiar model of tourist industry. Small entrepreneurs without capitals originated one of the most important tourism districts in the Mediterranean. This development model preceded somehow that of the industrial districts of the so-called *Third Italy* (Bagnasco, 1988; 1977) emerged in the years of the consolidation of the Riminese tourist industry. The common characteristics were the family business, the low starting capital, a great flexibility in the organization of the work that also implied average working hours of 8–14 hours a day without a weekly rest, salaries 40% below the standard contract, and half of the employees working illegally (Benini & Savelli, 1976; Mackun, 1998). This productive model applied to tourism originated a high customization of tourism supply targeted on a habitual clientele (Bonini, 2003; Benini & Savelli, 1976). These characteristics represented the strength and at the same time the weakness of the model. On the one hand, it offered a highly personalized service and a perfectly suited holiday, so that the Riminese mass tourism supply has never been rigidly standardized in line with the traditional tour operators Fordist supply (Ioannides & Debbage, 1998). On the other hand the model was not stimulated to the innovation of the management processes and to the acquisition of new customers.

Since the early 1980s it was universally evident that the seaside monoculture model was facing a relevant crisis. Several economic operators denounced the stagnation of the model and the need for a structural renewal based on significant economic investments. Rimini's mayor Chicchi (Dall'Ara, 2002) since the first half of the 1980s invited to a renewal and to structural investment. The first effective attempt to support a renewal process of small hotels quality standard started only in 1994. At the same time the Fair consolidated its leading position in the event and conference sector reaching in 1985 around 400,000 visitors. In 1987 the first Italian aquatic Park was created in Riccione. The Park called Aquafan strengthened the process leading to the constitution of a real Riminese district of the thematic and recreational parks. In 1988 the tourist tax was abolished opening a new crisis front in a system that shifted from stagnation to crisis.

The environmental and mass-media crisis of 1989[3] accelerated a process ongoing for a decade (Agertur, 1989). But 1989 was also the symbolic year of the collapse of the Socialist regimes of East Europe. In Rimini, as well as in the rest of the *red* Emilia–Romagna there changed the local political equilibriums and the leadership of the Communist Party faded away in favour of local centre-right wing governments for a short time. In 1991, PCI chose Rimini to celebrate the passage from the old PCI to the new *Partito Democratico di Sinistra*. Political equilibriums had to be reinvented and the traditional networking strategies grouping hoteliers and other tourism sectors started wavering no longer supported by the adhesion to the seaside tourism monoculture model but also to a shared ideology. The crucial issue set after 1989 has been the need to rebuild shared vision of both the town future and its place in the tourist market. If the seaside tourism monoculture and the adhesion to the political ideology have been the hinges on which Rimini has built its social, economic, and political relationships starting from the 1990s both cannot control the social and economic fragmentation tendencies. Today the social contract that made Rimini famous is breaking into pieces.

Reinventing Rimini Territory Vocation

We can symbolically choose 1989 crisis as the turning point between the monocultural evolutionary process of Rimini local economy and a new phase. This passage implied a new competition for the access to a new clientele oriented to emerging tourism sectors arisen before the 1989 crisis but never representing a sound alternative to the traditional tourism model. The new development poles became the Fair, the conventions, the marina, events tourism, and the inland. Some sectors like the discotheques in the Adriatic Riviera benefited of a boom during the 1990s with 90–100 thousand visitors each weekend but the sector lost its importance at the end of the decade. The entrepreneurial class delayed conforming to the radical transformation of the tourist demand, uncertain between the old development model, and the emergence of new forms of tourism (see Table 13.2).

The institutional actors on the other hand has been often much more willing to a strategic reflection than the economic operators supporting for instance the creation of a seat

---

[3] In July 1989 the campaign against mucilage presence in the Adriatic Sea broke out in national and European newspapers lasting during the all summer. Pollution was indicated as main reason for such a phenomenon. The state of national emergency was declared and Rimini applied to some international authorities, such as Peter Morris who had worked in Alaska to put an end to the damages provoked by the petroleum came out from the Exxon oil-tanker. Summer visitor presences fell from 7.069.935 in 1988 to 5.174.694 in 1989. On annual bases the fall is fixed on around 2.500.000 stays less (Dall'Ara, 2002). Successive studies will emphasize the recurrence of the mucilage presence, already certified for ages, and absence of connections between pollution and the phenomenon determined by other variables like water temperature and sea streams.

Table 13.2: Tourism diversification strategies after 1989 environmental crisis.

Development policies	Main architectural projects
Fair tourism	New trade fair district
Conferences tourism	New conference centre
Marine tourism	New Marina
Theme parks	
Cultural tourism	
Event tourism	
Nightlife and discotheque	
Old town regeneration	

of the University of Bologna in Rimini starting from 1992 education programmes in tourism-related issues. From a reactive reflection motivated by the stagnation of international tourism the political debate started focusing on the slow passage from the old tourist model of the seaside tourism monoculture to a new tourism vocation. The 1989 crisis marked a paradigmatic passage as reported by the words of the Mayor Luciano Chicchi:

"The algae of this summer 1989 [...] have only accelerated the process, by putting everyone with his back to the wall and compelling to a reaction, to a choice. From audience of a dragged agony, we need to become actors of a new development phase" (Dall'Ara, 2002; originally in Italian).

Considering the environmental impacts, real or alleged, the 1989 crisis marked a point of no return on the perception of the psychological and physical destination carrying capacity. In fact, although tourist presences collapsed and only in the past few years tourists stays went back to the levels reached before 1989 the bathers began to use the beach starting from the summer 1990. Nevertheless the idea of environmental risk started playing a part in the debate on the future of the destination. All problems related to the waste water treatment systems and swimming water quality have become a priority and the matter of environmental decay generally fed to a large extent the first antitourism demonstrations. During the 1990s a growing concern for the environmental and territorial criticalities together with the perception of tourism as threat and not as occasion for a strategic improvement of urban quality can be registered. At the same time, the Catholic Church has adopted a definite position regarding the changes of life style connected with tourism and the danger of a progressive transformation of the Riminese community identity (Dal'Ara, 2002).

Two surveys carried out in 1994 and 2001 emphasized the fact that citizens started showing signs of intolerance towards tourism. Between the two surveys such percentage rose from 14.5 up to over the 18% of the population with a progressive radicalization of the antitourism positions of those uncertain or just annoyed in the mid-1990s. If we analyse the motivations a certain degree of anxiety clearly appears for lack of tourism phenomena government and for its strongest impacts such as noise, traffic, rise in prices, and the overloaded urban infrastructures. Therefore it is not tourism that causes anxiety but rather the lack of a tourist planning strategies (Trademark, 2001). At the same time, a sea-sonal and often irregular employment with fewer prospects of winter job and the stagna-tion of arrivals leading to a consequent cut in profits for the operators marked a change in the perception of the economic and social sustainability of the tourism model.

Structural characteristics of the local tourism system and the evolution of the international tourism industry both on the demand and supply side as described by the Fordism/Post-Fordism debate (Amin, 1994; Ioannides & Debbage, 1998; Poon, 1993; Torres, 2002) have been relevant variables in the seaside tourism monoculture crisis. More generally during the 1990s (even if with some differences in the effectiveness of the process) the approach to local development policies in Europe has been evolving toward a plurality of decentralized forms of actions. According to Governa and Salone (2004) four main elements have been innovating the urban and territorial policies strategies in Italy, in some case leading to normative changes supporting the process:

- The emerging and general recognition of new forms for the representation of interests and the consequent legitimization of a plurality of actors supporting different interests in urban and territorial transformations.
- A new approach toward decision-making processes including more attention to negoti-ation, public–private partnerships and inter institutional cooperation.
- A new centrality of local authorities in supporting integrated strategies at the territorial scale and an acceptation of an international competition scenario.
- The increasing adoption of public competition systems in the distribution of financial resources on the national scale.

One of the main consequences of such an evolutionary process has been the centrality of local and territorial development strategies. Differently from the traditional top-down approach to development strategies local authorities at urban, provincial, and regional scale are more and more involved in supporting local economic actors and territorial vocations in the planning process. On the other hand we can observe the lack of a coherent reconsideration of planning and decision-making processes under the light of a systemic, complex, and flexible approach that the new centrality of *territory rhetoric* will implies. Short-term and business drove planning philosophy underline strategies and processes that most of the time makes refer-ence to value expression like strategy, integration, and system without accepting the con-sequent change in decision-making and planning paradigms (Dematteis & Governa, 2002).

At the same time the Italian tourism sector has known an evolution in the governing mechanisms at different levels. At the national level during the 1970s the regional Govern-ments have been starting to use the powers the Constitution assured them. Conflicting inter-ests opposing the regional Governments and the central one reduced the level of independence and innovation previewed by the reform supporting the progressive decentralization of powers on the regional scale even if different laws (1977; 1983) attempted to regulate the domain. In 1993 the Regions promoted a popular referendum for the abrogation of the Tourism Ministry. The success of the initiative created the conditions for an effective con-trol over tourism sector policies by regional authorities.

The emerging role of the Regions lasts until now even if in 2001 a new law aimed to reorganize the sector. The reform (Law no. 135, 2001) dealing with the *"Riforma della leg-islazione nazionale del turismo"* tried to introduce a new organizational body called Local

Tourism System defined in the Article no. 5 as "homogeneous or integrated tourist systems including territories even belonging to different regions, characterized by the integrated offer cultural, environmental goods of tourist attraction, including typical agriculture products or local handicraft products, or else characterized by a wide presence of both single and associated tourist enterprises". In Rimini experience the creation of a Local Tourism System organization is nowadays debated also for the perception of such an innovation as ineffective especially for budget constraint. A contested point is the regional direct financing of the Local Tourism Systems and the lack of coordination between the national law previsions and the regional norms not financing the Local Tourism Systems. The local-based institutions supporting local tourism marketing strategies and tourism policies implementation have been only partially supported by the regional norms. The principle of the distinction between marketing strategies (supported by the Region) and commercialization projects (supported by the operators associations) as expressed by the regional law regulating tourism financing has been criticized for the lack of coordination and the inadequacy in supporting the new integration phase of different tourism sectors and different territories under coherent strategies.

The municipality after the end of the PCI hegemony has been loosing the ability to support innovative development strategies different from the daily mediation between different interests. On the other hand the closure of the Tourism Office in 1986 (with the progressive transfer of functions to the regional level) and the abolition of the tourism tax in 1988 have been progressively reducing the capability to sustain effective policies at the urban scale. The two traditional protagonists of the local debate apparently have progressively lost their leading role of the local economic networks. New emerging influence poles like the Fair seems to represent in a more consistent way the most innovative expressions of the local economy.

Starting from 1995 another relevant actor has been continuously increasing its influence on the tourism sector in Rimini. The Province especially starting from 2002 has been the most influent supporters of the adoption of sustainable development as the key concept leading to a new broad consensus on local development strategies. The Province has also introduced in the local debate the sustainable tourism theme especially by means of the actions of an EU Life project[4] and has been supporting the experience of a Local Agenda 21 on the provincial base. The weakness generally related to LA21 processes (agenda setting

---

[4] The EU Life project *Strategies and tools toward sustainable tourism in the Mediterranean coastal areas* (Life 00/env/it-0067), promoted by the Province together with the Calvià City Council (Spain), Ambiente Italia, and Federalberghi (Italy). The project started in 2000 and ended in December 2003. Two international conferences dealing with themes of sustainable tourism, the adoption of administration plans based on the Integrated Coastal Zone Management (ICZM) of the UE and the Carrying Capacity Assessment (CCA) of the United National Environment Programme (UNEP) has been organized. Furthermore the project implied the diffusion of environmentally friendly management strategies among tourism sector operators, the activation of participative processes at the local level, such as Local Agenda 21 and the reinforcement of a network of cities for a sustainable tourism in cooperation with the International Council for Local Environmental Initiative (ICLEI). In Calvià the demolition of 16 hotels built in the early 1970s and the new planning strategies have given visibility to a possible reuse of edified areas often showing relevant impacts, in Rimini the project tried to put into action a process of divulgation on sustainable tourism themes.

modalities, reduced stakeholders representation, and decision-making process legitimacy) can be observed also in the Rimini experience.

Since June 2002 the LA21 forum tried to integrate within the Agenda 21 process the EU Life project cornerstones by mean of visible actions aiming to create the conditions for an alternative development view between local tourism operators. In this sense an interesting project has been the realization of a preliminary project for the design of beach establishments with low environmental impact (environmental friendly buildings materials, water saving, recycling, and alternatives energy sources). After the opening of the first establishment in the summer of 2003 the partial reduction of the establishment administration costs has been leading a small number of beach operators to implement the same actions. The impact on the sector is still reduced existing around 500 beach operators in Rimini and the surrounding destinations, nearly 10% of the national amount.

Poor success met the Local Agenda 21 process put in action in February 2003 by the municipality over the crucial themes of urban regeneration, mobility, and participated urban planning. In the light of this experience the provincial Local Agenda 21 has been choosing to avoid critical themes like mobility, tourism seasonality, limitations in hotels stays, eco-compatible agriculture, urban quality, alternative energy sources, and accessibility to the territory. The provincial authority if on the one hand has stimulated the adoption of good practices in the sustainable administration of tourist enterprises on the other hand has been able to create effective premises for the integrated promotion of the Riminese territory by means of the creation in 2001 of the *Agenzia per il marketing di distretto* (the District Marketing Agency).

By means of such agency the Province started adapting its strategies to the new national law on tourism introducing the Local Tourist Systems innovation. The agency thanks to the institutional and financial support of the Government, the Emilia–Romagna region ,and the Province has been equipped with the greatest freedom of action in order to represent a local reference for the sector. The new agency arose from the cooperation with the category associations, included in the board of directors. The promotion of the territory on a large scale is the strategic starting point for the building of the Riminese integrated tourist system by mean of new tourism seasonality and the diversification of the tourism supply; between the projects activated by the agency the financing of modernization projects for tourism sector activities.

Notwithstanding with the attempt of the Province to adopt sustainability principles as the key concept of Rimini new urban vocation and the incontestable impact of such a strategy on tourism marketing very challenging issues in terms of destination accessibility and local mobility have to be faced. The discussion over the opportunity to plan the construction of a surface railway has been involving the city for more than two decades and from 1996 the operative proposals has been discussed. The main issue has been represented by the choice of the localization of the new course in a city showing a very compact structure. An opportunity has been represented by the traditional railway infrastructure that if adapted showed interesting strength. On the one hand the reduction of the costs for the intervention, on the other the reuse of partially dismissed areas not in use. The choice has been different. In January 2006 the Province, The Mayors of Rimini and Riccione and the President of the TRAM Agency (the subject in charge of the project) presented the definitive plan for the building of a new surface railway only partially using existing structures advantages. A 93-million euro project for the construction of around 9 kilometre route with a capacity of around 3000 passengers per hour. The main constraint seems to be the mediation process with the owners of the properties that will be expropriated. Even reducing to 17 the number of stops to limit the impact of the main infrastructural works,[5] has been calculated that the mediation process will involve around 650 different stakeholders. The negotiation at the moment has been managed by the direction of the project and some solutions like for instance the reduction of the number of the railway tracks to two seems to indicate that an effective mediation process has been activated. The project will start in 2007 and the planned conclusion is 2011. The main issue can be represented by the length of the administrative processes in the eventuality of new conflicting positions during the expropriation process.

The surface railways construction is part of a more general strategy toward the theme of mobility involving National, Regional, and Local decision-making levels. The aim is to provide Rimini area with a new line for the A14 highway (from two lines to three) and the complete renewal of the SS 16, one of the most traffic-congested secondary roads. According to the President of Rimini Province the success of the integration of these three innovative solutions to mobility issues will be one of strategic resources supporting the provincial economic system. Starting from the summer 2005 some Rimini hotels have been supporting a project to reduce the use of cars from the main Italians cities to Rimini. The customers choosing the hotel supporting the initiatives has been travelling by train and the hotels covered the costs of the journey. Starting from summer 2006 the initiative will involve international customers by the organization of trains from the traditional zones of incoming (France, Germany, and Austria). Apart from these interesting initiatives the main issue at the moment seems to be represented by the tourism flows management strategies. During the summer 2005 for instance the traffic system has been near to collapse in different week ends (especially in June) for the number of excursionists or week end tourists arriving in Rimini. During the first week end of June for instance the highway has been blocked for hours and the impacts on the regional traffic system has been relevant. The new week end tourists mobility represent the new challenge for the local decision-makers and clarify the complexity of the contemporary phase in Rimini tourism development.

Tourism diversification process and the extension of the traditional seasonality can be considered as emerging trends. During the past years interesting growth rates are observables during the whole year especially in the conferences and events sector. The conferences tourism growth today is competing with the traditional seaside tourism attracting over 1 million stays each year and generating economic resources comparables with the summer season. Interestingly is the hotel sector that is retarding the innovation of organizational philosophy for instance opening the whole year. At the moment around a quarter of the hotels work on a annual base and in different cases out of the peak season the room supply has been lower than the demand limiting the growth potentiality of the event and congress sector.

The Fair is more and more influent in the local development dynamics. In 2005 for instance has been approved the project for the construction of the most important Italian conference centre in Rimini strategically supporting the sector as the main protagonist of the tourism diversification process. One of the main constraints in the rejuvenation process

---

[5] Spontaneous committee grouping citizens involved in the expropriation process has been created to contest the project but at the moment seems that an agreement has been reached.

at the destination level are represented by the real estate market dynamics. According to a real estate agent report in 2005 Rimini has been the most expensive real estate market in the Emilia–Romagna region and largely over the national average costs.[6]

The real estate speculation has been traditionally representing a relevant actor in the seaside tourism monoculture system. Nowadays the availability of building spaces in the urban area is extremely reduced and the building permissions are one of the most effective tools for the municipality to finance the realization of new tourism attractions. The basic idea of the so-called *motorini immobiliari* approach (that translated can sound like *building sector engines*) is to provide building permissions for a value similar to the costs of the property acquired by the municipality in order to finance it. The formula for instance has been adopted to partially cover the costs for a new stadium and for the new conferences centre. This approach is really attractive for building speculators. The urban structure is suffering traditionally unsolved questions in the mobility sector but also in terms of spaces available for public uses. In the new congress centre case the political opposition parties has been supporting a radical position against the consolidation of this approach to support public interventions costs. Furthermore representing the positions of the city centre commerce sector the protest has been focusing on the commercial destination of the new buildings that will be introducing new competitors in the traditional commerce scenario.

The same approach seems to be at the base of the most interesting scenario for the renewal of the hotel sector. In the attempt to create a wide consensus base during the 2005 summer the actual leading Party *Democratici di Sinistra* born from the transformation process of the former Communist Party tried to elaborate a discussion document (DS, 2005) on tourism development strategies. It's the first attempt of a relevant political actor to recreate the conditions of collective consensus that characterized Rimini before the 1989 crisis. Interestingly apart from the support to the new tourism seasonality and tourism products diversification processes in the framework of the Sustainability principles the document seems to lack strategic vision in imagining a new and innovative development strategy. Themes like the support to the growth of the immaterial culture resources like arts, fashion, and music and more generally the activities with strong innovation potentialities are largely underestimated and need more institutional support.

On the contrary great attention has been devoted to the proposal for the creation of a company supporting the hotel sector renewal process. The idea is based on the observation that around 45% of the hotels business are directed by managers that do not owns the hotels and as a consequence the lack of motivation to periodically renew the structures is evident. A company financed by relevant economic partners[7] and supporting the project has been involved in the feasibility study in collaboration with the hotel sector association. The project will finance the purchasing of the structure, the renewal or the demolition of the hotels out of market. This approach will represent an opportunity to renovate the local tourism supply and at the same time a chance for replace out of market hotels with other services. The main critics to the project observe that even aiming to increase the tourism sector structures standards it will finally increase the anomalies of the real estate market supporting the adoption of the so-called

---

[6] Data *Ufficio Studi Tecnocasa*.
[7] A national-based company with partners like *Sviluppo Italia* (51%) and *Banca Intesa, FIAT* and *Marcegaglia* collecting the 49% of the shares.

motorini immobiliari financing tool. The creation of urban transformation companies will provide the organizational framework supporting the single regeneration process and providing a
coherent strategy according to the characteristics of the city area interested by the project.

Interestingly a decentralization process involving the new tourism attractions and leaded
by the impossibility to find urban spaces adequate to the needs of the emerging tourism sectors is supporting the adoption of tourism policies focusing on the district scale. The association of the local theme parks for instance (now called *Riviera dei Parchi*) since 1988 has been
supporting the creation of a real tourism parks district and today involves the main attractions
of the Adriatic Riviera. The same approach can be observed in the attempts to integrate the
inland tourism attractions with the coastline tourism supply. The creation of the new brand
Signoria dei Malatesta is trying to support the integration of two tourism territories like the
coast and the inland traditionally not collaborating and now is starting supporting integration
processes even with other tourism systems outside the provincial and regional boundaries
adopting the philosophy of the new national law regulating Local Tourism System activities.

Tourism marketing strategies seem to represent a sector where the level of integration
between different decision-making levels starts to produce systemic strategies of promotion.
From 2001 the Agenzia per il Marketing di Distretto (Marketing District Agency) has been supporting the promotion activities on an integrated scale including the inland destinations and the
emerging niche tourism sectors (sport, food and wine, cultural tourism). The hotel sectors has
been creating Product Clubs grouping hotels targeting their supply on peculiar niche sectors
like sport tourism or showing typical characteristics like the hotels managed by women.

On the other hand the regional Tourism Office strategy has been focusing on the German
market target. The agency has been supporting the choice of the German low cost airlines
Hapag–Lloyd Express and DBA to increase the flight from the main German cities to Rimini
for the summer 2006. The local hoteliers associations have been ready to support the costs
of the operations by covering the eventual loss derived for the airlines by a reduced success of
the project. The local tourism sector associations have been participating also to the costs of
an annual-based marketing campaign in Germany to support the promotion strategy. The
attempt to inaugurate a new season of relationships with the international tourists flows can
be considered as a challenging test for the emerging policies supporting the increase of small
hotels quality standards and more generally the efforts to renovate Rimini destination image.

Tourism Monoculture and Governance Regime

The 1980s crisis of the traditional seasonal tourism supply involved the whole asset of the
decision-making process. Today different tourism sectors concur in sharing resources and
influence on decisional process for the presence of new stakeholders. On the other hand
political legitimacy depends on the capability to manage an increasingly complex network
of interests. We have described the scenario of the groups of interest supporting the
tourism monoculture development model. The coincidence of interests between tourism
sectors activities and building industry growth has been relevant at the point that we can
indicate this phase also as *tourism-real estate monoculture* model.

In Rimini the impressive capability of political realism showed by PCI in the post-war
period supported the peculiar formation of an entrepreneurial class without capitals and the

bills represented the only resource accessible for the new entrepreneurship. The key factor of Rimini success as a tourism destination has been the creation of thousand of boarding houses managed by former sharecroppers or craftsman's families. The city has been rebuilt around the tourism development project and this network of small businesses (around 1650 at the edge of the development cycle at the end of 1970s) has been part of what we can define as an *urban regime* scenario. The influence of the hotel sector in the decision-making process for around 40 years has been impressive. We can individuate in the dualism Municipality (expression of the local tourism industry) and the Tourism Office (representing the national Government priorities and detaining the relevant incomes determined by the local tourism tax) the main conflict area in the local decision-making process for a decade. The first supporting the Communist Party strategy, the second aiming to preserve the 1930s status of Rimini as elite destination. Nevertheless when the success of the tourism monoculture model appear complete (in less than 10 years), even the Tourism Office–Municipality conflicting positions have been coinciding.

If we consider some aspects described as constitutive of a regime we can find an interesting correspondence with the tourism monoculture system. First the level of consensus on shared development priorities and interests was nearly total. It was very clear that the city needed to be rebuilt in the first years after the Second World War without limiting the capacity of the new entrepreneurial class to reach enough money to own a parcel and build a boarding house. Supported by an exponential growth of the demand tourism represented an easy accessible driving force for local economic actors despite the crisis of other sectors. In this phase the ideological adhesion to the Communist Party development policy provided a supplementary consensus base on values and strategic visions. A growth-based approach was nearly universally accepted on the one hand limiting the debate over the city's strategic choices and on the other providing effectives and widespread consensus-based strategies for city development. The analysis of local press tourism development *discourse* provides interesting confirmation of the level of consensus in Rimini local debate. It shows that both government oriented and leftist local newspapers have been sharing for long time the same orientation toward tourism development priorities.

Second the influence of the tourism operators on local governments was high. Rimini municipality has been governed by the Communist Party for around 40 years and local governments founded in the Party an important vehicle of consensus. Even when the 1950 and 1960 boom has been reducing the tourism growth new forms of consensus and collaboration has been introduced in the local governing scenario. The Cooperative Societies provided the solution for the new development phase criticalities. The need to change governing approach in the passage from the uncontrolled expansion phase to the management of a complex tourism system reaching 6 millions stays each season created a new space for the first institutionalized networking strategies.

This consideration introduces the theme of the effective implementation of the governing strategy. In a first phase the resources has been mainly provided by local actors like the bank Cassa di Risparmio. At the same time the sold out seasons of the 1950s and 1960s supported those investments. Starting from the 1970s the Cooperative Societies and emerging development poles like the Fair has been supporting more effectively the tourism policies enlarging the governing network to new actors. The Tourism Office has been traditionally supporting continuous investments in urban renewal projects but also in tourism events, marketing campaigns and generally in tourism-related projects. Starting from 1988 local tourism policies has been facing the increasing difficulties of a financing system introducing elements of competition between different actors and a reduced freedom of movement in the spending policies.

Another interesting element of the tourism monoculture regime is the limited influence of the national Government in tourism policies implementation. The institutional framework of tourism government at the national level has been creating the condition for a reduced influence of national Government in local strategic choices. This process has been increasing the influence of both the local representatives of the Communist Party and of the Christian Democrat Party. Even with a continuous conflicting positioning on the implementation of tourism policies we can observe the existence of a consolidated consensus on strategic choices. Starting from the 1970s the increased influence of the regional government level on decision-making processes has been opening the scenario to a new actor. We can observe that until the end of the 1980s this evolutionary process has been only partially influencing the Rimini governing coalition. Furthermore can be interesting to note that the connections between the regional tourism authorities and the local politics have been traditionally relevant. The former Mayor Ceccaroni for instance has been in charge during the 1970s as regional Councillor for Tourism and the actual director of the regional Tourism Office has been in charge as Mayor of Rimini in the past.

A real turning point has been represented by the years from 1986 to 1989 (Dall'Ara, 1986). We identify in this period the end of the traditional tourism monoculture system and the passage from the traditional regime governing the city to new forms of governance. The abolition of the local Tourism Office (1986) and of the tourism tax (1988), the crisis of the former Communist regimes in east Europe and Asia united with the 1989 environmental crisis constituted a real fracture with the traditional governing scenario. Starting from the end of the 1980s we observe an interesting evolution in the local governance patterns. The tourism growth philosophy starts to be generally perceived as no more capable to support a monocultural development strategy based on the traditional tourism season. Rimini faces the challenge of a multiplication of development poles (in the tourism sector but also in the emerging manufacturing productions) and of legitimating their role in the traditional governing coalitions. The traditional tourism actors founded in local decision-makers like the Tourism Office and the municipality two perfect partners in building effective governing coalitions. The contemporary scenario seems to be characterized by the search for new equilibriums. In this picture traditional actors and emerging ones are competing in the definition of a new strategic agenda managing the contemporary complexity.

At the moment we can observe the lack of a shared development strategy. On the one hand the building sector and the local govern seem to constitute the most influent alliance and in some way the last manifestation of the partnership governing the city for around 40 years. All the main urban policies implemented during the last 10 years and planned for the future 10 seems to be inspired by the traditional urban growth philosophy lacking for instance planning schemes introducing a deep reflection on the strategic renewal of the urban structure. Very relevant projects like the new conferences centre and the new stadium are manifestations of such an approach. Others projects like the surface railways are interesting pioneering attempts to reorganize the urban mobility representing probably the main contemporary issue in the area.

On the other hand conflicting positions oppose traditional and emergent economic operators of the tourism sector but more generally different groups of interests. The debate over the impacts of informal commerce, over the Beach Scheme opposing traditionalist and innovates approaches to tourism services management, the continuous discussion over illegal working conditions in the tourism and buildings sectors, the emergence of antitourism manifestations increased by the impacts determined by new tourism flows are all manifestations of the multiplicity of views on destination future. A shared agenda is far to be individuated and the multiplication of conflicting positions clearly describe this process.

Sustainable Development of tourism constitutes the most relevant attempt to provide a unifying discourse in local development strategies. In this sense the role of the Province as an actor capable to coordinate the different interests can represent an interesting perspective even if not in a near future. At the moment sustainability has been adopted as a conceptual framework trying to provide a unifying strategic vision. The future will show to what extent sustainability discourses will really affect the complex scenario analysed.

Conclusions

This chapter adopts an urban regime approach to the study of governance processes in a traditional mass tourism destination showing development patterns originating a tourism monoculture system. In this sense we individuate a phase (around from 1948 to 1988) showing some peculiar aspects of a regime as described by the urban governance literature. The progressive lost of influence of such a governing partnership has been originated by several factors. The international literature focusing on global changing processes (Soja, 2000; Swyngedouw, 1997) has been introducing elements of reflections on the new relationships between local territories and global processes and the reshaping of local realities identities and vocations. In a word Complexity is more and more the conceptual framework characterizing these processes. This chapter focuses more on the local dimension of such a process of territorial change trying to analyse the consistency of local networking strategies in order to provide long-lasting governing coalitions. What emerges from our analysis is that the passage from tourism monoculture systems to multi-sectoral and multi-stakeholders scenarios characterising some traditional Mediterranean destinations implies new governing strategies and new discourses legitimating agenda setting processes.

The growth-based strategy supporting tourism monoculture in Rimini originated a broad consensus and at the same time a reduced opportunity for alternative views in some way reinforced by the peculiar approach to democracy of PCI inspired by *Democratic Centralism* principles. Today if on the one hand competition between territories is based on a larger scale and involves a broad spectrum of actors on the other traditional governing networks keep a certain influence on the decision-making processes. The emergence of a broadly accepted discourse of *public participation* on decision-making processes has been supporting for instance the implementation of Local Agenda 21 processes both on the municipal scale and the provincial one (Provincia di Rimini, 2003). Even if the Province LA21 has been reaching a certain visibility especially for the attention devoted the adoption of Sustainable Development as a key concept we observe a lack of effectiveness of the process but also some criticalities in the agenda setting and in the stakeholders selection processes. Furthermore the lack of coordination between LA21 suggestions and effective planning tools reduces the impact of such a strategic expansion of the decision-maker's base. The persistence of local elites control over governance processes testimony the need for new and more effective mechanisms of democratization of politics at the local level (Somerville, 2005).

At the moment the reshaping of the governing scenario by mean of the integration between different levels of government and different development poles supporting competing strategies is definitely leading to the end of the tourism monoculture phase and to the integration of traditional governing partnerships with emerging actors at different levels. This scenario that imply the evolution toward what has been described as a multi-level governance regime (Hooghe & Marks, 2001; Marks, 1996) redefining the role of traditional representatives institutions and networks of interests is nevertheless facing the resistances of a consolidated local oligarchies founding their interests in traditional governing coalitions. Tourism diversification and enlarged tourism seasonality are central variables in providing new resources supporting this evolutionary process.

Acknowledgements

We are grateful to Professor Luisanna Fodde for providing useful suggestions to our work.

References

Agarwal, S. (2002). Restructuring seaside tourism. The resort lifecyle. *Annals of Tourism Research*, *29*(1), 25–55.

Agertur Emilia–Romagna (1989). *L'estate Più Difficile*. Rimini: Chiamami Città.

Aguilo', E., Alegre, J., & Sard, M. (2005). The persistence of the sun and sand tourism model. *Tourism Management*, *26*, 219–231.

Airaldi, L. (1985). Pianificazione Urbanistica e Trasformazione del Territorio sulla Riviera Romagnola. *Storia Urbana*, *IX*, 32.

Amin, A. (1994). *Post-Fordism: A reader*. Oxford and Cambridge, MA: Blackwell.

Bagnasco, A. (1977). *Tre Italie. La Problematica Territoriale dello Sviluppo Italiano*. Bologna: Il Mulino.

Bagnasco, A. (1988). *La Costruzione Sociale del Mercato*. Bologna: Il Mulino.

Bagnasco, A. (1994). Regioni, Tradizione Civica, Modernizzazione Italiana: Un Commento alla Ricerca di Putnam. *Stato e Mercato*, *40*(11), 93–104.

Benini, E. (1976). Aspetti e Problematiche dello Sviluppo Turistico nella Riviera Romagnola. In: C. Stroppa (Ed.), *Sviluppo del Territorio e Ruolo del Turismo*. Bologna: Cooperativa Libraria Universitaria.

Benini, E., & Savelli, A. (1986). *Il Senso del Far Vacanza*. Milan: Franco Angeli.

Biagini, E. (1990). *La Riviera di Romagna. Sviluppo di un Sistema Turistico*. Bologna: Patron Editore.

Bianchi, R. (2003). Place and power in tourism development: Tracking the complex articulations of community and locality. Pasos. *Revista de turismo y patrimonio cultural*, *1*(1), 13–32.

Bianchi, R. (2004). Tourism restructuring and the politics of sustainability: A critical view from the European periphery (The Canary Islands). *Journal of Sustainable Tourism*, *12*(6), 495–529.

Boissevain, J., & Selwyn, T. (Eds) (2004). *Contesting the foreshore. Tourism, society and politics on the coast*. Amsterdam: Amsterdam University Press.

Bonini, A. (2003) La Visione dell'ospitalità Secondo la Scuola di Rimini. In: A. Rossini (Ed.), *Rimini e il Turismo. Saggi sul DistrettoTturistico Più Famoso d'Europa*. Milan: Franco Angeli.

Bramwell, B. (2004). Mass tourism, diversification and sustainability in Southern Europe's coastal regions. In: B. Bramwell (Ed.), Coastal mass tourism. Diversification and sustainable development in Southern Europe. Clevedon: Channel View Publications.

Bramwell, B., & Sharman, A. (1999). Collaboration in local tourism policymaking. *Annals of Tourism Research*, 26(2), 392–415.

Buhalis, D., & Cooper, C. (1998). Competition or co-operation? Small and medium sized tourism enterprises at the destination, In Laws, Faulkner & Moscardo (Eds), Embracing and managing change in tourism: International case studies. London: Routledge.

Burns, P. (2004). Tourism planning. A third way ? *Annals of Tourism Research*, 31(1), 24–43.

Butler, R. (1980). The concept of a tourist area cycle of evolution: Implications for the management of resources. *Canadian Geographer*, 24, 5–12.

Cheong, S., & Miller, M. L. (2000). Power and tourism. A foucauldian observation. *Annals of Tourism Research*, 27(2), 371–390.

Conti, G., & Pasini, P. G. (2000). *Rimini Città Come Storia* (Vol. 2). Rimini: Giusti.

Conti, G. (1986). *Rimini la Capitale Europea del Turismo*. Rimini: Azienda Autonoma di Soggiorno.

Convention Bureau della Riviera di Romagna (2003). Il Sistema Congressuale Riminese. Rimini.

Dall'Ara, G. (1986). Ma Cos'è Questa Crisi? In: G. Conti (Ed.), *Rimini la Capitale Europea del Turismo*. Rimini: Azienda Autonoma di Soggiorno.

Dall'Ara, G. (2002). *La Storia dell'industria Turistica Riminese Vista Attraverso Cinquanta Anni di Strategie*. Milan: Franco Angeli.

Davies, J. S. (2002a). Urban regime theory: A normative – empirical critique. *Journal of Urban Affairs*, 24(1), 1–17.

Davies, J. S. (2002b). The governance of urban regeneration: A critique of the 'Governing Without Government' Thesis. *Public Administration*, 80(2), 301–322.

Davies, J. S. (2003). Partnerships versus regimes: Why regime theory cannot explain urban coalitions in the UK. *Journal of Urban Affairs*, 25(3), 253–269.

Dematteis, G., & Governa, F. (2002). Ha Ancora Senso Parlare di Identità Territoriale? Paper presented at the *International Conference*, La Nuova Cultura delle Città, Accademia dei Lincei, 5–7, November, Rome, Italy.

De Grazia, V. (1981). *Consenso e Cultura di Massa nell'Italia Fascista*. Bari: Laterza.

De Salvo, P. (2003). *Il Processo di Formazione della Politica Turistica*. Milan: Franco Angeli.

Dowding, K. (2001). Explaining urban regimes. *International Journal of Urban and Regional Research*, 25(1), 7–19.

DS (2005). L'Analisi e le Proposte dei DS Riminesi sul Turismo, proceedings of the Direzione Federale and the Unioni Comunali of Bellaria-Igea Marina, Rimini, Riccione, Misano Adriatico and Cattolica meeting, Democratici di Sinistra Party, 27 June 2005, Rimini.

EEA (2003). Europe's environment: The third assessment. Environmental Assessment Report No. 10. Copenhagen: European Environment Agency.

Elkin, S. L. (1987). *City and regime in the American Republic*. Chicago: University of Chicago Press.

EU Commission (2004). *The European Tourism Industry. A Multi-Sector With Dynamic Markets. Structures, Developments and Importance for Europe's Economy*. Report prepared for the Enterprise Dg (Unit D.3) of The European Commission. Luxemburg : Enterprise publications.

Fabbri, R. (1992). *Intervista a Ceccaroni*. Rimini: Chiamami Città & Guaraldi Editore.

Farina, F. (1993). *La Riviera di Rimini 1790–1993*. Rimini: Centocinquanta Anni di Vita Balneare.

Farina, F. (1995). *Le Sirene dell'adriatico, 1850–1950*. Riti e Miti Balneari Attraverso i Manifesti Pubblicitari, Exposition Catalogue. Milan: Motta.

Focus Lab (2004). *Agenda 21 Locale in Italia 2004*. Indagine sull'attuazione dei Processi di Agenda 21. Focus Lab Italy.

Galli, G. (1966). *Il Bipartitismo Imperfetto*. Bologna: Il Mulino.

Getz, D. (1987). Tourism planning and research: Traditions, models and futures. *Proceedings of the Australian travel research workshop*, Bunbury, Western Australia, 5–6 November.

Gobbi, G., & Sica, P. (1982). *Rimini*. Bari: Laterza.

Governa, F., & Salone, C. (2004). Territories in action, Territories for action: The territorial dimension of Italian local development policies. *International Journal of Urban and Regional Research, 28*(4), 796–818.

Hall, C. M. (2000). *Tourism planning*. Harlow: Prentice Hall.

Harding, A. (1994). Urban regimes and growth machines: Towards a cross-national research agenda. *Urban Affairs Quarterly, 29*(3), 356–382.

Harding, A. (1997). Urban regimes in a Europe of cities. *European Urban and Regional Studies, 4*(4), 291–314.

Hooghe, L., & Marks, G. (2001). Multi-level governance and European integration. Oxford: Rowman & Littlefield Publication.

Ioannides, D., & Debbage, K. G. (1998). Neo-Fordism and flexible specialization in the travel industry: Dissecting the polyglot. In: D. Ioannides & K. G. Debbage (Eds), *The economic geography of the tourist industry. A supply – side analysis*. London: Routledge.

Jamal, T. B., & Getz , D. (1995). Collaboration theory and community tourism planning. *Annals of Tourism Research, 22*(1), 186–204.

John, P. (2001) *Local governance in Western Europe*. London: Sage.

Kearns, A., & Paddison, R. (2000). New challenges for urban governance. *Urban Studies, 37*(5–6), 845–850.

Knowles, T., & Curtis, S. (1999). The market viability of European mass tourist destinations. A post-stagnation life-cycle analysis. *International Journal of Tourism Research, 1*, 87–96.

Kousis, M. (2000). Tourism and the environment. A social movements perspective. *Annals of Tourism Research, 27*(2), 468–489.

Long, P. (1999). Tourism development regimes in the inner city Fringe: The case of discover Islington, London. *Journal of Sustainable Tourism, 8*(3), 190–206.

Lowndes, V., Pratchett, L., & Stoker, G. (2001). Trends in public participation: Part 1 – Local Government perspectives. *Public Administration, 79*(1), 205–22.

Mackun, P. (1998). Tourism in the third Italy: Labor and social – business networks. In: D. Ioannides & K. G. Debbage (Eds), The economic geography of the tourist industry. A supply – side analysis. London: Routledge.

Marcuse, P., & Van Kempen, R. (2000). *Globalizing cities. A new spatial order?* Oxford: Blackwell.

Marks, G. (1996). An actor-centred approach to multi-level governance. *Regional and Federal Studies, 6*(2), 20–40.

Mouritsen, P. (2003). What's the civil in civil society? Robert Putnam, Italy and the Republican tradition. *Political Studies, 51*, 650–668.

Murphy, P. E. (1985). *Tourism: A community approach*. New York: Methuen.

Pearce, P. L., Moscardo, G., & Ross, G. F. (1996). *Tourism community relationships*. Oxford: Pergamon Press.

Poma, L., & Bondi, M. (2001). *Il Sistema Turistico tra Tradizione e Nuova Competizione. Il Caso Rimini*. Milan : Franco Angeli.

Poon, A. (1993). *Tourism, technology and competitive strategies*. Wallingford, CAB international.

Priestley, G. K., & Mundet, L. (1998). The post-stagnation phase of the resort cycle. *Annals of Tourism Research, 25*(1), 85–111.

Provincia di Rimini (2003). *Piano d'Azione e Progetti Agenda 21 Locale*. Forum provinciale Agenda 21 Locale, Campagna Europea Città Sostenibili.

Putnam, R. D. (1993). *Making democracy work: Civic traditions in modern Italy*. Princeton, NJ: Princeton University Press.

Reed, M. G. (1997). Power relations and community-based tourism planning. *Annals of Tourism Research*, *24*(2), 566–591.

Regione Emilia–Romagna (2004). *Rapporto Annuale 2004*. Osservatorio Turistico Regionale dell'Emilia–Romagna.

Rhodes, R. A. W. (1997). *Understanding governance*. Buckingham: Open University Press.

Rhodes, R. A. W. (2000). Governance and public administration. In: J. Pierre (Ed.), *Debating governance. Authority, Steering and Democracy*. Oxford: Oxford University Press.

Rimini Fiera s.p.a. (2003). *Bilancio D'Esercizio e Bilancio Consolidato*. Rimini.

Rispoli, M. (2001). *Prodotti Turistici Evoluti. Casi ed Esperienze In Italia*. Turin: Giappichelli Editore.

Selwyn, T. (2000). The De-Mediterraneanisation of the Mediterranean? *Current Issues in Tourism*, *3*(3), 226–245.

Soja, E. W. (2000). *Postmetropolis. Critical studies of cities and regions*. Oxford: Blackwell.

Somerville, P. (2005). Community governance and democracy. *Policy and Politics*, *33*(1), 117–144.

Stoker, G., & Mossberger, K. (1994). Urban regime theory in comparative perspective. *Environment and Planning C: Government and Policy*, *12*, 195–212.

Stoker, G. (1995). Regime theory and urban politics. In: Judge, Stoker & Wolman (Eds), *Theories of urban politics*. London: Sage.

Stone, C. N. (1989). *Regime politics: Governing Atlanta, 1946–1988*. Lawrence, KS: University Press of Kansas.

Stone, C. N. (1993). Urban regimes and the capacity to govern. *Journal of Urban Affairs*, *15*(1), 1–28.

Stone, C. N. (2002). Urban regimes and problems of local democracy. Paper presented at the *ECPR Workshop No. 12*, The politics of metropolitan governance, Joint Sessions, Turin 22–27, March 2002.

Stone, C. N. (2004a). It's more than the economy after all: Continuing the debate about urban regimes. *Journal of Urban Affairs*, *26*(1), 1–19.

Stone, C. N. (2004b). Rejoinder: Multiple imperatives, or some thoughts about governance in a loosely coupled but stratified society. *Journal of Urban Affairs*, *26*(1), 35–42.

Swyngedouw, E. (1997). Neither global nor local: 'Glocalization' and the politics of scale. In: K. R. Cox (Ed.), *Spaces of globalization. Reasserting the power of the local*. London: The Guilford Press.

Thomas, R., & Thomas, H. (2005). Understanding tourism policy-making in urban areas, with particular reference to small firms. *Tourism Geographies*, *7*(2), 121–137.

Tintori, C. (1888). *I Bagni di Rimini*, Rimini: Racconto Storico.

Torres, R. (2002). Cancun's tourism development from a Fordist spectrum of analysis. *Tourist Studies*, *2*(1), 87–116.

Trademark Italia (2001). II° Rapporto sull'Antiturismo, Rimini.

Travaglini, C. (2003). Dal Congresso alla Città Congressuale. In: A. Rossini (Ed.). *Rimini e il Turismo. Saggi sul Distretto Turistico più Famoso d'Europa*. Milan: Franco Angeli.

Zaghini, P. (1999). *La Federazione Comunista Riminese (1949–1991)*. Rimini: Pietroneo Capitani Editore.

Chapter 14

The MTV Europe Music Awards Edinburgh03: Delivering Local Inclusion?

Gavin Reid

Introduction

In November 2003 Edinburgh hosted one of the largest cultural events ever held in Scotland: the MTV Europe Music Awards Edinburgh03. To public sector organisers and political leaders the event offered extensive local involvement and a series of unique opportunities to showcase Scotland's tourism and creative sectors to a potential global audience of 1 billion people. This chapter presents findings of a detailed case study critically assessing the positive and inclusive rhetoric surrounding this event. The chapter highlights how, despite the use of public subsidy, the delivery of social inclusion was not local policy-makers' central focus. Rather, the dominant rationales for attracting the event were global; notably its contribution to Edinburgh's tourism and event hosting credentials. When combined with other global realities – in this case MTV's desire for a spectacular television product and the promotion of global pop celebrities – this limited the visibility of local participation. It seems clear from this case study that, for small cities embracing the events of global corporations, literature relating to their use of cultural events for place marketing (Avraham, 2004; Balsas, 2004; Bianchinni, 1999; Evans & Shaw, 2004; Wilks-Heeg & North, 2004) downplays how their place features become part of transnational companies' marketing plans. Here, MTV's central position in global youth culture and larger budget meant they had editorial control of the event with social inclusion permitted providing it did not interfere with their organisation of a highly complex television show. Despite MTV's global power its event entered the realities of power within the local political framework, with their desire for control and exclusion of locals antagonising the powerful local newspaper whose right of centre political leanings meant they were already inclined to use the event to criticise public sector event organisers. The newspapers' negative event readings exasperated local organisers and tested relations between them and MTV. Conflict between local elites and residents over the former's choice of cultural identity symbols as indicators of local attractiveness (Hughes, 1999) was evident in this event but, in addition, tensions existed between MTV and local organisers over this. The power imbalance between local organisers and global event owners meant the former sometimes lost control of images emanating from the event, producing a tension between their place marketing intentions and MTV's definition of good television. To fully discuss the above issues the chapter is structured as follows. The next section outlines the politics of cultural events and city imaging to show the tensions involved when local political and policy frameworks focus on event-led regeneration. To counter the usual inclusive event rhetoric the local framework is then examined via an introduction to the divisions and inequalities within the city of Edinburgh. Next, the case study findings are outlined and related to event literature then, finally, the last section develops some concluding remarks.

Cultural Events and Contemporary Urban Policy

With global economic restructuring encouraging deindustrialisation, and New Right and New Labour governments promoting financial prudence, cities now increasingly compete for inward investment, tourists and the new service class. Within this "new realism" (Hughes, 1999) public officials market the city as a dynamic environment within which to live, work and play. Rojek and Urry (1997, p. 31) remark that, in this process, "Those cities with either low visibility or a poor image will not even be considered", while Essex and Chalkey (1998, p. 188) draw on Harvey (1989) when arguing that major events provide urban spectacles that enable cities to "express their personality, enhance their status and advertise their position on a global stage". Within this local framework, public agencies work with the private sector to deliver high-profile events that transform the city into a spectacular product with the symbolic capital (Bourdieu, 1984) of distinctiveness and pre-eminence that, they hope, will produce economic capital through increased tourism and business investment (Hall & Jenkins, 1995; Shaw & Williams, 2002). As the aforementioned authors remark, through events, "the city becomes identified – at least for a time – with a particular spectacle" (p. 267), with public agencies seeking to maximise the duration of this association via innovative marketing. With positive images from cultural events often receiving blanket global media coverage, both on cultural programmes and apparently unbiased news broadcasts (Smith, 2001), they are particularly attractive to industrial cities keen to rid themselves of their 19th century and/or 1970s manufacturing image to signify to tourists, inward investors and residents that the city is in the process of renewal and they should experience this vibrant new era (Weiler & Hall, 1992). As Rojek and Urry (1997, p. 37) argue, in this context, "it is not surprising that the entrepreneurial city is as proactive in seeking to capture mobile special events as it is in developing its own special events".

The process of symbolic regeneration (Hall & Hodge, 2000) has also been theorised within the context of postmodernism in that, while the time/space compression associated with this process reduces obstacles to physical distance, it increases the importance of real or imagined place characteristics to capital (Waitt, 1999) which can be delivered via cultural events. Postmodern theory has also been used to describe how cities, previously recognised as centres of production, are now repositioning themselves as centres of consumption: what Spink and Bramham (1998) term the postmodern "fun city", where emphasis is placed on the production and marketing of images and signs not goods. Eade (1997) believes that "In this contemporary urban context, popular and mass culture are regarded as legitimate sources of prestige and cultural and symbolic capital" and, to maximise this, "traditional forms of cultural consumption are being changed to attract wider audiences". Hughes (1999) agrees, arguing that, as local authorities shift from emphasising managerialism to entrepreneurialism, "this attitudinal change admitted the inclusion of pleasure as a formal objective of public sector intervention" (p. 123). While cities' incorporation of the arts previously suggested its civilised nature, now the urban context requires the promotion of excitement with cities actively embracing popular music in addition to the "high arts" (Rojek & Urry, 1997). However, the emphasis on event-led regeneration within local policy frameworks has attracted much criticism, notably over: their unproven long-term impact; whether benefits go to polit- ical and economic elites at the expense of ordinary taxpayers (Jones & Wilks-Heeg, 2004); the loss of the city as a source of personal identity (Bramham, Henry, Mommaas & van der Poel, 1989); whether public monies are better spent on less glamorous, but no less important, urban problems (Garcia, 2003); the lack of postevent analyses (Higham, 1999) and the methodological weaknesses of events' economic impact studies (Crompton, 2001). Others question whether local elites promote events, less for their contribution to local cultural par- ticipation, and more for the tourist industry (Garcia, 2004). This theme of the local policy framework being dominated by an economic view of culture has also been highlighted by Balibrea (2004) who criticises the current trend towards monumentalising the city via large projects. Critics of the dominant local framework of event-led regeneration highlight how events often lack any real connection to local culture (McCarthy, 2005), while the frame- work's celebratory discourses deflects from underlying socio-economic inequalities (Mooney, 2004; Wilks-Heeg & North, 2004). Critics argue that any informed analyses of events must consider the role of power politics which leads to the crucial questions of "whose culture" is being promoted (Wils-Heeg & North, 2004) and "whose story is dom- inating and whose is being marginalised" (Mooney, 2004).

Edinburgh: The Festival City

Edinburgh is currently undergoing an economic and cultural renaissance aided by: the decision to site the new Scottish Parliament there; an influx of young professionals; private sector investment in bars and restaurants; an unprecedented building boom; up-market retailers locating within its city centre; its iconic city centre skyline and global events' repu- tation from its International Festival and Fringe (Watson, 2003). Carlsen and Taylor (2003) argue that cities' attempts to re-image themselves using cultural events take place in the context of divided cities: a view pertinent here as, although branded Edinburgh03, the event took place two miles from the city centre in the port of Leith which, while officially part of Edinburgh, has a separate identity borne of a distinguished maritime heritage. Leith was an independent burgh between 1833 and 1920 when it amalgamated, amidst much bitterness, with Edinburgh, with much of this discontent stemming from the view that, for centuries, Edinburgh ran the port in its interests (Greig, Savage, Dargue & Kirkwood-Smith, 1989; Hutton, 1995; Marshall, 1983; Mowat, 1994; Wallace, 1985). Since the mid 1980s Leith has witnessed extensive regeneration via Edinburgh's Waterfront Development project which seeks to provide Scotland's capital city with the space and waterfront lifestyle capable of attracting the people needed to sustain its place in 21st century commerce. However, Hall and Jenkins (1995) argue that waterfront development schemes act as "props for large enter-prises and consumption" and, because they are "interconnected to the power relationships that exist within and outwith the community . . . the heritage of the losers is missing/ underrepresented". Edinburgh's economic growth and "Festival City" label have not deflected tensions surrounding the city's events strategy; notably whether it is excluding deprived peripheral housing estates and is overly corporate. This chapter therefore examines whether the MTV Awards heightened debate over the local politics of place.

Methodology

Owing to its ability to analyse contemporary issues within a real life context a case study approach (Yin, 2003) was used in this study. To appreciate the importance and complexity of the event's contextual conditions – and links between this and its organisation – a variety of methods were adopted. The research began by assessing literature relating to the politics of leisure events followed by an examination of historical relations between Leith and Edinburgh, the local economic and political context and MTV. Next, a content analysis of event literature stemming from event organisers was undertaken with the overall aim being to synthesise the academic and contextual into a series of issues to be put to relevant actors. These individuals – notably key organisers and prominent event critics – were deemed clos-est to the event's decision-making process and the politics behind it. They were identified via a content analysis of local newspaper and national television coverage of the event. To assess the politics of using the MTV Awards to re-image Edinburgh the research conducted twelve semi-structured interviews with representatives drawn from Edinburgh and Lothians Tourist Board (ELTB), the Edinburgh Convention Bureau, EventScotland, Scottish Enterprise, VisitScotland, Edinburgh Council, the local Conservative Group, the Leith Initiative for Tourism and a Leith historian. Seven telephone interviews were also conducted with MTV Europe's Senior Vice President, Director of Marketing and Chief Operating Officer; the Property Director of Forth Ports Plc, two journalists from the *Edinburgh Evening News* and one from *The Scotsman*. The interviews were conducted between June 2003 and January 2004 and covered: the reasons for the event subsidy; the partnership between MTV and local organisers; the extent of local involvement; media reporting and the event's contribution to the tourism and creative industries. Data analysis involved repeated readings of interview transcripts with the framework for this analysis primarily based on the literature review (Denzin & Lincoln, 1994; Marvasti, 2004). The research adopted a recursive and iterative approach where data collection and analysis occurred simultaneously with each informing the other (Blaikie, 2000; Bryman, 2001). The analysis moved beyond assessing the frequency of issues to interviewees' understanding of them (Denscombe, 1998), with the development of categories of meaning (Green, 2000) achieved through this continual revisiting of interview transcripts and academic literature. To assess the MTV Awards' promotional potential a content analysis was also undertaken of its televised programming, notably: the "Come to Scotland" travelogue; two "Road to Edinburgh" concerts; the Awards' on-line interactive game and the Award show. A limitation of the research was its focus on elite event producers and critics whose age stifled appreciation of young people's event readings. Greater balance would have been achieved by collecting the thoughts of locals actually involved in the event.

Discussion

While there was direct economic benefit to Edinburgh from MTV's decision to use it for its 10th anniversary show – with the occupancy of approximately 8000 city hotel rooms in the event week initially said to be worth £4 million – it was the event's indirect benefits that most appealed to public officials. In particular, they saw Edinburgh's location, for one night, at the centre of the entertainment universe as a unique opportunity to showcase it, and Scotland, as an exciting place to live, work, visit and invest in (Wilson, 2003). Local organisers stressed the benefits of Edinburgh's promotion as part of the Awards' package, seen as far more effective in reaching young potential repeat tourists than conventional tourism marketing. The ELTB official believed that, just by choosing Edinburgh, MTV propelled the city, almost instantly, into a leading European city break destination for young people which might have taken another 5 years with traditional marketing. Also appealing was the event's ability to shift Edinburgh's traditional label of "the Athens of the North" towards a contemporary fashion and leisure capital. The VisitScotland official saw the MTV collaboration as ideal because, like their preferred "wild timers" market segment, it had an aspirational image and the "MTV generation" were global travellers but elusive (Ward, 2003). Given the prominence of heritage and scenery in people's perceptions of Scotland, the VisitScotland official felt that developing a more contemporary brand required "surprising people" out of their traditional thinking, and MTV's decision to choose Scotland for their event did this. MTV's Vice President saw their company as representing "a cool and hip vision of the world" and thus Edinburgh's association with it loosened its conservative image which was useful from a marketing perspective. Countering those who felt the event was not required as Edinburgh was already well-known internationally (Jamieson, 2003), MTV's Chief Operating Officer argued that this was "a certain type of Edinburgh" – notably of the film Trainspotting and the Edinburgh International Tattoo – the former which, to him, the city was keen to distance itself from, while the latter appealed to an older market. In terms of priorities within the local policy framework it was clear that image making and tourism were more prominent than the event's contribution to local social inclusion.

Centrally important to local policy-makers was the event's contribution to Edinburgh's global place marketing. For instance, the council leader saw the event as great timing as it came just after the Edinburgh Festival and Fringe and before its winter festival (Edinburgh's Capital Christmas) and Hogmanay celebrations. Underpinning this was the desire to create a more dynamic city economy, youthful image and year-round tourism to meet the recent increase in hotel bed spaces, with the council's vision being to create the most prosperous northern European city by 2015. The council leader felt that "to do this you need to build the brand and the MTV Awards are consistent with that". While it will be seen later that local organisers were genuinely keen to deliver some local involvement in the event, it was MTV's inclusion of global celebrities that really appealed. As the ELTB representative stated, "we couldn't afford a Robbie or a Kylie but MTV can as their 'B list' is our 'A list' which will propel us into a different league". By this he meant elite European cities, such as London, Barcelona and Paris, deemed appropriate company for the dynamic and cosmopolitan Edinburgh but, as the council leader remarked, "not everyone understands this as they haven't been". The ELTB official argued that a feature of successful cities was their strong sense of place which wasn't apparent in Edinburgh as those who'd visited the city, and experienced its contemporary aspects, felt it rivalled Barcelona, Dublin and Paris, whilst those who hadn't, bracketed it with provincial cities like Chester, Bath, Stratford-upon-Avon and York. As he remarked, "If that's the way we're perceived we'll never persuade people to send their children here or locate their businesses here" (Brown & Lyons, 2003).

The MTV and Edinburgh Partnership

As Hall (1992) argues, questions of "why, for what, and for whom are these events held?" are key when assessing the politics of using major events for economic, tourism and image purposes. The council's Special Projects Officer described the event's public/private partnership as "very unusual" because MTV's £4.5 million budget gave it editorial control. While Scottish representatives' experience of working with MTV was overwhelmingly positive, communication problems arose because there wasn't, as one put it, "a single door to MTV". This was seen when MTV adopted Edinburgh's new "One City Trust" as its charity – an organisation supporting arts, education and social projects in the city's poorest areas – because, having thought they'd obtained agreement for this, local officials were told by another part of MTV that, as an international organisation, they were only committed to campaigning for international charities. However, after some negotiations, MTV agreed to: promote the charity on large screens at the Princes Street Gardens' concert; auction pop star memorabilia at the charity's launch and provide a donation from MTV UK. Despite a number of requests the research was unable to establish how much this donation actually was. The event's global realities were not lost on local organisers who believed it differed from others they'd staged because, rather than dealing with government departments or public organisations, this involved a global private company which exerted tight control on their public relations machine that arrived late at the event. This influenced the local organising framework as Scottish representatives couldn't initiate their communication plan as early as they'd like because MTV weren't ready and it was their event. This had negative repercussions because it prevented Scottish officials communicating early that this was a television show, not a live concert with thousands of public tickets available; with the result being raised public expectations towards seeing the show and controversy, given Edinburgh Council's (£125 k) subsidy, over the decision to sell only 50 of the 6000 tickets in Edinburgh and, instead, allocate many to the event's sponsors (American Express, Vodafone Live, Replay Blue Jeans, Foot Locker). This left local residents to compete with other European callers, via a single hotline number, for 2000 tickets that sold out in 14 minutes. An *Evening News'* journalist saw this as one of many public relations (PR) disasters surrounding the event with people having to sleep on the street for 24 hours to get tickets.

The council's Event Champion stated that they recognised early the dangers of press stories about "the MTV circus comes to Leith and nobody benefited", deemed unacceptable to a Labour council and a Scottish Executive keen on social inclusion. A range of local initiatives were therefore organised which MTV were happy to support as long, crucially, as it didn't interfere with organising their television show. These included: local companies with sought-after local knowledge delivering services such as hairdressing, security and plant hire; a simultaneous free "thank you" concert from MTV to 8000 people in Princes Street Gardens, with 750 tickets given to local charities; 1000 local youngsters from schools, colleges and universities used at rehearsals and at the Awards' show as the "pit" audience, red carpet "screamers", "seat-fillers for the stars", dancers and singers. The latter involvement was controlled by MTV via auditions to include the kind of lively youngsters needed for their television spectacular (Mooney & Halstead, 2003). An MTV press release stated that the "thank you" concert allowed those unable to attend the main event to experience the celebrations "MTV style". However, in reality, this live link to the main Awards served a number of purposes as the main show's compere – the film star Vin Diesel – was given "his most daring assignment ever" to get, by car, from Leith to Princes Street Gardens in 20 minutes to introduce a performance by the Flaming Lips and the Chemical Brothers. MTV's Chief Operating Officer felt this gave the show a narrative – could he do it? – which was better than viewers merely waiting to see who won awards. It also overcame Jones's (2001) contention that formal arenas can hinder host city showcasing as television footage of Diesel driving across the city showed famous Edinburgh landmarks with the actor remarking, "this place is beautiful, I wish we had more time to do some sightseeing". The contention that locals provide an essential backdrop to successful events by providing spectacle and dramatic occasion (Hall & Hodge, 2000) was evident here with cameras constantly panning to ecstatic young people in Princes Street Gardens; some holding a "thanks for the ticket" banner. MTV's Marketing Director felt that having "8000 other people on the street appreciating the show" gave the Awards "accessibility" compared with "the lucky few at the main event". However, it wasn't just exuberant local youngsters that provided the "essential backdrop" as the Gardens' concert also accessed Edinburgh's iconic city centre skyline. This was crucial because part of the event's local framework, the Leith venue, didn't offer the place imagery wanted by both sides – MTV for a spectacular television moment and Scottish officials for destination profiling of Edinburgh. However, the visual spectacle of a 4-minute pop performance encapsulating psychedelic imagery filmed against the backdrop of an illuminated Edinburgh Castle undeniably did. Thus, while marketed as a "thank you" concert to locals, an MTV official described it as "a good deal": thoughts shared by Scottish officials who believed it overcame charges that the event was elitist and a local historian's belief that watching the Leith show involved "watching an event not a place" (Farquarson, 2003). As Hinch and Higham (2004) argue, cities hosting events seek global recognition, but the local context must be highlighted for distinctiveness. While the Awards' economic impact study highlighted overwhelmingly positive feedback from 182 of those attending the Gardens' concert (SQW, 2004) the "thank you" concert often involved watching the main show on large screens and cheering rehearsals for the excellent 4-minute "live" television link to the main Awards.

The MTV Awards as a Marketing Vehicle

Discussing the marketing surrounding Sydney's Olympic bid, Waitt (1999) states that "the social, cultural and historical elements of a locality are mixed and matched by the playful antics of marketeers" (p. 1057). While this was seen by the "thank you" concert's unusual juxtaposition of ancient (Edinburgh Castle) and modern (technologically orientated pop performance), MTV's Vice President argued that the award show allowed them to "have fun with Scottish heritage". This included: the use of sporrans to deliver notification of the award winners; getting the Scottish football team's "Tartan Army" supporters to sing parts of the "Best Song" category and Vin Diesel being dressed in a leather kilt and singing "Flower of Scotland". While at one point Diesel asked, "Why are we allowing the Tartan Army to destroy that song", MTV's Chief Operating Officer saw such Scottishness as their "creative spur" which this local framework reinterpreted to give the show a "striking twist". For instance, the show's commercial breaks had short inserts showing images of Edinburgh buildings daubed with slogans such as "disposable icons", again, taking well-known local images but, as the aforementioned interviewee remarked, "changing the view". While Scottish officials felt MTV's use of Scottish culture had worked brilliantly, the show's best aspect – seen as invaluable for long-term tourism prospects – were the positive endorsements from global pop stars (45 in total) including: Justin Timberlake "You don't get nicer than you people"; Sean Paul "Edinburgh you've been a great host, it's a very beautiful place"; Beyonce "I would love to come back to Scotland. I've seen the castle, I've eaten in fantastic restaurants and the people are brilliant". Scottish officials' views mirrored McTernan's (2003) assessment that the Awards encapsulated the global currency of the age, celebrity. Local officials believed the event further enhanced Scotland's celebrity status, aided earlier by the Scottish weddings of Madonna and Stella McCartney. However, the global realities of celebrity culture also hindered local officials' tourist strategies as it was felt that the pop stars' image rights prevented use of their endorsements in traditional adverts. Officials argued that, if used in context, there was a chance of using them on the VisitScotland web site and, if careful, press stories.

Another promotional opportunity was a 30-minute "Come to Scotland" programme broadcast repeatedly on MTV in the days before the event. This combined destination sell and encouragement of voting and interest in the Awards. Scottish officials saw this as ideal because a conventional travelogue would be switched off by their target market. While the programme showed aspects of contemporary Edinburgh, with footage of its Hogmanay Party and a vox pop of young locals singing the city's praises from city centre locations, it disappointed some officials for lapsing into old Scottish stereotypes with the Scottish pop group Travis asking pop and film stars questions such as "what is a sporran?" and "what is tossing the caber?". Promoting a welcoming image of Scotland was also hindered by the band's decision to, albeit jokingly, warn viewers about shell-suited "neds" who caused trouble at bus and train stations. One tourist official saw the programme as a promotional opportunity that "got away from us" which could have been avoided if they had told the band their re-imaging intentions. There seems, here, to have been a tension between MTV's desire to create a television programme attractive to a global audience and Scottish public agencies' local re-imaging agenda. It appeared that MTV's creative personnel were reluctant to listen to local officials about programme content; a situation accentuated by local organisers' awareness of the global realities of power politics, heard in their comments: "they (MTV) know their audience, we wouldn't dream of telling them how to spend their money"; "MTV know what they're doing, they've got a track record" and "it's their gig . . . they're the professionals".

A tourist official believed that one promotional vehicle that worked well was the themed interactive on-line game (Monkey Mission) on the MTV web site. This sought to increase interest in the Awards by offering VIP tickets for the event if the user navigated an escaped monkey from Edinburgh Zoo "around Edinburgh's city centre trendy bars, shops and restaurants". The ELTB representative highlighted its benefit when arguing, "the game will engage millions of kids in a travelogue through Edinburgh and, in a clever, almost passive way, is going to force them to learn about Edinburgh in a way that bombarding them with images of the castle wouldn't achieve". This worked better than the "Come to Scotland" programme as Scottish officials worked closely with MTV's on-line Marketing Director to include suitable images. The initiative was seen as having long-term tourism benefits as they were hoping to include it on the ELTB web site. Another promotional opportunity was four concerts held in English cities (London, Birmingham, Manchester and Newcastle) entitled "The Road to Edinburgh" broadcast on MTV in the show's run-up. However, the two concerts examined (London and Birmingham) mainly consisted of: the top 20 moments from previous award ceremonies, low-key performances from various pop acts; brief showcasing of the English cities and adverts from the Awards' main sponsors (and others). Apart from a number of name checks for the Edinburgh show there was no wider destination profiling, although there was apparently press coverage of the concerts in the four English cities. However, the VisitScotland official saw them as a great opportunity to access key markets as 92% of trips to Scotland come from within the UK. VisitScotland also bought MTV advertising slots in the run-up to the Awards to showcase Scotland as an adventure sport destination. The organisation's official saw this as particularly important as it promoted the required contemporary image and had that sought-after ability to surprise people out of their traditional perceptions of Scottish tourism.

Local Tensions and Media Portrayals

Not surprisingly, given the event's high-profile and corporate emphasis, it initially attracted much criticism. Turning this volume's title on its head, much of this revolved around the belief that, in dancing to a global events' framework, this was ignoring local realities. For instance, a Leith historian described the MTV Awards as "a non-event" and a "30 second flash in the pan" with "locals paying for a party to which they weren't invited". The crucial aspect, to him, was that there were two populations in Leith: one stemming from the Edinburgh Waterfront project's new-build housing, the other a local population that had been in the area for centuries. He saw this event as being primarily for the former. Echoing Fredline et al.'s (2002, p. 37) argument that events cause dissatisfaction when "the theme does not fit the socio-cultural milieu of the community", and Waitt's (1999, p. 1058) point that events can be an "irrelevance to the realities of local histories, localities and culture", he argued that, because the MTV Awards had no cultural connection to Leith's maritime past, locals were indifferent to it: in contrast to the 1995 Tall Ships event which, because it was free and had this organic connection, created a "buzz" that was still talked about. He believed the council's event subsidy contradicted its social inclusion policy and urged Edinburgh politicians to show "the realities of life, rather than what they think the realities are" as there was too great an emphasis on large prestige projects for "the few" which weren't conducive to sustainable tourism involving smaller events connected to the area. *The Scotsman* journalist felt the event did little for Leith's problems of poverty, heroin addiction and prostitution and, like much of Edinburgh tourism, benefited city centre shops and hotels with their "Mcjobs". While MTV's Executive Director argued that they'd learned over the years not to stage the Awards with a fence around it, the local historian believed that, in reality, the event was about a global corporation and global pop stars promoting themselves and, to enable this, "a glass wall included the select few while excluding the great unwashed". He also saw this process as encapsulating local "power politics" with Edinburgh politicians and Forth Ports' "power brokers" using the event to promote their economically inspired Waterfront regeneration project which ignored indigenous Leithers' socio-economic problems. To him, the actual showcasing of Leith was minimal, with a few televised shots of the docks and Ocean Terminal, but nothing on local historical sites deemed underdeveloped from a tourist perspective. However, the Leith Initiative for Tourism representative felt the historian's views were "stuck in the dark ages" as the event made local bars and restaurants more attractive to young people, while the floodlighting of buildings during the event week gave the shore a safer feel, showing the waterfront's potential as a short-break destination. He did express disappointment however that stars chose to go into Edinburgh for their after show parties rather than stay in Leith. Highlighting again the symbolic benefits of events, the Forth Ports' Property Director argued that the association with a blue chip company like MTV gave a seal of approval to the area's regeneration, a view reiterated by another director who felt the event's scale – second only (he believed) to the Oscars in the entertainment industry – almost matched the scale of progress in the area's regeneration. On a more practical level, Forth Ports' officials felt the MTV link allowed them to reach a young audience – seen as a key shopping segment – and showcase Ocean Terminal to high-quality London retailers, both of which aided their ambition to be the city's premier shopping destination. One tourist official remarked that, while the event was a seminal moment in Leith's evolution, it was about promoting Edinburgh as the global brand with a rich waterfront in Leith. He believed that all great world cities had a waterfront but here residents and tourists had their back to Edinburgh's, with their gaze focusing on its iconic city centre skyline. This event was therefore conceptualised within a strategic local framework which sought to reconnect Edinburgh and the port of Leith to enhance Edinburgh's economic prospects within the realities of the global economy.

A key institution within Edinburgh's local political framework is the *Edinburgh Evening News* – part of a newspaper stable often critical of the public sector. A number of interviewees felt the *News*'s initially negative event coverage symptomatic of its long tradition of "council bashing" and annoyance at MTV's official sponsorship deal with the Glasgow-based *Daily Record*. While the council leader wrote to the *Evening News* stating that the event caused very little unwanted disruption and created an unprecedented buzz benefiting the whole city (Anderson, 2003) – a view largely confirmed by *News*' representatives – the paper printed articles such as: "Fury at Princes Street Closure for MTV" (24/10/03); "Tourism chiefs snap up city's MTV tickets" (29/10/03); "I want my MTV award tickets" ("Letters" 18/10/03); "Fans furious at awards tickets" ("Letters" 31/10/03); "City snubbed over MTV awards tickets" (7/10/03); "What a sell-out" ("Letters" 15/10/03); "Awards of little benefit to locals" ("Letters" 1/11/03); "Seeing red over MTV red carpet snub" (20/10/03); "Church facing MTV road chaos" (31/10/03); "City pays for MTV clean-up at hotels" (30/10/03); "Students miss out on lots of Di-dough at MTV awards" (1/11/03); "Paying for a party but no invitation" (4/11/03); "Fury as Edinburgh's bill for MTV soars to £230,000" (12/12/03); "Taxpayers hit with £45,000 MTV police bill" (26/2/04). *News*' representatives denied any political agenda, stating the paper was "independent" and was merely acting as a "watchdog" for Edinburgh residents. One *News* journalist attributed the negative coverage to MTV's desire for complete control which prevented the council and the newspaper publicising local initiatives, and organisers' "PR disasters"; notably VisitScotland selling 100 tickets for the Gardens' concert to tourists and the decision, on security grounds, to close the docks which prevented locals accessing the show's "red carpet". This led to MTV receiving pleas by the city's Lord Provost and council's Event Champion to change this strategy to maintain community support. An *Evening News'* editorial (20/10/03) argued that few ordinary members of the public would get tickets for the Gardens' concert, or main show, and thus the decision sent a message to Edinburgh residents that they'd get nothing more from the event than television viewers. The *News'* reporter stated that, when they contacted MTV about this "they wouldn't say anything … but eventually they did auditions for this too". A steering group official felt the newspaper's "VisitScotland" story unfair as they were only doing their job with a small amount of tickets.

The local Conservative Party's Cultural spokesperson expressed concerns about the event's exclusionary nature when arguing "This event may as well be held on the moon as far as the people of Edinburgh are concerned . . . It's obvious MTV don't want local people anywhere near", while a Liberal Democrat councillor stated "You can't just bring an event like the awards to Edinburgh and exclude local people . . . the city must do more to respond to the rights of those who live, work and worship in the city centre when they plan the event" (McEwan, 2003). The newspaper and opposition councillors were angered by the event's £75 k "hidden costs", funded out of existing council budgets, to finance extra cleansing, policing, traffic management, staffing and public safety: additional to the £125 k of council money part-financing the creation of the event arena and the £30 k used to part-fund banners in the city. Waitt's (1999) contention that place marketing requires a "pristine environment" received a political twist as the Conservative Group also expressed anger at the council spending £25 k cleaning city centre hotel fronts in preparation for the Awards a cost, they argued, which should have been met by the hotels. Ironically, these hotels hindered place promotion by lacking suitable ISDN or broadband technology which prevented the event's 700 accredited journalists sending large numbers of pictures to their overseas offices. Opposition councillors believed that the additional cleaning of hotels and Leith area showed the Labour administration making the city look attractive for tourists when, in the latter area, the issue was a low priority. Indeed, the chairman of a Leith residents association wrote to the *News* (4/11/03) – in response to this additional cleaning and claims that Leith was a potential worldwide tourist venue – to highlight a "different Leith" a few hundred yards from the MTV venue, one noted for graffiti, poor lighting and broken paving where the council's cleansing department rarely ventured. He concluded by stating "The council is quick to boast about its achievements but continues to ignore our pleas for a reasonable standard of living". The Liberal Democrat group secretary was equally critical about the additional money, especially for "hotels who would have made so much money out of the Awards but don't put a penny back in for us". The council leader however saw the Conservative and Liberal Democrat comments as political opportunism, pointing to the lack of opposition motions when the Awards were first mooted, while also arguing "if we hadn't spent money on additional cleaning" then opposition parties would say "Edinburgh wasn't a world class city – you can't win". He saw the *Evening News'* coverage as symptomatic of a thread that ran through Edinburgh that saw events for tourists not locals. To him this ignored that, alongside financial services, tourism was central to the city's economy employing over 25,000 people and, through their events strategy, they had delivered year-round tourism. Having had experience of the *Evening News'* approach, steering group members advised MTV – said by one official to have felt "angry and betrayed" by some of the *News'* coverage – to "hold their nerve" as "when the event comes to town the volume of positive stories will minimise criticism". Indeed, on the event day the *Evening News'* editorial stated that, given the economic benefit and the showcasing of Edinburgh with some of the world's biggest stars to future tourists, the public money "will prove to have been more than worth it".

News Management

While the above highlights the news management problems facing the steering group, they were allowed to influence how the event was perceived through a special colour supplement in the Glasgow-based *Sunday Herald*, published the weekend before the Awards. For £5000 the ELTB official was allowed to write the publication's editorial – obviously positive – and raise the profile of the public agencies involved as their logos appeared at the bottom of each page. Positive media profile was also provided by MTV's decision to give Edinburgh an award for putting on the best show in the event's 10 year history. However, of crucial importance in terms of news management was the publication, in March 2004, of the event's economic impact study. The report, undertaken by independent consultants who'd examined the impact of other events for the organisers assessed only "the direct economic and wider marketing *benefits* … generated by the *successful* staging of the Awards" (SQW, 2004, p. 1). Methodologically, the desk research covered a limited range and quality of sources, namely other economic impact studies – often seen as methodologically flawed (Crompton, 2001; Gratton, Dobson & Shibili, 2001) – and information from MTV, while consultations were mainly with major retailers and hotels who were key event beneficiaries. While the report admitted that estimating an event's media value is "notoriously difficult" (p. 29), "subject to some judgement" and "difficult to assess" (p. 31), assumptions were made that 5% of the Awards' television programming "mentioned Edinburgh and/or Scotland in some specific way" (p. 31), and that this should be classed as editorial coverage – not normal advertising – with the former seen to be three times more valuable. Rather than highlight the critical comments made in the *Edinburgh Evening News*, it was reported as contributing "*a* piece on tickets and the treatment of fans" (p. 37).

The economic impact study's methodological limitations served an important local political purpose by highlighting favourable event comments from the global media – notably the "influential" US Billboard magazine which reported "how the event can be used to showcase a city, or indeed a country to the world", the French Tele 7 Jours magazine that described Edinburgh as "the flamboyant capital of Scotland", Poland's Metro newspaper that stated "many Scottish accents gave splendour to the ceremony" and "one of Norway's foremost newspapers" (Dagbladet) that commented "Scotland makes it great on the night" (SQW, 2004; Ward, 2004). The use of particular multipliers highlighted that the Awards provided double the economic benefit (£9 million) to Edinburgh and Scotland than originally thought, thereby generating further positive media headlines (Cowie, 2004; Ferguson, 2004; Ward, 2004). The above passage hasn't meant to disparage the case for the event, or the efforts of event organisers, but highlight the limitations of its economic impact analysis. As some respondents argued, the most important benefits of these Awards couldn't be quantified such as: the creation of a more contemporary and dynamic image for Leith, Edinburgh and Scotland amongst potential tourists and inward investors; the "buzz" in the city in the run-up to the event and the excitement of local youngsters watching the events, dancing or singing next to their idols at the main show, or involved in one of the many local spin-offs.

Conclusion

While critics described the MTV Europe Music Awards as a media circus, this chapter highlights how it formed part of Edinburgh's attempt to become the most prominent northern European city by 2015. What is evident from the case study is that relationships between local frameworks and global realities are extremely complex, with local organisers and MTV representatives unable to determine the event's outcome. Local organisers clearly saw the event within a global reality which champions events' ability to position cities favourably within the increasingly competitive global tourism and inward investment market. Officials felt that Edinburgh's rise to a leading European tourism destination was enhanced by MTV's central place in global youth culture and the city's packaging within its unconventional marketing which encapsulated the 21st century's celebrity obsession. This prominent global reality – the central role played by transnational corporations – was also seen in MTV's editorial control of the event which meant local inclusion took place within their over-riding aim of producing a spectacular television show. While this created memorable *moments* for youngsters involved, longer-lasting benefits required social inclusion to be given greater priority within local event objectives. A local event framework based on tourism and image marketing, combined with MTV's global realities of television, celebrity and marketing itself, meant local inclusion was marginalised. Literature emphasising how local event organisers select positive city images for place marketing should therefore appreciate the realities of power in this global/local partnership because, here, images preferred by MTV for good television did, occasionally, contrast with organisers' place marketing objectives. Evidence of tensions between organisers and locals over images of cultural identity used in events (Hughes, 1999) must extend to tensions between local organisers and global event owners. Academic language of event-led re-imaging deflects from the imaging needs of powerful global event owners as Edinburgh's iconic place features and youngsters' enthusiasm re-imaged MTV's traditional award show. Of central importance in the local event framework is the local media (Atkinson & Laurier, 1995). Here, MTV's control of information antagonised the local newspaper which was already angered by the ticket allocation to corporate sponsors over locals. The newspaper's negative event reporting highlighted that, despite the realities of global power, the realities of local media power set the political agenda. Branding the event Edinburgh03, but staging it in the under-developed port of Leith, symbolised a key local political objective of reconnecting Edinburgh with its waterfront to aid its global economic prospects. However, critics within Leith felt the event benefited MTV, global pop stars, local political elites and affluent incomers, not locals. Their views echoed studies highlighting events' elite-driven exclusion of local work, historical and class realities (Atkinson & Laurier, 1995; France & Roche, 1998; Fredline, Jago & Deery, 2003; Waitt, 1999).

References

Anderson, D. (2003). A buzz that benefits the whole city. *Edinburgh Evening News*, 8th November.

Atkinson, D., & Laurier, E. (1995). A sanitised city: Social exclusion at Bristol's International Festival of the Sea. *Geoforum, 29*, 197–206.

Avraham, E. (2004). Media strategies for improving an unfavourable city image. *Cities, 21*(6), 471–479.

Balibrea, M.P. (2004). Urban culture and the post industrial city: challenging the Barcelona model. *Journal of Spanish Cultural Studies, 12*(2), 187–210.

Balsas, G. (2004). City centre regeneration in the context of the 2001 European capital of culture in Porto, Portugal. *Local Economy, 19*(4), 396–410.

Bianchinni, F. (1999). Cultural planning for urban sustainability. In: L. Nystrom (ed.), *City and culture — cultural processes and urban sustainability*. Stockholm: The Swedish Urban Environment Council.

Blaikie, N. (2000). *Designing social research: The logic of application*. Cambridge: Polity Press.

Bourdieu, P. (1984). *Distinction: A social critique of the judgement of taste*. London: Routledge.

Bramham, P., Henry, I., Mommaas, H., & van der Poel, H. (Eds) (1989). *Leisure and urban processes: critical studies of leisure policy in western European cities*. London: Routledge.

Brown, C., & Lyons, W. (2003). Brand new approach for Auld Reekie. *The Scotsman*, 3rd December.

Bryman, A. (2001). *Social research methods*. Oxford: Oxford University Press.

Carlsen, J., & Taylor, A. (2003). Mega events and urban renewal: The case of Manchester 2002 commonwealth games. *Event Management, 18*, 15–22.

Cowie, E. (2004). MTV's big Scottish night yields £9 million high notes. *The Herald*, 16th March.

Crompton, J. L. (2001). Public subsidies to professional team sport facilities in the USA. In: C. Gratton & I. Henry (Eds), *Sport in the city: The role of sport in economic and social regeneration*. London: Routledge.

Denscombe, M. (1998). *The good research guide*. Buckingham: Open University Press.

Denzin, N., & Lincoln, Y. S. (1994). *Handbook of qualitative research*. London: Sage Publications.

Eade, J. (1997). *Living in the global city: Globalisation as a local process*. London: Routledge.

Essex, S., & Chalkey, B. (1998). Olympic games: Catalyst of urban change. *Leisure Studies, 7*, 187–206.

Edinburgh Evening News (2003) Comment, 6th November.

Evans, G., & Shaw, P. (2004). *The contribution of culture to regeneration in the UK: A review of evidence*. A Report for the Department of Culture, Media & Sport, Leeds Metropolitan University.

Farquarson, K. (2003). Ready to rock. *Sunday Times*, 5th October.

Ferguson, B. (2004). MTV is an £8.9 million boost to Scotland. *Edinburgh Evening News*, 15th March.

France, A., & Roche, M. (1998). Sport meg-events, urban policy and youth identity: Issues of citizenship and exclusion in Sheffield. In: M. Roche (Ed.), *Sport, popular culture and identity* (Vol. 5). Chelsea School Research Centre/University of Brighton, Oxford: Meyer & Meyer Sport.

Fredline, L., Jago, L., & Deery, M. (2002). The development of a generic management scale to measure the social impact of events. *Event Management, 18*, 23–37.

Fredline, L., Jago, L., & Deery, M. (2003). The development of a generic scale to measure the social impact of events. *Event Management, 8*(1), 23–37.

Garcia, B. (2003). Urban regeneration, arts programming and major events. Glasgow 1990, Sydney 2000 and Barcelona 2004' Paper presented at the conference Journeys of Expression II: Cultural Festivals/Events and Tourism, Vienna, Austria (6–9 March).

Garcia, B. (2004). Cultural policy and urban regeneration in Western European cities: Lessons from experience, prospects for the future. *Local Economy, 19*(4) 312–326.

Gratton, C., Dobson, N., & Shibili, S. (2001). The economic impact of major sports events: A case study of six European and World championships. In: I. Henry & C. Gratton (Eds), *Sport in the city: The role of sport in economic and social regeneration*. London: Routledge.

Green, K. (2000). Exploring the everyday "philosophies" of physical education teachers from a sociological perspective. *Sport, Education and Society, 5*(2), 109–129.

Greig, J., Savage, B., Dargue, C., & Kirkwood-Smith, L. (1989). *Leith lives: A walk in the past*. Local History Project, Scottish Development Agency, Edinburgh.

Hall, C. M. (1992). *Hallmark tourist events: Impacts, management & planning*. London: Belhaven Press.

Hall, C. M., & Hodge, J. (2000). The politics of place and identity in the Sydney Olympics: Sharing the spirit of corporatism. In: M. Roche (Ed.), *Sport, popular culture and identity* (2nd ed., Vol. 5). Oxford: Chelsea School Research Centre, Meyer and Meyer Sport (UK) Ltd.

Hall, C. M., & Jenkins, J. (1995). *Tourism & public policy*. London: Routledge.

Harvey, D. (1989). *The condition of postmodernity*. Oxford: Blackwell.

Higham, J. E. S. (1999). Sport as an avenue of tourism development: An analysis of the positive and negative impacts of sports tourism. *Current Issues in Tourism, 2*(1), 82–90.

Hinch, T., & Higham, J. (2004). *Sport Tourism Development*. Clevedon: Channel View Publications.

Hughes, G. (1999). Urban revitalisation: The use of festive time strategies. *Leisure Studies, 18*, 119–135.

Hutton, G. (1995). *Old Leith*. Ayrshire: Stenlake.

Jamieson, B. (2003). If M is for music, I claim C is for curmudgeons. *The Scotsman*, 6th November.

Jones, C. (2001). Mega-events and host-region impacts: Determining the true worth of the 1999 Rugby World Cup. *International Journal of Tourism Research, 3*, 241–251.

Marshall, J. S. (1983). *The church in the midst: South Leith Parish Church through five centuries*. Edinburgh: Edina Press.

Marvasti, A. B. (2004). *Qualitative research in sociology*. London: Sage Publications.

McCarthy, J. (2005). Promoting image and identity in 'cultural quarters': The case of Dundee. *Local Economy, 20*(3), 280–293.

McEwan, A. (2003). Church facing MTV road chaos. *Edinburgh Evening News*, 31st October.

McTernan, J. (2003). Celebrity is the only religion that matters to today's youth. *Scotland on Sunday*, 9th November.

Mooney, C., & Halstead, S. (2003). MTV plea for 500 fans to star at awards show. *Edinburgh Evening News*, 25th October.

Mooney, G. (2004). Cultural policy as urban transformation? Critical reflections on Glasgow, European city of culture 1990. *Local Economy, 19*(4), 327–340.

Mowat, S. C. (1994). *The port of leith: Its history and its people*. Forth Ports Plc, John Donald Publishers Ltd, Edinburgh.

Rojek, C., & Urry, J. (1997). *Touring cultures: Transformations of travel and theory*. London: Routledge.

Shaw, G., & Williams, A. M. (2002). *Critical issues in tourism* (2nd ed.). Oxford: Blackwell Publishers Ltd.

Smith, A. (2001). Sporting a new image? Sport-based regeneration strategies as a means of enhancing the image of the city tourist destination. In: C. Gratton & I. Henry (Eds), *Sport in the city: The role of sport in economic and social regeneration*. London: Routledge.

Spink, J., & Bramham, P. (1998). The myth of the 24 hour city. In: P. Bramham & W. Murphy (Eds), *Policy and publics: Leisure, culture and commerce*. University of Brighton/LSA Publication No. 65, Eastbourne.

SQW (2004). *Economic impact of the MTV Europe Awards Edinburgh03*. Edinburgh: Scottish Enterprise.

Waitt, G. (1999). Playing games with Sydney: Marketing Sydney for the 2000 Olympics. *Urban Studies, 36*, 1055–1077.

Wallace, J. M. (1985). *Traditions of Trinity and Leith*. Edinburgh: John Donald Publishers.

Ward, S. (2003). Hooking up: VisitScotland targets MTV Awards. *The Scotsman*, 5th November.

Ward, S. (2004). MTV awards generate £9 million for the economy and put Edinburgh on world stage. *The Scotsman*, 16th March.

Watson, J. (2003). Back to the future. *Scotland on Sunday*, 30th November.

Weiler, B., & Hall, C. M. (1992). *Special interest tourism*. London: Belhaven Books.

Wilks-Heeg, S., & North, P. (2004). Cultural policy & urban regeneration. *Local Economy*, 19(4), 305–311.

Wilson, D. (2003). And the winner is … Edinburgh. *Edinburgh Evening News*, 8th November.

Yin, K. (2003). *Case study research: Design and methods* (3rd ed). Thousand Oaks, CA: Sage.

Chapter 15

The Lost Gardens and Airport Expansion: Focalisation in Heritage Landscapes

M. W. J. Spaul

Introduction

The attention of the traveller, taking off from London's Stansted Airport, is more likely to be fixated on the attractions of some distant destination than the cultural intricacies of the Essex countryside dropping away beneath the aircraft. However, a glance under the port wing would reveal the woodland pasture of Hatfield Forest, catering – under the steward-ship of the National Trust – for a steady flow of visitors drawn by the variegated pleasures of woodland walks, picnic places, and lakeside tea-rooms. A more awkward craning of the neck may just afford a glimpse, under the port tailplane, of the remnants of the Easton Lodge estate gathered around the site of its long-vanished focal house. The Gardens of Easton Lodge, in a heritage gesture similar to that of the highly publicised restoration of the Lost Gardens of Heligan (Samuel, 1998, pp. 125–131), have been partially reconstructed and opened to public view. Enjoying a status on the National Gardens Register as "of historical importance", the site is an established feature on the circuits of East Anglian heritage tourism. Unsurprisingly, both of these landscapes figure prominently in arguments over the proposed expansion of Stansted Airport, with a second runway and associated infrastructure projected to brush up against the boundaries of the Easton Lodge estate (CPRE, 2003a; Department for Transport, 2003). In the summer of 2003, visitors to the Gardens of Easton Lodge, as they passed into the remnants of an elaborate design created by Harold Peto in 1902, were entreated to petition against airport expansion (under the aegis of the local pressure group "Stop Stansted Expansion"). Oddly, at least from a certain viewpoint, this entreaty was supported by little more than the bare facts of the expansion plans and Stop Stansted Expansion's key visual signifier: the looming silhouettes of an endless stream of airliners. It was as if the landscape itself, a garden frozen in mid-restoration by the "threat" of the airport's encroachment on its tranquil precincts, was deemed sufficient argument; and that it marshalled – by dint of its fabric, lineage, and associations – all that can be reasonably said on the subject. Irrespective of whether it was conscious strategy to let the heritage landscape of the gardens stand *in lieu* of argument, there is much to be gained by testing the apparent assumption that this landscape may encode a socio-political position, can be made to speak, and can stand as an articulate element in a complex planning debate.

The Gardens of Easton Lodge constitute the centrepiece of a set of leisure sites and residential dwellings established among the fragments of what were once the estates of the Duke of Warwick: the manor house and tithe barn form a banqueting and conference facility; a caravan site has settled on a lakeside location by the old rectory; and a long-distance footpath weaves around the perimeter of the estate. The creation of an airfield during World War II ensured that Easton Lodge could not take its place alongside the manicured heritage sites of the National Trust. The declaration, in 1940, by the Secretary of State for War that "we are out to win this war and should not be put off by a desire to maintain intact the stately homes of England" (Smith, 1996, p. 142) was a prescient indication of the future of Easton Lodge. The oaks of the parkland were removed by explosives and bulldozer; the house could not economically be reoccupied after its use as a headquarters; and the gardens became overgrown. The contemporary landscape is the result of piecemeal renovation and re-use and, as such, has some of the schizoid quality of the urban fringe. The ensemble of old airfield buildings, concrete trackways cross-hatching prairie-scale arable fields, and stranded estate cottages still marked with the Warwick crest do not sit happily with conventional images of either rurality or the country house estate. The ambivalence of the landscape, and the attempts to enrol it in the circuits of contemporary heritage and leisure consumption, make its analysis problematic. Following Dixon Hunt's (2004, pp. 12–17) adaptations of literary theory to landscape analysis, the current study is conceived as an attempt to adapt aspects of narratology as analytical devices. In particular the idea of "focalisation" (or "point of view"), is used as a means of approaching a highly ambivalent "landscape text" and tracing some of the different "voices" with which it speaks.

Theoretical Context

The analytic standpoint of regarding a landscape as a text, and hence amenable to being probed by a range of semiotic techniques, is sufficiently well-established that it does not require a general justification. However, like all truisms, the principle that "a landscape is a text" must be rendered specific before it can be used to establish any clear results. The general orientation adopted here is that of, for example Bishop (1995), Cosgrove (1984) and Daniels (1993) with a landscape being viewed as a cultural construction which can be best understood by treating it as a text amongst, and in relation to, other cultural texts. Thus a landscape is drawn into a web of intertextual relationships (e.g. Allen, 2000) which reaches across boundaries of genre and medium, with the landscape's physical form having no privileged analytical significance. This is particularly apparent in landscapes which are consciously curated and presented as "heritage landscapes", and subject to the forms of cultural consumption associated with mobile, literate, leisure activities. In such cases there is no clear boundary between the heritage object and the various media objects which surround and interpret it. However, to establish a landscape as one amongst a web of cultural texts does not fully specify how that textual ensemble is to be conceived and analysed. As with the bare gesture towards "landscape as text" as a principle, so the bare gesture towards "semiotic techniques" is insufficiently specific; and any particular analysis requires the identification of a specific semiotic orientation, a conception of the text, and a specific set of analytic instruments.

This study is an attempt to apply narratological techniques (e.g. Bal, 1985; Genette, 1980; Prince, 1982) to heritage landscapes, hence treating a landscape as, textually, a narrative. There are a broad range of senses in which a landscape may be considered to be a narrative text. One of the most common is that current in landscape archaeology, of the sort popularised by Hoskins (1988, original 1955), in which a landscape is made to yield – with the aid of the historically informed interpretive skills of the archaeologist – the realist tale of its historical production, organised into a linear, developmental narrative. Another well-established sense is that of landscape conceived along the narrative lines of theatre, as a consciously produced spectacle to be experienced as an unfolding narrative by those passing through the landscape – a conception which guided the design of gardens in the early 18th century (Thacker, 1994, pp. 176–195) and some contemporary approaches to landscape design (e.g. Whiston Spirn, 1998). A typical heritage site – of which Easton Lodge may be considered an instance – may be seen to hover somewhere between these conceptions: an accumulation of historical traces consciously presented in a manner which dramatises the processes of their production, restoration, and current stewardship; and experienced by their visitors as set of narratives of historical change, present sense-making, and – in a reflexive mode – of leisure consumption itself.

As Bal (2001, p. 41) has pointed out, one does not identify some meaningful text as a narrative and then proceed to apply an established set of narratological techniques to release its meaning and the intricacies of its narrative construction. Rather, one acknowledges that any semiotic object may possess a narrative dimension, and in trying to articulate this dimension help to define and refine the instruments of narratology. This is particularly true for such texts as landscapes, which cannot straightforwardly be aligned with more conventional objects of narratological analysis such as novels, films, and narrative paintings. This study is concerned principally with a single aspect of narrative, that of "focalisation", a formalised version of the intuitive concepts of "point of view" or "perspective" as they occur in narratives; the ways in which the world of the story – the fabula – may be framed and rendered from the standpoint of a particular social identity (for a standard formulation see Genette, 1980, pp. 162–190, for some difficulties in this formulation, and some refinements, see Grishakova, 2000; Jahn, 1996). If the landscape of the Easton Lodge estate may be said to dramatise its past and its relationship with the present, then the question arises of how it does so, and whether this dramatisation is as univocal as seems to be assumed in the rhetoric of protest against the expansion of Stansted Airport. The question being pursued is whether the concept of focalisation, and the narratological theory which surrounds it, permits these questions to be posed in a revealing way; and also whether it can help to guide the assembling of the textual resources of the landscape into coherent standpoints.

To establish a sense in which heritage landscapes may function as narrative texts, it is useful to consider the practice of garden design in the early 18th century, the era in which "picturesque" gardening came into vogue. Gardens were created on an analogy with the landscape paintings of the day, which had strong narrative elements focused on classical themes (e.g. Andrews, 1999, pp. 94–105). Addison and Pope promulgated the maxim that "All gardening is landscape painting. Just like a landscape hung up". (quoted in Dixon Hunt, 1992, p. 106); and just as the paintings of Poussin and his many imitators blended Italianate landscapes with episodes from classical mythology, gardeners created linked series of walks and vistas punctuated by classical statuary and architecture. Such projects were also conceived in terms of theatre, with a succession of scenes constituting a narrative line; gardens were designed like stage sets, using the perspectival devices developed in the theatre of day. The text of the picturesque garden requires a considerable interpretative contribution from the viewer, presupposing a set of dispositions heavily dependent on class membership: a classical education which provided the resources to decode statuary, architecture and inscriptions, and the desire for the leisured exercise of "wit", taking delight in puzzle-solving and wry landscape "jokes" (Dixon Hunt, 1992, pp. 114–117) – without such a contribution the narratives degenerate into a succession of mystifying visual tableaux.

Extreme textuality fell out of favour as the "natural" landscape gardens of Brown and Repton displaced the classical picturesque (Dixon Hunt, 1992, p. 128) and the experience of the garden became one of personal response to natural forms. However, the picturesque garden remains a useful "thought figure" to apply in making sense of some aspects of contemporary heritage sites, since it dramatised the classical past and inserted it into an English present as the assertion of a social and political stance. Pope and other neo-classicists took seriously the idea that classical times could provide a working moral model for the England of their day. In a similar manner, heritage sites which dramatise their own past, presenting it as a sequence of interpreted scenes or tableaux, are driven by an underlying sense of the value of the site's past and its instructional or paradigmatic role in the present. The Gardens of Easton Lodge, typical in this respect, are consciously recreated from the relics and documents of the past in a process of reconstruction valuing authenticity, respect for tradition, and the marshalling of craft skills. Implicit in such a project is an evaluative framework which justifies the resurrection of specific elements of the past in the present, and in so doing comments on the present (Maleuvre, 1999, p. 12). The effect is akin to the "satiric" elements of picturesque gardens; those which – rather than directly narrating classical events – existed to point out and comment upon the inevitable disjunction between the classical past and the English present, to the detriment of the latter (see Dixon Hunt, 1992, pp. 112–114; Pugh, 1988, pp. 28–42).

The contribution from the viewer required for a heritage landscape to yield a narrative is, broadly, a condition of all texts. An interpreter of a text must bring an understanding of the appropriate codes to it, along with the background knowledge necessary to flesh out its meaning. However, this general contribution made by the viewer to a landscape masks a more subtle kind of contribution which must be made to certain landscapes; the kind required by a landscape which displays the lack of unity typified by the "historically damaged" Easton Lodge estate. This further contribution can be clarified by adapting a distinction applied by Barthes (1974) to literary texts; the distinction between the "readerly" and the "writerly" text. A readerly text is one which assumes its own self-containment in form and meaning, existing to be assimilated by the reader on its own terms. In landscape terms, a picturesque garden might be deemed a readerly text. Despite the contribution made by the viewer, it is conceived as a unity and largely determines – by means of its form and embedded signifiers – the codes, knowledge, and social dispositions which must be brought to it if it is to yield any articulated meaning. The same is true of heritage sites constructed from such unified landscapes: typically the intact country and house and grounds, with the addition of "designed" interpretative materials, such as those corporatised forms of presentation associated with

English Heritage or the National Trust. Such a site might reasonably be seen as a realist Victorian novel projected into landscape, with a clearly delineated story space, cast of characters, and historical plot – and, as such, providing a plotted, univocal experience for the visitor. Set against the "readerly text" is the "writerly text", a text which is manifestly incomplete and uncertain in its form and sense; a set of borrowed fragments which demands completion from the reader, who takes on the role of writer even in the act of reading. This characterisation seems appropriate for those landscapes – such as the Easton Lodge estate – which have been cross-hatched by historical upheavals, varied uses and ownership, and divergent interests. A heritage site established over such cross-hatching will inevitably take on the qualities of the experimental modernist novel rather than its realist forerunner; a landscape which more closely corresponds to the seemingly random fragments of a Joyce or a Beckett, than to the solid realities of a Trollope.

Methodology: Focalisation and Landscape

The privileged image in narratology is that of storytelling, exemplified by narrative transmission in the form of the printed novel, or of the oral storyteller with a co-present audience. Narratological models are populated by personified roles: historical and implied authors and readers, various levels of narrator and narrate, characters within the story, etc. (Rimmon-Kenan, 2002, pp. 87–106.) The barrier which this framework seems to place before the assimilation, as a narrative mode, of the encounter of a viewer with a landscape is more apparent than real, since many of these personified roles – at least in the narratological traditions stemming from structuralism (for a taxonomy of narrative theories, see McQuillan, 2000, pp. 309–347) – function as formal, analytical placeholders. Thus, there is no difficulty in following Dixon Hunt's informal account (see above) of the theatrical functioning of the picturesque garden, which assigns to the landscape the role of narrative materials and scenario, and to the viewer the dual role of actor and spectator. More generally, narratological models become applicable to an encounter with landscape when the viewer is interpreted as taking on a range of narrating functions as well as that of audience. This enactment of multiple narrative roles is a central feature in narrative or dialogical models of the self-developed in both social psychology (Fireman, McVay, & Flanagan, 2003; Leiman, 2002) and literary studies (Worthington, 1996), in which an apparently unified self is conceived as an "internal community" of semiotic positions which complement and comment on one another. Included in the multiple roles that may be played out by the viewer is that of enacting multiple centres of focalisation: having the competence to perceive and "enact the drama" of the landscape from a number of viewpoints, each defined as a specific aesthetic, social, and ideological location.

The cluster of ideas which are denoted by "perspective", "point of view", and "focalisation" are clearly ocular in origin; at root, they depend upon the metaphorical assimilation of all forms of perception and cognition to vision. However, if this assimilation is taken too literally as the physical vision of a character in a story, then it fails to capture all that is intuitively required of a "perspective", and naïve ocular models fall prey to a well-rehearsed range of objections: not all focalisation need be through identified and located characters, it can be achieved by a shift in discursive stance on the part of a narrator; a character may undergo transformative experiences and begin to perceive matters in a different way; the object of focalised description need not be a perceivable thing or event, it may be a set of abstract ideas or a socio-historical change beyond any direct perception; etc. (see the discussion in Jahn, 1996, pp. 243–251). In structuralist narratology these difficulties are sidestepped. Focalisation is detached from optical metaphors and interpreted discursively – a centre of focalisation is provided by a discursive framework, a conceptual orientation, and way of speaking. The marker of a distinct centre of focalisation is some set of principles which govern the selection of events from the fabula for reporting, language, and stylistic devices in which the report is framed, and the intertexts that provide a context for the interpretation of the report (Rimmon-Kenan, 2002, pp. 84–86).

This transposed sense of focalisation is directly serviceable for exploring multiple perspectives on heritage landscapes. In narratological models formulated by Greimas and Fontanille (cited in Grishakova, 2000, pp. 545–552) a centre of focalisation is a "conceptual focus" or "centre of orientation" which does not necessarily correspond to a person: a pure "observer" defined in conceptual terms. This conceptual focus is formed in the space of interaction between the observer and the observed; a space which is neither physical nor subjective, but rather semiotic in nature. Observer and observed exist in a relationship of mutual determination, with an exchange of semiotic materials between them, the flow of which is determined by the specific course of their interaction. Any real, historical viewer comes to a landscape equipped with a range of interpretative competences: a knowledge of a range of social roles and positions, and their associated languages (for the concept of a social language, see Bakhtin, 1981, pp. 275–300); a web of internalised texts (in the widest, semiotic sense of the term) ready to connect with aspects of the landscape; a set of desires and motivations which fuel the encounter with the landscape; and the social meaning of the activities in which that encounter is embedded. Meeting the viewer is a landscape with its features prepared by time and diverse hands, signposted (metaphorically, and perhaps literally) with markers and texts, and set in its own unique geographical, social, and economic context. The interaction between the viewer and the landscape has a specific course, serving as a syntactic structure which draws together semiotic resources from both. Those aspects of the meaning of this encounter which are dynamic in nature – those which involve the unfolding of historical or social processes – are envisaged as arising in narrative fragments framed by the viewer with the semiotic resources the encounter has assembled. Thus, the multiple centres of focalisation framing the fragmentary narratives experienced as the meaning of a heritage landscape, are formed in a flow of texts from viewer and landscape, set in motion and regulated by the course of interaction between them (e.g. see Dixon Hunt, 2003; Freytag, 2003). This flow of texts gives rise to the "compositional principles" which form each centre of focalisation: a structure of social languages, stylistic devices, compositional paradigms, and intertexts.

Analysis: Easton Lodge, Viewpoints, and Vignettes

The theoretical framework developed above only takes on substantial analytic force when it is shaped and made specific in concrete case studies. Thus, this section develops a pair of vignettes in which this loose model is given concrete form, providing specific – if limited – examples of semiotic flows and the formation of focal centres. In the first, a path is traced through some of the written texts which surround Easton Lodge; in particular, some focalisation devices are projected into the contemporary landscape from a novel written early last century. In the second, there is less emphasis on written texts, and more on the way images and landscape forms can direct a compositional framework; the vignette is structured around the opposition between different forms of stasis and mobility.

Vignette 1: Seeing Through Mr Britling

The visitor's perambulation around the Easton Lodge estate is punctuated by encounters with printed texts; these work – in part – to undo some of the processes of historical erasure of the past 70 years, and to create a sense of the life which once animated the repurposed fragments to be found on the site today. The guidebook to the gardens (Magnus & Spencer-Jones, n.d.), which the visitor is urged to purchase on arrival, and the detailed parish history – obtainable as the visitor wanders through both church and tea-shop – make much of the literary and dramatic associations of the estate. These are centred on H. G. Wells' lengthy occupation of the "Glebe House" – one manifestation of the aristocratic socialism practised, as patronage and community projects, by Frances Maynard, Countess of Warwick. With the Countess' conversion to socialism in the early 20th century the estate played host to a stream of writers, artists, politicians, and trade union activists. This social milieu became textualised in Wells' work, particularly in the novel *Mr Britling Sees It Through* – although in a form which, if followed far enough by a contemporary visitor, yields a surprising inversion of Edwardian certainties.

Mr Britling Sees It Through is set in a thinly fictionalised version of the Easton Lodge estate. The narrative begins in the late summer of 1914 and traces the events of World War I from the distance of the Essex countryside: "... this story is essentially the history of the opening and realisation of the Great War as it happened to one small group of people in Essex, and more particularly as it happened to one human brain". In Wells' fiction, Easton Lodge becomes "Claverings", the "Glebe" becomes "The Dower House", and Frances Maynard becomes "Lady Homartyn"; but the setting and cultural milieu is left substantially in place: the guests walk in Peto's Italian garden, not yet fallen into ruin, and the flower show is held in the Deer Park, yet to disappear under concrete runways in the urgency of another war. The novel opens with the arrival of an American visitor, an occasion for Britling – the principal centre of focalisation – to expand upon the character and countryside of Essex: old England preserved in rural aspic, untainted by the creeping suburbanisation infecting the Home Countries. He draws together landscape and life in a lyrical sweep: "There are oaks and hornbeams in the park about Claverings that have echoed to the howling of wolves and the clank of men in armour. ... Here in Essex we're as lax as the 18th century. ... Our roses and oaks are wonderful; that alone shows that this is the real England. ... If I wanted to play golf – which I don't, being a decent Essex man – I should have to motor ten miles into Hertfordshire" (Wells, 1933, p. 24).

The terms of Britling's account re-emerge in the Little Easton parish history (Spurrier, 1986). Despite the intervening 70 years – with its suburbanisation of market towns, gentrification of the countryside, radical changes in agriculture, and the advent of mass transport – the heart of Essex is still, in its pages, occupied by "contented people to whom London is anathema" and who, unhurried and dialect-speaking, "cannot bear to believe that Stansted's greater airport will yet be a reality" (Spurrier, 1986, pp. 1–2) – a reference to the last wave of airport expansion, not the current controversy. In pages printed decades earlier, the fictional Britling begins to question this place image. Even before the cataclysm of the Great War forces a painful self-redefinition, Britling has to abandon his image of rural Essex and his place within it. His American visitor – strangely prescient of the heritage critiques of the late 1980s, or perhaps simply aware of Quatremere de Quincy's writings of the early 19th century (Maleuvre, 1999, pp. 13–21) – bursts the bubble of old England by pointing out its already hollow artificiality. Despite the undeniable antiquity of the material trappings of the estate, its cottages and farmyards, and an outward appearance of historical stasis, the life of old England had been replaced by something thoroughly modern: "it looks and feels more like the traditional Old England than anyone could possibly have believed … in reality it is less like the traditional Old England than anyone could possibly have imagined" (Wells, 1933, pp. 26–27). This observation nags at Britling, and his perception that he occupies a living tradition is replaced by feelings of futility and guilt at living a life of self-indulgent fantasy. As he recognises the selectivity of the evidence on which he had based his construction of rural life, his Essex place image collapses: "His barn was a barn no longer, his farmyard held no cattle; he was just living laxly in the buildings that ancient needs had made, he was living on the accumulated prosperity of former times …" (Wells, 1933, p. 76). Britling's changed perception colours his interpretation of the life around him, and the imminence of war accelerates his growing sense of loss. The August Bank Holiday flower show and fete is held in the Deer Park at Claverings as Europe slides into general mobilisation: "The day was to live in Britling's memory with a harsh brightness like the brightness of that sunshine one sees at times at the edge of a thunderstorm" (Wells, 1933, p. 108). The pleasures of rural recreation are stripped of their innocence, and darkness seems to invade the festivities. Britling's doomed sons wins prizes at the sideshows to the background accompaniment of the rattle of rifle fire from the shooting gallery; and the starting gun which sets the balloon race in motion seems to echo a shot in Sarajevo. Britling has realised that a dream of England is no protection against the inexorable logic of modernity. Ironically, a form of warfare which Wells foresaw (in his prophecy of air-borne destruction *The War in the Air*) transformed Easton Lodge's contact with global conflict from the metaphorical to the real. The contemporary visitor to the Gardens of Easton Lodge – car-borne, hyper-mobile, and filling in a little leisure time between holidays in more distant climes – hearing the rumble of a distant aircraft counterpoint the light splashing of the fountain in Peto's Italian courtyard, is hard put to escape the reflection that civil modernity may be quite as destructive of tradition as its military counterpart.

Vignette 2: Stasis and Mobility

The country house garden, as Pugh (1988, pp. 4–5) characterises it, is a place of stasis. It purports to function outside the normal processes of change and exchange, and can do so persuasively because it exists outside the normal constraints of geographical place, creating – by enclosure and remodelling – a linguistic entity. The Gardens of Easton Lodge perform this rope trick by a rejection of the working countryside in which they are embedded (for a general account of this process of rejection, see Williamson, 1995, pp. 100–118). On approach they give the impression of an island of tall trees adrift in an arable sea, the dense barrier of the surrounding tree belt giving the garden the character of a *hortus conclusus* (van Zuylen, 1995, pp. 30–43) – a bounded zone in which the distinctions between the real and the symbolic have been flattened. The guidebook to the garden reproduces one of the RAF's last survey photographs from 1942, showing that the garden allowed itself one vista, onto the landscaped space of the deer park; but now, with nothing to gaze on but crops and concrete trackways, enclosure has been made complete. This act of withdrawal is now emphasised by a picket line of protest posters. This threshold may be read, at face value, as a schism between the tranquillity of rural England and the unthought aggression of economic imperatives; a reading which may crystallise around the striking visual design – all-consuming jet engines shredding a green and pleasant land – of the CPRE's pamphlet *Airports Destroy the Countryside* (CPRE, n.d.). Alternatively, and more obliquely, it may be read as the declaration of a secret complicity with the airport and its promise of cut-price escape to foreign lands. For, as Pugh (1988, p. 9) indicates, the garden is "the consummate image of holiday and travel to exotic places", promising "journeys of discovery", and pleasure without consequence, within a tightly defined symbolic space.

The symbolic space of a heritage site permits a certain erasure of the distinction between past and present, and Easton Lodge's guidebook, and small gallery museum permit the visitor to overlay, in imagination, the present form of the gardens with Peto's designs in their pristine state, frozen in sepia images. The visitor can metempsychotically (Seaton, 2002) take a place alongside the metropolitan blades of the "Marlborough House Set", arrested forever on the steps of the terrace in confident, late-Victorian poses; or stroll with earnest social reformers, plotting a new order in tree-shaded walks through the epitome of the old. The gallery offers the visitor the semiotic resources central to the site's principal "lost garden" trope, as the romantic contemplation of ruins is dependent on the capacity to conjure up the spirit of the past clinging to the ragged edges of physical relics (for the role of the ruin in romanticism see, e.g. Koerner, 1990, pp. 23–28). The relics of the Gardens of Easton Lodge occupy their rhetorical roles with varied success. The rotting ribs of Peto's tree-house – once a place of escape into an airy cage – function now as something akin to an Elizabethan memento mori; and the Shelley Pavilion, designed as a summer house, has decayed into a romantic ruin – a role which it plausibly might always have occupied. However, where once the visitor could stroll through the glade to a thatched Japanese tree-house, or lean on the balustrade of the sunken Italian garden, staring into the depths of the lily pond, the present state of the garden clouds any re-enactment. The tea house has been replaced by the gesture of a *tenboudai* – a viewing platform – jealously gazing over a lake withdrawn from the garden by the prosaic terms of a lease to an angling association; and the Italian garden is jarringly stuck in a half-restored state, losing any clear meaning as either ruin or complete artefact now that the airport's encroachment has made the site an uncertain investment. The compositional paradigm of the romantic ruin loses its shape when the dynamics of the contemporary world visibly have a hand in the process of decay.

Despite the promise of retreat and stasis held out by the Gardens of Easton Lodge, a probing of its form and interpretative materials reveals it as a characteristic product of a mobile culture. Peto, the son of a railway magnate, culled its forms from southern Europe and the Orient. He used his privileged mobility to travel to Japan in the late 19th century, and shaped his garden with a selection of the artefacts which flooded from Japan to the West at the height of *la Japonisme* – the vogue for all things Japanese. His favoured form, the Italianate, was rooted in English tastes formed by the aristocratic tradition of the grand tour and by the migration of Italian artworks to the centres of industrial and financial power. More practically, the materials of the garden and the labour which shaped it depended upon mobility: stone brought from Ham Hill in Somerset, the Shelley pavilion relocated from Sussex, and workers transported from an inebriates' home on the other side of the county. In general, the country house garden is the expression of a mobile, urban mentality, and its green mutations of urban forms – boulevards, alleys, squares – sit uneasily in a rural setting (Pugh, 1988, pp. 23). Easton Lodge, in its heyday, was a place of constant migration of guests and goods: from the principal Warwick estates in the midlands, from London. The degree of mobility this entailed is apparent in the travel arrangements which were made, with the Countess of Warwick paying for the construction of a halt on the branch line from Braintree to Bishop's Stortford, finding the existing nearby stations insufficiently convenient. Braintree station is now becalmed at the end of a single-track spur, and the line which led on to Easton Lodge now enjoys an afterlife as a long-distance footpath – for the energetic and ecologically sensitive it still provides a means of access for the estate. The contemporary warehousing on the site of Easton Lodge Halt is unlikely to inspire nostalgia for the age of steam, and the idyll of branch-line England. The station grew into a complex of sidings as the Countess of Warwick's guests gave way to the personnel and munitions of the USAAF's 386th Bomb Group; and the legacy of this operation lasted long enough to host one of the first waves of globalisation to lap against Easton Lodge, as bananas were brought from Avonmouth and Barry Docks to ripen on the outskirts of the estate. From this standpoint, the selection of the Gardens of Easton Lodge as a symbol of "holding the line" against the destructive demands of a hyper-mobile society seems a little perverse.

Conclusions

The vignettes above are hardly exhaustive of those which could be traced around the landscape of Easton Lodge, in particular, neither specifically horticultural or military themes have been explored. However, an attempt has been made to set up models of how contrasting viewpoints for the framing of narrative fragments may be constructed with materials from the semiotic space in which viewer and landscape meet. It is apparent in the second vignette that this process might be as well served by the use of something other than a written medium: that of the photo-essay, the film, or by interactive multimedia. The overall goal – the construction of a modernist mosaic of centres of focalisation – would remain unchanged. As for the substantive points of the planning controversy surrounding the expansion of Stansted Airport, these studies suggest that the discussion of policy against the background of realist cultural categories such as "tranquil countryside" (a combination of visual and aural qualities, CPRE, 2002; 2003b) is an oversimplification of the meaning of rural landscapes, and a denial of their multivocality (MacNaghten, 2003).

References

Allen, G. (2000). *Intertextuality*. London: Routledge.
Andrews, M. (1999). *Landscape and western art*. Oxford: Oxford University Press.

Bakhtin, M. (1981). *The dialogic imagination.* Austin, TX: University of Texas Press.

Bal, M. (1985). *Narratology: Introduction to the theory of narrative.* London: University of Toronto Press.

Bal, M. (2001). *Looking in: The art of viewing.* Amsterdam: Gordon and Breach.

Barthes, R. (1974). S/Z. London: Jonathan Cape.

Bishop, P. (1995). *An archetypal constable: National identity and the geography of Nostalgia.* London: Athlone.

Cosgrove, D. (1984). *Social formation and symbolic landscape.* Madison, WI: University of Wisconsin Press.

CPRE (2002). *Tranquillity.* London: CPRE.

CPRE (2003a). *The future development of air transport in the United Kingdom.* London: CPRE.

CPRE (2003b). *Plane crazy.* London: CPRE.

CPRE (n.d.). *Expanding airports destroy the countryside.* London: CPRE.

Daniels, S. (1993). *Fields of vision: Landscape imagery and national identity.* Cambridge: Polity.

Department for Transport (2003). The future of air transport (white paper). London: Department for Transport.

Dixon Hunt, J. (1992). Gardens and the picturesque: Studies in the history of landscape architecture. Boston, MA: MIT Press.

Dixon Hunt, J. (2003). The lordship of the feet: Toward a poetics of movement in the garden. In: M. Conan (Ed.), *Landscape design and the experience of motion.* Washington, DC: Dumbarton Oaks.

Dixon Hunt, J. (2004). *The afterlife of gardens.* London: Reaktion Books.

Fireman, G., McVay, T., & Flanagan, O. (2003). *Narrative and consciousness.* Oxford: Oxford University Press.

Freytag, A. (2003). When the railway conquered the garden: Velocity in Parisian and Viennese parks. In: M. Conan (Ed.), *Landscape design and the experience of motion.* Washington, DC: Dumbarton Oaks.

Genette, G. (1980). *Narrative discourse: An essay in method.* Ithaca: Cornell University Press.

Grishakova, M. (2000). The acts of presence renegotiated: Towards the semiotics of the observer and point of view. *Sign Systems Studies, 30*(2), 529–553.

Hoskins, W. G. (1988). The making of the English landscape. London: Hodder and Stoughton.

Jahn, M. (1996). Windows of focalization: Deconstructing and reconstructing a narratological concept. *Style, 30*(2), 241–267.

Koerner, J. (1990). *Caspar David Friedrich and the subject of landscape.* London: Reaktion Books.

Leiman, M. (2002). Toward semiotic dialogism: The role of sign mediation in the dialogical self. *Theory and Psychology, 12*(2), 221–235.

MacNaghten, P. (2003). Contested countrysides and planning futures. *Planning Theory and Practice, 4*(1), 96–100.

Magnus, I., & Spencer-Jones, R. (n.d.). *The history of Easton Lodge.* Little Easton: The Gardens of Easton Lodge.

Maleuvre, D. (1999). *Museum memories: History, technology, art.* Stanford: Stanford University Press.

McQuillan, M. (2000). *The narrative reader.* London: Routledge.

Prince, G. (1982). *Narratology: The form and functioning of narrative.* Berlin: Mouton.

Pugh, S. (1988). *Garden, nature, language.* Manchester: University of Manchester Press.

Rimmon-Kenan, S. (2002). *Narrative fiction.* London: Routledge.

Samuel, R. (1998). *Island stories: Unravelling Britain.* London: Verso.

Seaton, A. (2002). Tourism as metempsychosis and metemsomatosis: The personae of eternal recurrence. In: G. Dann (Ed.), *The tourist as metaphor of the social world.* Oxford: CAB International.

Smith, G. (1996). *Essex airfields in the Second World War.* Newbury: Countryside Books.

Spurrier, F. (1986). *Beyond the forest.* Little Easton: Five Parishes.

Thacker, C. (1994). *The genius of gardening: The history of gardens in Britain and Ireland*. London: Weidenfeld and Nicolson.

Van Zuylen, G. (1995). *The garden: Visions of paradise*. London: Thames and Hudson.

Wells, H. G. (1933). *Mr. Britling sees it through*. London: Waterlow and Sons.

Whiston Spirn, A. (1998). *The language of landscape*. New Haven, CT: Yale University Press.

Williamson, T. (1995). *Polite landscapes: Gardens and society in eighteenth-century England*. Stroud: Sutton.

Worthington, K. (1996). *Self as narrative: Subjectivity and community in contemporary fiction*. Oxford: Oxford University Press.

SECTION III:

CIRCULATION, FLOWS AND SECURITY

Chapter 16

The War Is Over So Let the Games Begin

Adrian Devine, Robert Connor and Frances Devine

Introduction

For more than 30 years "Northern Ireland" has been a war zone with an ongoing cycle of protest and violence fuelled by sectarian division and hatred. Not surprisingly, given the negative media coverage, tourism in Northern Ireland has been adversely affected. According to Buckely and Klemm (1993) the presence of terrorism has been the key factor as to why Northern Ireland has not developed its full tourism potential. "The continuing political instability and frequent violence have influenced tourist numbers and occupancy levels. This has resulted in a small tourism base in terms of receipts and visitors; unsuitable tourist developments because of a poor economic and social image; and a lack of a suitable infra-structure". (Wilson, Smyth, Murray & Black, 1997, p. 26)

On Good Friday, 10 April 1998, after 30 years of a bloody civil war in which over 3600 people had been killed and over 30,000 injured, the negotiations that resulted in the Good Friday Agreement were finally concluded. "The 1998 Good Friday Agreement was designed to manage political tensions within a framework of devolved and all-island institutions" (Tonge, 2005, p.1). It provided a historic opportunity for Unionists and Nationalists to put aside the divisions and violence of the past and to move forward and build a stable future together. However the Agreement has always had its critics. The Unionist Party was deeply divided over the Agreement with many thinking that too much had been conceded to republicans. At the time of writing the Northern Ireland Assembly has been suspended until the stalemate is resolved between Unionist demands for an unqualified disbanding of the Irish Republican Army (IRA) and Nationalist demands for full implementation of policing reform, demilitarisation and a return to local institutions. Nevertheless, the Good Friday Agreement (1998) and the peace process have delivered changes which were almost unimaginable to Northern Ireland a decade earlier.

Tourism and politics
Copyright © 2007 by Elsevier Ltd.
All rights of reproduction in any form reserved.
ISBN: 0-08-045075-X

The Peace Process and Tourism Performance

The Good Friday Agreement has generated a sense of relief and optimism within the tourism industry. Indeed the peace dividend is already evident for the Northern Ireland economy. Despite major obstacles such as the outbreak of foot and mouth, the impact of 11/9 on outbound travel from the USA and the strength of the sterling pound, visitor spending and numbers in Northern Ireland has increased every year since the Good Friday Agreement 1998.

There is, however, a major cause for concern if the purpose of why people visit is analysed. Despite the peace process the number of pure holiday visitors to Northern Ireland is still only 17% (NITB, 2004). Tourism contribution to the Northern Ireland GNP in 2004, 7 years after the Good Friday Agreement was signed, was still a mere 2.1% compared to 6% and 7% for its neighbours Scotland and the Republic of Ireland, respectively which have a very similar natural infrastructure (NITB, 2005). These figures would suggest a weakness in Northern Ireland's tourism product to attract the pure holiday visitor. O'Neill and Fitz (1996) would support the claim that the troubles have severely stifled the development of the tourism product. Baum (1995) referred to the period from 1969 when political tension escalated as the "lost years" in terms of tourism development. Leslie (1999), on the other hand, is more direct in his criticism and accused the NITB of not doing enough in terms of promoting the region.

Now it is time to look to the future rather than trying to attribute blame for this poor performance. Tourism in Northern Ireland is now at a crossroads, with the opportunity to map out a new vision for itself, but this is no easy task in what has become a very competitive market. Advances in transport and the emergence of new markets, particularly in the Asia Pacific region and Eastern Europe, means that today's tourists are spoilt for choice and, as a result, are more demanding, selective and discerning. Considering its temperate climate and location on the periphery of Western Europe Northern Ireland must differentiate its tourism product through diversification and the development of niche markets in order to compete in the international market and attract the overseas holidaymaker.

A number of alternative forms of tourism have been suggested including heritage tourism (Boyd, 2000) and cultural tourism which the NITB continues to support despite Belfast's unsuccessful bid for the "European City of Culture 2008". The conference market is another example of diversification which has the added advantage of not being affected by seasonality. There are other areas with potential such as genealogy and rural tourism but the remainder of this chapter will concentrate on one particular market in Northern Ireland – "sports tourism".

Sports Tourism

The concept of sports tourism is problematic due to it resulting from a fusion of two separate terms, both of which are complex in their own right (Weed & Bull, 2004). Jackson and Glyptis (1992) delineate two types of sports-related tourism: the first where the sport is consciously used by destinations seeking to develop their tourism profile and the second where tourism has emerged more or less as a result of sports activity. Standeven and De Knop (1999, p. 12) define sport tourism as: "All forms of active and passive involvement in sporting activity, participated in casually or in an organised way for non-commercial or business/commercial reasons, that necessitate travel away from home and work locality". The Canadian Sport Tourism Alliance describes it as "any activity in which people are attracted to a particular centre as a sport event participant, or an event spectator, or to attend sports attractions or business meetings" (Loverseed, 2001, p. 26).

Regardless of how sports tourism is defined, it is a rapidly growing market that represents a huge revenue generator at local, national and international level. Sports facilities and events are now being used by a considerable number of tour operators, accommodation providers and destinations to "add value" to their tourism offering (Standeven & De Knop, 1999). The opportunities to be gained from the development of sports tourism relate to the growing importance of sport within society (Weed & Bull, 2004). In 1999 a report based on a survey conducted by *SportTravel Magazine* estimated that Sports Travel in the USA is worth at least US$118.3 billion per year (Loverseed, 2001). In 2001 a total of 1.8 million overseas visitors to the UK either watched a sporting event or participated in amateur sport during their stay. This is approximately 8% of the total of 22.8 million overseas visitors to the UK in 2001. These visitors spent £1.4 billion during their stay, some 12% of total spending of all overseas visitors (British Tourist Authority, 2003). Although these figures do not relate specifically to Northern Ireland, it is still part of the UK and would therefore lend support to the argument that sports tourism is a niche market with huge potential.

Sports Tourism In Northern Ireland

In its simplest form "sports tourism" involves sport as part of a general holiday undertaken on a casual, informal basis and this has been part of holidaymaking for many years. However, there is growing evidence to show that sport is now seen as a more important part of the general holiday, if not the most important part, and as a result many resorts, destinations and countries are specifically promoting sporting opportunities. In 1998 the NITB identified walking, cycling, angling, equestrianism and golf as key products which would attract the more active visitor (NITB, 1999). Walking and cycling product marketing groups were established in 1999 and the NITB assisted in the development of two long distance coast-to-coast cycling routes and the launch of the Waymarked Ways Network. The angling and equestrian product marketing groups have also been active producing product literature and organising familiarisation trips for tour operators and journalists. The golf product continues to be generically marketed and promoted by the NITB at international specialist shows and at major golf tournaments with the Golfers Passport Scheme now covering 45 golf courses offering discounted fees. In 2001 the International Association of Golf Tour Operators awarded Northern Ireland the title of " Established Golf Destination of the Year".

The fact that five key activities have been identified and developed would, suggest that the NITB does recognise the benefits that can be gained from the sport–tourism link. Yet in terms of promotion and product development, it would seem that the NITB has failed to acknowledge that the sports tourist may be either participative or non-participative (Glyptis, 1982). In 2001 1.2 million visitors to the UK watched a sporting event spending £832 million (British Tourist Authority, 2003), yet the only spectator sport that is mentioned on the NITB web site is ice hockey! It could be argued that the NITB is naive and unaware of the benefits of attracting spectators to watch sport, but this is not the case as the NITB has supported a wide range of national and international events such as the North West 200 Motor Bike Weekend and the Irish Masters Golf Tournament. As with many issues relating to Northern Ireland the reason for the NITB's reluctance to promote local spectator sports as part of the tourism product lies deep rooted in the country's troubled political past.

Sport and Politics In Northern Ireland

Sport in Northern Ireland is used as an expression of cultural identity and the type of sports people participate in and the teams they support usually reflect their community background and perceived political and cultural allegiances (McGingley, Kremer, Trew & Ogle, 1998). Catholics are more likely to participate in sports which celebrate the Irish tradition (Gaelic games) whereas Protestants are more likely to engage in sports which celebrate the British tradition (soccer, rugby, hockey and cricket). Sugden (1995) argues that the games curriculum in schools in Northern Ireland is highly dependent on whether the school is Catholic or Protestant. Gaelic Games predominate in Catholic schools while rugby, cricket and hockey are predominately played in Protestant schools. Sugden and Harvie (1995) found that the majority of sports governing bodies do not include and have no desire to include community relations themes in their constitution or coaching programmes.

Rugby functions in an all-Ireland context in Northern Ireland despite being a Protestant/Unionist dominated sport. Even though Ireland fields a rugby team consisting of players from both the North and the South, tension still remains in relation to which flag should be flown at matches, which anthem should be aired and where international matches should be played (Sugden, 1995). Cricket and hockey are also played in Northern Ireland but are not popular amongst the Catholic community for a number of reasons. Firstly, they are perceived to be culturally British sports, secondly, they are rarely played in Catholic schools and lastly, cricket and hockey clubs are mainly located in Protestant areas which are frequently inaccessible to Catholics (Sugden and Harvie, 1995).

The majority of the research which exists regarding the issue of sectarianism and sport in Northern Ireland concentrates on two of Northern Ireland's largest sporting bodies – the Irish Football Association (soccer) and the Gaelic Athletics Association (GAA). A survey commissioned by the Northern Ireland Sports Council (1999) revealed that 67% of people in Northern Ireland believe that sectarianism is rife in sport within the province. Almost two thirds of respondents (63%) either "agreed" or "strongly agreed" that religious tension was associated with sport in Northern Ireland, whilst 66% believed sport was troubled with spectator violence. When asked the question, "are there any sports which you would see as having reinforced divisions between the communities?" 42% stated Gaelic Games (Gaelic football 27% and hurling 15%) and 14% stated soccer.

According to Bairner (2000) soccer in Northern Ireland reflects the political divisions which were established by the partition of the country. Only 3 of the 14 clubs, which play in the Premier League in Northern Ireland have a large Catholic following. Catholic supporters often feel intimidated by the loyalist sectarian chants for loyalist paramilitaries at matches. The Irish Football Association has attempted to address the problem by appointing a Community Relations Officer but the sectarian abuse directed at the Catholic player Neil Lennon at a recent international match plus a death threat which forced him to actually retire from international football would suggest that sectarianism is still rife in the sport.

Gaelic games are also surrounded with controversy due to its nationalist ethos. The GAA was founded at a time when there was a revival in Irish political and cultural nationalism in the last quarter of the 19th century. The GAA was viewed as an important opportunity to nurture the sense of an Irish national identity and an important vehicle to halt the popularity of British sports in Ireland. The GAA is perceived by the Unionist community as a sectarian organisation because of its ban on the security force personnel from membership (Rule 21) and also because of its past association with political issues such as the IRA hunger striker (1981). Unionists feel alienated from the GAA because of its nationalist aspirations and because of factors such as the flying of the Irish Tricolour at matches, the naming of GAA grounds and clubs after republican heroes (e.g. Casement Park Belfast) and also because of arms caches on GAA property (Sudgen, 1995).

Despite the Northern Ireland Sports Council's campaign "Sport without Prejudice" (1997) sectarianism has had an impact on various sports in Northern Ireland. As a result of this link between sport and politics public bodies such as the Northern Ireland Sports Council and the NITB have found themselves in a very precarious situation, having to be very careful not to be seen as biased towards one particular sport. This explains why the only spectator sport promoted on the NITB web site is the North American sport of ice hockey. The Belfast Giants was formed in 2000 to play in the UK's ice hockey Superleague. Unlike the traditional spectator sports in Northern Ireland, the team and sport has been marketed as something totally non-secular, and appealed to people who were sick and tired of politics and religious bigotry. In their first season of operations (2001–2002) the Giants drew an average crowd of 6448 fans which was easily the best in the league and the eleventh best in Europe (IIHF, 2003). These fans are devotees of what Bairner (2003) described as "consumer sport"– it is without roots in local traditions, an argument that could be easily supported given that there is only one ice rink in Northern Ireland.

The Peace Process and Local Sport

Since the signing of the Good Friday Agreement in 1998 attitudes within Northern Ireland are changing. The Nationalist and Unionist communities are beginning to accept each other's culture, of which sport is an integral part. "There appears to be a diminution of sectarianism in the sporting arena" (Tonge, 2005, p. 209). This thawing of tensions was evident among Irish league soccer supporters to such an extent that, in 1998, the Catholic-supported Cliftonville team in North Belfast was allowed to stage home matches against Protestant-supported Linfield for the first time since the 1970s. In 1999 Nationalist Sinn Fein leaders joined Unionist politicians and the chief constable of the RUC at Lansdowne road to support Ulster in the Rugby Union European Cup final. At the end of 2001, the GAA removed its controversial ban on British security forces to play Gaelic games (Rule 21). This was followed in August 2004 by another landmark decision by the GAA to share the proposed new national stadium with rugby and soccer.

It could be argued that with a more peaceful climate the NITB and the newly created Tourism Ireland Limited (responsible for overseas marketing) are now in a stronger position to promote local sports without being accused of political bias. With this in mind it is important to note that although the non-active element of sports tourism may be a lucrative market it is also very competitive. In order to encourage the overseas visitor to come and watch a sporting event it must offer the tourist at least one of the following:

- Excitement
- Sporting excellence
- A unique experience

Hockey and cricket remain minority sports in Northern Ireland. Crowds are small and the standard at both club and international level is rather poor compared to some countries. Since turning professional the standard of local rugby has improved and this was reflected in Ulster's performance in the European Cup and Ireland's third place ranking for the 2003 World Cup. Unfortunately, this success has not increased interest at club level and matches in Northern Ireland do not attract large crowds. Consequently, the atmosphere at matches is rather subdued compared to that in ruby stadiums in other parts of the British Isles. Sudgen (1995) states that rugby is a middle class sport played mainly in middle class grammar schools in Northern Ireland. This may help to explain the poor gate receipts. There is a semi-professional soccer league in Northern Ireland but the standard compared to the English and Scottish professional leagues is very poor and this is reflected in the atmosphere and attendance at local games. In 2004 the Northern Ireland soccer team had the misfortunate of setting a new world record in International football by not scoring a goal in 1298 minutes of play! This has certainly not helped the sport at grass roots level.

Despite the fact that it is still amateur the most professionally organised sport in Northern Ireland is Gaelic Games. There are a number of reasons why Gaelic Games would appeal to the overseas visitor as a sports tourism event. The first is the sheer size and scale of the sport in Northern Ireland. The GAA is dedicated to promoting the games of Gaelic football, hurling, handball, rounders and camogie. Gaelic football could be described as a cross between soccer and rugby and is played by 51,270 men and 8541 women, making it not only the most popular Gaelic sport but the most popular sport in Northern Ireland. There are 2063 teams in Northern Ireland and each county operate senior and underage leagues (Ulster Council GAA, 2004). At the elite level there is an inter-county league and championship. In 2004 the average attendance at the Ulster Gaelic Football championship game was 25,594 (www.gaa.ie/ulster, 2004). For the first time ever, the all-Ireland final was contested between two counties from Northern Ireland and was watched live by 80,000 spectators while TV viewing figures for the match reached 148,000 (BBC, 2003) – impressive figures considering Northern Ireland's population is a mere 1.7 million!

As a spectacle Gaelic Football embodies the type of fast paced, skilled high scoring events that any sports fan will respond to. Local fans are passionate about their sport and at both club and elite matches there is intense rivalry that creates an electric atmosphere. There is, however, a strong link between the Catholic Church and Gaelic games which ensures that there is a family atmosphere at matches and crowd control and hooliganism have never been an issue.

Gaelic football is something that is unique to the island of Ireland and therefore should add value to the tourism offering. Besides seeking escape and a break in their daily routines, tourists also use sport as a means of relaxation and as an opportunity to discover something new. Weed and Bull (2004) refer to "curiosity" spectators who are a feature at many league matches in sports such as American Football and baseball in the USA, Korfball in the Netherlands and Australian Rules football in Australia. Reeves (2000) and Train (1994) found that a significant group of tourists, mostly families with children, attend a sporting event while on holiday because it provided a unique and novel experience. Kick boxing in Thailand, martial arts in Japan and bull fighting in Spain are examples of sports associated with a particular country and there is no reason why Gaelic Football should not be promoted in a similar way in Northern Ireland.

Boyd (2000) states that the culture tourism product in Northern Ireland must include attractions that cover both the Nationalist and Unionist communities allowing visitors to experience a diversity of cultures reflective of very different histories. He makes reference to the tourism potential of the Orange Order marches which are so important in Unionist heritage. This author agrees with Boyd (2000) and recommends that Gaelic football and hurling, handball, rounders and camogie should also be promoted as they are a celebration of the nationalist traditions and heritage in Northern Ireland. The GAA was set up to nurture a sense of Irish identity and throughout Northern Ireland the local GAA club is at the heart of the community. It is not just a form of recreation but an expression of the people and their culture.

The commitment and the passion of the GAA members are not just confined to sport but they also promote the Irish language, music and dance. The Official Guide of the GAA (Rule 4) states that: "The Association shall actively support the Irish language, traditional Irish dancing, music, song and other aspects of Irish culture" (www.gaa.ie accessed 16 March 2004). Through an organisation called Scor, which means "large gathering" in Irish, the GAA runs talent competitions at various venues around the country. Although the Scor was intro- duced by the GAA in the late 1960s to encourage club members to enjoy other aspects of Irish culture competitions are not exclusive to GAA members and therefore has tourism potential.

The appeal and reputation of Gaelic games are spreading throughout the world. The GAA and the Australian Rules Association, for example, have organised an International Rules series combining the rules of the two sports which encourages fans from both coun- tries to travel with the national team. Technological advances and the wider scope of TV and radio communications plus the GAA's new web site allows Irish immigrants to watch inter-county matches and keep up to date with the latest club results. In many cases Gaelic games serve as a tangible tie with home for those who might otherwise drift away from their Irish heritage as they build lives in other countries and cultures. According to Getz (1997) much spectator tourism involves travel to watch a family member or friend com- pete. An old club playing in the county final or a brother or sister representing the county in an Ulster final may be enough to persuade an expatriate to holiday in Northern Ireland. There has been a tendency in the wider tourism literature to underplay the importance of the visiting, friends and relatives market (VFR), but the reality in Northern Ireland is that it represents the largest proportion of total visitors.

Weed and Bull (2004) have suggested that some people who visit a sporting event while on holiday may fall into the category of "associated experience sports tourist". Their pri- mary motivation for participation/spectating relates to some aspect of the experience other than the activity itself. In the case of Gaelic games overseas visitors to Northern Ireland may be attracted by the social aspect of the game. The "warm welcome" and the "craic" which the Irish are so famous for is never more prevalent than in the local GAA club after the match and, unlike some sports in Northern Ireland such as Golf and Rugby, access is not restricted to members.

Methodology – Testing the Demand for Gaelic Games

In order to determine the appeal and reputation of the GAA among tourists to Northern Ireland a survey was conducted during the peak tourism months of June, July and August 2004. The study involved direct contact with overseas visitors at four different types of venue: (1) The Giant's Causeway in County Antrim, Cookstown; (2) Tourist Information Centre, County Tyrone; (3) Mount Errigal Hotel, Letterkenny, County Donegal (4) and Hillrest Youth Hostel, Bushmills, County Derry.

Tourists were invited to participate on a voluntary basis in the self-completion of a questionnaire. The response was excellent. Four hundred and fourteen questionnaires were completed.

General Characteristics of the Respondents

Of the 414 respondents 50.7% were male and 49.3% female. Almost 45% of the respondents were aged 20–29 years, 25.3% fell within the age group of 30–49 years, 15.1% were 50 years plus and the remainder were between 16–19. The majority of the respondents were European 55.8%. Other nationalities included: British at 15.2%; the Americas and Australia 29%. The main purpose of visit to Ireland was for a holiday (Table 16.4).

Awareness of the GAA

Only a disappointing 12.3% of the respondents stated that they were familiar with the GAA and the activities it organised (Table 16.1). British and American visitors were more aware of Gaelic games than Australians, which was surprising considering the media attention surrounding the International Rules series between Ireland and Australia (Table 16.2).

Table 16.3 highlights the tourism potential of Gaelic games with 68.8% of respondents either interested in playing or watching a sport that is unique to the Island of Ireland. Fifty one percent of the sample would prefer to watch while 11% would want to participate (Table 16.4).

Similar to what Gibson, Wiiming and Holdnak (2002) found in his analysis of college football in the USA, an increasing number of females were including sport in their holiday

Table 16.1: Awareness of GAA.

Aware of GAA	Number (*n* = 414)	Valid (%)
Yes	51	12.3
No	363	87.7

itinerary either to watch (52%) or participate (20%) (see Table 16.5). It is also interesting to note that, although they represent a relatively small proportion of this study, 100% of the business tourists surveyed stated that they would like to watch a Gaelic football or hurling match during their stay (Table 16.6).

Table 16.2: Nationality and awareness of GAA.

| | | | What is your nationality? | | | | |
			British	**European**	**American**	**Canadian/ Australian**	**Total**
Are you aware of the GAA	Yes	% within are you aware of the GAA	29.4	47.1	17.6	5.9	100
		% within nationality	23.8	10.4	27.3	3.4	12.3
	No	% within are you aware of the GAA	13.2	57.0	6.6	23.1	100
		% within nationality	76.2	89.6	72.7	96.6	87.7
Total		% within are you aware of the GAA	15.2	55.8	8.0	21.0	100
		% within nationality	100	100	100	100	100

Table 16.3: Respondents interested in playing or watching a sport unique to the Island of Ireland.

Interested in playing or watching a sport	Number ($n = 414$)	Valid (%)
Yes	285	68.8
No	129	31.2

Table 16.4: Respondents who are interested in a sport.

Level of involvement	Number ($n = 285$)	Valid (%)
To watch	144	51
To participate	30	11
Both	111	38.9

Table 16.5: Sex of respondents and interest in sport.

			If Yes!			
			To watch	To participate	Both	Total
Sex of respondent	Male	% within sex	47.9	16.7	35.4	100
		% within if yes	47.9	80.0	45.9	50.5
	Female	% within sex	53.2	4.3	42.6	100
		% within if yes	52.1	20.0	54.1	49.5
Total		% within sex	50.5	10.5	38.9	100
		% within if yes	100	100	100	100

Table 16.6: Purpose of visit and interest in sport.

			What is the purpose of your visit?				
			VFR	Business	Pure Holiday	Other	Total
Would you be interested in watching,	Yes	% within would you be interested	13.7	5.3	80.0	1.1	100
		% within purpose of visit	61.9	100	68.5	100	68.8
participating	No	% within would you be interested	18.6		81.4		100
		% within purpose of visit	38.1		31.5		31.2
Total		% within would you be interested	15.2	3.6	80.4	0.7	100
		% within purpose of visit	100	100	100	100	100

Questions 11 and 12 of the questionnaire referred to the social-cultural dimension of the GAA – the Scor. An impressive 89.8% of the respondents stated that they would be interested in attending a talent competition, which would include Irish dance, Irish music, story telling and Irish language. It was no surprise, however, to find that females would be more interested in attending the Scor than males (Tables 16.7 and 16.8).

Discussion – Marketing Gaelic Games and the Scor as a Tourism Product

The main conclusion that can be drawn from this survey was that overseas tourists would certainly be interested in the activities offered by the GAA. Unfortunately awareness of

Table 16.7: Respondents interested in the Scor.

Level of interest	Number ($n = 414$)	Valid (%)
Extremely	114	27.5
Very	147	35.5
Moderately	111	26.8
Not	42	10.2

Table 16.8: Sex of respondent and their interest in the Scor.

			Sex of the respondent		
			Male	Female	Total
Would	Extremely	% within would be interested	42.1	57.9	100
you be		% within sex	22.9	32.4	27.5
interested	Very	% within would be interested	44.9	55.1	100
in Scor		% within sex	31.4	39.7	35.5
	Moderately	% within would be interested	59.5	40.5	100
		% within sex	31.4	22.1	26.8
	Not	% within would be interested	71.4	28.6	100
		% within sex	14.3	5.9	10.2
Total	% within would be interested		50.7	49.3	100
	% within sex		100	100	100

such activities is a problem. The remainder of this chapter will address this issue by discussing how Tourism Ireland and the NITB could incorporate the activities of the GAA into their marketing strategy. A marketing mix consisting of the four basic elements – product, price promotion and place – will be used to help Gaelic games and the Scor create a place image that will differentiate and sell Northern Ireland as a tourism destination.

1 Product

The product decision involves deciding what could be offered to a group of customers and how this could be packaged. In the USA, for example, 26.9% of members of the National Tour Operators Association provide spectator sports tours (Hudson, 2003). Some of these specialise in a specific sport such as baseball or American football and they arrange packages for tourists that would include the travel, match ticket, guided tours of the stadium, a visit to a hall of fame or sports museum and in some cases even a visit to the team changing rooms or a post match drink with the coach and players. At present there are no tour operators which focus specifically on the Gaelic games.

This link with tour operators should not only involve selling tickets for matches or visiting a GAA museum but should include a package that would provide the opportunity to learn how to play Gaelic sports. Tourists are now more active and are keen to learn new skills. Swarbrooke, Beard, Leckie and Pomfret (2003) for example, included training with Thai boxers in Thailand as one of the great adventure holidays for 2002. The GAA employs development officers in each county and their primary role is to develop Gaelic games in schools. There is no reason why these development officers could not work during the summer months with tour operators and hold introductory classes for visiting tourists. Not only would this offer the tourist a unique and enjoyable experience but it would also provide the important foundation stage in the sports development continuum as outlined by Weed and Bull (2004).

For the dedicated fan at home and abroad the GAA should also consider organising fantasy sports camps. These provide an opportunity for adults to train with their favourite sports stars, with the coach of a popular team and/or at a famous sport venue. In the USA almost every major league baseball team offers a fantasy camp and in England retired premiership soccer stars are tapping into this lucrative market.

In an attempt to improve the spatial spread of tourism the NITB has stated that Northern Ireland must offer the tourist a more broadly defined heritage-cultural tourism product (NITB, 2004). As various writers such as Bourdieu (1978) and Hargreaves (1982) have pointed out "sport is a culture form". As an integral part of community life in Northern Ireland the Gaelic games should therefore be promoted with culture tourism. The Scor should also be promoted as part of this cultural package as it has played a significant part in the revival of Irish culture and is ideal for the tourist who wants to experience and learn more about the traditions and pastimes of the Irish people.

Closely linked to culture tourism is the niche market of genealogy. In Northern Ireland tracing roots is very popular especially with the American, English, Welsh and Scottish markets, which are major generators of tourism in Northern Ireland. These tourists are intrigued by the history of their ancestors, the traditional way of life, thatched cottages, mass rocks and, of course, the pastimes of their ancestors. For decades Gaelic games have been the pivot around which community life evolves especially in rural areas and therefore they could be marketed alongside genealogy, and, in some cases, part of the genealogy package.

2 Promotion

Weed and Bull (2004) refer to the "incidental sports tourist" those for whom sport is not the prime purpose of the trip but rather an opportunistic decision, often made on the spur of the moment while at a destination. According to Jackson and Glyptis (1992) the capture of potential incidental participants is largely about ensuring that information is available at the right place and at the right time. The results of this survey highlight that with only 12.3% of the overseas visitors being aware of the GAA and the activities which it offers it still remains one of Northern Ireland's best-kept secrets. This is not a major issue for the VFR market as they are more likely to be familiar with the sport and attend a match with friends and relatives but for the pure holidaymaker the lack of publicity is a problem in any country. If a tourist to Northern Ireland visits a local pub they may see pictures of Gaelic teams, old match programmes, newspaper clippings and signed shirts on the wall but this is not enough to promote the games to overseas visitors.

There are tourist information centres located in every town in Northern Ireland and as these are often the first port of call for overseas visitors they should display a calendar listing Gaelic matches that are taking place in the local community plus contact details and directions to local pitches. Posters and leaflets should also be distributed to local accommodation providers and shops. GAA interpretative centres are another possibility, providing information about players, grounds, fixtures, results, the history of the GAA, the rules of the games and details and dates of Scor competitions.

Like many other sporting bodies, the GAA has recently set up a very professional web site which will bring a new dimension to participation and interest in Gaelic games on a world stage. It provides some very useful information for the tourist and therefore should be included under "useful links" on the Tourism Ireland and the NITB web site. Likewise, the GAA web site should have direct links to the Tourism Ireland and the NITB web sites. The GAA has also launched two videos "What is hurling?" and "What is Gaelic football?". The video initiative is designed principally for consumption abroad so as to give people who are unfamiliar with Gaelic games a basic understanding and insight into them. These videos should be promoted and available at the Tourism Ireland limited overseas offices. Tour operators should also have access to these videos and a Gaelic football or hurling match should be part of the familiarisation trips organised by the Tourism Ireland and the NITB for incoming tour operators to Northern Ireland.

Green (2001) highlights the advantages of co-operative marketing and recommends that each sport should see other sporting events as a prime marketing opportunity to promote their event. While it may be too early in the peace process to expect Gaelic Games to be advertised at a soccer or rugby match in Northern Ireland without political opposition the fact that the GAA, IRFU (Rugby) and the IFA (Soccer) have agreed to share the proposed National Stadium in Belfast is certainly a step in the right direction.

According to Chalip (2004) there is a strong link between a sporting event and its host destination. If promoted properly the link between the GAA and the image it portrays can be exploited to attract overseas visitors to Northern Ireland. All Gaelic games are amateur, drug-free and family orientated – admirable qualities in today's sporting arena. In terms of the physical attributes of the games Gaelic football and hurling in particular are fast paced, rugged, exciting – all qualities which encapsulate the image Tourism Ireland and the NITB is trying to project overseas. Guinness has already used Hurling to great effect in its international advertising campaign so there is no reason why Tourism Ireland and the NITB cannot do the same. It would be mutually beneficial as it would reinforce Northern Ireland's brand image overseas as a unique, authentic, rugged and undiscovered country while the GAA would receive international publicity.

3 Place

Place involves decisions concerning the location of games and important elements include the availability and standard of accommodation, transport, ancillary attractions and tourist activities.

According to Boulton, Libert and Samek (2000) the process through which the economic benefits of sporting events are maximised are called "leveraging". Event leveraging begins by encouraging visitor spending, and by retaining visitor spending within the host community.

This can be achieved by fostering spending during the event, as well as by lengthening visitor stays.

An increasing number of inter-county Gaelic Football Championship matches are played in Clones, a small rural border town in County Monaghan. Many of these matches attract in excess of 20,000 spectators yet the town has limited accommodation and leisure facilities to cater for overnight visitors. The GAA's recent decision to use the proposed National Stadium, which will be located in Belfast, should have positive repercussions for the tourism industry. If properly marketed, domestic visitors will be encouraged to stay overnight and overseas visitors will be encouraged to extend their stay in Northern Ireland's capital city.

It is noteworthy at this stage that the author is not suggesting that only Gaelic games played in cities have tourism potential. The GAA has roots in the rural community and clubs are the lifeblood of the GAA. Although they may not have the atmosphere of a large stadium on cup final day, club matches will provide the tourist with an equally distinct experience and insight into Irish life. Moreover, by promoting the activities of local GAA clubs the regional tourist boards will help bring about a more balanced spread of tourism which at present is a key objective of Tourism Ireland and the NITB (2004).

To achieve this regional spread it is important for services and facilities to be placed in locations that tourists can easily travel to. Obviously it is not possible for local GAA clubs, which are parish based, to move their sports grounds to a more accessible location. The clubs and the local tourism organisation must ensure that there is adequate signposting, as this is an issue that continues to frustrate all types of visitor travelling in rural Ireland (Tourism Ireland, 2005).

4 Price

Pricing is another important factor in the overall marketing strategy especially since Gaelic games are relatively unknown outside of Ireland. Standevan and De Knop (1999, p. 34) make reference to the "casual spectators who simply enjoy watching a sport and who usually happen to come across it rather than plan their visit to attend it". For this particular visitor the price and the simplicity of the booking process will have a major bearing on whether they will make the effort to come and spectate.

The GAA must therefore consider cost and offer discounted rates for tourists, especially families which according to Train (1994) and Reeves (2000) are more likely to attend a sporting event while on holiday. A sponsorship deal with an airline or a tour operator could be a feasible option with free publicity in return for reduced ticket prices for overseas customers. This could be a lucrative venture for companies catering for business tourists who have time to spare while in Northern Ireland and have shown a keen interest in Gaelic games.

Conclusion

Since the late 1960s Northern Ireland has suffered conflict and bloodshed. The "troubles" have had an impact on every facet of life. Policymaking in areas not normally associated with politics and sectarianism have all been directly affected and this includes sport, tourism and consequently sports tourism.

The signing of the Good Friday Agreement 1998 heralded a new era of peace and optimism for the tourism industry in Northern Ireland. However, the percentage of pure holidaymakers visiting Northern Ireland since 1998 has decreased. This is a lesson for other countries that are recovering from similar political problems – peace does not guarantee tourism growth. In an increasingly competitive market tourists must not only be convinced that a destination is safe but that it is also worth visiting.

In order to attract the overseas tourist in an increasingly competitive environment each destination must differentiate their tourism product and develop niche markets. Sports tourism is a lucrative market but only if properly developed and promoted. Gaelic games in Northern Ireland are an example of a tourism product with latent potential. They are exciting and unique but unfortunately this chapter has shown that although overseas tourist would be interested in the activities offered by the GAA awareness is a pressing issue.

One of the official conclusions of the Sport and Tourism 1st World Conference (2001) was the lack of formal collaboration between sport and tourism organisations. Although sport and tourism can both do well managed as separate entities, substantial co-ordination and cohesion between the two areas are needed if sports tourism is to prosper at any destination. Gaelic games have never featured prominently in a tourism marketing strategy document in Northern Ireland. The GAA has launched a new marketing strategy but it does not mention tourism. If Gaelic games are to become a sports tourism event in Ireland the GAA must forge closer links with Tourism Ireland and the NITB and together manipulate the 4 P's to their mutual advantage. Ultimately, however, like many other aspects of tourism in Northern Ireland their true potential depends on the peace process, the commitment of the politicians, and, of course, the reliability of the terrorists to respect and maintain their cease-fire!

References

Bairner, A. (2000). After the war? Soccer, masculinity and violence in Northern Ireland. In: A. Messner & D. Sabo (Eds), *Masculinities, gender relations and sport* (pp. 176–194). California: Sage.

Bairner, A. (2003). *Studies an Irish Quarterly Review*. Available at http://www.jesuit.ie/studies/articles (Accessed 2 November).

Baum, T. (1995). Ireland – the peace dividend. *Insight*, July, 9–14.

Boulton, R., Libert, B., & Samek, S. (2000). A business model for the new economy. *Journal of Business Strategy, 21*(4), 29–35.

Bourdieu, P. (1978). Sport and social class. *Social Science Information, 18*(6), 820–833.

Boyd, S. W. (2000). "Heritage" Tourism in Northern Ireland: Opportunity under peace. *Current Issues in Tourism, 3*(2), 150–174.

British Tourism Authority (2003). *Tourism Intelligence Quarterly, 23*(4), 65–70.

Buckely, P., & Klemm, M. (1993). The decline of tourism in Northern Ireland. *Tourism Management*, June, 185–194.

Chalip, L. (2004). Beyond impact: A general model for sport event leverage. In: B. Ritchie & D. Adair (Eds), *Sport tourism interrelationships, impacts and issues* (pp. 226–252). Great Britain: Channel View.

Getz, D. (1997). Trends and issues in sport event tourism. *Tourism Recreation Research, 22*(2), 61–62.

Gibson, H., Willming, C., & Holdnak, A. C. (2002) Small-scale event sport tourism: College sport as an attraction. In: S. Gammon & J. Krutzman (Eds), *Sport tourism: Principles and practice* (pp. 3–18). Eastbourne: Leisure Studies.

Glyptis, S. A. (1989). Leisure and Patterns of Time Use. Paper presented at the *Leisure Studies Association Annual Conference, Bournemouth, England*, 24–26 April 1987. Eastbourne: Leisure Studies Association.

Green, B. C. (2001). Leveraging subculture and identity to promote sport events. *Sport Management Review, 4*(1), 1–19.

Hargreaves, J. (1982). Sport, culture and ideology. In: J. Hargreaves (Ed.), *Sport, culture and ideology*. London: Routledge.

Hudson, S. (2003). *Sport and adventure tourism*. New York: Haworth.

IIHF News Letter (2003). Available at http://www.iihf.com/news/iihfpr5402.htm (29 September).

Jackson, S., Batty, R., & Scherer, J. (2001). Transnational sport marketing at the global/local nexus: The Adidasification of the New Zealand all blacks. *International Journal of Sports Marketing and Sponsorship, 3*(2), 185–201.

Leslie, D. (1999). Terrorism and tourism: The Northern Ireland situation – A look behind the veil of certainty. *Journal of Travel Research, 38*, 37–40.

Loverseed, H. (2001). Sports tourism in North America. *Travel and Tourism Analyst, 3*, 25–42.

McGinley, M. Kremer, J. Trew, K., & Olge, S. (1998). Socio-cultural identity and attitudes to sport in Northern Ireland. *The Irish Journal of Psychology, 19*(4), 464–471.

Northern Ireland Sports Council (1999). *Sectarianism in Sport*.

Northern Ireland Tourist Board (NITB) (1999). *Tourism Marketing Plan 1999–2000*.

Northern Ireland Tourist Board (NITB) (2004). *Tourism in Northern Ireland a Strategic Framework for Action 2004–2007*.

Northern Ireland Tourist Board (NITB) (2004). *Annual Report:* 2001–2002.

Northern Ireland Tourist Board (NITB) (2004). *Tourism Facts:* 2001.

Northern Ireland Tourist Board (NITB) (2005). *Tourism Facts:* 2001.

O'Neill, M., & Fitz, F. (1996). Northern Ireland tourism: What chance now? *Tourism Management, 17*(3), 161–163.

Reeves, M. R. (2000). Evidencing the sport–tourism interrelationship. Paper presented at *Sports Conference*, Loughborough University, 20 August.

Standeven, J., & De Knop, P. (1999). *Sport Tourism*. Champaign, IL: Human Kinetics.

Sugden, J. (1995). Sport, community relations and community conflict in Northern Ireland. In: Seamus Dunn (Ed.), *Facets of the conflict in Northern Ireland* (pp. 199–214). London: MacMillan Press Ltd.

Sugden, J., & Harvie, S. (1995). *Sport and community relations in Northern Ireland*. Report to the Centre for the Study of Conflict, Belfast, 6 January.

Swarbrooke, J., Beard, C., Leckie, S., & Pomfret, G. (2003). *Adventure Tourism the new frontier*. Oxford: Butterworth-Heinemann.

Tonge, J. (2005). *The new northern Irish politics*. Hampshire: Palgrave MacMillan.

Tourism Ireland (2005). *Challenge: Focus: Action – Marketing the Island of Ireland Overseas in 2005*.

Train, P. (1994). Tourism and economic impacts of staging a special event: the European Cup, Birmingham. Unpublished MSc thesis. Loughborough University.

Ulster Council GAA (2004). *Strategic Plan 2004–2006*.

Ulster Football Championship (2004). Available at www.gaa.ie/ulster (Accessed 15 December).

Weed, M., & Bull, C. (2004). *Sports tourism: participants, policy and providers*. Oxford: Butterworth-Heinemann.

Wilson, M., Smyth, S., Murray, A., & Black, M. (1997). The future of the Northern Ireland accommodation sector. *International Journal of Contemporary Hospitality Management, 9*(1), 25–30.

Chapter 17

Hostile Meeting Grounds: Encounters between the Wretched of the Earth and the Tourist through Tourism and Terrorism in the 21st Century

Freya Higgins-Desbiolles

Introduction

> *"Injustice anywhere is a threat to justice everywhere. We are caught in an inescapable network of mutuality, tied in a single garment of destiny. Whatever affects one directly, affects all indirectly" Martin Luther King, 1963.*

It is now a cliché to note that tourism has been severely impacted by the events of the 11th of September 2001 and its aftermath. It was on that day that American and United Airlines aircraft were used to attack the World Trade Centre's Twin Towers in New York and the Pentagon in Washington, DC. Subsequently, one of the most pervasive questions asked is what meaning to attribute to these cataclysmic moments. While some have claimed it represents Huntington's (1996) prophesised "clash of civilisations", others maintained it was the act of madmen. This chapter asks if the space occupied by the tourists and the terrorists on these four aircraft represent new "meeting grounds", coining MacCannell's (1992) term, which forewarn us the transformation of patterns of contact across the perilous divides and shaky bridges of globalisation and tourism. Using Fanon's characterisation of the "wretched of the earth" (1967), are the "empty meeting grounds" giving way to "hostile meeting grounds"? Are the marginalised and the poor realising the hollowness of the promises of development that emanate from both tourism and globalisation as they jostle with the privileged on the playgrounds of tourism and the battlegrounds of terrorism? These questions will be explored by examining a series of moments in recent history which are illustrative of these encounters and the dilemmas they illuminate. These include the maintenance of the right to travel but the abandonment of the right to development, the Bali bombing of 2002 which consolidated the war of terrorism as a war on tourism, the deaths during deportation of rejected asylum seekers and the oxymoron that is sustainable tourism in the current era predicated on endless growth. The conclusion drawn from this survey is that a battle is being waged to secure the "new world order" which pits supporters of the status quo against the myriad of opponents that it inspires due to its inequities and environmental damages. This results in an "us" versus "them" dichotomy which in effect separates the "tourists" from the "terrorists" according to whether you "buy into" the consumer role assigned to you in our marketised societies. However, tourism can be a force for change in the world if it is viewed as more than just an "industry" and its leadership rises to the challenges with which contemporary events present us.

Context

The Meaning of September 11th

In terms of the loss of human life, the attacks of the 11th of September 2001 were shocking but not unprecedented in an age where high-technology weaponry can render large-scale death and destruction (often at a distance).[1] Yet any discussion of proportionality such as this statement implies was and is almost unspeakable. What was so shocking about these events recorded in acute detail and televised globally and then etched into our consciousnesses? Was it perhaps the weapons used, the sites attacked and the nation targeted? Terrorism has long been familiar but we had never even dreamed that the tools of our business and leisure, civilian airplanes, could be wielded as weapons against us so devastatingly. The World Trade Centre and the Pentagon are potent images of American power, one representing economic might that underpins the global-trading system and the other representing military might which protects it. Lastly, there is the shocking fact that large scale and swift suffering was brought to American soil which had remained largely free of fear in its own home. In the shock of the aftermath, as people strived to understand, numerous

---

[1] In fact, an interesting comparison can be made to Saddam Hussein's gas attack on the Kurds of Halabja which resulted in some 4000 dead within 2 days in March, 1988. The US saw Saddam's Iraq as a bulwark against revolutionary Iran and it had been supporting him in the bloody 8-year war with Iran (1980–1988). The US and its allies failed to denounce or do anything about this terrorist attack at the time in pursuit of its own national interests. It was only after the US committed itself to ousting Saddam's regime some 15 years later that this incident has been used to denounce him as a terrorist and justify an invasion of Iraq in March, 2003. Admittedly, this example involves a domestic case of state-sponsored terrorism (if you do not accept the assertion of Kurdish nationhood). Alternatively, one can point to the US attack on Panama instigated to remove General Manuel Noriega for his role in drugs trafficking. An aerial bombardment of Panama City hit the shanty towns leading to the loss of 20,000 homes and perhaps thousands of people – we do not know because they were not important enough to quantify let alone name unlike the innocents of "9/11". Interestingly the innocent civilians killed in the invasion of Iraq have also not been important enough to count or name as the US military leadership said "we do not do body counts" (of Iraqis that is) and have left it to concerned civilians to try to account for the civilian toll (see http://www.iraqbodycount.net/ which placed civilian deaths above 10,000 in 2003). Walden Bello has made the same point but with reference to mass killings conducted in World War II (Hiroshima, Nagasaki, Dresden, Hamburg and Tokyo), the Korean War and the Vietnam War, making the point that the US cannot claim the "… high ground in the current moral equation" (Bello, n.d.).

authorities claimed that these were the acts of madmen or the acts of criminals. Only later did a more coherent pronouncement evolve from the American President:

> "… an act of war was declared on the United States of America … these people can't stand freedom; they hate our values; they hate what America stands for".[2]

New York City Mayor Rudolf Giuliani actually chastised those who called for a deeper examination of the roots of the violence.[3] At a presentation to the UN's General Assembly he said:

> Those who say we must understand the reasons for terrorism, come with me to the thousands of funerals we're having in New York City, thousands, and explain those insane maniacal reasons to the children who grow up without fathers and mothers and to the parents who have their children ripped from them for no reason at all. Instead, I ask each of you to allow me to say at those funerals that your nation stands with America in making a solemn promise and pledge that we will achieve unconditional victory over terrorism and terrorists (van Wagtendonk, 2001).[4]

This is perhaps a less crude way of saying what US President Bush stated as "you are either with us or against us in the fight against terror".[5] This sentiment has been inflated to the category of the "Bush Doctrine". The "Bush Doctrine" is very simple: "Every nation in every region now has a decision to make. Either you are with us, or you are with the terrorists" (Bush, 2001).[6] The message is unmistakeably clear; there is no neutrality in this era. The world that was being constructed in the wake of the collapse of communism built on "consensual" commitment to free markets and globalised economies is looking perilously in danger, effectively symbolised by the replacement of the buzzword of "globalisation"

---

[2] President Bush, 13/09/01 at: http://www.whitehouse.gov/news/releases/2001/09/20010913-4.html.

[3] A diverse range of voices were calling for reflection. Kofi Annan, UN Secretary General, called for dedicated work towards development. Noam Chomsky said "The people in the advanced countries now face a choice: we can express justified horror, or we can seek to understand what may have led to these crimes. If we refuse to do the latter, we will be contributing to the likelihood that much worse lies ahead" (Mitchell & Schoeffel, 2002, p. xiii). Jean Baudrillard claimed that ultimately it is about globalisation: "At a pinch, we can say that they [the terrorists] *did it*, but we *wished for* it, … . Terrorism is immoral. The World Trade Centre event, that symbolic challenge is immoral, and it is a response to a globalisation which is itself immoral" (2002, p. 5, 12).

[4] This is a strong exhortation to not think, just feel the emotions well up and give vent to the guttural chant "USA! USA!", the one that greeted President Bush's speech at "ground zero". And as is apropos of our consumer culture, rather than invite solemn reflection on these momentous events, both President Bush and Mayor Giuliani were inviting Americans, only a few days after the event, to go out and spend their way to this "unconditional victory" by patronising the Broadway shows, restaurants, bars and hotels who were feeling the economic pinch that the terrorist-inspired fear brought. This in fact reveals the hidden fragility of the global market system.

[5] CNN, 6/11/01 at http://www.cnn.com/2001/US/11/06/gen.attack.on.terror/.

[6] In addition, the "Bush Doctrine" is backed up with the threat of "preventative attack" from the US acting unilaterally (if it must). This is quite different from former "pre-emptive policy" which necessitated some proof of an eminent threat; this new policy merely requires a perceived threat to be identified by the US. See: http://www.cooperativeresearch.org/wot/foreignpolicy/generalforeignpolicy.html.

with the buzzword of "terrorism", as bombings and attacks occur along invisible fault lines, including Bali in 2002, Madrid in 2003 and Bali, London and Egypt in 2005. Tourism is not immune to these pressures and the luxury it has been afforded previously of sheltering behind the "neutrality" of "business" will no longer remain an option.

The hope of a multilateral system built upon the rule of international law is giving way to the dictates of a *pax Americana*.[7] The US made a positional declaration when it stated at the 1992 Earth Summit in Rio that "the American way of life is not negotiable" (Sustainable Development Commission, n.d.), and it has followed through by opposing key environmental protocols such as Kyoto, undermining the development of international law with its opposition to being subject to the International Criminal Court and its re-dedication to militarisation by opposing the anti-ballistic missile (ABM) treaty so that it can pursue its "Son of Star Wars" project, among others. "9/11" merely exacerbated trends already well underway as American was already seeking to shape a world if not in accordance with its own image, certainly in accordance to its interests. Yet, the Universal Declaration of Human Rights provides the logic for the universal respect of human rights when it states: "… it is essential, if man is not to be compelled to have recourse, as a last resort, to rebellion against tyranny and oppression, that human rights should be protected by the rule of law" (UN, 1948). Could current dynamics in the so-called "War on Terrorism" be considered as rebellion against the tyranny and oppression of the *pax Americana* also known as the "Washington Consensus"[8] and the "market fundamentalism" it has inspired, much as Baudrillard has suggested (2002)? Could it be that the failure of 50 years of rhetoric that promised that all of humanity would enjoy the security and prosperity of development has finally rung hollow? Could Fanon's classic liberation text *The Wretched of the Earth* illuminate current events? And is tourism's role central to these cataclysmic events? These are the questions that concern this chapter.

Positioning and Methodology

As MacCannell's *Empty Meeting Grounds* inspires this work, I heed his concern to deal with the demands of scholarly objectivity when addressing the political nature of tourism. He asserts:

> The one path that still leads in the direction of scholarly objectivity, detachment, and neutrality is exactly the one originally thought to lead away from

---

[7] If you feel your interests coincide with the Americans', *pax Americana* does not sound so threatening, nor does its previous epithet, global policeman. However the imperialism behind such a vision can be glimpsed by examining the writings on the "Project for a New American Century" (as if one was not enough; see: http://www.newamericancentury.org). Left wing critics have irreverently referred to the US as "globocop" (NI, 2003, p. 8).

[8] The term Washington Consensus was coined by John Williamson of the Institute for International Economics in 1990 for the increasingly common view held by financial players that economic and trade liberalisation were the keys to financial prosperity (Williamson, 2000). Thomas argues "by "Washington" Williamson meant not only the US government, but all those institutions and networks of opinion leaders centred in the world's defacto capital – the IMF, the World Bank, think-tanks, politically sophisticated investment bankers, and worldly finance ministers, all those who meet each other in Washington and collectively define the conventional wisdom of the moment …" (1999, p. 225). The nature of the consensus is that free markets and strict fiscal policies are the keys to future economic development.

these classic virtues: that is an openly autobiographical style in which the subjective position of the author, especially on political matters, is presented in a clear and straightforward fashion. At least this enables the reader to review his or her own position to make the adjustments necessary for dialogue (1992, pp. 9–10).

I will follow his example in facilitating a useful exchange on what is a political domain by revealing my positioning. I am a humanist with cosmopolitan leanings. I am an American who gained critical insight into my country of birth by both travel and Peace Corps service, experiences which sent me on the trajectory of expatriate and "global soul". I am politically interested and hold degrees in politics and international relations.[9] I am a reluctant and late-blooming activist who gained insights into the injustices, inequities and sufferings both from the books I read during my studies, experiences in my journeys and specific meetings in my life path. These include my involvement with the Ngarrindjeri Aboriginal community of South Australia, the Circle of Friends based at my university who formed to try to persuade the Australian government to release an asylum-seeking family from their desert detention centre and my long-term involvement with "global education". I am a new Australian citizen who is disappointed at my poor timing of migrating to this country just as the Howard government led it on a backward looking path away from multiculturalism and reconciliation. I am also a lecturer and a researcher in the tourism discipline who brings a concern with social justice to this field of endeavour. This brief autobiography will contextualise the broad-ranging nature of this polemic work and the inspiration of its uncomfortable questions. I have already begun to explore these issues in a magazine article written shortly after the 11th of September 2001 (Higgins-Desbiolles, 2001). The format of the polemic essay is selected to facilitate the raising of challenging questions that have remained largely unasked in the realm of academic discourse in tourism which is frequently conservative due to its observance of the constraints of scholarly "objectivity" required in the positivist tradition.[10] Thus it is an attempt at opening the dialogue that MacCannell invites in the quotation above, for surely dialogue across divides is what is called for in the "hostile meeting grounds" created in the aftermath of "9/11".

Discussion

The Wretched and the Rich

Frantz Fanon's *The wretched of the earth* has been described as "the greatest masterpiece of the anti-colonial struggle" (Sartre, 1967). It possesses poignant analysis of not only the

---

[9] My Masters thesis focused on management of terrorism in the European Union in the aftermath of the Schengen Agreement's implementation of free movement of people.

[10] It is with trepidation that I discuss such diverse topics and trends because I know that critical readers will be able to pick at the fabric of the argument and find weaknesses in the technique of its weaver. What I would ask is that the critical reader judge its tapestry as an impressionistic artwork best looked at from the perspective of the broad brush of the artist and not at the individual points on the weave.

political and economic effects of colonisation but more importantly the psychological effects. His analysis of the violence of colonialism and the counter-violence it inspires from the colonised is both rooted within the context that Fanon was working but applicable more generally. With awareness of Gates' warning against a "too uncritical appropriation" of Fanon (1992, p. 465), this chapter dares to ask if his classic work of revolutionary philosophy *The Wretched of the Earth* (1967) might illuminate contemporary events. The text is dated[11] – the peoples of the Third World[12] have almost universally thrown off the yoke of colonialism. Capitalism has won the epic battle against socialism and the market guides us all, First and Third World alike, down the path of "progress" and "development". What value has Fanon now? Post-September 11th does his characterisation of the "wretched of the earth" hold resonance? After all, bin Laden and his team of hijackers were by no means poor and without privilege. Important analysts such as terrorism expert Walter Laqueur have been at pains to point out that the connection between terrorism and poverty is spurious (2003, pp. 11–29). But the point is not that the terrorists do or do not come from the "wretched", because logically contemporary terrorists need to be educated and able to blend in on the global "meeting grounds" thus making more likely their middle class roots; and alternatively, the poor are bound in the grip of grim survival and so their struggle is more localised. What Laqueur is missing is that terrorism by its very nature is an appeal to the hearts and minds of others – whether to instil terror or inspire support.[13] Thus it matters whether justice that has been repeatedly promised is still continually and insultingly denied.

Fanon's "wretched of the earth" know their situation; "… on the level of immediate experience, the native, who has seen the modern world penetrate into the furthermost corners of the bush, is most acutely aware of all the things he does not possess" (1967, p. 58). Fanon claims that the colonised he spoke of knew that their oppression could only be overturned by a resort to violence; "we have seen that it is the intuition of the colonised masses that their liberation must, and can only, be achieved by force" (1967, p. 57). Does the new form of domination (whether called neo-imperialism, *pax Americana* or the Washington Consensus) require a similar resort to violence?

---

[11] *The Wretched of the Earth* by Frantz Fanon (1967) was written while he served as a psychiatrist at an Algerian hospital during its bloody war for freedom from France in the 1950s. Much of its content is specific to this conflict and to this historical era of liberation from colonialism. However, its philosophical basis holds wider relevance and interest.

[12] This chapter uses the unsatisfactory but well familiar terminology of "First" and "Third" Worlds to represent the divide between the "developed" and the "developing" nations in the global community. One must recognise that there exists a First World within the third and a Third World within the first; most of the nations of the "Second World", that is socialist, have now merged into the Third World category or form part of a "new Second World" according to Sklair (2002) as they are adapting to the market but have not yet attained First world status.

[13] My definition of terrorism is the use of violence or the threat of violence against one target in order to instil terror and to influence the opinions or actions of third party others for a political purpose. It is this act of influence on a third party and its political nature which distinguish it from ordinary crime. Frequently in the past, the goal of terrorism had been to influence governments, and so many terrorist acts were committed against politicians, state institutions or other symbols of the state (such as assassinations, kidnappings and bombings). However, with the growth in democracies during the 20th century, terrorists have increasingly used terror against civilians as leverage against the governments who are accountable to them. I would argue that the rampant pace of globalisation now means that terrorists can see their actions as occurring on a global stage. Could the hearts and minds of the "wretched of the earth" be the new battleground that the terrorists seek to seize?

Today, the people Fanon talks about, "the wretched of the earth", are not only acutely aware of what they do not possess, they are increasingly aware of their loss of ability to ensure their own survival as they are induced to grow cash crops for export, supply cut flowers to the rich nations and serve the rich tourists, all in an effort to appease the International Monetary Fund (IMF) and World Bank and alleviate crippling dept regimes irregardless of the effects such activities have on their subsistence capabilities, cultural survival, ecological integrity and children's future.[14] I will not elaborate on this when activists and analysts such as Vandana Shiva, Amartya Sen, Walden Bello, Anita Pleumarom, Arundhati Roy, Deborah McLaren and others have contributed much insight.

Sartre, in his preface to Fanon's text, states that Fanon lays bare concealed liberal hypocrisy that not only is the prologue to the liberation of the oppressed but also can enable the oppressed to regain their humanity by facing the unpalatable truth of oppression (1967, pp. 12–13). Is our world not cursed by a similar hypocrisy which enables us to comfortably continue our consumerist endeavours while intolerable suffering occurs not very far from us in our "global village"?[15] Such hypocrisy includes the idea that starving people in the Third World can climb their way out of poverty by catering to rich tourists from the First World (*á la* the "Sustainable Tourism – Eliminating Poverty" (ST – EP) Programme of the United Nation World Tourism Organization (UNWTO). Or that ecotourism can save environments, deliver development and spiritually uplift while using jumbo jet aircraft for transporting ecotourists (ego-terrorists?) to the last "pristine" and "untouched" wildernesses remaining on our heavily burdened planet. Lastly, we all can get on the market "merry-go-round" and fulfil our consumer duty to keep the economy growing by spending continuously and still have the natural environment to enjoy on our holidays despite our best efforts to suck economic profits out of every last ounce of it. This is patent nonsense. Quotes could be garnered from the likes of David Suzuki (a scientist), Herman Daly (an economist) or David Korten (a globalisation analyst), but perhaps the words of the United Nations Environment Program (UNEP) are authoritative enough to convince. The UNEP's *Global Environment Outlook 2000* claimed:

> The continued poverty of the majority of the planet's inhabitants and excessive consumption by the minority are the two major causes of environmental degradation. The present course is unsustainable and postponing action is no longer an option (UNEP, 1999).

If the link between environmental destruction, poverty and over-consumption was not confrontational enough, Dr Klaus Toepfer, Director of the UNEP stated "a 10-fold reduction in resource consumption in the industrialised countries is a necessary long-term target if

---

[14] This does not even take into account the lessons that peoples of the Third world can draw from Iraq where a crippling sanctions regime and an unjustified invasion have led to the deaths of thousands of civilians.

[15] Or even worse, we go to tour this poverty and suffering in our perverse voyeurism. Examples include "war tourism" (thanks to recent violence, destinations abound from Serbia, to Afghanistan to Iraq), "terrorism tourism" (it was reported in 2003 that Gush Etzion Tourism Association of Israel was organising tours focused on the US market to introduce the "world of terrorism" and a chance to train with the experts from the Israeli Defence Forces, see O'Loughlin, 2003) and lastly, the "poverty tourism" well described by Hutnyk (1996).

adequate resources are to be released for the needs of developing countries" (Kirby, 1999). But not only do former President Bush's words of 1992 ("The American way of life is not negotiable") forewarn us that Toepfer's words are unlikely to have any meaningful effect, but the consumers around the world who have bought the dream of the "American way of life" in both the First and Third Worlds present powerful obstacles to such change. Globalisation analyst Leslie Sklair has called this phenomenon the "culture-ideology of consumerism" and it is one of the main pillars that upholds the dominance of "capitalist globalisation" (2002).[16] We have all, almost, literally "bought" into the system.[17] Tourism is an integral component of this system as its uptake as a "cultural-ideological" practice has not been difficult to advance since it is touted as delivering peace, development, conservation as well as consumer happiness simultaneously.

Tourism as Ideology: The Right to Travel

While much of the discussion of tourism focuses upon its ability to provide fun and/or fulfilment (Butcher, 2003) or focuses upon its characteristics as an "industry"(Gee, Makens & Choy, 1997; Smith, 1988), some critical analyses focus on the ideological dimension of tourism (e.g. Goldstone, 2001; MacCannell, 1992; Mowforth & Munt, 2003). A tourism management text provides the following definition of tourism:

> Tourism can be defined as the theories and practices of travelling and visiting places for leisure-related purposes.
> Tourism comprises the ideas and opinions people hold which shape their decision about going on trips, about where to go (and where not to go) and what to do or not do, about how to relate to other tourists, locals and service personnel. And it is all the behavioural manifestations of those ideas and opinions (Leiper, 1995, p. 20).

This innocuous definition illuminates the ideology behind contemporary tourism and travel. The "theories", "ideas", "opinions" and "practices" that Leiper (1995) refers to could be taken at one level to relate to our social practices of dividing leisure from work, the beliefs about what are appropriate "re-creative" activities and personal desires and actions that collectively comprise the larger phenomenon of tourism. However at another level, Leiper's definition can

---

[16] In fact it is the aspiration to live the "American dream" on the part of ordinary people around the globe that has allowed the rise of American hegemony through the "Washington Consensus" (while the actual agenda has been pushed by the "transnational capitalist class" (to use Sklair's terminology). If Baudrillard is right and the meaning of "9/11" does represent a war over globalisation rather than a "war on terrorism" (2002), what we are seeing now is an abandonment of the tactic to obtain acquiescence to the market agenda through the promise of the "American dream" for a tactic to obtain acquiescence through the threat from the "American war machine".

[17] So being "anti-American" or "anti-globalisation" does nothing to alleviate the problem, because we are all implicated. Our task is not to imagine how we are going to convince the Americans to not invade Iraq or to cut back on its own consumption or ratify the Kyoto protocol, but rather we must convince ourselves to do without (the "live simply, so others can simply live" philosophy). The former is perhaps much easier for most non-Americans to engage with than the latter.

be read to refer to ideological attributes that adhere to contemporary tourism such as the practice of First world tourists wielding their financial power to holiday in Third World locations, the belief that tourism is subject to individual preferences and not properly the subject of "moralisation" (Butcher, 2003) and particularly, a conceptualisation of a "right" to tourism and travel.

Because holiday time has been legislated and compensated for in many First World countries since the early years of the 20th century, many of their citizens view travel as a right rather than as a privilege. This has led to the right to travel being incorporated in key international documents including the Universal Declaration of Human Rights of 1948, the International Covenant on Economic, Social and Cultural Rights of 1966, the UNWTO's Tourism Bill of Rights and Tourist Code of 1985 and the Global Code of Ethics for Tourism of 1999. The Universal Declaration of Human Rights has two passages that underpin the right to travel, Articles 13 (2) and 24. Article 13, Section 2 states "Everyone has the right to leave any country, including his own, and to return to his country" (UN, 1948), which O'Byrne describes as underpinning the human right to travel (2001, pp. 411–413). Combined with Article 24 which states "everyone has the right to rest and leisure, including reasonable limitation of working hours and periodic holidays with pay" (UN, 1948), this fundamental document of international law is credited with situating travel and tourism as part of human rights. The justification for asserting such new rights can be gleaned from the words of the UNWTO who declare tourism's potential value in "contributing to economic development, international understanding, peace, prosperity and universal respect for, and observance of, human rights and fundamental freedoms for all ..." (UNWTO, 1999). Making such important and varied contributions to the human good, tourism and travel are uniquely worthy among "industries" of elevation to a human rights status. However, it is obvious that this human right is not universally enjoyed and there is a clear divide between the First and Third Worlds in this respect, resulting in the former providing the vast bulk of international tourists and the latter increasingly serving as their hosts. We have largely forgotten in this era of the ascendancy of the market that important international tourism declarations acknowledged the need to bridge this divide between the First and Third Worlds' ability to fulfil the human right to travel and tourism. For example, the Manila Declaration of the UNWTO in 1980 declared in its opening statements:

> Convinced ... that world tourism can contribute to the establishment of a new international economic order (NIEO) that can *help to eliminate the widening economic gap between developed and developing countries* and ensure the steady acceleration of economic and social progress, in particular of the developing countries,
>
> Aware that world *tourism can only flourish if based on equity* ... and if its ultimate aim is the improvement of the quality of life and the creation of better living conditions *for all peoples* ... (emphasis added, UNWTO, 1980).

The more recent code promulgated is the Global Code of Ethics for Tourism (UNWTO, 1999), which follows in the line of its predecessors but adds value by enunciating the roles and responsibilities of all of the various stakeholders in tourism. This code was forged in the new era brought with the demise of communism and the triumph of the "Washington consensus"; and so not surprisingly, its preamble states:

> ... the world tourism industry as a whole has much to gain by operating in an environment that favours the market economy, private enterprise and free trade and that serves to optimise its beneficial effects on the creation of wealth and employment (UNWTO, 1999).

Also reflecting concerns contemporaneous with its development, it acknowledges the need to balance economic development with environmental protection and alleviation of poverty, and thus is informed by the sustainability discourse of the 1990s. However, the code's passage on the right to travel found in Article 7 proves interesting in that it not only reiterates the right to travel and tourism already stated in other key documents such as the Universal Declaration of Human Rights, but it also advocates government support of initiatives such as "social tourism" and other processes to promote access to tourism for potential disadvantaged groups in their societies such as the disabled, youth, seniors and families. While it was not surprising that preceding codes and declarations, such as the Manila Declaration of 1980, contained similar statements and concerns because they were forged at the height of the Cold War when the rhetoric of the First World's commitment to Third World development was used in the ideological struggle for the hearts and minds of the Third World, it is surprising that such rhetoric has survived into the era of the Washington Consensus. But because there is no mention of the NIEO[18] in this document (unlike the Manila Declaration), one can assume that each government's ability to fulfil its "social tourism" obligations to its citizenry and thus make real their citizens exercise of their "right to tour" is dependent upon them obtaining sufficient levels of development to make conditions possible to fulfil such obligations. The only statement this code makes about obligations to development in the countries of the Third World is a call that:

> Multinational enterprises of the tourism industry should not exploit the dominant positions they sometimes occupy ... they should involve themselves in local development, avoiding, by the excessive repatriation of their profits or their induced imports, a reduction of their contribution to the economies in which they are established (UNWTO, 1999, Article 9).

Thus this code effectively abandons the agenda of development through tourism to market forces.

---

[18] The NIEO was demanded by the decolonised countries of the developing world in the 1970s as a way to overcome the inequitable legacy of colonialism on their communities. It was set as the agenda of the UN in the 1970s and included such policies as technology transfer, fairer trade rules and aid policies which would secure development for developing countries. Unfortunately the ability of developing countries to leverage support for the NIEO from powerful developed countries receded with the collapse of socialism in the 1990s. Since this time development has moved from the justice agenda found in the NIEO to a marketised phenomenon based on developing countries ability to secure foreign investment and engage in the free trade system.

The debate about whether the free market delivers development is the key debate of our times and the statistics that are rolled out by the World Bank with its *World Development Indicators* and then refuted by opponents is not essential to this argument.[19] It is intuitive that a universal right to tourism and travel have no real meaning when the vast majority of the world's population must struggle to secure their own survival, including finding the means of subsistence, accessing safe drinking water, ensuring adequate health to subsist and trying to maintain culture and family on the land to which one belongs. This contrasts strongly with the experience of wealthy, First World tourists who can travel to places of poverty or danger in order to enhance their status as "intrepid" travellers or to "find themselves" again. Should these tourists get into trouble in the tour zone–war zone (or battleground–playground), the full apparatus of their rich state is called upon to diplomatically protect their interests, to medivac them out of harm's way *toute de suite* and to financially compensate them for any losses they might incur (subject to the provisions of their insurance policies).[20]

In his discussion of the "empty meeting grounds" of tourism, MacCannell (1992) sees a dichotomy between those travellers who use the tourism encounter to construct dialogue with others and those travellers who want to travel the world but with all the accoutrement and comforts of home. The latter he describes as:

> … an overturned nomadic consciousness in which the ultimate goal of travel is to set up sedentary housekeeping in the entire world, to displace the local peoples, or at least to subordinate them in the enterprise, to make them the "household" staff of global capitalists (1992, p. 66).

The former represent the hope of tourism's contribution to a better world and demonstrate that any assertion of a "right" such as the right to tourism also entails an accompanying "responsibility", that is a necessity to utilise the privilege to achieve a meaningfully beneficial outcome. The latter are perhaps responsible for the "empty meeting grounds" of tourism transforming into "hostile meeting grounds" as the "wretched" and the "rich" encounter each other on an ideological site where the pleasures of the "rich" are paid for by the sufferings of the "wretched". We have somehow forgotten in the market era that a truly universal notion of a right to travel and tourism could only be predicated on a foundation of a right to development for all.

---

[19] Though I would commend Sklair's treatment of these issues in his globalisation analysis where he presents his argument that development has given way to the aims of capitalist globalisation; a system which by its very nature causes "class polarisation" (vast disparities between groups) and a crisis of ecological unsustainability (2002, see pp. 48–53 where he specifically addresses the indicators of development/underdevelopment).

[20] These brief sentences remind me of a television show which brilliantly presents this contrast quite poignantly. *Worlds Apart* is an American series which recently aired in Australia. It shows four American families travelling to other parts of the world for an experience of "another world". I recently viewed one where a well-to-do New York family spends 9 days with a rural family in India. While the Indian hosts were by no means poor, the American visitors found the difficulties in obtaining water, the endless work to be done, the lack of "proper" sanitation and the general struggle for daily survival to be confronting initially. By the end of the visit, both families had bonded very strongly and their shared experiences had a profound impact on all. However, at the end of the 9 days, the Americans boarded their plane for their return to their luxurious lifestyle without a thought for the possibility of a reciprocal visit from their new Indian friends. The ideological assumption behind this show – that it is the "rich" who visit and are moved by the "wretched" – gives pause for cynicism on the rhetoric of tourism as a force for peace and tolerance.

Transits, Terrorists, Tourists and the Wretched: Airports as Icons of Our World

Airports and airlines have long been subject to the attention of terrorists for a number of reasons, including their symbolic value as a state asset, their high media value and the fact that their transportation capacity can be used to good effect. Examples include the attacks on airports in the 1970s and 1980s including Israel's Lod airport in 1972, Athens and Rome airports in 1973, Orly airport in France in 1983 and Madras airport in India in 1984. Terrorists have also attacked planes with bombs and rockets, including an Air India flight over the Atlantic in 1985, a Pan Am flight over Lockerbie, Scotland in 1983, a UTA flight over Niger in 1989 and an El Al flight at Mombasa airport, Kenya in 2002. At the height of the terrorism of the late 1960s and early 1970s, terrorists hijacked planes for escape to friendly countries or political leverage against enemy governments; examples include the spectacular event of September, 1970 when the Popular Front for the Liberation of Palestine (PFLP) held three planes and their passengers at Jordan's airport and the collaborative effort of the PFLP and the Baader-Meinhof gang of Germany who together hijacked an Air France plane which was diverted to Entebbe, Uganda and led to a famous raid by Israel's special forces in 1976. Lastly, the al Qaeda terrorists turned hijacked planes into potent and symbolic weapons to wield against the Twin Towers and the Pentagon, which were both actual and symbolic targets. That airports and airlines are contested spaces must be readily apparent from this brief outline despite their ordinary and mundane appearances to most users at most times.

But airports and airlines are also contested spaces in less spectacular fashion as the "wretched" and the "rich" transit past each other in their travels. We know how the "rich", both tourists and business people, frequently use the infrastructure of airports and airplanes in their globe-trotting through our "global village". What may be less familiar is how these same facilities are used to "deport" the less desirable globetrotters, the unwanted asylum seekers and economic migrants. As globalisation's favours and famines fall unevenly across the breadth of the globe, individuals and families are forced to leave their homelands in search of asylum or survival in other lands, sometimes resorting to airplanes and airports if they are fortunate,[21] oftentimes forced into leaky and dangerous boats, unsafe cargo crates and perilous trucks and other road vehicles. However, when they arrive at their destination anticipating haven and opportunity, they sometimes find themselves greeted with hostility, bureaucratic mazes and perhaps ultimately rejection and deportation back to their origin.[22] In fact, some rejected asylum seekers have died in forced repatriation back from whence they came, accidentally suffocated through the sedation drugs, pillows and duct tape that have been used to silence them, as they are detained on the back rows of airplanes, so that they do not "discomfort" the "rich" who are the proper clients of these services.[23]

---

[21] This is not the case for those that use the technique of stowing away in the undercarriage of planes. Africa has provided many such cases but one example is the 16-year old who froze to death as the plane went from Brazzaville, Congo to Paris in 2003.

[22] Because the rules of contemporary globalisation allow free movement of capital, goods, services, business-people and tourists but not the poor seeking job opportunities.

[23] For example, Mariame Guru-Hagos of Somalia was asphyxiated during deportation from Paris to Johannesburg in 2003. In 1999, Aamir Mohamed Ageeb of Sudan suffocated under a motorcycle helmet during deportation from Frankfurt airport, Khaled Abuzarifeh of Palestine suffocated under a gag during deportation from Zurich airport and Marcus Omofuna of Nigeria suffocated because of a taped mouth during deportation from Vienna (see: http://www.united.non-profit.nl/pdfs/listofdeaths.pdf).

The airport presents the stark differences between the "wretched" and the "rich" quite vividly as they use these "meeting grounds" of the airport. Asylum seekers dream of greeting their loved ones one day at this airport as they join them for asylum in their chosen country; in contrast the "rich" tourists or business people buzz about the airport with their trainers on or their laptops in tow, completely oblivious to the privilege that they are enjoying and complaining about the inconvenience of security measures or the tediousness of long journeys and their jet lag. The airport and the airplane are in fact "hostile meeting grounds" as the "rich" and the "wretched" jostle for access to use them for the fulfilment of their right to travel, even if they rarely actually "encounter" each other in the process. In Australia, where the government has abandoned many of its obligations under the Refugee Convention, and makes asylum a very arduous status to obtain, the refugee supporters who have taken up the moral conscience of a nation have organised antideportation awareness-raising rallies at major airports such as Melbourne's and petitioned airlines such as Qantas and Malaysian Airlines to not cooperate with the government's efforts at forced returns of rejected asylum seekers. These anti-deportation rallies are an attempt to make visible those "wretched" that the "rich" do not want to see, as it might make their enjoyment of their right to travel a little less comfortable.[24] These encounters across the "hostile meeting grounds" of the airport and airplane between "rich", "wretched" and now "activist" are a microcosm of the dynamics of our world and are as disturbing and illuminating as the events of "9/11" even if less spectacular. Recently it was reported that France, Germany, Italy, Spain and the UK are cooperating on an initiative to create a specially chartered air service for deportations of "illegal immigrants" nicknamed "Migrant Air" in order to keep such encounters out of our consciousness and off our consciences making the operations more economical as a "bonus" (Travis, 2005, p. 7).

Bali's Hostile Meeting Grounds

The Bali bombing of the 12th of October 2002 marked an attack on a major tourism site as Paddy's Bar and the Sari Club located at Kuta Beach were decimated by a suicide bomb attack conducted by supporters of Jemaah Islamiah (JI). The devastation was remarkable

---

[24] This effort is not always embraced by the targets of enlightenment. In 2004, the Australian series of Big Brother reality show was thrown into turmoil when a young housemate used his eviction to make a silent protest against the government's treatment of asylum seekers by holding a sign that read "free the refugees". He refused to chat with the shows hostess as is custom and received boos from the audience for his actions. The media buzzed in the following days with criticism of Merlin's "stunt" with public opinion declaring him a little odd but with no discussion of the issue. Merlin also had to apologise to children in the audience watching his eviction show for "upsetting" them with his protest. This one incident illuminates how the media works to support the "culture-ideology of consumption" by anaesthetising us to any interest in "real" issues by drip feeding us on a diet of consumer desires, inane gossip and fruitless play. The ironies abound in this incident as the last thing that "reality" TV wants to give its consumers is any look at any uncomfortable reality. Also interesting is that the reality show participants are voluntarily detained and the asylum seekers are involuntarily detained, both perhaps similarly traumatised in their seeking of improvements in their life situation.

and 190 people died,[25] among them 88 Australians. This event impacted on Australians particularly strongly who have long viewed Bali as its slice of the "pleasure periphery" as it has offered inexpensive holiday packages of the mass variety. Kuta has long conjured a particular image in mind as a place for young, particularly Australian, tourists to sun by day and party by night; Picard quotes the 1990 Lonely Planet guide book as stating "Kuta is a good place to get a suntan, definitely a good place to get pissed and supposedly a good place to get laid" (1996, p. 80). Because of the presence of comparatively wealthy tourists who seek a variety of hedonistic pleasures, including drugs and sex, Kuta has attracted migrants from around Indonesia who seek wealth from the opportunities that this offers, including the "Kuta cowboys" who provide "romance tourism" services to young women on holiday. It is this "playground" that the JI terrorists decided to make their "battleground" in their war against Western decadence. As the "War on Terror" heated up and southeast Asia became a focus, al Qaeda trained, JI terrorist Hambali decided to target bars, cafes or night-clubs "frequented by Westerners" for bombing (Neighbour, 2003). While it is not fashionable to listen to the terrorists, Imam Samudra gave 13 reasons for the Bali bombing[26] and ratio-nalised the selection of these particular sites at Kuta:

> The reason I chose Paddy's and the Sari Club in Jalan Legian, Kuta, Bali as targets for the jihad bombing is because I saw a lot of foreigners there engaged in immoral acts; and that place is the biggest centre of immoral activities in Bali, compared to other places (Samudra, 2002).

In the aftermath of these devastating bombs, Bali and Kuta have undergone some startling transformations. Bali has changed from Australia's "pleasure periphery" to an offshore part of Australia[27]; the major national newspaper *The Australian's* headline read "Special

---

[25] An interesting footnote can be made that a young Indonesian woman named Endang was severely injured in the blast, while her husband was detained in Baxter detention centre in South Australia (an Iranian man without legal status in Indonesia who came to Australia by boat-seeking asylum) and their two children stayed on Java with family. She was not medivac-ed to Australia for emergency treatment and he was not allowed transit to Bali to be with her, so she died without her family. South Australian magistrate Brian Deegan lost his son in the Bali bombing and during his involvement with those issues learned of the Sammaki's family's plight (father "detained" and children without him). He offered to sponsor the children's visit to South Australia if they could get temporary visas in order for the family to have a brief reunion after years apart without success. However, when the Sammaki children were photographed holding hands with the Australian Prime Minister in his brief visit to Bali a year later, circumstances quietly shifted. Before long, the family was reunited and living out in the Australian community with permanent protection visas. This is a singular incident with many quite amazing intersections and full of rich meanings for understanding dynamics within our global village (see Gearin, 2003).

[26] These included such reasons as opposing the "US army of the cross and its allies", revenge for the 2001 bombing of Afghanistan, Australia's role in East Timor, Muslim suffering in such diverse places as Kashmir, Bosnia and Ambon and Jewish and Christian occupation of two Islamic holy lands (for the full statement and complete list see Samudra, 2002).

[27] Interesting how the islands off Australia's shore have been recently embraced and repelled in short order. As we see here Bali becomes a part of Australia while at the same time other islands belonging to Australia to the north of Australia's mainland have been excised in order to ensure that Australia's protection regimes for asylum seekers do not apply to "illegal" boat people who arrive there (such as Ashmore reef, Christmas Island, Melville Island and the Torres Strait Islands). Other islands further afield belonging to other states such as Manus Island, Papua New Guinea and Nauru are commandeered for detaining these repelled asylum seekers.

edition – Carnage hits Australia's Holiday Island – Terror hits home" (Greenlees, 2002, p. 1). Kuta has changed from a rather notorious and seedy playground for tourists to a battleground for terrorists. Another transformation is underway as the site of the two clubs is becoming a battleground monument for more serious and contemplative tourists with the building of a memorial in 2003; a similar, yet different Australian appropriation of this Balinese space.

Another more metaphorical battle was soon raging on the implications of this event for tourism. Ten days after the bomb attack, *The Australian* carried an interesting article under the headline "Cleansing of foreign evils a "good thing" (Ellis, 2002, p. 4). Here it was reported that a well-respected Balinese academic, Luh Ketut Suryani said that the effects of the bombing was a "good thing" and that she had advised local authorities to leave the bombsite untouched as a memorial to the evils of tourism (an altogether different meaning to the monument than the one described above). In her interview she said:

> This is the punishment of God because we have not developed cultural tourism but we have brought in many things outside our Balinese culture. We now have prostitution, gambling, paedophilia, drugs and casino. These things are not Balinese. These things are brought in by foreigners. It disturbs our culture. It is good for us that Australians will not come back to Bali for a few months or a year. Our people can go back to their land, to their paddy. Bali will learn from this. I am not against tourism, but many Balinese now think the dollar is more important than maintaining culture (Ellis, 2002, p. 4).

The Australian made a note that she was not known as a "nationalist firebrand" and her comments reflect a belief of a growing Balinese lobby, but this did not assuage those that saw her comments as "insensitive" and "anti-Australian". From another angle, Coward wrote in *The Ecologist* (2002, p. 24) that the backpacking clubber attracted to Bali was unacceptably oblivious to the hostility that their partying could arouse in a traditional society. She stated "This kind of tourism, which views the world as its playground and other cultures as the backdrop for the same lifestyles as back home, is highly problematic. It's a form of casual imperialism …" (Coward, 2002, p. 24). She makes a point of saying she does not condone the bombing; rather that she wishes us to reflect on the issues the experience raises:

> If nothing else, these attacks should be used to cultivate some cultural self-awareness that our consumerist lifestyles are not what all people aspire to. Until this is realised, many young peoples won't see how at risk they are (Coward, 2002, p. 24).

Her article raised a response from O'Neill (2003) of the *Christian Science Monitor* in an article titled "Don't blame the backpacking victims". O'Neill claimed that such sentiments expressed by Coward and others are only "a short step to viewing them as legitimate terrorist targets" and reflect a long-standing antipathy to tourism on the part of "western" environmentalists, academics and other tourism critics (2003). His assessment was:

> This all looks like a bad dose of Western self-loathing, where environmental commentators in the West are projecting their own prejudices onto the

events in Bali ... it was terrible enough that the Bali victims were cut down while travelling and enjoying themselves, without commentators spouting that there is something sinister about seeing the world with a backpack and a pair of dancing shoes (O'Neill, 2003).

This is a similar dynamic to that in the aftermath of "9/11" in resisting reflection. O'Neill said let's not look beyond the immediate issues of these young people happily enjoying themselves in their right to travel the world and the evil bombers who shattered their innocence. O'Neill accused an article by Nicholson-Lord of also placing culpability on the victims; admittedly this work is very critical of tourism but O'Neill failed to engage with Nicholson-Lord's clear message to both the tourists and the travel industry that facilitates them that they can no longer ignore "that much of the planet is in turmoil or despair and that to go on partying in the midst of it all, or trying to 'find oneself', is at the very least in questionable taste" (Nicholson-Lord, 2002, p. 23). He made a plain case for the industry and for travellers to educate themselves about the issues and the risks because the world is increasingly more dangerous for not only the "wretched" but now also for the "rich".

The concern is that the act of enjoying this right to travel is an ideological act which is predicated on a system of inequity and therefore may invite another ideological act, terrorism, as a response. This is not sympathising with terrorism but saying that the hubris of First World tourists asserting their right to travel freely, with maximum comfort and guaranteed safety is "sinister" when others cannot even ensure the means of survival for themselves, their families and their ways of life. It is an obscene and intolerable situation and the efforts of commentators such as O'Neill is to shield us from thinking about the ideological baggage that is packed in our backpacks and the dirt and blood that is adhering to our dancing shoes. This invocation to not think beyond the role of ourselves as carefree backpackers on the open road is not dissimilar to the New York appeal to see shows and visit restaurants. It hints at the sedating affect that our consumerist culture performs us: we stubbornly refuse to consider that our free movement may be related somehow to the asylum seekers imprisonment at Baxter Detention Centre in Australia, our silence in the illegal invasion of Iraq in 2003 might be a catalyst to the bombs in Madrid and London and the others that are to follow,[28] our tourist hedonism might be implicated in the poverty of the destitute and our consumerist lifestyle might contribute to the loss of biological diversity and ecological integrity and so threaten our very long-term existence.

Meeting Grounds of Denial: Tourism and the Environment

One last topic for exploration in this challenging of tourism, is the issue of tourism, the environment and sustainability. From the 1980s when the discourse of environmentalism impacted on businesses and their ability to appropriate the environment and its resources, sustainability became a buzzword on everyone's lips. Business has been won over by the argument that sustainable business practices are not only good for the environment but also

---

[28] Not to mention the failure to pay any attention to, let alone deal with the "Palestinian question" for decades despite the fact that almost the entire Middle East considers it a fundamental human rights issue of vital importance and thus remains an outstanding grievance in the international arena.

good for business. Ecotourism promises even more; it promises not only profits for the tourism industry, a special experience to the tourist, development for host communities but also conservation and even enhancement of nature. It would seem that the conundrum of development and the environment is not difficult at all, with a little human ingenuity and goodwill. But sustainability discourse has been with us for a very long time now, and all creatures great and small, from the World Bank, the UNWTO, national governments, transnational corporations to the local business and the lone individual, are seemingly converted. But an examination of the tourism industry reveals a great disjuncture between rhetoric and reality.

One example is the implementation of the Balearic Islands "eco-tax". The Balearics are iconic for overdeveloped mass tourism; with a total population of 800,000 hosting 11 million tourists per year (Templeton, 2003). The stresses that tourism places on these sensitive islands is not difficult to imagine. As a result of recognised environmental pressures, an "eco-tax" was implemented in May 2002 which levied a 1 euro fee on hotel occupants per day of their stay contributing some 21 million euros in its first year for an environmental fund (Templeton, 2003). However, this small initiative met with heated opposition from significant players in the British tourism industry. These included the Association of Business Travel Agents, the Federation of Tour Operators and Thomas Cook travel agency (travelmole.com, 2002). Tourism Concern, a British non-governmental organisation (NGO) focused on ethical tourism, has said:

> We think the tourism industry should put its green words into action. On the one hand they are saying they want to sign up to sustainable tourism and on the other they are doing everything they can to oppose it. Unfortunately, their actions are speaking louder than their words (travelmole.com, 2002).

However, it was lack of political support that has seen its withdrawal. Local government elections in May 2003 brought in a centre–right government of the Popular Party and ousted the Socialist party that had implemented the tax (Templeton, 2003). It was reported that British tour operators "overwhelmingly welcomed" this action; the Association of British Travel Agents stated:

> We are very pleased to see that the new Balearic government will be scrapping the so-called eco-tax. It was always an unfair burden, in particular for families on a tight budget, and we hope the government will look to better sources of revenue to continue improving the environment (Templeton, 2003).

While travel industry players said that potential tourists to the Balearics had been diverted to other destinations to avoid paying the levy, Templeton cites statistics that UK visitation had risen in fact by 8% during the period and only a handful of complaints about the tax had been submitted to the government (2003). The fact that the eco-tax only costs the average holidaymaker perhaps 7 euros per holiday and that British travel research has shown that 64% of British tourists surveyed were willing to pay up to 5% more for an environmentally sound holiday (travelmole.com, 2002), indicates that in this instance, the tourists were being used as an excuse. This particular case study illustrates that important tourism industry leaders show a demonstrable gap between their rhetoric and their actions when it comes to a meaningful environmental agenda with real ramifications on their interests.

Moving from a micro-example to a macro and fundamental one, lies the issue of reconciling sustainability discourse in tourism and the widespread use of unsustainable transport technologies in the tourism endeavour. Few tourism analysts have engaged with this issue at all, with Cater and Goodall (1997) providing a rare exception in their discussion of sustainable tourism entitled "Must tourism destroy its resource base?" Tourism's use of travel technologies, and in particular the aviation required for some international travel, contributes to global warming. Cater and Goodall ask whether conventional tourism can be made more sustainable under these conditions:

> Currently tourist transport uses too much fuel. Public transport could be substituted for private transport, short-haul travel to nearer destinations for long-haul holiday journeys, high-occupancy charter flights for scheduled flights and flight refuelling stops planned to minimise the need to tanker extra fuel. It is, however, questionable whether tourism can adopt measures which will reduce significantly emissions from the use of transport services and other energy resources. Staying at home appears to be the "greenest" way to holiday (1997, pp. 88–89).

In an effort to ensure that the environmental costs of aviation transport is calculated into the total ticket price, an environmental group in the UK has proposed that passengers pay an eco levy of Great Britain Pounds (GBP) 28 per 1000 kilometres travelled (travelmole.com, 2003). Airport Watch advocated the plan in order to raise funds to offset environmental damage induced by aviation emissions and as a catalyst to a new "holiday culture" where air travel comes to be viewed as a precious luxury to be rationed and not as an frequent occurrence that one can seize on whenever cheap offers come through the letterbox. Focusing upon the popular British destination of Spanish Majorca which would attract an extra cost of Great Britain Pounds 90 with the levy and thus no longer be the cheap holiday destination that it now is, one managing director of a British travel company said it was not a viable plan as tourists would prove unwilling to pay; instead he proposed "Tourists can help solve problems around the world. In Kenya, for example, people are much more interested in the bigger issues, for example, tourist cash helping to treat people dying of malaria" (travelmole.com, 2003).[29] This is indicative of an obstinate refusal by some in the industry to accept measures that are anything other than voluntary in nature and without costs to their bottom lines. Big players, such as British Airways, may find that carbon-trading schemes may be worth while pursing, but it is still an effort to head off threats of such tax and penalty schemes that could be imposed upon them by governments.

Cater and Goodall (1997) are pessimistic in their assessment of the likelihood of the tourism industry effectively addressing this thorny issue. This has left the issue to

---

[29] It is ironic that he points to malaria as his higher concern considering that it is rich world tourists who use the most up-to-date anti-malarial drugs which most Kenyans cannot afford and which contributes to the growing resistance of the disease and thus the ineffectiveness of the prophylactics.

environmentalists and NGOs who have not only called for government regulation of the industry as described above but also pioneered efforts to educate the tourists about the size of their "ecological footprint" (i.e. environmental impacts) when they undertake certain transport modes for their journeys. One effort is the web site called "Choose Climate"[30] which has an interactive model created by a climate engineer that allows the user to plot a journey and the programme will calculate the amount of greenhouse gas emissions this journey will contribute per passenger. In the section entitled "Flying off to a warmer climate",[31] a dedicated effort is made to educate the traveller about the true costs of airline travel.[32] For example, using the interactive map on this web site to plot a journey from Australia to the UK indicates this approximate 16,000 kilometres journey would contribute total greenhouse gas emissions to a warming effect equivalent to 10,749 kilograms of CO_2. The web site facility then places this information in a context that the user can understand, for instance, stating that this trip would utilise 2.43 years of your total sustainable carbon emissions budget. Another section offers alternative choices, which advise the user to consider other modes of transport than cheap flights, use of communications technologies such as video-conferencing[33] and holidaying closer to home.

The environmental issues surrounding tourism actually illuminate some of the major problems with the current tourism system and have been well explored by analysts such as Mowforth and Munt (2003). One of the sources of the problem is the "freedom" taken for granted in the tourism arena. Tourists assert their "right" to travel where they wish and how they wish (if they have the economic means to support their demand) and the tourism industry manages to appropriate resources such as not only airspace, but also the world's beautiful places, people's exotic cultures and there very acts of living in order to service this tourist demand. What the environmental aspects of tourism reveal is that these "rights" must be balanced with their attendant responsibilities, including real limitations on growth and provisions that contribute to equity and social justice. But considering tourism's fundamental role in the "culture-ideology of consumerism" which is predicated on continual economic growth[34] through continual consumer consumption (Sklair, 2002), it is highly unlikely that such requirements will be accepted. This discourse of sustainability is engaged

---

[30] Accessible at http://www.chooseclimate.org.

[31] The icon for the cursor on the computer screen is a jumbo jet which is "chased" around by CO_2, NO_2 and H_2O emissions as the user manipulates the cursor to navigate the sight.

[32] In a powerful subsection entitled "cheap flights", the web site informs the viewer that airline flights are cheap for a number of reasons including: the atmosphere is a global commons and thus access is free; aviation fuel is untaxed (unlike fuel for land transport); oil is cheaply priced despite the fact that it is a finite resource; and air transport is a "prestige" sector that is subsidised by state governments. The message is that cheap holidays are cheap because they do not reflect the true costs of the service and it is at a cost to the environment whose bill will be served in the distant or not-so-distant future. The title "choose climate" means that we make choices as to whether we will live in a warmer climate with the attendant ravages of the effects of global warming, just that many of us are unaware of this.

[33] On the issue of unsustainable transport and international conferences, another response has come from those who do not wish to curtail travel as they implement carbon offset programmes such as funding the creation of new tree plantations. This occurred at the 2002 UN Johannesburg World Summit on Sustainable Development (see: http://www.greeningthewssd.com/).

[34] Ceaseless growth could be referred to as the "logic of cancer". Also highly recommended is Clive Hamilton's analysis in *Growth Fetish* (2003).

with by industry in order to continue business as usual and has the taint of hypocrisy much as ST-EP mentioned earlier. However, if you simply juxtapose the images of the "rich" continuing to enjoy their global jet-setting lifestyles into the indefinite future, while the "wretched" Pacific Islanders such as the people of Kiribati and Tuvalu who will have to seek asylum in other countries because soon their homelands will disappear under the rising waters of global warming, you can see that the hypocrisy of "sustainability" will soon be exposed and that such inequity cannot be indefinitely ignored.

Alternatives to the Hostile Meeting Grounds of Tourism and Globalisation

> *"Tourism has a role to play in building peace. Diplomacy cannot do it alone, politics is not adequate, but enlightened tourism, that is intellectually inspiring and spiritually uplifting can help the world" – Dr. Surin, PATA conference, Bali, April, 2003 (quoted in Muqbil, 2003a).*

Tourism does not have to be the damaging and exploitative force that is herein described. Advocates of peace through tourism, responsible tourism, volunteer tourism and the like have long argued that tourism is powerful force for understanding and tolerance that is vital for dissipating the hostilities across the divides in the global community. Vital and innovative contributions in this effort are occurring more and more. Ryan (2002) has proposed the application of the principles of stakeholder theory and social tourism to improve the meaning of sustainability and improve outcomes of balancing the competing and complex interests of the various stakeholders in tourism. Reid's (2003) text on tourism planning challenges tourism to contribute to distributive justice and thereby create a more equitable world. Wearing (2001) has explored volunteer tourism for an analysis of tourism that promotes experiences that "make a difference". Scheyvens' (2002) text on "tourism *for* development" also casts a critical eye to contemporary tourism and explores some new areas such as "justice tourism" where tourism can be made to work for the community good.

Inayatullah (1995) has provided an analysis of tourism that may be very timely to return to at this particular historical moment in the development of tourism. In an article entitled "Rethinking Tourism" he applied an Islamic perspective to tourism as an offering to a topic that has been analysed overwhelmingly from a "Western" perspective. This analysis results in a tourism checklist with a difference. He asks:

> How does tourism affect the distribution of wealth? Does tourism create conditions where economic growth is sustaining? Does tourism reduce structural violence (poverty, ill-health and racism caused by the system) or does it contribute to the further impoverishment of the periphery? Does tourism reduce personal direct violence? Can we create types of tourism that enhance individual and social peace? Does tourism create the possibilities for cultural pluralism, that is, conditions where one culture understands the categories of the other culture … ? Can knowledge of the other reduce intolerance, creating the possibility of a multicultural peaceful world? Does tourism help create economic democracy? Is tourism progressive? Is there a progressive

use of resources, from physical to mental to cultural–spiritual? (1995, p. 413).

Inayatullah's analysis supports my view that tourism is much more than an industry, it is a social force (Higgins-Desbiolles, 2006). Its power has been co-opted by the tourism industry which has chained it to the market paradigm and harnessed its energies for private profit and the wealth accumulation of a few. It cannot and must not remain this way for much longer. Tourism has long promised much more than it has delivered but it has been allowed to appropriate resources according to this promise. The players in the tourism industry have sheltered behind the protection of "neutrality" in business. Few leaders have been willing to engage in the bigger issues of our day, fearing the repercussions of getting into "politics". Imtiaz Muqbil of *Travel Impact Newswire* is the rare exception and he has been prodding the conscience of the industry relentlessly.[35]

The effect of the "War on Terror" is to exacerbate an increasingly divided world. The American leadership and those allied with it increasingly see a world divided between "us" and the "terrorists".[36] In effect we could use metaphorical language that you are either a "tourist" or a "terrorist" according to your choice to buy into the "civilised" world. You are an acceptable component of the "civilised" world according to whether you "buy into" the consumer role assigned to you in our marketised world.[37] This is clearly not a desirable situation for tourism which sells itself best in a peaceful world where people of difference meet (if even superficially) across divides. Futurists must clearly see a tourism phenomenon where tourism circuits get narrowed to friendly territories, and so it would seem likely tourism leaders will step up the rhetoric of peace and tolerance to forestall such eventualities which may pinch their economic bottom line.[38] This will not be good enough. As Muqbil has advocated repeatedly (for instance 2003a,b), tourism leaders must think bigger than this and embrace issues that they have long chosen to avoid. They must commit themselves to a real agenda for change that embraces the lofty principles that they have already committed themselves to in the various declarations discussed earlier. Hypocrisy invites the actions and reactions that Fanon (1967) warned us about so many years ago. The "wretched" and the "rich" must come to terms across the divides of these "hostile meeting grounds" for a

---

[35] Particularly recommended was his paper "Terrorism, more resilient than tourism" in which he exhorted the industry to look at the root causes of terrorism and commit themselves to engagement with some of the big issues (Muqbil, 2003b).

[36] Not only do the words of the "Bush Doctrine" clearly declare this but military advice demonstrates that this thinking goes very deep. See Barnett's analysis in "Pentagon's New Map" in which the world is divided between those of us in the market and therefore "civilised" and the rest, who are described as "the gap" (2003).

[37] An interesting headline in The Ecologist read "Environmentalists are the new terrorists", in reference to American legislation in some states under the title of the Animal and Ecological Terrorism Act (see Ecologist, 2003, p. 11).

[38] Thus Weissmann in Travel Weekly predicted that not only are people from the Middle East deciding to only travel to "friendly countries" (now Malaysia and not the US for instance), but Americans may need to do so as well (2004, p. 57). While the tourists circuits are changing patterns according to political friendliness, interestingly a "terrorist" travel circuit has developed with "tours" for training in friendly states such as Afghanistan and Pakistan.

future in which we can all survive and perhaps even thrive; "business as usual" is not an option.[39]

Conclusion

> *"We are one more September 11th away from the end of the Open Society"* –
> Thomas Friedman, New York Times, 2002

"9/11" indicated major fault lines in global "meeting grounds" that had been hypocritically ignored for far too long. The promise of development has rung hollow in the globalisation era as contributions to development aid have withered and countries have been left to market mechanisms which disproportionately allocates benefits to the "rich" while frequently reaping wholesale environmental devastation in the process. Nowhere is this more effectively symbolised than the "rich" tourist enjoying their holidays among some of the poorest places in the world. The rhetoric of the "right" to tourism and travel is premised on the impressive contributions that tourism can make to peace, understanding, development and sustainability. This brief investigation of tourism's role in over-consumption in the First world, the lack of facilitation of a universal right to travel due to the absence of the fulfilment of the right to development and the "greenwash" of the sustainability debate indicates that tourism's *raison d'etre* is open to challenge.

Resorting to the language of the "war on terror", tourism has a choice to make. It can either encamp itself with the market fundamentalists and secure itself a world that is increasingly dangerous and fragmented, or it can encamp itself with humanity and take up the reins that it has as such a powerful social force. The hypocrisy of ST-EP, the Global Code of Ethics in Tourism and sustainable tourism is growing increasingly intolerable in a world where poverty and suffering is growing rather than abating. These initiatives will not be able to mask the fact that tourism is failing to live up to its promises and therefore is not worthy of the allowances, subsidies and support that it is given in a world where resources are increasingly stretched. Tourism must serve the "wretched" as well as the "rich" if it is to continue to enjoy the open access it has been given to the world's resources and the faith that has been instilled in it to improve the lives of people.

Acknowledgements

An earlier version of this chapter has been published by the Ecumenical Coalition on Tourism in their Perspectives in Tourism series.

---

[39] That this is true is clear by the growing gathering of the civil society movement through the World Social Forum (WSF) which has gathered to challenge the dominance of the Washington Consensus through the meetings it holds under the auspices of the World Economic Forum. In conjunction with the assertion of Third World clout at the Cancun summit of the World Trade Organisation in 2003, it is clear that the "wretched" are seeking systemic change. At their 2004 meeting in Mumbai, the WSF put the tourism industry in its crosshairs with a Global Summit on Tourism. The theme of this tourism session was "who really benefits from tourism?" and a call to "democratise tourism!" was released. One NGO participant, the Ecumenical Coalition on Tourism (ECOT) called for the WSF to advocate for a tourism that is "pro-people" (ECOT, 2003).

Comments and feedback received from Dr. Olga Gostin, Vesper Tjukonai and an anonymous referee are gratefully acknowledged. Kate Leeson provided editiorial assistance.

References

Barnett, T. P. M. (2003). The Pentagon's New Map. *Esquire*, March. Retrieved 01 April 2003, from http://www.nwc.navy.mil/newrulesets/ThePentagonsNewMap.htm

Baudrillard, J. (2002). *The spirit of terrorism, and Requiem for the Twin Towers*. London: Verso.

Bello, W. (n.d.). *Endless war? Focus on the Global South*. Retrieved on 2 February 2002, from http://www.focusweb.org/publications/2001/endless_war.html.

Bush, G. W. (2001, 20 September). Address to a Joint Session of Congress and the American People. Retrieved 23 February 2004, from http://www.whitehouse.gov/news/releases/2001/09/20010920-8.html

Butcher, J. (2003). *The moralisation of tourism*. London: Routledge.

Cater, E., & Goodall, B. (1997). Must tourism destroy its resource base? In: L. France (Ed.), *Earthscan reader in sustainable tourism* (pp. 85–89). London: Earthscan Publications.

Coward, R. (2002). Bali, bombs and backpackers. *The Ecologist*, December, 24.

Ecologist (2003). Environmentalists are the new terrorists. July/August, 11.

Ecumenical Coalition on Tourism (ECOT) (2003). *Concept paper for World Social Forum*. Unpublished document.

Ellis, E. (2002, 22 October). Cleansing of foreign evils a "good thing". *The Australian*, 4.

Fanon, F. (1967). *The wretched of the earth*. London: Penguin Books.

Gates, H. L. (1992). Critical fanonism. *Critical Inquiry*, *17*, 457–470.

Gearin, S. (2003, 6 November). Sammaki granted permanent residency. *The 7:30 Report*. Retrieved 3 March 2004, from http://www.abc.net.au/7.30/content/2003/s984031.htm

Gee, C. Y., Makens, J. C., & Choy, D. J. L. (1997). *The travel industry* (3rd ed.). Honolulu: University of Hawaii.

Goldstone, P. (2001). *Making the world safe for tourism*. New Haven, CT: Yale University Press.

Greenlees (2002, October 14). Terror hits home. *The Australian*, 1.

Hamilton, C. (2003). *Growth fetish*. Crows Nest, NSW: Allen & Unwin.

Higgins-Desbiolles, F. (2001). The wretched of the earth and the newest "new world order". *Dissent*, *7*, 21–23.

Higgins-Desbiolles, F. (2006). More than an "industry": The forgotten power of tourism as a social force. *Tourism Management*, *27*(5), in press.

Huntington, S. (1996). *The clash of civilizations*. New York: Simon & Schuster.

Hutnyk, J. (1996). *The rumour of Calcutta: Tourism, charity, and the poverty of representation*. London: Zed books.

Inayatullah, S. (1995). Rethinking tourism: Unfamiliar histories and alternative future. *Tourism Management*, *16*(6), 411–415.

Kirby, A. (1999). UN urges rich to slash consumption. *BBC News Online*, September 15. Available at http://news.bbc.co.uk/1/hi/sci/tech/447078.stm (accessed 10 November 2003).

Laqueur, W. (2003). *No end to war: Terrorism in the twenty-first century*. New York: Continuum.

Leiper, N. (1995). *Tourism management*. Melbourne, Vic.: RMIT Press.

MacCannell, D. (1992). *Empty Meeting Grounds*. London: Routledge.

Mitchell, P. R., & Schoeffel, J. (2002). *Understanding power: The indispensable Chomsky*. Melbourne, Vic.: Scribe Publications.

Mowforth, M., & Munt, I. (2003). *Tourism and sustainability: New tourism in the Third World* (2nd ed.). London: Routledge.

Muqbil, I. (2003a). It's the food chain, stupid. *Travel Impact Newswire*, April 23, 15.

Muqbil, I. (2003b). *Terrorism, more resilient than tourism*. Unpublished position paper.

Neighbour, S. (2003). The Bali confessions. Transcript of *Four Corners*, Australian Broadcasting Corporation. Retrieved 11 February 2003, from http://www.abc.net.au/4corners/content/2003/transcripts/s780910.htm.

New Internationalist (NI) (2003). Globocops unleashed. *New Internationalist, 355,* 8.

Nicholson-Lord, D. (2002). Against the western invaders. *New Statesman,* 9 December, 22–23.

O'Byrne, D. (2001). On passports and border controls. *Annals of Tourism Research, 28*(2), 399–416.

O'Loughlin, E. (2003, 8 March). Terrorism tourism for holiday of a lifetime. *Sydney Morning Herald.* Retrieved 15 November 2003, from http://www.smh.com.au/articles/2003/03/07/1046826529967.html?oneclick=true

O'Neill, B. (2003). Don't blame the backpacking victims. *Christian Science Monitor,* January 6. Retrieved 15 March 2004, from http://www.csmonitor.com/2003/0106/p.09s01-coop.htm

Picard, D. (1996). *Bali: Cultural tourism and touristic culture.* Singapore: Archipelago Press.

Reid, D. G. (2003). *Tourism, globalization and development: Responsible tourism planning.* London: Pluto Press.

Ryan, C. (2002). Equity, management, power sharing and sustainability – Issues of "new tourism". *Tourism Management, 23,* 17–26.

Samudra, I. (2002). Transcript of confession, 29 November. *Four Corners.* Retrieved 11 February 2003, from http://www.abc.net.au/4corners/content/2003/20030210_bali_confessions/target_bali.htm.

Sartre, J. P. (1967). Preface. In: F. Fanon (Ed.), *The wretched of the earth.* London: Penguin Books.

Scheyvens, R. (2002). *Tourism for development: Empowering communities.* Harlow, UK: Prentice-Hall.

Sklair, L. (2002). *Globalization: Capitalism and its alternatives* (3rd ed.). Oxford: Oxford University Press.

Smith, S. L. J. (1988). Defining tourism: A supply-side view. *Annals of Tourism Research, 15,* 179–190.

Sustainable Development Commission (SDC) (n.d.). Redefining prosperity: Resource productivity, economic growth and sustainable development. Retrieved 5 June 2004, from http://www.sd-commission.gov.uk/pubs/rp/annex.htm

Templeton, T. (2003, 8 June). A kick in the Balearics for eco-tax. *The Observer.* Retrieved 9 October 2003, from http:www.travel.guardian.co.uk/news/story/0,7445,972821,00.html

Thomas, C. (1999). Where is the world now? *Review of International Studies, 25,* 225–244.

Travelmole.com (2002, 19 February). Tourism concern criticises industry reaction to Balearics eco-tax. Retrieved 23 February 2003, from http://travelmole.com/news_detail.php?news_id=72535

Travelmole.com (2003, 23 June).Plans for a new eco-tax condemned. Retrieved 23 June 2003, from http://travelmole.com

Travis, A. (2005, 7 July). New European airline to send deportees home. *Sydney Morning Herald,* 7.

United Nations (1948). Universal declaration of human rights. Retrieved 17 January 2003, from http://www.fourmilab.ch/etexts/www/un/udhr.html

United Nations Environment Program (UNEP) (1999). GEO 2000 Press release. Retrieved 10 November 2003, from http://www.unep.org/geo2000/pressrel/index.htm

United Nations World Tourism Organization (UNWTO) (1980). Manila declaration on world tourism. Retrieved 13 February 2003, from http://www.world-tourism.org/sustainable/concepts

United Nations World Tourism Organization (UNWTO) (1999). Global code of ethics for tourism. Retrieved 8 March 2000, from http://www.world-tourism.org/pressrel/CODEOFE,htm

Van Wagtendonk, R. (2001). Joining forces against terrorism. Radio Netherlands web site. Retrieved 14 December 2003, from http://www.rnw.nl/hotspots/html/un011002.html

Wearing, S. (2001). *Volunteer tourism: Experiences that make a difference.* Oxon: CABI.

Weissmann, A. (2004). Ugly travelers. *Travel Weekly,* May 17, 57.

Williamson, J. (2000). What should the World Bank think about the Washington consensus? *The World Bank Research Observer, 15*(2), 251–264. Retrieved 13 June 2004, from http://www.worldbank.org/research/journals/wbro/obsaug00/pdf/%286%29Williamson.pdf

Chapter 18

Defending Voyeurism: Dark Tourism and the Problem of Global Security

Debbie Lisle

Introduction

In late 1992, Italian travel agent Massimo Beyerle offered an "October War Zone Tour" in Bosnia. For $25,000 a piece, clients could spend 2 weeks in the battlefield accompanied by doctors and security forces. Beyerle's general aim was to take tourists "where the fighting has just ended, such as the South of Lebanon, Dubrovnik or Vukovar, as close as possible to the places shown on the television news, so that our clients can see and speak with the people, and see for themselves the damages caused by war" (Keenan, 1994, p. 136). Four months after the Dayton Accords were signed, several more "terror tourists" arrived in Sarajevo to see the remnants of conflict and purchase shrapnel, shell casings and discarded UN helmets as souvenirs (Lisle, 2000, p. 106). While the "October War Zone Tour" seems like a bizarre form of extreme travel, it reveals a significant development in the tourism industry. In a number of post-conflict areas, an increasing number of visitors are interested in encountering the remnants of recent conflict. Think, for example, of the millions of visitors who flocked to Ground Zero following the 9/11 attacks, or those who make a special effort to visit Nelson Mandela's prison cell on Robben Island (Lisle, 2004; Strange & Kempa, 2003). These developments clarify difficult decisions for local authorities: should they preserve and display sites of recent conflict as part of their rebuilt tourist infrastructure? Or should they bulldoze these terrible reminders and replace them with "normal" tourist attractions that don't focus on the conflict?

The tourist's desire to encounter sites of conflict has recently been understood as part of the wider phenomena of Dark Tourism – a fascination with visiting sites of "death, disaster and atrocity" (Conforti, 1996; Lennon & Foley, 2000; Miles, 2002; Strange & Kempa, 2003). Seaton initially described these developments as "Thanatourism", or, "travel to a location wholly, or partially, motivated by the desire for actual or symbolic encounters with death" (Dann & Seaton, 2002; Seaton, 1999, p. 131; 1996). Dark Tourism, of course, has a long and varied history which takes in such historical spectacles Roman gladiator battles, public hangings and aristocrats visiting the Battle of Waterloo (Seaton, 1999, pp. 131–132). Moreover,

Dark Tourism encompasses all forms of "death, disaster and atrocity", from famous sites of celebrity death (e.g. the JFK site in Dallas, the Princess Diana site in Paris) to more established museums dealing with war and genocide (Lennon & Foley, 2000). This chapter is specifically concerned with those aspects of Dark Tourism that pertain to the visiting of war zones, battle-fields and other man-made conflicts. It develops a critical reading of the Dark Tourism literature – especially Lennon and Foley's *Dark Tourism* – in order to show how conventional understandings of this practice align with a problematic and outdated notion of global secur-ity. This geopolitical alignment is supported by more general problems in Lennon and Foley's argument: they do not engage with important literature on voyeurism and the consumption of danger; their numerous and potentially interesting case studies are rendered superficial by their resistance to theorizing, and they frame the figure of the tourist as entirely passive. By crit-ically reading *Dark Tourism*, this chapter goes on to dispute one of the central claims of Tourism Studies in general, namely, that the practices of tourism and conflict can be separated. To take proper account of the intersections and overlaps between tourism and conflict, this chapter argues that a much more critical and transnational formulation of global security is required.

The Rise of Dark Tourism

It is not difficult to explain the increase in Dark Tourism to conflict zones over the past 15 years. Firstly, the intensification of globalization has made every part of the world instantly recognizable, accessible and understandable. This is especially the case with sites of conflict – the repetitive framing and circulation of war zone imagery within the news media (especially since the television war of Vietnam), means audiences are as familiar with images of Mogadishu and Sarajevo as they are of London and New York. Indeed, Lennon and Foley site the popular media as a primary reason for the popularity of all forms of Dark Tourism (2000, pp. 8–20). Secondly, a dramatic increase in the total number of people travelling has been both an engine and consequence of the larger forces of globalization. For example, tourism has grown exponentially since the 1980s, and although the events of September 11th, 2001 adversely affected tourism numbers, the industry is now recovering (Bonham, Edmonds & Mak, 2006; Leisure Report, 2004; World Tourism Organization, 2002). Thirdly, as a conse-quence of the huge growth of tourism worldwide, the industry has fragmented into a number of smaller niche markets catering to special interests. In effect, tourism is no longer restricted to its traditional forms (e.g. 2 weeks in the sun, a cruise, a safari, a cultural experience in London or Paris), but now encompasses almost all human activity – food tourism, sex tourism, sports tourism, literary tours, city breaks, trekking holidays, eco-tourism, scuba diving, singles holidays, train and plane spotting, etc. As Robinson argues, "The fragmentation of the tourist industry, involving millions of individual businesses together with governments, public and voluntary agencies and regulators, owners and shareholders, makes it difficult to speak of tourism as a single industrial sector" (2001, p. 35). With this in mind, it is not difficult to see how Dark Tourism to sites of conflict has become another "niche market" in the growing tourism industry.

While mediation, globalization and fragmentation offer compelling reasons for the rise of Dark Tourism, none reveal the most significant reason: the shifting ground of authenticity.

As many scholars have argued, the myth of modern tourism is centred on the possibility of encountering authentic difference – seeing the "real" Bali, engaging with the "real" Spaniards, having "real" adventures by getting off the beaten track (Cohen, 1988; MacCannell, 1992; 1976; Taylor, 2001; Wang, 1999). But as tourism became a truly global industry in the 1990s, that myth of authenticity became more difficult to maintain. As every part of the globe became quickly commodified and re-designed for the enjoyment of global tourists, the "real" soon disappeared into a staged, mediated and "fake" version of itself. Indeed, as Bauman has argued, we now live in a global theme park (1997; 1996). It is not the case that only intrepid travellers can access the "real" while passive tourists are content with the "fake" – in the global theme park, there is no difference between the real and the fake, between the authentic and the staged, and indeed, between the tourist and the traveller. And this is precisely why sites of recent conflict – war zones, battlefields, mass graves, camps – function as the last remaining "real" in an otherwise commodified world. For what is more "real" than death, atrocity, warfare and violence? In short, tourists are motivated to see places like Belfast, Beirut and Cambodia because these are the *only places left* where it is possible to experience an unmediated and authentic encounter with "the real".

The Geopolitics of Dark Tourism

While it would be easy to dismiss these "trouble tourists" as voyeurs, this chapter contends that the judgement of voyeurism requires some theoretical and analytical unpacking. Within psychoanalysis the voyeur attains sexual pleasure from gazing upon what is hidden from view within the private sphere, for example, a Peeping Tom gazes through a window in order to watch someone undress. By extension, the Dark Tourist gains satisfaction by accessing areas of conflict and violence that most tourists would classify as "off limits" (Lisle, 2004, p. 16). The claim here is that those who derive pleasure, satisfaction or comfort from gazing at sites of recent violence and conflict somehow deviate from "proper" and "respectable" tourist practice. Lennon and Foley try to refute this charge by suggesting that visiting sites of death and atrocity is primarily commemorative rather than voyeuristic or disrespectful. They argue that although sites of death are commodified as tourist products, they differ from more conventional tourist attractions because they are primarily shaped by messages of remembrance and education. Therefore, it is perfectly acceptable to visit sites of death in order to (a) show respect for the dead and properly mourn them, or (b) learn lessons about a terrible historical event so that it never happens again (Lennon and Foley, 2000, pp. 10–11). In other words, one is not being a "voyeur" when visiting the camps at Auschwitz-Birkenau, one is learning about the Holocaust and also commemorating it. Lennon and Foley's examination of Dark Tourism suggests that while practices of public commemoration are usually restricted to established institutions like cemeteries and museums, increased mobility means that these practices can now occur in many different sites.

By rescuing Dark Tourism from the charge of voyeurism, Lennon and Foley force these practices to conform to the parameters of the tourist gaze (MacCannell, 1992; 1976; Urry, 1990). The work of MacCannell and Urry is significant firstly because it places tourism within larger discourses of leisure and consumption, and secondly because it distinguishes the practices of travelling, visiting and holiday-making from the everyday practices of work. But what is seldom acknowledged about the tourist gaze is its underlying geopolitics. In suggesting that tourism happens in places that are physically separate from where we live and work, MacCannell and Urry reproduce a familiar claim that the world is divided into spatial containers we call home (i.e. those national communities that grant us citizenship) and those places we call foreign (i.e. where we go for holidays). Despite their critical insights, neither MacCannell nor Urry examine how the bifurcation of the world into "home" and "away" is constructed by a powerful discourse of danger. In other words, the division of the world into home/away is overlaid by an attending cartography of danger that contains tourism within global spaces that are above all *safe*. This geopolitical alignment makes sense within a conventional understanding of authenticity: a tourist's desire to encounter the real will always be trumped by his/her desire for safety and security (Lisle, 2000, pp. 94–95). For example, tourists might want to visit the Pyramids and sail down the Nile, but they will forego this experience if the political and religious tensions in North Africa threaten their vacation.

What, then, do the practices of Dark Tourism reveal about the discursive alignment between the tourist gaze and geopolitics? Lennon and Foley's work is crucial here, for in forcing the practices of Dark Tourism to conform to the spatial categories of the tourist gaze, they *moralize* the binary pairings of home/away and safety/danger. Even Lennon and Foley recognize that there are some truly voyeuristic practices that are unacceptable – primarily those that glorify rather than properly commemorate a tragic past (2000, pp. 27–45). Simply put, Lennon and Foley are not interested in those "deviant" figures operating outside the moral boundaries enshrined in the tourist gaze. Indeed, these travellers are "not significant" in the larger world of Dark Tourism (Lennon & Foley, 2000, p. 23). In naming, excluding and judging this deviant behaviour, Lennon and Foley reaffirm the conventional geopolitics of the tourist gaze and jettison what is most provocative and challenging about Dark Tourism. Indeed, Dark Tourists visiting conflict zones are important *precisely because* they transgress and therefore call into question the spatial and moral distinctions of the tourist gaze. By failing to pursue the significance of these transgressions – theoretically, ethically and politically – Lennon and Foley consign their work to mere observation, and dismiss these "voyeuristic" and "deviant" practices as simply another niche market in a continually fragmenting tourist industry. Rather than depoliticize these practices like Lennon and Foley do, this chapter suggests that the presence of tourists in sites of conflict requires a profound shift in the way we understand the relationship between danger and tourism. Helpful in this endeavour are critical voices in International Relations that question the conventional positioning of safety and danger on the globe.

The Civilizational Framing of Global Security

The discipline of International Relations has a long history of mapping how sovereign nationstates achieve security, order and justice within an anarchical international system. Traditional accounts of global security foreground the status, power and territorial integrity of the nationstate, and argue that strong states are the best way to ensure global security and stability. Since the end of the Cold War, International Relations scholars have had to shift their focus on sovereign nation-states in order to take account of the forces of globalization. The problem with this shift is that it did not go far enough: discourses of danger proliferate *even though* the primary actors in global security are civilizations rather than nation-states. This "new ortho-doxy" in International Relations is clarified in two important arguments. Firstly, Francis Fukuyama's claim that capitalist liberal democracies constitute the most successful, pros-perous and peaceful civilization (as opposed to regimes that are "mired" in the ideological struggles of the past) suggests that the extension of liberal democracy is also the best way to ensure global security and order. Indeed, Fukuyama draws on a tradition of "Democratic Peace" theories which claim that liberal democracies do not go to war with each other (Doyle, 1999; 1995; Russett, 1993). Secondly, Samuel Huntington claims that the new "fault lines" of global politics – the places where conflicts will occur – are civilizational rather than national (2002). Huntington was one of the first scholars to suggest that the next great global conflict will be between the West and Islam and that the civilizational family of the West should co-operate to protect themselves from the threat posed by Islam. The problem with Dark Tourism is that it uncritically reproduces this new orthodoxy in International Relations. Acceptable practices of commemoration in museums, cemeteries, graveyards, etc. bolster "our" privileged civilizational identities and histories that must be protected from "them". Consequently, Lennon and Foley cannot see how the intersections between tourism and security always exceed their civilizational framings. To properly address the geopolitics of Dark Tourism and show how they disrupt conventional accounts of global security, a more transnational framework is required. Since the end of the Cold War, a number of critical scholars in International Relations have pointed out the limitations of both national and civ-ilizational accounts of global security (Buzan, Waever & de Wilde, 1997; Krause & Williams 1997). This work locates the nation-state alongside competing international authorities (e.g. NGOs, social movements) and illustrates how security has fundamentally changed with the current forces of globalization. It also critically reveals how conventional accounts of global security perpetuate a discourse of danger by creating and protecting a homogenous identity *inside* while projecting otherness and difference *outside* (Campbell, 1998; Der Derian & Shapiro, 1989; Shapiro & Alker, 1996; Walker, 1993). Moreover, as R.B.J. Walker has argued, these conventional framings of global security are dangerous because they per-petuate "the impossible dream of absolute invulnerability" (1997).

Critical work in International Relations asks three important questions about the changing nature of global security in the context of globalization. Firstly, *what is to be secured?* Because the transnational character of global politics has revealed the porous nature of the nation-state's borders, security issues are no longer restricted to military defence of the state or the pursuit of national interest. For example, no place is impermeable to environmental threats (e.g. famine, drought, floods), large population migrations (e.g. refugee movements, asylum seekers, migrant labour), biological contamination (e.g. SARS, HIV, Avian Flu) or the trans-fer of illegal goods (e.g. drugs, weapons, endangered species). Because the *variety* of threats has dramatically increased, a number of political issues outside of war, violence and conflict are now candidates for "securitization" (Buzan et al., 1997). Secondly, *who is in charge of global security if the state is no longer the primary authority in a globalized world?* It is no longer just soldiers, politicians and diplomats responding to security threats. Rather, coord-inated responses to "complex emergencies" now involve a host of non-state actors such as aid workers, charities, UN agencies, civil society groups, scientists, doctors and the media. The ongoing War on Terror is instructive here: just as Al Qaeda use modern technologies and extensive networks to create new forms of transnational terror, Western governments have been forced to coordinate an equally transnational response. Not only does this mean orchestrating militaries of different abilities and sizes, it also means employing private security firms and companies to take over secondary tasks (e.g. running prisons, protecting diplomats, securing oil fields). This is not a conventional war in any sense: we now live in an era of network centric warfare where forces are highly flexible, mobile and technologically equipped (Dillon, 2002). Thirdly, *who is being secured if "citizens" are no longer the primary subject of International Relations?* With increasing mobility, it is unclear who is responsible for the security of "non-citizens" (e.g. migrants, refugees, guest workers) and whether "we" have a responsibility to protect citizens of nations where human rights are routinely being violated. This has led to fierce debates over humanitarian intervention. What are the "universally accepted" conditions that would automatically trigger a multilateral humanitarian intervention? Why was there an intervention in Kosovo but not Rwanda? Not only do these debates invoke rigid subject positions of "saviour" and "victim", they fail to take account of how technology has completely re-defined the subject of security. Foucault (2003) and Agamben (1998) have articulated this shift most clearly by arguing that it is no longer "individuals" who are being secured, but rather, life itself. Information about our DNA, our tissues, our organs, our cells – our very genetic make up – is now subject to intense surveillance, regulation and control. For example, biometric technologies (e.g. facial and gait recognition, retina and fingerprint scans, identity cards, racial profiling) have made the targeting and apprehension of "dangerous" subjects much easier.

While these transformations in the way we understand global security are now accepted in International Relations, they are ignored when tourism is the object of study. And this is precisely the problem with Lennon and Foley's argument: they suggest that the rise of Dark Tourism is in part the result of increased mobility and globalization, but they fail to see how these same forces have utterly transformed conventional notions of geopolitics and security. It is as if they have mapped a "new" practice onto an "old" world. They maintain this juxtaposition by uncritically reproducing a discourse of danger that aligns neatly with problematic arguments about bounded civilizations in conflict. In short, Lennon and Foley do acknowledge that we are living in a thoroughly transnational world where subjects, objects and information are constantly crossing established boundaries – whether these are national or civilizational. The point here is that many of the subjects who cross these borders are tourists. But by framing Dark Tourism through such an outdated conception of geopolitics and security, Lennon and Foley contain these potentially transgressive travellers within *safe* borders. In this way, Lennon and Foley miss how Dark Tourists tap us into the transnational circuits that constitute our current geopolitical landscape.

The Separation of Tourism and Conflict

Lennon and Foley's inability to take account of the transnational world we now live in is not surprising, for they are simply reproducing a wider assumption evident in Tourism Studies. When Tourism Studies comes to discuss the difficult issues of war, violence and conflict, they rely on a simplistic post-war model which insists upon a clear separation between the social phenomena of conflict and tourism. This separation was forged in the aftermath of World War II (WWII) when the modern tourism industry developed as an engine of post-war growth

SECURITY	Peace	Conflict	Peace
TIME	→	→	→
TOURISM	Tourism	No Tourism	Tourism again

Figure 18.1: The post-war model of conflict and tourism.

and prosperity. The idea here is simple: if there is peace tourism prospers, and if there is conflict tourism suffers. As Pizam and Mansfield conclude, "safety, tranquillity and peace are a necessary condition for prosperous tourism"(1996, p. 1). Figure 18.1 sets out the logic of the post-war model in which the cycles of peace and conflict endemic to global security map neatly onto the cycles of growth and stagnation endemic to the tourist industry. Thus, when peace reigns in the world, tourism prospers – but when conflict erupts, tourism stagnates and even stops completely.

The logic of the post-war model is clear: there is an unambiguous demarcation between conflict and peace, and tourist practices are always subservient to this division. Indeed, tourism and conflict are not equally weighted within the model: conflict is always privileged because it determines when tourist activity can develop (in peace) and when it must cease (in war). Pizam and Mansfield argue that Tourism Studies frames questions of conflict with two goals in mind: firstly, to examine the "causes and effects" of conflict on tourism, and secondly, to suggest "possible measures to contain and minimize the negative effects" (1996, p. 2). The assumption here is that once a community has come through a conflict, they must work to jettison their "war-zone" status and develop a more inviting image of a holiday destination that can guarantee security alongside authenticity and difference. Consequently, much of the work within Tourism Studies that engages with questions of conflict focuses primarily on the latter stages of the post-war model where tourism encourages peace and vice versa.

The post-war model of conflict and tourism is certainly not a timeless or universal frame-work, and must therefore be understood in its proper historical context. As Valene Smith explains, the experience of WWII established the historical parameters for the relationship between tourism and conflict:

> The penetration of war into the fabric of human life makes it *the time-marker of society*. People know that life has changed perceptibly, and they chronicle the differences in their lives as three eras: "before the war," "during the war," and "after the war." This pervasive impact of warfare figures prominently in the tourist involvement with memories and monuments (1996, p. 253).

But the cyclical nature of conflict and peace does more than simply temporalize society into before, during and after the war. It also determines the appropriate length of time that must pass before practices of tourism can begin after conflict. This time lag was easier to control after WWII because mass tourism was developing in tandem with the more general re-building of welfare states in the Western world. This established a particular tempo for the development of Dark Tourism, for example, as American commercial airlines began flying across the Atlantic, ex-servicemen returned to the beaches of Normandy and the battlefields of Europe as *tourists* rather than soldiers. However, it was 1957 by the time airplanes eclipsed ships as the preferred method of travel across the Atlantic, and by then the Cold War was already in full swing (Smith, 1998, p. 217). This historical context is crucial for it reveals how the measured development of Dark Tourism is determined by wider geopolitical goals. Very simply, monuments, memorials, exhibits and installations about conflict always project backwards into the time they are commemorating, but their construction is determined largely by *present-tense* geopolitical concerns. For example, visiting WWII monuments and memorials became an important part of the patriotic mobilization of American citizens during the Cold War – these tourist sites harkened back to a "Good War" and reinforced images of a triumphant nation. It is not difficult to see how the present framing of the past within the post-war model frames Dark Tourism within wider discourses of patriotism and national identity: "we" go to museums, monuments and memorials to learn about "our" role in a particular conflict, and "we" take comfort in tales of victory, sacrifice and heroism that can sustain us as we face contemporary threats. Unsure about the "red scare"? Go to the Phoenix memorial at Pearl Harbour, or the USS Intrepid in Manhattan, and be reassured about the glory, strength and courage of the American military.

By reproducing the post-war model assumed within Tourism Studies, Lennon and Foley are forced to hang onto an outdated geopolitical framework *despite* the overwhelming evidence of globalization. But they are not alone in their belatedness; indeed, many scholars in Tourism Studies use the "civilizational" framing of global security to argue that tourism encourages peace (D'Amore & Jafari, 1998; Hill, Gibbons, Illurn & Var, 1995; Karshenas, 1996). As Louis D'Amore explains, tourism operates

> by spreading information about the personalities, beliefs, aspirations, perspectives, culture and politics of the citizens of one country to the citizens of another … Through tourism we can come rather to an appreciation of the rich human, cultural, and ecological diversity that our world mosaic offers' to evolve a mutual trust and respect for one another and the dignity of all life on earth (1988, pp. 38–39).

It is not difficult to hear the echoes of Fukuyama here: tourists from an "enlightened" Western civilization are important messengers of peace. But as Askjellerud rightly argues, D'Amore's arguments ignore the complex and mutual constitution of these terms: "if tourism expects to be, or not to be, a force for peace, conflict needs to be included in the debate" (2003, p. 742). This is especially the case in a context of globalization where the practices of both tourism and conflict exceed the post-war model. Indeed, every place on earth is now a potential security target *and* a potential tourist destination. In places like Jerusalem, Belfast and Beirut, the orbits of security and tourism collide in explicit ways. Here you find tourists, terrorists and soldiers occupying the *same* space. In places like Bali, Mombassa, Luxor and Columbia, tourists have become explicit targets in the ongoing War on Terror. But this spatial collapse has a temporal component: conflict is no longer a temporary condition like the post-war model suggests. In places like the Middle East, conflict has become a "normal" way of life. And it is not just the duration of conflict that has changed – "war" has been replaced by terrorism, multilateral humanitarian intervention and civil unrest that have no clear start or end points. More importantly, the rapid influx of tourists immediately after a conflict blurs the neat end of violence and the arrival of peace enshrined in the post-war model. The ease of travel in the global theme park makes it possible for war zones to immediately re-enter the orbit of the tourist gaze as the next hotspot. Very simply, the separation of conflict and tourism makes little sense in a context of perpetual global insecurity and increased mobility.

The Complicity of Tourism Studies

Writing almost 10 years after the fall of the Berlin Wall, Valene Smith argued that we should maintain the post-war model that separates tourism and conflict: "war, or its threat, is at the cost of tourism, and is both an economic and political tool. The avoidance of war through intervention, if successful, preserves political hegemony and tourism revenues" (Smith, 1998, p. 220). Smith's argument helps to make sense of the post-war model's resuscitation after the events of September 11th, 2001. As Goodrich argues, issues of security are now central to the tourism industry which willingly participates in a variety of government efforts to make travellers feel safe (2002). What is particularly significant about these efforts to restore a correlation between tourism and safety is that they are driven by a discourse of managerial rule. More and more, the industry is practicing "risk assessment" and "crisis management" in order to keep conflict as far away from tourism as possible (Blake & Sinclair, 2003; Faulkner, 2001; Lepp & Gibson, 2003; Poirier, 1997). The problem with the discourse of managerial rule is that it enables a clear reproduction of the new orthodoxy of International Relations. Not only does it activate a very clear understanding of what it means to be "civilized" and "free" in a new world order, it also activates strategies by which "we" can identify terrorists who mean to do harm to "our" civilization. Think, for example, of how passenger profiling at airports has become a key component of security within the tourist industry, despite compelling arguments about racism and the erosion of civil liberties. In order to "preserve political hegemony" as Smith argues, it is necessary to uncritically reproduce problematic geopolitical distinctions between "us" and "them". In effect, September 11th, 2001 has displaced WWII as the new *time-marker of society* so that we are now working within a new "post-9/11" model that invokes new discourses and strategies to separate tourism and conflict.

By privileging tourist revenue above any ethical questions about intervention and war, Smith justifies any disagreeable or violent actions undertaken by a political hegemony. In effect, Smith's claim foregrounds economics as the *raison d'etre* of tourism, and therefore the primary focus of Tourism Studies. And in this she is right, for Tourism Studies *is* dominated by a positivist and rather narrow approach that seeks to quantify behaviour (e.g. by examining the "motivations" of certain tourists) and measure market forces (e.g. by detailing the "revenue" generating potential of a certain destination). As Jamal and Hollinshead argue, the tendency for Tourism Studies to separate subjects (tourists) and institutions (the industry) reveals a reliance on "positivism and scientism" that makes it difficult, if not impossible, to address the changing forms of security, warfare and intervention that are currently at work in the global sphere (2001). The problem, here, is that the methodologies used to address the intersection of tourism and conflict are part of the problem because they uncritically assume that the post-war model separating these two practices is an accurate and truthful description of the real world rather than a normative construction. But the hermeneutic tradition, among others, explains that positivism is never neutral or objective because it always smuggles in normative claims. This uncritical positivist orientation is the biggest problem with the way that Tourism Studies examines issues of security and conflict. This is especially clear in Lennon and Foley's *Dark Tourism*. As one critic explains, Lennon and Foley "position themselves as defenders of historical truth and against the commodification of 'Dark Tourism' sites" (Smith, 2002, p. 1189). Instructive, here, is Keith Hollinshead's challenge to scholars within Tourism Studies who should:

> reflect on the degree to which they themselves are currently held captive under the particular panoptic surveillance of institutional thought and action, and of the extent to which they themselves serve as self-regulating agents-of-normalcy of those carceral outlooks upon peoples, places, and pasts (1999, p. 8).

Hollinshead's challenge must be extended to those scholars who are currently framing the relationship between tourism and conflict to see how their arguments serve as "self-regulating agents-of-normalcy" with respect to the prevailing civilizational agenda of global security.

Conclusion

More than any other travellers, Dark Tourists tell us a great deal about the relationship between tourism and conflict. They illustrate that places of conflict are not excised by the tourist gaze, but are instead integral to it. The problem, however, is that the literature on Dark Tourism exemplified by Lennon and Foley's *Dark Tourism* is constrained in its observations because it makes problematic assumptions about geopolitics and security. This literature draws from a powerful new orthodoxy that installs civilizational distinctions between "us" and "them" and devises strategies through which "they" can be punished for contravening or intruding on "our" liberal values of tolerance and freedom. This normative reproduction results in a post-war model that continually separates the practices of tourism and conflict so that tourism can be equated with peace, security and prosperity. But rather than reinforcing this correlation, the civilizational distinctions between "us" and "them" so uncritically adopted by Dark Tourism end up producing hostility and antagonism rather than peace. Lennon and Foley's reliance on the post-war model prevents them from acknowledging the transnational character of our globalized world. Consequently, they miss the transgressive potential of Dark Tourism: by travelling to spaces that are "off limits", Dark Tourists actually disturb and critique the civilizational codes that underscore Tourism Studies. In part, Lennon and Foley cannot see this transgressive potential because they are handcuffed to a positivist research agenda. By starting an interdisciplinary conversation with critical scholarship in International Relations, this chapter has made an effort to disrupt that positivist consensus. By examining Dark Tourists from an alternative position, it has foregrounded more critically attuned vocabularies that do not automatically assume a world divided into conflicting civilizations.

Acknowledgements

For insightful critical comments on the paper, the author would like to thank an anonymous reviewer; participants in the "Tourism, Politics and Democracy" conference hosted by

CENTOPS in September 2004; and participants in the Design History Society Conference hosted by the University of Ulster and the Design History Society in September 2004.

References

Agamben, G. (1998). *Homo Sacer: Sovereign power and bare life*, Trans. D. Heller-Roazen. Stanford: Stanford University Press.

Askjellerud, S. (2003). The tourist: A messenger of peace? *Annals of Tourism Research, 30*(3), 741–744.

Bauman, Z. (1996). From pilgrim to tourist – or a short history of identity. In: S. Hall & P. du Gay (Eds), *Questions of cultural identity* (pp. 18–36). London: Sage.

Bauman, Z. (1997). *Postmodernity and its discontents.* Cambridge: Polity Press.

Blake, A., & Sinclair, M. T. (2003). Tourism crisis management: US response to September 11. *Annals of Tourism Research, 30*(4), 813–832.

Bonham, C., Edmonds, C., & Mak, J. (2006). *The impact of 9/11 and other terrible global events on tourism in the US and Hawaii.* East-West Center Working Papers: Economics Series, No. 87, February. Available http://www.eastwestcenter.org/stored/pdfs/ECONwp087.pdf (Accessed 17-03-06).

Buzan, B., Waever, O., & de Wilde, J. (1997). *Security: A new framework for analysis.* Boulder: Lynne Reinner.

Campbell, D. (1998). *Writing security: United States' foreign policy and the politics of identity.* Manchester: Manchester University Press.

Cohen, E. (1988). Authenticity and commoditization in tourism. *Annals of Tourism Research, 15,* 371–386.

Conforti, J. M. (1996). Ghettos as tourism attractions. *Annals of Tourism Research, 23*(4), 830–842.

D'Amore, L. (1988). Tourism – the world's peace industry. *Journal of Travel Research, 27,* 35–40.

D'Amore, L., & Jafari, J. (1988). *Tourism: A vital force for peace.* Montreal: D'Amore and Associates Ltd.

Dann, G., & Seaton, A. V. (2002). *Slavery, contested heritage and Thanatourism.* Binghampton: Haworth Hospitality Press.

Der Derian, J., & Shapiro, M. (Eds) (1989). *International/intertextual relations: Postmodern readings of world politics.* Lexington: Lexington Books.

Dillon, M. (2002). Network society, network-centric warfare and the state of emergency. *Theory, Culture and Identity, 19*(4), 71–79.

Doyle, M. (1995). On the democratic peace. *International Security, 19*(4), 164–184.

Doyle, M. (1999). A liberal view: Preserving and expanding the liberal Pacific union. In: T. V. Paul & J. A. Hall (Eds), *International order and the future of world politics* (pp. 41–66). Oxford: Oxford University Press.

Faulkner, B. (2001). Towards a framework for tourism disaster management. *Tourism Management, 22*(2), 135–147.

Foucault, M. (2003). *Society must be defended: Lectures at the college de France, 1975–1976*, Trans. David Macey. London: Picador.

Fukuyama, F. (1993). *The end of history and the last man.* New York: Penguin.

Goodrich, J. N. (2002). September 11, 2001 attack on America: A record of the immediate impacts and reactions in the USA travel and tourism industry. *Tourism Management, 23*(6), 573–580.

Hill, B., Gibbons, D., Illurn, S., & Var, T. (1995). International institute for peace through tourism. *Annals of Tourism Research, 22*(3), 709.

Hollinshead, K. (1999). Surveillance of the worlds of tourism: Foucault and the eye-of-power. *Tourism Management, 20*(1), 7–23.

Huntington, S. (2002). *The clash of civilizations and the remaking of world order*. New York: Free Press.

Jamal, T., & Hollinshead, K. (2001). Tourism and the Forbidden Zone: the undeserved power of qualitative inquiry. *Tourism Management, 22*(1), 63–82.

Karshenas, M. (1996). A step towards other cultures to give a chance for peace. In: M. Robinson, N. Evans & P. Callaghan (Eds), *Tourism and cultural change*. Sunderland: British Educational Publishers.

Kennan, T. (1994). Live from … In: E. Diller & R. Scofidio (Eds), *Back to the front: Tourisms of war* (pp. 130–163). F.R.A.C. Basse-Normandie: Princeton Architectural Press.

Krause, K., & Williams, M. (Eds) (1997). *Critical security studies: Concepts and cases*. London: UCL Press.

Leisure Report (2004). Record number visitors point to UK tourism recovery. *The Leisure Report*, 1st December, p. 8.

Lennon, J., & Foley, M. (2000). *Dark Tourism: The attraction of death and disaster*. London: Continuum.

Lepp, A., & Gibson, H. (2003). Tourist roles, perceived risk and international tourism. *Annals of Tourism Research, 30*(3), 606–624.

Lisle, D. (2000). Consuming danger: Re-imagining the war/tourism divide. *Alternatives: Local, Global, Political, 25*(1), 91–116.

Lisle, D. (2004). Gazing at ground zero: Tourism, voyeurism and spectacle. *Journal for Cultural Research, 8*(1), 3–21.

MacCannell, D. (1976). *The tourist: A new theory of the leisure class*. New York: Shocken.

MacCannell, D. (1992). *Empty meeting ground: The tourist papers*. London: Routledge.

Miles, W. F. S. (2002). Auschwitz: Museum interpretation and Darker Tourism. *Annals of Tourism Research, 29*(4), 1175–1178.

Pizam, A., & Mansfield, Y. (Eds) (1996). *Tourism, crime and international security issues*. Chichester: John Wiley & Sons.

Poirier, R. A. (1997). Political risk analysis and tourism. *Annals of Tourism Research, 24*(3), 675–686.

Robinson, M. (2001). Tourism encounters: Inter- and intra-cultural conflicts and the world's largest industry. In: N. Alsayyad (Ed.), *Consuming tradition, manufacturing heritage: Global norms and urban forms in the age of tourism*. London: Routledge.

Russett, B. (1993). *Grasping the democratic peace: Principles for a post-cold war world*. Princeton: Princeton University Press.

Seaton, A. V. (1996). From Thanatopsis to Thanatourism: Guided by the dark. *Journal of International Heritage Studies, 2*(2), 234–244.

Seaton, A. V. (1999). War and Thanatourism: Waterloo, 1815–1914. *Annals of Tourism Research, 26*(1), 130–158.

Shapiro, M., & Alker Jr, H. (Eds) (1996). *Challenging boundaries*. Minneapolis, MN: University of Minnesota Press.

Smith, V. (1996). War and its tourist attractions. In: A. Pizam & Y. Mansfield (Eds), *Tourism, crime and international security issues* (pp. 247–264). Chichester: John Wiley & Sons.

Smith, V. (1998). War and tourism: An American ethnography. *Annals of Tourism Research, 25*(1), 202–227.

Smith, W. W. (2002). Book review of Dark Tourism. *Annals of Tourism Research, 29*(4), 1188–1189.

Strange, C., & Kempa, M. (2003). Shades of Dark Tourism: Alcatraz and Robben Island. *Annals of Tourism Research, 30*(2), 386–405.

Taylor, J. P. (2001). Authenticity and sincerity in tourism. *Annals of Tourism Research, 28*(1), 7–26.

Urry, J. (1990). *The tourist gaze: Leisure and travel in contemporary societies*. London: Sage.

Walker, R. B. J. (1993). *Inside/outside: International relations as political theory*. Cambridge: Cambridge University Press.

Walker, R. B. J. (1997). The subject of security. In: K. Krause & M. Williams (Eds), *Critical security studies: Concepts and cases*. London: UCL Press.

Wang, N. (1999). Rethinking authenticity in tourism experience. *Annals of Tourism Research, 26*(2), 349–370.

World Tourism Organization (2002). World Tourism Recovery Committee. Available at www.world-tourism.org/market_research/recovery/menu.html (Accessed 26-07-04).

Chapter 19

Rethinking Globalization Theory in Tourism*

Ana María Munar

The New World Order and the Door to Touristhood

The contemporary era has seen a great increase in global flows, trans-national networks and interconnections that have quantitatively and qualitatively contributed to the widening of globalization (Held, Mc Grew, Goldblatt & Perraton, 1999). This development of intensified globalization took a step further at the end of the 1980s with the beginning of the post-Cold War era. The ninth of November 1989 was to be a new date in the annals of the history of the old European continent. Like domino pieces the countries, satellites of the Soviet Empire, threw their communist parties out of power and started a long journey towards democracy and a market economy. During this period the international economic institutions were gaining political power and economic influence through the policies of the Washington Consensus (Stiglitz, 2002). A neo-liberal vision was to be implemented and promoted globally (Held et al., 1999; Stiglitz, 2002). The wall fell and citizens openly declared their right to be tourists. Tourism was to be included in the new range of products and services that were to become available to the population of the world.

The dream of escaping from the ordinary (Jafari, 1987) was no longer stopped by the forbidden sign of a military frontier. Frontiers became deterritorialized (Held et al., 1999). They disappeared from the geographical map and became reincarnated again in the form of an empty credit card. The exclusion of touristhood was to be dictated by a competitive new social order, with new norms of inclusion and exclusion (Held et al., 1999). The places of the sacred (Wang, 2000) were to become an exclusive club of the haves, unavailable to the have-nots.

---

*At time of publication this chapter had been also accepted for publication in the *Journal of Tourism, Culture and Communication* (late 2006).

At the same time as the New World Order was making its entrance on the global scene, tourism was becoming available to the new millions who were entering the consumer society. The market was expanding globally (Castells, 1996). According to the study conducted by Matthew Bentley, and quoted in the book *The State of the World 2004* of the World Watch Institute, 1.700 million people are part of the consumer society. Nearly half of them are living in the developing world, in China alone, they account for 240 million (World Watch Institute, 2004). The Pacific and Eastern Asia became new commercial centres showing the highest-growth percentage in tourism of the last decade, with 16% of the global market quota in the year 2000 (WTO, 2002). A sign that things had changed was the celebration of the World Travel Fair in Shanghai in February 2004.

In the meantime the widening of globalization did not prevent stratification. There were millions of people without the basic requirements for a decent life. In the developing world 1.2 billion people (almost a quarter of the world's population) were classified by the World Bank as living in absolute poverty (World Watch Institute, 2003).

The reality of the non-consumers was described by the sociologist Zygmunt Bauman as the world of the vagabonds (Bauman, 1998). Globalization was also the landscape of the ones having the right to enter the touristhood scene and the ones that do not. This reality became another way of demonstrating global inequalities. In the large metropolis of the world a short geographical distance and an immense social distance could exist between the ones that could be tourists and the ones that only could be vagabonds. The meeting with "the other" was just around the corner. Ning Wang claims that tourist's experiences of "strangehood" are similar to the more general experiences of modern urban dwellers who must regularly deal with strangers (Wang, 2000).

The New World Order was correctly called new, and it certainly became a reality to most of the world but it is extremely questionable to what extent it could be called order. If order is to be identified with structure, rules and harmony, the reality of the end of the 20th century made it clear that this was not the case. Chaos seemed to be gaining ground day by day, making more of a certainty the idea of living in a risk society (Beck, 2000); in geopolitical terms with new forms of terrorism and in personal terms in each individual life. Now tourism had to deal with intensive globalization (Held et al., 1999) and new risks emerging in new places. This was a challenge to the tourism industry and for tourism planners. Considering that one of the factors of international development of the tourism industry was based on avoiding political and economic problems (Martorell, 2002). Then these tasks have become more difficult than ever. Therefore, a better understanding of the inter-relation between globalization and tourism is a crucial matter in order to analyse the present and the future of tourism and of those who are at the core of the subject of the study of tourism; the tourists.

The aim of this chapter is through qualitative research to rethink the relationship between tourism and globalization by placing tourism research in the broader theoretical frame of globalization theory. This is done by answering the following question: Is it possible through the three approaches method used in globalization theory bring to light the different approaches and theoretical contradictions that exist in the understanding of globalization and tourism and determine a proper understanding and definition of globalization to be used in tourism research?

Dammed to Popularity: The Paradox of Inclusiveness

Globalization, a word that in the 1970s and the early 1980s had been discussed between academic professors and scientific experts, thus became an extraordinary instrument to describe the new world born from the ruins of the Soviets. For decades, Social Sciences have been developing languages that relate to each other, in an everlasting internal dialogue only opened to the members of the club.

Terms such as second modernity (Beck, 2000), linguistic turn (Habermas, 1987), glocalization (Robertson, 1995), spatialization (Bauman, 1998), poliarchy (Dahl, 1989) McDonalization (Ritzer, 1996) are well known to social scientists and intellectuals but are completely unknown to the great majority of society. The academic system suffers from a historical autopoiesis that has kept many of the scientific analyses out of general public debate and civil society (Habermas, 1987; 1998). Specific and autopoietic languages are part of today's systems of social inclusion and exclusion. The distinctive language of science, and in this case of social sciences, can be considered as a powerful tool of exclusion.

Globalization became the exception to the rule. In 1960 the term had yet to be invented (in English) (Ghemawat, 2001), and in just three decades the term jumped out of the academic books and scientific journals and experienced an explosion of popularity. At least one term of the latest century social sciences had opened the door to inclusiveness. The society at the end of the millennium chose the word and made it popular. Globalization, could be heard in radio music programs, and read in sports journals and ladies' magazines. It became "in", and by the very expansion of its use seemed to prove its ability to describe the changes experienced by the people of the world. Debates of all kinds and at all levels were held to discuss if globalization was good or bad (Bhagwati, 2004). The phenomenon was blamed for all the catastrophes that the satellites beamed directly to television sets in comfortable living rooms at home. It became a phenomenon about which everyone held an opinion (Held et al., 1999). The discussion of the meaning of the word transformed into an enormous trans-national forum with two major groups, pro-globalization and anti-globalization (Bhagwati, 2004).

Paradoxically at the same the time that the term was exemplifying social inclusion and social science was becoming popular, it became more and more institutionalized in academic circles. The institutional recognition and the preference of the academic community for this issue can be seen by looking at the academic production of books or articles on the topic. If in 1980, 300 books on globalization appeared or articles were published, by the second half of the 1990s, the annual publication rate exceeded 3000 (Guillen, 1999, quoted by Ghemawat, 2001, p. 2). According to Professor Pankaj Ghemawat from Harvard Business School, looking at these numbers "in stock rather than flow terms, interpolation and extrapolation suggest that about 1–2000 such books or articles had been published by 1980, and 40,000 by 2000" (Ghemawat, 2001, p. 2).

The explosion in its use made it more and more difficult for globalization to be used to analyse the changes of our world, at the same time that the scientific community of the world devoted more efforts than ever before to include this phenomenon as part of the core knowledge of all social sciences and thus creating a paradoxical situation. So much had been said about its meaning and consequences at the beginning of the 21st century, that the contours of the term ended by losing its form and became extended and shadowy. An academic term was suffering after becoming "last year's hit". With hundreds of definitions and ways of using the word, it was dammed to social success and scientific confusion.

Globalists and Anti-Globalists: The Misleading Debate

The term was used to explain many different fields of the social sciences, for some authors globalization did mean the removals of barriers to free trade (Stiglitz, 2002, p. ix) and the hegemony of the liberal economy (De la Dehesa, 2000), for others the existence of new global companies (Keohane, 1984, quoted by Held et al., 1999), for those focusing on the civil society, the birth of social relations through time and space (Giddens, 1990) the creation of new imagined communities (Appadurai, 1990, quoted in Beck, 2000), and the birth of a network society (Castells, 1996). For political scientists' globalization denoted the losing of power and political control by the nation states and the restructuring of national representative democracies (Held, 1997). The general picture was a melting pot of diverse definitions competing with each other. The result: A lack of accuracy and rigour when the term had to be used for research purposes.

To make the debate even more complex, several authors (Gray, 1998; Hirst, 1997) denied that globalization really existed, and accused other social scientists of giving too much importance to new technologies and new markets, forgetting how deep rooted local cultures are, how national states are still the most powerful political institutions and how the market was only bringing prosperity to some parts of the world while leaving behind huge geographical areas.

While this was happening in the academic world, the civil society became itself an important player in the globalization debate. As the international agencies, international experts and powerful personalities were getting closer, organizing meetings, creating new forums of dialogue, such as the famous Davos meeting in Switzerland established for the political and economic elites of the world (Beck, 2000), some part of the civil society was starting to organize itself as a general and vague movement against the New World Order. Surprisingly a political issue could again mobilize thousands of people on the streets, in a massive expression of discontent with the international institutions (Bhagwati, 2004). The transport industry and the fall in the cost of airfares have helped not only an ever-increasing number of international tourists, but have also made it possible for young people of different countries to become global activists (Anheier, Glasius & Kaldor, 2001; Held et al., 1999).

Many different voices were raised during the mobilizations in Seattle, Prague, Washington, Geneva, Cancun, but the general motto was that another globalization was possible (Anheier et al., 2001; Bhagwati, 2004). The movements came to be commonly known as the anti-globalization movement. Although some visible heads of the movements talked about the need for another kind of globalization or globalization with a human face, the anti-globalist label was put on the movement from the very beginning (Bhagwati, 2004).

The traditional division between left and right was now to be reproduced between the globalists and the anti-globalists. In general terms the globalists were identified as the defenders of the neo-liberal economic policy and the anti-globalists as the defenders of the use of political power to control economic capitalism (Beck, 2000). In even more general terms the globalists had become by then mostly rightwing, and the anti-globalists mostly leftwing. The division would prove to be as useless and misleading as the traditional dichotomies good–bad, we-the others, etc. (Beck, 2000; Burns, 2004). As the word globalization became more and more blurred, this division of the debate not only did not help to clarify what globalization was about, but in fact created a greater confusion.

This approach which placed authors, politicians, activists, writers, economists, etc. on the two sides of the pro-contra debate, became inadequate as soon as one took a closer look at what these authors and other important participants in the debate were saying. The black and white picture became full of shadows and nuances that the dichotomy of the debate did not allow. A closer look at the anti-globalization movement showed that the great majority of the participants, acknowledged some positive aspects of the closer interconnectedness of the people of the globe (Anheier et al., 2001; Beck, 2000). No one denied the benefits or advantages of the increasing amount of information available, or the trade in medicines that could save children lives. Their strongest critique was against some economic effects of globalization, and the behaviour of international institutions that had written the rules making economic globalization possible. They were not against globalization but against some aspects of the economic and cultural globalization. Differences inside the anti-globalization movement were many, from the anarchist-autonomous groups that desired to annihilate any kind of authoritative system or structural power, to the defenders of the model of the welfare state, together with extreme right nationalists who did not have the legitimacy of any power over the nation, the ones that defended the rights of native communities (Held et al., 1999) or others related to a wider environmental movement (Beck, 2000).

The globalists saw positive aspects in the economic globalization process but they also found tendencies that should be changed, some blamed the liberalization of capital (Stiglitz, 2000), some the lack of prudence in opening domestic financial markets to global integration (Bhagwati, 2004), some the double moral standards of the western countries in trade policies (UNDP, 2003) and others became critics as soon as the focus was for example on political globalization and global governance (De la Dehesa, 2000). The conclusion of the previous analysis is that many times the actors in the debate were not talking about the same realities and did not share a common definition of globalization. If the meaning of such a debate was to clarify, to structure a body of knowledge around the globalization phenomenon, then the conclusion is that this division had proved to be a misleading one bringing more chaos to the massive use of the term.

The Three Approaches Method and Tourism: Hyperglobalists, Traditionalists and Transformationalists

Beyond the unfruitful debate between globalists and anti-globalists another way of classifying the efforts of the academic community in describing globalization appeared in the methodological analysis of David Held, Anthony McGrew, David Goldblatt and Jonathan Perraton in their book *Global transformations. Politics, economics and culture* (Held et al., 1999).

As a way of breaking the dichotomy of the debate, the methodology of the three approaches allows one to clarify what the different tendencies have been saying on globalization. It moves away from an either-or talk and into a debate between theories and understandings.

The approaches that have been considered are: the hyperglobalist, the traditionalist and the transformationalist (Held et al., 1999). The three approaches were identified by how they answer the five principal sets of arguments in the globalization debate. These five issues are: conceptualization, causal dynamics, socio-economic consequences, implications for state power and governance and historical trajectory. The idea of this classification is not to give a throughout account of what every thinker has been saying about globalization. The intention of such a method of classification is to highlight not only the main trends but also the principal problems in the current literature on globalization (Held et al., 1999).

Problems of confusion and misunderstandings in the study of globalization can also be seen in the way tourism experts use it. Some authors tend to identify globalization with economic globalization, in a narrow understanding of the phenomenon (Brown, 1998; Knowles, Diamantis & Bey El-Mourhabi, 2001; Reid, 2003; Sugiyarto, Blake & Sinclair, 2003), some have a much broader understanding of the term (Teo & Li, 2003; Wang, 2000; Wood, 2000). Through a qualitative review of the tourism literature related to globalization it is intended to find the different arguments and positions of the three approaches to globalization.

The Hyperglobalists Approach

Conceptualization and historical trajectory   The hyperglobalist approach understands globalization as a particularity, or a singular condition. Their view of social change tends to be a linear one, to this view, humanity is on a long journey and globalization is the next stop. Globalization is to be understood as a new époque in human history and the nation states as the old structures of the last (De la Dehesa, 2000; Ohmae, 1990). Globalization entails a fundamental reconfiguration of the framework of human action (Albrow, 1996, quoted in Held et al., 1998). In this new époque humanity will see the arrival of a global market and a global society. Globalization becomes a new daybreak that some receive with joy and some with fear. The positive ones are the authors of a neo-liberal tendency (De la Dehesa, 2000). They see all the promises of a new global market free at last of the restrictions of national politics, and a new emancipation era based on human autonomy. Their general opinion is that during the last decades humanity has benefited greatly from the globalization process (Santamaría, 2003). The time has come for the practical ideals that through globalization will replace the fight of the old ideologies (De la Dehesa, 2000).

The negative hyperglobalists follow a neo-Marxist or radical tendency. They agree with the description of globalization presented by the neo-liberals and that is precisely what makes it terrifying. They see all the catastrophes of untamed global market capitalism without any possible control by the welfare states. Globalization becomes then the power of the free capital looking for the best location without any obligation to follow labour laws or tax legislation. It is like a step back to 19th century capitalism, with no social rights and no social security networks (Sernau, 2000).

Both the neo-liberals and the neo-Marxists-radicals although having very different normative basis have in common the fact that they already share a pre-idea of what the final globalization is.

Causal dynamics   This tendency follows the logic of economics. The main motor of globalization is formed by the changes and developments that happen in the world economy. It is mono-causal and expression of a one-dimensional thinking (Beck, 2000). In general terms, they think that globalization consists in the restructuring of the world economic system, in the way of further international integrations of the markets (Déniz Espinós, 2003).

For the hyperglobalists the principal agents of globalization are the global companies that make the extension of the global market possible (De la Dehesa, 2000; Ohmae, 1990). Trans-national corporations have become more relevant for the future of global affairs than nations (Barber, 1995). Other globalization processes, such as cultural or political processes, are a consequence of the developments of the economy. Ulrich Beck defines this economic logic as globalism (Beck, 2000). It is a revival of the idea of progress and modernity. The hyperglobalists understand globalization as a high-speed train where the economy is the engine.

Socio-economic consequences   The hyperglobalizers share the conviction that globalization is changing the north–south relations creating a new pattern of winners and losers in the world. This happens between countries as well as within each one (Held et al., 1999). The citizens who are not able to follow up with the technological development and the new rules of the global market, are left behind, having only an ever more fragile state to support them (Gray, 1998; Stiglitz, 2000).

Globalization is the expansion of the McWorld (Barber, 1995). Global society becomes the expression of a single global market, and this one is identified as the final form of the Enlightenment's project of a universal civilization (Gray, 1998; Rodrik, 2001). It is the American model turned into a "one size fits all" model of civilization.

The idea of a national homogeneity and culture is being eroded by the increased infrastructures of communication and information technology (Castells, 1996). People are becoming increasingly aware of the many common interests and common problems, from the environment to music hits, and a global civil society is emerging (Mulgan, 1998).

Implications for state power and governance   The state power is losing control over the development of society and the national economy (De la Dehesa, 2000). For the neo-liberal tendencies, globalization is a good strategy to roll back the state and give the free-market society the fullest scope possible. To the neo-Marxistic-radical tendencies of the hyperglobalists the nation state is due to globalization suffering in agony (Barber, 2003). Globalization means that, in the future, solidarity and taxation will only be imposed on the citizens that are left behind in the latest capitalist society, and that the grounds of the welfare state will disappear (Daly, 1996). National governments are relegated to a secondary role by increasingly powerful forces at local, regional or international level.

Hyperglobalizers and tourism   In tourism research it is also possible to find this hyperglobalist position (Brown, 1998; Holjevac, 2003; Martorell, 2002; Reid, 2003; Sernau, 2000; Sugiyarto et al., 2003). For some the global market is a world of new opportunities and tourism will benefit greatly from such a development (Holjevac, 2003). Tourism is for the hyperglobalists a force working in favour of the global market and the global society. Tourism is the recipe for growth. For some globalization is understood as being the reality of increasing trade liberalization and lowering domestic taxation, and within this scenario the combination of tourism growth and globalization is a beneficial one (Sugiyarto et al., 2003). Others agree with the view that this next stop of humanity is a wonderland; growth without limits and a booming industry are the perspectives for the future (Holjevac, 2003; Martorell, 2002). Others are so optimistic that their prognosis is that only a global war can stop this enormous growth from becoming a reality (Go & Ritchie, 1990).

Hyperglobalizers in tourism put the economy as the centre of the understanding of tourism and the tourist. In the *Encyclopedia of Tourism* globalization is explained mainly from an economic perspective (Jafari, 2000). There is no mention of the transformations of society, power relations, culture, etc. through globalization and how they can affect the future of tourism.

The tourism global market is seen as the opposite of regionalization. Globalization is changing the nature of international tourism in such a way that it will make tourism the most important economic sector on a world scale (Peter Keller, quoted in Ryan, 1997). Globalization is decreasing the importance of the regional market share in world tourism (Smeral, 1998).

The hyperglobalist tendency has also affected the views on tourism policy and development, and can be identified as the understanding of tourism as a new outward-oriented growth sector and the expression of the rise of neo-liberal outward-oriented strategies (Brohman, 1996).

Tourism becomes also an important contribution to the rising of a global society. The growth of tourism for the hyperglobalists can be a way of enhancing international understanding and harmony between the people of the world (Askjellerud, 2003) and promoting relatively peaceful international environment (Wang, 2000).

Hyperglobalizers in tourism focus on the process of globalization and its standardizing impact in those products, services and institutions first offered domestically and now supplied on a world scale (Smeral, 1998). Tourists are, to this view, global consumers. The global culture of consumerism reaches through globalization all kinds of leisure related activities that have been increasingly commodified (Smeral, 1998). They are the face of global capitalism wherever they go. They will bring developing countries into the consumer society of the new century. It is the reality of millions of humans that see "mass consumption as a part of their pursuit of happiness" (Aramberri, 2001, p. 757).

Other hyperglobalizers in tourism consider the growth of the tourism global market and the birth of a global "harmonic" society, as a problem (Reid, 2003; Sernau, 2000). They represent the pessimistic hyperglobalizers. They agree with the other positive hyperglobalizers that tourism will grow and expand all over the planet. They are aware that the prognosis of the UNWTO for the number of international tourists is 1 billion international tourists by the year 2010 (WTO, 1999). With tendencies that could be classified as neo-Marxists or radicals the defenders of this negative view look at the dangers that millions of tourists may present to the environment, the local culture and society, etc. Tourists for them are in most cases still just golden hordes (Reid, 2003; Turner & Ash, 1975).

The pessimists share with the other hyperglobalizers the understanding that tourists are not more than global consumers. They help to expand the global society that represents the western culture dominating the world. Globalization is blamed for being an "accomplice of ethnocentric nationalization in the eradication of difference" (Wang, 2000, p. 132).

Tourism is seen as a force of homogenization of the world, and as Donald Reid puts it: "It is a world wide phenomenon dominated by trans-national corporations, which both exports the culture of the west to the developing countries, and perhaps more importantly, drains the developing world of its resources, including capital. (...) This exploitation is supported by the mantra of development, supposedly for the benefit of those who are left behind by the economic advances and increased standards of living created in the industrialized world. (...) The tourism sector is tied closely to the globalizing force which pursues profits over justice. (...) While globalization is made possible by the drive of capitalism to expand and grow, and by the development and pervasiveness of new technologies, tourism is one of the important beneficiaries and vehicles of its expression." (Reid, 2003, pp. 2–3).

For all the hyperglobalizers, tourism is a way to reach a global society. However for this pessimistic position the outcome does not bring understanding but instead homogenization, not peace but the conquering by means of economic dependency. The global civilization is the western civilization becoming global (Smeral, 1998).

The Traditionalist Approach

Conceptualization and historical trajectory   This is an approach which prevails mainly as a reaction to the hyperglobalist tendencies (Held et al., 1999). They share the same conceptualization that the hyperglobalizers have on globalization. Globalization is conceived as a particularity and as the emergence of a global market and a global civil society. Taking this conceptualization for good they accuse the hyperglobalizers of elaborating theories based on a series of myths (Hirst, 1997). They argue that globalization is not a reality, because some empirical data shows that there is not a perfect global market with the law of one price, and that there are not market interactions throughout the entire globe on a high scale and extension.

The argument is based on a series of statistical data to prove that the hyperglobalizers are exaggerating the changes in a form for current "hysteria" (Krugman, 1996, p. 208). Even more, this tendency argues that the extension of the market was even greater in the golden age of trade from the end of the 20th century until World War I (Hirst, 1997). The pretension of the hyperglobalists that the current situation of the global economy is unprecedented is another "silly claim" (Krugman, 1996, p. 120).

Causal dynamics   The traditionalist approach relies primarily on an economical conception of globalization (Beck, 2000; Held et al., 1999). Globalization is conceived as a perfect integrated global market, and the empirical evidence shows that this total integration is not a reality. Therefore, globalization is nothing more than a myth taught by hysterical speakers.

Socio-economic changes   The economic activity is undergoing not a process of globalization but of regionalization (Hirst, 1997). Economies of the modern cities show a process of localization (Krugman, 1996). The regionalization process and globalization appear as opponents in the future economic development. The difference of wealth between the regions of the world is still the reality of the world economy, and the patterns of inequality and hierarchy are not the exception but the rule during the last century (Hirst, 1997).

The world is not becoming a place for understanding or peaceful collaboration, but the arena for the fight between civilizations (Huntington, 2004). Many traditionalists also accuse hyperglobalizers of underestimating the power of the national cultures and traditions.

Implications for state power and governance   This approach argues that the nation state is not dying (Krugman, 1996). On the contrary, the nation state policies are crucial to the development of the internationalization of the economy. National governments have been deeply implicated in the recent intensification of global trade (Callinicos et al., 1994, quoted in Held et al., 1999). Even the trans-national corporations that for the hyperglobalists are the primary agents of globalization maintain 2/3 of their actives in their home region or country and sell more or less the same portion of their goods or services (Hirst, 1997).

Global governance is another myth as the inequalities of the world have prevailed at the beginning of the 21st century. For the traditionalists the reality is that coordinated actions undertaken by the national states and the international institutions are a determining factor in maintaining control over the economy of the world (Hirst, 1997).

Traditionalists and tourism   The traditionalist approach in tourism also has the economy as its main analytic framework. From this point of view authors point out that domestic tourism represents 80% of all tourism movements, compared to international tourism (Vellas & Bécherel, 1995).

For authors like François Vellas and Lionel Bécherel what characterizes tourism at the end of the 20th century is regionalization and not global tourism. Europe has the dominant position due to the concentration of the travel flows to certain destinations in the region and to the effects of international travel towards the region itself. This is the effect of regionalism (Vellas & Bécherel, 1995). As shown previously regionalism is understood to be the opposite of globalization.

It is worth noticing that in the book written by Vellas and Bécherel and published in 1995 under the title of *International Tourism*, there is not even a mention in the index about globalization.

In much of the tourism literature and research there is a preference for the use of the term international tourism and not global tourism. The word international stresses the importance of the national framework. Nations are regarded as containers of homogenized tourists, in interrelation with each other as opposed to the global borderless capital, images or ideas of the hyperglobalists. This view does not reflect the changing reality of the nation state or the interconnections and flows that are not representative of any nation (Beck, 2000; Held et al., 1999; Wang, 2000).

Traditionalists tend to consider a tourist as a consumer of one country consuming in another one. In general terms human beings are the consumers of mass culture and tourism products. This tendency advocates that it is actually focusing on "real life" and "the real world" (Aramberri, 2001). As consumerism is a phenomenon born in the western countries, the expansion of tourism is also seen as the expansion of the West, and not the birth of a new global society.

The Transformationalist Approach

Conceptualization and historical trajectory[1] "At the heart of the transformationalist thesis is a conviction that, at the dawn of a new millennium, globalization is a central driving force behind the rapid social, political and economic changes that are reshaping modern societies and world order" (Held et al., 1999, p. 7).

In the transformationalist account globalization is responsible for the deep transformation of all spheres of human activity at the beginning of the new century. In this respect the transformationalist thesis is not responding to a linear logic as it does not claim to know an ideal model of globalization or the globalization last stage (Held et al., 1999). In comparison with the hyperglobalizers it does not understand globalization as a perfect global market, or a global civilization. But on the other hand, this approach does not agree with the traditionalists in their statement that globalization is just a myth or global hysteria. The transformationalists share the conviction that the changes in contemporary economic, social and political aspects of the world are "historically unprecedented" (Held et al., 1999, p. 7), and that such changes make global life today more complex than ever before in history (Beck, 2000). The world has never been so interdependent and interconnected, and our actions affect others as never before (Mulgan, 1998). Globalization is to be understood as a deeply rooted historical process, not a linear one, but one that is discontinues and that pulls societies in many directions. It is not a macro process coming from nowhere, such as the free capital, but the evolving of modernity in the history of humanity. Globalization is in this respect not a particularity but a set of processes that structure a global system. Any account of globalization relies on some kind of historical narrative (Held et al., 1999).

Globalization refers to spatio-temporal processes of change. "Accordingly, the concept of globalization implies first and foremost, a stretching of social, political and economic activities across frontiers such that events, decisions and activities in one region of the world can come to have significance for individuals and communities in distant regions of the world. In this sense, it embodies trans-regional interconnectedness, the widening reach of networks of social activity and power and the possibility of action at distance." (Held et al., 1999, p. 15).

Causal dynamics   The transformalists hold a critical stand point towards the narrower economic conceptualization of the phenomenon. Unlike the traditionalists this perspective points out that even though statistical data are important, they do not necessarily capture the qualitative shifts in the nature of societies. Globalization has to be conceived as a "highly differentiated process which finds expression in all the key domains of human activity" (Held et al., 1999, p. 12).

The driver of the processes of globalization is not only economic change and technological discoveries, although both questions are important. There is a complex intersection

---

[1]Although Held et al. in their work "*Global Transformations. Politics, Economics and Culture*" 1999, propose an analytical framework out of the three approaches, their framework can easily be connected to the transformationalist approach in such crucial issues as conceptualization and causal dynamics of globalization. Therefore, the presentation of their analytical framework for globalization is integrated as part of the transformationalists approach. We understand their analytic proposal not as a new school of thought about globalization but like a proposal inside the transformationalist's approach.

between a multiplicity of driving forces economical, political, cultural and technological that are experiencing change.

For the transformationalist approach modernity and globalization are linked together and interconnected in such a way that the understanding of the first will enlighten the understanding of the other and vice versa (Beck, 2000; Held et al., 1999; Sernau, 2000).

Socio-economic consequences   The impacts of globalization for the transformationalists are many and of great importance. The increased interconnectedness of globalization means that a complex global system connects the fate of one community to the fate of other communities around the globe (Held et al., 1999). These processes are not granting a greater convergence or homogeneity between the peoples of the world. On the contrary they structure *new forms of social inclusion and exclusion* (Bauman, 1998) inside every country as well as in global power relations. The North and the South are not longer geopolitical identities, globalization recasts traditional patterns of inclusion and exclusion forging new hierarchies that penetrate all the societies of the globe (Held et al., 1999). The classical divisions between the North and the South, the First World and the Third World are no longer only a macro level reality, they are now crossing and trespassing the geographical divisions as well as the levels of the territorial system and becoming a reality in all the major world cities. There is a *deterritorialization* and a new *reterritorialization* of economic activity that is at the core of the expansion of *global stratification* through all the territorial levels, local, regional, national and global (Bauman, 1998; Castells, 1996). The study of the stretching of human activities across frontiers explains the intensification, the extensity and the velocity patterns of such connections.

On the socio-cultural side the transformationalist approach sees the intensification of mutual dependence beyond national boundaries (Beck, 2000) not only as a matter of objectivity and action but as the *conscious reflexivity* on such action. The awareness of the world as a common home and a single place (Robertson, 1995). The transformation of the human condition by the conscious attention on globality. The local and the global are not to be understood as two mutually exclusive features. *Glocalization* is the transformationalist way of understanding cultural globalization (Robertson, 1995). Global culture is not a static phenomenon, in the same way that globalization in general is not a static particularity. The contradictory elements of universalism and particularism, connection and fragmentation, happen at the same time in human history, glocally. Surpassing the dichotomy of the understanding of the world the transformationalist approach is based on *the inclusive mode of distinction* (Beck, 2000). The exclusive mode of distinction uses the either-or logic, the inclusive mode of distinction understands the social, political and economical realities that fall out of the closed categories or separate worlds not as strange incidents but as new regular expressions (Beck, 2000).

Implications for the state power and governance   For most transformationalists globalization presents a new and unprecedented challenge to the modern nation states. The nation state is therefore in a process of reconstruction and re-invention. They challenge the traditionalists opinion that the state still remains sovereign in terms of power, functions or authority (Castells, 1996). The nation state has to share the monopoly of power with other political structures both at trans-national and local levels, "the primacy of the state in global politics is increasingly challenged, both from below and above" (Beck, 2000, p. 94). The methodology of the national order, for which nations were homogenous units with the same legal, economic and cultural order and autonomous from the rest of the world, can be a claim but is no longer a reality (Anheier & Katz, 2005; Held et al., 1999).

At the core of the transformationalists' thesis is the belief that a new sovereign regime is emerging, with deep implications for the future of democracy in our times, and this is a challenge to the enhancement in the world of political democratic principles such as accountability and legitimacy. Powerful new non-territorial forms of economic, social and political organizations push for greater influence and create new sites of power.

What About the People?

At the centre of the transformationalist way of understanding the world there is also a way of conceiving the human being in the world. These comments are only an introduction to a much wider discussion and debate in the realm of the social sciences about the linguistic turn, the critical theory, discourse theory, etc. (Giddens, 1984; Harvey, 1989), and it is an essential part of the transformationalist approach.

To clarify what human beings are, it is easier to specify first what human beings are not. Human beings are not only consumers, or examples of the economic rationality (economicism). Human beings are not only national citizens having homogenous and identical culture, language, beliefs and rights within their regional or national boundaries (nationalism). Human beings are not to be regarded as atoms floating in the world, unattached to one another, nature and technique (individualism). Human beings are not only acting through principles of rationality (rationalism).

Human beings are persons in interaction with the world. Human life is a life of interconnections. Humans only persist as long as the interconnections are a reality, as long as the lungs breathe air and the human brain perceives the reality surrounding it. In this sense "the constitution of the 'I' is created only through the 'discourse of the other' " (Giddens, 1984, p. 43). It is only in a dialogical (Habermas, 1987; 1998) and not dichotomical relation with the world that we can perceive and reflect on ourselves.

In a transformationalist understanding the human being is self-interpreting. All this cognitive endeavour involves interpretation, with a particular framework of concepts, beliefs and standards. There is not a theory-neutral observation language in social sciences (Wang, 2000). All our self-understandings, as well as all our understandings of other things are rooted in history. This process of self-understanding and understandings relates back to ourselves and lays the path for the transformation of the conditions of our own life.

A Transformationalist Understanding of Globalization in Tourism

Ning Wang in his book *Tourism and Modernity. A Sociological Analysis*, understands globalization as the next stage of modernity. He shares the idea of the transformationalists that the root to globalization is already present in modernity, first through imperialism and colonialism and now as the "villagization" of the earth (Wang, 2000, p. 125). Inbound tourism characterizes the first modernity and the expansion of international tourism is the core of the last modernity. Globalization is an expression of the development from the first modernity to the late modernity and its social-spatial strategy (Wang, 2000).

Globalization, through transformationalism, is understood as a process deep rooted in history and as a face of the late modernity project and subsequently is to the understanding of tourism an expression of modernity. "The modern subject is a subject on the move. Central to the idea of modernity is that of movement, that modern societies have brought about striking changes in the nature and experience of motion or travel. (…) In many ways the modern world is inconceivable without these new forms of long-distance transportation and travel. It is not the pedestrian flâneur who is emblematic of modernity but rather, the train-passenger, car driver and jet plane passenger" (Urry, 1995, p. 141).

Tourism is an interdisciplinary field of study, and as such the academic community has repeatedly approached this study by focusing on parts of the phenomenon rather than considering it as a part of a whole system, in the way that during decades a narrower specialization in different fields has become the rule in the academic world (Brown, 1998; Jafari, 1987). The claim of a systemic perspective is also a claim of the transformationalist approach.

The understanding of the relationship between the development of the world system and the development of tourism is also the focus of other authors who present the understanding of non-linear methods as something fundamental in the study of complex systems (Farrell & Twining-Ward, 2003; Milne & Ateljevic, 2001). Dirk Reiser in his study of the Otago Peninsula makes a claim for the plural understanding of globalization as well as for a historical approach to the phenomenon (Reiser, 2003). These positions agree with the critique of the transformationalists to the linear approach of both traditionalists and hyperglobalists. The transformationalists' spatio-temporal awareness as well as their historic perspective is reflected in the demand of Farrell and Twining-Ward of commitment to the principles of complex adaptative systems within tourism (Farrell & Twining-Ward, 2003).

Several authors have pointed to the need of surpassing the everlasting dichotomy of local-global, particular-universal, we-others (Brown, 1998; Burns, 2004; Teo & Li, 2003; Teo & Yeoh, 1997) similar to the tranformationalists they use new ways of understanding social change through glocalization, inclusive distinctions, reflexivity, etc.

John Urry in the second edition of his book *The tourist gaze* devotes a whole chapter to the globalization issue. His perspective on globalization mainly inspired by the idea of Bauman of the "liquid modernity" (Bauman, 2000, quoted in Urry, 2002, p. 141) shares the transformationalist focus on flows and networks rather than fixed particular conditions: "There are not two separate entities, the 'global' and 'tourism' bearing some external connections with each other. Rather they are part and parcel of the same set of complex and interconnected processes" (Urry, 2002, p. 144). The question of deterritorialization explored in the transformationalist debate is also to be seen in Urry's "end of tourism" theory (Urry, 2002, p. 161), when he argues that the specific time–space in tourism is changing towards a mobile "economy of signs" (Urry, 2002, p. 161). Deterritoralization is also one of the important issues of the study made by Robert Wood on globalization in cruise tourism (Wood, 2000).

The feature, stressed by the traditionalists and in this case shared by the transformationalists that global interaction not only brings harmony and homogeneity but also fragmentation and conflict, is nothing new to many of the authors on tourism and globalization. Many researchers define tourism as a phenomenon with light and dark sides, and tourism is very often expressed as being a double-edged sword (Brohman, 1996).

The state is still an important player in tourism policy, even if the hyperglobalists argue that the importance of the nation state has diminished to a minimum. Authors such as Milne and Ateljevic write that "from a tourism perspective national governments often appear to be playing a more active role in coordinating the tourism marketing campaigns and broad-based product development that play such an important role in shaping tourism demand and behaviour" (Milne & Ateljevic, 2001, p. 373). The pressure towards the nation state also comes from local areas as the transformationalists suggested. In two research articles about tourism planning the focus of attention is zonal development through the local community (Burns, 2004; Russell, 2003). The question is to what extent this "very" local approach tends to diminish the importance of the nation state as a force for planning and structuring inside its territory? When looking at the pressure coming from above and below, there are many authors that have identified multinational corporations or international institutions as crucial to the understanding of the restructuring of power relations in tourism (Brown, 1998; Smeral, 1998; Teo & Li, 2003; Wang, 2000; Wood, 2000).

In tourism theory the idea of tourism as a recent phenomenon is generally accepted even though there have been tourists throughout the époques of human history. It is the increase in intensity and in extensity of the phenomenon that makes a difference between the pre-modern and the late modern tourism. From a transformationalist point of view this relates to the understanding of the relationship between globalization and tourism as deeply rooted in history, and with a clear spatio-temporal dimension (Wang, 2000).

Other authors such as C. Michael Hall or Peter Burns (2001) stand for a transformationalist approach to globalization in the book *Tourism in the Age of Globalization* (Wahab & Cooper, 2001). The book in its totality cannot give a common perspective on the phenomenon. In the first chapter of the book entitled *Tourism, Globalization and the Competitive Advantage of Nations* Salah Wahab and Chris Cooper go through several definitions of globalization in a row, from Ohmae, a clear hyperglobalist to McGrew a transformationalist, not taking into account the very different methodological implications that each approach has for the research presented.

Rethinking the Concept of the Tourist from a Transformationalist Perspective

Globalization theory has to refer to the human being, as much as Tourism theory has to refer to the tourist. Linked to the transformationalists theories of globalization regarding the people is the relating concept of the tourist in a globalized world.

In a traditional political and social theory, the questions of which kind of political and legal implications touristhood should have do not correspond to the answers. For traditionalists the conceptualization of citizenship relies on the Westphalian understanding of political life (Held, 1997). The rule of law is a national conquest. From a Westphalian view (Held, 1997) tourists leave their political dimension at home while packing for their trip. A traditionalist nationalist understanding of tourism and the tourist in globalization also has a problematic normative dimension. A tourist without a political dimension, without rights and duties, can never be the grounds for sustainability. It is an issue that is not only about conserving the environment or enhancing the local culture, but fighting for human dignity. Although the question of the relationship between the host and the guest has been treated largely in tourism literature, its predominant visions are from a cultural, social and economical perspective, the political dimensions of such relations remains mainly unexplored (Tosum, 2002; WTO, 1998).

The transformationalist approach challenges the traditionalist understanding by criticizing the nationalism methodologies (Beck, 2000), and opens the door to the understanding of tourists as global citizens. From a transformationalist approach to globalization theory citizenship moves to where the person moves. Rights and duties are not rooted but mobile. The realms of law are not in geography but in the same human being. The host–guest relationship is not to be regarded as a private one, not only as a question of the exchange of money for service, but as a contractual relationship with a clear public, civic dimension. The rule of law can also be trans-nationalized through globalization forces as well as commodities, technology and capital. Transformationalism brings a new understanding for political transfer (Held et al., 1999). By the simple act of becoming a tourist, a person gains some rights but also some duties. From this thesis, a new understanding of conflict resolution may be formed between the guest and the host.

According to Reiser all definitions of tourism evolve around "one or more of the following elements: tourism as the movement of people, tourism as a sector of the economy; tourism as a broad system of interaction relationship of people and their need to travel. Therefore involving a time dimension, a space dimension (people moving) and the exclusion/inclusion of people" (Reiser, 2003, p. 310). The transformationalist understanding of globalization connects with this last part of the text of Reiser.

The tourist should not be understood in a narrow manner. Again it is clearer to explain what tourists are not in a transformationalist perception. Tourists are not only consumers, not only national representatives of their country of residence, they are not only atomized individuals. *The tourist is the reflexive knowledgeable person moving out of its ordinary space for a relatively short period of time and reincorporating him/herself again to its ordinary space.* The ordinary (Jafari, 1987) is what the tourist reflexively understands at her/his "home", the relative short period is again a reflexive variable.

Final Considerations

A summary of the contributions of the different approaches has been structured in Table 19.1. The three approaches to globalization are classified in the table by the dominant features of the theory which are the causal dynamics underlying the relation of tourism in the global system, the historical trajectory of tourism compared to the understanding of the historical trajectory of globalization, the conceptualization of the individual or human being in the case of globalization and of the individual as tourist, the general definition of globalization and its reflection on the understanding of tourism and globalization, the dominant motive of some particular issues or images that in that approach represent globalization as such or globalization and tourism and finally the conceptualization based on a linear or non-linear methodology.

Table 19.1: The three approaches method and tourism.

The three approaches	Globalization's						
	Dominant features	Causal dynamics	Historical trajectory	Human dimension	Definition	Dominant motive	Conceptualization
Hyperglobalizers	Global market and global society	Capitalism and technology	Global civilization	Global consumers	A new framework for human action	Mcdonalds, Hollywood, etc.	Linear development fixed particularity
Hyperglobalizers and tourism	Tourism as a global market tourist as consumer	Capitalism and technology	Global tourism	Everybody can become a tourist	A new framework for tourism development	Standarization, theme parks, disneyfication	Linear development fixed particularity
Traditionalists	World less interdependent than in 1890	States and markets	Clash of civilizations and regional blocks	National consumers	Internationalization and regionalization	National interest	Linear development fixed particularity
Traditionalists and tourism	Tourism as different regional markets and tourists as national citizens	National, local and regional tourism policies and national and regional tourists markets	International tourism development dependent of the regions	Inbound tourists and national typification of the tourist when abroad	Internationalization of tourism and regionalization of international tourism	Inbound tourism, national interest	Linear development fixed particularity
Transformationalist	"Thick", extensive and intensive globalization	Combined forces of modernity	Indeterminate: global inter-action and fragmentation	Global citizens	The reordering of interregional relations and action at distance	Transformation of political community	Open-ended historical process differentiated process
Transformationalists and tourism	"Thick" intensive and extensive global tourism	Combined forces of modernity	Indeterminate: tourism as a double edged sword	Global tourists as global citizens	Understanding of tourism system as part of the reordering of international relations and action at distance	Every item of culture becomes "Touristifiable," glocalization	Open-ended historical process differentiated process

Conclusion: A New Landscape for Research in Tourism

Through the study of the literature of globalization and specifically the one studying globalization and tourism these are some of the answers to the question addressed in this chapter.

1 The method of the three approaches has been shown to be useful in clarifying the different positions that tourism researchers have on globalization and several conclusions can be drawn from this theoretical analysis.

Two important critiques can be opposed to the hyperglobalist as well as to the traditionalist approach. They both rely on a methodology with a linear approach and a pre-conceptual idea of the final reality of globalization. In this way they share a "metaphysical component". Their analysis remains in the domains of the dichotomy of the either-or logic; nation-global, regional-global, in this sense one particularity excludes the other. This methodology fails because it ignores the possibilities of the overlapping of particularities (inclusive distinctions) and of a glocalization approach.

Although during recent years many researchers of tourism have included the study of globalization in their analysis, no one has intended to present a complete systemic understanding of globalization. Most contributions are a collection of views of different positions on globalization, a sum of theories and statements, however a global understanding of the phenomenon has not yet emerged from within the community of researchers in tourism.

Through the literature review of globalization and tourism there are examples and positions that can be categorized as belonging to the three different approaches, but the hyperglobalist approach happens to be more common than the traditionalist or transformationalist approach in the literature addressed in this chapter. Further research could focus on the implications of the methodological problems related to hyperglobalists and traditionalist position when used in tourism.

2 Other relevant issues in relation to the normative conclusions regarding the relevance of a proposal of a methodology based on the transformationalist approach to globalization for tourism research are:

The sum of the undertaken study of the globalization theory in tourism emphasized the understanding of globalization as a deep rooted historical phenomenon and as a force for change in our modern world. This argument follows the transformationalist approach as opposed to the hyperglobalist or traditionalist. Transformationalism does not have a pre-conceptual and ideal picture of what globalization is. It is an approach that takes into consideration the spatio-temporal dimensions such as the levels of extensity, intensity and velocity of the globalization processes, the organizational dimensions as well as the historical periods of globalization, in a dynamic framework, which changes in time and space. Future research related to this analysis may focus on the study of the stretching of the human activities across frontiers related to tourism analysing for example the intensity, the extensity, the impact propensity and the velocity patterns of such connections.

Many authors in tourism do not conceptualize globalization in an all evolving explanation but when describing global development and tourism they refer to many aspects related to the transformationalist approach. They can be considered as partial but very important contributions to the transformationalist understanding of globalization and its relation to tourism. In this sense the most important feature is that several researchers in tourism agree in the use of the same methodology, non-linear and historically rooted, the relevance of spatio-temporal dimensions, as well as, the conceptualization of modernity to understand the process of social transformation.

The transformationalist understanding of the human being enlightens the concept of the tourist. The conclusion is that the reflexive tourist in his/her movement away from home brings his/her self-understanding and interpretations with him/her. In this sense, all the processes of becoming and being a tourist can be understood as making a contribution to the arena of global discourse. Therefore, a shadow of a global citizenship in practice can be seen in the action of becoming and being a tourist as well as in the inter-relation of all other men and women with the tourists. The dialectic relationship of the ordinary and non-ordinary world (Jafari, 1987) has a political dimension. This has clear implications for the way that the tourism academic world understands tourism policy. To have a transformationalist globalization approach to tourism policy will demand that tourists are seen as active participants together with both the local population and local and national institutions, when deciding what the future for tourism should look like. Much further research can be used to analyse the political dimension of tourists in globalization.

References

Anheier, H., & Katz, H. (2005). Network approaches to global civil society. In: H. Anheier, M. Glasius, & M. Kaldor (Eds), *Global Civil Society 2004/5* (pp. 206–221). London: Sage.

Anheier, H., Glasius M., & Kaldor, M. (Eds). (2001). *Global civil society 2001*. New York: Oxford University Press.

Aramberri, J. (2001). The host should get lost. Paradigms in the tourist theory. *Annals of Tourism Research*, *28*(3), 738–761.

Askjellerud, S. (2003). The tourist: A messenger of peace? *Annals of Tourism Research*, *30*(3), 741–744.

Barber, B. R. (1995). *Jihad vs. McWorld*. New York: Times Books.

Barber, B. R. (2003). *Fear's empire: war, terrorism, and democracy*. New York: W.W. Norton & Ci.

Bauman, Z. (1998). *Globalization. The human consequences*. Cambridge, UK: Blackwell Publishers.

Beck, U. (2000). *What is globalization*. Cambridge, UK: Polity Press.

Bhagwati, J. (2004). *In defense of globalization*. New York: Oxford University Press.

Brohman, J. (1996). New directions in tourism for third world development. *Annals of Tourism Research*, *23*(1), 48–70.

Brown, F. (1998). *Tourism reassessed. Blight or blessing?* Oxford: Butterworth-Heinemann.

Burns, P. (2001). Brief encounters. Culture, tourism and the local-global nexus. In: S. Wahab & C. Cooper (Eds), *Tourism in the age of globalization* (pp. 290–305). London: Routledge.

Burns, P. (2004). Tourism planning: A third way. *Annals of Tourism Research*, *31*(1), 24–43.

Castells, M. (1996). *The information age: economy, society and culture*. Oxford Chicago: Blackwell.

Dahl, R. A. (1989). *Democracy and its critics*. New Haven and London: Yale University Press.

Daly, H. E. (1996). *Efter Væksten*. Denmark: Hovedland.

De la Dehesa, G. (2000). *Comprender la globalización*. Madrid: Alianza Editorial.

Déniz Espinós, J. (2003). La globalització i el desenvolupament a l'Amèrica Llatina. In: C. Groizard (Ed.), *Globalització i Desenvolupament* (pp. 101–126). Palma: Universitat de les Illes Balears.

Farrell, B. H., & Twining-Ward, L. (2003). Reconceptualizing tourism. *Annals of Tourism Research*, *31*(2), 274–295.

Ghemawat, P. (2001). *Globalization as market integration and the future of international business.* Working paper. Harvard Business School, Boston, United States.

Giddens, A. (1984). *The constitution of society.* Cambridge: Polity Press.

Giddens, A. (1990). *The consequences of modernity.* Cambridge: Polity Press.

Go, F., & Ritchie, J. R. B. (1990). Tourism and transnationalism. *Tourism Management, 11*(4), 287–290.

Gray, J. (1998). *False down. The delusions of global capitalism.* London: Granta Publications.

Habermas, J. (1987). *Samtalens fornuft.* Charlottenlund, DK: Rosinante.

Habermas, J. (1998). *Facticidad y validez.* Madrid: Trotta.

Hall, C. M. (2001). Territorial economic integration and globalization. In: S. Wahab & C. Cooper (Eds), *Tourism in the age of globalization* (pp. 22–44). London: Routledge.

Harvey, D. (1989). *The condition of postmodernity.* Oxford: Blackwell.

Held, D. (1997). *La democracia y el orden global.* Barcelona: Paidós.

Held, D., Mc Grew, A., Goldblatt, D., & Perraton, J. (1999). *Global transformations. Politics, economics and culture.* Cambridge, UK: Polity Press.

Hirst, P. (1997). *Globalisering, Demokrati og det Civile Samfund.* Copenhagen: Hans Reitzels Forlag.

Holjevac, I. A. (2003). A vision of tourism and the hotel industry in the 21st century. *Hospitality Management, 22,* 129–134.

Huntington, S. (2004). El reto hispano a EEUU. *Foreign Policy Edición Española.* April/May 2004, 20–35.

Jafari, J. (1987). Tourism models: the sociocultural aspects. *Tourism Management, 8*(2), 151–159.

Jafari, J. (Ed.) (2000). *Encyclopedia of tourism.* London: Routledge.

Knowles, T., Diamantis, D., & Bey El-Mourhabi, J. (2001). *The globalization of tourism and hospitality. A strategic perspective.* Trowbridge, UK: Cromwell Press.

Krugman, P. (1996). *Pop internationalism.* Cambridge, Massachusetts: The Massachusetts Institute of Technology Press.

Martorell Cunill, O. (2002). *Cadenas hoteleras. Analisis del top 10.* Barcelona: Ariel.

Milne, S., & Ateljevic, I. (2001). Tourism, economic development and the global-local nexus: Theory embracing complexity. *Tourism Geographies, 3*(4), 369–393.

Mulgan, G. (1998). *Connexity: responsibility, freedom, business and power in the new century.* London: Vintage.

Ohmae, K. (1990). *The borderless world.* London: Collins.

Reid, D. (2003). *Tourism, globalization, and development. Responsible tourism planning.* London: Pluto Press.

Reiser, D. (2003). Globalisation: An old phenomenon that needs to be rediscovered for tourism? *Tourism and Hospitality Research, 4*(4), 306–320.

Ritzer, G. (1996). *La Macdonalización de la Sociedad.* Barcelona: Ariel.

Robertson, R. (1995). Glocalization: Time–space and homogeneity-heterogeneity. In: M. Featherstone, S. Lash & R. Robertson (Eds), *Global modernities.* London: Sage.

Rodrik, D. (2001). *The global governance of trade as if development really mattered.* United Nations Development Programme publications.

Russell, R. V. (2003). Tourists and refugees. Coinciding sociocultural impacts. *Annals of Tourism Research, 30*(4), 833–846.

Ryan, C. (1997). Reports: limits to globalization – A review of "Globalization and Tourism" – The 46th Congress of the International Association of Scientific Experts in Tourism (AIEST), Rotorua, New Zealand – September, 1996. *Tourism Management, 18*(3), 184–186.

Santamaría, A. (2003). L'Impacte de la Globalització a l'Africa. In: C. Groizard (Ed.), *Globalització i Desenvolupament* (pp. 127–144). Palma: Universitat de les Illes Balears.

Sernau, S. (2000). *Bound: Living in the globalized world*. Connecticut: Kumarian Press.

Smeral, E. (1998). The impact of globalization on small and medium enterprises: New challenges for tourism policies in the European countries. *Tourism Management, 19*(4), 371–380.

Stiglitz, J. (2002). *Globalization and its discontents*. New York: W.W. Norton.

Sugiyarto, G., Blake, A., & Sinclair, T. (2003). Tourism and globalization. Economic impact in Indonesia. *Annals of Tourism Research, 30*(3), 683–701.

Teo, P., & Li, L. H. (2003). Global and local interactions in tourism. *Annals of Tourism Research, 30*(2), 287–306.

Teo, P., & Yeoh, B. (1997). Remaking local heritage for tourism. *Annals of Tourism Research, 4*(1), 192–213.

Tosum, C. (2002). Host perceptions of impacts. A comparative tourism study. *Annals of Tourism Research, 29*(1), 231–253.

Turner, L., & Ash, J. (1975). *The golden hordes. International tourism and the pleasure periphery*. London: Constable.

United Nations Development Programme (UNDP) (2003). *Human development report 2003*. New York: Oxford University Press.

Urry, J. (1995). *Consuming places*. New York: Routledge.

Urry, J. (2002). *The tourist gaze* (2nd ed.). London: Sage.

Vellas, F., & Bécherel, L. (1995). *International tourism*. New York: St. Martin's Press.

Wahab, S., & Cooper, C. (Eds). (2001). *Tourism in the age of globalization*. London: Routledge.

Wang, N. (2000). *Tourism and modernity. A sociological analysis*. Tourism Social Sciences Series. Oxford: Elsevier Science Ltd.

Wood, R. (2000). Caribbean cruise tourism. Globalization at sea. *Annals of Tourism Research, 27*(2), 345–370.

World Tourism Organization (WTO) (1998). *Introducción al turismo*. Madrid: WTO.

World Tourism Organization (WTO) (1999). *Tourism: 2020 vision*. Madrid: WTO.

World Tourism Organization (WTO) (2002). *Tendencias de los mercados turísticos: panorama mundial y actualidad del turismo-2002*. Madrid: WTO.

World Watch Institute (2003). *The state of the world*. London: Earthscan.

World Watch Institute (2004). *L'estat del món*. Barcelona: Centre Unesco de Catalunya.

Chapter 20

The End of Tourism, the Beginning of Law?

Brian Simpson and Cheryl Simpson

Introduction

This chapter seeks to investigate how law constructs tourism. What we mean by this is that law has to be seen as not some simple regulatory mechanism within which travel and tourism takes place, but that it can be read as text which sends powerful messages about how tourism is to be understood. The messages are powerful because of the privileged position which law occupies in the social order. But this does not mean that law cannot be analysed as another expression of cultural understandings about social phenomenon and critiqued on the same basis.

We propose to conduct this analysis in the first instance through an examination of how legal discourse has been engaged to construct what we suggest are "new" understandings of tourism. In the main this has been done through embracing the language of human rights and environmental sustainability in framing laws – more usually at the level of international law – which are designed to regulate and construct tourism and the tourist experience. This process can be broadly recognised in what has become known as "ethical tourism". The problem for the law has been that this recasting of tourism around ethics has created dilemmas akin to other areas of law which invoke notions such as the "public interest" in pursuit of socially just outcomes. The major dilemma is, of course, to define precisely which set of values is to be used to determine what is socially just.

This dilemma is not simply a problem "for" law but is, we argue, a problem "of" law. Law tends to present itself to the world as a unified body of rules which can be applied to particular situations or phenomenon. We agree with Smart however who rejects this idea of law. As she says, "law operates with conflicting principles and contradictory effects at every level from High Court judgements to administrative law" (Smart, 1989, p. 4). However, traditional legal method denies this view of law and presents law as a discipline which can affect change for the better in the world. As Smart says:

> Law sets itself outside the social order, as if through the application of legal method and rigour, it becomes a thing apart which can in turn reflect upon the world from which it is divorced. (Smart, 1989, p. 11)

Smart's project is to demonstrate how law constructs a particular view of women's lives as "truth" and then presents the (legal) solution to that "reality". In effect she argues that as law is the product of patriarchal relationships, then how can we expect that it will deliver real benefits to women's lives. But there is also a broader point here about how law responds to the plight of those who suffer disadvantage. As Smart writes:

> [I] refer to the assumption that law functions to right wrongs, to create more rights, and hence to empower the disadvantaged. I drew a comparison with medicine which has also been presumed to cure ills and make whole the infirm. However, we are also aware of the iatrogenic potential of medicine, namely its ability to create illness and disease in the process of striving for cures. It is time we extended this insight to the field of law. We need to consider the extent that in exercising law we may produce effects that make conditions worse, and that in worsening conditions we make the mistake of assuming that we need to apply more doses of legislation. (Smart, 1989, p. 161)

Feminist legal academics have utilised such an approach to identify the manner in which the contradictions in law support the broad arguments of scholars such as Smart. Their concern is primarily with the disadvantage and discrimination suffered by women and how law constructs and deals with that disadvantage. It is our argument that tourism too has in recent years been constructed in law as a problem of disadvantage and that law has presented the solution in terms of granting more rights to those disadvantaged by tourism. But in the tradition of Smart, we also ask whether the assumption that such rights actually improve the lives of those affected is well founded. It is our suspicion that the interests that sit behind law have been able to construct a definition of tourism which actually disempowers the disadvantaged under the guise of improving their lives.

It is at this point that one may come to the conclusion that law is not so much the solution to "unethical" or "harmful" tourism as part of the problem. Notions such as "ethical" tourism probably do more to disguise rather than address the problems created by exploitation within tourism, or perhaps more precisely what may be regarded as the "essence" of tourism. As Crick argues, citing Boorstin and Fussell:

> Boorstin ... stresses the difference between 'travelling' [with its etymological connection to the notion of work (*travail*)] and 'tourism' (the apotheosis of the pseudo, where passivity rather than activity reigns). Tourism is a form of experience packaged to prevent real contact with others, a manufactured, trivial, unauthentic way of being, a form of travel emasculated, made safe by commercialism.... For Fussell, to write about tourism is necessarily to write satire, for the 'travel industry' is a contradiction in terms: Exploration is discovering the undiscovered; travel is at least intended to reveal what history has discovered; tourism, on the other hand, is merely about a world discovered (or even created) by entrepreneurs, packaged and then marketed. (Crick, 1989, p. 308)

Crick bemoans the lack of social science research on tourism and thus a lack of evidence upon which to base any understanding of the impact of tourism on local communities (Crick, 1989, p. 310). We shall return to Crick's ideas, but this point is significant here for thinking about the role of the law in constructing tourism. If Crick is correct and there is limited social scientific data about the impacts of tourism on communities, then how can the law protect society from the negative aspects of tourism when the negative consequences have not been properly identified? The short answer can be found in Teubner's application of autopoietic theory to law. This is the idea that law is a self-referential system which can construct its own reality about social phenomenon albeit drawing on other bodies of knowledge:

> Interference of law and other social discourses does not mean that they merge into a multi-dimensional super discourse, nor does it imply that information is 'exchanged' among them. Rather, information is constituted anew in each discourse and interference adds nothing but the simultaneity of two communicative events. (Teubner, 1989, p. 745, cited in King & Piper, 1990, p. 18)

In other words law can construct its own meaning of the tourist experience and then present its "legal" solution. The problem is that in construing the world in its particular way, it may also misconstrue. As King and Piper note:

> Law's *raison d'être* is as a body which conceptualises the world into rights and duties on which it can adjudicate and which swings into action when an individual, personal or corporate, wishes to activate a right or impose a duty. The law's actions are largely reactive. They are determined by the nature of rights and duties embodied in law, which, in civil law jurisdictions and increasingly in common law jurisdictions, is made by external agencies, notably the legislature. (King & Piper, 1990, p. 11)

Although King and Piper are addressing themselves to the manner in which law confronts child welfare, the approach seems similarly apt for how law deals with the problem of the impact of tourism, given Crick's stance on the lack of social science data on the impact of tourism on communities. This might suggest that law has even greater latitude to construct a "reality" around tourism than in other areas where more science exists, suggesting that the law's response to tourism is even more problematic. King and Piper's point is:

> not that science is superior in any absolute terms but rather that, while law's truths may be effective within law's own normative domain, their idiosyncratic nature and dependence upon normative operations may make them highly inappropriate as a basis for reality construction… (King & Piper, 1990, p. 6)

We would suggest that this passage can be applied to the area of tourism and its impacts. If we combine Smart's analysis of law as a package of contradictions – though presented as a unitary discipline – with Teubner's and King and Piper's notion that law is self-referential and can construct its own discourse, we come to the law which regulates and defines tourism as a problem rather than a solution, full of contradictions and inconsistencies which far from making sense of tourism, blur, confuse, and even destroy it.

If one accepts that tourism is by definition exploitative (Crick, 1989) and advances certain interests over others, then where the law seeks to construct tourism as something which can be pursued in an ethical manner we need to ask whether this is a deception. What we propose is that law has to be analysed and critiqued for the role it plays in providing a smokescreen within which tourism pursues patterns of exploitation. It is at this point that our discussion intersects with the theme of the "end of tourism", and our example of laws which regulate the free movement of people and capital which are as much a part of discussions about tourism as they are about immigration control. The consequence of an examination of the function of law from this broader perspective is that all laws relating to the movement and regulation of people become part of the discussion of the tourist/ traveller in the modern world. The "end of tourism" then is also a consequence of this approach for "tourism" is no more than a legal construction which ebbs and flows according to prevailing ideas of what is "appropriate" travel. In this sense, there can be no "ethical tourism" because tourism can be regarded as intrinsically "unethical" and so the role of the law is not to "fix" bad practice in tourism but to allow the exploitative practices of tourism to continue under the guise of "lawful cover".

In other words, the social forces which produce travel and mobility around the world (along with the exploitative and oppressive practices which underpin that mobility) are the same forces which produce the legal framework within which this occurs. For that reason, law has to be seen as flowing from that oppression and not something that sits outside and regulates it (Smart, 1989). Thus to understand how law regulates movement is to understand how it constructs tourism. In that sense there is no tourism law, only laws which relate to movement, surveillance and control of those who travel, making the label "tourist" a malleable and transitory state.

Reconstructing Tourism around Human Rights Discourse and Global Tolerance

The past three decades in particular have witnessed the increased articulation of tourism in terms of the human rights of people affected by its impacts. This discourse contains a mix of human rights and sustainability concerns. Much of this discourse has emanated from the offices of the World Tourism Organisation (WTO) – an agency of the United Nations – and is supported by a series of "legal" documents. The basis of what we would call this "legal discourse" can be found in the Statutes of the WTO which state that the:

> fundamental aim of the Organization shall be the promotion and development of tourism with a view to contributing to economic development, international understanding, peace, prosperity, and universal respect for, and observance of, human rights and fundamental freedoms for all without distinction as to race, sex, language or religion. The Organization shall take all appropriate action to attain this objective. (WTO Statutes, Art 3(1))

One action taken by the WTO in furtherance of these objectives has been the sponsorship of a number of conferences which have led to various statements and declarations. In 1980, for example, a conference in Manila gave rise to the *Manila Declaration on World Tourism* which proclaimed that:

> world tourism can develop in a climate of peace and security which can be achieved through the joint efforts of all States in promoting the reduction of international tension and in developing international cooperation in a spirit of friendship, *respect for human rights*, and understanding among all States. (Manila Declaration on World Tourism, Preamble) (our emphasis)

The Declaration also proclaimed its faith in the ability of tourism to "contribute to a new international economic order" that would "help to eliminate the widening gap between developed and developing countries" (Manila Declaration on World Tourism, Preamble). The Declaration further stated the primacy of spiritual over technical and material factors in tourism, which referred to:

(a) the total fulfilment of the human being;
(b) a constantly increasing contribution to education;
(c) equality of destiny of nations;
(d) the liberation of man in a spirit of respect for his dignity and destiny;
(e) the affirmation of the originality of cultures and respect for the moral heritage of peoples (Manila Declaration on World Tourism, Article 21).

Further documents have built upon these themes of respect for human rights and tourism's role in promoting global tolerance: the *Acapulco Documents on the Rights to Holidays 1982, Tourism Bill of Rights and Tourism Codes 1985, The Hague Declaration on Tourism 1985*, and the *Manila Declaration on the Social Impacts of Tourism 1997*.

An important underpinning of these documents has always been the free movement of people, as it is clear that tourism – and thus access to its perceived benefits – requires the movement of people around the globe and within countries. The Acapulco document recognised that the objectives and goals of world tourism can only be achieved "within the general framework of freedom of movement and travel" (*Acapulco Documents on the Rights to Holidays 1982*, Article 9(d)). This principle was to operate within the limitations imposed by "the existing social and economic conditions of each country, its sovereignty, legislation and traditions as well as the rights and duties of its citizens" (*Acapulco Documents on the Rights to Holidays* 1982, Article 9(d)(iv)). But herein lies the problem – where is the line between facilitating the free movement of tourists and the protection of national sovereignty to be drawn? And what interests will determine how this line is drawn?

This becomes a critical issue for the role of law in tourism as it will be called on to define what is "acceptable" movement and what is not. Indeed, this is expressly stated in the Acapulco document itself where it calls for "national legislative, statutory and financial bodies (and other relevant organisations)" to harmonise "the easing, wherever practicable, of travel formalities in respect of entry into and exit from the territory, customs, and currency and health regulations." (*Acapulco Documents on the Rights to Holidays 1982,* Article 17(d))

The *Tourism Bill of Rights and Tourist Code 1985* also develops the notion of free movement for tourists through its provisions which call for the free movement of domestic and international tourists "without prejudice to any limitative measures taken in the national interest concerning certain areas of the territory" (Article V). It also emphasises the right of tourists to free access to places of tourist interest, and "freedom of movement in places of transit and sojourn." (Article XIII)

What is the role of the law in giving effect to this principle of freedom of movement? Once translated into a legal matter, the issue of who is a "tourist" becomes a matter of definition and it is through the process of definition that the law can in effect remove from those who fall outside the definition the "human right" that is being claimed, while supporting it for those who fall within the definition. Thus, as we will see, the question of whether one is a "tourist", "refugee", or "asylum seeker" will determine how one's freedom of movement is to be determined.

The principles of human rights referred to above have also become embedded in one of the most recent expressions of the WTO's aims: the *Global Code of Ethics for Tourism*. This document proclaims a "right to tourism" which in itself demands freedom of movement:

> The prospect of direct and personal access to the discovery and enjoyment of the planet's resources constitutes a right equally open to all the world's inhabitants; the increasingly extensive participation in national and international tourism should be regarded as one of the best possible expressions of the sustained growth of free time, and obstacles should not be placed in its way. (*Global Code of Ethics For Tourism*, Article 7)

This then leads to support for freedom of movement in the following terms:

> Tourists and visitors should benefit, in compliance with international law and national legislation, from the liberty to move within their countries and from one State to another, in accordance with Article 13 of the Universal Declaration of Human Rights; they should have access to places of transit and stay and to tourism and cultural sites without being subject to excessive formalities or discrimination. (*Global Code of Ethics For Tourism*, Article 7)

Yet one can see a contradiction within the terms of this document itself. This statement of "ethical" principle for tourism contains within it the potential for discrimination, for it is apparent that the principles of respect and tolerance are to be proffered to those who are "tourists". For those who fall outside that definition it is presumably justifiable to indeed discriminate, and this will become apparent in the analysis of a recent House of Lords decision which we conduct below. It is the tourist who possesses the human rights according to this document. Of course, it may be said that this document is only addressed to tourists and so it does not preclude the human rights of others. But it is implicit in the document that free movement is not the norm and that tourists should not suffer the same level of control afforded to others.

Ethical Tourism: Contradictions and Continuities

Our argument has been that the law both contains and reflects the contradictions contained within tourism, while claiming to produce an "appropriate" legal solution to the "reality" of tourism. The above WTO documents reflect an increasing role for tourism in promoting human rights and mutual understanding. Crick responds to this claimed "peace and under-standing" benefit of tourism by referring to the very 1980 conference in Manila (which produced the *Declaration on World Tourism* above) and in which the need to preserve Philippine culture was asserted while at the same time the city was said to have 10,000 prostitutes "at the disposal of international tourists and members of the local elite" (Crick, 1989, p. 328). This point suggests a quite different reality than that envisaged by the law. As Crick notes further:

> Tourism is very much about *our* culture, not about *their* culture or our desire to learn about it. This explains the presence in guidebooks of sites and signs that have little genuine historic or living connection to a culture but that exist simply as markers in the touristic universe. As Barthes remarks, perceptively, travel guidebooks are actually instruments of blindness. They do not, in other words, tell one about another culture at all. (Crick, 1989, p. 328)

He also refers to the suggestion that international tourism narrows the mind rather than broad-ens it. The claim here is that travellers are indifferent to the social reality of their hosts and empirical evidence is that individual perceptions are replaced with stereotypes. Crick sug-gests that the mystifying images promoted by the tourism industry are part of the industry itself and should not prevent a "realistic and empirical analysis of this industry and its con-sequences" (Crick, 1989, p. 329). Crick's analysis makes us confront the extent to which tourism is by definition exploitative and repressive. In this context the notion of "ethical tourism" seems to be a contradiction, yet the law – at least through the various documents produced by the WTO and endorsed by the UN and national governments – suggests that tourism can be made ethical and its negative impacts moderated or eliminated.

The notion that there exists a contradiction between this discourse of tourism based on human rights and global tolerance concerns and the discourse of tourism as one which is in essence opposed to understanding others is also supported by work on the experience of tourists in cities who seek out "pre-packaged" and sanitised presentations of cities they visit. Boniface and Fowler seem optimistic that there is a role for a discourse on tourism that challenges more orthodox ideas of what tourists want:

> Maybe the average tourist does not want to know: but maybe the average tourist should be made to become acquainted with urban reality, which is after all rather more a product of history than a soft-focus, sanitized heritage alone.... In a curiously vivid way, the sociologies of contemporary urban societies are arguably as much 'historical', and can certainly be made as interesting in presentation, as any old building or patriotic tomb. (Boniface & Fowler, 1993, p. 71)

Yet in their hope for a "better" form of tourism there also lies the chagrin that the current nature of tourism is not about understanding and tolerance but about consumption:

> In essence, so far, too much tourist attention is being concentrated upon too little of the whole world collection of urban heritage and the significant historical processes of which it is, at one and the same time, product and witness. For many, many reasons, some of which we have tried to indicate, the tourist is not being allowed the opportunity to see visually, and 'see' in the sense of 'perceive intellectually', all that he, or she, might. Towns and cities are actually much more interesting than the tourist is often allowed to appreciate – and there is no need for the visitor's experience of *urbanitas* to be effectively short-changed. Tourism may thrive, but tourists are constrained. Selection and ignorance inhibit the quality of the urban heritage itself; they bottle the potential of the experience of an urban visit both for the individual and for our better collective appreciation of urbanity as a very remarkable world phenomenon. (Boniface & Fowler, 1993, pp. 76–77)

Of course, this "packaged" city is about the commodification of tourism. As Fainstein and Gladstone note:

> Ideally, tourism would genuinely enlarge the mind of the traveler by bringing him or her into contact with an authentic "other". Instead, however, tourist locales simply become products to be exchanged within the confines of advanced capitalism; the resulting process inevitably means that "tourism is the chance to go and see what has been made trite. (Fainstein & Gladstone, 1999, p. 28 citing Debord, 1994, p. 120)

Thus while there does exist a legal discourse that attempts to locate tourism within the context of the promotion of human rights and mutual understanding, many of the texts on tourism question, explicitly or implicitly, this construction of tourism. Krippendorf thus maintains that tourism leads to greater misunderstanding or at least confirmation of the stereotypes held by tourists and their hosts. He regards travel as promoting "mutual misunderstanding" (Krippendorf, 1987, p. 61).

This may suggest a much more confused understanding of tourism and its objectives than that which is posited by the WTO and the documents which have arisen from its work. Yet those documents represent a strand of legal discourse on tourism which has much currency. How do we reconcile these competing discourses on tourism? What can the law tell us about how we construct tourism now?

From Tourists to Travellers: Free Movement as a Human Right

As we have seen above, the underpinning of the various rights asserted by the law in the context of tourism rests on freedom of movement for tourists. As we have suggested this makes the definition of "tourist" critical in order to attract that right. But it is also at this point that legal discourse becomes even more confused and contradictory. The notion that freedom of movement is a fundamental human right conflicts with the sovereignty of nations to control immigration and the flow of people over its borders. This is manifested in contemporary times in the notion of "border protection" which has become something of a mantra for politicians who are concerned with international terrorism.

And it is clearly a combination of terrorism, the displacement of people globally due to war and famine, and global economic shifts in production which create this anxiety about control of the movement of people. Of course, this can also be understood as part of the tensions and contradictions surrounding "global" versus "local" issues (see e.g. Robertson, 1995, p. 33) played out in what some call a "new world disorder" where on the one hand the imperatives of the market push us in the direction of globalisation, while the response to such forces tends to be in terms of the re-assertion of national identity. Barber regards neither of these forces as necessarily democratic and in a world where "Jihad" stands for national and religious faiths and "McWorld" stands for world capitalism he suggests the challenge is whether democratic institutions:

> can secure new foundations either in the parochialism of ethnic identity (and its accompanying politics of resentment) or in the universalism of the profit motive (and its accompanying politics of commodities)... (Barber, 1995, pp. 219–220)

These forces particularly affect the cities in which we live, cities which have become places of difference because of historical movements of people into them, but which now produce the context within which the forces described by Barber play out. As Sandercock says:

> Cities and regions of the 21st century are multiethnic, multiracial, multiple. The cultural diversity which has emerged in cities in the West, and will continue to insert itself as a distinguishing characteristic of cities the world over, is also producing what I call a new world disorder. The multicultural city/ region is perceived by many as more of a threat than an opportunity. The threats are multiple: psychological, economic, religious, cultural. It is a complicated experiencing of fear of 'the Other' alongside fear of losing one's job, fear of a whole way of life being eroded, fear of change itself. These fears are producing rising levels of anxiety about and violence against those who are different, who are not seen as belonging, 'not my people'. This fear is as great a threat to the future stability of cities and regions as the much more talked about economic forces. In the first year of the new millennium, such fears have produced race riots in three British cities; the re-emergence of Le Pen in France as the standard-bearer for a coalition of the fearful; the strengthening of right-wing, anti-immigrant parties in most European countries; and in Australia, an immigration backlash which has given rise to the 'Pacific Solution', the notion of buying a small island away from the mainland on which to dump unwelcome refugees – out of sight, out of mind. (Sandercock, 2003, p. 4)

The consequences of such fears naturally impacts on tourism in a number of ways. The effect of the racist policies of Pauline Hanson's One Nation party in Australia in the late 1990s was to immediately make Australia less attractive as a tourist destination for Asian tourists (Litvin, 1999). Fear of the "other" in overseas destinations also reinforces the idea that "seeing one's own country first" is safer and more desirable. In this way what occurs within tourism is part of broader patterns of social dislocation. In this climate the notion that individuals should be free to move about the world as a basic human right is hard to maintain.

It can be stated at the outset that the human right to "free movement" asserted above is a legal construct. Nations have always maintained their right to restrict entry to persons who present themselves at their borders. What does seem to vary are the "categories of suspicion" upon which officials determine who may enter a particular country. For example, eligibility for the visa waiver programme when entering the United States (which is the pathway to the most convenient tourist visa available) relies on the foreign national not only him or herself not being a security threat but also coming from a country which has a "low non-immigrant visa refusal rate" and which the United States has "evaluate[d] the effect that the country's designation [as a country to which the visa waiver programme may apply] would have on the law enforcement and security interests of the United States" (*Immigration and Nationality Act* (US), s.217). Clearly, the purpose of the law is to screen "real" tourists from potential threats to the interests of the United States. The problem is that in doing so it places under suspicion potentially all visitors while assuming that there is a clear distinction between "tourists" and "others."

The increasing number of travellers be they tourists, or refugees seeking asylum in other countries has brought with it a spate of new legislation and resulting case law. Reading cases and legislation as text which tells a story over and above the strict legal analysis of the meaning of words provides another dimension in the understanding of how different the impact of law has become depending on how the traveller is defined. Both Australia and the UK have in recent years introduced new legislation which could be fairly described as punitive in its application to particular travellers, specifically those wanting asylum.

The recent decision of the House of Lords in *R. v. Immigration Officer at Prague Airport; ex parte European Roma Rights Centre* [2004] UKHL 55 was concerned with the lawfulness of the procedures adopted by British immigration officers stationed at Prague airport in screening Czech nationals who wished to enter the UK. Their specific task was to reduce the numbers of Czech nationals seeking asylum in the UK, specifically targeting Roma Czechs. The plight of the Roma has been widely reported in recent years. That they have suffered discrimination in regard to employment and education within Czech society as well as persecution is commonly known (Lord Bingham of Cornhill, *R. v. Immigration Officer at Prague Airport*, 2–4).

In this particular case the six appellants who were all of Romani ethnic origin challenged the procedures of the British immigration officers which had resulted in them being denied entry to the United Kingdom on the grounds that the procedures offended various human rights laws: the 1951 Geneva Convention on Refugees and the 1967 Protocol relating to the Status of Refugees; principles of customary international law; and that they constituted unjustifiable discrimination on racial grounds and so breached the *Race Relations Act* 1976 (*R. v. Immigration Officer at Prague Airport*, para.1). The Court of Appeal had denied their claims and they then appealed to the House of Lords.

Racial Discrimination and Prospective Travellers

The appellate committee of the House of Lords as a whole addressed all three points but it was the claim of unjustifiable discrimination on racial grounds which held sway with the court and determined the case. Lord Bingham justified the right of the UK to turn away prospective refugees or asylum seekers in certain circumstances. His comments on the convention and international law issue took an historical perspective where he commented that "[t]he power to admit, exclude and expel aliens was among the earliest and most widely recognised powers of the sovereign state" (*R. v. Immigration Officer at Prague Airport*, para.11).

He went on to discuss the 1951 Convention and customary law as it developed in response to the major displacement and persecution of people during the 1930s and 1940s [at 14]. He explained that:

> [f]irst it was a convention relating to the status of refugees. The focus of the convention was on the treatment of refugees within the receiving state. Secondly, and like most international conventions, it represented a compromise between competing interests, in this case between the need to ensure humane treatment of the victims of oppression on the one hand and the wish of sovereign states to maintain control over those seeking entry into the territory on the other. (*R. v. Immigration Officer at Prague Airport*, para. 14)

In articulating the basis of the Convention Lord Bingham also reflects the legal discourse embedded in the WTO documents on tourism – the protection and advancement of human rights and mutual understanding and respect. Following this discourse the majority of the committee agreed that there had been racial discrimination towards the Romani at the Prague airport by British immigration officials. The judgement of Baroness Hale sums up the decision of the court:

> the object is to establish a case that the Prague operation was carried out in a discriminatory fashion. All the evidence before us, other than the intentions of those in charge of the operation, which intentions were not conveyed to officers on the ground, supports the inference that Roma were, simply because they were Roma, routinely treated with more suspicion and subjected to more intensive and intrusive questioning than non-Roma. There is nothing surprising about this. Indeed, the Court of Appeal considered it 'wholly inevitable'. This may be going too far. But setting up an operation like this, prompted by an influx of asylum seekers who are overwhelmingly from one comparatively easily identifiable racial or ethnic group, requires enormous care if it is to be done without discrimination. This did not happen. The inevitable conclusion is that the operation was inherently and systematically discriminatory and unlawful. (*R. v. Immigration Officer at Prague Airport*, para. 97)

On the face of it the decision appears to suggest that the targeting of the Roma visitors was unlawful on the basis that it breached the *Race Relations Act* 1976. In fact, the Act (under

Section 19D) permits discrimination on racial grounds for immigration or nationality purposes if there has been an express authorisation issued by the Minister. An authorisation had been issued in this case directing immigration officers to subject to "more rigorous examination than other persons" Roma persons who wished to travel to the United Kingdom (*Race Relations (Immigration and Asylum) (No 2) Authorisation* 2001). The Immigration Department's position was that the Authorisation did not apply to the officer's stationed in Prague and so did not rely on that document to defend their actions. It claimed that the officials did not discriminate at all (*R. v. Immigration Officer at Prague Airport*, para.80, per Hale, B.) Hale, B. explained the Court of Appeal's decision (by a majority of 2:1) which had upheld the immigrations officer's actions:

> The Court of Appeal accepted that the judge was entitled to find that the immigration officers tried to give both Roma and non-Roma a fair and equal opportunity to satisfy them that they were coming to the United Kingdom for a permitted purpose and not to claim asylum once here. But they considered it 'wholly inevitable' that, being aware that Roma have a much greater incentive to claim asylum and that the vast majority, if not all, of those seeking asylum from the Czech Republic are Roma, immigration officers will treat their answers with greater scepticism, will be less easily persuaded that they are coming for a permitted purpose, and that 'generally, therefore, Roma are questioned for longer and more intensively than non-Roma and are more likely to be refused leave to enter than non-Roma' (Simon Brown LJ, paras 66–67). Laws LJ referred to the last of these propositions as 'plainly true on the facts of this case' (para 102). Simon Brown LJ, with whom Mantell LJ agreed, held that nevertheless this was not less favourable treatment, or if it was, it was not on racial grounds. The Roma were not being treated differently *qua* Roma but *qua* potential asylum seekers. Laws LJ considered it 'inescapable' that this was less favourable treatment (para 102). (*R. v. Immigration Officer at Prague Airport*, para. 81)

Hale, B. agreed with the dissenting judge in the Court of Appeal that the treatment of the Roma travellers was discriminatory:

> The Roma were being treated more sceptically than the non-Roma. There was a good reason for this. How did the immigration officers know to treat them more sceptically? Because they were Roma. That is acting on racial grounds. (*R. v. Immigration Officer at Prague Airport*, para. 82)

Hale, B. then spent some time explaining that the Authorisation which did not apply to the Prague based immigration officers actually had created an impression in the minds of the officials that they had to target Roma visitors. If the Authorisation had applied to the officials then the discrimination would have been lawful, but as it did not apply, it was its existence and the impression it created that led the officials to act in a discriminatory manner. (*R. v. Immigration Officer at Prague Airport*, para. 86, per Hale, B.)

Refugees, Tourists and Human Rights: Cases as Text

One can read *R. v. Immigration Officer at Prague Airport* for the legal precedent it sets for the relatively narrow point it decided. But a broader reading will see that it demonstrates a remarkable convergence of issues between refugees and tourists. It also demonstrates the manner in which the law operates in a confused and contradictory manner. The first point to make is of course that many of the Roma seeking to enter the United Kingdom were in effect tourists or visitors coming for a short trip to visit friends or relatives (*R. v. Immigration Officer at Prague Airport*, para. 94). Yet at no point do the judges refer to "tourists" or to any of the documents which assert freedom of movement for tourists.

There is however reference in the case to terrorists – albeit by way of reference to the Court of Appeal's judgement with which a majority of the House of Lords disagreed. Nevertheless as a piece of text the quote from the Court of Appeal says much about the connections made by the law. In justifying the approach taken towards the Romas at Prague airport as being non-discriminatory the Court of Appeal had said:

> because of the greater degree of scepticism with which Roma applicants will inevitably be treated, they are more likely to be refused leave to enter than non-Roma applicants. But this is because they are less well placed to persuade the immigration office that they are not lying in order to seek asylum. That is not to say, however, that they are being stereotyped. Rather it is to acknowledge the undoubtedly disadvantaged position of many Roma in the Czech Republic. Of course it would be wrong in any individual case to assume that the Roma applicant is lying, but I decline to hold that the immigration officer cannot properly be warier of that possibility in a Roma's case than in the case of a non-Roma applicant. If a terrorist outrage were committed on our streets today, would the police not be entitled to question more suspiciously those in the vicinity appearing to come from an Islamic background? (*R (European Roma Rights Centre) v. Immigration Officer at Prague Airport* [2004] QB 811. per Simon Brown LJ at 840)

In the House of Lords, Lord Steyn remarked that "at first glance" this reasoning seemed to have "the attractiveness of common sense" (*R. v. Immigration Officer at Prague Airport*, para. 37) but he resiled from that view when considering how this introduced into the law a justification for direct discrimination which the Race Relations Act expressly does not allow. Nevertheless, one may ask how is it that the Courts considered the implications of this decision for police powers and the handling of terrorism while ignoring the place of tourism in legal discourse?

The case also shows how fragile are notions of human rights in legal discourse. As Lord Bingham quoted Lord Hoffman from *R v Secretary of State for the Home Department, Ex p Simms*:

> Parliamentary sovereignty means that Parliament can, if it chooses, legislate contrary to fundamental principles of human rights. The Human Rights Act 1998 will not detract from this power. The constraints upon its exercise by

Parliament are ultimately political, not legal. ([2000] 2 AC 115 at 131, cited at para. 29 in *R. v. Immigration Officer at Prague Airport*)

The point of the decision in *R. v. Immigration Officer at Prague Airport* is that the actions of the official were clearly discriminatory, but if the Authorisation had applied then the acts would not have been unlawful. The case in effect supplied the blueprint for future acts of discrimination.

The Roma case also highlights the type of legislative change which has been introduced in a number of countries since the flow of asylum seekers has increased around the globe. The refugees of today come from many countries who are at war with other countries, some who have been caught up in civil war, and many who are the recipients of overt discrimination because they are from minority groups. The ready availability and greater affordability of mass global transport has seen the mobilisation of people in unprecedented numbers. Travel to far away destinations is certainly no longer the exclusive domain of the "well heeled middle classes". Nor is travel exclusive to those seeking to experience destinations which are described in the most inviting and enticing terms. Those persons who suffer discrimination and oppression within their own country can, for the price of an air fare or other mode of transport well believe they will find themselves as travellers on the path to a better way of life.

The accessibility of countries for many travellers has become a two edged sword for many governments. The tourists are most welcome, the asylum seekers most unwelcome. Countries such as the UK and Australia have introduced laws to make the entry of asylum seekers far more difficult than for any other form of traveller. For asylum seekers it would seem that balancing the scales of competing interests between the state and its border protection on the one hand and the human rights of the asylum seeker on the other, are in some countries very much tipped toward the state securing its borders. The introduction of legislation favoring such an approach tends to occur in a political climate of fear.

The aim of all such legislation is to deter would be asylum seekers from entering the country. Australia has particularly draconian laws in place which ensure that any one entering the country without a valid visa must be subject to mandatory detention (*Migration Act* 1958, Cth. (Aus)). The aim of dealing with asylum seekers in this way is also meant to send a strong message to those who would be asylum seekers who would chose to come to the country without a visa. The government's approach it could be argued has been successful to a large extent as the number of asylum seekers arriving by boat has diminished in recent times.

But this approach also reinforces the notion that the "refugee" (or asylum seeker) is distinct from the "tourist." What we ask is whether this distinction is more artificial than real, and whether the role of law has more to do with constructing artificial boundaries which actually operate to promote inequalities rather than protect human rights. To begin with, the practical distinction between refugees and tourists is a fine one, at least inasmuch as both groups have similar impacts on culture. As Russell has argued:

> According to his worst critics, tourism is an invasion that takes over the host
> culture and transforms it into a spectacle. The infusion of outside capital
> takes away local autonomy and laces economic power in the hands of the

developers and investors. Likewise, refugee impact in countries and regions of asylum has become significant. In the past refugees were a temporary phenomenon. They came they went, either returning home, settling where they were, or moving on to yet another country where they could resettle. Now, however millions of refugees stay displaced for longer. They are people who live out their lives in camps in foreign countries with little promise for a stable future, and their reliance on the resources there has resulted in changes to both cultures. (Russell, 2003, p. 835)

In law, both groups have their interests articulated in terms of human rights. For the tourist it is the human right to travel and visit other places, for the refugee it is the human right to travel to escape persecution. In an interesting sense, both groups converge legally in claiming the right of free movement. Both groups are also regarded as having an impact on the cultures they "invade" – thus calls for ethical tourism, and demands that refugees be located away from the rest of the community play to the politics of fear discussed above. In other words there is created a legal discourse which is designed to justify containment of both tourism and asylum seeking. It is these legal convergences and apparent contradictions with which we are concerned.

The Mishap of Unwanted Travellers

These convergences and contradictions play out in one further example. In recent times Australia has adopted a draconian approach to those persons seeking asylum in Australia, particularly those arriving by boat. To combat the increasing numbers of illegal boat arrivals the government introduced an amendment to the Migration Act 1958. The amendment excised certain Australian island territories (Ashmore and Cartier islands, Christmas island, Cocos (Keeling) Island, offshore resource and other installations (Australian Immigration Fact Sheet, April 2003).

The excise provision has the effect of barring "unauthorised arrivals at these places from applying for a visa (Section 46A). It allows Commonwealth officials to move those people to a declared safe country (Section 198A), and it provides officials with discretion on whether to detain these people when in that offshore place (Subsections 189(3) and (4))." (Australian Immigration Fact Sheet, April 2003) The result of the amendment in effect means that once a person enters the designated excised place they are barred from making any visa application as a result of entering Australia in that area illegally. It is clear that the amendment was passed in response to the perceived threat of growing numbers of unwanted travellers arriving on Australian shores and seeking asylum.

Australian immigration figures provide a "snapshot overview" of unauthorised boat arrivals as follows: There were 4175 unauthorised boat arrivals in 1999–2000, compared with 926 in 1998–1999, and 157 in 1997–1998. Of the 75 unauthorised boats in 1999–2000, 73 (97%) were embarked in Indonesia. The main landing site for unauthorised boat arrivals in 1999–2000 were the Ashmore Islands and Christmas Island. The top three countries or territories of citizenship for unauthorised boat arrivals in 1999–2000 were Iraq with 2297 arrivals, Afghanistan with 1263 and Iran with 227 unauthorised boat arrivals. (Australian Immigration, 2003)

It is clear from the amendment to the Migration Act 1958 that it is particular types of travellers that the government is anxious to deter. The Roma case provides a similar parallel in many respects. In both instances we have governments regulating the movement of groups of people through the implementation of legislation which in reality has impacted on particular groups of persons. The Roma case demonstrated the outright discrimination against Roma gypsies who "might" seek asylum in the UK if given the opportunity to land at an airport in the United Kingdom. Australia has also stemmed the tide of asylum seekers. The amendment to the Migration Act ensures that asylum seekers arriving by boat have limited opportunity to apply for asylum as they, like the Roma have been "headed off at the post" before being given the right to apply for asylum. Like the British government, the Australian government is also very aware of which groups of people are most likely to seek asylum within their respective countries. On analysis, rather than a discourse which speaks to two distinct groups, what we can observe is an interweaving of issues which relate to tourism and asylum seeking which obscures rather than elucidates the stated concerns with human rights in order to support – in our view – quite different objectives to do with populist fears and advanced capitalism.

The excising of Christmas Island is a good example of how the government chooses to portray the regulation of the movement of travellers for a specific political purpose.

Christmas Island has also been promoted to a very different group of travellers in recent times for quite a different political purpose. It has been marketed as an ideal tourist destination. Today one can peruse the web site of the Christmas Island Tourism Association for guidance on accommodation and interesting pursuits for the pleasure-seeking tourist while on the island (www.christmas.net.au).

Just a few short years ago in 1993 a casino complex and resort was opened in anticipation of enticing wealthy Asian tourists. As one press report on ways that the government had considered attracting travellers to the island noted:

> the Howard [Federal] government's minister for territories even urged Immigration minister Amanda Vandstone to allow Asian gamblers to visit the island without having to obtain visas. (Murdoch (*The Age*, Melbourne), 21 July 2004)

A former manager of the casino, interviewed for a national current affairs programme, maintained that the first weekend of operation of the casino saw an $A15 million profit. Aeroplanes went to and from Christmas Island and Jakarta as the wealthy elite of Indonesia visited the Casino bringing plenty of spending money with them. It was even claimed in the programme that president Suharto had given the Casino his personal blessing. (Australian Broadcasting Commission, 4 Corners, 1 July 2002)

In 1998, the casino on Christmas Island was closed when the former owner was forced into bankruptcy thus ending the flow of Asian tourists flying into Christmas Island for the specific purpose of visiting the casino. Today Christmas Island is better known as the place where 433 asylum seekers in an old wooden boat were destined when the Norwegian ship the *Tampa* rescued them and then found itself in the middle of a major political controversy.

The Australian government went to great lengths to ensure that the asylum seekers taken on board the *Tampa* for humanitarian reasons did not under any circumstances come into Australian waters to land on Christmas Island. Peter Mares sums the situation up thus:

> On the afternoon and evening of Monday, 3 September, more than eight days after being rescued at sea, the asylum seekers were transferred from the open deck of the *Tampa*, to the Australian naval vessel HMAS *Manoora*. Only the four Indonesian crew members of the *Palapa 1* were taken to the Australian mainland, where they would face prosecution for people-smuggling. The week-long deployment of elite SAS commandos to Christmas Island cost $3 million per day, or about $50,000 for each of the Tampa's rescued passengers, more than the cost of detaining all the asylum seekers in a mainland camp for a full year. This marked the beginning of a huge spending spree, as the government made it clear that it would spare no cost to counter the 'threat' posed by unarmed civilians seeking sanctuary in Australia. (Mares, 2002, p. 126)

The role of law has been most significant in these two very different aspects of people movement in regard to Christmas Island. On both counts the legal construction of the different forms of movement of people has played a major role in how the travellers are to be perceived and treated in terms of their human rights. Travellers who are perceived to be threatening to the "new global order" receive close scrutiny and their movement is regulated in a manner which bears little resemblance to the traveller who achieves the status of tourist. The important point of course, is that the status of "tourist" is not a simple matter for the traveller to claim. As the House of Lords decision discussed above demonstrates, the relevant authorities may simply ignore the issue of tourism and proceed to accord to the traveller the label of suspicion. So too in the story of Christmas Island, the law aids in shifting that location from that of an entry barrier to a tourist destination. In this sense, there is no more tourism, simply constantly changing notions of movement around which the law varies the legal status of the individual.

Conclusion: The Legal Construction of Movement and Mobility

We have argued that law constructs tourism in increasingly various ways to achieve different outcomes, and that this process is essentially about the legal construction of "movement". When the movement (or travel) is acceptable it may be defined as tourism and attract various human rights to free movement. However, travel for other reasons, such as seeking refuge from persecution, may be legally constructed as suspicious, illegitimate or legitimate, depending on various criteria, with a consequent restriction or allowance of movement into (and around) a country. In this context, the labels are constantly moving and the protection accorded by various human rights standards is not fixed and pre-determined. In this sense the law does not simply respond to the need to regulate and control the global movement of individual. The law, produced by the culture which is both suspicious and wary of difference, becomes part of the process which constructs that difference and so assists in disguising the various power inequalities which lie beneath the phenomenon of global mobility.

Is there a difference between the tourist and the refugee? Or are we all "travellers" – the particular label dependent on how the law wishes to view us? To answer this requires and understanding of who has the power to control the law and impose their political aims on others. The law then is merely part of the process which may result in the "sex tourist" being recast as the "economic saviour" or "sexual predator", the "heritage vandal" as the "cultural explorer", or the "tourist" as the "asylum seeker" or "terrorist". The point is that in the world of the law, there is no "tourism", simply the beginning of a legal discussion centred on constantly shifting notions about movement, mobility and the powerful forces which drive them.

References

Australian Broadcasting Commission, 4 Corners (1 July 2002). *The Christmas Party.* Available at www.abc.net.au/4corners/archives/2002b_Monday1July2002.htm
Australian Immigration (2003). Available at http://www.immi.gov.au/illeglas/border2000.border20.htm (Accessed 8-07-2003).
Australian Immigration Fact Sheet (2003). Australia's excised offshore places. Available at http://www.immi.gov.au/facts/81excised.htm (Accessed 14-07-2003).
Barber, B. R. (1995). *Jihad vs. McWorld.* New York: Ballantine.
Boniface, P., & Fowler, P. J. (1993). *Heritage and tourism in "the global village"* London: Routledge.
Christmas Island Tourism Association – http://www.christmas.net.au
Crick, M. (1989). Representations of international tourism in the social sciences: Sun, sex, sights, savings, and servility. *Annual Review of Anthropology, 18,* 307–313.
DeBord, G. (1994). *The society of the spectacle.* New York: Zone.
Fainstein, S. S., & Gladstone, D. (1999). Evaluating urban tourism. In: D. R. Judd & S. S. Fainstein (Eds), *The tourist city.* New Haven, CT and London: Yale University Press.
King, M., & Piper, C. (1990). *How the law thinks about children.* Aldershot: Gower.
Krippendorf, J. (1987). *The holiday makers.* Oxford: Butterworth-Heinemann.
Litvin, S. (1999). Tourism and politics: The impact of Pauline Hanson's one nation party on Australian visitor arrivals. *The Journal of Tourism Studies, 10*(1), 51–60.
Mares, P. (2002). *Borderline: Australia's response to refugees and asylum seekers in the wake of the Tampa.* Sydney: UNSW PRESS.
Murdoch, L. (2004). Casino ruling will destroy our future. *The Age (Melbourne),* July 21.
Robertson, R. (1995). Globalization: Time–space and homogeneity–heterogeneity. In: M. Featherstone, S. Lash & R. Robertson (Eds), *Global modernities.* London: Sage.
Russell, R. V. (2003). Tourists and refugees: Coinciding sociocultural impacts. *Annals of Tourism Research, 30*(4), 833–846.
Sandercock, L. (2003). *Mongrel cities.* London and New York: Continuum.
Smart, C. (1989). *Feminism and the power of law.* London: Routledge.
Teubner, G. (1989). How the law thinks: Toward a constructive epistemology of law. *Law and Society Revue, 23*(5), 727–756.

Legal Documents

Acapulco Documents on the Rights to Holidays 1982
Global Code of Ethics for Tourism 1999

Manila Declaration on World Tourism 1980
World Tourism Organization Statutes
Tourism Bill of Rights and Tourism Codes 1985
The Hague Declaration on Tourism 1985
Manila Declaration on the Social Impacts of Tourism 1997
Migration Act 1958 (Cth.) (Australia)
Immigration and Nationality Act (US)
Race Relations Act 1976 (UK)
Race Relations (Immigration and Asylum) (No 2) Authorisation 2001
R. v. Immigration Officer at Prague Airport; ex parte European Roma Rights Centre [2004] UKHL 55

Author Index

Abraham, S., 195
Abromeit, H., 35
Agamben, G., 338
Agarwal, S., 235
Ahmad, R., 197, 203, 205
Alker Jr, H., 337
Allee, J. G., 7
Allen, G., 280
Amin, A., 249
Anastasiadou, C., 63, 68
Anderson, D., 272
Andrew, D., 116–117
Andrews, M., 281
Anheier, H., 350–351, 359
Ap, J., 151, 164
Aramberri, J., 354, 356
Arrighi, G., 178–179
Asami, T., 75
Asamizu, M., 80
Ash, J., 354
Askjellerud, S., 340, 354
Ashley, C., 152
Aspinwall, M., 60, 61
Ateljevic, I., 176, 360–361
Atkinson, D., 275
AU/NEPAD 184
Austin, G., 75
Avraham, E., 263
Axford, B., 59–60

Bagnasco, A., 246
Bähre, H., 34–35, 40–41, 44–46, 51, 53
Baidal, J. A., 12
Bairner, A., 296–297
Bakhtin, M., 284
Bal, M., 281

Balasubramaniam, V., 205
Balibrea, M.P., 265
Balsan, F., 116
Balsas, G., 263
Barber, B. R., 353, 377
Barker, A., 96
Barron, G., 211
Barthes, R., 282
Battle, G., 215
Baudrillard, J., 119, 311, 312, 316
Baum, T., 294
Bauman, Z., 1, 335, 348–349, 358
Beard, C., 304
Beavon, K. S. O., 152
Bécherel, L., 356
Beck, U., 348–351, 353, 355–359, 362
Befu, H., 75–77
Bell, D., 94
Benins, E., 246
Beppu Foreign Tourists Information
    Bureau, 72
Bernholz, P., 34
Beteille, A., 116
Bey El–Mourhabi, J., 352
Bhagwati, J., 349–351
Bianchi, R. V., 183, 187
Bianchi, R., 235–236
Bianchinni, F., 263
Bieger, T., 54
Binns, T., 178, 185
Bishop, P., 280
Black, M., 293
Blaikie, N., 266
Blake, A., 215, 341, 352–354
Blum, U., 34
Boissevain, J., 236

Bonham, C., 334
Boniface, P., 119–120, 153, 163, 375–376
Bonini, A., 246
Bonvillain, N., 111, 115
Boulton, R., 305
Bourdieu, P., 118–119, 264, 304
Boyd, S. W., 294, 299
Boyle, A., 73
Bradfield, R., 211–215, 222, 231
Bramham, P., 264–265
Bramwell, B., 169, 235–236
Bremkes, W., 43
Breyer, F., 34
Brimmel, J. H., 196
Briscoe, J., 156
Britton, S. G., 176
Brodie, V., 95–97
Brohman, J., 179, 354, 361
Brown, C., 268
Brown, F., 151, 352–353, 360–361
Brunt, P., 21, 151, 180
Bryman, A., 266
Brysk, A., 86
Buckely, P., 293
Buhalis, D., 236
Bull, C., 294–295, 299, 304
Bunkers, S., 212
Burke, A., 115–117
Burns, P., 1, 5, 151, 236, 351, 360–361
Burnstick, E., 113
Burt, G., 211–215, 222, 231
Buruma, I., 76
Busby, G., 180
Busche, J., 39
Bush, G. W., 311
Butcher, J., 86, 316–317
Butler, B., 88
Butler, R., 235
Buzan, B., 337

Cairns, G., 211–215, 222, 231
Callaghan, R., 150, 151, 155, 156, 172
Campbell, D., 337
Carlsen, J., 265

Carr, S., 73
Carrier, J., 13
Cartier, C. L., 195, 200
Castells, M., 348, 350, 353, 358
Cater, E., 326
CEC 62
Chalip, L., 305
Chalkey, B., 264
Chang, T. C., 10, 176
Chapman, K., 150–151, 156
Cheah, B. K., 195
Cheong, S., 19, 236
Cheyne, J., 21, 25
Choy, D. J. L., 316
City of Johannesburg 151, 155
CNN–TravelGuide 151
Coen, D., 61–62
Cohen, E., 335
Community Aid Abroad 87–88, 91
Conforti, J. M., 333
Connell, J., 180
Consult 43, 45
Conti, G., 241–242
CONTOURS 6
Cooper, C., 236, 361
Cooper, M. J., 71, 79
Corbett, R., 61
Cosgrove, D., 280
Courtney, P., 21, 151
Coward, R., 323
Cowie, E., 274
CPRE 279, 288
Craik, M., 194
Crick, M., 370–372, 375
Crompton, J. L., 265, 274
Curley, M. G., 197
Curtis, S., 235
Czada, R., 35, 37–40

Dahl, R. A., 349
Dale, P. N., 75–77
Dall'Ara, G., 243, 246–248, 256
Daly, H. E., 353
Damer, B., 150
Damgaard, G., 212

Daniels, S., 280
Dann, G., 333
Dargue, C., 265
Davies, J. S., 237–238
Day, P., 193
D'Amore, L., 340
De Grazia, V., 242
De Knop, P., 294–295
De la Dehesa, G., 350–353
De Salvo, P., 244
de Wilde, J., 337
Debbage, K. G., 246, 249
Debelle, P., 100
DeBord, G., 376
Deery, M., 271, 275
Dematteis, G., 249
Déniz Espinós, J., 353
Denscombe, M., 266
Denzin, N. K., 84, 266
Department for Transport 279
Der Derian, J., 337
Devarajan, S., 215
Diamantis, D., 352
Dieke, P. U. C., 176
Dillon, M., 338
Din, K. H., 196
Dinan, C., 63, 67–68
DIW 36
Dixon Hunt, J., 280–282, 284
Dobson, N., 274
Dowling, R. K., 169
Dondolo, L., 150, 156, 162–163
Dowding, K., 237
Doyle, M., 337
DS 253
Dubarry, R., 215
Du Cros, H., 169
Duffy, R., 85–86
Dumbraveanu, D., 140
Duval, D., 2
Dye, T., 6

Eade, J., 264
Eades, J. S., 71
Earnshaw, D., 61

Eastern Cape Province 187
Ecologist 329
Eco–tourism coup 99
Edmonds, C., 334
Edwards, E., 110
EEA 235
Elkin, S. L., 237
Elliot, J., 64
Elliott, J., 178, 194
Ellis, E., 323
Emerson, S., 97
Enloe, C., 2
Equations 183
Eriksen, T. H., 112
ESI 141–143
Essex, S., 264
ETP 66
Eugenio–Martin, J., 215
Evans, C., 215
Evans, G., 263

Fabbri, R., 242, 245
Fainstein, S. S., 376
Fanon, F., 314, 329
Farquarson, K., 269
Farrell, B. H., 360
Farrow, P., 156
Faulkner, B., 21–22, 341
Fawcett, C., 113
Ferguson, B., 274
Fireman, G., 283
Fisher, D., 6
Fitz, F., 294
Fitzpatrick, M., 115–117
Fladmark, F.M., 153
Flanagan, O., 283
Flood, R. A., 213
Flowers, B. S., 214
Foley, M., 333–336
Forde, D. C., 117
Foucault, M., 180, 338
Fowler, P., 119–120, 375–376
France, A., 275
Franke, W., 113
Franklin, A., 1

Fredline, E., 21–22
Fredline, L., 271, 275
Freedom House 7
Freytag, A., 284
Fukuyama, F., 337
Furniss, L., 215

Gaeble, T., 8
Galli, G., 244
Ganesan, V., 197
Garcia, B., 265
Garrett, L., 6, 9
Gauci, A., 184
Gauteng Tourism Authority 149, 155
Gearin, S., 322
Gee, C. V., 316
Genette, G., 281
Gerosa, V., 184
Getz, D., 235, 236, 299
Ghemawat, P., 349
Gibbons, D., 340
Gibney, M., 14
Gibson, H., 300, 341
Giddens, A., 350, 359
Gladstone, D., 376
Glasius M., 350–351
Go, F., 354
Godau, A., 41
Goh, B. L., 206
Gold Reef Guides 150, 156
Goldblatt, D., 347–353, 355–359, 362
Goldstone, P., 316
Goodall, B., 326
Goodrich, J. N., 341
Gooroochurn, N., 215
Gosovic, B., 181, 185, 187, 189
Goudie, S. S., 149, 152
Goulet, D., 176
Governa, F., 249
Gratton, C., 274
Gray, J., 350, 353
Green, B. C., 305
Green, K., 266
Greenlees 323
Greenway, P., 115–117

Greenwood, J., 60–64, 67
Greig, J., 265
Greiner, U., 53
Grishakova, M., 281, 284
Gunaratnam, S., 201
Gursoy, D., 5, 22

Habermas, J., 349, 359
Hall, C. M., 2, 14, 59, 62, 194, 213,
    235, 264, 268–269, 361
Hall, D., 140
Hall, M. C., 175
Halstead, S., 269
Hanel, U., 34
Hansen, M., 88
Hardin, P. K., 214
Harding, A., 237–238
Hargreaves, J., 304
Harvey, D., 179, 264, 359
Harvie, S., 296
Hawkins, D., 176
Hay, B., 212, 215
Hebbert, M., 78
Hegge, M., 212
Heijden, K., 211–215, 222, 231
Held, D., 347–353, 355–359,
    361–362
Hellyer, R., 74
Hemming, S., 94
Hempel, R., 42
Heng, P. K., 195–196
Henry, I., 265
Heuschmid, W., 49
Higgins–Desbiolles, F., 94, 96, 98,
    313, 329
Higham, J. E. S., 265
Higham, J., 269
Hill, B., 340
Hinch, T., 269
Hirst, P., 350, 355–356
Ho, K. C., 176
Ho, K. L., 199
Hodge, J., 264, 269
Hodgson, A. M., 214
Hoffmann, L., 38

Holden, A., 162
Holjevac, I. A., 353–354
Holdnak, A. C., 300
Hollinshead, K., 341
Honey, M., 183–184, 189
Hong, C., 197
Hooghe, L., 258
Horrocks, C., 119
Hoskins, W. G., 281
Howard, B. R., 111
Hudson, S., 303
Hughes, G., 263–265, 275
Hüning, H., 40
Hunter, L., 116–117
Huntington, S. P., 177, 337, 356
Hutnyk, J., 315
Hutton, G., 265

Ian, F., 151–152
Ibrahim, Z., 196
ICVA 142
Illurn, S., 340
IMF 185
Inayatullah, S., 328
Ioannides, D., 246, 249
Ismail, F., 75–77

Jacobs, F., 61
Jafari, J., 340, 347, 354, 360, 362, 365
Jago, L., 271, 275
Jahn, M., 281, 284
Jamal, T. B., 236, 341
Jamieson, B., 267
Jamieson, W., 176
Jan Osmanczyk, E., 111–112
Japan Association of Travel Agents 76, 79
Jenkins, J., 59, 62, 213, 264
Jevtic, Z., 119
Joburg Gateway to Africa 151, 156
John, P., 237
Johnson, R., 21
Johnston, A. M., 92
Jones, M., 214

Judge, D., 61
Jurowski, C., 5, 22

Kahn, J. S., 198, 206
Kaiser, C., 44
Kajimoto, T., 76, 78
Kaldor, M., 350–351
Kapferer, S., 39–40
Karshenas, M., 340
Katz, H., 359
Kawasaki, T., 76
Keal, P., 91
Keitumetse, S., 109, 114
Kempa, M., 333
Kenny, S. J., 95–96
Kerr, B., 211
Khan, F., 149, 152
Khalifah, Z., 196
Killian D., 149, 152
Kincheloe, J. L., 84
King, M., 371
King, V. T., 193, 206
Kirby, A., 316
Kirkwood–Smith, L., 265
Kirsten, M., 185
Klemm, M., 293
Klump, R., 35
Knoke, D., 36
Knowles, T., 235, 352
Koerner, J., 287
Kohl, P. L., 113
Korostelina, K., 73
Kousis, M., 236
Krannich, R., 21
Krause, K., 337
Kreilkamp, E., 54
Krippendorf, J., 376
Kropotkin, P., 189
Krugman, P., 355–356
Kuppusamy, B., 198, 201
Kuru Development Trust 114

Lane, B., 169
Langewiesche, W., 10
Langton, M., 98

Lawrence, B., 195
Lasswell, H., 14
Latherwick, P., 151
Lau, L., 197, 204
Laumann, E.O., 36
Laurier, E., 275
Lawrence, B., 195
Lawson, R., 21
Lawton, L., 22, 86
Leckie, S., 304
Lederer, P., 211
Lefebvre, H., 180
Lehmbruch, G. , 35–38
Leiman, M., 283
Leiper, N., 316
Leipold, H., 35
Leisen, B., 213
Leisure Report 334
Lembke, D., 46
Lennon, J., 215, 333–336
Lepp, A., 341
Leslie, D., 294
Li, L. H., 352, 360–361
Libert, B., 305
Lickorish, L. J., 59
Liew, L., 201
Liew, W. C., 201
Light, D., 140
Lincoln, Y. S., 84, 266
Lindberg, K., 21, 176
Lippard, L., 2
Lisle, D., 333, 335–336
Litvin, S., 378
Liu, H., 198
Liu, J. H., 195
Lockyer, T., 79
Long, P., 238
Loverseed, H., 295
Lubbe, B. A., 149
Lyons, W., 268

Mabogane, M., 150, 151, 155, 156, 172
MacCannell, D., 153, 163, 316, 319, 335
Macey, D., 177
Mackun, P., 246

MacNaghten, P., 288
Madrigal, R., 19, 21–22
Mak, J., 334
Makens, J. C., 316
Maleuvre, D., 282, 286
Mandal, S. K., 198
Mann, M., 169
Mansfield, Y., 339
Mares, P., 385
Marks, G., 258
Marshall, J. S., 265
Martorell Cunill, O., 348, 353, 354
Marvasti, A. B., 266
Mashinini, V., 187
Mason, P., 21, 25
Mathieson, A., 85
Mayo, P., 177
Mazey, S., 59–61
Mbeki, T., 187
Mc Grew, A., 347–353, 355–359, 362
McCarthy, J., 265
McDonough, B., 75
McEwan, A., 273
McGraw, C., 215
McKay, I., 73
McKercher, B., 169
McLaren, D., 92, 94
McLaren, P., 84
McMahon–Beattie, U., 211, 222
McQuillan, M., 283
McVay, T., 283
Meethan, K., 72, 110, 120
Melzow, J., 47
Mercer, D., 21
Meyer–Schwieckerath, M., 50
Miles, W. F. S., 333
Miller, M., 19, 236
Milne, S., 176, 360–361
Mitchell, P. R., 311
Molstad, A., 176
Mommaas, H., 265
Mooney, C., 269
Mooney, G., 265
Moore, M., 7
MorningStorm, B., 113

Moscardo, G. M., 153, 236
Mossberger, K., 237
Mowat, S. C., 265
Mowforth, M., 85, 179, 182, 316, 327
Mulgan, G., 353, 357
Mundet, L., 235
Murdoch, L., 384
Munro, C., 222
Munt, I., 85, 179, 182, 316, 327
Muqbil, I., 328–329
Murphy, A., 115–117
Murphy, P., 5, 236
Murray, A., 293
Mwalwanda, C., 184

Nash, D., 153
Neighbour, S., 322
Neugebauer, G., 40
Neumayer, E., 6–7, 14
Ngarrindjeri Ramsar Working Group 104
Nian, Y. S., 196
Nicholson–Lord, D., 324
Nolan, R., 110
North, P., 263, 265
Northern Ireland Sports Council 296
Norton, P., 186
Nugent, N., 61–62

O'Loughlin, E., 315
O'Neill, B., 323–324
O'Neill, M., 294
O'Sullivan, V., 14
Ohmae, K., 352–353
Osborne, D. E., 8
Ott, M., 197

Page, S. J., 180
Parenti, M., 14
Parker, S., 149
Parsons, N., 114
Partidario, P. J., 215
Pasini, P. G., 241–242
Passeron, J., 118–119
Passow, U., 47

Patterson, T., 12
Pearce, P., 21–22, 151, 153, 236
Peet, R., 176–177, 180–181, 189
Pera, L., 92
Perraton, J., 347–353, 355–359, 362
Peters, G. B., 62
Pforr, C., 12
Pijnenburg, B., 61
Picard, D., 322
Piper, C., 371
Pizam, A., 339
Poirier, R. A., 341
Pomfret, G., 304
Poon, A., 150, 249
Potter, R. B., 178
Priestley, G. K., 235
Prince, G., 281
Pritchard, S., 115, 118
Provincia di Rimini 257
Pugh, S., 282, 286–288

Radebe, W., 155
Ramchander, P., 150–151, 156, 163–164
Ratz, T., 151
Reed, M. G., 236
Reeves, M. R., 299, 306
Reid, D., 352–355
Reiser, D., 360, 362
Rhodes, R. A. W., 237
Richards, G., 163
Richards, L., 214
Richardson, J., 59–61
Richmond, S., 115–117
Richter, L. K., 5–6, 8–11, 13–14, 194, 196
Richter, L., 8, 9, 14
Richter, W. L., 5, 6, 8, 13, 14
Rimini Fiera, S. P. A., 259
Rimmon–Kenan, S., 283–284
Ringland, G., 213, 231
Ritchie, J. R. B., 354
Ritzer, G., 180, 349
Roberts, L., 140
Robertson, J. M., 194
Robertson, R., 349, 358, 377

Robinson, M., 86, 153, 163, 334
Robinson, S., 215
Roche, M., 275
Roe, D., 152
Rodrik, D., 353
Rogers, S., 215
Rogerson, C. M., 185
Rojek, C., 264–265
Romm, N. R. A., 213
Roorda, N., 215
Ross, G. F., 236
Russell, R. V., 361, 383
Russett, B., 337
Ryan, C., 107, 213, 328, 354

SA Tourism 155
Said, E. W., 194
Salone, C., 249
Samek, S., 305
Samudra, I., 322
Samuel, R., 279
Sandercock, L., 377
Santamaría, A., 352
Santiago, A. M., 20
Sartre, J. P., 313
Saugestad, S., 111, 115
Sautter, E. T., 213
Savage, B., 265
Scheyvens, R., 105, 182, 328
Schneider, O., 42
Schoeffel, J., 311
Schor, J., 8
Schütz, W., 52
Schwarz, G., 35
Scraton, P., 1
Seaton, A., 287, 333
Seers, D., 176
Seibel, W., 39–40
Selwyn, T., 1, 235–236
Sernau, S., 352–354, 358
Shackleton, M., 61
Shapiro, M., 337
Sharman, A., 169, 236
Shaw, G., 264
Shaw, P., 263

Shibili, S., 274
Shiota, M., 79
Simons, M., 95–96
Simpson, F., 140
Sinclair, M. T., 215, 341
Sinclair, T., 352–354
Sing, S., 169
Sirikaya, E., 19, 22
Sithole, K., 150–151
Sklair, L., 314, 327
Smart, C., 369–370, 372
Smeral, E., 354–355, 361
Smith, A. D., 112, 206
Smith, A., 264
Smith, D., 178
Smith, G., 280
Smith, L. T., 83
Smith, L., 8
Smith, M., 21, 85–86
Smith, R., 211
Smith, S. L. J., 316
Smith, V. L., 110, 116, 162
Smith, V., 153, 340–341
Smith, W. W., 342
Smyth, S., 293
Snow, S. G., 93
Söderbaum, F., 186
Sofield, T. H. B., 176, 186, 188
Soholt, D., 212
Soja, E. W., 257
Somerville, P., 258
Sonmez, S., 19, 22
South Africa Online Travel Guide 150,
    156
Soweto SA., 150, 155
Soweto Tours 150, 156
Sparrow, J., 214
Spink, J., 264
Spurrier, F., 285–286
SQW 269, 274
Standeven, J., 294–295
Stevens, I., 96
Stewart–Harawira, M., 94
Stiglitz, J., 347, 350
Stockwell, A. J., 195

Stoker, G., 237–238
Stoll, G., 51
Stone A., 115–117
Stone, C. N., 237–238
Strange, C., 333
Sugden, J., 296
Sugiyarto, G., 215, 352–354
Suryadinata, L., 198
Swaney, D., 115–117
Swarbrooke, J., 304
Swyngedouw, E., 257

Tahir, S., 196
Tan, C. C., 200
Tan, E., 196
Tan, J., 197
Tyler, D., 63, 67, 68
Taylor, A., 265
Taylor, J. P., 335
Taylor, J., 120
Templeton, T., 325
Teo, P., 176, 352, 360–361
Teuber, J., 35
Teubner, G., 371
Teye, V., 19, 22
Thacker, C., 281
Thomas, C., 312
Thomas, H., 238
Thomas, R., 238
Timothy, D., 2, 169
Tonge, J., 293, 297
Torres, R., 249
Tosum, C., 362
Tourism Ireland 306
Train, P., 299, 306
Travis, A., 321
Trevorrow, T., 97, 100
Tsing, M. C., 196
Tsuda, T., 71, 74
Turner, L., 354
Twining–Ward, L., 360
Tyler, D., 63, 67–68

Ulster Council GAA 298
UNESCO 111, 114

Urry, J., 152, 264–265, 335, 360
Uysal, M., 22

Vaisutis, J., 115–117
Van der Poel, H., 265
Van der Post, L., 120
Van Wagtendonk, R., 311
Van Zuylen, G., 287
Var, T., 340
Vellas, F., 356
Vergragt, P., 215

Waever, O., 337
Wahab, S., 361
Waitt, G., 116, 264, 269, 275
Walker, R. B. J., 337
Wall, G., 85
Wallace, J. M., 265
Wang, G., 195–196
Wang, N., 335, 347–348, 352, 354, 356, 359–361
Ward, C., 195
Ward, S., 267, 274
Watson, J., 265
Watts, M., 181
Wearing, S., 328
Weaver, D., 22, 86
Weed, M., 294–295, 299, 304
Wegner, M., 38
Weiler, B., 264
Weissmann, A., 329
Welfens, P. J. J., 38
Wells, H. G., 285–286
Whiston Spirn, A., 281
Wildman, K., 115–117
Wilks–Heeg, S., 263, 265
Williams, A. M., 264
Williams, J., 21
Williams, M., 337
Williams, R., 189
Williams, T., 100
Williamson, J., 312
Williamson, O. E., 36
Williamson, T., 286
Willming, C., 300

Wilson, D., 267
Wilson, M., 293
Witz, L., 156, 162
Wolf, L., 150–151, 153
Wong, P. N., 197
Wood, R., 211, 352, 360–361
Woods, M. J., 155
Worden, N., 195–196, 200
World 6
World Tourism Organization
    334
World Watch Institute 348
Worth, O., 180
Worthington, K., 283

Woulde, D., 212
Wright, G., 211–215, 222, 231
Wrobel, R. M., 34–35
WTTC 186

Yamashita, S., 80
Yeoh, B., 360
Yeoman, I., 211, 215, 222
Yin, K., 266
Yoneyama, L., 74

Zaghini, P., 243–244
Zeigler, H., 6
Zissu, A., 204

Subject Index

Airlines/airports, as terrorists target, 320
ASEAN (Association of Southeast Asian Nations), 10, 196
Asia, South Asia, 10
Asylum seekers, *see* Refugees
Atlanta, 13
Australia, 378
Azienda di Soggiorno, tourism office, 244

Bali, 340
Banja-Luka, 124, 137
Barnett formula, 211
Beppu, spa tourism city, 72
1997 Berlin Declaration on Sustainable Tourism, 92
Bhutan, 11
BiH (Bosnia-Herzegovina) tourism and culture
  and EC TEMPUS project, 123–145,
    see also separate entry
  Bosnian institutions in, 127
  Development Planning Unit (DPU), 128
  governmental agencies in, 128, 130
  institutions beyond the consortium, 129–132
  inter-governmental agencies in, 129–130
  international agencies in, 129
  international financial bodies in, 130
  local and international media and publishers, 131–132
  local and regional institutions in neighbouring countries and the UK, 130
  non-governmental sector in, 128–129
  private sector in, 128
  tourism enterprises and attractions, 131
  university sector in, 128
Bologna, 124
Botswana, 109, 112, 114
  San/Basarwa/Bushmen, 114
  Tsodilo World Heritage site, 114
Bourdieu's cultural capital theory, 117–119

Canada, 89
Cancun, 350
CARDS (Community Assistance for Reconstruction, Development and Stabilisation) Programme, 130
CBD (Convention on Biological Diversity), 92
CEI (Central European Initiative), 130
Cervia, 130
Cesenatico, 130
CGE (Computable general equilibrium) modeling, 215
China, 11, 14, 230
Christmas Island, 384–385
Colonialism and tourism 195–196
Columbia, 340
Croatia, 127, 140–141
CSR (Corporate social responsibility), 84
Cuba, 11

Dark tourism and global security problem, 333–343
  9/11 attacks, 333
  geopolitics of, 335–336
  global security, civilizational framing of, 336–338
  media on, 334

positivist approach, 341
post-war model of, 339–340
rise of, 334–335
tourism and conflict, separation of,
    338–341
tourism studies, complicity of, 341–342
World War II (WWII), 338–339
Dayton Accords, 127, 140, 333
Decision explorer, 214
Delphi technique, 215
Democracy
    and tourism, 5–14
    defined and evolved, 6–9
    in the popular media, 7
    political definitions of, 9
Developing countries, globalisation and
        tourism policies in, 175–189, *see also*
        under Hegemony
Doxey's Irridex model, 168
Draft Declaration, on indigenous peoples
        rights, 87
    implementation procedures, difficulties,
        91
    importance, 89–90
    principles, 88
Dubai, 222

EC TEMPUS project and tourism and
        culture in Bosnia-Herzegovina,
        123–145, *see also under* BiH
    building the project consortium,
        127–129
    de-centralised co-operation principle in,
        126
    ethnic dissonance and divisions in,
        143–144
    European Co-operation, as background
        to, 124–125
    expurgated version, 132–135
    initial stages, 125–127
    institutional network building for,
        124–132
    institutions role in, 144
    interpretations and conclusions,
        143–145

lessons about institutions from, 140–143
    modules, 134–135
    nature and organisation of, 144
    TEMPUS Institution Building (TIB)
        projects, 124
    training, networking, mobilising
        support, and strategic planning,
        132–140
    unexpurgated version, 136–139
    universities role in, 144
Economic and tourism policy
    and the role of the state, 34–35
    economic framework of a market
        economy in tourism, 33–54
ECOT (Ecumenical Coalition on Tourism),
        85
Ecotourism, 325
ECPAT (End Child Prostitution, Child
        Pornography and Trafficking of
        Children for Sexual Purposes), 85
Edinburgh, MTV Europe music awards in,
        263–275, *see also individual entry*
    as the festival city, 265–266
    Edinburgh and Lothians Tourist Board
        (ELTB), 266
    global marketing growth due to, 267
    location advantages, 267
Ella Stewart Family Centres, 226
Emilia–Romagna region, 130–131,
        251–253
Enterprise tourism, 116
Environmentalism and tourism, 324–328
    climate issue and, 327
Estonia, 218
Ethical tourism, 369–370, 374
Ethnic Chinese spaces in Malaysia,
        193–206, *see also under* Politics of
        tourism
EU (European Union) level
    complex policy environment, 59–68, *see*
        also Tourism interest groups
    political thinking and the expansion of,
        60
Europe, eastern Europe, as tourist
        attraction, 8

European Commission's (EC's) Trans-
European mobility scheme for
university studies (TEMPUS)
Programme, *see* EC TEMPUS project

First World War, 241
Focalisation in heritage landscapes,
279–288, *see also under* Heritage
landscapes
transposed sense of, 284
FRG (Federal Republic of Germany), 35,
41, 53

GAA (Gaelic Athletics Association), of
northern Ireland
and the Scor as a tourism product,
302–306, *see also* Scor
awareness of, 300
contribution to tourism, 296–297
marketing strategy, 302–306
nationality and awareness, 301
place, marketing strategy, 305–306
pricing, marketing strategy, 306
product decision, marketing strategy,
303–304
promotion, marketing strategy, 304–305
respondents characteristics, 300–301
testing the demand for, 300–302
GATT (General Agreement and Tariffs and
Trade), 183
Gardens, 281–282
GDR (German Democratic Republic),
35–49, 51–53
child and youth tourism institutions in, 41
Germany, unification, and travel
industry boom, 41–42
hotel and restaurant industry, 45–48
hotel industry, 46
restaurant industry, 45–46
restaurants, privatisation, 45
three-sector model in, 36
transportation sector, reorganisation,
44–48
Gemeinschaftsaufgabe (Joint Task)
assistance programme, 48–51

Geneva, 350
Germany, eastern
accommodation market, 50
collective property transformation, 39
hotel industry, *Gemeinschaftsaufgabe*
(Joint Task) assistance programme
and the bedding boom in, 48–51
market transformation of, disposal and
property rights in, 38–40
municipal property, 39
property of parties and organisations, 39
property of private persons and legal
persons, 39
transformational result in, 38
travel agencies in 1991, 43
versus western German tourism
destinations, 47
Germany, western, 36–53
hotel industry reputation, 49
GLA (Greater London Assembly), 135
Global Code of Ethics for Tourism, 317
Global security problem and dark tourism,
333–343, *see also under* Dark
tourism
and international relations, 337
capitalist liberal democracies, 337
'fault lines' of global politics, 337
Globalisation and tourism policies in
developing countries, 175–189, *see
also under* Hegemony
cultural globalisation, 177
economic globalisation, 177
global tourism, hegemony structure in,
182
political globalisation, 178
Globalization theory in tourism,
rethinking, 347–365
and regionalization, 354
antiglobalization movement, 350–351
globalists and anti-globalists, 350–351
New World Order and the door to
touristhood, 347–348
paradox of inclusiveness, 349–350
three approaches method and tourism,
351–359, *see also individual entry*

Good Friday Agreement, 293–294, 297, 307
Group politics and tourism interest
representation at the supranational
level, 59–68, *see also* Tourism
interest group

Hegemony, globalisation and tourism
policies in developing countries,
175–189, *see also under*
Globalisation
and divergence/convergence, 177–181
and globalisation, divergence and
tourism, 181–184
cultural convergence, 178
cultural hegemony, 177
divergence concept, 178
economic hegemony, 177
hegemony levels, 182
political hegemony, 177
possible ways forward, 186
southern African context and
comparative examples, 184–186
tourism and development, 176
Helsinki Accords, on travel, 5
Heritage landscapes, focalisation in,
279–288
focalisation and landscape, 283–284
Gardens of Easton Lodge, 279–281
Gardens of Easton Lodge, viewpoints,
and vignettes, 284–288
Mr Britling Sees It Through narrative,
285
narratological techniques, 281–282
stasis and mobility, 286–288
symbolic space of, 287
theoretical context, 280–283
viewer's contribution to, 282
Heritage tourism, 199
Hexagons, visual thinking technique, 214
HIB (Hindmarsh Island Bridge) conflict,
90, 95–97, 99–100
Human rights and tourism, 84–86,
372–374
academia weighing into, 85
contradictions and continuities, 375–376

free movement as a human right,
376–378
Hyperglobalists approach, 351–359
causal dynamics, 352–353
conceptualization and historical
trajectory, 352–355
socio-economic consequences, 353
state power and governance, 353

IBSA (India–Brazil–South Africa)
dialogue forum, 186
Iceland, 217
IDONS software package, 214
ILO (International Labour Organisation),
109–118
IMF (International Monetary Fund), 179,
182, 315
Inbound tourism in Japan
challenges for, 79
ethnocentrism affecting, 73
geographical affecting, 79
globalization impact on, 72, 80
high domestic prices affecting, 79
international and domestic marketing
and visitor acceptance strategies
affecting, 79
Japanese cultural reactions and the
government's desire in, 71–81
Nihonjinron affecting, 74–78, *see also*
separate entry
politics of exclusion, 72–74
Visit Japan Campaigns, 78–80
Welcome Plan 21, 78–80
xenophobia, 72–73
India, 12, 230
Indigeneity concept/ indigenous
communities, 109
1957 convention, 112
and African politics, global–local
connections, 111–115
and enterprise tourism, 115–117
and ethnicity, 112
as North–South debate, 113
Bourdieu's cultural capital theory,
117–119

commodification of, 110
cultural consumption of, 110
indigenous communities, representation,
    115
indigenous Indians, 113
local and global perceptions, 110
Southern Africa indigenous
    communities, 115
Indigenous rights checking unbridled
    tourism, 83–105, *see also* Draft
    Declaration
and globalisation, 94
formulation, 86
human rights and tourism,
    84–86
in Panama, 93
indigenous Hawaiians, 93
Ngarrindjeri effort to tame tourism, 94,
    see also individual entry
theoretical perspective and
    methodology, 83–84
International Year of Ecotourism
    2002, 98
IRA (Irish Republican Army), 293
Ireland, northern Ireland, tourism in,
    293–307
Good Friday Agreement, 293–294,
    297, 307
peace process and tourism performance,
    294
sports tourism, 294–295, *see also*
    separate entry
tourism contribution to economy, 294
Irritation Index (Irridex) Model, 21
Israel, 14
Italian tourism, 245
urban and territorial policies strategies,
    249

Japan
foreign residents in, 73
Gaijin tourists in, 74
inbound tourism in, 71–81, *see also*
    Inbound tourism
Jugendtourist, youth travel organiser, 42

Kansas City, 13
Kenya, 326
Kiribati, 328
Korea, 11
Kuala Lumpur, 200
Kuala Lumpur Infrastructure University
    College (KLIUC), 197
Kyushu, 80

Law, constructing tourism, 369–386
Acapulco document, 373
feminist legal academics, 370
mishap of unwanted travellers, 383–385
racial discrimination and prospective
    travellers, 379–380
refugees, tourists and human rights,
    381–383, *see also separate entry*
tourism around human rights discourse
    and global tolerance, 372–374
*Tourism Bill of Rights and Tourist Code
    1985*, 374
Leith, 265–266, 272–273
Lesotho, 187
Libya, 11
Luxor, 340

Madrid, 217
Malacca, 199–201
Baba Nyonya Heritage Museum, 200
Cheng Hoon Teng Temple, 200–201
Malacca Chinese Assembly Hall
    (MCAH), 202
Malaysia, ethnic Chinese spaces in,
    193–206
Cahaya dan Bunyi (Light and Sound),
    201–202
Malaysia Truly Asia, tourism slogan, 204
Memorial Pengistyharan Kemerdekaan
    (Memorial Hall of Independence),
    201
Muzium Budaya (Cultural Museum),
    201
Peranakans, 195, 198, 200
Stadthuys museum, 203
Zheng He Gallery, 202–205

Market economy transformation,
    privatisation during, 33–54
  'Governance Principle', 36
  complexity, 34
  description, 34
  outcome, 51–53
  privatisation and institutional change
    within, 35
  sector concept, political fields and the
    explanation of sector transformation
    paths, 36–38
  state-owned forestry property,
    privatisation, 41
  system transformation, the reform of
    property rights and tourism politics,
    33–34, *see also* Systems theory
MCP (Malayan Communist Party), 195
Mecklenburg-West Pomerania's Baltic, 51
Mediterranean mass tourism destinations
    and governance networks, 235–258,
    see also Rimini
  boosterism, 236
  defining urban regimes, 237–239
  in 1970s, 246
  in 1980s, 246
  industry-oriented approaches, 236
  Local Agenda 21 (LA21) process, 240,
    250–251, 257–258
  methodology remarks, 239–240
  network agreement, nature, 237–238
  networking experiences, emerging role,
    246
  regime analysis, 238
  seaside tourism monoculture, formation,
    240–242
  tourism monoculture and governance
    regime, 254–257
  tourism policies and planning strategies,
    235
Miami, 13
Migration Act 1958, 383–384
Mombassa, 340
Montenegro, 140–141
Morocco, 222
Mostar, 133, 137

MSPW (Munro Satellite Positioning
    Watch), 218
MTV Europe music awards, Edinburgh03,
    263–275, *see also* Edinburgh
  'Come to Scotland' programme, 270
  'thank you' concert, 268–269
  as a marketing vehicle, 269–271
  cultural events and contemporary urban
    policy, 264–265
  local policy framework, 265
  local tensions and media portrayals,
    271–274
  methodology, 266
  MTV and Edinburgh partnership,
    268–269
  news management, 274–275
  to showcase Scotland's tourism,
    263–275
Myanmar, 13

Neo-colonialism, 180–188
NEPAD (New Economic Partnership for
    Africa's Development), 184
New Orleans, 13
Ngarrindjeri, Aboriginal people, 94–105
  'secret women's business', 95–96
  Alexandrina Council, 100–101
  Coorong National Park (CNP), 95
  Goolwa town, 100
  Heritage Protection legislation, 95–96
  Hindmarsh Island Bridge (HIB) conflict,
    95–97
  in securing their indigenous rights,
    99–104
  indigenous rights assertion by, 95–105
  Kumarangk/Hindmarsh Island, 99
  Kungan Ngarrindjeri Yunnan
    Agreement, 100–103
NGOs (Nongovernment organisations), in
    tourism development, 84, 126
Nihonjinron (a theory of Japanese identity)
    concept, 74–78
  and the future outlook for tourism,
    77–78
  definition, 75

purpose of, 76–77
to defend Japanese economic growth
uniqueness, 76
to group unification, 77
to recreate Japanese identity, 76
North-Mediterranean mass tourism
destinations, 235
Nvivo, 214

Oaxaca Declaration, 93
OECD (Organization of Economic
Cooperation and Development), 10
Okinawa, 80
OSCE (Organisation of European Co-
operation and Development), 129
Otago Peninsula, 360
Ownership economic system, 34

Pakistan, 14
Paris, 217
PAS (Parti Islam Se Malaysia), 198
PATA (Pacific Area Travel Association), 10
People Power Tour, in Philippines, 13
PFLP (Popular Front for the Liberation of
Palestine), 320
Philippines, 13, 19–20
intramuros, 20, 23–25
Mardi Gras Festival, 20
People Power Tour in, 13
respondent voting data, 26
sampled respondents by barangay, 25
WOW Philippines, 20, 23–26
WOW Philippines, positive impacts, 29
WOW Philippines, statistical analyses,
24
Picturesque garden, 281–283
Pilgrimage tourism, 14
Planning economic systems, 34
Poland, 217
Political platform, tourism as, 19–30, *see
also* Philippines
background, 19–20
factor analysis, 27
findings, 25–29
impacts data analysis, 28

literature review, 21–22
methodology, 22–25
voting behaviour, 22–23, 27
Politics of tourism, ethnic Chinese spaces
in Malaysia, 193–206
broadening horizons and accelerating
transitions, 205–206
colonial legacy, 195–196
courting the Chinese vote through
heritage tourism, 199
discussion and analysis, 195–205
economic reforms (*perestroika*), 197
international politics affecting local
responses, 197
literature, 194
local political alignments, 198–199
Malacca, 199–201, *see also separate
entry*
methodology, 194–195
political openness (*glasnost*), 197
Prague, 350
Promozione Alberghiera, Cooperative
Society, 245–246
PRSPs (Poverty Reduction Strategy
Papers), 185

Racial discrimination and prospective
travellers, 379–380
Refugees, tourists and human rights,
381–383
*R. v. Immigration Officer at Prague
Airport*, 381–382, 384
Reisewelt, east German state travel agency,
42
Rimini, Italian coastal destination, 130,
236–240
after Second World War, 242
and 1989 crisis, 247–248
and decentralization process, 254
and Province, 250–251
Bipolarismo Imperfetto, political phase,
244
boarding houses in, 255
Communist Party, Rimini tourism under,
244

development phase, 242
Emilia–Romagna region, 251–253
evolutionary process of, 245
Fair in, 252
in 1922, 242
Italian conference centre in, 252
local tourism system, structural
   characteristics, 249
mass tourism boom of, 241
motorini immobiliari approach,
   253–254
Rimini model creation, and mass
   tourism, 242–247
Rimini territory vocation, reinventing,
   247–254
surface railways construction in, 252
Rome, 217
Russia, 8, 230

Salt Lake City, 13
San/Bushmen/Basarwa communities, 116
Sarajevo, 124, 133
SATC tourism, 98–100, 103–104
Saudi Arabia, 14
Scenario planning
  in Scotland tourism, 212
  key to the success of, 213
  principles and history of, 212
  scenario construction, 213–215
Schmenner project, 218
Scor organisation, 302–306
  respondents interested in, 303
  sex of respondents in, 303
Scotland, tourism in, *see* Scottish tourism
Scottish tourism, *see also* MTV Europe
  music awards
  accommodation sector, 219
  actions and outcomes, 222
  ageing population affecting, 220
  building a strategic conversation, 226
  business tourism, 217, 220
  by 2015, total value of, 230
  challenges in, 220, 212
  continuous investment programme for,
    218

demographic problem impact on, 211
domestic market growth due to, 217
economic growth due to, 217
employment due to, 217
Estonia Centre of Excellence, 218
future for tourism up to 2015, 211–231
health tourism and small family centres,
  220
investment in quality assurance, 230
making tourism everyone's business,
  218
opportunities and challenges for,
  222–226
required actions for future, 226–231
required policy actions, 226–231
scenario-planning methodology,
  212–215, *see also separate entry*
Scotland 2015, contributors to, 214
Scottish tourism industries, 219
Scottish tourism proposition,
  development of, 230
Short Break Destination, 212, 216, *see
  also separate entry*
strategy map, 229
Tourism Development Act of 2014, 219
tourism organization, 212
two plausible futures, 215–216
UK market based tourism destination,
  230
Weekend getaway 2015, 223–225
Yesterday's Destination, 212, *see also
  separate entry*
yield management strategy for the
  economy, 231
Seaside tourism monoculture,
  consolidation process of, 243
Seattle, 350
SECC (Scottish Exhibition and
  Conference Centre), 230
Sector concept, political fields and sector
  transformation paths, 36–38
  large-scale technical infrastructure
    sectors, 37
  manufacturing industry, 37–38
  sector property rights, restructuring, 39

sector types, 36–37
sector-specific property rights, 36
service sectors, 37–38
state-organised sectors, 37
three-sector model, 36
Serbia, 137
Shell International, 212
Short break destination scenario, in
    Scotland. 212, 215–216
spending patterns, 216
value of tourism in 2015, 216
SI (Socialist International), 187
SI (Survival International), 109
Singapore, 10, 200
Slovenia, 127
SMEs (small and medium enterprises), 65
SMME (Small, Medium and Micro-
    Enterprises) development, 185
South Africa, *see also* Soweto; Township
    tourism
cultural resources post-1994, 149–150
social impacts of tourism on local
    communities in, 152
urban black townships in, 150
Soviet Union, 11
Soweto, 153–154
as tourism destination, impact on local
    residents, 168
children's condition, 159–160
Credo Mutwa Cultural Village, 156
everyday life and historical landmarks,
    157–161
getting world's attention, 153
Hector Peterson Memorial site, 155–157
informal settlement, 158
living conditions, 158
Orlando power station, 158
reasons for selecting Soweto as study
    area, 154–155
Regina Mundi Catholic Parish Church,
    156–157
Soweto township tourism trail, 156–161
traditional healer, 159
Wandies tavern, 159
wealth and poverty, 158

Spain, 11
and Greek mass tourism destinations,
    245
Sports tourism, in northern Ireland,
    294–296
and politics, 296–297
as cultural identity, 296
Belfast Giants, 297
Canadian Sport Tourism Alliance, 295
definition, 294
Gaelic games, 296–297, *see also* Gaelic
    Athletics Association
Golfers Passport Scheme, 295
non-active element of, 298
peace process and local sport, 297–300
Rugby functions, 296, 298
soccer, 296, 298
visiting, friends and relatives market
    (VFR), 299
Waymarked Ways Network, 295
Sustainable Tourism – Eliminating Poverty
    (ST–EP) Programme, 315, 328
Systems theory, transformation research
    and tourism science, 33–34

Taiwan, 11
Terrorism and tourism, in the 21st century,
    309–331
'Bush Doctrine', 311
anti-ballistic missile (ABM) treaty, 312
Bali bombing of 2002, 310
context, 310–312
Kuta, 322–323
meaning of September 11th, 310–312
Pentagon, attacks on, 310, 320
positioning and methodology, 312–313
The Wretched of the Earth work, 314
transits, terrorists, tourists and the
    wretched, 320–321
Twin Towers, 320
World Trade Centre, attacks on, 310
Wretched and the Rich, 313–316
Third Italy, 246
Three approaches method and tourism,
    351–359, 363

hyperglobalists, traditionalists and
transformationalists, 351–359, *see*
also under individual entries
TIC (Tourism Information Centre)
network, 231
Tourism industry
and civil actors, 126
capital and raw material, 126
disposal and property rights in,
reconstruction, 40
for economic production, 36
implications for, 92–94
indigenous rights regime for the
processes and conduction of, 92
intra-sector transformation paths in,
40–41
market transformation, *see* Market
economy transformation
Tourism interest groups, 59–68
agenda setting, 67
and government, reciprocal relationship,
60
at European level, 63
at the supranational level, 59
characteristics, 62–63
classifications, 60
communication and co-operation
among, 65–66
findings, 64–67
in England, 63
non-producer groups, 62
of a small size, 64, 68
problem area, 63–64
producer groups, 62
representativeness, overlap and issues, 65
single interest groups, 62
study context, 60–62
Tourism programmes
extrinsic variables, 21
intrinsic variables, 21
social exchange theory, 22
social representations theory, 22
socioeconomic variables, 21
Tourism, see also individual entries
and democracy, *see under* Democracy

and globalization, 328–330
and international order, 9
and terrorism in the 21st century,
309–331, *see also under* Terrorism
as ideology, 316–319
as political platform, 19–30, *see also*
under Political platform
commodification of, 376
creation, international rights
organisations, national governments
in, 109–120, *see also* International
Labour Organisation (ILO)
eco-tourism, 189
environmental issues affecting, 10,
324–328, *see also* Environmentalism
in development programme, 151–152
Islamic perspective to, 328
law constructing, 369–386, *see also*
individual entry
perspectives, 5–6
pilgrimage tourism, 14
politics of, *see under* Politics of tourism
privatization, 12
single voice versus multi voice, 65–66
social science research on, lack of, 371
spiritual over technical and material
factors in, 373
stakeholder theory on, 328
tourism survival, scarcity principle in,
116
Township tourism, socio-cultural impact
of, management, 149–171, *see also*
South Africa
authenticity in, 163
blessing or blight?, 162–164
data analysis, 165
most positively perceived socio-
cultural impacts, 165–166
most negatively perceived socio-
cultural impacts, 165–168
Likert scale, 164
problem investigated, 152–153
profile of respondents, 164
research methodology, 164–165
research objectives, 153

Soweto, 153–154, *see also separate entry*
traditional mass tourism, 189
Traditionalist approach, 351–359
  causal dynamics, 355
  conceptualization and historical
    trajectory, 355
  socio-economic changes, 355–356
  state power and governance,
    implications for, 356
Transformation, *see also* Market economy
  transformation
  endogenous and exogenous institutional
    change, 35
Transformationalist approach, 351–359
  and deterritoralization, 360
  causal dynamics, 357–358
  conceptualization and historical
    trajectory, 357
  of globalization in tourism, 359–361
  on tourism concept, 361–362
  socio-economic consequences, 358
  state power and governance,
    implications for, 358–359
Travel industry, 41
Treuhandanstalt agency, 37–42, 44–48
TSA (Tourism satellite account) approach,
  226
Turkey, 230
Tuvalu, 328

UMNO (United Malays National
  Organization), 195
UN Economic and Social Council
  (ECOSOC), 87
UNDP (United Nations Development
  Programme), 125
UNEP (United Nations Environment
  Program), 129, 315

UNESCO (United Nations Educational
  Scientific and Cultural Organisation),
  110–115, 200
UNWTO (United Nation World Tourism
  Organization), 9, 84, 315
United Nations Draft Declaration on the
  Rights of Indigenous Peoples, *see*
  Draft Declaration
Universal Declaration of Human Rights of
  1948, 317–318
US tourism, 9, 11, 378

VisitScotland tourism organization, 212,
  267, 273

Warsaw, 217
Washington, 350
WB (World Bank), 176, 179, 182, 315
WGIP (Working Group on Indigenous
  Populations), 87–88
WHO (World Health Organization), 9
WTO (World Tourism Organisation), 9,
  186, 222, 372, 379
WTO (World Trade Organisation), 180
WTTC (World Travel and Tourism
  Council), 183, 186

Yemen, 11
Yesterday's destination scenario, in
  Scotland, 212, 215–216, 219–221
  1970s command and control economy,
    219–220
  opportunities and challenges, 227–228
  spending patterns, 221
  tourism in 2015, 220–221, 222–226
Yugoslavia, 127, 142

Zambia, 185